lonely planet

D0249104

Munich, Bavaria
& the Black Forest

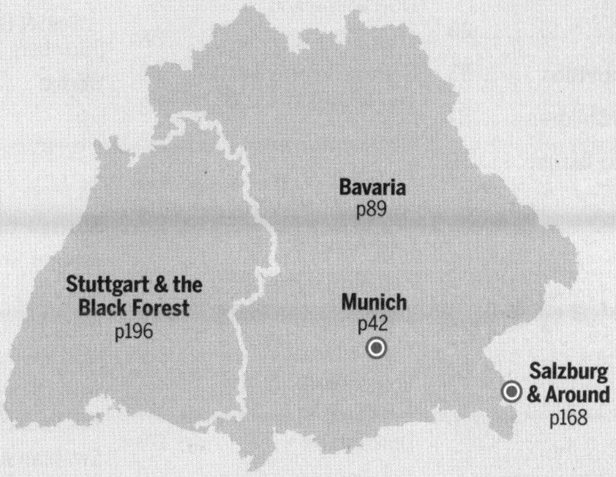

Bavaria
p89

Stuttgart & the
Black Forest
p196

Munich
p42
◎

Salzburg
◎ & Around
p168

THIS EDITION WRITTEN AND RESEARCHED BY

Kerry Christiani, Marc Di Duca

FCADOU / GETTY IMAGES ©

OKTOBERFEST P24

Contents

TRAVELSTOCK44 - JUERGEN HELD / GETTY IMAGES ©

HOFBRÄUHAUS, MUNICH
P78

WITHDRAWN

Welcome to Munich, Bavaria & the Black Forest

Hilltop castles and green energy, beer halls and luxury cars, Alps and edgy art – southern Germany blends thigh-slapping tradition with clear-headed modernity like nowhere else on earth.

Southern Comfort

The Germans have a word for it – *Gemütlichkeit* – that untranslatable blend of cosiness, well-being and a laid-back attitude. Nowhere does this mood permeate deeper than in the prosperous south where it awaits you in a region of fairy-lit beer gardens, Alpine views, medieval towns and rousing hilltop castles. But there's another facet to *Gemütlichkeit:* it's also a marble-smooth autobahn of luxury cars speeding to gourmet restaurants and chic Alpine spas, Munich's high-brow cultural scene robed in black, and cappuccinos at dawn on intercity expresses. The two southern Germanys coexist side-by-side, an incongruous mix packed with the unexpected.

Alpine Air & Munich Flair

Bavaria is definitely a place for those who prefer their air fresh rather than freshened. Though the Alps only tickle Germany's underbelly, locals know how to get the most out of their peaks, stringing cable cars up the vertical reality of the Alps; marking out entire atlases of cycling, hiking and cross-country skiing trails; even running a train up the inside of the Zugspitze, Germany's highest mountain. Yet all this is just a short ride from the urban *joie de vivre* of Munich, a sassy, sophisticated and self-confident city with a nonchalant, almost Mediterranean feel.

Cuckoo Clocks & Lederhosen

If you're in search of strapping Alpine types in Lederhosen, big-bosomed wenches juggling platters of pork, tipsy oompah bands and lanes of Hänsel-and-Gretel cottages, you'll be pleased to hear that Germany's south keeps all its clichéd promises. Nowhere is this truer than on the Romantic Road, a 350km-long route from Würzburg to the Alps stringing centuries' worth of quaint walled towns along a ribbon of history and tweeness. And if you think the folksy fuss is just for the tourists you'd be wrong – many Bavarians keep a pair of Lederhosen or a Dirndl in their closets for special occasions.

King of the Castle

Southern Germany is famed for its castles, from medieval fortresses to the 19th-century follies commissioned by Bavaria's most celebrated king, Ludwig II. Mad about Versailles (and some claim just plain mad) he 'single-handedly' launched Bavaria's tourist industry and even stirred Walt Disney with his story-book Neuschwanstein Castle. You could spend a month zig-zagging between sugary palaces, stuccoed baroque residences, wind-cracked Gothic ruins and vista-rich chateaux. Palace fatigue? Then retreat to a cosy tavern and raise a tankard to this marvellous corner of Europe.

Why I Love Southern Germany

By Marc Di Duca, Writer

Is it the sap-scented hills and trails in forests Black and Bavarian, the Franconian beer and dark tourism of Nuremberg or the emotions stirred by the tragic Ludwig II story? Or is it a mildly envious admiration for southern Germany's knack of producing cars that work, the galleries packed with modern art or the awe I feel for the German intellect as I face yet another devilishly complex Deutsche Bahn ticket machine (perhaps not)? I suppose it's all the above and heaps more that have me returning time and again to this quirky yet level-headed chunk of Europe.

For more about our writers, see page 320

Above: Geroldsee and Mt Karwendel (p102)

Munich, Bavaria & the Black Forest

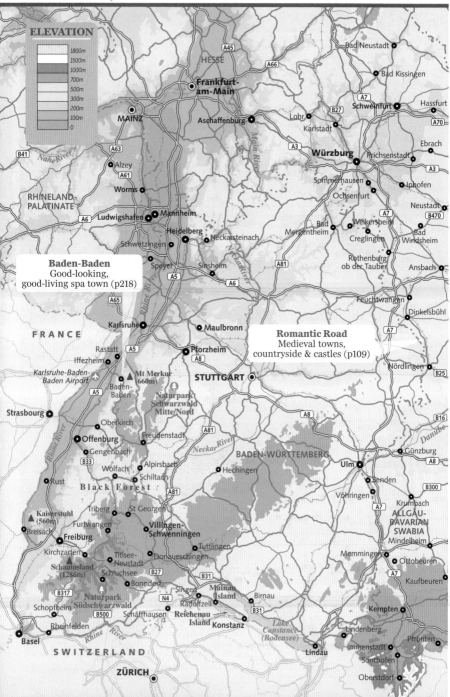

ELEVATION

1800m
1500m
1000m
700m
500m
300m
200m
100m
0

Baden-Baden
Good-looking,
good-living spa town (p218)

Romantic Road
Medieval towns,
countryside & castles (p109)

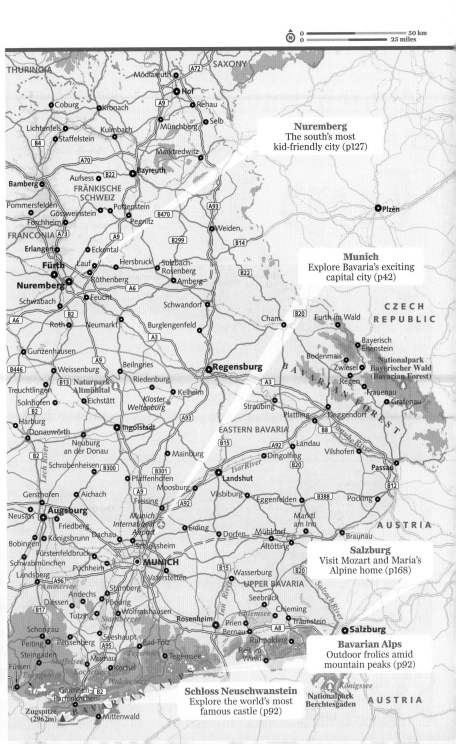

Munich, Bavaria &
the Black Forest's
Top 10

Munich

1 Confident and cutting edge, traditional and twee, Bavaria's capital takes all the state's quirky variety and condenses it into one of Europe's most intriguing destinations. The 'city of art and beer' wows with its world-beating collections of old masters, Gothic sculpture and pop art; but when the high-brow day ends, Munich (p42) retreats to the beer hall to savour a hop-infused culture like no other. Factor in some intense nightlife, world-class museums and easy-going locals and it's plain to see there's much more to Munich than just Oktoberfest.

Oktoberfest

2 Social barriers evaporate, strangers become friends and everybody sings too loudly, drinks in excess and has way too much fun at the world's biggest beer bash (p24) in Munich. The event lures a global posse of hedonists, but there's a quieter, folksier side, with less-raucous beer tents and time-honoured traditions teleporting visitors back to its early 19th-century beginnings. So squeeze into your Lederhosen or Dirndl and get on down to the Theresienwiese – it's an experience you won't forget, if you can remember it at all, that is.

MICHAEL FELLNER / GETTY IMAGES ©

DENNIS K. JOHNSON / GETTY IMAGES ©

Beer Halls & Gardens

3 Munich and Bavaria are synonymous with the beer hall, a time-warped institution of towering tankards; tightly trussed, strong-armed waitresses; and resident oompah bands. The (grand)daddy of all beer halls is central Munich's Hofbräuhaus (p78), but there are plenty of equally characterful, and perhaps less touristy, spots throughout the south. If you prefer your watering holes al fresco, Munich's beer gardens have been plonking down wet ones for over 200 years, and this summertime passion certainly has another two centuries' worth of elbow bending to come.
Hofbräuhaus, Munich

Romantic Road

4 As roads go, Western Bavaria's Romantic Road (p109) is something pretty special – a 350km-long ribbon of higgledy piggledy walled towns and soothing country-side. However, it's not all medieval quaintness; the route passes block-buster Harburg castle, the Unesco-listed baroque Wieskirche and Ludwig II's Neuschwanstein. Yes, it's tourist-clogged, and yes, the renovation can be more Technicolor than Teutonic, but come in the snow, stroll after the tourist buses depart or tackle the route by bike, and the Romantic Road begins to live up to its name. Rothenburg ob der Tauber

Baden-Baden

5 Some 2000 years ago the Romans raved about *baden* (bathing) in Baden-Baden's therapeutic waters, and the spring-fed town (p218) still hasn't lost its touch. Royalty and celebrities from Queen Victoria to Victoria Beckham have put this classy Black Forest spa town on the global map, but its merits speak for themselves. Nestled snugly at the foot of thickly wooded hills, this is a good-looking, good-living town of pristine belle époque villas and sculpture-strewn gardens, cupola-crowned spas, and ritzy boutiques, cafes and restaurants.

Hiking

6 If you're a fan of *wandern* (hiking), boy are you in for a treat – the hiking in southern Germany is about as good as it gets. Whether you want to ramble among the mythical mountains of Berchtesgaden (p107), splashed with jewel-coloured lakes, crest the country's highest peak, 2962m Zugspitze (p98), or trek from hut-to-hut in the Alps, there is a trail with your name on it. Edging west brings you to the wonderful solitude, bristling spruce forests and mile after glorious mile of footpaths in the Black Forest. Zugspitze

Nuremberg

7 The beer is as dark as the tourism in buzzing Nuremberg (p127), where some of the region's most evocative Nazi heritage sites, including the mammoth rally grounds where the faithful came en masse to Heil Hitler, draw those on the Third Reich trail. So with all its Nazi and WWII associations, you may be surprised to hear that Bavaria's second city is also its most child-friendly, with heaps for the kids to do. It's also sticky flypaper for Renaissance art fans, enticed to the city by Dürer, who was born here.

DENNIS K. JOHNSON / GETTY IMAGES ©

SCANRAIL / GETTY IMAGES ©

Schloss Neuschwanstein

8 Bavaria's best-known castle (p92) emerges from hilltop woodland above Füssen like a bedtime storybook vision. Commissioned by Ludwig II, 19th-century king of Bavaria, Neuschwanstein is top of the league when it comes to Germany's tourist attractions and it's easy to see why. What would have been a private royal residence is a reflection of Ludwig II's longing to retreat into his own cloistered fantasy world, a secluded realm in which the operas of Richard Wagner played a pivotal role. No wonder Walt found inspiration here for his Disney World creations.

Salzburg

9 At times Salzburg (p170) can feel like a Hollywood film set, with its theatrical alpine backdrop, exuberant baroque architecture, and Mozart and Maria everywhere. But here's the good news: it's real. History seeps through the Altstadt's maze of narrow lanes, crowned by a formidable fortress and sprinkled with churches and abbeys. Pathways thread along river banks and cliff ridges, allowing you to survey the city from every photogenic angle. By night, locals pour into palatial concert halls for chamber concerts, and chestnut-canopied beer gardens for monastic brews.

PUTT SAKDHNAGOOL / GETTY IMAGES ©

Christmas Markets

10 It's Advent so pull on your woollies, grab a mug of mulled wine and a wedge of festive gingerbread and set out to discover southern Germany's fabled Yuletide markets. Sprawled across ancient town squares in a Christmassy ruck of fairy lights, handmade ornaments, live nativity scenes and irresistible treats, they arouse a bagful of season's cheer as you hunt down those not-made-in-China (though look to make sure) gifts for folks back home. Nuremberg has the biggest fair (p132), but Munich and Freiburg also get in on the act.

Need to Know

For more information, see Survival Guide (p293)

Currency
Euro (€)

Language
German

Visas
Generally not required for stays of up to 90 days; some nationalities will need a Schengen visa.

Money
ATMs widely available. Credit and debit cards accepted at most hotels and shops but not all restaurants.

Mobile Phones
Phones from most other countries work in Germany but attract roaming charges. Local SIM cards cost as little as €10.

Time
Central European Time (GMT/UTC plus one hour)

When To Go

Warm to hot summers, mild winters
Warm to hot summers, cold winters
Mild summers, cold winters
Cold climate

Nuremberg
GO Apr–Oct

Stuttgart
GO Apr–Oct

Munich
GO Any Time

Freiburg
GO Apr–Oct

Salzburg
GO Any Time

High Season
(May–Sep)

➡ Best time to travel: skies are bright and temperatures comfortable.

➡ Good for hiking and other outdoor pursuits, hanging out in beer gardens and attending festivals.

Shoulder
(Mar–May & Oct)

➡ Fewer tourists means lower prices and less crowded sights.

➡ Surprisingly pleasant weather and a riot of colour: wildflowers in spring, foliage in autumn.

Low Season
(Nov–Feb)

➡ With the exception of winter sports, activities focus more on culture and city life.

➡ Reduced opening hours or seasonal closures at museums, other sights and smaller guesthouses.

Websites

City of Munich (www.muenchen.de) Official tourism site.

Bavarian Tourism Association (www.bayern.by) Bavaria's official tourism site.

Black Forest Tourism (www.blackforest-tourism.com) Black Forest's official tourism site.

Castles in Bavaria (www.schloesser.bayern.de) Bavaria's palaces and castles.

State of Bavaria (www.bayern.de) Official Bavarian government site.

Lonely Planet (www.lonelyplanet.com/Germany) Destination information, hotel bookings, traveller forum and more.

Important Numbers

Omit the area code if you are inside that area. Drop the initial 0 if calling from abroad.

Country code	☏ +49
International access code	☏ 00
Emergency (police, fire, ambulance, mountain rescue)	☏ 112

Exchange Rates

Australia	A$1	€0.67
Canada	C$1	€0.71
Japan	¥100	€0.73
New Zealand	NZ$1	€0.60
UK	UK£1	€1.40
USA	US$1	€0.90

For current exchange rates see www.xe.com

Daily Costs

Budget: less than €70

➡ Dorm beds: €15–30

➡ Lots of relatively cheap supermarkets for self-caterers; avoid overpriced markets

➡ In Munich, visit museums and galleries on Sundays when many charge €1 admission

Midrange: €70–€200

➡ Double room in a midrange hotel: around €80

➡ Main course in a midrange restaurant: €8–18

➡ Economy car rental from around €30 per day (less if booked online in advance)

Top End: over €200

➡ Luxury hotel room from €160

➡ Three-course meal in a good restaurant: around €45

Opening Hours

Opening hours don't vary much across the year.

Banks 8.30am–4pm Mon-Fri, limited opening Sat

Restaurants 11am–11pm

Cafes 7.30am–7pm

Bars and Clubs 6pm–1am minimum

Shops 9.30am–8pm Mon-Sat

Arriving in the Region

Munich Airport (p85) Shuttle bus every 20 minutes to the Hauptbahnhof from 5am to 8pm. S-Bahn every 20 minutes, almost 24 hours. Taxi to city centre €50 to €70.

Nuremberg Airport (p138) U-Bahn every few minutes to the city centre. Taxi to city centre €16.

Salzburg Airport (p191) City bus every 10 to 20 minutes to the Hauptbahnhof from 5.30am to 11pm. Taxi to city centre €20.

Getting Around

Southern Germany's transport system is efficient though does tend to serve the local population more than tourists (no buses on Saturday evenings and Sundays for instance). For timetables across the region head to www.bahn.de.

Train The most efficient way of getting around with a dense network of lines and stations.

Car Good for travelling at your own pace and without the ticket time constraints of the public transport system. Motorways are good, things slow down considerably off the Autobahn.

Bus Most journeys in the Alps and some on the Romantic Road are by bus. Otherwise the least efficient way of seeing the region.

Bike A cheap and green way of seeing the region's cities. Bike paths are plentiful in Munich and Nuremberg.

For much more on **getting around**, see p302

PLAN YOUR TRIP NEED TO KNOW

First Time

For more information, see Survival Guide (p293)

Checklist

➡ Ensure your passport is valid for another four months after arrival in Germany

➡ Check budget airline baggage restrictions carefully

➡ If possible, inform your bank/credit card company you'll be travelling in Germany

➡ Make sure your travel insurance covers all planned activities

➡ Find out what you need to provide to hire a car

What to Pack

➡ Hiking boots and other walking gear for Alpine trails

➡ Phrasebook or translation app

➡ European plug adaptor for charging up gadgetry – you won't find them in Germany

➡ A sweater or fleece even in summer for evenings in the Alps

Top Tips for Your Trip

➡ Try to start your day trips and journeys by public transport after 9am and use a Bayern Ticket – you'll save hundreds of euros, especially if you're not travelling alone.

➡ Holidays such as Easter or Christmas aren't good times to travel to Germany. Things are often completely dead, businesses closed for days and public transport skeletal.

➡ Schedule some time away from southern Germany's big cities to sample life at a slower, more traditional pace.

What to Wear

In general, Germans are fairly laid back about clothing and you'll only need to think about apparel in certain specific situations. Smart casual will do for the vast majority of evening occasions and outside of more fashion-conscious Munich, you may be surprised how informally Germans dress to smart restaurants, the theatre and for other special occasions. Only the most upmarket establishments may insist on jackets for men, but these are rare. For sightseeing take sturdy shoes for all those cobbled streets and a waterproof coat; walking boots or trail shoes are essential if you are heading to the Alps or even for a walk around one of the region's many lakes. Even at the height of summer long sleeves are a must in the evenings, especially at altitude.

Sleeping

Booking ahead is always a good idea in Germany's south – you never know what obscure festival or event might be going on in the place you are heading to that could fill every bed with visitors.

➡ **Hotels** These are of a good to excellent standard across the board but rates are generally high.

➡ **B&Bs & Guesthouses** The accommodation of choice in rural areas often with high standards and hearty breakfasts.

➡ **Hostels** Independent hostels can be found in tourist hotspots such as Munich and Nuremberg. Classic youth hostels are widespread and often occupy historic buildings.

Saving Money

Southern Germany is an expensive place, but there are ways of preventing your stash of euros from being depleted too rapidly.

➡ Germany's public transport systems offer myriad ways of saving cash – hardly anyone pays full fare. The best place to start is www.bahn.de.

➡ Making accommodation reservations on popular booking websites can save you a lot, especially at quiet times in the big cities.

➡ Take advantage of big buffet breakfast and cheap lunch menus to fill up on the cheap.

Bargaining

Bargaining is not acceptable in any situation in southern Germany.

Tipping

➡ **When to tip** You could get through an entire trip around southern Germany without giving a single tip. Few service industry employees expect them these days, though most still appreciate a little extra when it comes their way.

➡ **Hotels** Generally €1 per bag.

➡ **Pubs** Leave a little small change for the barman.

➡ **Restaurants** Round up the bill to the nearest €5 (or €10) if you were satisfied with service.

➡ **Taxis** Round up to the nearest €5 so the driver doesn't have to hunt for change.

➡ **Toilet Attendants** €0.50 usually keeps these guys happy unless a price list states exact rates.

WESTEND61 / GETTY IMAGES ©

Siegestor, Munich (p42)

Etiquette

Southern Germans are a pretty rigid bunch, with elderly people in particular expecting lots of set behaviour and stock phrases. It's easy to make a mistake, but the following should help you avoid red-faced moments.

➡ **Greetings** Until noon say '*Guten Morgen*'; from noon until early evening this becomes '*Gruss Gott*'. '*Guten Abend*' is used from around 6pm onwards until it's time to say '*Gute Nacht*'. Use the formal '*Sie*' with strangers, and the informal '*du*' and first names if invited to. If in doubt, use '*Sie*'.

➡ **At the Table** Tucking in before the '*Guten Appetit*' starting gun is fired is regarded as bad manners. When drinking wine, the toast is '*Zum Wohl*', with beer it's '*Prost*'.

➡ **When meeting up** Punctuality is appreciated – never arrive more than 15 minutes late.

Language

It's just about possible to get by in Germany's south without speaking any German whatsoever, but learning a few simple words and phrases will pay dividends in all kinds of situations from the restaurant table to the booking office. In big cities, such as Munich and Nuremberg, English is spoken by those who come into regular contact with foreigners, but this may not be the case in rural locations.

What's New

Black Forest National Park

Finally approved in 2014, Germany's newest national park located between Baden-Baden and Freudenstadt is 100 sq km of moorland, glacial lakes, deep valleys, mountains and unspoilt stretches of coniferous forest in the heart of the Black Forest. Ideal for hiking and cycling and set up as a family-friendly attraction, the main information centre is Ruhestein, the best place to start when striking out into this wonderful piece of European landscape.

Hot Hostels

New hostels are springing up across Bavaria with particularly good newcomers in Nuremberg (Five Reasons; p133), Füssen (Old Kings; p94) and Augsburg (Übernacht; p124).

Dom St Kilian

Würzburg's top temple has undergone complete renovation, adding tasteful modern elements to one of Germany's most unusual cathedral interiors. (p111)

KIBALA

The new kiddies' area at Nuremberg's excellent Deutsche Bahn Museum is a must for any choo-choo-loving little'un with lots of interactive railway fun and a ride-on train to enjoy. (p128)

Richard Wagner Museum

The paint might still be wet on Bayreuth's fully revamped Richard Wagner Museum, housed in the building the great composer inhabited, his unmarked grave concealed behind. (p142)

Vegan Victuals

Counterbalancing the current craze for burgers, newcomers Selly's (p164) in Passau and Bodhi (p77) in Munich's Westend are meat- and dairy-free archipelagos in Bavaria's pork-crazed ocean.

Monument to the Victims of National Socialism

This newly minted monument in Munich's city centre is a powerful memorial to those who died at the hands of the Nazis. (p54)

Kaiserburg Museum

The exhibition at Nuremberg's top attraction, its medieval hilltop castle, has been given a multimillion-euro upgrade. (p128)

Lenbachhaus New Wing

The Lenbachhaus in Munich has a spanking new wing designed by none other than British architect Norman Foster. (p57)

Burgers for the Burgers

Burgers are in danger of replacing sausages as the traditional snack of choice in the Bavarian capital with countless burger joints sprouting up and almost every restaurant including a version in its menu. (p73)

BMW's Esszimmer

Not only do BMW make the best cars in Germany's south, they also serve the best food – this Michelin-star restaurant perched above the four-wheeled actions has quickly become the city's finest. (p77)

For more recommendations and reviews, see lonelyplanet.com/bavaria

If You Like...

Castles & Palaces

Love castles? Then Bavaria is your place with some blockbuster piles hugging hilltops and hogging city centre plots. And three cheers for King Ludwig II for commissioning the region's most charming chateaux.

Neuschwanstein King Ludwig's – and the world's – most celebrated castle is Bavaria's top must-see. (p92)

Residenz (Munich) The former residence of the Bavarian royal family is essential viewing in the Bavarian capital. (p51)

Linderhof Versailles-inspired, it occupies a remote site surrounded by snow-capped peaks and moody pine forests. (p95)

Herrenchiemsee Another of Ludwig II's 'Versailles in miniature' located on an island in the Chiemsee. (p105)

Nymphenburg Munich's grandest pile is famous for its 'Gallery of the Beauties' and stately gardens. (p64)

Residenz (Würzburg) Würzburg's Residenz was home to the local prince-bishops and boasts the world's largest ceiling fresco. (p110)

Cars & Trains

Germany and Bavaria are synonymous with high-tech industries, particularly when it comes to cars. Explore the past and present of Bavaria's motor industry and discover its railway heritage at high-velocity museums.

BMW Welt & Museum Experience BMW's high-octane present then cross the bridge to the company's exciting car museum. (p64)

Deutsche Bahn Museum A wonderful repository of Germany's choo-choo past containing some of its best-known locos. (p128)

Audi Forum Ingolstadt is home to Audi and the company's museum will get a petrolhead's pulse racing. (p158)

Bayerisches Eisenbahnmuseum Nördlingen's railway museum is a retirement home for Deutsche Bahn's steam locos of yesteryear. (p121)

Mercedes-Benz Museum Complete your luxury car museum collection at this shrine to the Mercs of yesterday in Stuttgart. (p199)

Museums

Bavaria's ruling Wittelsbach family certainly liked their art and their world-class collections now pack Munich's museums and galleries. Countless other repositories of the past tell southern Germany's tale with imagination and flair.

Münchner Stadtmuseum An innovatively conceived overview of Munich's past created in 2008 to mark the city's 850th birthday. (p46)

Alte Pinakothek The finest art from the Wittelsbachs' extensive collections and the high-brow highlight of Munich's Kunstareal. (p54)

Pinakothek der Moderne Chunky retro design and artwork, plus temporary shows, pack out this minimalist, purpose-built Munich museum. (p55)

Deutsches Museum This great museum has experiments and demonstrations that bring out the boffin in everyone, especially kids. (p60)

Germanisches Nationalmuseum Nuremberg's contribution to the Bavarian museum scene is this journey through Germany's cultural past. (p129)

Museum der Bayerischen Könige A stunning location on the Alpsee and a must for all Bavarian royalty fans. (p94)

Deutsche Bahn Museum One of Europe's best railway museums with lots for kids to see and do. (p128)

Salzburg Museum In the baroque Neue Residenz Palace, this flagship museum takes you on a historical romp through the history of Salzburg. (p171)

ALLAN BAXTER / GETTY IMAGES ©

Antiquarium, Munich Residenz (p51)

WWII Heritage

Southern Germany certainly has its fair share of sites made infamous by the Nazis during their rise to power and subsequent demise at the hands of the Allies.

Hitler's Eagle's Nest Soar into the Alps to this high perch built as Hitler's mountain retreat. (p107)

Dachau Concentration Camp The Nazis' first concentration camp is a moving memorial to the inmates that suffered and died here. (p86)

Memorium Nuremberg Trials Visit the courtroom where many top-ranking Nazis were tried and sentenced for their crimes against humanity. (p128)

Reichsparteitagsgelände Ever wondered where all that footage of a ranting Hitler and Sieg-Heiling masses was filmed? (p129)

Dokumentation Obersalzberg Learn how Obersalzberg in the Berchtesgadener Land became the Nazis' headquarters. (p107)

White Rose Memorial This small memorial within Munich's Ludwig-Maximilians-Universität commemorates students executed for anti-Nazi activities. (p61)

Churches

From baroque riots to Gothic restraint, round-arched Romanesque to red-brick marvels, southern Germany's steadfast Catholic tradition has bequeathed the region a posse of show-stopping churches, often bejewelled with exquisite works of art.

Freiburg Münster A sandstone colossus presiding over Freiburg's historical core. The tower affords views as far as France. (p233)

Wieskirche This Unesco-listed barrage of baroque ornamentation enjoys a pretty setting amid idyllic Alpine meadows. (p95)

Asamkirche Munich's baroque masterpiece created by the Asam brothers as their private chapel. (p46)

Frauenkirche No building in the city centre may rise higher than the spires of Munich's famous church. (p43)

St Martin Church The spire of Landshut's basilica is the world's tallest brick structure at 130m. (p161)

Ulmer Münster Ulm's massive cathedral may just prove that size *is* everything. (p213)

Michaelskirche The crypt at this newly renovated church is the final resting place of King Ludwig II. (p47)

Dom Salzburg's cathedral stands out as a masterpiece of baroque art. (p174)

Spas & Pools

Perhaps not instantly synonymous with spas and pools, southern Germany offers a surprising number of places to get pampered and pummelled, tossed around by a wave machine or just wet.

Baden-Baden The grand dame of central Europe's spa towns and still a magnet for royalty and celebrity. (p220)

Alpamare Bad Tölz is home to Europe's longest waterslide and an indoor surfing wave. (p104)

Watzmann Therme Berchtesgaden's spa complex offers wellness, sport and saunas galore against a pristine Alpine backdrop. (p108)

Badeparadies Palm trees in the Black Forest? Not the only surprise at this spa and water park. (p241)

Müller'sches Volksbad Munich's most characterful swimming pool still bedecked in original *Jugenstil* decoration. (p68)

Local Food & Drink

It would seem Southern Germany has a beer and a sausage for every day of the year. And you can round off a Teutonic feast with possibly the world's most scrumptious cake.

Beer Every tipple has its home – whisky belongs to Scotland, wine to France, beer to Bavaria. (p286)

Sausages You could easily put together a sausage-themed tour of southern Germany. (p284)

Snowballs & Gingerbread Rothenburg's sugar-dusted snowballs and Nuremberg's peppery gingerbread are just two of the region's tooth-rotters. (p285)

Black Forest Gateau A mouthwatering combination of choco-late sponge, whipped cream and black cherries, infused with cherry brandy. (p285)

Wine Southern Germany's finest wines come from the south-facing slopes around Würzburg. (p287)

Viktualienmarkt By far southern Germany's best open-air market in the heart of Munich's city centre. (p46)

Lakes & Mountains

Bavaria claims just a sliver of the Alps but packs a lot into its mountains. Between the peaks glisten glacier-fed lakes providing stop-and-stare vistas and ample opportunities for water-borne fun.

Zugspitze You won't need crampons to tackle Germany's highest peak – just a ticket for the train! (p98)

Starnbergersee A watery weekend destination for Munich folk and the place King Ludwig II met his end. (p88)

Garmisch-Partenkirchen The German Alps' premier resort has the state's longest skiing season and heaps of hiking. (p34)

Königssee Bavaria's most picturesque lake is a great starting point for flits into the Alpine backcountry. (p107)

Lake Constance Shared between Germany, Switzerland and Austria and by millions of snap-happy tourists. (p247)

Shopping

For every chain store and out-of-town megamall in Germany's south there's an independent boutique or family-run emporium selling those special items you just won't find back home.

Christmas Markets Packing the centres of Munich, Nuremberg and Salzburg among others, the region's Yuletide bazaars are legendary. (p132)

Dirndl & Lederhosen If you're planning a session in a beer tent, you may as well look the part. (p279)

Yuletide decorations It's Christmas every day of the year at Rothenburg's Weihnachtsdorf (Christmas Village). (p118)

Cuckoo clocks Triberg is cuckoo central, though these inimitable timepieces are available across the region. (p243)

Outdoor gear Munich has some of the best outdoor kit stockists in the Alpine region. (p83)

Toys Southern Germany has given mankind Ravensburger jigsaws, the world of Playmobil and Käthe-Kruse dolls. (p135)

Music & Literature

Some of the biggest heavyweights of the Germanic musical and literary worlds hail from this neck of the *wald* or spent long periods of time here.

Wagner Germany's most controversial composer had Bayreuth's Festspielhaus built specially for his operas. (p142)

Mozart Salzburg is Mozart central, though associations do pop up in several other places across southern Germany. (p170)

Goethe Drop into Tübingen's Cottahaus, once the home of Goethe's first publisher. (p209)

Sound of Music Take a *Sound of Music* film location tour around Salzburg's city centre. (p180)

Bayreuther Festspiele Bayreuth hosts the world's greatest Wagner festival each August. (p148)

Brecht Visit the Augsburg house where Germany's greatest 20th-century playwright and poet was born. (p124)

Month by Month

January

With the last corks of New Year popped, it's time to clear your head on the ski slopes of the Alps. Winter bites coldest in January so wrap up snug while sightseeing.

✯ Hornschlittenrennen

Fun celebration (www.horn schlitten.de) on 6 January in Garmisch-Partenkirchen with locals racing downhill on period sleds once used for bringing hay and wood down to the valleys.

✯ Mozartwoche

Since 1956 Salzburg has held a Mozart Week (p181) in late January to mark the great composer's birthday on the 27th of the month. The event lures a spectacular list of internationally renowned conductors, soloists and orchestras.

February

The skiing season reaches its zenith with clogged pistes and queues at the ski lifts. Down in the valleys and on the plains you can probably kiss goodbye to the snow as the very first hints of spring appear.

✯ Fasching (Carnival)

During the six-week pre-Lent period (January to February) preceding Ash Wednesday, many towns celebrate with silly costumes, waving parades, incomprehensible satirical shows and drunken revelry, especially in Munich (p69). Rio it ain't.

May

Spring has well and truly *gesprungen*! The cable cars are heaving hikers instead of skiers up the mountainsides, the beer garden season kicks off under flowering chestnut trees and asparagus features on every menu.

✯ Maifest

On the eve of 1 May, the May Festival celebrates the end of winter with villagers chopping down a tree to make a *Maibaum* (maypole), painting, carving and decorating it, then partying around it.

June

Summer is on the way and this is one of the most comfortable months in which to travel before the worst of the heat hits. The solstice (21st) sees bonfires lit on mountaintops throughout Bavaria.

✯ Africa Festival

Bongo drums, hot rhythms and fancy costumes turn the banks of the Main River in Würzburg into Europe's largest international festival of African-origin music. The event (p113) is held in late May or early June and draws around 100,000 visitors.

July

Fleeing the city heat is as easy as buying a train ticket to the cooler air of the Alps. Return to an urban setting in the evenings as the festival season swings into action.

✯ Tollwood Festival

Crowds flock to Munich's Olympiapark for this popular month-long world-culture festival (p69) with concerts, theatre, circus acts, readings and other fun events. It's held from late June to late July, and also has a winter incarnation in December.

✨ Christopher Street Day

Gay, lesbian, straight or transgender – everybody comes out to party at Munich's flashy gay parade (p69) held over two days in mid-July and attracting 50,000 revellers. Provocative costumes, rainbow flags, techno music and naked torsos guaranteed.

✨ Samba Festival

This unlikely orgy of song and dance in mid-July draws a quarter of a million people to normally sedate Coburg for three days of exotically colourful carnival costumes, high-energy music and a procession of gyrating backsides (p145).

✨ Wagner Festival

This prestigious festival (p148) held in Bayreuth from late July to August is *the* Wagner event of the year, attracting opera-goers from every continent. Tickets are hard to come by.

August

Summer is at its peak, the kids are off school, campsites fill with an international fleet of campervans, and the Alpine meadows reach their floral peak.

✨ Sommerfest

Join in four days of gigs, food and partying by the River Neckar in Stuttgart. Held in early August, if the weather is hot the event

(p201) attracts half a million revellers.

✨ Salzburg Festival

One of the most important classical-music festivals in Europe, this premier event (p181) runs from late July to the end of August and features everything from Mozart to contemporary music, opera and theatre. Special performances for children also dot the program.

✨ Gäubodenvolksfest

This epic Oktoberfest-style drink-up and occasion for much red-faced revelry draws around 1.2 million people to little Straubing for 11 days starting on the second Friday of August. Expect lots of oompah music and traditional costumes as well as a fun fair for the little 'uns (p165).

🔒 Stuttgarter Weindorf

Beginning on the last weekend in August, this 10-day event (p201) sees winemakers from the region sell the year's vintages from hundreds of booths on Schlossplatz and the Oberer Schlossgarten.

September

Autumn delivers its first nip, especially at altitude. Pupils return to their schools, students to uni and small-town Germany reverts to its reassuringly predictable central European normality.

✨ Oktoberfest

Oktoberfest should be under October, right? Wrong. It actually takes place more

in September than October. The world's most celebrated guzzle fest (p24) is Bavaria's top event with five million raising a tankard or ten. *Prost!*

✨ Cannstatter Volksfest

Very similar to Oktoberfest, Stuttgart's biggest beer festival (p201) takes place for two weeks from late September to mid-October and features processions, a fairground and a huge firework display to round things off.

🏃 Munich Marathon

Bavaria's top mass-participation running event (p69) wisely takes place just after Oktoberfest, keeping at least the runners sober in the weeks leading up to the race. The course skips through the historical centre before ending in a grandstand finish at the Olympic Stadium.

December

An eventful month with the ski season beginning in earnest and the 5 December visit by St Nick. Bavarian New Year's Eve celebrations see fireworks launched by thousands of amateur (pyro)maniacs.

🔒 Christmas Markets

Celebrate the holidays at glittery Christmas markets with mulled wine, gingerbread cookies and shimmering ornaments. The markets in Munich, Nuremberg, Freiburg and Salzburg are the most famous, but smaller ones sometimes have more local flavour. Open from late November to 24 December (p132).

Plan Your Trip
Oktoberfest

The world's largest drink-a-thon and the traditional highlight of Bavaria's annual events calender, Oktoberfest is one of the best-known fairs on earth. No other event manages to mix such a level of crimson-faced humour, drunken debauchery and excessive consumption of beer with so much tradition, history and oompah music.

Need to Know

Where
At the Theresienwiese to the west of the city centre. Poccistrasse and Theresienwiese are the nearest U-Bahn stations.

When
For 16 days up to the first (or occasionally second) Sunday in October.

2016: 17th September to 3rd October

2017: 23rd September to 8th October

2018: 22nd September to 7th October

Hours
Beer is served from 10am to 10.30pm Monday to Friday, 9am to 10.30pm Saturday and Sunday.

Other attractions and facilities open longer hours.

Costs
Admission to the Oktoberfest: free

Price of a 1L *Mass* of beer: around €10

Half a roast chicken: around €9

Stats
Visitors: between six and seven million

Amount of beer consumed: between six and seven million litres

Beer tents: 35 (14 large, 21 small)

Mass Hysteria

As early as mid-July the brewery crews move in to start erecting the tents which almost fill the Theresienwiese, a gravelly open space in the western reaches of Munich city centre known locally as the Wiesn. When the canvas is taut, the space-age technology is in place to deliver millions of litres of beer to the taps, the Ferris wheel is ready to roll and tens of thousands of chickens are rotating on grills. The Wiesn is ready to welcome the millions of people who arrive annually to toast Germany's 'city of beer'.

During the 16 days of festivities, most travellers dip in for a few days or perhaps a week, taking time off from the *Mass* (the towering 1L mugs of beer) to see Munich's sights and perhaps a castle or two. Whatever you decide to do, be sure to book everything up to a year in advance. And if you can't make it for Oktoberfest, fear not. Throughout the summer and autumn the region hosts countless other fests, often with more traditional, less commercial atmospheres (and cheaper beer). Erding and Straubing have particularly good events.

A Bit of History

The world's biggest foam fest has its origins in a simple horse race. In 1810 Bavarian crown prince Ludwig, later King

Ludwig I, married Princess Therese of Saxe-Hildburghausen, and following the wedding a horse race was held at the city gates. The six-day celebration was such a galloping success that it became an annual event, was extended and moved forward to start in September so that visitors could enjoy warmer weather and lighter nights. The horse race, which quickly became a sideshow to the suds, ended in 1960, but an agricultural show is still part of the Oktoberfest, albeit a small one.

Ozapft ist's!

Starting at 10.45am on the first day, the brewer's parade (the Festzug) travels through the city centre from the River Isar to the fairgrounds. This involves many old, brightly decorated horse-drawn carriages once used to transport kegs from brewery to pub and countless felt-hatted tag alongs. When the procession reaches the Wiesn, focus switches to the Schottenhamel beer tent and the mayor of Munich who, on the stroke of noon, takes a mallet and knocks the tap into the first keg. As the beer flows forth and the thirsty crowds cheer, the mayor exclaims: *'Ozapft ist's!'* (literally 'It's tapped' in Bavarian dialect). If you want to witness this ceremonial opening of the Oktoberfest, be sure to get there as early as 9am to bag a seat.

The Beer

Let's get down to the real reason most come to Oktoberfest – the beer. All the suds pulled at Oktoberfest must have been brewed within Munich's city limits which restricts the number of breweries permitted to wet your whistle to six: Hofbräu-München (of Hofbräuhaus fame), the world famous Paulaner, Löwenbräu, Augustiner, and the less well-known Hacker-Pschorr and Spaten.

The famous 1L *Mass* brought to your table by a Dirndl-trussed waitress, contains pretty strong stuff as the breweries cook up special concoctions for the occasion (usually known as *Oktoberfestbier*). The percentage of alcohol starts at around 5.8% which makes a single *Mass* the equivalent of almost 3.5 pints of most regular ales in Britain, Australia and the US. Traditionally the most potent brews are piped to the Wiesn by Hofbräu, the weakest by Hacker Pschorr.

TOP 10 TIPS

➡ No cash changes hands within the beer tents – to be served beer, buy special metal tokens (*Biermarken*) from outside the tents. If you have tokens left over at the end of your session, you can spend them in some Munich pubs.

➡ No glass bottles are allowed at the Oktoberfest due to countless injuries over the years.

➡ Food at Oktoberfest is as pricey as the beer, so bring your own snacks. These can be consumed on the outside terraces of the beer tents but not inside.

➡ Beer tents are elbow to elbow all day on Saturday and Sunday, but for lighter traffic try a weekday afternoon. Until Friday of the first week the evenings tend to be slightly less swamped as well.

➡ Don't even think of lighting up in any of the beer tents. Anti-smoking laws mean your time in the tent will be up and you could face a fine.

➡ If you pop out of a beer tent during the busy times, don't expect your seat to be free when you return.

➡ Don't drink in excess – the beer at Oktoberfest is strong stuff, and probably much more potent than your local brew back home.

➡ The vast majority of the beer tents have their last call at 10.30pm.

➡ The Wiesn has its own post office, left luggage office and childcare centre.

➡ You can reserve a seat at some of the beer tents up to a year in advance – see the tents' individual websites to find out how.

OKTOBERFEST'S ASTOUNDING STATS

➡ The biggest ever beer tent was the Bräurosl of 1913 which held a whopping 12,000 drinkers.

➡ Munich's biggest bash of the year has been cancelled an amazing 24 times, mostly due to cholera epidemics and war. There was no Oktoberfest during either world wars and in 1923 and 1924 inflation put paid to the festivities.

➡ If you are your party's nominated driver, don't think you're getting off lightly when it comes to the bill. A litre of water costs almost as much as a *Mass* of beer!

➡ Some 90,000L of wine are supped over the 16 days of Wiesn frolics.

➡ It takes around 10 weeks to erect the beer tents and five weeks to dismantle them.

➡ Around 12,000 waiters and waitresses are employed at Oktoberfest.

➡ Around 75% of the Munich Red Cross' annual workload occurs during Oktoberfest.

➡ Around 900 passports are handed into the lost property office each year.

Not Just Beer

The Oktoberfest is not called the world biggest fair for nothing, and while most visitor's focus is on the *bier*, there's quite a lot going on away from the tents.

The funfair with its big wheel, ye-olde test-your-strength booths and scarier 21st-century rides are obvious attractions but magic performances, an agricultural show (it's more interesting than it sounds) and stalls selling everything from Oktoberfest souvenirs to waffles constitute other minor diversions. The first Sunday sees an impressive costumed procession wend its way through Munich city centre, a tradition going back to 1835, and the customary religious Oktoberfest mass is held in the Hippodrom beer tent on the first Thursday. A brass band concert huffs and puffs beneath the Bavaria statue on the morning of the second Sunday near the spot from where the gun salute is fired on the last Sunday. These events are mostly attended by locals, but give a more traditional insight into the origins and customs of this blockbuster fair for those with a deeper, less inebriated interest.

Sleeping It Off

Your chances of scoring a room in Munich once the mayor has driven the tap into the famous first keg are next to nil, and even a bed in the dingiest of dorms will come with an absurd price tag. However, with Munich's excellent transport links to the rest of Bavaria, and the proximity of the Hauptbahnhof to the Theresienwiese, commuting in from Augsburg, Garmisch-Partenkirchen or Ingolstadt, or even Salzburg and Nuremberg, is feasible. This secret got out long ago, and accommodation providers across Bavaria hitch up their rates from mid-September, but not as much as in Munich. Book accommodation just as the previous Oktoberfest is finishing if possible. If you decide to stay out of town, make sure you know when the last train back is, or you'll be spending a potentially chilly night at the Hauptbahnhof!

Camping is a fun and relatively inexpensive way to get around the accommodation shortage. Wiesn Camp (www.munich-oktoberfest.com) sets up shop every year at the Olympic Equestrian Centre in München-Riem, a 20-minute S-Bahn ride from the Hauptbahnhof. The site offers four-man tent hire for between €59 and €79 a night. Another place you won't need your own rustling nylon is The Tent (www.the-tent.com) where you can bed down in the communal FloorTent for as little as €15 a night!

Family Fun

The two Tuesday afternoons (from noon to 6pm) are dedicated family days with reduced charges for funfair rides, special family oriented events, and lots of balloons and roasted almonds. Away from these days, the Augustiner Festhalle is regarded as the most family-friendly beer tent, but children are allowed into all the others. All tots under six must be out by 8pm every day. The tents have become better places for

Above: Hofbräu-
Festzelt at Oktoberfest

Right: Horses and cart,
Oktoberfest parade

children since the music was turned down (until 6pm) and smoking was banned.

Dirndl & Lederhosen

Part of the fun at the Wiesn is looking the part: traditional Bavarian Dirndl for the gals, Lederhosen and felt hat for the guys. Dirndl consists of a figure-squeezing bodice, a frilly blouse, a skirt that ends just below the knee and an apron. The real deal costs a Hellenic bailout of euros but Munich has countless discount *Trachten* (folk costume) shops where cheaper versions can be bought. For second-hand Dirndl and Lederhosen, try Holareidulijö (p83).

Top Beer Tents

Here is our selection of the Wiesn's finest marquees:

➡ **Hippodrom** (www.hippodrom-oktoberfest. de) Seating 3200 inside, this popular tent attracts a young crowd and the odd German celebrity. Spatenbräu and Löwenbräu beers and top-notch Bavarian food, plus lots of gobsmackingly pricey champagne.

➡ **Hofbräu-Festzelt** (www.hb-festzelt.de) Including the beer garden and standing room, this tent can accommodate almost 10,000 drinkers. A favourite among English-speaking visitors.

➡ **Schottenhamel** (www.festzelt. schottenhamel.de) Where Munich's mayor kicks off the whole caboodle with a little mallet.

➡ **Käfers Wiesen Schänke** Exellent food, longer opening hours (to 1am) and Paulaner beer make this a popular tent with partying celebs and wannabes.

➡ **Glöckle Wirt** (www.gloeckle-wirt.de) If you fancy something a bit different, this is one of the most attractive, most intimate and smallest of the beer tents, bedecked with antiques and knickknacks of yesteryear.

Online Resources

➡ **Oktoberfest** (www.oktoberfest.de) The definitive Oktoberfest website containing a wealth of facts, figures and maps.

➡ **City of Munich** (www.oktoberfest.eu) The official Oktoberfest pages from the City of Munich website.

IMPORTANT OKTOBERFEST NUMBERS

Don't forget that when calling from a mobile, the dialling code for Munich is 089.

➡ **Security Point** ☏5022 2366
➡ **First-aid post** ☏5022 2424
➡ **Oktoberfest police station** ☏500 3220
➡ **Guided tours of the Oktoberfest** ☏232 3900
➡ **Oktoberfest Lost & Found office** ☏2338 2825
➡ **Taxi** ☏21 610

➡ **Oktoberfest-TV** (www.oktoberfest-tv.de) Webcam coverage of the event plus heaps of info.

➡ **Bavarian Tourist Portal** (www.bavaria. by) General information in English on the Oktoberfest from the Bavarian Tourist Board.

➡ **Wiesn Countdown** (www.wiesn-countdown. com) Find out exactly how many seconds remain until the next Oktoberfest.

Dangers & Annoyances

Seven million litres of strong Oktoberfest beer equates to a lot of intoxicating ethanol and, as you might expect, drunkenness is the main source of danger during Oktoberfest. Things tend to be pretty calm within the beer tents themselves, but it's late at night, when the elbow bending is over, that trouble can flare up as the inebriated masses stagger to the Hauptbahnhof and other stations. Stay well clear of any bother.

For problems at the Wiesn itself, the Oktoberfest has its own dedicated police force, lost and found office, first-aid post and fire brigade.

Aktion Sichere Wiesn für Mädchen und Frauen (www.sicherewiesn.de) offers free multilingual assistance at Oktoberfest to women who have been sexually harassed or feel otherwise unsafe. It is located below the Bavaria statue in the Service Centre (Servicezentrum in German) and is open from 6pm to 1am.

There have been rare cases of drink spiking at Oktoberfest.

Itineraries

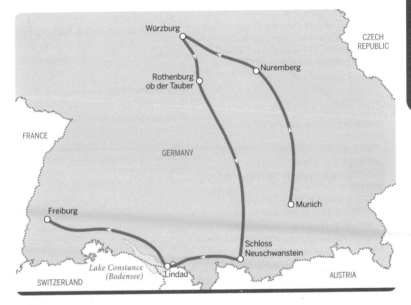

 **Southern Germany Highlights**

This itinerary takes in the best of the region in a whistle-stop tour of southern Germany's must-sees. You could spend months exploring the region but 10 days is just enough to tick off the essentials.

Kick off your southern odyssey in **Munich** where three days is barely enough time to sample the Bavarian capital's art and beer. A short hop north by train brings you to **Nuremberg**, the bustling capital of Franconia and a major draw for fans of both dark tourism and dark beer. Another train, another historic city, this time university town **Würzburg** well known for its wines and the famous prince-bishop's residence. You're now at the northern terminus of the 350km-long Romantic Road. The most engaging stop along the route is **Rothenburg ob der Tauber**, a labyrinth of medieval streets and lanes with heaps of sugary architecture. The Romantic Road ends at the gates of **Schloss Neuschwanstein**, Bavarian King Ludwig II's fairy-tale pad and one of the world's most iconic 19th-century follies. Stop off at **Lindau** on the shores of Lake Constance en route to **Freiburg** in the southern Black Forest, where you can follow a tour of the Münster with a slab of the famous local gateau.

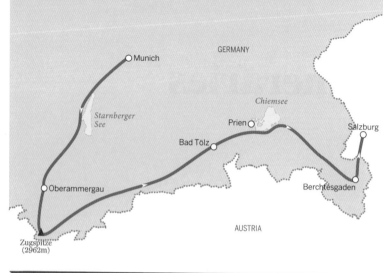

Munich & the Alps

10 DAYS

The Alps are one of the definite highlights of Bavaria and almost every visitor makes at least one trip to these famous peaks. This itinerary includes the best stop-offs and includes everything from lakes in the foothills to a train ride to the top of the highest peak.

This itinerary can be tackled as a point-to-point trip or as day trips from Munich; the German Alps are easily reachable by train from there. Beginning in **Munich**, you'll need at least three days to cover the essential viewing in this vibrant metropolis, perhaps reserving a bit of time for a spot of shopping and to visit some of the city's lesser known sights such as the Olympiapark and BMW Welt. If there's time, gobsmackingly beautiful **Starnberger See** is an S-Bahn ride away. Pretty **Oberammergau**, famous for its once-a-decade passion play, is just over two hours (with changes) on the train from Munich's Hauptbahnhof and makes a superb base for visiting King Ludwig II's Schloss Linderhof, an easy going 12km hike. Then it's time to stand on the roof of Germany: the **Zugspitze** above Garmisch-Partenkirchen, the Bundesrepublik's highest peak. If you don't have your own wheels you'll have to backtrack all the way to Munich to reach the spa town of **Bad Tölz**, home to Alpamare, the region's best water park. Heading east, more train connections bring you to the **Chiemsee** in no time. Water sports are one of the big draws here, though most come for another of Ludwig II's palaces, Schloss Herrenchiemsee, set on an island (the Herreninsel) in the lake and accessible by ferry from the town of **Prien**. After a day of messing around on the *wasser* (water) it's back into the mountains, this time the ranges around **Berchtesgaden** in Germany's extreme southeastern tip. Some intriguing Nazi history, particularly Hitler's mountain perch, the Eagle's Nest, now a seasonal restaurant, draws many visitors. For an equally photogenic escapade, take one of the electric boats from Berchtesgaden along the stunningly picturesque Königssee, surrounded by the Berchtesgaden National Park. From Berchtesgaden it's a short bus ride into Austria and a day or two of *Sound of Music*–mania in achingly beautiful **Salzburg**.

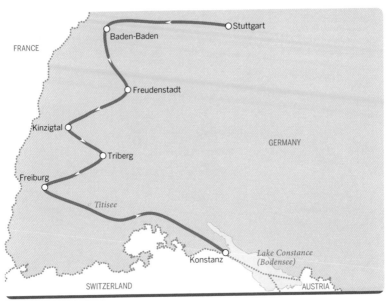

Stuttgart & Black Forest

1 WEEK

This zigzagging canter through Germany's southwest is one for those who like a varied time when on their travels – the route is a mix of cuckoo clocks and state-of-the art luxury car museums, half-timbered villages and the big-city vibe of Stuttgart.

Begin with a couple of days exploring the galleries, stately plazas and vibrant nightlife of regional capital **Stuttgart**. High on your agenda should be the city's regal heart, Schlossplatz, the Staatsgalerie's art treasures and evenings spent sampling local rieslings in a *Weinstube* (wine tavern) or hanging out in Theodor-Heuss-Strasse's lounge bars. Car fans should race to the space-age Mercedes-Benz and Porsche museums. On day three, head west to **Baden-Baden**, a swish art-nouveau spa town picturesquely nestled at the foot of the Black Forest's spruce-cloaked hills. Here you can wallow in thermal waters, saunter through the sculpture-speckled Lichtentaler Allee gardens and try your luck in the casino. Day four takes you south along the serpentine Schwarzwald-Hochstrasse, or B500, with tremendous forest and mountain panoramas at every bend. Stop to glimpse Germany's largest square in **Freudenstadt** on your way to the curving **Kinzigtal**, the prettiest valley in this neck of the woods, with its orchards, vineyards and cluster of half-timbered villages. Your fifth day takes you to the Black Forest's most storied town, **Triberg**, where Germany's highest waterfall flows, the world's biggest cuckoo clock calls, and Claus Schäfer bakes *the* best Black Forest gateau using the original 1915 recipe. Work off the cake with a walk or cross-country ski in the wooded heights of Martinskapelle or Stöcklewaldturm. A scenic hour's drive from Triberg brings you to the sunny university city of **Freiburg**, close to the French border. Spend the day absorbing its easygoing flair in the Altstadt's quaint lanes, watched over by a monster of a medieval minster. Wind out your final day by the lake. Swinging east brings you to forest-rimmed **Titisee** en route to the watery expanse of **Lake Constance**, Central Europe's third largest lake, flanked by quaint villages, vineyards, wetlands and beaches. An afternoon in **Konstanz** is just long enough to get a taste of this Roman-rooted city, where the historic alleys of the Altstadt wend down to a relaxed lakefront promenade.

Romantic Road
Nuremburg & Franconia

1 WEEK Romantic Road

1 WEEK Nuremberg & Franconia

Germany's most popular tourist route winds its way for 350km through Bavaria's western reaches.

The Romantic Road begins at **Würzburg** where two days are enough to tour the impressive Baroque Residenz and sample the region's wines. From here carve your way south to magical **Rothenburg ob der Tauber** where you can lose yourself in the tangle of medieval lanes and celebrate Christmas every day. Your next destination is quaint little **Dinkelsbühl**, a medieval gem ringed by a complete set of town walls. More medieval defences ring **Nördlingen**, a less touristy but equally attractive stopover. Then set aside some time to check out the storybook castle guarding the half-timbered village of **Harburg**, and to stroll through twee **Donauwörth** before hitting the energetic city of **Augsburg**, the Romantic Road's biggest city with countless attractions. Many a church graces the Romantic Road but, to Augsburg's south, the one packing the mightiest punch is the luminous Wieskirche, a true baroque masterpiece. Contemplate King Ludwig II's flights of fancy at his whimsical castle, **Schloss Neuschwanstein**, where the route comes to a fittingly fairy-tale climax.

Franconia has a quite different feel to it than southern Bavaria and this itinerary gives a taste of what the region is all about.

The lively capital of Franconia, **Nuremberg** has bags to see and do – including the Nuremberg trials courtroom, the Germanisches Nationalmuseum and the Deutsche Bahn Railway Museum – and an embarrassment of eateries to choose from when you return from exploring the region. A close second in Franconia's pecking order is Unesco-listed **Bamberg**, a confusion of ancient bridges, winding cobbled streets and riverside cottages, the air perfumed by numerous breweries producing the town's unique *Rauchbier* (smoked beer). An hour's train ride brings you to **Bayreuth**, famous for its annual Wagner Festival but a pleasant place to stroll any time of year. Around 100km north of Nuremberg, **Coburg** is memorable for its fortress, its British Royal family connections and the longest sausages you'll ever eat served in the smallest bread buns. Round off your time in Franconia with a hike, bike or canoe trip (requiring more time) through the glorious **Naturpark Altmühltal**.

Plan Your Trip

Outdoor Activities

Bavaria and the Black Forest certainly live up to their reputations as first-rate outdoor destinations. There's plenty to do year-round, with each season offering its own special delights, be it hiking among spring wildflowers, swimming in an Alpine lake warmed by the summer sun, biking among a kaleidoscope of autumn foliage or celebrating winter by skiing through deep powder.

Hiking & Mountaineering

Der Weg ist das Ziel (the journey is the reward) could be the perfect strapline for Bavaria and the Black Forest. No matter whether you want to peak-bag in the Alps, stroll gently among fragrant spruce and pine with the kids or embark on multiday treks over hill and forested dale, this region is brilliant for exploring on foot.

Trails are usually well signposted, sometimes with symbols quaintly painted on tree trunks. To find a route matching your fitness level and time frame, pick the brains of local tourist office staff, who may also be able to supply you with maps and tips. Some offer multiday 'hiking without luggage' packages that include accommodation and luggage transfer between hotels.

The sky-scraping peaks of the Bavarian Alps are Germany's mountaineering heartland. Here you can pick between day treks and multiday hut-to-hut clambers, though you'll need to be reasonably fit and come equipped with the right gear and topographic maps or GPS. Trails can be steep and narrow, with icy patches lingering well into early summer. Before heading out, seek local advice on routes, equipment and weather. If you're inexperienced, ask tourist offices about local outfitters offering instruction, equipment rental and guided tours.

Best...

Skiing
Garmisch-Partenkirchen – A holy grail for downhill skiers, with titanic peaks, groomed slopes and an impeccable snow record.

Hiking
Black Forest National Park – Mile after pine-scented mile of trails weaving through forests, mist-enshrouded valleys and half-timbered villages that look like something from a bedtime storybook.

Mountaineering
Bavarian Alps – Grapple with limestone peaks in this mountaineering wonderland.

Windsurfing
Walchensee – Let your sail catch the breeze on this jewel-coloured, mountain-rimmed lake.

Cycling
Altmühltal Radweg – A 'Best of Bavaria' bike ride, taking in river bends and dense forests, ragged limestone cliffs and castle-topped villages.

The **Deutscher Alpenverein** (DAV; ☑089 140 030; www.alpenverein.de) is a mine of information on hiking and mountaineering, and has local branches in practically every town. It maintains hundreds of Alpine mountain huts, where you can spend the night and get a meal. Local DAV chapters also organise courses (climbing, mountaineering etc) as well as guided treks. If you're planning multiday treks, becoming a member of the organisation can yield a 30% to 50% discount on Alpine huts and other benefits, including insurance.

For climbing routes, gear, walls and more, visit www.dav-felsinfo.de, www.klettern.de and www.climbing.de (all in German).

When to Walk

The summer months are the best for walking in the Alps, when snow retreats to the highest peaks, and wildflowers carpet the slopes. Rush hour is from July to August when you'll need to book hut accommodation well in advance. Autumn has its own charm, with fewer crowds and a riot of colour in deciduous forests. Snow makes it impossible to undertake high-altitude walks during the rest of the year. Many of the big resorts, however, are criss-crossed with winter walking trails, and crunching through snow with a crisp blue sky overhead certainly has its own magic.

Resources

➡ **German National Tourist Office** (www.germany.travel) Your first port of call, with information in English on walking in Bavaria and the Black Forest.

➡ **Kompass** (www.kompass.de, in German) Has a reliable series of 1:25,000 scale walking maps, which come with booklets listing background information on trails.

➡ **Wanderbares Deutschland** (www.wanderbares-deutschland.de) Features the lowdown on dozens of walking trails and has a handy interactive map. Some routes are also detailed in English.

➡ **Wandern ohne Gepäck** (www.wandern-ohne-gepaeck-deutschland.de, in German) Touch base with the 'hiking without luggage' specialists.

Winter Sports

Modern lifts, primed ski runs from easy-peasy blues to death-wish blacks, solitary cross-country trails, log huts, steaming mulled wine, hearty dinners by a crackling fire – these are the hallmarks of a German skiing holiday.

The Bavarian Alps, only an hour's drive south of Munich, offers the best downhill slopes and most reliable snow conditions. The most famous and ritzy resort is **Garmisch-Partenkirchen** (☑4931, 74260; www.skischule-gap.de; Am Hausberg 8; 1-day group lessons €35, ski gear €25), which hosted the FIS Alpine Skiing World Championship 2011 and is but a snowball's throw from Germany's highest peak, 2962m Zugspitze. The resort has 60km of slopes to pound, mostly geared towards intermediates.

STAR TREKS FOR...

➡ **Alpine hikers** Swoon over views of colossal mountains and jewel-coloured lakes hiking in the Berchtesgaden National Park (p108) and Oberstdorf (p102).

➡ **Family ramblers** Kiddies love the wondrous Partnachklamm gorge (p98) and red squirrel-spotting on the trail shadowing the 163m Triberger Wasserfall (p243), Germany's highest waterfall.

➡ **Serious mountaineers** One word: Zugspitze (p98). The tough ascent and phenomenal four-country views are breathtaking in every sense of the word.

➡ **Long-distance hikers** Trek Bavaria's beautiful 200km Altmühltal-Panoramaweg (p148) or the 280km Westweg (p226), the ultimate walk in the Black Forest.

➡ **Wildlife spotters** Wander silently for the chance to see deer, otters, and woodpeckers in the Bavarian Forest National Park (p166) and eagles, chamois, marmots and salamanders in Berchtesgaden National Park (p108).

➡ **Escapists** Seek solace hiking in the fir-cloaked hills of the Black Forest and the Bavarian Forest National Park (p166).

TOP FIVE BIKE TOURING TRAILS

➡ **Altmühltal Radweg** (160km) Easy to moderate route from Rothenburg to Beilngries, following the Altmühl River through the Altmühltal Nature Park.

➡ **Donauradweg** (434km) Travelling from Neu-Ulm to Passau, this is a delightful, easy to moderate riverside trip along one of Europe's great streams.

➡ **Romantische Strasse** (359km) Würzburg to Füssen; this easy to moderate route is one of the nicest ways to explore Germany's most famous holiday route, though it can get busy during the summer peak season.

➡ **Bodensee-Königssee Radweg** (418km) Lindau to Berchtesgaden; a moderate route running along the foot of the Alps with magnificent views.

➡ **Bodensee Cycle Path** (273km) Mostly flat, well-marked, tri-country route, which does a loop of Europe's third largest lake, taking in vineyards, meadows, orchards, wetlands, historic towns and Alpine vistas.

Picture-book pretty Oberstdorf in the Allgäu Alps forms the heart of the Oberstdorf-Kleinwalsertal ski region, where 125km of slopes are covered by a single ski pass. It's a good pick for boarders, with snow parks and a half-pipe to play on, and cross-country skiers who come to glide along 75km of classic and 55km of skating tracks. For low-key skiing and stunning scenery, there is **Jenner** (p108) near Berchtesgaden, with vertical drops up to 600m and truly royal vistas of the emerald Königssee, and family-magnet Kranzberg in Mittenwald.

Elsewhere in the country, the mountains may not soar as high as in the Alps, but assets include cheaper prices, smaller crowds, and resorts with a low-key atmosphere suited to families. The Bavarian Forest and the Black Forest have the most reliable snow levels, with moderate downhill action on the Grosser Arber and Feldberg mountains respectively.

At higher elevations, the season generally runs from late November/early December to March. Resorts have equipment-hire facilities. Skis, boots and poles cost around €20/12 for downhill/cross-country gear. Group lessons cost €30 to €45 per day.

Resources

➡ **Bergfex** (www.bergfex.com) A handy website with piste maps, snow forecasts of the Alps and details of German ski resorts.

➡ **On the Snow** (www.onthesnow.co.uk) Reviews of Germany's ski resorts, plus snow reports, webcams and lift pass details.

➡ **Skiresort** (www.skiresort.de) Ski resorts searchable by map and region, with piste details, pass prices and more.

Cycling & Mountain Biking

Strap on your helmet! Bavaria and the Black Forest are superb cycling territory, whether you're off on a leisurely lakeside spin or a multiday bike touring adventure. Practically every town and region has a network of signposted bike routes. For day tours, staff at the local tourist offices can supply you with ideas, maps and advice.

Mountain biking is hugely popular in the Black Forest and in the Alpine region, especially around Garmisch-Partenkirchen (p99), Berchtesgaden (p108) and Freudenstadt (p226). The Bavarian Forest is another top destination for mountain bikers with more than 450km of challenging routes and climbs. The mountain-bike elite comes to the Black Forest for several international MTB races, including the Black Forest Ultra Bike Marathon (www.ultra-bike.de) in June, the Worldclass MTB Challenge (www.womc.de) in July and the Vaude Trans Schwarzwald (www.trans-schwarzwald.com) in August.

Southern Germany is criss-crossed by dozens of long-distance trails, making it ideal for *Radwandern* (bike touring). Routes are well signposted and typically are a combination of lightly travelled back roads, forestry tracks and paved highways with dedicated bike lanes.

Bike Rental

Most towns have at least one bike-hire station (often at or near the train station), usually with a choice of city, mountain, electro and children's bikes. Depending on the

THE BIG CHILL

If climbing mountains or whizzing down slopes has left you frazzled and achy, a trip to a day spa may be just the ticket. Every place has its own array of massages and treatments. Not a stitch of clothing is worn in German saunas, so leave your modesty in the locker, and always bring or hire a towel.

➡ **Friedrichsbad** (p220) The crown jewel of Baden-Baden's spas, with its Roman Irish bath and Carrera marble pool.

➡ **Alpamare** (p104) Great family all-rounder with surfing, water slides and a wave pool for kids, mineral baths, saunas and treatments for grown-ups.

➡ **Watzmann Therme** (p108) Perfect for a soak in the Bavarian Alps.

➡ **Sanitas Spa** (p243) Snuggled in the Black Forest, this Triberg spa has first-class treatments, a pool with views of forest-draped hills and, ahhh... blissfully few crowds.

➡ **Kaiser-Friedrich-Therme** (www.wiesbaden.de; Langgasse 38-40; per hr May-Aug €4.50, Sep-Apr €6; ⊙10am-10pm, to midnight Fri & Sat Sep-Apr, women only Tue) Splash around as the Romans once did at this regal-looking spa in Wiesbaden, where spring water bubbles up at 66.4°C.

➡ **Rupertustherme** (☎01805-606 706; Friedrich-Ebert-Allee 21; 4hr ticket €14, incl sauna €19; ⊙9am-10pm) Saline-spring day spa with big Alpine views.

model, you'll pay between €10 to €40 per day or €50 to €120 per week, plus a deposit.

Route Planning

For inspiration and route planning, check out www.germany-tourism, which provides (in English) an overview of routes, helpful planning tips, a route finder and free downloads of route maps and descriptions. For more detailed route descriptions German readers can consult www.schwarzwald-bike.de, www.blackforest-tourism.com and www.bayernbike.de. The Galli Verlag (www.galli-verlag.de) publishes a variety of bike guides sold in bookshops and by the publisher.

Maps & Resources

For basic route maps, order or download the free *Bayernnetz für Radler* (Bavarian Cycling Network) from www.bayerninfo.de. For on-the-road navigating, the best maps are those published by the national cycling organisation Allgemeiner Deutscher Fahrrad Club (www.adfc.de). They indicate inclines, track conditions and the location of repair shops. GPS users should find the UTM grid coordinates useful.

ADFC also publishes a useful online directory called Bett & Bike (www.bettundbike.de) that lists thousands of bicycle-friendly accommodations. Bookstores stock the printed version.

Water Sports

There's no sea for miles but southern Germany's lakes and rivers offer plenty of water-based action. The water quality is high, especially in the glacier-fed Alpine lakes, but the swimming season is relatively short (June to September) since water temperatures rarely climb above 21°C. Steady breezes, deep water and good visibility attract windsurfers and divers to the dazzlingly turquoise, mountain-backed Walchensee in Tölzer Land. Starnberger See, Lake Constance, the fjordlike Schluchsee and Chiemsee offer great windsurfing, sailing and boating in lovely surroundings.

Kayaking and canoeing are great fun and easy to get the hang of. One of the most popular areas to absorb the slow, soothing rhythm of waterways is the Altmühltal Nature Park (p148), where the mellow Altmühl River meanders past steep cliffs, willow-fringed banks and little beaches.

Canyoning is growing in popularity across Europe and southern Germany is no exception. Suitable sites have been identified across the region – contact **Xconcepts** (☎0151 1143 6890; www.xconcepts.de) near Oberstdorf for guided canyoning excursions.

Plan Your Trip

Travel with Children

With its tradition of lager, beer halls, Lederhosen and tipsy oompah ensembles, you'd be excused for thinking southern Germany is a wholly unsuitable place to bring the little'uns. But you'd be wrong. Germany's south, especially its larger cities, lays on lots of tot-focused activities. In fact, having kids on board can make your holiday a more enjoyable experience and bring you closer to the locals than a few tankards of ale ever could.

On the Ground

In Transit

Trains are preferable to buses when travelling with toddlers as they can leave their seats and wander around quite safely. All trains have at least half a carriage dedicated to carrying prams (and bikes and wheelchairs) and copious amounts of luggage.

Most forms of city transport – such as Munich's trams, trains and underground – are pram-friendly and lifts are ubiquitous. Various discounts are available for families.

Most car-hire companies provide child booster and baby seats. They are often free but must be reserved in advance.

Feeding Frenzy

When it comes to feeding the pack, Germany's south is one of Europe's easier destinations. Most restaurants welcome young diners with smaller portions, special menus and perhaps even a free balloon.

Youngsters under 16 are allowed into pubs and bars at any time, as long as they are accompanied by a parent. This includes beer halls and gardens, the latter being particularly popular with families who can bring their own picnics. Thanks

Best Places for Kids

Nuremberg

Bavaria's most child-friendly city with attractions as diverse as the Deutsche Bahn Museum, a school museum and a zoo.

Munich

Plenty of hands-on and high-octane diversions as well as a classic toy museum and fantastic trams to ride all day.

Rothenburg ob der Tauber

Edible snowballs and Christmas tree lights in the heat of the summer holidays – pure magic if you're six.

Europa Park

Europe in miniature and Welt der Kinder (Children's World) at Germany's biggest theme park.

Ulm

Most kids love Lego and most adults love the fact Legoland keeps them occupied for a few hours.

Triberg

Some kids will burst into tears at the sight of a titchy bird lurching out of a clock, others will go cuckoo at the very thought.

to Germany's smoking ban, fume-filled premises are a thing of the past.

Breastfeeding in public is perfectly acceptable.

All Change

City centres can be a headache for parents of nappy-wearing children – your best bet is to dip into a department store, though these usually position their toilets as far away from the entrance as possible, on the very top floor. Things are better at places of interest, and at child-centric attractions nappy-changing amenities are first rate. In emergencies you can pop into the nearest pub or restaurant – staff rarely object.

Discounts

Family tickets are available at the vast majority of sights. It's always worth asking if there's a discount, even if none is advertised.

Children's Highlights

Museums

➡ **Deutsches Museum, Munich** (p60) The KinderReich at Munich's science museum is hands-on fun.

➡ **Deutsche Bahn Museum, Nuremberg** (p128) Germany's top railway museum has a huge interactive section for choo-choo enthusiasts.

➡ **Children & Young People's Museum, Nuremberg** (p135) Heaps of hands-on experiments.

➡ **Weihnachtsdorf, Rothenburg ob der Tauber** (p118) This Romantic Road institution houses a hands-off museum meaning kids are usually more interested in the adjacent Yuletide superstore.

➡ **Spielzeugmuseum, Munich** (p47) An I-had-that-in-1974 kinda museum, so not just for kids.

KINDERLAND BAVARIA

Overseen by the Bavarian tourist board, the Kinderland Bavaria program (www.bavaria.by) guarantees the good standard of children's facilities as well as rating amenities used by holidaying families. Businesses sporting the Kinderland Bavaria logo have been checked for everything from toy safety to availability of pram storage.

➡ **Bayerisches Eisenbahnmuseum, Nördlingen** (p121) Retired locos to clamber around on and seasonal steam train rides.

➡ **Spielzeugmuseum, Salzburg** (p182) Classic toy museum with Punch and Judy shows and free tea for the adults.

Fresh-Air Fun

➡ **Playground of the Senses, Nuremberg** (p135) Education by stealth at this large open-air experiment park.

➡ **Englischer Garten, Munich** (p57) Large playground, ice creams, boat rides and acres of grass.

➡ **Steinwasen Park, Black Forest** (p238) Alpine animals, rides and a huge hanging bridge.

➡ **Tierpark Hellabrunn, Munich** (p68) Themed playgrounds, a cafe, feeding sessions and a special children's zoo.

Rainy Day Sights

➡ **Playmobil, Nuremberg** (p135) Head-quartered in Zindorf just outside Nuremberg, the adjoining fun park is one of the city's best family attractions.

➡ **Münchner Marionetten Theater, Munich** (p65) Bavaria's top puppet theatre.

➡ **BMW Welt, Munich** (p64) Grip the wheel of BMW's latest models and wish you were old enough to have a driver's licence.

➡ **Alpamare, Bad Tölz** (p104) Aqua-fun for all the family at Bavaria's best water park.

Planning

When to Go

The best times to visit are spring and early autumn. Summer temperatures see the niggle factor climb and central Europe's subzero winters are no fun.

Sleeping

The majority of hotels and guesthouses are pretty kid-friendly and the higher up the food chain you ascend, the more facilities (baby-sitting, laundry) there are likely to be. Small-hotel and guesthouse owners are generally willing to supply extra beds and even cots for babies. Of course campsites are the most entertaining places to stay; some have playgrounds and kids' clubs.

Regions at a Glance

Munich

History
Museums
Beer

Historic Sights

Losing yourself in the House of Wittelsbach's opulent Residenz, taking a guided tour of Nazi-related sites or discovering the city's recent sporting past at the Olympiapark and Allianz Arena are just some of the history-rich experiences on offer.

Well-Rounded Culture

From the hands-on fun of the Deutsches Museum to the high-brow, hands-off masterpieces of the Alte Pinakothek, the outrageous pop art of the Museum Brandhorst to the waxed classics of the BMW Museum, Munich has a repository of the past for every rainy day, and one for most sunny ones, too.

Oktoberfest Ales

Mammoth beer halls swaying to the oompah beat, chestnut-canopied beer gardens and Oktoberfest, proud breweries striving to out-brew their rivals and breakfasts of Weissbier and *Weisswurst* – Munich is the unchallenged beer capital of the world.

p42

Bavaria

Castles
Romance
Mountains

Fairy-Tale Palaces

From spectacular hilltop follies such as Neuschwanstein to medieval strongholds like Nuremberg's Kaiserburg, visits to castles and palaces provide some of Bavaria's most memorable days out.

Romantic Scenery

Whether it be the panorama from an Alpine peak or a lazy cruise along the Danube, Bavaria packs in a lot of dreamy encounters. But the biggest chunk of romance comes in the form of the Romantic Road, a mostly rural route meandering from one time-warped medieval town to the next.

Alpine Magic

Compared to its neighbours, Bavaria possesses but a scant sliver of the Alps, but there's still bags of dramatic scenery out there to enjoy. Clearly visible and easily reachable from Munich, winter skiing and summer hiking are the main draws.

p89

Salzburg & Around

Music
Architecture
Outdoor Activities

Mozart & Maria

In the city that sired Mozart, music is in Salzburg's blood. *Sound of Music* bike tours rattle through the tangled lanes, while classical music climaxes during August's Salzburg Festival.

Baroque Treasures

They broke the baroque mold when they refashioned Salzburg following the counter-reformation, and it's all thanks to some high-minded prince-archbishops. Ramble among architectural riches like the lordly Residenz and Dom in the Unesco World Heritage–listed Altstadt.

Mountains

Mother Superior sang about climbing every mountain, but now cable cars zip up Salzburg's peaks. Take in the full sweep of the city from Mönchsberg and Kapuzinerberg; hike, ski and paraglide at Untersberg and Gaisberg; or delve into the Alps for serious outdoor action.

p168

Stuttgart & the Black Forest

Landscapes
Outdoor Activities
City Life

Lyrical Landscapes

The Black Forest is fairy-tale Germany in a nutshell. This forested patchwork of hills and valleys, where waterfalls and brooks run swift and clear, is one of the region's greatest escapes. Tiptoe off the beaten track to half-timbered villages and tucked-away farmhouses.

Skiing & Hiking

Big views, bracing air and well-marked trails lure you outdoors here. Strap on boots for some of Germany's best hiking or swish through snowy woodlands on cross-country skis. Lake Constance is perfect cycling terrain.

Cultured Cities

Stuttgart woos with outstanding galleries, concert halls and high-tech temples to the automobile, but there's more. Soak in the spas of Baden-Baden, hang out in Roman-rooted Konstanz, and spy the world's tallest steeple in Ulm.

p196

On the Road

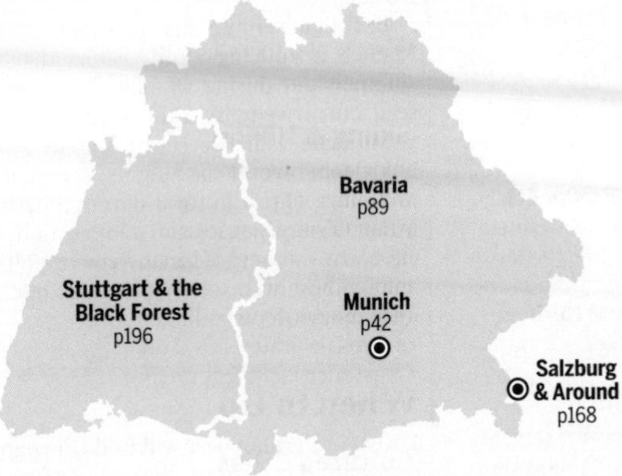

Bavaria
p89

Stuttgart & the Black Forest
p196

Munich
p42
⊙

Salzburg & Around
⊙
p168

Munich

🖉089 / POP 1.38 MILLION

Best Places to Eat

➡ Fraunhofer (p75)

➡ Königsquelle (p74)

➡ Tantris (p76)

➡ Prinz Myshkin (p74)

➡ Esszimmer (p77)

Best Places to Drink

➡ Alter Simpl (p79)

➡ Augustiner Bräustuben (p81)

➡ Hofbräuhaus (p78)

➡ Hirschgarten (p80)

➡ Baader Café (p79)

Why Go?

The natural habitat of well-heeled power dressers and Lederhosen-clad thigh-slappers, Mediterranean-style street cafes and Mitteleuropa beer halls, highbrow art and high-tech industry, Germany's unofficial southern capital is a flourishing success story that revels in its own contradictions. If you're looking for Alpine clichés, they're all here, but the Bavarian metropolis has many an unexpected card down its Dirndl.

But whatever else this city is, it's popular. Statistics show Munich is enticing more visitors than ever, especially in summer and during Oktoberfest, when the entire planet seems to arrive to toast the town.

Munich's walkable centre retains a small-town air but holds some world-class sights, especially art galleries and museums. Throw in royal Bavarian heritage, an entire suburb of Olympic legacy and a kitbag of dark tourism, and it's clear why southern Germany's metropolis is such a favourite among those who seek out the past but like to hit the town once they're done.

When to Go

Lovers of German beer will find true happiness in Munich's beer halls during Stark Bier Zeit (strong beer season). This popular festival takes place for three weeks in February or March and is the time to sup the strong ale monks once brewed to sustain themselves through the Lenten fast.

September to October is the best time to amble in the Englischer Garten (English Garden) as its trees fire off an autumnal salute.

In December, pretty Marienplatz at the city's heart fills with Christmassy stalls, lights and enough yuletide cheer to share among its international gaggle of shoppers.

History

It was Benedictine monks, drawn by fertile farmland and the closeness to Catholic Italy, who settled in what is now Munich. The city derives its name from the medieval *Munichen* (monks). In 1158 the Imperial Diet in Augsburg sanctioned the rule of Heinrich der Löwe, and Munich the city was born.

In 1240 the city passed to the House of Wittelsbach, which would govern Munich (and Bavaria) until the 20th century. Munich prospered as a salt-trading centre but was hit hard by plague in 1349. The epidemic subsided only after 150 years, whereupon the relieved *Schäffler* (coopers) initiated a ritualistic dance to remind burghers of their good fortune. The Schäfflertanz is performed every seven years but is re-enacted daily by the little figures on the city's Glockenspiel (carillon) on Marienplatz.

By the 19th century an explosion of monument building gave Munich its spectacular architecture and wide Italianate avenues. Things got out of hand after King Ludwig II ascended the throne in 1864, as spending for his grandiose projects (such as Schloss Neuschwanstein south of Munich) bankrupted the royal house and threatened the government's coffers. Ironically, today they are the biggest money-spinners of Bavaria's tourism industry.

Munich has seen many turbulent times, but the 20th century was particularly bumpy. WWI practically starved the city to death, while the Nazis first rose to prominence here and WWII nearly wiped Munich off the map.

The 1972 Olympic Games began as a celebration of a new democratic Germany but ended in tragedy when 17 people were killed in a terrorist hostage-taking incident. In 2006 the city won a brighter place in sporting history when it hosted the opening game of the FIFA World Cup.

Today Munich's claim to being the 'secret capital' of Germany is well founded. The city is recognised for its high living standards – with more millionaires per capita than any other German city except Hamburg – and for haute couture that rivals that of Paris and Milan. Having celebrated its 850th birthday just short of a decade ago, this great metropolis is striding affluently forward into the 21st century.

⊙ Sights

Munich's major sights cluster around the Altstadt, with the main museum district just north of the Residenz. However, it will take another day or two to explore bohemian Schwabing, the sprawling Englischer Garten, and trendy Haidhausen to the east. Northwest of the Altstadt you'll find cosmopolitan Neuhausen, the Olympiapark and another of Munich's royal highlights – Schloss Nymphenburg.

⊙ Altstadt

Marienplatz SQUARE
(Map p48; ⑤ Marienplatz, ⓤ Marienplatz) The epicentral heart and soul of the Altstadt, Marienplatz is a popular gathering spot and packs a lot of personality into a compact frame. It's anchored by the **Mariensäule** (Mary's Column; Map p48), built in 1638 to celebrate victory over Swedish forces during the Thirty Years' War. This is the busiest spot in all Munich, with throngs of tourists swarming across its expanse from early morning till late at night.

Neues Rathaus HISTORIC BUILDING
(New Town Hall; Map p48; Marienplatz; ⓤ Marienplatz, ⑤ Marienplatz) The soot-blackened façade of the neo-Gothic Neues Rathaus is festooned with gargoyles, statues and a dragon scaling the turrets; the tourist office is on the ground floor. For pinpointing Munich's landmarks without losing your breath, catch the lift up the 85m-tall **tower** (adult/concession €2.50/1; ⊙10am-7pm daily).

The **Glockenspiel** (⊙11am, noon, 5pm & 9pm) has 43 bells and 32 figures that perform two historical events. The top half tells the story of a tournament held in 1568 to celebrate the marriage of Duke Wilhelm V to Renata of Lothringen, while the bottom half portrays the Schäfflertanz (cooper's dance).

Frauenkirche CHURCH
(Church of Our Lady; Map p48; www.muenchner-dom.de; Frauenplatz 1; ⊙7am-7pm Sat-Wed, to 8.30pm Thu, to 6pm Fri; ⑤ Marienplatz) The landmark Frauenkirche, built between 1468 and 1488, is Munich's spiritual heart and the Mt Everest among its churches. No other building in the central city may stand taller than its onion-domed twin towers, which reach a skyscraping 99m. The south tower can be

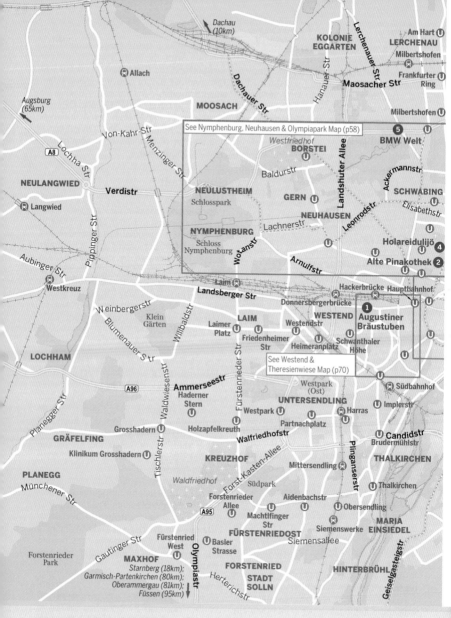

Munich Highlights

❶ Raising a 1L stein of *Bier* at an authentic beer hall, such as the **Augustiner Bräustuben** (p81)

❷ Feeling your brow growing higher among the world-class art collections at the **Alte Pinakothek** (p54)

❸ Revelling in the blingfest that is the **Schatzkammer der Residenz** (p53)

❹ Squeezing Alpine style into Lederhosen or a Dirndl at a

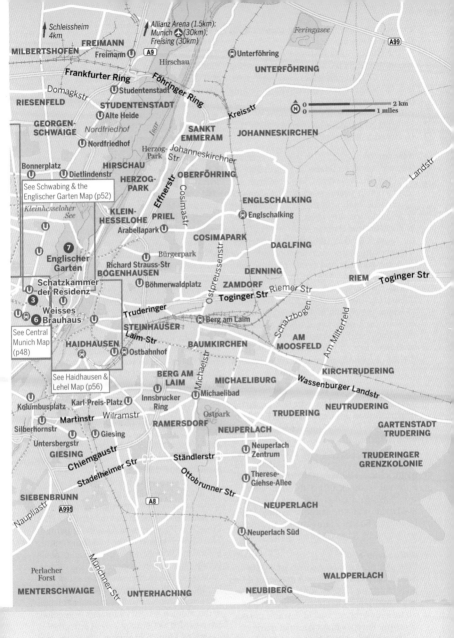

folk-costume emporium, such
as **Holareidulijö** (p83)

5 Getting under the high-
octane hood of **BMW Welt**
(p64)

6 Enjoying a brunch of
traditional *Weisswurst* (veal
sausage), a pretzel and a
Weissbier (wheat beer) at
Weisses Brauhaus (p75)

7 Watching daredevil surfers
negotiate an urban wave on
the artificial stream in the
Englischer Garten (p57)

climbed but was under urgent renovation at the time of writing.

The church sustained severe bomb damage in WWII; its reconstruction is a soaring passage of light but otherwise fairly spartan. Of note are the epic cenotaph (empty tomb) of Ludwig the Bavarian, just past the entrance, and the bronze plaques of Pope Benedict XVI and his predecessor John Paul II, affixed to nearby pillars.

Asamkirche   CHURCH
(Map p48; Sendlinger Strasse 32; ☺9am-6pm Sat-Thu, 1-6pm Fri; ⓢSendlinger Tor, ⓊSendlinger Tor) **FREE** Though pocket sized, the late-baroque Asamkirche, built in 1746, is as rich and epic as a giant's treasure chest. Its creators, the brothers Cosmas Damian Asam and Egid Quirin Asam, dug deep into their considerable talent box to swathe every inch of wall space with gilt garlands and docile cherubs, false marble and oversized barley twist columns.

The crowning glory is the ceiling fresco illustrating the life of St John Nepomuk, to whom the church is dedicated (lie down on your back on a pew to fully appreciate the complicated perspective). The brothers lived next door and this was originally their private chapel; the main altar could be seen through a window from their home.

St Peterskirche   CHURCH
(Church of St Peter; Map p48; Rindermarkt 1; church free, tower adult/concession €2/1; ☺tower 9am-6pm Mon-Fri, from 10am Sat & Sun; ⓊMarienplatz, ⓢMarienplatz) Some 306 steps divide you from the best view of central Munich from the 92m tower of St Peterskirche, Munich's oldest church (1150). Inside awaits a virtual textbook of art through the centuries. Worth a closer peek are the Gothic St-Martin-Altar, the baroque ceiling fresco by Johann Baptist Zimmermann and rococo sculptures by Ignaz Günther.

Viktualienmarkt   MARKET
(Map p48; ☺Mon-Fri & morning Sat; ⓊMarienplatz, ⓢMarienplatz) Fresh fruit and vegetables, piles of artisan cheeses, tubs of exotic olives, hams and jams, chanterelles and truffles – Viktualienmarkt is a feast of flavours and one of central Europe's finest gourmet markets.

The market moved here in 1807 when it outgrew the Marienplatz and many of the stalls have been run by generations of the same family. Put together a picnic and head for the market's very own beer garden for an al fresco lunch with a brew and to watch the traders in action.

Heiliggeistkirche   CHURCH
(Church of the Holy Spirit; Map p48; Im Tal 77; ☺7am-6pm; ⓊMarienplatz, ⓢMarienplatz) Gothic at its core, this baroque church on the edge of the Viktualienmarkt has fantastic ceiling frescoes created by the Asam brothers in 1720, depicting the foundation of a hospice that once stood next door. The hospice was demolished to make way for the new Viktualienmarkt.

Münchner Stadtmuseum   MUSEUM
(City Museum; Map p48; www.muenchner-stadtmuseum.de; St-Jakobs-Platz 1; adult/concession/child €6/3.50/free, audioguide free; ☺10am-6pm Tue-Sun; ⓊMarienplatz, ⓢMarienplatz) Installed for the city's 850th birthday (2008), the Münchner Stadtmuseum's Typisch München (Typical Munich) exhibition – taking up the whole of a rambling building – tells Munich's story in an imaginative, uncluttered and engaging way. Exhibits in each section represent something quintessential about the city; a booklet/audioguide relates the tale behind them, thus condensing a long and tangled history into easily digestible themes.

Set out in chronological order, the exhibition kicks off with the founding monks and ends in the postwar-boom decades. The first of five sections, Old Munich, contains a scale model of the city in the late 16th century (one of five commissioned by Duke Albrecht V; the Bayerisches Nationalmuseum (p60) displays the others), but the highlight here is the *The Morris Dancers*, a series of statuettes gyrating like 15th-century ravers. It's one of the most valuable works owned by the city.

Next comes New Munich, which charts the Bavarian capital's 18th- and 19th-century transformation into prestigious royal capital and the making of the modern city. The *Canaletto View* gives an idea in oil paint of how Munich looked in the mid-18th century, before the Wittelsbachs (the German noble family that ruled Bavaria) launched their makeover. The section also takes a fascinating look at the origins of Oktoberfest and Munich's cuisine, as well as the phenomenon of the 'Munich Beauty' – Munich's womenfolk are regarded as Germany's most attractive.

City of Munich examines the weird and wonderful late 19th and early 20th centuries, a period known for Jugenstil architecture and design, Richard Wagner and avant-garde rumblings in Schwabing. Munich became the 'city of art and beer', a title many are likely to agree it still holds today.

The fourth hall, Revue, becomes a little obscure but basically deals with the aftermath of WWI and the rise of the Nazis. The lead-up to war and the city's suffering during WWII occupy the Feuchtwangersaal, where a photo of a very determined Chamberlain stands next to the other signatories to the Munich Agreement. This is followed by a couple of fascinating rooms that paint a portrait of the modern city, including nostalgic TV footage from the last 40 years.

Though the Typical Munich exhibition touches on the period, the rise of the Nazis has been rightly left as a powerful separate exhibition called Nationalsozialismus in München. This occupies an eerily windowless annexe.

Jüdisches Museum   MUSEUM

(Jewish Museum; Map p48; www.juedisches-museum-muenchen.de; St-Jakobs-Platz 16; adult/child €6/3; ⊙10am-6pm Tue-Sun; ⓓSendlinger Tor, ⓤSendlinger Tor) Coming to terms with its Nazi past has not historically been a priority in Munich, which is why the opening of the Jewish Museum in 2007 was hailed as a milestone. The permanent exhibition offers an insight into Jewish history, life and culture in the city. The Holocaust is dealt with, but the focus is clearly on contemporary Jewish culture.

The museum is part of the Jewish complex on St-Jakobs-Platz that also includes a community centre with a restaurant and a bunker-like synagogue that's rarely open to the public. Munich has the second-largest Jewish population in Germany after Berlin's: around 9300 people.

Michaelskirche   CHURCH

(Church of St Michael; Map p48; Kaufingerstrasse 52; crypt admission €2; ⊙crypt 9.30am-4.30pm Mon-Fri, to 2.30pm Sat & Sun; ⓓKarlsplatz, ⓢKarlsplatz, ⓤKarlsplatz) It stands quiet and dignified amid the retail frenzy out on Kaufingerstrasse, but to fans of Ludwig II, the Michaelskirche is the ultimate place of pilgrimage. Its dank crypt is the final resting place of the Mad King, whose humble tomb is usually drowned in flowers.

Completed in 1597, St Michael's was the largest Renaissance church north of the Alps when it was built. It boasts an impressive unsupported barrel-vaulted ceiling, and the massive bronze statue between the two entrances shows the archangel finishing off a dragon-like creature, a classic Counter Reformation–era symbol of Catholicism triumphing over Protestantism. The building has been fully renovated in recent years and has never looked more impressive.

Altes Rathaus   HISTORIC BUILDING

(Old Town Hall; Map p48; Marienplatz; ⓤMarienplatz, ⓢMarienplatz) The eastern side of Marienplatz is dominated by the Altes Rathaus. Lightning got the better of the medieval original in 1460 and WWII bombs levelled its successor, so what you see is really the third incarnation of the building designed by Jörg von Halspach of Frauenkirche fame. On 9 November 1938 Joseph Goebbels gave a hate-filled speech here that launched the nationwide *Kristallnacht* pogroms.

Today the church houses the adorable Spielzeugmuseum (Toy Museum; Map p48; www.toymuseum.de; Marienplatz 15; adult/child €4/1; ⊙10am-5.30pm; ⓢMarienplatz, ⓤMarienplatz), with its huge collection of rare and precious toys from Europe and the US.

Bier & Oktoberfestmuseum   MUSEUM

(Beer & Oktoberfest Museum; Map p48; www.bier-und-oktoberfestmuseum.de; Sterneckerstrasse 2; adult/concession €4/2.50; ⊙1-6pm Tue-Sat; ⓓIsartor, ⓢIsartor) Head to this popular museum to learn all about Bavarian suds and

---

MUNICH'S BEST MUSEUMS

Munich has almost 50 museums, some so vast and containing so many exhibits you could spend a whole day shuffling through a single institution. Gallery fatigue strikes many a visitor and it's easy to get your *pinakotheks* in a twist. Here we list Munich's best museums – be selective and take your time.

Curious kids KinderReich at the Deutsches Museum (p60)

Petrol heads BMW Welt (p64)

Tech types Deutsches Museum (p60)

Design devotees Pinakothek der Moderne (p55)

Dino hunters Paläontologisches Museum (p65)

Sovereign stalkers Residenzmuseum (p52)

Art-ficionados Alte Pinakothek (p54)

History seekers Bayerisches Nationalmuseum (p60)

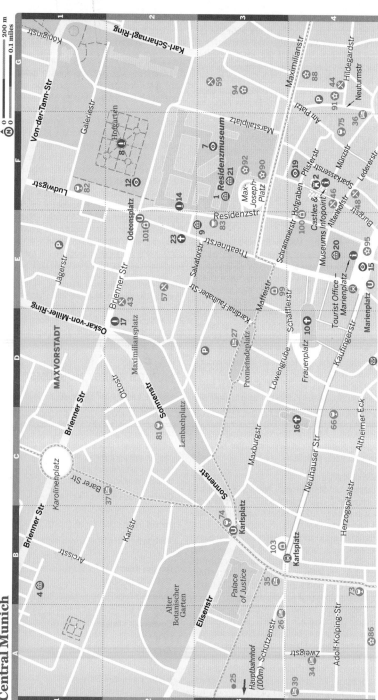

48

MUNICH

Central Munich

200 m
0.1 miles

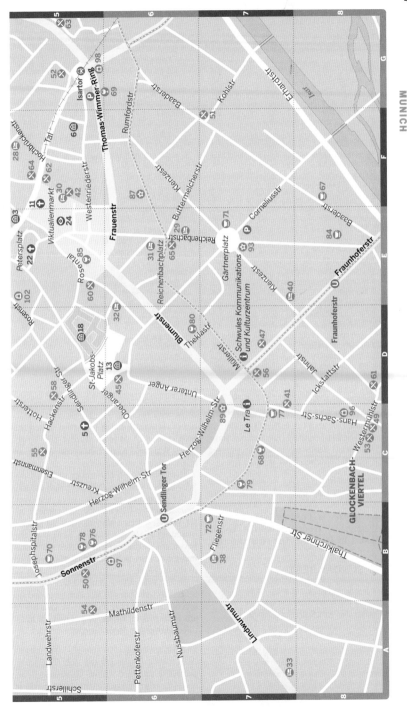

Central Munich

the world's most famous booze-up. The four floors heave with old brewing vats, historic photos and some of the earliest Oktoberfest regalia. The 14th-century building has some fine medieval features, including painted ceilings and a kitchen with an open fire.

Feldherrnhalle   HISTORIC BUILDING
(Field Marshalls Hall; Map p48; Residenzstrasse 1; U Odeonsplatz) Corking up Odeonsplatz' southern side is Friedrich von Gärnter's Feldherrnhalle, modelled on the Loggia dei Lanzi in Florence. The structure pays homage to the Bavarian army and positively drips with testosterone; check out the statues of General Johann Tilly, who kicked the Swedes out of Munich during the Thirty Years' War; and Karl Philipp von Wrede, an ally-turned-foe of Napoleon.

It was here on 9 November 1923 that police stopped the so-called Beer Hall Putsch, Hitler's attempt to bring down the Weimar Republic (Germany's government after WWI). A fierce skirmish left 20 people, including 16 Nazis, dead. A plaque in the pavement of the square's eastern side commemorates the police officers who perished in the incident.

Hitler was subsequently tried and sentenced to five years in jail, but he ended up serving a mere nine months in Landsberg am Lech prison, where he penned his hate-filled manifesto, *Mein Kampf.*

ℹ **SUNDAY BEST**

Save yourself a bailout of euros by visiting the Alte Pinakothek, Neue Pinakothek, Pinakothek der Moderne, Bayerisches Nationalmuseum, Museum Brandhorst, the Glyptothek, Archäologische Staatssammlung and several other less-visited museums and galleries on a Sunday, when admission to each is reduced to a symbolic €1.

Theatinerkirche   CHURCH
(Map p48; Theatinerstrasse 22; S Odeonsplatz) The mustard-yellow Theatinerkirche, built to commemorate the 1662 birth of

Prince Max Emanuel, is the work of Swiss architect Enrico Zuccalli. Also known as St Kajetan's, it's a voluptuous design with two massive twin towers flanking a giant cupola. Inside, an ornate dome lords over the Fürstengruft (royal crypt), the final destination of several Wittelsbach rulers, including King Maximilian II (1811–64). The building was receiving much-needed renovation at the time of research but was still open to the public.

Alter Hof
PALACE
(Map p48; Burgstrasse 8; Ⓢ Marienplatz, Ⓤ Marienplatz) Alter Hof was the starter home of the Wittelsbach family and has its origins in the 12th century. The Bavarian rulers moved out of this central palace as long ago as the 15th century. Visitors can only see the central courtyard, where the bay window on the southern facade was nicknamed Monkey Tower in honour of a valiant ape that saved an infant Ludwig the Bavarian from the clutches of a ferocious market pig. Local lore at its most bizarre.

Münzhof
ARCHITECTURE
(Map p48; Hofgraben 4; Ⓤ Marienplatz, Ⓢ Marienplatz) The former Münzhof (mint) has a pretty courtyard, remarkable for its three-storey Renaissance arcades dating from 1567. An inscription on the western side of the building reads Moneta Regis (Money Rules), particularly apt words for this well-heeled part of Europe. The building now houses the agency charged with protecting Bavaria's many historical monuments.

⊙ Residenz & Around

The Residenz is a suitably grand palace that reflects the splendour and power of the Wittelsbach clan, the Bavarian rulers who lived here from 1385 to 1918. The edifice dwarfs Max-Joseph-Platz along with the grandiose Nationaltheater (p82), home to the Bavarian State Opera. Its museums are among the jewels in Munich's cultural crown and are an unmissable part of the Bavarian experience.

Four giant bronze lion statues (Map p48; Residenzstrasse; Ⓤ Odeonsplatz) guard the

Schwabing & the Englischer Garten

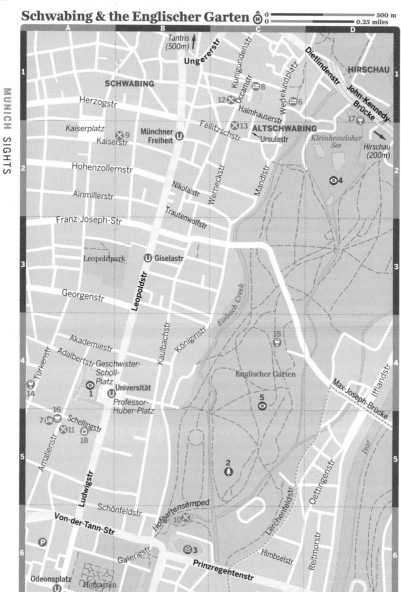

entrance to the palace, supported by pedestals festooned with a half-human, half-animal face. Note the creatures' remarkably shiny noses. If you wait a moment, you'll see the reason for the sheen: scores of people walk by and casually rub one or all four noses. It's supposed to bring wealth and good luck.

★ **Residenzmuseum** MUSEUM
(Map p48; ☎089-290 671; www.residenz-
muenchen.de; Residenzstrasse 1; adult/concession/

Schwabing & the Englischer Garten

under 18yr €7/6/free; ⊘9am-6pm Apr–mid-Oct, 10am-5pm mid-Oct–Mar, last entry 1hr before closing; ⓤOdeonsplatz) Home to Bavaria's Wittelsbach rulers from 1508 until WWI, the Residenz is Munich's number one attraction. The amazing treasures, as well as all the trappings of their lifestyles over the centuries, are on display at the Residenzmuseum, which takes up around half of the palace. Allow at least two hours to see everything at a gallop.

Tours are in the company of a rather long-winded audioguide (free), and gone are the days when the building was divided into morning and afternoon sections, all of which means a lot of ground to cover in one go. It's worth fast forwarding a bit to where the prescribed route splits into short and long tours, taking the long route for the most spectacular interiors. Approximately 90 rooms are open to the public at any one time, but as renovation work is ongoing, closures are inevitable and you may not see all the highlights.

When wandering the Residenz, don't forget that only 50 sq metres of the building's roof remained intact at the end of WWII. Most of what you see today is a painstaking postwar reconstruction.

The tours kick off at the Grottenhof (Grotto Court), home of the wonderful Perseusbrunnen (Perseus Fountain), with its namesake holding the dripping head of Medusa. Next door is the famous Antiquarium, a barrel-vaulted hall smothered in frescoes and built to house the Wittelsbachs' enormous antique collection. It's widely regarded as the finest Renaissance interior north of the Alps.

Further along the tour route, the neo-Byzantine Hofkirche was built for Ludwig I in 1826. After WWII only the red-brick walls were left; it reopened as an atmospheric concert venue in 2003.

Upstairs are the Kurfürstenzimmer (Electors Rooms), with some stunning Italian portraits and a passage lined with two dozen views of Italy, painted by local romantic artist Carl Rottmann. Also up here are François Cuvilliés' Reiche Zimmer (Rich Rooms), a six-room extravaganza of exuberant rococo carried out by the top stucco and fresco artists of the day; they're a definite highlight. More rococo magic awaits in the Ahnengallery (Ancestors Gallery), with 121 portraits of the rulers of Bavaria in chronological order.

The Hofkapelle, reserved for the ruler and his family, fades quickly in the memory when you see the exquisite Reichekapelle, with its blue and gilt ceiling, inlaid marble and 16th-century organ. Considered the finest rococo interiors in southern Germany, another spot to linger is the Steinzimmer (Stone Rooms), the emperor's quarters, awash in intricately patterned and coloured marble.

Schatzkammer der Residenz MUSEUM
(Residence Treasury; Map p48; Residenzstrasse 1; adult/concession/under 18yr €7/6/free; ⊘9am-6pm Apr–mid-Oct, 10am-5pm mid-Oct–Mar, last entry 1hr before closing; ⓤOdeonsplatz) The Residenzmuseum entrance also leads to the Schatzkammer der Residenz, a veritable banker's bonus worth of jewel-encrusted bling of yesteryear, from golden toothpicks to finely crafted swords, and miniatures in ivory to gold-entombed cosmetics trunks. The 1250 incredibly intricate and attractive items on display come in every precious material you could imagine, including lapis lazuli, crystal, coral and amber.

Definite highlights are the Bavarian crown insignia and the ruby-and-diamond-encrusted jewellery of Queen Therese (1792–1854).

MAXIMILIANSTRASSE

It's pricey and pretentious, but no trip to Munich would be complete without a wander along Maximilianstrasse, one of the city's swishest boulevards. Starting at Max-Joseph-Platz, it's a 1km-long ribbon of style where well-heeled shoppers browse for Breguet and Prada and bored bodyguards loiter by Bentleys and Rolls Royces. Recently it's also become a haunt for Munich's many beggars. Several of the city's finest theatrical venues, including the Nationaltheater, the Kammerspiele and the GOP Varieté Theater, are also here.

Built between 1852 and 1875, Maximilianstrasse was essentially an ego trip for King Max II. He harnessed the skills of architect Friedrich von Bürklein to create a unique stylistic hotchpotch ranging from Bavarian rustic to Italian Renaissance and English Gothic. It even became known as the Maximilianic Style. That's the king gazing down upon his boulevard – engulfed by roaring traffic – from his perch at the centre of the strip. Clinging to the base are four rather stern-looking children holding the coats of arms of Bavaria, Franconia, Swabia and the Palatinate.

Cuvilliés-Theater
THEATRE

(Map p48; Residenzstrasse 1; adult/concession/under 18yr €3.50/2.50/free; ⊙2-6pm Mon-Sat, 9am-6pm Sun Apr-Jul & Sep–mid-Oct, 9am-6pm daily Aug, 2-5pm Mon-Sat, 10am-5pm Sun Nov-Mar; 🚇Nationaltheater) Commissioned by Maximilian III in the mid-18th century, François Cuvilliés fashioned one of Europe's finest rococo theatres. Famous for hosting the premiere of Mozart's opera *Idomeneo,* the theatre was restored to its former glory by means of a restoration in the mid-noughties, and its stage once again hosts high-brow musical and operatic performances.

Access is limited to the auditorium, where you can take a seat and admire the four tiers of *loggia* (galleries), dripping with rococo embellishment, at your leisure.

Monument to the Victims of National Socialism
MONUMENT

(Map p48; Brienner Strasse; ⓤOdeonsplatz) This striking monument is made up of four Ts holding up a block-like cage in which an eternal flame flutters in remembrance of those who died at the hands of the Nazis due to their political beliefs, race, religion, sexual orientation or disability. Moved to this spot in 2014, it's a sternly simple reminder of Munich's not-so-distant past.

Hofgarten
GARDENS

(Map p48; ⓤOdeonsplatz) Office workers catching some rays during their lunch break, stylish mothers pushing prams, seniors on bikes, a gaggle of chatty nuns – everybody comes to the Hofgarten. The formal court gardens, with fountains, radiant flower beds, lime tree–lined gravel paths and benches galore, sit just north of the Residenz. Paths converge at the **Dianatempel** (Map p48), a striking octagonal pavilion honouring the Roman goddess of the hunt. Enter the gardens from Odeonsplatz.

⊙ Maxvorstadt, Schwabing & the Englischer Garten

Visitors spending even just a few hours in the city are likely to find themselves in Maxvorstadt at some point, as the district is home to Munich's Kunstareal (art district), an entire neighbourhood of top-drawer museums.

Alte Pinakothek
MUSEUM

(Map p58; ☑089-238 0526; www.pinakothek.de; Barer Strasse 27; adult/child €4/2, Sun €1, audioguide €4.50; ⊙10am-8pm Tue, to 6pm Wed-Sun; 🚇Pinakotheken, 🚌Pinakotheken) Munich's main repository of Old European Masters is crammed with all the major players that decorated canvases between the 14th and 18th centuries. This neoclassical temple was masterminded by Leo von Klenze and is a delicacy even if you can't tell your Rembrandt from your Rubens. The collection is world famous for its exceptional quality and depth, especially when it comes to German masters.

The oldest works are altar paintings, among which Michael Pacher's *Four Church Fathers* and Lucas Cranach the Elder's *Crucifixion* (1503), an emotional rendition of the suffering Jesus, stand out.

A key room is the Dürersaal upstairs. Here hangs Albrecht Dürer's famous Christ-like *Self-Portrait* (1500), showing the gaze of an artist brimming with self-confidence. His final major work, *The Four Apostles,* depicts

John, Peter, Paul and Mark as rather humble men, in keeping with post-Reformation ideas. Compare this to Matthias Grünewald's *Sts Erasmus and Maurice,* which shows the saints dressed in rich robes like kings.

For a secular theme, inspect Albrecht Altdorfer's *Battle of Alexander the Great* (1529), which captures in dizzying detail a 6th-century war pitting Greeks against Persians.

There's a choice bunch of works by Dutch masters, including an altarpiece by Rogier van der Weyden called *The Adoration of the Magi,* plus *The Seven Joys of Mary* by Hans Memling, *Danae* by Jan Gossaert and *The Land of Cockayne* by Pieter Bruegel the Elder. At 6m in height, Rubens' epic *Last Judgment* is so big that Klenze custom-designed the hall for it. A memorable portrait is *Hélène Fourment* (1631), a youthful beauty who was the ageing Rubens' second wife.

The Italians are represented by Botticelli, Rafael, Titian and many others, while the French collection includes paintings by Nicolas Poussin, Claude Lorrain and François Boucher. Among the Spaniards are such heavy hitters as El Greco, Murillo and Velázquez.

The Alte Pinakothek is under much-needed renovation until mid-2018, with parts of the building taking turns to close while work is carried out.

Pinakothek der Moderne   MUSEUM

(Map p58; ☑089-2380 5360; www.pinakothek.de; Barer Strasse 40; adult/child €10/7, Sun €1; ⊙10am-6pm Tue, Wed & Fri-Sun, to 8pm Thu; ▣Pinakotheken, ▣Pinakotheken) Germany's largest modern-art museum unites four significant collections under a single roof: 20th-century art, applied design from the 19th century to today, a graphics collection and an architecture museum. It's housed in a spectacular building by Stephan Braunfels, whose four-storey interior centres on a vast eye-like dome through which soft natural light filters throughout the blanched white galleries.

The State Gallery of Modern Art has some exemplary modern classics by Picasso, Klee, Dalí and Kandinsky and many lesser-known works that will be new to most visitors. More recent big shots include Georg Baselitz, Andy Warhol, Cy Twombly, Dan Flavin and the late enfant terrible Joseph Beuys.

In a world obsessed by retro style, the New Collection is the busiest section of the museum. Housed in the basement, it focuses on applied design from the industrial revolution via art nouveau and Bauhaus to today. VW Beetles, Eames chairs and early

Apple Macs stand alongside more obscure interwar items that wouldn't be out of place in a Kraftwerk video. There's lots of 1960s furniture, the latest spool tape recorders and an exhibition of the weirdest jewellery you'll ever see.

The State Graphics Collection boasts 400,000 pieces of art on paper, including drawings, prints and engravings by such craftsmen as Leonardo da Vinci and Paul Cézanne. Because of the light-sensitive nature of these works, only a tiny fraction of the collection is shown at any given time.

Finally, there's the Architecture Museum, with entire studios of drawings, blueprints, photographs and models by such top practitioners as baroque architect Balthasar Neumann, Bauhaus maven Le Corbusier and 1920s expressionist Erich Mendelsohn.

Neue Pinakothek   MUSEUM

(Map p58; ☑089-2380 5195; www.pinakothek.de; Barer Strasse 29; adult/child €7/5, Sun €1; ⊙10am-6pm Thu-Mon, to 8pm Wed; ▣Pinakotheken, ▣Pinakotheken) The Neue Pinakothek harbours a well-respected collection of 19th- and early-20th-century paintings and sculpture, from rococo to *Jugendstil* (art nouveau). All the world-famous household names get wall space here, including crowd-pleasing French impressionists such as Monet, Cézanne and Degas as well as Van Gogh, whose boldly pigmented *Sunflowers* (1888) radiates cheer.

Perhaps the most memorable canvases, though, are by Romantic painter Caspar David Friedrich, who specialised in emotionally charged, brooding landscapes.

There are also several works by Gauguin, including *Breton Peasant Women* (1894), and Manet, including *Breakfast in the Studio* (1869). Turner gets a look-in with his dramatically sublime *Ostende* (1844).

Local painters represented in the exhibition include Carl Spitzweg and Wilhelm von Kobell of the Dachau School and Munich society painters such as Wilhelm von Kaulbach, Franz Lenbach and Karl von Piloty. Another focus is work by the Deutschrömer (German Romans), a group of neoclassicists centred on Johann Koch, who stuck mainly to Italian landscapes.

Museum Brandhorst   GALLERY

(Map p58; www.museum-brandhorst.de; Theresienstrasse 35a; adult/child €7/5, Sun €1; ⊙10am-6pm Tue, Wed & Fri-Sun, to 8pm Thu; ▣Maxvorstadt/Sammlung Brandhorst, ▣Pinakotheken) A big,

Haidhausen & Lehel

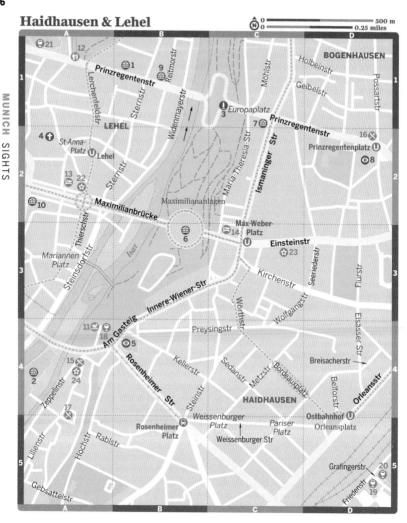

bold and aptly abstract building, clad entirely in vividly multihued ceramic tubes, the Brandhorst jostled its way into the Munich Kunstareal in a punk blaze of colour mid-2009. Its walls, its floor and occasionally its ceiling provide space for some of the most challenging art in the city, among it some instantly recognisable 20th-century images by Andy Warhol, whose work dominates the collection.

Pop art's 1960s poster boy pops up throughout the gallery and even has an entire room dedicated to pieces such as his punkish *Self-Portrait* (1986), *Marilyn* (1962) and *Triple Elvis* (1963).

The other prevailing artist at the Brandhorst is the lesser-known Cy Twombly. His arrestingly spectacular splash-and-dribble canvases are a bit of an acquired taste, but this is the place to acquire it if ever there was one.

Elsewhere Dan Flavin floodlights various corners with his eye-watering light installations and other big names such as Mario Merz, Alex Katz and Sigmar Polke also make an appearance. Damien Hirst gets a look-in here and there.

Haidhausen & Lehel

Lenbachhaus MUSEUM
(Municipal Gallery; Map p58; ☑089-2333 2000; www.lenbachhaus.de; Luisenstrasse 33; adult/concession incl audioguide €10/5; ☉10am-9pm Tue, to 6pm Wed-Sun; ☐Königsplatz, ⓤKönigsplatz) Reopened in 2013 to rave reviews after a four-year renovation that saw the addition of a new wing by noted architect Norman Foster, this glorious gallery is once again the go-to place to admire the vibrant canvases of Kandinsky, Franz Marc, Paul Klee and other members of ground-breaking modernist group Der Blaue Reiter (The Blue Rider), founded in Munich in 1911.

Contemporary art is another focal point. An eyecatcher is a glass-and-steel sculpture by Olafur Eliasson in the soaring new atrium. Many other big names are also represented, including Gerhard Richter, Sigmar Polke, Anselm Kiefer, Andy Warhol, Dan Flavin, Richard Serra and Jenny Holzer.

Tickets are also valid for special exhibits at the nearby Kunstbau, a 120m-long tunnel above the Königsplatz U-Bahn station.

Glyptothek MUSEUM
(Map p58; www.antike-am-koenigsplatz.mwn. de; Königsplatz 3; adult/concession €6/4, Sun €1; ☉10am-5pm Fri-Sun, Tue & Wed, to 8pm Thu; ☐Königsplatz, ⓤKönigsplatz) If you're a fan of classical art or simply enjoy the sight of naked guys without noses (or other pertinent body parts), make a beeline for the Glyptothek. One of Munich's oldest museums, it's a feast of art and sculpture from ancient Greece and Rome amassed by Ludwig I between 1806 and 1830, and it opens a surprisingly naughty window onto the ancient world. Tickets for the museum are also valid for the Antikensammlungen.

Museum Reich der Kristalle MUSEUM
(Map p58; Theresienstrasse 41; adult/concession €4/2; ☉1-5pm Tue-Sun; ☐Maxvorstadt/ Sammlung Brandhorst, ☐Pinakotheken) If diamonds are your best friends, head to the Museum Reich der Kristalle, with its Fort Knox-worthy collection of gemstones and crystals, including a giant Russian emerald and meteorite fragments from Kansas.

Antikensammlungen MUSEUM
(Map p48; www.antike-am-koenigsplatz.mwn. de; Königsplatz 1; adult/concession €6/4, Sun €1; ☉10am-5pm Fri-Sun, Tue & Wed, to 8pm Wed; ☐Königsplatz, ⓤKönigsplatz) This old-school museum is an engaging showcase of exquisite Greek, Roman and Etruscan antiquities. The collection of Greek vases, each artistically decorated with gods and heroes, wars and weddings, is particularly outstanding. Other galleries present gold and silver jewellery and ornaments, figurines made from terracotta and more precious bronze, and super-fragile glass drinking vessels. Tickets for the museum are also valid for the Glyptothek.

Englischer Garten PARK
(Map p52; ⓤUniversität) The sprawling English Garden is among Europe's biggest city parks – it even rivals London's Hyde

Nymphenburg, Neuhausen & Olympiapark

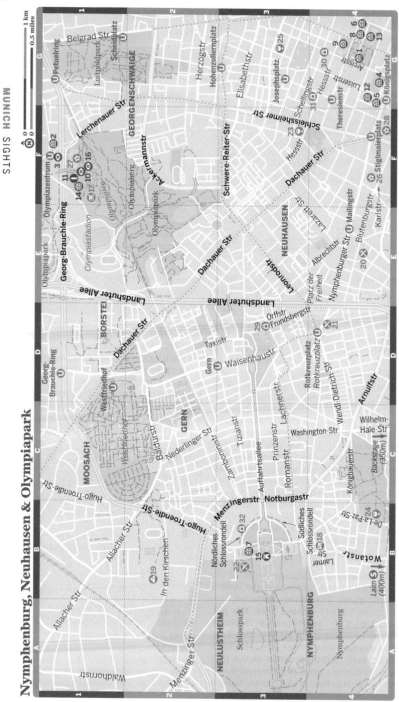

Nymphenburg, Neuhausen & Olympiapark

MUNICH SIGHTS

Park and New York's Central Park for size – and is a popular playground for locals and visitors alike. Stretching north from Prinzregentenstrasse for about 5km, it was commissioned by Elector Karl Theodor in 1789 and designed by Benjamin Thompson, an American-born scientist working as an adviser to the Bavarian government.

Paths wander through dark stands of mature oak and maple before emerging into sunlit meadows of lush grass. Locals are mindful of the park's popularity and tolerate the close quarters of cyclists, walkers and joggers. Street musicians dodge balls kicked by children and students sprawl on the grass to chat about missed lectures.

Sooner or later you'll find your way to the **Kleinhesseloher See** (Map p52), a lovely lake at the centre of the park. Work up a sweat while taking a spin around three little islands, then quaff a well-earned foamy one at the **Seehaus beer garden** (Map p52; Kleinhesselohe 3; [♿]; [Ⓢ] Münchner Freiheit).

Several historic follies lend the park a playful charm. The wholly unexpected **Chinesischer Turm** (Chinese Tower; Map p52; [☎]089-383 8730; www.chinaturm.de; Englischer Garten 3; [⊙]10am-11pm; [🚌]Chinesischer Turm, [🚌]Tivolistrasse), now at the heart of Munich's oldest beer garden, was built in the 18th century during a pan-European craze for all things oriental. Further south, at the top of a

gentle hill, stands the heavily photographed **Monopteros** (Map p52) (1838), a small Greek temple whose ledges are often knee-to-knee with dangling legs belonging to people admiring the view of the Munich skyline.

Another hint of Asia awaits further south at the **Japanisches Teehaus** (Japanese Teahouse; Map p52; Englischer Garten), built for the 1972 Olympics by an idyllic duck pond. The best time to come is for

NO WAVE GOODBYE

At the southern tip of the Englischer Garten you'll see scores of people leaning over a bridge to cheer on wetsuit-clad daredevils as they 'hang 10' on an artificially created wave at **Surfing in the Eisbach** (Map p56; Prinzregentenstrasse; [🚌]Nationalmuseum/Haus der Kunst) . It's only a single wave, but it's a damn fine one. The surfers are such an attraction that the tourist office includes them in its brochures.

A few years ago park authorities attempted to ban this watery entertainment, but a successful campaign by surfers saw plans to turn the wave off shelved.

To find out more about Munich's urban surfers, see www.eisbachwelle.de.

an authentic tea ceremony celebrated by a Japanese tea master.

Bayerisches Nationalmuseum   MUSEUM

(Map p56; www.bayerisches-nationalmuseum. de; Prinzregentenstrasse 3; adult/concession €7/6, Sun €1; ☺10am-5pm Tue, Wed & Fri-Sun, to 8pm Thu; ☐Nationalmuseum/Haus Der Kunst, ☐Nationalmuseum/Haus Der Kunst) Picture the classic 19th-century museum, a palatial neoclassical edifice overflowing with exotic treasure and thought-provoking works of art, a repository for a nation's history, a grand purpose-built display case for royal trinkets, church baubles and state-owned rarities – this is the Bavarian National Museum, a good old-fashioned institution for no-nonsense museum lovers. As the collection fills 40 rooms over three floors, there's a lot to get through here, so be prepared for at least two hours' legwork.

Most visitors start on the 1st floor, where hall after hall is packed with baroque, mannerist and Renaissance sculpture, ecclesiastical treasures (check out all those wobbly Gothic 'S' figures), Renaissance clothing and one-off pieces such as the 1000-year-old St Kunigunde's chest fashioned in mammoth ivory and gold. Climb to the 2nd floor to move up in history to the rococo, *Jugendstil* and modern periods, represented by priceless collections of Nymphenburg and Meissen porcelain, Tiffany glass, Augsburg silver and precious items used by the Bavarian royal family. Also up here is a huge circular model of Munich in the first half of the 19th century, shortly after it was transformed into a capital fit for a kingdom.

It's easy to miss, but the building's basement also holds an evocatively displayed collection of Krippen (nativity scenes), some with a Cecil B DeMille–style cast of thousands. Retold in paper, wood and resin, there are Christmas-story scenes here from Bohemia, Moravia and Tyrol, but the biggest contingent hails from Naples. Also here is the excellent museum shop.

☺ Haidhausen & Lehel

Deutsches Museum   MUSEUM

(Map p56; ☎089-217 9333; www.deutsches-museum.de; Museumsinsel 1; adult/child €11/4; ☺9am-5pm; ☐Deutsches Museum) If you're one of those people for whom science is an unfathomable turn-off, a visit to the Deutsches Museum might just show you that physics and engineering are more fun than you thought. Spending a few hours in this temple to technology is an eye-opening journey of discovery and the exhibitions and demonstrations will certainly be a hit with young, sponge-like minds.

There are tons of interactive displays (including glass blowing and paper making), live demonstrations and experiments, model coal and salt mines, and engaging sections on cave paintings, geodesy, microelectronics and astronomy. In fact, it can be pretty overwhelming after a while, so it's best to prioritise what you want to see.

The place to entertain children aged three to eight is the fabulous KinderReich, where 1000 activities, from a kid-size mouse wheel to interactive water fun, await. Get the litties to climb all over a fire engine, build things with giant Lego, construct a waterway with canals and locks, or bang on a drum all day in a – thankfully – soundproof instrument room. Note that KinderReich closes at 4.30pm.

Sammlung Schack   MUSEUM

(Map p56; www.sammlung-schack.de; Prinzregentenstrasse 9; adult/concession €4/3; ☺10am-6pm Wed-Sun; ☐Reitmorstrasse/Sammlung Schack) Count Adolf Friedrich von Schack (1815–94) was a great fan of 19th-century Romantic painters such as Böcklin, Feuerbach and von Schwind. His collection is housed in the former Prussian embassy, now the Schack-Galerie. A tour of the intimate space is like an escape into the idealised fantasy worlds created by these artists.

Haus der Kunst   MUSEUM

(House of Art; Map p52; www.hausderkunst.de; Prinzregentenstrasse 1; adult/concession €12/10; ☺10am-8pm Fri-Wed, to 10pm Thu; ☐Nationalmuseum/Haus Der Kunst, ☐Nationalmuseum/Haus Der Kunst) This stern art deco edifice was built in 1937 to showcase Nazi art, but now the Haus der Kunst presents works by exactly the artists whom the Nazis rejected and deemed degenerate. Temporary shows focus on contemporary art and design.

Staatliches Museum für Völkerkunde   MUSEUM

(State Museum of Ethnology; Map p56; www. voelkerkundemuseum-muenchen.de; Maximilianstrasse 42; adult/concession €5/4, Sun €1; ☺9.30am-5.30pm Tue-Sun; ☐Maxmonument) With a bonanza of art and objects from Africa, India, the Americas, the Middle East and Polynesia, the State Museum of Ethnology has one of the most prestigious and

THE WHITE ROSE

Open resistance to the Nazis was rare during the Third Reich; after 1933, intimidation and the instant 'justice' of the Gestapo and SS served as powerful disincentives. One of the few groups to rebel was the ill-fated Weisse Rose (White Rose), led by Munich University students Hans and Sophie Scholl.

The nonviolent White Rose began operating in 1942, its members stealing out at night to smear 'Freedom!' and 'Down with Hitler!' on the city's walls. Soon they were printing anti-Nazi leaflets on the mass extermination of the Jews and other Nazi atrocities. One read: 'We shall not be silent – we are your guilty conscience. The White Rose will not leave you in peace'.

In February 1943, Hans and Sophie were caught distributing leaflets at the university. Together with their best friend, Christoph Probst, the Scholls were arrested and charged with treason. After a summary trial, all three were found guilty and beheaded the same afternoon. Their extraordinary courage inspired the award-winning film *Sophie Scholl – Die Letzten Tage* (Sophie Scholl – The Final Days; 2005).

A memorial exhibit to the White Rose, DenkStätte (Map p52; Geschwister-Scholl-Platz 1; ⊘10am-4pm Mon-Fri, noon-3pm Sat ; Ⓤ Universität) FREE is within the Ludwig-Maximilian-Universität.

---

complete ethnological collections anywhere. Sculpture from West and Central Africa is particularly impressive, as are Peruvian ceramics, Indian jewellery, mummy parts, and artefacts from the days of Captain Cook.

Klosterkirche St Anna im Lehel CHURCH
(Map p56; St-Anna-Platz 21; ⊘6am-7pm; ⓐLehel, Ⓤ Lehel) The Asamkirche may be more sumptuous, but the Klosterkirche St Anna im Lehel is actually a collaboration of the top dogs of the rococo. Johann Michael Fischer designed the building, and Cosmas Damian Asam painted the stunning ceiling fresco and altar.

Maximilianeum HISTORIC BUILDING
(Map p56; Max-Planck-Strasse 1; ⓐMaximilianeum) Maximilianstrasse culminates in the glorious Maximilianeum, completed in 1874, a decade after Max II's sudden death. It's an imposing structure, drawn like a theatre curtain across a hilltop, and bedecked with mosaics, paintings and other artistic objects. It's framed by an undulating park called the Maximiliananlagen, which is a haven for cyclists in summer and tobogganists in winter.

Kulturzentrum Gasteig CULTURAL CENTRE
(Gasteig Culture Centre; Map p56; ☑089-480 980; www.gasteig.de; Rosenheimer Strasse 5; ⊘8am-11pm; ⓐAm Gasteig) One of Munich's top cultural venues, the Kulturzentrum Gasteig caused quite a controversy a generation ago due to its postmodern, boxy, glass-and-brick design. The complex harbours four concert halls, including the 2400-seat

Philharmonie, the permanent home of the Münchner Philharmoniker.

◉ Bogenhausen

Museum Villa Stuck MUSEUM
(Map p56; www.villastuck.de; Prinzregentenstrasse 60; adult/concession €9/4.50; ⊘11am-6pm Tue-Sun; ⓐFriedensengel/Villa Stuck) Franz von Stuck was a leading light in Munich's art scene around the turn of the 20th century and his residence is one of the finest *Jugendstil* homes you'll ever see. Stuck came up with the intricate design, which forges tapestries, patterned floors, coffered ceilings and other elements into a harmonious work of art. Today his pad is open as a museum with changing exhibitions.

Friedensengel STATUE
(Map p56; ⓐFriedensengel/Villa Stuck) Just east of the Isar River, the *Friedensengel* (Angel of Peace) statue stands guard from its perch atop a 23m-high column. It commemorates the 1871 Treaty of Versailles, which ended the Franco-Prussian War, and the base contains some shimmering golden Roman-style mosaics.

Prinzregententheater THEATRE
(Map p56; ☑089-218 502; www.prinzregententheater.de; Prinzregentenplatz 12; ⓢPrinzregentenplatz) One of Bogenhausen's main landmarks is the Prinzregententheater. Its dramatic mix of art nouveau and neoclassical styles was conceived under Prince Regent Luitpold as a festival house for Richard Wagner operas.

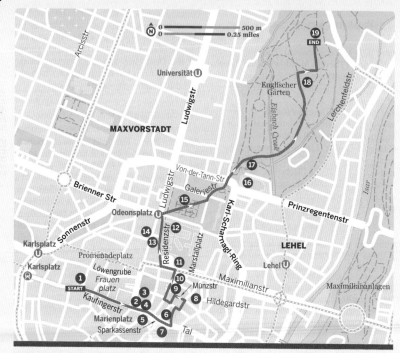

City Walk
Munich's Altstadt

START MICHAELSKIRCHE
END CHINESISCHER TURM
LENGTH 5KM, 2½ HOURS

This circuit takes in the key sights in Munich's historic centre. Commence at ❶ **Michael-skirche** (p47), final resting place of King Ludwig II. Proceed east along the main shopping drag, passing by Munich's landmark Frauenkirche. The way opens into Marienplatz, punctuated by the ❷ **Mariensäule** (p43) in front of the neo-Gothic ❸ **Neues Rathaus** (p43). The ❹ **Fischbrunnen** gushes peacefully near the entrance. The steeple of ❺ **St Peterskirche** (p46) affords a great vista of the old town, including the ❻ **Altes Rathaus** (p47). To see Asam frescoes, peek inside the ❼ **Heiliggeistkirche** (p46).

Head east on Im Tal, taking a left into Maderbräustrasse to Orlandostrasse, site of the ❽ **Hofbräuhaus** (p78), Munich's most (in)famous beer hall. Then go west on Münzstrasse, left into Sparkassenstrasse and then into the alley Ledererstrasse. At Burgstrasse, turn right into the courtyard of the ❾ **Alter**

Hof (p51), the Wittelsbachs' early residence in Munich. Exit north and proceed along Hofgraben, past the former ❿ **Münzhof** (p51). The street opens into Maximilianstrasse and Max-Joseph-Platz, address of the grand ⓫ **Nationaltheater** (p82) and fine opera. The ⓬ **Residenz** (p52) was the seat of the Wittelsbach rulers for over four centuries.

Stroll north on Residenzstrasse to reach Odeonsplatz, site of the Nazis' first lunge at power. Here looms the ⓭ **Feldherrnhalle** (p50), a hulking shrine to war heroes. The mustard-yellow ⓮ **Theatinerkirche** (p50) contains the Wittelsbachs' family crypt. Head into green territory from here, starting with the neoclassical ⓯ **Hofgarten** (p54). Cross it diagonally and go through the underpass to enter the Englischer Garten. Proceed past the ⓰ **Haus der Kunst** (p60). The route winds past the ceremonial ⓱ **Japanisches Teehaus** (p59). A little hill with a classical folly, the ⓲ **Monopteros** (p59), completes the leisurely scene. At the end, take a seat in the beer garden alongside the multitiered ⓳ **Chinesischer Turm** (p59).

⊙ Westend & Theresienwiese

Theresienwiese PARK

(Map p70; U Theresienwiese) The huge Theresienwiese (Theresa Meadow), better known as Wies'n, southwest of the Altstadt, is the site of the Oktoberfest. At the western end of the 'meadow' is the Ruhmeshalle (Hall of Fame; Map p70; Theresienhöhe 16; U Theresienwiese) FREE guarding solemn statues of Bavarian leaders, as well as the Bavariastatue (Statue of Bavaria; Map p70; Theresienhöhe 16; adult/concession €3.50/2.50; ⊙ 9am-6pm Apr–mid-Oct, to 8pm during Oktoberfest; U Theresienwiese), an 18m-high Amazon in the Statue of Liberty tradition, oak wreath in her hand and lion at her feet.

This iron lady has a cunning design that makes her seem solid, but actually you can climb via the knee joint up to the head for a great view of the Oktoberfest. At other times, views are not particularly inspiring.

Verkehrszentrum MUSEUM

(Map p70; www.deutsches-museum.de/verkehrszentrum; Theresienhöhe 14a; adult/concession €6/3; ⊙ 9am-5pm; S Theresienwiese) Sheltered in a historic trade-fair complex, the Verkehrszentrum features some fascinating exhibits, with hands-on displays about pioneering research and famous inventions, plus cars, boats and trains, and the history of car racing. Another section shows off the Deutsches Museum's entire vehicle collection, from the first motorcars to high-speed ICE (inter-city express) trains.

⊙ Olympiapark & Around

Olympiapark STADIUM

(Olympic Park; Map p58; www.olympiapark.de; stadium adult/child €3/2, stadium tour adult/concession €7.50/5; ⊙ stadium tours 11am, 1pm & 4pm Apr-Oct; U Olympiazentrum) The area to the north of the city where soldiers once paraded and the world's first Zeppelin landed in 1909 found a new role in the 1960s as the Olympiapark. Built for the 1972 Olympic Summer Games, it has quite a small-scale feel and some may be amazed that the games could once have been held at such a petite venue.

The complex draws people year-round with concerts, festivals and sporting events, and its swimming hall and ice-skating rink are open to the public.

A good first stop is the Info-Pavilion, which has information, maps, tour tickets

---

OKTOBERFEST

It all started as an elaborate wedding toast – and turned into the world's biggest collective booze-up. In October 1810 the future king, Bavarian Crown Prince Ludwig I, married Princess Therese and the newlyweds threw an enormous party at the city gates, complete with a horse race. The next year Ludwig's fun-loving subjects came back for more. The festival was extended and, to fend off autumn, was moved forward to September. As the years rolled on, the racehorses were dropped and sometimes the party had to be cancelled, but the institution called Oktoberfest was here to stay.

Nearly two centuries later, this 16-day extravaganza draws more than six million visitors a year to celebrate a marriage of good cheer and outright debauchery. A special dark, strong beer (Wies'nbier) is brewed for the occasion, and Müncheners spend the day at the office in Lederhosen and Dirndl in order to hit the festival right after work. No admission fee is charged, but most of the fun costs something.

On the meadow called Theresienwiese (Wies'n for short), a temporary city is erected, consisting of beer tents, amusements and rides – just what drinkers need after several frothy ones! The action kicks off with the Brewer's Parade at 11am on the first day of the festival. The parade begins at Sonnenstrasse and winds its way to the fairgrounds via Schwanthalerstrasse. At noon, the lord mayor stands before the thirsty crowds at Theresienwiese and, with due pomp, slams a wooden tap into a cask of beer. As the beer gushes out, the mayor exclaims, *O'zapft ist's!* (It's tapped!). The next day resembles the opening of the Olympics, as a young woman on horseback leads a parade of costumed participants from all over the world.

Hotels book out very quickly and prices skyrocket, so reserve accommodation as early as you can (a year in advance). The festival is a 15-minute walk southwest of the Hauptbahnhof, and is served by its own U-Bahn station, Theresienwiese. Trams and buses have signs reading Zur Festwiese (literally 'to the Festival Meadow').

> **DON'T MISS**
>
> ## BMW PLANT TOURS
>
> If you like cars, be sure not to miss a tour of BMW's state-of-the-art plant. BMW Plant Tours (☑089-125 016 001; www.bmw-welt.com; adult/concession €8/5; ⊙9am-6.15pm Mon-Fri; Ⓤ Petuelring) in English and German last 2½ hours and take in the entire production process. Booking well ahead is essential, especially in summer.

and a model of the complex. Staff also rent out MP3 players for a self-guided audio tour.

Olympiapark has two famous eye-catchers: the 290m Olympiaturm (Olympic Tower; Map p58; adult/child €5.50/3.50; ⊙9am-midnight; Ⓤ Olympiazentrum) and the warped Olympiastadion. Germans have a soft spot for the latter because it was on this hallowed turf in 1974 that the national soccer team – led by 'the Kaiser' Franz Beckenbauer – won the FIFA World Cup.

When the sky is clear, you'll quite literally have Munich at your feet against the breathtaking backdrop of the Alps from the top of the Olympiaturm.

BMW Welt
NOTABLE BUILDING

(BMW World; Map p58; ☑089-125 016 001; www.bmw-welt.de; Am Olympiapark 1; tours adult/child €7/5; ⊙7.30am-midnight; Ⓤ Olympiazentrum) **FREE** Next to the Olympiapark, the glass-and-steel, double-cone tornado spiraling down from a dark cloud the size of an aircraft carrier holds BMW Welt, truly a petrol head's dream. Apart from its role as a prestigious car pick-up centre, this king of showrooms acts as a shop window for BMW's latest models and a show space for the company as a whole.

Straddle a powerful motorbike, marvel at technology-packed saloons and estates (no tyre kicking, please), browse the 'lifestyle' shop or take the 80-minute guided tour. On the Junior Campus, kids learn about mobility, fancy themselves car engineers and even get to design their own vehicle in workshops. Hang around long enough and you're sure to see motorbike stunts on the staircases and other petroleum-fuelled antics.

BMW Museum
MUSEUM

(Map p58; www.bmw-welt.de; Am Olympiapark 2; adult/concession €10/7; ⊙10am-6pm Tue-Sun; Ⓤ Olympiazentrum) This silver bowl-shaped museum comprises seven themed 'houses'

that examine the development of BMW's product line and include sections on motorcycles and motor racing. Even if you can't tell a head gasket from a crankshaft, the interior design – with its curvy retro feel, futuristic bridges, squares and huge backlit wall screens – is reason enough to visit.

The museum is linked to two more architecturally stunning buildings: the BMW headquarters (closed to the public) and the BMW Welt showroom.

Rock Museum
MUSEUM

(Map p58; www.rockmuseum.de; Besucherplattform des Münchner Olympiaturms; adult/child €4.50/3.50; ⊙9am-midnight; Ⓤ Olympiazentrum) Your lift ticket to the Olympiaturm also buys access to the small if quirky Rock Museum. Ozzie Osbourne's signed guitar, a poem penned by Jim Morrison and Britney Spears' glitter jeans jostle for space with letters, photos and concert tickets, all the result of three decades of collecting by a pair of rock fans.

◉ Outer Districts

Schloss Nymphenburg
PALACE

(Map p58; www.schloss-nymphenburg.de; adult/concession €6/5; ⊙9am-6pm Apr–mid-Oct, 10am-4pm mid-Oct–Mar; ⬛ Schloss Nymphenburg) This commanding palace and its lavish gardens sprawl around 5km northwest of the Altstadt. Begun in 1664 as a villa for Electress Adelaide of Savoy, the stately pile was extended over the next century to create the royal family's summer residence. Franz Duke of Bavaria, head of the once royal Wittelsbach family, still occupies an apartment here.

The main palace building consists of a large villa and two wings of creaking parquet floors and sumptuous period rooms. Right at the beginning of the self-guided tour comes the high point of the entire *Schloss*, the Schönheitengalerie, housed in the former apartments of Queen Caroline. Some 38 portraits of attractive females chosen by an admiring King Ludwig I peer prettily from the walls. The most famous image is of Helene Sedlmayr, the daughter of a shoemaker, wearing a lavish frock the king gave her for the sitting. You'll also find Ludwig's beautiful, but notorious, lover Lola Montez, as well as 19th-century gossip-column celebrity Lady Jane Ellenborough and English beauty Lady Jane Erskin.

Further along the tour route comes the Queen's Bedroom, which still contains the sleigh bed on which Ludwig II was born, and the King's Chamber, resplendent with three-dimensional ceiling frescoes.

Also in the main building is the **Marstallmuseum**, displaying royal coaches and riding gear. This includes Ludwig II's fairy tale–like rococo sleigh, ingeniously fitted with oil lamps for his crazed nocturnal outings. Upstairs is the world's largest collection of porcelain made by the famous Nymphenburger Manufaktur. Also known as the Sammlung Bäuml, it presents the entire product palette from the company's founding in 1747 until 1930.

The sprawling park behind Schloss Nymphenburg is a favourite spot with Münchners and visitors for strolling, jogging or whiling away a lazy afternoon. It's laid out in grand English style and accented with water features, including a large lake, a cascade and a canal, popular for feeding swans and for ice skating and ice curling when it freezes over in winter.

The park's chief folly, the **Amalienburg**, is a small hunting lodge dripping with crystal and gilt decoration; don't miss the amazing **Spiegelsaal** (hall of mirrors). The two-storey Pagodenburg was built in the early 18th century as a Chinese teahouse and is swathed in ceramic tiles depicting landscapes, figures and floral ornamentation. The Badenburg is a sauna and bathing house that still has its original heating system. Finally, the **Magdalenenklause** was built as a mock hermitage in faux-ruined style.

Allianz Arena   STADIUM
(☑ tours 089-6993 1222; www.allianz-arena.de; Werner-Heisenberg-Allee 25, Fröttmaning; tour

---

MUNICH FOR CHILDREN

(Tiny) hands down, Munich is a great city for children, with plenty of activities to please even the most attention span–challenged tots. There are plenty of parks for romping around, swimming pools and lakes for cooling off, and family-friendly beer gardens with children's playgrounds for making new friends.

Deutsches Museum (p60) Many of the city's museums have special kid-oriented programs, but the highly interactive KinderReich at the Deutches Museum specifically lures the single-digit set.

Tierpark Hellabrunn (p68) Petting baby goats, feeding pelicans, watching falcons and hawks perform or even riding a camel should make for some unforgettable memories at the city zoo.

SeaLife München (Map p58; www.visitsealife.com; Willi-Daume-Platz 1; adult/child gate prices €16.95/13.50; ☉ 10am-7pm; Ⓢ Olympiazentrum) For a fishy immersion, head to this new attraction in the Olympiapark.

Paläontologisches Museum (Palaeontological Museum; Map p58; www.palmuc.de; Richard-Wagner-Strasse 10; admission free; ☉ 8am-4pm Mon-Thu, to 2pm Fri; Ⓠ Königsplatz, Ⓤ Königsplatz) **FREE** Dino fans will gravitate here.

Museum Mensch und Natur (Museum of Humankind & Nature; Map p58; www.mmn-muenchen.de; Schloss Nymphenburg; adult/child €3/2; ☉ 9am-5pm Tue, Wed & Fri, to 8pm Thu, 10am-6pm Sat & Sun; Ⓠ Schloss Nymphenburg) Budding scientists will find plenty to marvel at in this museum within the Schloss Nymphenburg.

Spielzeugmuseum (p47) The Spielzeugmuseum is of the look-but-don't-touch variety, but kids might still get a kick out of seeing what toys grandma used to pester for.

Münchner Marionettentheater (Map p48; ☑ 089-265 712; www.muema-theater.de; Blumenstrasse 32; ☉ 3pm Wed-Sun, 8pm Sat) The adorable singing and dancing marionettes performing here have enthralled generations of wee ones.

Münchner Theater für Kinder (Map p58; ☑ 089-594 545; www.mtfk.de; Dachauer Strasse 46) This theatre offers budding thespians a chance to enjoy fairy tales and children's classics in the style of *Pinocchio* and German children's classic *Max & Moritz*.

Brauseschwein (Map p58; Frundsbergstrasse 52; ☉ 10am-1pm & 3pm-6.30pm Mon-Fri, 11am-2pm Sat) This wacky toy shop near Schloss Nymphenburg sells everything from penny candy to joke articles and wooden trains.

PEARL BUCKNALL / GETTY IMAGES ©

1. Rothenburg ob der Tauber (p115) 2. Hitler's Eagle's Nest (p107)
3. Wieskirche interior (p95)

ALTRENDO TRAVEL / GETTY IMAGES ©

A Historical Journey

To sample the region's history is essentially the main reason most head to Germany's south and there really is something for everyone here. Churches, palaces, Nazi sights and whole medieval towns preserved in historical aspic are the main draws.

Nazi Past

Despite all the chocolate box scenery, Bavaria hides a dark past. From Dachau concentration camp to Hitler's Eagle's Nest, Nuremberg's courthouse and Reichsparteitagsgelände to Berchtesgaden's Dokumentation Obersalzberg, there are plenty of opportunities across the state to reflect upon this most sinister chapter in history.

Romantic Road

If you like your history quaint, efficiently well-preserved, varied and drawn up into an orderly queue, get yourself onto the Romantic Road, Germany's most popular touring route. From Würzburg to the Alps, this 350km route takes in medieval walled towns, baroque churches and palaces, a thousand half-timbered houses and some of Germany's best castles.

The House of Wittelsbach

They ruled for well over 700 years, bequeathed modern Bavaria a wealth of architecture, art and other trinkets, and one of their number, 'mad' King Ludwig II, launched the state's tourist industry with his architectural flights of fancy and Wagner obsession – the Wittelsbachs did more to shape Bavaria than any other family.

Magnificent Churches

Whether you are fan of stern Romanesque, flowery rococo, sugary baroque or pompous neo-Gothic, southern Germany has a church for you. Top temples to include on any ecclesiastically themed itinerary include the remote Wieskirche, Munich's Asamkirche, the Münsters of Freiburg and Ulm and Landshut's brick colossus.

adult/child €10/6.50; ⊘ tours in English 1pm; Ⓤ Fröttmaning) Sporting and architecture fans alike should take a side trip to the northern suburb of Fröttmaning to see the ultraslick €340-million Allianz Arena, Munich's dramatic football stadium. The 75-minute stadium tours are hugely popular (no tours on match days). Tickets can be booked online.

Nicknamed the life belt and the rubber boat, the stadium has walls made of inflatable cushions that can be individually lit to match the colours of the host team (red for 1 FC Bayern, blue for TSV 1860, and white for the national side).

Tierpark Hellabrunn   ZOO
(Hellabrunn Zoo; ☐ 089-625 080; www.tierpark-hellabrunn.de; Tierparkstrasse 30; adult/child €14/5; ⊘ 9am-6pm Apr-Sep, to 5pm Oct-Mar; ☐ 52 from Marienplatz, ☐ Tiroler Platz, Ⓤ Thalkirchen) Some 6km south of the city centre, Tierpark Hellabrunn has 5000 furry, feathered and finned friends that rarely fail to enthral the little ones. The zoo was one of the first to organise animals by continent, with enclosures aiming to mimic natural habitats as closely as possible.

🏃 Activities

Boating
A lovely spot to take your sweetheart for a spin is on the Kleinhesseloher See (p59) in the Englischer Garten. Rowing or pedal boats cost around €8 per half-hour for up to four people. Boats may also be hired at the Olympiapark (p63).

Cycling
Munich is an excellent place for cycling, particularly along the Isar River. Some 1200km of cycle paths within the city limits make it one of Europe's friendliest places for two-wheelers.

Swimming
Bathing in the Isar River isn't advisable, due to strong and unpredictable currents (especially in the Englischer Garten), though many locals do. Better to head out of town to one of the many nearby swimming lakes, including the popular **Feringasee** (by car, take the S8 to Unterföhring, then follow signs), where the party never stops on hot summer days; the pretty **Feldmochinger See**, which is framed by gentle mounds and has a special area for wheelchair-bound bathers (by car, take the S1 to Feldmoching); and the **Unterföhringer See** (☐ S8, bicyclevia

the Isarradweg), which has warm water and is easily reached by bicycle via the Isarradweg or via the S8 to Unterföhring.

The best public swimming-pool options, both indoors, are the **Olympia Schwimmhalle** (Map p58; www.swm.de; Coubertinplatz 1; 3hr pass adult/concession €4.60/3.40; ⊘ 7am-11pm; Ⓢ Olympiazentrum), where Mark Spitz famously won seven gold medals in 1972, and the spectacular **Müller'sches Volksbad** (Map p56; www.swm.de; Rosenheimer Strasse 1; adult/child €4.30/3.30; ⊘ 7.30am-11pm; ☐ Am Gasteig), where you can swim in art-nouveau splendour.

🧭 Tours

For a budget tour of Munich's high-brow collections, try **bus 100 Museenlinie**, which runs from the Hauptbahnhof to the Ostbahnhof (east station) via 21 of the city's museums and galleries, including all the big hitters. As this is an ordinary bus route, the tour costs no more than a public-transport ticket.

★ Radius Tours & Bike Rental   TOUR
(Map p70; ☐ 089-543 487 7720; www.radiustours.com; Arnulfstrasse 3; Ⓢ Hauptbahnhof, ☐ Hauptbahnhof, Ⓤ Hauptbahnhof) Entertaining and informative English-language tours include the two-hour Discover Munich walk (€13), the fascinating 2½-hour Hitler and the Third Reich tour (€15), and the three-hour Bavarian Beer tour (€29.50). The company also runs popular excursions to Neuschwanstein, Salzburg and Dachau and has hundreds of bikes for hire (€14.50 per day).

Mike's Bike Tours   BICYCLE TOUR
(Map p48; ☐ 089-2554 3987; www.mikesbiketours.com; Bräuhaus Strasse 10; tours from €30; Ⓢ Marienplatz, Ⓤ Marienplatz) This outfit runs various guided bike tours of the city as well as a couple of other themed excursions. The standard tour is around four hours long (with a one-hour beer-garden break; lunch is not included); the deluxe tour goes for seven hours and covers 16km.

New Europe Munich   WALKING TOUR
(www.newmunichtours.com; ⊘ tours 10am, 10.45am & 2pm; Ⓢ Marienplatz, Ⓤ Marienplatz) Departing from Marienplatz, these English-language walking tours tick off all Munich's central landmarks in three hours. Guides are well informed and fun, though they are under pressure at the end of the tour to get as much as they can in tips. The

company also runs (paid) tours to Dachau (€22) and Neuschwanstein (€37).

Grayline Hop-On-Hop-Off Tours   BUS TOUR
(www.grayline.com/Munich; adult/child €15/10; ☺ hourly) This tour-bus company offers a choice of three tours, from one-hour highlights to the 2½-hour grand tour, as well as excursions to Ludwig II's castles, the Romantic Road, Dachau, Berchtesgaden, Zugspitze and Salzburg. All tours can be booked online and the buses are new. The **main departure point** (Map p48; Ⓢ Hauptbahnhof, Ⓤ Hauptbahnhof) is outside the Karstadt department store opposite the Hauptbahnhof.

✮✮ Festivals & Events

Munich always has something to celebrate. For details, check www.muenchen-tourist.de.

Fasching   CARNIVAL
Beginning on 7 January and ending on Ash Wednesday, this carnival involves all kinds of merriment, such as costume parades and fancy-dress balls.

Starkbierzeit   BEER
Salvator, Optimator, Unimator, Maximator and Triumphator are not the names of gladiators but potent *doppelbock* brews dekegged only between Shrovetide and Easter. Many of Bavaria's breweries take part.

Frühlingsfest   BEER
(www.fruehlingsfest-muenchen.de) This mini-Oktoberfest kicks off the outdoor-festival season with two weeks of beer tents and attractions starting in mid-April.

Maidult   CULTURAL
The first of three dult fairs (traditional fairs with rides and food) held on the Mariahilfplatz. Starts on the Saturday preceding 1 May.

Filmfest München   FILM
(www.filmfest-muenchen.de) This festival presents intriguing and often high-calibre fare by newbies and masters from around the world.

Tollwood Festival   CULTURAL
(www.tollwood.de) Major world-culture festival with concerts, theatre, circus, readings and other fun events held from late June to late July. Also throughout December on the Theresienwiese.

Christopher Street Day   GAY & LESBIAN
(www.csd-munich.de) Gay festival and parade culminating in a big street party on Marien-

platz. Usually held on the second weekend in July.

Jakobidult   CULTURAL
The second dult festival (traditional fair with rides and food) of the year starts on the Saturday following 25 July and continues for one week.

Opernfestspiele   MUSIC
(Opera Festival; www.muenchner-opern-festspiele.de) The Bavarian State Opera brings in top-notch talent from around the world for this month-long festival, which takes place at numerous venues around the city throughout July.

Oktoberfest   BEER
(www.oktoberfest.de) Legendary beer-swilling party running from mid-September to the first Sunday in October. Held on the Theresienwiese.

Munich Marathon   SPORTS
(www.muenchenmarathon.de) More than 10,000 runners from around the world take to the streets in mid-October, finishing after just over 42km at the Olympiastadion.

Christkindlmarkt   CHRISTMAS MARKET
(www.christkindlmarkt.de; ☺ late Nov-Christmas Eve) Traditional Christmas market on Marienplatz.

🛏 Sleeping

Room rates in Munich tend to be high, and they skyrocket during the Oktoberfest. Book well ahead. Budget travellers are spoilt for choice around the Hauptbahnhof, where the majority of hostels congregate, while the Altstadt has the most top-end hotels. Hostels are widespread but tend to be big, professionally run affairs that lack atmosphere.

Altstadt & Around

Hotel Blauer Bock   HOTEL €€
(Map p48; ☎ 089-231 780; www.hotelblauerbock.de; Sebastiansplatz 9; s/d from €47/79; ☎; Ⓤ Marienplatz, Ⓢ Marienplatz) A pretzel's throw from the Viktualienmarkt, this simple hotel has cunningly slipped through the net of Atlstadt gentrification to become one of the city centre's best deals. The cheapest, unmodernised rooms have shared facilities, the updated en-suite chambers are of a 21st-century vintage, and all are quiet, despite the location. Superb restaurant.

Westend & Theresienwiese

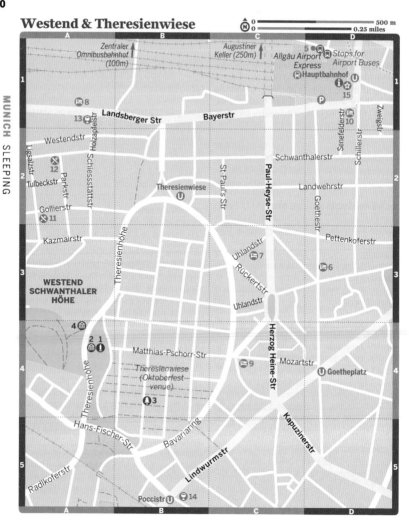

Westend & Theresienwiese

Hotel am Viktualienmarkt HOTEL €€
(Map p48; ☎089-231 1090; www.hotel-am-viktualienmarkt.de; Utzschneiderstrasse 14; s/d from €59/129; ☎; Ⓤ Marienplatz, Ⓢ Marienplatz) Elke and her daughter Stephanie run this good-value property with panache and a sunny attitude. The best of the up-to-date 26 rooms have wooden floors and framed poster art. All this, plus the city-centre location, makes it a superb deal.

Hotel am Markt HOTEL €€
(Map p48; ☎089-225 014; www.hotel-am-markt.eu; Heiliggeiststrasse 6; d from €112; ☎; Ⓢ Marienplatz, Ⓤ Marienplatz) As super central as you could wish, this slender, medieval-style hotel occupies a gabled and turreted building overlooking the Viktualienmarkt. Bedrooms are midrange business standard, some with cheap flatpack, others with vaguely antique-style furniture. Bathrooms are also a mixed bag, but the general standard is good. There's a restaurant on site.

★**Bayerischer Hof** HOTEL €€€
(Map p48; ☎089-21 200; www.bayerischerhof.de; Promenadeplatz 2-6; r €250-450; ❄☎☎; Ⓖ Theatinerstrasse) Around since 1841, this is one of the grande dames of Munich hotels. Rooms come in a number of styles, from busy Laura Ashley to minimalist cosmopolitan. The super-central location and pool come in addition to impeccably regimented staff. Marble, antiques and oil paintings abound, and you can dine till you burst at any of the five fabulous restaurants.

Cortiina HOTEL €€€
(Map p48; ☎089-242 2490; www.cortiina.com; Ledererstrasse 8; s €120-269, d €150-309; ℙ❄☎; Ⓤ Marienplatz, Ⓢ Marienplatz) Tiptoeing between hip and haute, this hotel scores best with trendy, design-minded travellers. The street-level lounge usually buzzes with cocktail-swigging belles and beaus, but all traces of hustle evaporate the moment you step into your minimalist, feng shui-inspired room. Breakfast is an unappetising €22.50 extra.

Hotel Mandarin Oriental Munich HOTEL €€€
(Map p48; ☎089-290 980; www.mandarinoriental.com; Neuturmstrasse 1; d from €625; ℙ❄@☎☎; Ⓤ Marienplatz, Ⓢ Marienplatz) These magnificent neo-Renaissance digs lure the world's glamorous, rich, powerful and famous with opulently understated rooms and top-notch service. Paul McCartney, Bill Clinton and Prince Charles have

crumpled the sheets here. Service is polite almost to a fault, but – incredibly – breakfast and internet access are extra.

🏠 Gärtnerplatzviertel & Glockenbachviertel

Pension Gärtnerplatz GUESTHOUSE €€
(Map p48; ☎089-202 5170; www.pensiongaertnerplatz.de; Klenzestrasse 45; s/d €82/130; ☎; Ⓤ Fraunhoferstrasse) Flee the urban hullabaloo to an Alpine fantasy land where rooms entice with carved wood, painted bedsteads, woollen rugs and crisp, quality bedding. In one room a portrait of Ludwig II watches you as you slumber; breakfasts are honestly organic.

Deutsche Eiche HOTEL €€
(Map p48; ☎089-231 1660; www.deutsche-eiche.com; Reichenbachstrasse 13; s/d from €99/159; ☎; Ⓖ Reichenbachplatz) The rainbow flag flutters alongside the usual national pennants outside this traditionally gay outpost that invites style junkies of all sexual orientations to enjoy the slick rooms and first-class restaurant. There's a sauna on the premises.

🏠 Around the Hauptbahnhof

Wombats City Hostel Munich HOSTEL €
(Map p70; ☎089-5998 9180; www.wombats-hostels.com; Senefelderstrasse 1; dm €23-32, d €84; ℙ@☎; Ⓖ Hauptbahnhof, Ⓤ Hauptbahnhof) Munich's top hostel is a professionally run affair with a whopping 300 dorm beds plus private rooms. Dorms are painted in cheerful pastels and outfitted with wooden floors, ensuite facilities, sturdy lockers and comfy pine bunks, all in a central location near the train station. A free welcome drink awaits in the bar. Buffet breakfast costs €4.30.

Meininger's HOSTEL, HOTEL €
(Map p70; ☎089-5499 8023; www.meininger-hostels.de; Landsbergerstrasse 20; dm/s/d without breakfast from €16/50/66; ☎; Ⓖ Holzapfelstrasse) About 800m west of the Hauptbahnhof, this energetic hostel-hotel has basic, clean, bright rooms with big dorms divided into two for a bit of privacy. Room rates vary wildly depending on the date, events taking place in Munich, and occupancy. Breakfast is an extra €6.90; bike hire costs from €8 per day.

Hotel Cocoon DESIGN HOTEL €€
(Map p48; ☎089-5999 3907; www.hotel-cocoon.de; Lindwurmstrasse 35; s/d from €69/89; ☎☎; Ⓖ Sendlinger Tor, Ⓤ Sendlinger Tor) Fans of

retro design will strike gold in this central lifestyle hotel. Things kick off in reception, with its faux-'70s veneer and dangling '60s ball chairs, and continue in the rooms. All are identical, decorated in retro oranges and greens and equipped with LCD TV, iPod dock and a 'laptop cabin'. Breakfast costs €9.

The glass showers stand in the sleeping area, with only a kitschy Alpine-meadow scene veiling life's vitals.

Hotel Eder   HOTEL €€

(Map p48; ☎089-554 660; www.hotel-eder. de; Zweigstrasse 8; s €55-180, d €65-230; ⊜🛜; 🚇Hauptbahnhof, ⓢHauptbahnhof, ⓤHauptbahnhof) A slice of small-town Bavaria teleported to the slightly seedy area south of the Hauptbahnhof, this rustic oasis has its chequered curtains, carved-wood chairs and Sisi/Ludwig II portraits firmly in place for those who didn't come all this way for the cocktails. The unevenly sized rooms are slightly vanilla, but when rates are midrange to low, this is a nifty deal.

Hotelissimo Haberstock   HOTEL €€

(Map p48; ☎089-557 855; www.hotelissimo. com; Schillerstrasse 4; s/d from €74/104; 🛜; 🚇Hauptbahnhof, ⓢHauptbahnhof, ⓤHauptbahnhof) The cheery decor at this value-for-money pick reflects the vision of the owners, a husband-and-wife team with a feel for colour, fabrics and design. Easy-on-the-eye gold, brown and cream tones dominate the good-sized rooms on the lower floors, while upper ones radiate a bolder, Mediterranean palette.

Hotel Müller   HOTEL €€

(Map p48; ☎089-232 3860; www.hotel-muellermuenchen.de; Fliegenstrasse 4; s/d from €79/109; 🛜; ⓢSendlinger Tor) This friendly hotel has big, bright, business-standard rooms and a good price-to-quality ratio, with five-star breakfasts and polite staff. Despite the city-centre location, the side-street position is pretty quiet.

Hotel Königshof   HOTEL €€€

(Map p48; ☎089-55 1360; www.koenigshofhotel.de; Karlsplatz 25; d from €190; ✳🛜; 🚇Karlsplatz, ⓢKarlsplatz, ⓤKarlsplatz) Over-the-top luxury and obsessive attention to detail make the 'King's Court' a real treat. Rooms range from better-than-average business standard to sumptuous belle époque–style quarters. A Michelin-starred restaurant and a stylish bar are on the premises, and some of the rooms have views of busy Karlsplatz (Stachus), giving the place a heart-of-the-action feel.

Anna Hotel   DESIGN HOTEL €€€

(Map p48; ☎089-599 940; www.geiselprivathotels.de; Schützenstrasse 1; s €160-215, d €175-235; ✳🛜; 🚇Karlsplatz, ⓤKarlsplatz, ⓢKarlsplatz) Urban sophisticates love this well-positioned designer den, where you can retire to rooms dressed in sensuous Donghia furniture and regal colours or tempered by teakwood, marble and mosaics and offering a more minimalist feel. The swanky restaurant-bar is a hive of dining activity.

🛏 Schwabing

La Maison   DESIGN HOTEL €€

(Map p52; ☎089-3303 5550; www.hotel-lamaison.com; Occamstrasse 24; s/d from €110/125; 🅿✳🛜; ⓤMünchner Freiheit) Discerningly retro and immaculate in shades of imperial purple and uber-cool grey, this sassy number wows, its rooms flaunting heated oak floors, jet-black washbasins and starkly contrasting design throughout – though the operators can't resist putting a pack of gummy bears on the expertly ruffed pillows! Cool bar on ground level.

Gästehaus Englischer Garten   GUESTHOUSE €€

(Map p52; ☎089-383 9410; www.hotelenglischergarten.de; Liebergesellstrasse 8; s €75-205, d €87-205; 🅿@🛜; ⓤMünchner Freiheit) Cosily inserted into a 200-year-old ivy-clad mill, this small guesthouse on the edge of the Englischer Garten offers a Bavarian version of the British B&B experience. Not all rooms are en suite, but the breakfast is generous and there's cycle hire (€12 per day).

Hotel Marienbad   HOTEL €€

(Map p48; ☎089-595 585; www.hotelmarienbad.de; Barer Strasse 11; s €55-135, d €120-155; 🛜; 🚇Ottostrasse) Back in the 19th century, Wagner, Puccini and Rilke shacked up at the Marienbad, which once ranked among Munich's finest hotels. The place is still friendly and well maintained, and the 30 rooms flaunt an endearing jumble of styles, from playful art nouveau to floral country Bavarian to campy 1960s utilitarian. Amenities, fortunately, are of more recent vintage.

Hotel Hauser   HOTEL €€

(Map p52; ☎089-286 6750; www.hotel-hauser. de; Schellingstrasse 11; s €80-165, d €118-225; 🛜; ⓤUniversität) The ageing woody rooms here date back to the optimistic days of the economic miracle (the 1950s) but are pristinely maintained, if small. Unexpected extras include a sauna and solarium.

Nymphenburg, Neuhausen & Around

Tent   CAMPGROUND €
(Map p58; ☑089-141 4300; www.the-tent.com; In den Kirchen 30; tent bunks/floor space €10.50/7.50, campsites from €11; ☺ Jun-Nov; ⊕ Botanischer Garten) A kilometre north of Schloss Nymphenburg, this youth-oriented camping ground has classic tent pitches as well as a 160-bunk main tent with floor space and foam mats for shoestring nomads. It's by far the cheapest sleep in town during the Oktoberfest.

★**Hotel Laimer Hof**   HOTEL €€
(Map p58; ☑089-178 0380; www.laimerhof. de; Laimer Strasse 40; s/d from €65/75; P@☎; ⊕Romanplatz) Just a five-minute amble from Schloss Nymphenburg, this superbly tranquil refuge is run by a friendly team who take time to get to know their guests. No two of the 23 rooms are alike, but all boast antique touches, oriental carpets and golden beds. Free bike rental, and coffee and tea in the lobby. Breakfast costs €10.

Haidhausen & Lehel

Hotel Ritzi   HOTEL €€€
(Map p56; ☑089-414 240 890; www.hotel-ritzi. de; Maria-Theresia-Strasse 2a; s/d from €100/149; ☎; ⊕Maxmilianeum) At this charming art hotel next to a little park, creaky wooden stairs (no lift) lead to rooms that transport you to the Caribbean, Africa, Morocco and other exotic lands. But it's the *Jugendstil* features of the building that really impress, as does the much-praised restaurant downstairs, with its Sunday brunch and well-chosen wine list.

Hotel Opéra   HOTEL €€€
(Map p56; ☑089-210 4940; www.hotel-opera. de; St-Anna-Strasse 10; d from €230; ☺☎; ⊕Maxmonument, Ⓤ Lehel) Like the gates to heaven, a white double door opens at the touch of a tiny brass button at the Hotel Opéra. Beyond awaits a smart, petite cocoon of quiet sophistication with peaches-and-cream marble floors, a chandelier scavenged from the Vatican and uniquely decorated rooms.

Westend & Theresienwiese

Pension Westfalia   B&B €
(Map p70; ☑089-530 377; www.pension-westfalia.de; Mozartstrasse 23; s/d from €38/50; ☎; Ⓤ Goetheplatz) Literally a stumble away from the Oktoberfest meadow, this stately four-storey villa conceals a cosy, family-run guesthouse that makes a serene base for sightseeing (outside the beer fest). Rooms are reached by lift; the cheaper ones have corridor facilities.

Hotel Mariandl   HOTEL €€
(Map p70; ☑089-552 9100; www.mariandl. com; Goethestrasse 51; s €68-98, d €88-128; ☎; ⊕Sendlinger Tor, Ⓤ Sendlinger Tor) If you like your history laced with quirkiness, you'll find both aplenty in this rambling neo-Gothic mansion. It's an utterly charming place where rooms convincingly capture the *Jugendstil* period with hand-selected antiques and ornamented ceilings. Breakfast is served until 4pm in the Vienna-style downstairs cafe, which also hosts frequent live jazz or classical-music nights.

Hotel Uhland   HOTEL €€
(Map p70; ☑089-543 350; www.hotel-uhland. de; Uhlandstrasse 1; s/d incl breakfast from €75/95; P☎; Ⓤ Theresienwiese) The Uhland is an enduring favourite with regulars who like their hotel to feel like a home away from home. Free parking, a breakfast buffet with organic products, and minibar drinks that won't dent your budget are just some of the thoughtful features. Rooms have extra-large waterbeds.

Eating

Munich's food was once described by Viennese actor Helmut Qualtinger as 'garnish for the beer', and while that may still ring true in traditional beer halls and eateries, where the menu rarely ventures beyond the roast-pork-and-sausage routine, elsewhere Munich can claim to have southern Germany's most exciting restaurant scene. There's lots of innovation going on in Munich's kitchens, where the best dishes make use of fresh regional, seasonal and organic ingredients. The Bavarian capital is also the best place between Vienna and Paris for a spot of internationally flavoured dining, especially when it comes to Italian, Afghan and Turkish food, and even vegetarians can look forward to something other than noodles and salads. The latest craze is for burgers: if you do plump for this non-traditional fare, at least go for the 100%-Bavarian-beef version.

Altstadt & Around

Küche am Tor   GERMAN, ITALIAN €
(Map p48; Lueg Ins Land 1; mains around €8.50; ☺noon-5pm Mon-Fri; ☑; ⊕Isartor, Ⓢ Isartor)

No-nonsense, blink-and-you'd-miss-it lunch stop for local office workers with a comfortingly short menu of mostly German fare, but containing little Mediterranean touches such as pesto, tuna and *salsiccia* (Italian sausage).

Hans im Glück
BURGERS €

(Map p48; Sonnenstrasse 24; burgers €8; ⊘11am-midnight Mon-Thu, to 2am Fri & Sat; 🚇Karlsplatz, Ⓢ Karlsplatz, Ⓤ Karlsplatz) Plugging into Munich's current obsession with the burger, this new joint in the old post office building serves a juicy selection of meat in buns amid a forest of real birch trunks that grow straight out of the floor. Takeaway and veggie versions available.

Schmalznudel
CAFE €

(Cafe Frischhut; Map p48; Prälat-Zistl-Strasse 8; pastries €1.70; ⊘8am-6pm; ⓊMarienplatz, Ⓢ Marienplatz) This incredibly popular institution serves just four traditional pastries, one of which, the *Schmalznudel* (an oily type of doughnut), gives the place its local nickname. Every baked goodie you munch here is crisp and fragrant, as they're always fresh off the hotplate. They're best eaten with a steaming pot of coffee on a winter's day.

Königsquelle
EUROPEAN €€

(Map p48; ☑089-220 071; www.koenigsquelle. com; Baaderplatz 2; mains €9-21; ⊘5pm-1am Sun-Fri, from 7pm Sat; 🚇Isartor, 🚇Isartor) This Munich institution is well loved for its attentive service, expertly prepared food and dark, well-stocked hardwood bar containing what must be the Bavarian capital's best selection of malt whiskies. The hardly decipherable handwritten menu hovers somewhere mid-Alps, with anything from schnitzel to linguine and goat's cheese to cannelloni to choose from.

Refettorio
ITALIAN €€

(Map p48; ☑089-2280 1680; www.refetto riomuenchen.de; Marstallplatz 3; mains €11.50-28.50; ⊘noon-midnight Tue-Fri, 10am-midnight Sat, 10am-6pm Sun; 🛜; 🚇Nationaltheater) The latest recruit to Munich's army of Italian eateries is this colourful, fresh-feeling and utterly 21st-century place near the opera and the Residenztheater. Every table and chair is a different colour, Greek mosaics hang at strategic points and bits of art are dotted like pepperoni on a pizza. The menu is expertly executed and commendably brief.

Fedora
ITALIAN €€

(Map p48; www.fedorabar.de; Ledererstrasse 3; mains around €12, pizzas €10-15; ⊘10am-1am Mon-Thu, to 2am Fri & Sat, 4pm-midnight Sun; ⓊMarienplatz, Ⓢ Marienplatz) Occupying the vaulted spaces of the 13th-century Zerwirkgewölbe, this Italian job named after the famous hat does a decent pizza and has an open kitchen where you can watch cooks load it up. Tables bearing chequered tablecloths spread out from a big bar, and there's plenty of sunny street-side seating.

Conviva
INTERNATIONAL €€

(Map p48; www.conviva-muenchen.de; Hildegardstrasse 1; 3-course lunch €8-10, dinner mains €10-15; ⊘11am-1am Mon-Sat, from 5pm Sun; ☑; 🚇Kammerspiele) The industrially exposed interior and barely dressed tables mean nothing distracts from the great food at this theatre restaurant. The daily-changing menus make the most of local seasonal ingredients and are reassuringly short.

Prinz Myshkin
VEGETARIAN €€

(Map p48; ☑089-265 596; www.prinzmyshkin. com; Hackenstrasse 2; mains €10-19; ⊘11am-12.30am; ☑; ⓊMarienplatz, Ⓢ Marienplatz) This place is proof, if any were needed, that the vegetarian experience has left the sandals, beards and lentils era. Occupying a former brewery, Munich's premier meat-free dining spot is an vaulted and open-plan but intimate space. Health-conscious eaters come to savour imaginative dishes such as curry-orange-carrot soup, unexpectedly good curries and 'wellness desserts'.

Bratwurstherzl
FRANCONIAN €€

(Map p48; Dreifaltigkeitsplatz 1; mains €7-16; ⊘10am-11pm Mon-Sat; ⓊMarienplatz, Ⓢ Marienplatz) Cosy panelling and an ancient vaulted brick ceiling set the tone of this Old Munich tavern with a Franconian focus. Homemade organic sausages are grilled to perfection on an open beechwood fire and served on heart-shaped pewter plates. They're best enjoyed with a cold one from the Hacker-Pschorr brewery.

OskarMaria
INTERNATIONAL €€

(Map p48; www.oskarmaria.com; Salvatorplatz 1; mains €8-26; ⊘10am-midnight Mon-Sat, to 7pm Sun; ⓊOdeonsplatz) The cafe at the Literaturhaus cultural centre is a commendably stylish spot, with bookishly high ceilings, rows of small central European cafe tables and sprightly waiters. The highbrow atmosphere will be appreciated by those who prefer their eateries (virtually) tourist free and the menu features international staples plus several Bavarian favourites.

Cafe Luitpold CAFE €€
(Map p48; www.cafe-luitpold.de; Briennerstrasse 11; mains €11-20; ⏰8am-7pm Mon, to 11pm Tue-Sat, 9am-7pm Sun; ⓤOdeonsplatz) A cluster of pillarbox-red street-side tables and chairs announces you've arrived at this stylish but not uber-cool retreat. It offers a choice of three spaces: a lively bar, a less boisterous columned cafe and a cool palm-leaved atrium. Good for a daytime coffee-and-cake halt or a full evening blowout with all the trimmings.

Weisses Brauhaus BAVARIAN €€
(Map p48; ☑089-290 1380; www.weisses-brauhaus.de; Tal 7; mains €7-20; ⓤMarienplatz, ⓢMarienplatz) One of Munich's classic beer halls, in the evenings this place is charged with red-faced, ale-infused hilarity, with Alpine whoops accompanying the rabble-rousing oompah band. The *Weisswurst* (veal sausage) here sets the standard for the rest to aspire to; sluice down a pair with the unsurpassed Schneider *Weissbier*. It's understandably very popular and reservations are recommended after 7pm.

Tegernseer Tal BAVARIAN €€
(Map p48; Tal 8; mains €9-20; ⏰9.30am-1am Sun-Wed, to 3am Thu-Sat; ☎; ⓤMarienplatz, ⓢMarienplatz) A blond-wood interior illuminated by a huge skylight makes this a bright alternative to Munich's dark-panelled taverns. And with Alpine Tegernseer beer on tap and an imaginative menu of regional food, this is generally a lighter, calmer beer-hall experience with a less raucous ambience.

Einstein JEWISH €€
(Map p48; St-Jakobs-Platz 18; mains €10-19; ⏰noon-3pm & 6pm-midnight Sat-Thu, 12.30-3pm Fri; ⓡMarienplatz, ⓤMarienplatz) Reflected in the plate-glass windows of the Jewish Museum, this is the only kosher eatery in the city centre. The ID and bag search entry process is worth it for the restaurant's uncluttered lines, smartly laid tables, soothing ambience and menu of well-crafted Israeli dishes.

Lemar AFGHANI €€
(Map p48; ☑089-2694 9454; Brunnstrasse 4; mains €12.50-15; ⏰6-11pm; ⓡSendlinger Tor, ⓤSendlinger Tor) Lemar provides an excellent introduction to this little-known but tasty cuisine, serving scrumptious Afghan dishes such as spicy lentil soup, chicken kebabs, fried basmati rice with raisins and pistachios, and *mantu* (pasta balls filled with meat and yoghurt). Rave reviews from all who eat in the authentic cushion-strewn dining space mean bookings may be necessary.

Galleria ITALIAN €€€
(Map p48; ☑089-297 995; www.ristorante-galleria.de; Sparkassenstrasse 11; 2/3 courses €16/25; ⏰noon-2.30pm & 6-11pm; ⓢMarienplatz, ⓤMarienplatz) Munich has a multitude of Italian eateries, but Galleria is a cut above the rest. The compact interior hits you first, a multihued, eclectic mix of contemporary art and tightly packed tables. The menu has a few surprises, such as turbot with lentil curry and coconut foam. Reservations are pretty much essential in the evening.

✖ Gärtnerplatzviertel & Glockenbackviertel

Götterspeise CAFE €
(Map p48; Jahnstrasse 30; snacks from €3; ⏰8am-7pm Mon-Fri, 9am-6pm Sat; ⓡMüllerstrasse) The name of this cafe translates as 'food of the gods' and the food in question is that most addictive of treats, chocolate. Here it comes in many forms, both liquid and solid, but there are also teas, coffees and cakes and little smokers' perches outside for Germany's many puffing chocoholics.

Wiener Cafe CAFE €
(Map p48; cnr Reichenbachstrasse & Rumfordstrasse; snacks €1.50-5; ⏰8.30am-6pm Mon-Fri, 8am-5pm Sat; ⓡReichenbachplatz) The only cool thing about this delightfully old-fashioned central European coffeehouse is the marble table tops.

★ Fraunhofer BAVARIAN €€
(Map p48; ☑089-266 460; www.fraunhofer-theater.de; Fraunhoferstrasse 9; mains €7-25; ⏰4.30pm-1am Mon-Fri, 10am-1am Sat; ☎; ⓡMüllerstrasse) With its screechy parquet floors, stuccoed ceilings, wood panelling and virtually no trace that the last century even happened, this wonderfully characterful inn is perfect for exploring the region with a fork. The menu is a seasonally adapted checklist of southern German favourites but also features at least a dozen vegetarian dishes and the odd exotic ingredient.

The tiny theatre at the back stages great shows and was among the venues that pioneered a modern style of *Volksmusik* (folk music) back in the '70s and '80s.

Bamyan AFGHANI €€
(Map p48; www.bamyan.de; Hans-Sachs-Strasse 3; mains €8-16; ⏰3pm-1am Mon-Sat, from 6pm Sun; ⓡMüllerstrasse) The terms 'happy hour', 'cocktail' and 'chilled vibe' don't often go together with the word 'Afghan', but that's

exactly the combination you get at this exotic hang-out, named after the Buddha statues infamously destroyed by the Taliban in 2001. Central Asian soups, kebabs, rice and lamb dishes and big salads are eaten at handmade tables inlaid with ornate metalwork.

MC Müller
BURGERS €€

(Map p48; www.mcmueller.org; cnr Müllerstrasse & Fraunhoferstrasse; burgers €7.20-15.50; ⊙6pm-2am Mon-Thu, to 4am Fri & Sat; 🚇Müllerstrasse) Retro '60s looks and triple duty as bar, DJ lounge and burger joint until the wee hours.

Sushi & Soul
SUSHI €€

(Map p48; Klenzestrasse 21; mains €12-20; ⊙6pm-1am; 🚇Reichenbachplatz) This popular sushi joint serves up piscine morsels and creative cocktails to a Japanese-pop soundtrack.

La Bouche
FRENCH €€€

(Map p48; ☑089-265 626; www.restaurant-la-bouche.de; Jahnstrasse 30; mains €14.50-30; ⊙noon-3pm Mon-Fri, 6pm-midnight Mon-Sat; 🚇Fraunhoferstrasse) Expect good Gallic goings-on at this French-inspired port of call, where tables are squished as tight as lovers and the accent is on imaginative but gimmick-free fare, such as truffle ravioli, veal liver with caramelised apple, and plenty of fish. It's much bigger than first meets the eye: there's a second room at the back.

🍴 Schwabing & Maxvorstadt

Pommes Boutique
FAST FOOD €

(Map p52; Amalienstrasse 46; fries €3.20; ⊙10am-10pm Mon-Sat, noon-8pm Sun; 🚇Universität) This funky lunch halt serves cheap-as-chips Belgian-style fries made from organic potatoes, 30-odd finger-licking dips to dunk them in and *Currywurst* to die for.

Chopan
AFGHANI €€

(Map p58; Elvirastrasse 18A; mains €7-17.50; ⊙6pm-midnight; 🚇Maillingerstrasse) Munich has a huge Afghan community, whose most respected eatery is this much-lauded restaurant done out Central Asian caravanserai style with rich fabrics, multihued glass lanterns and geometric patterns. In this culinary Aladdin's cave you'll discover an exotic menu of lamb, lentils, rice, spinach and flatbread in various combinations, but there are no alcoholic beverages to see things on their way.

Potting Shed
BURGERS €€

(Map p52; Occamstrasse 11; mains €6-17; ⊙from 6pm; 🚇Münchner Freiheit) This relaxed hang-out serves tapas, gourmet burgers and cocktails to an easy-going evening crowd. The burger menu whisks you round the globe, but it's the house speciality, the 'Potting Shed Special', involving an organic beef burger flambéed in whisky, that catches the eye on the simple but well-concocted menu.

Ruff's Burger
BURGERS €€

(Map p52; Occamstrasse 4; burgers €7-15; ⊙11.30am-11pm Mon-Wed, to midnight Thu-Sat, to 10pm Sun; 🚇Münchner Freiheit) Munich's obsession with putting a fried bit of meat between two buns continues at this Schwabing joint, where the burgers are 100% Bavarian beef – except, of course, for the token veggie version. Erdinger and Tegernseer beer and mostly outdoor seating.

★ Tantris
INTERNATIONAL €€€

(☑089-361 9590; www.tantris.de; Johann-Fichte-Strasse 7; menu from €80; ⊙noon-3pm & 6.30pm-1am Tue-Sat; 🕾; 🚇Dietlindenstrasse) Tantris means 'the search for perfection' and here, at one of Germany's most famous restaurants, they're not far off it. The interior design is full-bodied '70s – all postbox reds, truffle blacks and illuminated yellows – with sublime food and service sometimes as unobtrusive as it is efficient. The wine cellar is probably Germany's best. Reservations are essential.

Cochinchina
ASIAN €€€

(Map p52; ☑089-3898 9577; www.cochinchina.de; Kaiserstrasse 28; mains around €20; ⊙11.30am-2.30pm & 6pm-midnight; 🚇Münchner Freiheit) Bearing an old name for southern Vietnam, this cosmopolitan Asiatic fusion restaurant is Munich's top place for Vietnamese and Chinese concoctions, consumed in a dark, dramatically exotic space devoted to the firefly and splashed with the odd bit of colour in the shape of Chinese vases and lamps. The traditional *pho* soup is southern Germany's best.

🍴 Nymphenburg, Neuhausen & Around

Eiscafé Sarcletti
GELATERIA €

(Map p58; www.sarcletti.de; Nymphenburger Strasse 155; ⊙9am-11.30pm May-Aug, slightly shorter hours Sep-Apr; 🚇Volkartstrasse) Ice-cream addicts have been getting their gelato fix at this Munich institution since 1879. Choose from more than 50 mouth-watering flavours, from not-so-plain vanilla to coconut milk and lime.

Schlosscafé Im Palmenhaus
CAFE €€

(Map p58; www.palmenhaus.de; Schloss Nymphenburg 43; mains €9-15; ⏲11am-6pm Tue-Fri, from 10am Sat & Sun; ⓟSchloss Nymphenburg) The glass-fronted 1820 palm house where Ludwig II used to keep his exotic house plants warm in winter is now a high-ceilinged and pleasantly scented cafe serving soups, salads, sandwiches and other light meals. It's just behind Schloss Nymphenburg.

Esszimmer
MEDITERRANEAN €€€

(Map p58; ☎089-358 991 814; www.bmw-welt.com; BMW Welt, Am Olympiapark 1; 4/5 courses €90/110; ⏲from 4pm Tue-Sat; ❄ⓢ; ⓤOlympiazentrum) It took Bobby Bräuer, head chef at the gourmet restaurant at BMW World, just two years to gain his first Michelin star. Munich's top dining spot is the place to sample high-octane French and Mediterranean morsels, served in a trendily dark and veneered dining room above the i8s and 7 Series. Life in the gastronomic fast lane.

🍴 Haidhausen & Lehel

Wirtshaus in der Au
BAVARIAN €€

(Map p56; ☎089-448 1400; Lilienstrasse 51; mains €10-16; ⏲5pm-midnight Mon-Fri, from 10am Sat & Sun; ⓟDeutsches Museum) This Bavarian tavern's simple slogan is 'Beer and dumplings since 1901', and it's that time-honoured staple (the dumpling) that's the speciality here (the tavern even runs a dumpling-making course in English). Once a brewery, the space-rich dining area has chunky tiled floors, a lofty ceiling and a crackling fireplace in winter. When spring springs, the beer garden fills.

Dreigroschenkeller
BAVARIAN €€

(Map p56; Lilienstrasse 2; mains €10-19; ⏲5pm-1am Sun-Thu, to 3am Fri & Sat; ⓟDeutsches Museum) A cosy and labyrinthine brick-cellar pub with rooms – based upon Bertolt Brecht's *Die Dreigroschenoper* (The Threepenny Opera) – ranging from a prison cell to a red satiny salon. There are nine types of beer to choose from and an extensive menu of hearty international and Bavarian favourites.

Vegelangelo
VEGETARIAN €€

(Map p48; ☎089-2880 6836; www.vegelangelo.de; Thomas-Wimmer-Ring 16; mains €10-19, set menu €24-30; ⏲noon-2pm Tue-Thu, 6pm-late Mon-Sat; ⓢ; ⓟIsartor, ⓢIsartor) Reservations are compulsory at this petite vegie spot, where Indian odds and ends, a piano and a small Victorian fireplace distract little from the superb meat-free cooking, all of which can be converted to suit vegans. There's a set-menu-only policy Friday and Saturday. No prams allowed.

Swagat
INDIAN €€

(Map p56; Prinzregentenplatz 13; mains €10.50-22.50; ⏲11.30am-2.30pm & 5.30pm-1am; ⓢ; ⓟPrinzregentenplatz, ⓤPrinzregentenplatz) Swagat fills every nook of an intimate cellar space with Indian fabrics, cavorting Hindu gods and snow-white tablecloths. The curry is as hot as Bavarians can take it, and there's plenty to please non-carnivores.

🍴 Westend

★ Marais
CAFE €

(Map p70; Parkstrasse 2; dishes €5-13; ⏲8am-8pm Tue-Sat, 10am-6pm Sun; ⓢ; ⓟHolzapfelstrasse) Is it a junk shop, a cafe or a sewing shop? Well, Westend's oddest coffeehouse is in fact all three, and everything you see in this converted haberdashery – the knick-knacks, the cakes and the antique chair you're sitting on – is for sale.

Bodhi
VEGAN €€

(Map p70; Ligsalzstrasse 23; mains €10-17; ⏲from 5pm Mon-Fri, from noon Sat, 10am-2pm Sun; ⓢ; ⓤSchwanthalerhöhe) This new vegan restaurant has an uncluttered, wood-rich interior where health-conscious diners feast on meat-and-dairy-free pastas, burgers, salads, soya steaks and tofu-based dishes. Whether those same wellness fanatics swill it all down with the large selection of cocktails and whisky, we'll never know.

La Vecchia Masseria
ITALIAN €€

(Map p48; Mathildenstrasse 3; mains €9-18, pizzas €7-8.50; ⏲11.30am-12.30am; ⓟSendlinger Tor, ⓢSendlinger Tor) One of Munich's longest-established Italian *osterie*, this earthy, rurally themed place has chunky wood tables, antique tin buckets, baskets and clothing irons, all conjuring up the ambience of an Apennine farmhouse. There's a small beer garden out the front, but this only operates until 9.30pm.

🍸 Drinking & Nightlife

Munich is a great place for boozers. Raucous beer halls, snazzy hotel lounges, chestnut-canopied beer gardens, hipster DJ bars, designer cocktail temples – the variety is so huge that finding a party den to match your mood is not exactly a tall order. Generally speaking, student-flavoured places abound in Maxvorstadt and Schwabing, while traditional beer halls and taverns cluster in the Altstadt; Haidhausen attracts trendy types, and the Gärtnerplatzviertel and Glockenbachviertel are alive with gay bars and hipster haunts.

No matter where you are, you won't be far from an enticing cafe to get a java-infused pick-me-up. Many also serve light fare and delicious (often homemade) cakes and are great places to linger, chat, write postcards or simply watch people on parade.

Bavaria's brews are best sampled in a venerable *Bierkeller* (beer hall) or *Biergarten* (beer garden). People come primarily to drink, although food is usually served. In beer gardens you are usually allowed to bring your own picnic as long as you sit at tables without tablecloths and order something to drink. Sometimes there's a resident brass band pumping oompah music. And don't even think about sitting at a *Stammtisch* (a table reserved for regulars; look for a brass plaque or some other sign)! Beer gardens are, for the most part, very family friendly, with play areas and kids' menus.

Munich has a thriving club scene, so no matter whether your musical tastes run to disco or dance hall, house or punk, techno or punk-folk, you'll find a place to get those feet moving. To get the latest from the scene, peruse the listings mags or sift through the myriad flyers in shops, cafes and bars. This being Munich, expect pretty strict doors at most venues. Dance floors rarely heat up before 1am, so showing up early may increase your chances of getting in without suffering the indignities of a ridiculous wait and possible rejection. If you look under 30, bring ID. Cover charges rarely exceed €15.

🍺 Altstadt & Around

Hofbräuhaus
BEER HALL

(Map p48; ☎089-290 136 100; www.hofbrauhaus.de; Am Platzl 9; 1L beer €8, mains €10-20; ⊙9am-11.30pm; 🎭Kammerspiele, Ⓢ Marienplatz, Ⓤ Marienplatz) Every visitor to Munich should make a pilgrimage to this mothership of all beer halls, if only once. There is a range of spaces in which to do your mass lifting: the horse chestnut–shaded garden, the main hall next to the oompah band, tables opposite the industrial-scale kitchen and quieter corners.

Harry Klein
CLUB

(Map p48; www.harrykleinclub.de; Sonnenstrasse 8; ⊙from 11pm; 🎭Karlsplatz, Ⓢ Karlsplatz, Ⓤ Karlsplatz) Follow the gold-lined passageway off Sonnenstrasse to what some regard as one of the best *Elektro-clubs* in the world. Nights here are an amazing alchemy of electro sound and visuals, with live video art projected onto the walls Kraftwerk style blending to awe-inspiring effect with the music.

MilchundBar
CLUB

(Map p48; www.milchundbar.de; Sonnenstrasse 27; 🎭Sendlinger Tor, Ⓤ Sendlinger Tor) This relative newcomer is one of the hottest addresses in the city centre for those who like to spend the hours between supper and breakfast boogieing to an eclectic mix of nostalgia hits during the week and top DJs at the weekends.

Rote Sonne
CLUB

(Map p48; www.rote-sonne.com; Maximiliansplatz 5; ⊙from 11pm Thu-Sun; 🎭Lenbachplatz) Named for a 1969 Munich cult movie starring It-Girl Uschi Obermaier, the Red Sun is a fiery nirvana for fans of electronic sounds. A global roster of DJs keeps the wooden dance floor packed and sweaty until the sun rises.

Viktualienmarkt
BEER GARDEN

(Map p48; Viktualienmarkt 6; ⊙9am-10pm; Ⓤ Marienplatz, Ⓢ Marienplatz) After a day of sightseeing or stocking up on tasty nibbles at the Viktualienmarkt, find a table at this chestnut-shaded beer garden, a Munich institution since 1807. The breweries take turns serving here, so you never know what's on tap.

Schumann's Bar
BAR

(Map p48; ☎089-229 060; www.schumanns.de; Odeonsplatz 6-7; ⊙8am-3am Mon-Fri, 6pm-3am Sat & Sun; Ⓢ Odeonsplatz) Urbane and sophisticated, Schumann's shakes up Munich's nightlife with libational flights of fancy in an impressive range of concoctions. It's also good for weekday breakfasts.

Braunauer Hof
PUB

(Map p48; Frauenstrasse 42; ⊙11.30am-11pm Mon-Sat; 🎭Isartor, Ⓢ Isartor) Near the Isartor, drinkers can choose between the traditional Bavarian interior or the beer garden out the back that enjoys a surprisingly tranquil setting despite its city-centre location. Most come for the Paulaner beer of an eve, but the €8.50 lunch menu is good value for money.

Stereo Cafe
CAFE

(Map p48; www.stereocafe.de; Residenzstrasse 25; ⊙10am-8pm Mon-Sat; 🎭Theatinerstrasse) Right opposite the Residenz, with bar stools looking out of huge windows at its western flank, this light, airy, vaguely Portuguese place (port, *pastel de nata,* Atlantic fish dishes) is a real gem and a nice spot for a pre-theatre aperitif or mid-sightseeing/shopping timeout. It's accessed through the downstairs men's-accessory emporium.

Café Cord CAFE
(Map p48; ☎089-5454 0780; www.cafe-cord. tv; Sonnenstrasse 19; mains €10-20; ⊙11am-1am Mon-Sat; 🕾; 🚊Karlsplatz, ⑤Karlsplatz, ⑪Karlsplatz) Set back from busy Sonnenstrasse in a modern precinct, clean-cut Cord is good stop for a light lunch or coffee or an ideal first pit stop before a long night on the club circuit. In summer, the delicious global fare tastes best on the romantic, twinkly courtyard.

Heart CLUB
(Map p48; www.h-e-a-r-t.me; Lenbachplatz 2a; 🚊Lenbachplatz) Exclusive dine-dance-flirt club ensconced somewhat fittingly in the old stock exchange and aimed at well-heeled over-25s who like their beef tartar served at 5am. Dress to impress for the cool, well-illuminated, mirror-ceilinged hall and other impressively designed chill spaces.

⊙ Gärtnerplatzviertel & Glockenbackviertel

Baader Café CAFE
(Map p48; Baaderstrasse 47; ⊙9.30am-1am; 🕾; 🚊Fraunhoferstrasse) Around since the mid-'80s, this literary think-and-drink place lures all sorts, from short skirts to tweed jackets, who linger over daytime coffees and nighttime cocktails. It's normally packed, even on winter Wednesday mornings, and is popular for Sunday brunch.

Trachtenvogl CAFE
(Map p48; Reichenbachstrasse 47; ⊙10am-1am Sun-Thu, to 2am Fri & Sat; 🕾; 🚊Fraunhoferstrasse) At night you'll have to shoehorn your way into this buzzy lair favoured by a chatty, boozy crowd of scenesters, artists and students. Daytimes are mellower – all the better to sample its hot-chocolate menu and check out the incongruous collection of cuckoo clocks and antlers, left over from the days when this was a traditional garment shop.

Del Fiori CAFE
(Map p48; Gärtnerplatz 1; ⊙10am-midnight; 🕾; 🚊Reichenbachplatz) Come to this buzzing Italian coffeehouse for the outdoor seating on the Gärtnerplatz, where there's standing room only from the first rays of late winter to the last of autumn. Great people-watching possibilities all day long.

⊙ Schwabing & Maxvorstadt

★**Alter Simpl** PUB
(Map p52; www.eggerlokale.de; Türkenstrasse 57; ⊙11am-3am Mon-Fri, to 4am Sat & Sun; 🚊Schellingstrasse) Thomas Mann and Hermann Hesse used to knock 'em back at this well-scuffed and wood-panelled thirst parlour. A bookish ambience still pervades, making this an apt spot to curl up with a weighty tome over a few Irish ales. The curious name is an abbreviation of the satirical magazine *Simplicissimus.*

Hirschau BEER GARDEN
(Gysslingstrasse 15; ⊙11.30am-11pm Mon-Fri, from 10am Sat & Sun; ⑪Dietlindenstrasse) This monster beer garden can seat 1700 quaffers and hosts live music almost every day in the summer months. Dispatch the kids to the excellent playground and adjacent minigolf course while you indulge in some tankard caressing.

Salon Иркутск BAR
(Map p58; www.salonirkutsk.de; Isabellastrasse 4; ⊙5pm-late; ⑪Josephsplatz) Escape the sugary cocktails and belly-inflating suds to one of Munich's more cultured watering holes, which touts itself as a Franco-Slavic evening bistro. You'll soon see this is no place to get slammed on Russian ethanol or cheap Gallic plonk – Monday is piano night, Wednesday is French evening and the green-painted, wood-panelled interior hosts exhibitions of local art.

Black Bean CAFE
(Map p52; Amalienstrasse 44; ⊙7am-7pm Mon-Fri, from 8am Sat & Sun; 🕾; ⑪Universität) If you thought the only decent brew Bavarians could mash was beer, train your Arabica radar to this regional retort to Starbucks. The organic coffee gets tops marks, as do the muffins.

Eat the Rich BAR
(Map p58; www.eattherich.de; Hessstrasse 90; ⊙7pm-1am Wed & Thu, to 4am Fri & Sat; ⑪Theresienstrasse) Strong cocktails served in half-litre glasses quickly loosen inhibitions at this sizzling nightspot, a great place to crash when the party's winding down everywhere else. Food is served till 3am on weekends.

News Bar CAFE
(Map p52; www.newsbarmunich.de; Amalienstrasse 55; ⊙10am-midnight Sun-Thu, to 1am Fri &

Sat; 📶; Ⓤ Universität) From tousled students to young managers and greying professors, everybody loves their news, especially at this stylish cafe that sells international papers and mags. It's an ideal breakfast spot before embarking on a day of Pinakothek museum hopping.

🍷 Nymphenburg, Neuhausen & Around

Hirschgarten   BEER GARDEN
(Map p58; www.hirschgarten.de; Hirschgarten 1; ⊙ 11.30am-1am; 🚋 Kriemhildenstrasse, Ⓢ Laim) The Everest of Munich beer gardens can accommodate up to 8000 Augustiner lovers

but still manages to feel airy and uncluttered. It's in a lovely spot in a former royal hunting preserve and rubs up against a deer enclosure and a carousel. Steer here after visiting Schloss Nymphenburg – it's only a short walk south of the palace.

Augustiner Keller   BEER GARDEN
(Arnulfstrasse 52; ⊙ 10am-1am Apr-Oct; 🚗; 🚋 Hopfenstrasse) Every year this leafy 5000-seat beer garden, about 500m west of the Hauptbahnhof, buzzes with fairy-lit thirst-quenching activity from the first sign that spring may have *gesprungen*. The ancient chestnuts are thick enough to seek refuge under when it rains,

---

OUT & ABOUT IN MUNICH

Munich's gay and lesbian scene is the liveliest in Bavaria but tame compared to that of Berlin, Cologne or Amsterdam. The rainbow flag flies especially proudly along Müllerstrasse and the adjoining Glockenbachviertel and Gärtnerplatzviertel. To plug into the scene, keep an eye out for freebie mags *Our Munich* and *Sergej*, which contain up-to-date listings and news about the community and gay-friendly establishments around town. Another source of info is www.gaytouristoffice.com.

Sub (Map p48; 📞 089-856 346 400; www.subonline.org; Müllerstrasse 14; ⊙ 7-11pm Sun-Thu, to midnight Fri & Sat; 🚋 Müllerstrasse) is a one-stop service and information agency; lesbians can also turn to **Le Tra** (Map p48; 📞 089-725 4272; www.letra.de; Angertorstrasse 3; ⊙ 2.30-5pm Mon & Wed, 10.30am-1pm Tue; 🚋 Müllerstrasse).

The main street parties of the year are Christopher Street Day (p69), held on Marienplatz on the second weekend in July, and the Schwules Strassenfest (www.schwules-strassenfest.de), held in mid-August along Hans-Sachs-Strasse in the Glockenbachviertel. During Oktoberfest, lesbigay folks invade the Bräurosl beer tent on the first Sunday and Fischer-Vroni on the second Monday.

Bars & Clubs

Ochsengarten (Map p48; www.ochsengarten.de; Müllerstrasse 47; 🚋 Müllerstrasse) The first bar to open in the Bavarian capital where to get in you have to be clad in leather, rubber, lycra, neopren or any other kinky attire you can think of. Gay men only.

Edelheiss (Map p48; www.edelheiss.de; Pestalozzistrasse 6; 🚋 Sendlinger Tor, Ⓤ Sendlinger Tor) A laid-back cafe by day, Edelheiss has vibrant party nights.

Nil (Map p48; www.cafenil.com; Hans-Sachs-Strasse 2; meals €3.50-8; ⊙ 3pm-3am; 🚋 Müllerstrasse) A construct in wood and marble with a vaguely Egyptian theme, this chilled-out cafe-bar is open till 3am and is a good place to crash after the party has stopped elsewhere.

NY Club (Map p48; www.nyclub.de; Sonnenstrasse 25; ⊙ Fri & Sat; 🚋 Sendlinger Tor, Ⓤ Sendlinger Tor) After a complete revamp, it's again 'Raining Men' at Munich's hottest gay dance temple, where you can party away with Ibiza-style abandon on the cool, back-lit main floor.

Bau (Map p48; www.bau-munich.de; Müllerstrasse 41; 🚋 Müllerstrasse) Bi-level bar that's party central for manly men, with plenty of leather, Levi's and uniforms on show. Foam parties take place in the small cellar darkroom.

Prosecco (Map p48; www.prosecco-munich.de; Theklatstrasse 1; 🚋 Müllerstrasse) Fun venue for dancing, cruising and drinking that attracts a mixed bunch of party people with quirky decor and a cheesy mix of music (mostly '80s and charts).

or else lug your mug to the actual beer cellar. Small playground.

☺ Haidhausen & Lehel

Biergarten Muffatwerk BEER GARDEN
(Map p56; www.muffatwerk.de; Zellstrasse 4; ☺from noon; 🖾Am Gasteig) Think of this one as a progressive beer garden with reggae instead of oompah, civilised imbibing instead of brainless guzzling, organic meats, fish and vegetables on the grill, and the option of chilling in lounge chairs. Opening hours are open-ended, meaning some very late finishes.

P1 CLUB
(Map p56; www.p1-club.de; Prinzregentenstrasse 1; 🖾Nationalmuseum/Haus der Kunst) If you make it past the notorious face control at Munich's premier late spot, you'll encounter a crowd of Bundesliga reserve players, Q-list celebs and quite a few Russian speakers too busy seeing and being seen to actually have a good time. But it's all part of the fun, and the decor and summer terrace have their appeal.

Kultfabrik CLUB
(Map p56; www.kultfabrik.de; Grafingerstrasse 6; ⑤Ostbahnhof) This former dumpling factory on the wrong side of the Ostbahnhof has more than a dozen, mostly mainstream, venues as well as numerous fast-food eateries, making it the best place in Munich to *carpe noctem* if you like that sort of thing.

Optimolwerke CLUB
(Map p56; www.optimolwerke.de; Friedenstrasse 10; ⑤Ostbahnhof) Just behind Kultfabrik, Optimol is another clubber's nirvana, with around 10 venues after dark. Latin lovers flock to **Do Brasil**, while **Die Burg** keeps the party hits and classics booming till 6am.

☺ Westend

★Augustiner Bräustuben BEER HALL
(Map p70; ☏089-507 047; www.braeustuben. de; Landsberger Strasse 19; ☺10am-midnight; 🖾Holzapfelstrasse) Depending on the wind, an aroma of hops envelops you as you approach this traditional beer hall inside the Augustiner brewery. The Bavarian fare is superb, especially the *Schweinshaxe* (pork knuckle). Due to the location the atmosphere in the evenings is slightly more authentic than that of its city-centre cousins, with fewer tourists at the long tables.

Backstage CLUB
(www.backstage.eu; Reitknechtstrasse 6; ⑤Hirschgarten) Refreshingly non-mainstream, this groovetastic club has a chilled night beer garden and a shape-shifting line-up of punk, nu metal, hip hop, dance hall and other alternative sounds, both canned and live.

Substanz CLUB
(Map p70; www.substanz-club.de; Ruppertstrasse 28; Ⓤ Poccistrasse) About as alternative as things get in Munich, this low-key, beery lair gets feet moving from house to indie to soul and brings out the city's edgy wordsmiths for regular poetry slams. Also hosts unusual events for a club, such as vinyl flea markets and soccer tournaments.

☆ Entertainment

Tickets to cultural and sporting events are available at venue box offices and official ticket outlets, such as **Zentraler Kartenvorverkauf** (Map p48; ☏089-5450 6060; www.zkv-muenchen.de; Marienplatz; ☺9am-8pm Mon-Sat; Ⓤ Marienplatz). Outlets are also good for online bookings, as is **München Ticket** (Map p70; ☏089-5481 8181; www.muenchen-ticket.de; Bahnhofplatz 2; ☺10am-8pm Mon-Sat; Ⓤ Hauptbahnhof), which shares premises with the tourist office at the Hauptbahnhof.

Websites useful for tuning into the local scene include www.munig.com, www. munichx.de, www.ganz-muenchen.de and www.muenchengehtaus.com. All are in German but are not too hard to navigate with some basic language skills. *In München* (www.in-muenchen.de), a freebie mag available at bars, restaurants and shops, is the most detailed print source for what's on in Munich. *Munich Found* (www.munichfound.de) is an English-language magazine geared towards expats and visitors. For glossy weekly lifestyle and entertainment news, consult *Prinz München* (http://prinz. de/muenchen/).

Cinemas

For show information check any of the listings publications. Movies presented in their original language are denoted in listings by the acronym OF *(Originalfassung)* or OV *(Originalversion)*; those with German subtitles are marked OmU *(Original mit Untertiteln)*.

Museum-Lichtspiele CINEMA
(Map p56; ☏089-482 403; www.museum-lichtspiele.de; Lilienstrasse 2; 🖾Deutsches Museum) Cult cinema with wacky interior

MUNICH ENTERTAINMENT

ℹ CITY TOUR CARD

The **Munich City Tour Card** (www.citytourcard-muenchen.com; 1/3 days €10.90/20.90) includes all public transport in the *Innenraum* (Munich city – zones 1 to 4, marked white on transport maps) and discounts of between 10% and 50% for over 50 attractions, tours, eateries and theatres. These include the Residenz Musuem (p52), the BMW Museum (p64) and the Bier & Oktoberfestmuseum (p47). It's available at some hotels, tourist offices, Munich public transport authority (MVV) offices and U-Bahn, S-Bahn and DB vending machines.

and screenings of the *Rocky Horror Picture Show* (11pm Friday and Saturday nights). Shows English-language movies.

Cinema　　　　　　　　　　　CINEMA
(Map p58; ☑ 089-555 255; www.cinema-muenchen.de; Nymphenburger Strasse 31; Ⓤ Stiglmaierplatz) Cult cinema with all films in English, all the time.

Classical & Opera

Bayerische Staatsoper　　　　　OPERA
(Bavarian State Opera; Map p48; ☑ 089-218 501; www.staatsoper.de; Max-Joseph-Platz 2; Ⓜ Nationaltheater) One of the world's best opera companies, the Bavarian State Opera performs to sell-out crowds at the **Nationaltheater** (Map p48; www.staatstheater.bayern.de; Max-Joseph-Platz 2; Ⓜ Nationaltheater) in the Residenz and puts the emphasis on Mozart, Strauss and Wagner. In summer it hosts the prestigious Opernfestspiele (p69). The opera's house band is the Bayerisches Staatsorchester, in business since 1523 and thus Munich's oldest orchestra.

Münchner Philharmoniker　　CLASSICAL MUSIC
(Map p56; ☑ 089-480 985 500; www.mphil.de; Rosenheimer Strasse 5; ⊘ mid-Sep–Jun; Ⓜ Am Gasteig) Munich's premier orchestra regularly performs at the Gasteig Cultural Centre (p61). Book tickets early, as performances usually sell out.

BR-Symphonieorchester　　CLASSICAL MUSIC
(www.br-so.com) Charismatic Lithuanian maestro Mariss Jansons has rejuvenated this orchestra's playlist and often performs with its choir at such venues as the Gasteig (p61) and the Prinzregententheater (p61).

Staatstheater am Gärtnerplatz　　CLASSICAL MUSIC
(Map p48; ☑ 089-2185 1960; www.gaertnerplatztheater.de; Gärtnerplatz 3; Ⓜ Reichenbachplatz) Spruced up for its 150th birthday in November 2015, this grand theatre specialises in light opera, musicals and dance.

Jazz

Jazzclub Unterfahrt im Einstein　　LIVE MUSIC
(Map p56; ☑ 089-448 2794; www.unterfahrt.de; Einsteinstrasse 42; Ⓤ Max-Weber-Platz) Join a diverse crowd at this long-established, intimate club for a mixed bag of acts ranging from old bebop to edgy experimental. The Sunday open-jam session is legendary.

Jazzbar Vogler　　　　　　JAZZ
(Map p48; www.jazzbar-vogler.com; Rumfordstrasse 17; Ⓜ Reichenbachplatz) This intimate watering hole brings some of Munich's baddest cats to the stage. You never know who'll show up for Monday's jam session, and Tuesday to Thursday are live piano nights, but the main acts are on Friday and Saturday.

Theatre

Bayerisches Staatsschauspiel　　THEATRE
(☑ 089-2185 1940; www.residenztheater.de) This leading ensemble has a bit of a conservative streak but still manages to find relevance for today's mad, mad world in works by Shakespeare, Schiller and other tried-and-true playwrights. Performances are in the **Residenztheater** (Map p48; Max-Joseph-Platz 2; Ⓜ Nationaltheater), the **Theater im Marstall** (Map p48; Marstallplatz 4; Ⓜ Kammerspiele) and the now fully renovated Cuvilliés-Theater (p54).

Münchner Kammerspiele　　THEATRE
(Map p48; ☑ 089-2339 6600; www.muenchner-kammerspiele.de; Maximilianstrasse 26; Ⓜ Kammerspiele) A venerable theatre with an edgy, slightly populist bent, the Kammerspiele delivers provocative interpretations of the classics as well as works by contemporary playwrights. Performances are in a beautifully refurbished art nouveau theatre at Maximilianstrasse 26 and in the **Neues Haus** (Map p48; Falckenbergstrasse 1), a new glass cube nearby.

Deutsches Theater　　　　THEATRE
(Map p48; ☑ 089-5523 4444; www.deutsches-theater.de; Schwanthalerstrasse 13; Ⓤ Hauptbahnhof, Ⓢ Hauptbahnhof) Munich's answer to London's West End hosts touring road

shows such as *The Rocky Horror Show,* *Spamalot* and *Mamma Mia.*

GOP Varieté Theater
THEATER

(Map p56; ☑089-210 288 444; www.variete.de; Maximilianstrasse 47; ⌂Maxmonument) Hosts a real jumble of acts and shows, from magicians to light comedies to musicals.

Spectator Sports

FC Bayern München
FOOTBALL

(☑089-6993 1333; www.fcbayern.de; Allianz Arena, Werner-Heisenberg-Allee 25, Fröttmaning; ⌂Fröttmaning) Germany's most successful team both domestically and on a European level plays home games the impressive Allianz Arena, built for the 2006 World Cup. Tickets can be ordered online.

EHC München
ICE HOCKEY

(Map p58; www.ehc-muenchen.de; Olympia Eishalle, Olympiapark; ⌂Olympiazentrum) It's not one of Germany's premier ice-hockey outfits, but EHC München's games at the Olympic ice rink are exciting spectacles nonetheless, plus the team features several Canadian and American players.

🔒 Shopping

Munich is a fun and sophisticated place to shop that goes far beyond chains and department stores. If you want those, head to Neuhauser Strasse and Kaufingerstrasse. Southeast of there, Sendlinger Strasse has smaller and somewhat more individual stores, including a few resale and vintage emporia.

To truly unchain yourself, though, you need to hit the Gärtnerplatzviertel and Glockenbachviertel, the bastion of well-curated indie stores and local designer boutiques. Hans-Sachs-Strasse and Reichenbachstrasse are especially worth visiting. Maxvorstadt, especially Türkenstrasse, also has an interesting line-up of stores with merchandise you certainly won't find back home.

Globetrotter
OUTDOOR EQUIPMENT

(Map p48; www.globetrotter.de; Isartorplatz 8-10; ⊙10am-8pm Mon-Sat; ⌂Isartor, Ⓢ Isartor) Munich's premier outdoor and travel stockist is worth a browse even if you've never pulled on a pair of hiking boots. The basement boasts a lake for testing out kayaks and there's a cafe, a travel agent and even a branch of the Alpenverein, as well as every travel and outdoor accessory you could ever possibly need.

Manufactum
HOMEWARES

(Map p48; www.manufactum.de; Dienerstrasse 12; ⊙9.30am-7pm Mon-Sat; Ⓢ Marienplatz, ⌂Marienplatz) Anyone with an admiration for top-quality design from Germany and further afield should make a beeline for this store. Last-a-lifetime household items compete for shelf space with retro toys, Bauhaus lamps and times-gone-by stationery. The stock changes according to the season.

Munich Readery
BOOKS

(Map p58; www.readery.de; Augustenstrasse 104; ⊙11am-8pm Mon-Fri, 10am-6pm Sat; ⌂Theresienstrasse) With Germany's biggest collection of secondhand English-language titles, the Readery is the place to go in Bavaria for holiday reading matter. The shop holds events such as author readings and there's a monthly book club. See the website for details.

Holareidulijö
CLOTHING

(Map p58; www.holareidulijoe.com; Schellingstrasse 81; ⊙noon-6.30pm Tue-Fri, 10am-1pm Sat; ⌂Schellingstrasse) Munich's only secondhand traditional-clothing store (the name is a phonetic yodel) is worth a look even if you don't intend buying. Apparently, wearing hand-me-down Lederhosen greatly reduces the risk of chafing.

Words' Worth Books
BOOKS

(Map p52; www.wordsworth.de; Schellingstrasse 3; ⊙9am-8pm Mon-Fri, 10am-4pm Sat; ⌂Schellingstrasse) You'll find tons of English-language books, from secondhand novels to the latest bestsellers, at this excellent and long-established bookstore.

Porzellan Manufaktur Nymphenburg
CERAMICS

(Map p58; www.nymphenburg.com; Nördliches Schlossrondell 8; ⊙10am-5pm Mon-Fri; ⌂Schloss Nymphenburg) Traditional and contemporary porcelain masterpieces by the royal manufacturer. Also in the Altstadt at **Odeonsplatz 1** (Map p48; ☑089-282 428; Odeonsplatz 1; ⊙10am-6.30pm Mon-Fri, to 4pm Sat; ⌂Odeonsplatz).

7 Himmel
CLOTHING

(Map p48; Hans-Sachs-Strasse 17; ⊙11am-7pm Mon-Fri, 10am-6pm Sat; ⌂Müllerstrasse) Female cool-hunters will be in seventh heaven (a translation of the boutique's name) when browsing the assortment of fashions and accessories by hip indie labels sold at surprisingly reasonable prices.

Flohmarkt Riem MARKET
(www.flohmarkt-riem.com; Willy-Brandt-Platz;
⊘6am-4pm Sat; Ⓤ Messestadt-Ost) Play urban
archaeologist and sift through heaps of junk
to unearth the odd treasure at Bavaria's largest flea market. It's located outside the city
centre by the trade-fair grounds in Riem.
Take the U2 to Messestadt-Ost.

Schuster OUTDOOR EQUIPMENT, SPORTS
(Map p48; Rosenstrasse 1-5; ⊘10am-8pm Mon-
Sat; Ⓢ Marienplatz, Ⓤ Marienplatz) Get tooled
up for the Alps at this sports megastore
boasting seven shiny floors of equipment,
including cycling, skiing, travel and camping paraphernalia.

Loden-Frey CLOTHING
(Map p48; www.lodenfrey.com; Maffeistrasse
5-7; ⊘10am-8pm Mon-Sat; 🚋 Theatinerstrasse)
The famous cloth producer stocks a wide
range of Bavarian wear and other top-end
clothes. The Lederhosen and Dirndl outfits
are a cut above the discount night-out versions and prices are accordingly high.

Foto-Video-Media Sauter ELECTRONICS
(Map p48; Sonnenstrasse 26; ⊘9.30am-8pm
Mon-Fri, to 7pm Sat; Ⓤ Sendlinger Tor) The largest
camera and video shop in town.

Stachus Passagen MALL
(Map p48; www.stachus-passagen.de; Karlsplatz/
Stachus; ⊘9.30am-8pm Mon-Sat; 🚋 Karlsplatz,
Ⓢ Karlsplatz, Ⓤ Karlsplatz) Europe's biggest underground shopping mall, with 36 escalators
and 250,000 shoppers a day wandering its 58
mainstream shops.

🛈 Information

DANGERS & ANNOYANCES

During Oktoberfest crime and staggering drunks
are major problems, especially around the
Hauptbahnhof. It's no joke: drunks in a crowd
trying to make their way home can get violent,
and there are around 100 cases of assault
every year. Leave early or stay cautious – if not
sober – yourself.

Strong and unpredictable currents make
cooling off in the Eisbach creek in the Englischer
Garten more dangerous than it looks. Exercise
extreme caution; there have been deaths.

Even the most verdant öko-warrior might
interrupt his/her yoghurt pot of rainwater to
agree with you that fast-moving bikes in central
Munich are a menace. Make sure you don't
wander onto bike lanes, especially when waiting
to cross the road and when alighting from buses
and trams.

INTERNET ACCESS

As across the rest of Europe, internet cafes are generally a thing of the past. Wi-fi is widespread though
rarely free. Most public libraries offer internet
access to non-residents. Check www.muenchner-
stadtbibliothek.de (in German) for details.

MEDICAL SERVICES

The US and UK consulates can provide lists of
English-speaking doctors.
Ärztlicher Hausbesuchdienst (☑089-555
566; www.ahd-hausbesuch.de) Doctor home
and hotel visits.
Bereitschaftsdienst der Münchner Ärzte
(☑089-116 117; ⊘24hr) Evening and weekend nonemergency medical services; English-speaking doctors.
Chirurgische Klinik (☑089-856 931 234;
www.chkmb.de; Nussbaumstrasse 20; Ⓤ Sendlinger Tor) Emergency room.
Emergency dentist (☑089-7233 093)
Emergency pharmacy (www.apotheken.de)
Online referrals to the nearest open pharmacy.
Most pharmacies have employees who speak
passable English, but there are several des-
ignated international pharmacies with staff
fluent in English, including **Ludwigs-Apotheke**
(Neuhauser Strasse 11; ⊘8am-6.30pm Mon-
Fri, 8.30am-1pm Sat; Ⓤ Marienplatz) and
Guten Tag Apotheke (Bahnhofplatz 2; ⊘7am-
8pm Mon-Fri, from 8am Sat; 🚋 Hauptbahnhof,
Ⓤ Hauptbahnhof, Ⓢ Hauptbahnhof).
Schwabing Hospital (☑089-30 680; Kölner
Platz 1; Ⓤ Scheidplatz) Accident and Emer-
gency.

MONEY

ATMs abound in the city centre, though not all
take every type of card.
Reisebank (Bahnhofplatz 2; ⊘7am-10pm;
🚋 Hauptbahnhof, Ⓤ Hauptbahnhof, Ⓢ Hauptbahnhof) Best place to change and withdraw
money at the Hauptbahnhof.

POST

Post office (Map p48; Sattlerstrasse
1; ⊘9am-6pm Mon-Fri, to 12.30pm Sat;
Ⓤ Marienplatz, Ⓢ Marienplatz) For additional
branches, search www.deutschepost.de.

TOURIST INFORMATION

Tourist Office – Marienplatz (Map p48;
☑089-2339 6500; www.muenchen.de; Marienplatz 2; ⊘10am-8pm Mon-Fri, to 4pm
Sat, to 2pm Sun Apr-Dec, closed Sun Jan-
Mar; Ⓤ Marienplatz, Ⓢ Marienplatz) There's
another branch at the Hauptbahnhof (Map
p70; ☑089-2339 6500; www.muenchen.de;
Bahnhofplatz 2; ⊘9am-8pm Mon-Sat, 10am-
6pm Sun; 🚋 Hauptbahnhof, Ⓤ Hauptbahnhof,
Ⓢ Hauptbahnhof).

Castles & Museums Infopoint (Map p48; 089-2101 4050; www.infopoint-museen-bayern.de; Alter Hof 1; 10am-6pm Mon-Sat; Marienplatz, Marienplatz) Central information point for museums and palaces throughout Bavaria.

Getting There & Away

AIR

Munich Airport (089-975 00; www.munich-airport.de), also known as Flughafen Franz-Josef Strauss, is second in importance only to Frankfurt for international and domestic connections. The main carrier is Lufthansa, but there are over 80 other companies operating from the airport's two runways, from major carriers such as British Airways and Emirates to minor operations such as Luxair and Air Malta.

Only one major airline from the UK doesn't use Munich's main airport – Ryanair flies into Memmingen's **Allgäu Airport** (FMM; 08331-984 2000; www.allgaeu-airport.de), 125km to the west.

BUS

Europabus links Munich to the Romantic Road. For times and fares for this service and all other national and international coaches, contact **Sindbad** (089-5454 8989; www.sindbad-gmbh.de; Hackerbrücke 4-6 (ZOB); Hackerbrücke).

The bold new **Zentraler Omnibusbahnhof** (Central Bus Station, ZOB; www.muenchen-zob.de; Arnulfstrasse 21; Hackerbrücke) located next to the Hackerbrücke S-Bahn station handles the vast majority of international and domestic coach services. There's a Eurolines/Touring office, a supermarket and various eateries on the 1st floor; buses depart from ground level.

The main operator out of the ZOB is now low-cost coach company **Meinfernbus/Flixbus** (0180 515 9915; www.meinfernbus.de; Zentraler Omnibusbahnhof, Arnulfstrasse 21), which links Munich to countless destinations across Germany and beyond.

A special Deutsche Bahn express coach leaves for Prague (€61, five hours, four daily) from the ZOB.

CAR & MOTORCYCLE

Munich has autobahns radiating in all directions. Take the A9 to Nuremberg, the A8 to Salzburg, the A95 to Garmisch-Partenkirchen and the A8 to Ulm or Stuttgart.

Naturally, Munich Airport has branches of all major car-hire companies. Book ahead online for the best rates.

TRAIN

Train connections from Munich to destinations in Bavaria are excellent and there are also numerous services to more distant cities within Germany and around Europe. All services leave from the Hauptbahnhof (Central Station).

Staffed by native English speakers, **Euraide** (www.euraide.de; Desk 1, Reisezentrum, Hauptbahnhof; 10am-7pm Mon-Fri Mar-Apr & Aug-Dec, to 8pm May-Jul; Hauptbahnhof, Hauptbahnhof, Hauptbahnhof) is a friendly agency based at the Hauptbahnhof that sells all DB products, makes reservations and can create personalised rail tours of Germany and beyond.

Connections from Munich:

→ **Augsburg** €13.30 to €20.50, 30 minutes, three hourly

→ **Baden-Baden** €87, four hours, hourly (change in Mannheim)

→ **Berlin** €130, 6½ hours, hourly

→ **Cologne** €142, 4½ hours, hourly

→ **Frankfurt** €101, 3¼ hours, hourly

→ **Freiburg** €93, 4½ hours, hourly (change in Mannheim)

→ **Nuremberg** €19 to €55, one hour to one hour 40 minutes, twice hourly

→ **Paris** from €142, six hours, daily

→ **Prague** €74, 6¼ hours, three daily

→ **Regensberg** €27.50, 1¾ hours, hourly

→ **Vienna** €93, 4½ hours, every two hours

→ **Würzburg** €71, two hours, twice hourly

→ **Zürich** €83, 4¼ hours, three daily

Getting Around

Central Munich is compact enough to explore on foot. The outlying suburbs are easily reachable by public transport, which is extensive and efficient, if showing its age slightly.

TO/FROM THE AIRPORT

Munich's airport is about 30km northeast of the city and linked by S-Bahn (S1 and S8) to the Hauptbahnhof. The trip costs €10.80, takes about 40 minutes and runs every 20 minutes almost 24 hours a day.

The Lufthansa Airport Bus shuttles at 20-minute intervals between the airport and Arnulf-strasse, next to the Hauptbahnhof, between 5.15am and 7.55pm. The trip takes about 45 minutes and costs €10.50 (return €17).

If you've booked a flight from Munich's 'other' airport at Memmingen (around 125km to the west), the **Allgäu Airport Express** (Map p70; www.aaexpress.de; single €17, €12 if prebooked online) also leaves from Arnulfstrasse at the Hauptbahnhof, making the trip up to seven times a day. The journey takes one hour 40 minutes and the fare is €13 (return €19.50).

A taxi from Munich Airport to the Altstadt costs €50 to €70.

CAR & MOTORCYCLE

Driving in central Munich can be a nightmare; many streets are one way or pedestrian only, ticket enforcement is Orwellian and parking is a nightmare. Car parks (indicated on the tourist-office map) charge about €1.70 to €2.20 per hour.

PUBLIC TRANSPORT

Munich's efficient public-transport system is composed of buses, trams, the U-Bahn and the S-Bahn. It's operated by MVV (www.mvv-muenchen.de), which maintains offices in U-Bahn stations at Marienplatz, the Hauptbahnhof, Sendlinger Tor, the Ostbahnhof and Poccistrasse. Staff hand out free network maps and timetables, sell tickets and answer questions. Automated trip planning in English is best done online. The U-Bahn and S-Bahn run almost 24 hours a day, with perhaps a short gap between 2am and 4am. Night buses and trams operate in the city centre.

Tickets & Fares

The city-of-Munich region is divided into four zones, with most places of visitor interest (except Dachau and the airport) conveniently clustering within the white *Innenraum* (inner zone).

Short rides (*Kurzstrecke*; four bus or tram stops, or two U-Bahn or S-Bahn stops) cost €1.40; longer trips cost €2.70. Children aged between six and 14 pay a flat €1.30 regardless of the length of the trip. Day passes are €6.20 for individuals and €11.70 for up to five people travelling together; a weekly pass called an IsarCard costs €14.10. Bikes cost €2.60 to take aboard and may only be taken on U-Bahn and S-Bahn trains, but not during the 6am to 9am and 4pm to 6pm rush hours.

Bus drivers sell single tickets and day passes, but tickets for the U-Bahn and S-Bahn and other passes must be purchased from vending machines at stations or MVV offices. Tram tickets are available from vending machines aboard. Most tickets must be stamped (validated) at station platform entrances and aboard buses and trams before use. The fine for getting caught without a valid ticket is €40.

TAXI

Taxis cost €3.50 at flag fall plus €1.50 to €1.80 per kilometre and are not much more convenient than public transport. Luggage is charged at €1.20 per piece. Ring a taxi on ☑216 10 or ☑194 10. Taxi ranks are indicated on the city's tourist map.

AROUND MUNICH

Dachau

KZ-Gedenkstätte Dachau   MEMORIAL

(Dachau Concentration Camp Memorial Site; ☑08131-669 970; www.kz-gedenkstaette-dachau.de; Peter-Roth-Strasse 2a, Dachau; museum admission free; ⊙9am-5pm Tue-Sun) Officially called the KZ-Gedenkstätte Dachau, this was the Nazis' first concentration camp, built by Heinrich Himmler in March 1933 to house political prisoners. All in all, it 'processed' more than 200,000 inmates, killing at least 43,000, and is now a haunting memorial. Expect to spend two to three hours here to fully absorb the exhibits. Note that children may find the experience too disturbing.

The place to start is the visitors centre, which houses a bookshop, a cafe and a tour-booking desk where you can pick up an audioguide (€3). It's on your left as you enter the main gate. Two-and-a-half-hour tours (€3) also run from here from Tuesday to Sunday at 11am and 1pm (extra tours run at 12.15pm on Sunday between August and September).

You pass into the compound itself through the Jourhaus, originally the only entrance. Set in wrought iron, the infamous, chilling slogan *Arbeit Macht Frei* (Work Sets You Free) hits you at the gate.

The museum is at the southern end of the camp. Here, a 22-minute English-language documentary runs at 10am, 11.30am, 12.30pm, 2pm and 3pm and uses mostly post-liberation footage to outline what took place here. Either side of the small cinema extends an exhibition relating the camp's harrowing story, from a relatively orderly prison for religious inmates, leftists and criminals to an overcrowded concentration camp racked by typhus, and its eventual liberation by the US Army in April 1945.

Disturbing displays include photographs of the camp, its officers and prisoners (all male until 1944), and of horrifying 'scientific experiments' carried out by Nazi doctors. Other exhibits include a whipping block, a chart showing the system of prisoner categories (Jews, homosexuals, Jehovah's Witnesses, Poles, Roma and other 'asocial' people) and documents on the persecution of 'degenerate' authors banned by the party. There's also a lot of information on the rise of the Nazis and other concentration camps around Europe, a scale model of the camp at its greatest extent and numerous uniforms and everyday objects belonging to inmates and guards.

Outside, in the former roll-call square, is the International Memorial (1968), inscribed in English, French, Yiddish, German and Russian, which reads 'Never Again'. Behind the exhibit building, the bunker was the notorious camp prison where inmates were tortured. Executions took place in the prison yard.

Inmates were housed in large barracks, now demolished, which used to line the main road north of the roll-call square. In the camp's northwestern corner is the crematorium and gas chamber, disguised as a shower room but never used. Several religious shrines, including a timber Russian Orthodox church, stand nearby.

Dachau is about 16km northwest of central Munich. The S2 makes the trip from Munich Hauptbahnhof to the station in Dachau in 21 minutes. You'll need a two-zone ticket (€5.20). Here change to frequent bus 726 (direction Saubachsiedlung) to get to the camp. Show your stamped ticket to the driver. By car, follow Dachauer Strasse straight out to Dachau and follow the KZ-Gedenkstätte signs.

Schleissheim

When you've exhausted all possibilities in central Munich, the northern suburb of Schleissheim is well worth the short S-Bahn trip for its three elegant palaces and a high-flying aviation museum – a great way to entertain the kids on a rainy afternoon.

To get to Schleissheim, take the S1 (direction Freising) to Oberschleissheim (€5.20), then walk along Mittenheimer Strasse for about 15 minutes towards the palaces. On weekdays only, bus 292 goes to the Mittenheimer Strasse stop.

By car, take Leopoldstrasse north until it becomes Ingolstädter Strasse. Then take the A99 to the Neuherberg exit, at the southern end of the airstrip.

◉ Sights

Neues Schloss Schleissheim PALACE
(New Palace; www.schloesser-schleissheim.de; Max-Emanuel-Platz 1; adult/concession €4.50/3.50, all 3 palaces €8/6; ⊙9am-6pm Apr-Sep, 10am-4pm Oct-Mar, closed Mon year-round; 🚆Mittenheimer Strasse) The crown jewel of Schleissheim's palatial trio is the Neues Schloss Schleissheim. This pompous pile was dreamed up

Around Munich

by Prince-Elector Max Emanuel in 1701 in anticipation of his promotion to emperor. It never came. Instead he was forced into exile for over a decade and didn't get back to building until 1715. Cash-flow problems required the scaling back of the original plans, but given the palace's huge dimensions and opulent interior, it's hard to imagine where exactly the cuts fell.

Some of the finest artists of the baroque era were called in to create such eye-pleasing sights as the ceremonial staircase, the Victory Hall and the Grand Gallery. There are outstanding pieces of period furniture, including the elector's four-poster bed, and intricately inlaid tables, and a particularly impressive ceiling fresco by Cosmas Damian Asam.

The palace is home to the Staatsgalerie (State Gallery), a selection of European baroque art drawn from the Bavarian State Collection, including works by such masters as Peter Paul Rubens, Anthony van Dyck and Carlo Saraceni. The most impressive room here is the Grand Galerie.

Flugwerft Schleissheim MUSEUM
(www.deutsches-museum.de/flugwerft; Ferdinand-Schulz-Allee; adult/child €6/3; ⊙9am-5pm; 🚆Mittenheimerstrasse) The Flugwerft Schleissheim, the aviation branch of the Deutsches

Museum, makes for a nice change of pace and aesthetics from Schleissheim's regal palaces. Spirits will soar at the sight of the lethal Soviet MiG-21 fighter jet, the Vietnam-era F-4E Phantom and a replica of Otto Lilienthal's 1894 glider, with a revolutionary wing shaped like Batman's cape. Kids can climb into an original cockpit, land a plane and even get their pilot's licence.

Altes Schloss Schleissheim
PALACE

(www.schloesser-schleissheim.de; Maximilianshof 1; adult/concession €3/2, all 3 palaces €8/6; ⊙9am-6pm Apr-Sep, 10am-4pm Oct-Mar, closed Mon year-round; 🚌Mittenheimer Strasse) The Altes Schloss Schleissheim is a mere shadow of its Renaissance self, having been altered and refashioned in the intervening centuries. It houses paintings and sculpture depicting religious culture and festivals all over the world, including an impressive collection of more than 100 nativity scenes.

Schloss Lustheim
PALACE

(www.schloesser-schleissheim.de; adult/concession €3.50/2.50, all 3 palaces €8/6; ⊙9am-6pm Apr-Sep, 10am-4pm Oct-Mar, closed Mon year-round; 🚌Mittenheimer Strasse) While construction of Prince-Elector Max Emanuel's Neues Schloss Schleissheim was going on, the elector and his retinue resided in the fanciful hunting palace of Schloss Lustheim, on a little island in the eastern Schlosspark. It now provides an elegant setting for porcelain masterpieces from Meissen.

Starnberg

Around 25km southwest of Munich, glittering Lake Starnberg (Starnberger See) was once the haunt of Bavaria's royal family but now provides a bit of easily accessible R and R for anyone looking to escape the hustle of the Bavarian capital.

At the northern end of the lake, the affluent, century-old town of Starnberg is the northern gateway to the lake district but lacks any lasting allure, meaning most visitors head straight on to other towns or sites along the lake's edge. The train station is just steps from the lake's shore, where you'll find cruise-boat landing docks, pedal-boat hire and lots of strolling day-trippers. Besides Lake Starnberg, the area comprises the Ammersee and the much smaller Pilsensee,

Wörthsee and Wesslinger See. Naturally, the region attracts water-sports enthusiasts, but it also has enough history to satisfy those who enjoy exploring the past.

◉ Sights

Berg
VILLAGE

(Starnberger See) Those on the King Ludwig II trail should make a beeline for this tiny village on the eastern shore of Lake Starnberg. It was here that he famously (and mysteriously) drowned along with his doctor in just a few feet of water. The spot where his body was found is marked with a large, solumn cross backed by a *Votivkapelle* (Memorial Chapel). Berg is 5km from Starnberg and can be reached on foot in around an hour.

Museum Starnberger See
MUSEUM

(www.museum-starnberger-see.de; Possenhofener Strasse 5, Starnberg; adult/child €3/2; ⊙10am-5pm Tue-Sun) You may have to duck your head when touring this 400-year-old farmhouse that offers a glimpse of life on the lake as it once was. It also boasts a precious Ignaz Günther sculpture in the little chapel. The modern extension showcases a fancy royal barge and a section on its construction.

❶ Information

Starnberger Fünf-Seen-Land Tourist Office
(☑08151-906 00; www.sta5.de; Wittelsbacherstrasse 2c, Starnberg; ⊙8am-6pm Mon-Fri year round, 9am-1pm Sat May–mid-Oct) Just north of Starnberg's Bahnhofsplatz, this tourist office has a free room-finding service and offers trip planning to other lake towns. The website has links to all tourist offices in the local communities.

❶ Getting There & Around

Starnberg is a half-hour ride on the S6 train from Munich Hauptbahnhof (€5.20).

From Easter to mid-October **Bayerische-Seen-Schifffahrt** (www.seenschifffahrt.de) runs boat services from Starnberg to other lakeside towns as well as offering longer cruises. Boats dock behind the S-Bahn station in Starnberg.

If you'd rather get around the lake under your own steam, Bike It hires out two-wheelers. **Paul Dechant** (☑08151 121 06; Hauptstrasse 20), near the S-Bahn station, hires out rowing, pedal and electric-powered boats from €15 per hour.

Bavaria

POP 12.6 MILLION

Best Places to Eat

➜ Albrecht Dürer Stube (p136)

➜ Le Ciel (p109)

➜ Bürgerspital Weinstube (p114)

➜ Mittermeier (p118)

➜ August (p125)

Best Places to Stay

➜ Hotel Herrnschlösschen (p118)

➜ Petit Hotel Orphée (p153)

➜ Dom Hotel (p125)

➜ Hotel Deutscher Kaiser (p133)

➜ Elements Hotel (p153)

Why Go?

From the cloud-shredding Alps to the fertile Danube plain, the Free State of Bavaria is a place that keeps its clichéd promises. Story-book castles bequeathed by an oddball king poke through dark forest, cowbells tinkle in flower-filled meadows, the thwack of palm on lederhosen accompanies the clump of frothy stein on timber bench, and medieval walled towns go about their time-warped business.

But diverse Bavaria offers much more than the chocolate-box idyll. Learn about Bavaria's state-of-the-art motor industry in Ingolstadt, discover its Nazi past in Nuremberg and Berchtesgaden, sip world-class wines in Würzburg, get on the Wagner trail in Bayreuth or seek out countless kiddy attractions across the state. Destinations are often described as possessing 'something for everyone', but in Bavaria's case this is no exaggeration.

And, whatever you do in Germany's southeast, every occasion is infused with that untranslatable feel-good air of *Gemütlichkeit* (cosiness) that makes exploring the region such an easygoing experience.

When to Go

A winter journey along an off-season, tourist-free Romantic Road really sees the snow-bound route live up to its name. Come the spring, tuck into some seasonal fare as Bavaria goes crazy for asparagus during *Spargelzeit* (from late March). The summer months are all about the beer garden, and this is obviously the best time to savour the region's unsurpassed brews in the balmy, fairy-lit air. Autumn is the time to experience the dreamy haze of the Bavarian Forest and the bustle of Bavaria's cities, revived after the summer's time-out.

Bavaria Highlights

1 Indulging your romantic fantasies at fairy-tale **Schloss Neuschwanstein** (p92)

2 Rack-and-pinioning your way to the top of the **Zugspitze** (p98), Germany's highest peak

3 Perching at the Eagle's Nest in **Berchtesgaden** (p108) to enjoy show-stopping Alpine vistas

4 Striking a trail through the tranquil wilds of the **Bavarian Forest National Park** (p166)

5 Going full circle around the town walls of quaint **Dinkelsbühl** (p119)

6 Messing around on the waters of the achingly picturesque **Königssee** (p107)

7 Revisiting Bavaria's Nazi past in **Nuremberg** (p127)

8 Going frothy at the mouth in the hundreds of superb **beer gardens, breweries and brewpubs** across the region (p137)

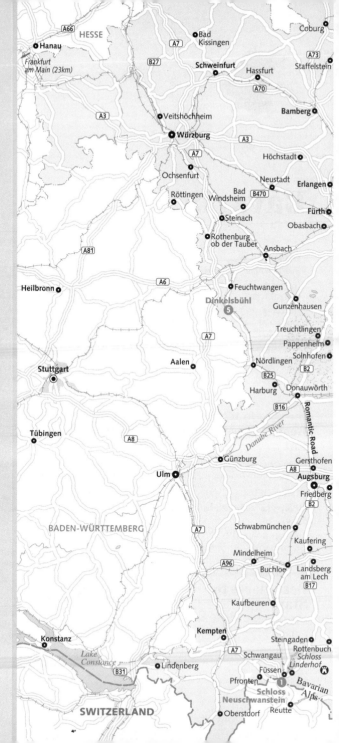

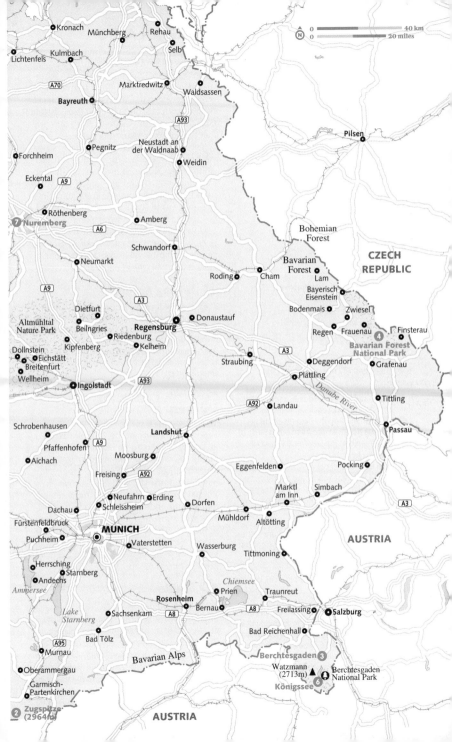

History

For centuries Bavaria was ruled as a duchy in the Holy Roman Empire, a patchwork of nations that extended from Italy to the North Sea. In the early 19th century, a conquering Napoleon annexed Bavaria, elevated it to the rank of kingdom and doubled its size. The fledgling nation became the object of power struggles between Prussia and Austria and, in 1871, was brought into the German Reich by Bismarck.

Bavaria was the only German state that refused to ratify the Basic Law (Germany's near constitution) following WWII. Instead, Bavaria's leaders opted to return to its pre-war status as a 'free state', and drafted their own constitution. Almost ever since, the *Land* (state) has been ruled by the Christlich-Soziale Union (CSU) the arch-conservative party that is peculiar to Bavaria. Its dominance of the politics of a single *Land* is unique in postwar Germany, having ruled for all but five of the last 50 years without the need to form a coalition with anyone else. Its sister party, the CDU, operates in the rest of the country by mutual agreement.

ℹ Getting There & Around

Munich is Bavaria's main transport hub, second only to Frankfurt in flight and rail connections. Rail is the best way to reach Munich from other parts of Germany, and the best means of getting from the Bavarian capital to other parts of Bavaria. Air links within Bavaria are much less extensive.

Without your own set of wheels in Eastern Bavaria and the Alps, you'll have to rely on bus services, which peter out in the evenings and at weekends. Trips along the Romantic Road can be done by tour bus, although again a car is a better idea. Several long-distance cycling routes cross Bavaria and the region's cities are some of the most cycle-friendly in the world, so getting around on two wheels could not be easier.

If you're travelling in a group, or can assemble one (as some people do pre-departure), you can make enormous savings with the Bayern-Ticket (€23, plus €5 per additional passenger). This allows up to five adults unlimited travel on one weekday from 9am to 3am, or from midnight to 3am the next day on weekends. The single version, costing €23, is also a good deal and means that all fares in Bavaria are basically capped at that price, as long as you don't leave before 9am. Both are good for 2nd-class rail travel across Bavaria (regional trains only, no ICs or ICEs), as well as most public transport.

BAVARIAN ALPS

Stretching west from Germany's remote southeastern corner to the Allgäu region near Lake Constance, the Bavarian Alps (Bayerische Alpen) form a stunningly beautiful natural divide along the Austrian border. Ranges further south may be higher, but these mountains shoot up from the foothills so abruptly that the impact is all the more dramatic.

The region is pocked with quaint frescoed villages, spas and health retreats, and possibilities for skiing, snowboarding, hiking, canoeing and paragliding – much of it year-round. The ski season lasts from about late December until April, while summer activities stretch from late May to November.

One of the largest resorts in the area is Garmisch-Partenkirchen, one of urban Bavaria's favourite getaways. Berchtesgaden, Füssen and Oberstdorf are also good bases.

ℹ Getting Around

There are few direct train routes between main centres, meaning buses are the most efficient method of public transport in the Alpine area. If you're driving, sometimes a short cut via Austria works out to be quicker (such as between Garmisch-Partenkirchen and Füssen or Oberstdorf).

Füssen

📞 08362 / POP 14,600

Nestled at the foot of the Alps, tourist-busy Füssen is the southern climax of the Romantic Road, with the nearby castles of Neuschwanstein and Hohenschwangau the highlight of many a southern Germany trip. But having 'done' the country's most popular tourist route and seen Ludwig II's fantasy palaces, there are other reasons to linger longer in the area. The town of Füssen is worth half a day's exploration and, from here, you can easily escape the crowds into a landscape of gentle hiking trails and Alpine vistas.

◉ Sights

★ **Schloss Neuschwanstein**   CASTLE

(📞 tickets 08362-930 830; www.neuschwanstein.de; Neuschwansteinstrasse 20; adult/concession €12/11, incl Hohenschwangau €23/21; ⊙ 9am-6pm Apr–mid-Oct, 10am-4pm mid-Oct–Mar) Appearing through the mountaintops like a mirage, Schloss Neuschwanstein was the model for Disney's *Sleeping Beauty* castle. King Ludwig II planned this fairy-tale pile himself, with the help of a stage designer rather than an architect. He envisioned it as a giant stage on which to recreate the world of Germanic mythology, inspired by the operatic works of his friend Richard Wagner. The most impressive room is the **Sänger-saal** (Minstrels' Hall), whose frescos depict scenes from the opera *Tannhäuser*.

Built as a romantic medieval castle, work started in 1869 and, like so many of Ludwig's grand schemes, was never finished. For all the coffer-depleting sums spent on it, the king spent just over 170 days in residence.

Completed sections include Ludwig's Tristan and Isolde–themed bedroom, dominated by a huge Gothic-style bed crowned with intricately carved cathedral-like spires; a gaudy artificial grotto (another allusion to *Tannhäuser*); and the Byzantine-style **Thronsaal** (Throne Room) with an incredible mosaic floor containing over two million stones. The painting opposite the (throneless) throne platform depicts another castle dreamed up by Ludwig that was never built. Almost every window provides tour-halting views across the plain below.

The tour ends with a 20-minute film on the castle and its creator, and there's a reasonably priced cafe and the inevitable gift shops.

For the postcard view of Neuschwanstein and the plains beyond, walk 10 minutes up to **Marienbrücke** (Mary's Bridge), which spans the spectacular Pöllat Gorge over a waterfall just above the castle. It's said Ludwig enjoyed coming up here after dark to watch the candlelight radiating from the Sängersaal.

Schloss Hohenschwangau CASTLE
(☏08362-930 830; www.hohenschwangau.de; Alpseestrasse 30; adult/concession €12/11, incl Neuschwanstein €23/21; ☉8am-5.30pm Apr–mid-Oct, 9am-3.30pm mid-Oct–Mar) King Ludwig II grew up at the sun-yellow Schloss Hohenschwangau and later enjoyed summers here until his death in 1886. His father, Maximilian II, built this palace in a neo-Gothic style atop 12th-century ruins left by Schwangau knights. Far less showy than Neuschwanstein, Hohenschwangau has a distinctly lived-in feel where every piece of furniture is a used original. After his father died, Ludwig's main alteration was having stars, illuminated with hidden oil lamps, painted on the ceiling of his bedroom.

It was at Hohenschwangau where Ludwig first met Richard Wagner. The **Hohenstaufensaal** features a square piano where the hard-up composer would entertain Ludwig with excerpts from his latest oeuvre. Some

---

ⓘ CASTLE TICKETS & TOURS

Schloss Neuschwanstein and Schloss Hohenschwangau can only be visited on guided tours (in German or English), which last about 35 minutes each (Hohenschwangau is first). Strictly timed tickets are available from the **Ticket Centre** (☏08362-930 830; www.hohenschwangau.de; Alpseestrasse 12; ☉8am-5.30pm Apr–mid-Oct, 9am-3.30pm mid-Oct–Mar) at the foot of the castles. In summer, come as early as 8am to ensure you get in that day.

Enough time is left between tours for the steep 30- to 40-minute walk between the castles. Alternatively, you can take a horse-drawn carriage, which is only marginally quicker.

Tickets for the **Museum of the Bavarian Kings** (p94) can be bought at the Ticket Centre and at the museum.

All Munich's tour companies run day excursions out to the castles.

---

rooms have frescos from German mythology, including the story of the Swan Knight, *Lohengrin*. The swan theme runs throughout.

Hohes Schloss CASTLE, GALLERY
(Magnusplatz 10; adult/concession €6/4; ☉galleries 11am-5pm Tue-Sun Apr-Oct, 1-4pm Fri-Sun Nov-Mar) The Hohes Schloss, a late-Gothic confection and one-time retreat of the bishops of Augsburg, lords it over Füssen's compact historical centre. The north wing of the palace contains the **Staatsgalerie** (State Gallery), with regional paintings and sculpture from the 15th and 16th centuries. The **Städtische Gemäldegalerie** (City Paintings Gallery) below is a showcase of 19th-century artists.

The inner courtyard is a masterpiece of illusionary architecture dating back to 1499; you'll do a double take before realising that the gables, oriels and windows are not quite as they seem.

Museum Füssen MUSEUM
(Lechhalde 3; adult/concession €6/4; ☉11am-5pm Tue-Sun Apr-Oct, 1-4pm Fri-Sun Nov-Mar) Below the Hohes Schloss, and integrated into the former Abbey of St Mang, this museum highlights Füssen's heyday as a 16th-century violin-making centre. You can also view the abbey's festive baroque rooms, Romanesque cloister and the St Anna Kapelle (AD 830) with its famous 'Dance of Death' paintings.

DON'T MISS

MUSEUM OF THE BAVARIAN KINGS

Museum der Bayerischen Könige (Museum of the Bavarian Kings; www. museumderbayerischenkoenige.de; Alpseestrasse 27; adult/concession €9.50/8; ☉10am-6pm) Palace-fatigued visitors often head straight for the bus stop, coach park or nearest beer after a tour of the castles, most overlooking this worthwhile museum, installed in a former lakeside hotel 400m from the castle ticket office (heading towards Alpsee lake). The architecturally stunning museum is packed with historical background on Bavaria's first family and well worth the extra legwork.

The big-window views across the stunningly beautiful lake (a great picnic spot) to the Alps are almost as stunning as the Wittelsbach bling on show, including Ludwig II's famous blue-and-gold robe.

A detailed audioguide is included in the ticket price.

Tegelbergbahn   CABLE CAR
(www.tegelbergbahn.de; one-way/return €12.40/ 19.40; ☉9am-5pm) For fabulous views of the Alps and the Forggensee, take this cable car to the top of the Tegelberg (1730m), a prime launching point for hang-gliders and parasailers. From here it's a wonderful hike down to the castles (two to three hours; follow the signs to Königsschlösser). To get to the valley station, take RVO bus 73 or 78 (www.rvo-bus.de) from Füssen Bahnhof.

🛌 Sleeping

Accommodation in the area is surprisingly good value and the tourist office can help track down private rooms from as low as €30 per person.

Old Kings Hostel   HOSTEL €
(☑08362-883 7385; www.oldkingshostel.com; Franziskanergasse 2; dm €22, d €52-58) This new design hostel tucked away in the mesh of lanes in the old town has two dorms and three doubles, all with a different quirky, but not overplayed, theme. Kitchen, continental breakfast (€5), laundry service and local beer are all available and the whole place is kept very neat and tidy.

Steakhaus   GUESTHOUSE €
(☑08362-509 883; www.steakhouse-fuessen. de; Tiroler Strasse 31; s/d €30/74; ℗🛜) These budget rooms above a restaurant a 10-minute walk south of Füssen town centre, towards the border with Austria, will win no prizes for decor or character, but the location at the Lechfall gorge, with uncluttered views of the Alps, River Lech and surrounding forests, is pure magic.

★Hotel Sonne   DESIGN HOTEL €€
(☑08362-9080; www.hotel-sonne.de; Prinzregentenplatz 1; s/d from €89/109; ℗🛜) Although traditional looking from outside, this Altstadt favourite offers an unexpected design-hotel experience within. Themed rooms feature everything from swooping bed canopies to big-print wallpaper, huge pieces of wall art to sumptious fabrics. The public spaces are littered with pieces of art, period costumes and design features – the overall effect is impressive and unusual for this part of Germany.

Altstadthotel Zum Hechten   HOTEL €€
(☑08362-916 00; www.hotel-hechten.com; Ritterstrasse 6; s €59-69, d €94-100; ℗🛜) This is one of Füssen's oldest hotels and one of its friendliest. Public areas are traditional in style, while the bedrooms are bright and modern with beautifully patterned parquet floors, a large bed and sunny colours. The small but classy spa is great for relaxing after a day on the trail.

Fantasia   DESIGN HOTEL €€
(☑08362-9080; www.hotel-fantasia.de; Ottostrasse 1; s €39-79, d €49-99; @🛜) This late-19th-century former holiday home for nuns and monks has been converted into a quirky design-hotel. The lounge is straight out of a design magazine; the rooms are slightly less wild, but still boast huge ceiling prints of Neuschwanstein Castle and idiosyncratic furniture. There's a pleasant garden in which to unwind after a hard day's sightseeing.

🍴 Eating

Vinzenzmurr   BAVARIAN €
(Reichenstrasse 35; all dishes under €6; ☉8am-6pm Mon-Fri, to 1pm Sat) Füssen branch of the Munich butcher and self-service canteen offering no-nonsense portions of *Leberkäse* (meatloaf) in a bun, goulash soup, *Saures Lüngerl* (goat or beef lung with dumplings), bratwurst and schnitzel as well as something for those crazy vegetarians. No coffee or desserts.

Beim Olivenbauer AUSTRIAN, ITALIAN €€
(Ottostrasse 7; mains €6.50-16; ⊙11.30am-11.30pm) The Tyrol meets the Allgäu at this fun eatery, its interior a jumble of Doric columns, mismatched tables and chairs, multi-hued paint and assorted rural knick-knackery. Treat yourself to a wheel of pizza and a glass of Austrian wine, or go local with a plate of *Maultaschen* (pork and spinach ravioli) and a mug of local beer.

There's a kids corner and a sunny beer garden too. Takeaway pizza service available.

Zum Hechten BAVARIAN €€
(Ritterstrasse 6; mains €8-19; ⊙10am-10pm) Füssen's best hotel restaurant keeps things regional with a menu of Allgäu staples like schnitzel and noodles, Bavarian pork-themed favourites, and local specialities such as venison goulash from the Ammertal. Post-meal, relax in the wood-panelled dining room caressing a König Ludwig Dunkel, one of Germany's best dark beers, brewed by the current head of the Wittelsbach family.

Zum Franziskaner BAVARIAN €€
(Kemptener Strasse 1; mains €6-19.50; ⊙noon-11pm) This revamped restaurant specialises in *Schweinshaxe* (pork knuckle) and schnitzel, prepared in more varieties than you can shake a haunch at. There's some choice for noncarnivores such as *Käsespätzle* (rolled cheese noodles) and salads, and when the sun shines the outdoor seating shares the pavement with the 'foot-washing' statue.

❶ Information

Tourist Office (☑08362-938 50; www.fuessen.de; Kaiser-Maximilian-Platz; ⊙9am-6pm Mon-Fri, 10am-2pm Sat, 10am-noon Sun) Can help find rooms.

❶ Getting There & Away

BUS

The **Deutsche Touring** (www.touring.de, www.romantic-road.com), the Romantic Road Coach (p110), leaves from outside Füssen train station at 8am. It arrives in Füssen at 8.30pm.

TRAIN

If you want to do the castles in a single day from Munich, you'll need to start early. The first train leaves Munich at 5.53am (€26.20; change in Buchloe), reaching Füssen at 7.52am. Otherwise, direct trains leave Munich once every two hours throughout the day.

❶ Getting Around

The brand-new train and bus stations are just a short stroll from the historical centre. The castles are around 3.5km away across the River Lech, so in theory are reachable on foot.

BUS

RVO buses 78 and 73 (www.rvo-bus.de) serve the castles from Füssen Bahnhof (€4.40 return, eight minutes, at least hourly). Tickets from the driver.

TAXI

Taxis to the castles are €10 each way and can be picked up at Füssen Bahnhof.

Wieskirche

Wieskirche CHURCH
(☑08862-932 930; www.wieskirche.de; ⊙8am-8pm Apr-Oct, to 5pm Nov-Mar) FREE Located in the village of Wies, just off the B17 between Füssen and Schongau, the Wieskirche is one of Bavaria's best-known baroque churches and a Unesco-listed heritage site. About a million visitors a year flock to see its pride and joy, the monumental work of the legendary artist-brothers, Dominikus and Johann Baptist Zimmermann.

In 1730, a farmer in Steingaden, about 30km northeast of Füssen, witnessed the miracle of his Christ statue shedding tears. Pilgrims poured into the town in such numbers over the next decade that the local abbot commissioned a new church to house the weepy work. Inside the almost circular structure, eight snow-white pillars are topped by gold capital stones and swirling decorations. The unsupported dome must have seemed like God's work in the mid-17th century, its surface adorned with a pastel ceiling fresco celebrating Christ's resurrection.

From Füssen, regional RVO bus 73 (www.rvo-bus.de) makes the journey four times daily. The Romantic Road Coach (p110) also stops here long enough in both directions to enable a brief look round and then get back on. By car, take the B17 northeast and turn right (east) at Steingaden.

Schloss Linderhof

Schloss Linderhof CASTLE
(www.schlosslinderhof.de; adult/concession €8.50/7.50; ⊙9am-6pm Apr–mid-Oct, 10am-4pm mid-Oct–Mar) A pocket-sized trove of weird treasures, Schloss Linderhof was Ludwig II's smallest but most sumptuous palace, and

the only one he lived to see fully completed. Finished in 1878, the palace hugs a steep hillside in a fantasy landscape of French gardens, fountains and follies. The reclusive king used the palace as a retreat and hardly ever received visitors here. Linderhof was inspired by Versailles and dedicated to Louis XIV, the French 'sun king'.

Linderhof's myth-laden, jewel-encrusted rooms are a monument to the king's excesses that so unsettled the governors in Munich. The **private bedroom** is the largest, heavily ornamented and anchored by an enormous 108-candle crystal chandelier weighing 500kg. An artificial waterfall, built to cool the room in summer, cascades just outside the window. The **dining room** reflects the king's fetish for privacy and inventions. The king ate from a mechanised dining board, whimsically labelled 'Table, Lay Yourself', that sank through the floor so that his servants could replenish it without being seen.

Created by the famous court gardener Carl von Effner, the gardens and outbuildings, open April to October, are as fascinating as the castle itself. The highlight here is the oriental-style **Moorish Kiosk**, where Ludwig, dressed in oriental garb, would preside over nightly entertainment from a peacock throne. Underwater light dances on the stalactites at the **Venus Grotto**, an artificial cave inspired

LUDWIG II, THE FAIRY-TALE KING

Every year on 13 June, a stirring ceremony takes place in Berg, on the eastern shore of Lake Starnberg. A small boat quietly glides towards a cross just offshore and a plain wreath is fastened to its front. The sound of a single trumpet cuts the silence as the boat returns from this solemn ritual in honour of the most beloved king ever to rule Bavaria: Ludwig II.

The cross marks the spot where Ludwig died under mysterious circumstances in 1886. His early death capped the life of a man at odds with the harsh realities of a modern world no longer in need of a romantic and idealistic monarch.

Prinz Otto Ludwig Friedrich Wilhelm was a sensitive soul, fascinated by romantic epics, architecture and music, but his parents, Maximilian II and Marie, took little interest in his musings and he suffered a lonely and joyless childhood. In 1864, at 18 years old, the prince became king. He was briefly engaged to the sister of Elisabeth (Sisi), the Austrian empress, but, as a rule, he preferred the company of men. He also worshipped composer Richard Wagner, whose Bayreuth opera house was built with Ludwig's funds.

Ludwig was an enthusiastic leader initially, but Bavaria's days as a sovereign state were numbered, and he became a puppet king after the creation of the German Reich in 1871 (which had its advantages, as Bismarck gave Ludwig a hefty allowance). Ludwig withdrew completely to drink, draw up castle plans and view concerts and operas in private. His obsession with French culture and the Sun King, Louis XIV, inspired the fantastical palaces of **Neuschwanstein** (p92), **Linderhof** (p95) and **Herrenchiemsee** (p105) – lavish projects that spelt his undoing.

Contrary to popular belief, it was only Ludwig's purse – and not the state treasury – that was being bankrupted. However, by 1886 his ever-growing mountain of debt and erratic behaviour had put him at odds with his cabinet. The king, it seemed, needed to be 'managed'.

In January 1886, several ministers and relatives arranged a hasty psychiatric test that diagnosed Ludwig as mentally unfit to rule (this was made easier by the fact that his brother had been declared insane years earlier). That June, he was removed to Schloss Berg on Lake Starnberg. A few days later the dejected bachelor and his doctor took a Sunday evening lakeside walk and were found several hours later, drowned in just a few feet of water.

No one knows with certainty what happened that night. There was no eyewitness nor any proper criminal investigation. The circumstantial evidence was conflicting and incomplete. Reports and documents were tampered with, destroyed or lost. Conspiracy theories abound. That summer the authorities opened Neuschwanstein to the public to help pay off Ludwig's huge debts. King Ludwig II was dead, but the myth, and a tourist industry, had been born.

by a stage set for Wagner's *Tannhäuser*. Now sadly empty, Ludwig's fantastic conch-shaped boat is moored by the shore.

Linderhof is about 13km west of Oberammergau and 26km northwest of Garmisch-Partenkirchen. Bus 9622 travels to Linderhof from Oberammergau nine times a day. If coming from Garmisch-Partenkirchen change in Ettal or Oberammergau. The last service from Linderhof is just before 6pm but, if you miss it, the 13km vista-rich hike back to Oberammergau is an easygoing amble along the valley floor through shady woodland.

Oberammergau

📞 08822 / POP 5100

Quietly quaint Oberammergau occupies a wide valley surrounded by the dark forests and snow-dusted peaks of the Ammergauer Alps. The centre is packed with traditional painted houses, woodcarving shops and awestruck tourists who come here to learn about the town's world-famous Passion Play. It's also a great budget base for hikes and cross-country skiing trips into easily accessible Alpine back country.

◎ Sights & Activities

Passionstheater   THEATRE
(📞 08822-945 8833; www.passionstheater.de; Othmar-Weis-Strasse 1; combined tour & Oberammergau Museum entry adult/concession €8/7; ⊙ tours 10am & 2pm in German, 11pm in English Apr-Oct & Dec) The Passionstheater, where the Passion Play is performed, can be visited as part of a guided tour. The tour provides ample background on the play's history and also lets you peek at the costumes and sets.

Ask at the tourist office about music, plays and opera performances that take place here over the summer.

Pilatushaus   NOTABLE BUILDING
(Ludwig-Thoma-Strasse 10; ⊙ 1-5pm Tue-Sat mid-May–mid-Oct) FREE Aside from the Passion Play, Oberammergau's other claim to fame is its Lüftmalerei, the eye-popping house facades painted in an illusionist style. The pick of the crop is the amazing Pilatushaus, whose painted columns snap into 3-D as you approach. It contains a gallery and several workshops.

Oberammergau Museum   MUSEUM
(📞 08822-941 36; www.oberammergaumuseum. de; Dorfstrasse 8; combined museum entry & Passiontheater tour adult/concession €8/7; ⊙ 10am-

5pm Tue-Sun Apr-Oct) This is one of the best places to view exquisite examples of Oberammergau's famously intricate woodcarving art. The village has a long tradition of craftspeople producing anything from an entire nativity scene in a single walnut shell to a life-size Virgin Mary. If you get the urge to take some home, plenty of specialist shops around town sell pricey pieces.

⚡ Festivals & Events

Passion Play   THEATRE
(www.passionplay-oberammergau.com) A blend of opera, ritual and Hollywood epic, the Passion Play has been performed every year ending in a zero (plus some extra years for a variety of reasons) since the late 17th century as a collective thank-you from the villagers for being spared the plague.

Half the village takes part, sewing amazing costumes and growing hair and beards for their roles (no wigs or false hair allowed). The next performances will take place between May and October 2020, but tours of the Passionstheater enable you to take a peek at the costumes and sets anytime.

The next performances will take place between May and October 2020, but tours of the Passionstheater enable you to take a peek at the costumes and sets anytime. The theatre doesn't lie dormant in the decade between Passion Plays – ask at the tourist office about music, plays and opera performances that take place here over the summer.

🛏 Sleeping & Eating

DJH Hostel   HOSTEL €
(📞 08822-4114; www.oberammergau.jugendherberge.de; Malensteinweg 10; dm from €22.90) This hostel provides immaculate en suite rooms, a guest kitchen and a filling Alpine breakfast.

Gästehaus Richter   B&B €
(📞 08822-935 765; www.gaestehaus-richter.de; Welfengasse 2; s/d €39/70; 🛜) The best deal in Oberammergau, this family-run guesthouse offers well-maintained rooms with some traditional Alpine elements, a guest kitchen and a hearty breakfast.

Hotel Turmwirt   HOTEL €€
(📞 08822-926 00; www.turmwirt.de; Ettalerstrasse 2; s/d from €75/99; 🛜) This recently updated hotel next to the church has pristine business-standard rooms, some with Alpine views from the balconies and bits of woodcarving art throughout.

ℹ ALPINE GUEST CARDS

Overnight anywhere in Garmisch-Partenkirchen and Oberammergau and your hotel or guesthouse should issue you with a free *Gästekarte,* which gives free bus travel anywhere between Garmisch-Partenkirchen and Füssen as well as many other discounts.

Mundart   BAVARIAN €€
(☑ 08822-949 7565; www.restaurant-mundart.de; Bahnhofstrasse 12; mains €11.60-17.90; ⊙ 11am-11pm Wed-Sun; ☎) Mouth-wateringly light, 21st-century versions of Bavarian classics await at this trendy, baby-blue and grey themed restaurant near the train station. The menu is reassuringly brief, prices reasonable and the service the best in the village. Always a choice of dishes for noncarnivores.

ℹ Information

Tourist Office (☑ 08822-922 740; www.ammergauer-alpen.de; Eugen-Papst-Strasse 9a; ⊙ 9am-6pm Mon-Fri, 9am-1pm Sat & Sun, closed Sat & Sun Nov-Mar) The tourist office can help find accommodation.

ℹ Getting There & Around

Hourly trains connect Munich with Oberammergau (change at Murnau; €19.80, 1¾ hours). Hourly RVO bus 9606 goes direct to Garmisch-Partenkirchen via Ettal; change at Echelsbacher Brücke for Füssen.

Ettal

Kloster Ettal   MONASTERY
(www.kloster-ettal.de; Kaiser-Ludwig-Platz 1; ⊙ 8.30am-noon & 1.15-5.45pm Mon-Sat, 9-10.45am & 2.30-5.30pm Sun) FREE Ettal would be just another bend in the road were it not for this famous monastery. The highlight here is the sugary rococo basilica housing the monks' prized possession, a marble Madonna brought from Rome by Ludwig der Bayer in 1330. However, some might argue that the real high point is sampling the monastically distilled Ettaler Klosterlikör, an equally sugary herbal digestif.

Ettal is 5km south of Oberammergau, an easy hike along the Ammer River. Otherwise take bus 9606 from Garmisch-Partenkirchen or Oberammergau.

Garmisch-Partenkirchen

☑ 08821 / POP 26,000
An incredibly popular hang-out for outdoorsy types, skiing fans and day trippers from Munich, the double-barrelled resort of Garmisch-Partenkirchen is blessed with a fabled setting a snowball's throw from the Alps. To say you 'wintered in Garmisch' still has an aristocratic ring, and the area offers some of the best skiing in the land, including runs on Germany's highest peak, the Zugspitze (2964m).

The towns of Garmisch and Partenkirchen were merged for the 1936 Winter Olympics and, to this day, host international skiing events. Each retains its own distinct character: Garmisch has a more 21st-century feel, while Partenkirchen has retained its old-world Alpine village vibe.

Garmisch-Partenkirchen also makes a handy base for excursions to Ludwig II's palaces, including nearby Schloss Linderhof (p95) and the lesser-known Jagdschloss Schachen, as well as Oberammergau (p97) and even, at a push, Neuschwanstein (p92) and Hohenschwangau (p93) castles.

◉ Sights

Zugspitze   MOUNTAIN
(www.zugspitze.de; return adult/child €51/29.50; ⊙ train 8.15am-2.15pm) On good days, views from Germany's rooftop extend into four countries. The round trip starts in Garmisch aboard a cogwheel train (Zahnradbahn) that chugs along the mountain base to the Eibsee, an idyllic forest lake. From here, the Eibsee-Seilbahn, a super-steep cable car, swings to the top at 2962m. When you're done admiring the views, the Gletscherbahn cable car takes you to the Zugspitze glacier at 2600m, from where the cogwheel train heads back to Garmisch.

The trip to the Zugspitze summit is as memorable as it is popular; beat the crowds by starting early in the day and, if possible, skip weekends altogether.

Partnachklamm   CANYON
(www.partnachklamm.eu; adult/concession €4/2.50; ⊙ 8am-6pm) A top attraction around Garmisch is this narrow and dramatically beautiful 700m-long gorge with walls rising up to 80m. The trail hewn into the rock is especially spectacular in winter when you can walk beneath curtains of icicles and frozen waterfalls.

Around Garmisch-Partenkirchen

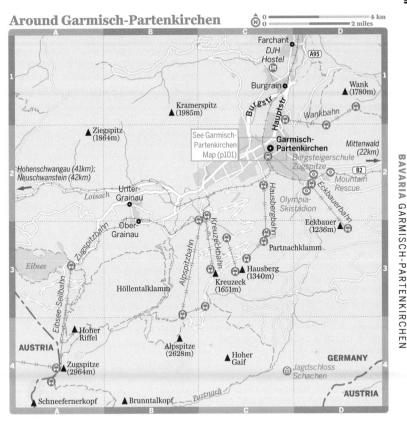

Jagdschloss Schachen   CASTLE
(☑08822-920 30; adult/concession €4.50/3.50;
☺tours 11am, 1pm, 2pm & 3pm Jun-Sep) A popular hiking route is to King Ludwig II's hunting lodge, Jagdschloss Schachen, which can
be reached via the Partnachklamm in about
a four-hour hike (10km). A plain wooden hut
from the outside, the interior is surprisingly
magnificent; the Moorish Room is something straight out of *Arabian Nights*.

🏃 Activities

Garmisch has two big ski fields: the Zugspitze plateau (2964m) and the Classic Ski
Area (Alpspitze, 2628m; Hausberg, 1340m;
Kreuzeck, 1651m; day pass per adult/child
€39.50/23). Local buses serve all the valley
stations. Cross-country ski trails run along
the main valleys, including a long section
from Garmisch to Mittenwald. If you're a be-
ginner, expect to pay around €60 per day for
group ski lessons, around €45 per hour for
private instruction.

The area around Garmisch-Partenkirchen
is also prime hiking and mountaineering
territory. The tourist office's website has a
superbly interactive tour-planning facility to
help you plot your way through the peaks on
foot, and many brochures and maps are also
available with route suggestions for all levels. Qualified Alpine guides are also on hand
at the tourist office between 4pm and 6pm
Monday and Thursday to answer questions
and provide all kinds of information. Hiking
to the Zugspitze summit is only possible in
summer and is only recommended for those
with experience in mountaineering.

Skischule   SKIING
(Map p101; ☑08821-4931; www.skischule-gap.
de; Am Hausberg 8) Ski hire and courses.

> ### ⓘ TOP SNOW
>
> A **Top Snow Card** (two days, adult/child €82.50/43.50) covers all the slopes around Garmisch as well as over the border in the Tyrol (an incredible 207km of pistes and 89 ski lifts).

Alpensport Total — SKIING

(Map p101; ☑ 08821-1425; www.alpensporttotal. de; Marienplatz 18) Winter ski school and hire centre that organises other outdoor activities in the warmer months.

Bergsteigerschule Zugspitze — HIKING

(☑ 08821-589 99; www.bergsteigerschule-zugspitze.de; Am Kreuzeckbahnhof 12a) A mountaineering school, offering guided hikes and courses. Located at the lower station of the Alpspitzbahn, southwest of the town.

Deutscher Alpenverein — HIKING

(Map p101; ☑ 08821-2701; www.alpenverein-gapa.de; Carl-Reiser-Strasse 2; ⊙ 2-6pm Mon & Tue, 10am-noon & 4-7pm Wed & Thu, 8am-1pm Fri) The German Alpine Club offers guided hikes and courses and its website is a mine of detailed, expertly updated local information, albeit in German only.

🛏 Sleeping

The tourist office operates a 24-hour outdoor room-reservation noticeboard.

Hostel 2962 — HOSTEL €

(Map p101; ☑ 08821-909 2674; www.hostel2962-garmisch.com; Partnachauenstrasse 3; dm/d from €20/60; 🛜) Touted as a hostel, the somewhat vibe-less 2962 is essentially a typical Garmisch hotel with seven dorms, but a good choice nonetheless. If you can get into one of the four- or five-bed rooms, it's the cheapest sleep in town. Breakfast is an extra €6 if you stay in a dorm.

DJH Hostel — HOSTEL €

(☑ 08821-967 050; www.garmisch.jugendherberge. de; Jochstrasse 10; dm from €24.90; P@🛜) The standards at this smart, immaculately maintained hostel are as good as at some chain hotels. Rooms have Ikea-style furnishings and fruity colour schemes, and there are indoor and outdoor climbing walls if the Alps are not enough. Located 4.5km north of the town. Arrange a free transfer from the train station.

Hotel Garmischer Hof — HOTEL €€

(Map p101; ☑ 08821-9110; www.garmischer-hof.de; Chamonixstrasse 10; s €59-80, d €98-138;

🛜⛵) In the ownership of the Seiwald family since 1928, many a climber, skier and Alpine adventurer has creased the sheets at this welcoming inn. Rooms are elegant and cosy with some traditional Alpine touches, the buffet breakfast is served in the vaulted cafe-restaurant, and there's a spa and sauna providing après-ski relief.

Gasthof zum Rassen — HOTEL €€

(☑ 08821-2089; www.gasthof-rassen.de; Ludwigstrasse 45; s €32-53, d €52-90; P🛜) This beautifully frescoed 14th-century building is home to a great option in this price bracket, where the simply furnished, contemporary rooms contrast with the traditionally frilly styling of the communal areas. The cavernous event hall, formerly a brewery, houses Bavaria's oldest folk theatre.

Reindl's Partenkirchner Hof — HOTEL €€€

(Map p101; ☑ 08821-943 870; www.reindls. de; Bahnhofstrasse 15; d incl breakfast €140-230; P@🛜) Though Reindl's doesn't look like five stars from the outside, this elegant luxury hotel is stacked with perks, a wine bar and a top-notch gourmet restaurant. Rooms are studies in folk-themed elegance and some enjoy gobsmacking mountain views.

🍴 Eating

Hobi's — BAKERY €

(Map p101; Zugspitzstrasse 2; snacks €2-5.50; ⊙5.45am-12.30pm & 2.30-5.30pm Mon-Fri, 5.45am-noon Sat, 6.30-11am Sun; 🛜) G-P's best bakery piles the cakes and sandwiches high and ladles out soup throughout the day. Lots of seats and good wi-fi.

★ Gasthof Fraundorfer — BAVARIAN €€

(www.gasthof-fraundorfer.de; Ludwigstrasse 24; mains €8-19; ⊙7am-midnight Thu-Mon, from 5pm Wed) If you came to the Alps to experience yodelling, knee slapping and red-faced locals in lederhosen, you just arrived at the right address. Steins of frothing ale fuel the increasingly raucous atmosphere as the evening progresses and monster portions of plattered pig meat push belt buckles to the limit. Decor ranges from baroque cherubs to hunting trophies and the 'Sports Corner'. Unmissable.

Zum Wildschütz — BAVARIAN €€

(Map p101; Bankgasse 9; mains €9-20; ⊙11.30am-10pm) The best place in town for fresh venison, rabbit, wild boar and other seasonal game dishes, this place is, not surprisingly, popular with hunters. The Tyrolean and south Bavarian takes on schnitzel

Garmisch-Partenkirchen

aren't bad either. If you prefer your victuals critter free, look elsewhere.

Zirbel   PUB FOOD €€
(Map p101; Promenadestrasse 2; mains €8-20; ⊙5pm-1am) Slightly away from the tourists and guarded by a grumpy-looking wood-carved bear, this popular, low-beamed and rustically themed pub serves noodle dishes, salads and schnitzel, all swilled down with Hofbräu beer. Sadly, only open in the evenings.

Bräustüberl   GERMAN €€
(Map p101; ☑ 08821-2312; www.braeustueberl-garmisch.de; Fürstenstrasse 23; mains €6-19; ⊙10am-1am) This quintessentially Bavarian tavern is the place to cosy up with some local nosh, served by dirndl-trussed waitresses, while the enormous enamel coal-burning stove revives chilled extremities. Live music and theatre take place in the upstairs hall.

Hofbräustüberl   BAVARIAN, YUGOSLAV €€
(Map p101; Chamonixstrasse 2; mains €11-20; ⊙11.30am-3pm & 5-11pm) Balkan spice meets south German heartiness at this Bavarian-Yugoslav restaurant right in the thick of things. Despite the seemingly echt-Bayern (authentic Bavarian) name, the long menu is a mixed bag of Alps and Adriatic, the interior understated and quite formal, the service top-notch. The Yugoslav wines are a rare treat.

Colosseo   ITALIAN €€
(Map p101; Klammstrasse 7; pizzas €4-9, other mains €5-20; ⊙11.30am-2.30pm & 5-11.30pm) If you fancy an Alpine take on *la dolce vita*, with mountain views and a bit of faux archaeology thrown in, this much-lauded pas-

Garmisch-Partenkirchen

ta and pizza parlour with a mammoth menu is the place to head.

❶ Information

Mountain Rescue (☑ 08821-3611, 112; www.bergwacht-bayern.de; Auenstrasse 7) Mountain rescue station.

Post Office (Map p101; Bahnhofstrasse 31)

Tourist Office (Map p101; ☑ 08821-180 700; www.gapa.de; Richard-Strauss-Platz 2; ⊙9am-6pm Mon-Sat, 10am-noon Sun) Friendly staff hands out maps, brochures and advice.

❶ Getting There & Around

Garmisch-Partenkirchen has hourly connections from Munich (€20.70, one hour 20 minutes); special packages, available from Munich Hauptbahnhof, combine the return trip with a Zugspitze day ski pass (around €50).

RVO bus 9606 (www.rvo-bus.de) leaves at 9.40am, reaching the Füssen castles at Neuschwanstein and Hohenschwangau two hours later. On the way back take the 4.13pm bus 9651 and change onto the 9606 at Echelsbacher Brücke or take the direct service at 5.18pm. The 9606 also runs hourly to Oberammergau (40 minutes).

The A95 from Munich is the direct road route. The most central parking is at the Kongresshaus (next to the tourist office).

Bus tickets cost €1.50 for journeys in town. For bike hire, try **Fahrrad Ostler** (Map p101; ☑ 08821-3362; Kreuzstrasse 1; per day/week from €10/40).

Mittenwald

☑ 08823 / POP 7300

Nestled in a cul-de-sac under snowcapped peaks, sleepily alluring Mittenwald, 20km southeast of Garmisch-Partenkirchen, is the most natural spot imaginable for a resort. Known far and wide for its master violin makers, the citizens of this drowsy village seem almost bemused by its popularity. The air is ridiculously clean, and on the main street the loudest noise is a babbling brook.

The **tourist office** (☑ 08823-339 81; www.mittenwald.de; Dammkarstrasse 3; ⊙ 8.30am-6pm Mon-Fri, 9am-noon Sat, 10am-noon Sun mid-May–mid-Oct, shorter hours rest of the year) has details of excellent hiking and cycling routes. Popular hikes with cable-car access will take you up the grandaddy Alpspitze (2628m), as well as the Wank, Mt Karwendel and the Wettersteinspitze. Return tickets to Karwendel, which boasts Germany's second-highest cable-car route, cost €26.50 per adult and $16.50 per child return.

The Karwendel ski field has one of the longest runs (7km) in Germany, but it is primarily for freestyle pros. All-day ski passes to the nearby Kranzberg ski fields, the best all-round option, cost €27 per adult and €20 per child. For equipment hire and ski/snowboard instruction contact the **Erste Skischule Mittenwald** (☑ 08823-3582; www.skischule-mittenwald.de; Bahnhofsplatz 14).

The only classic off-piste sight in town is the **Geigenbaumuseum** (www.geigenbaumuseum-mittenwald.de; Ballenhausgasse 3; adult/concession €4.50/3.50; ⊙ 11am-4pm Tue-Sun), a collection of over 200 locally crafted violins and the tools used to fashion them. It's also the venue for occasional concerts.

Behind a pretty facade, **Hotel-Gasthof Alpenrose** (☑ 08823-927 00; www.alpenrose-mittenwald.de; Obermarkt 1; s €30-59, d €77-97) has cosy, old-style rooms, a restaurant and live Bavarian music almost nightly. A short walk from the Obermarkt, **Gaststätte Römerschanz** (Innsbrucker Strasse 30; mains €7-17; ⊙ 10am-midnight Wed-Mon) has Mittenwald's tastiest food.

Mittenwald is served by trains from Garmisch-Partenkirchen (€4.40, 20 minutes, hourly), Munich (€24.20, 1¾ hours, hourly) and Innsbruck (€10.10, one hour, seven daily), across the border in Austria. Otherwise RVO bus 9608 connects Mittenwald with Garmisch-Partenkirchen (30 minutes) several times a day.

Oberstdorf

☑ 08322 / POP 9570

Spectacularly situated in the western Alps, the Allgäu region feels a long, long way from the rest of Bavaria, both in its cuisine (more *Spätzle* than dumplings) and the dialect, which is closer to the Swabian of Baden-Württemberg. The Allgäu's chief draw is the car-free resort of Oberstdorf, a major skiing centre a short hop from Austria.

🏃 Activities

Oberstdorf is almost ringed by towering peaks and offers some top-draw hiking. Skiers value the resort for its friendliness, lower prices and less-crowded pistes. The village is surrounded by 70km of well-maintained cross-country trails and three ski fields: the Nebelhorn, Fellhorn/Kanzelwand and Söllereck. For ski hire and tuition, try **Alpin Skischule** (☑ 08322-952 90; www.alpinskischule.de; Am Bahnhofplatz 1a) opposite the train station or **Erste Skischule Oberstdorf** (☑ 08322-3110; www.skischule-oberstdorf.de; Freiherr-von-Brutscher-Strasse 4).

Gaisalpseen HIKING
(single/return €31.50/24.50; ⊙ 9am-5pm daily) For an exhilarating day walk, ride the Nebelhorn cable car to the upper station, then hike down via the Gaisalpseen, two lovely alpine lakes (six hours).

Eissportzentrum Oberstdorf ICE SKATING
(☑ 08322-700 510; www.eissportzentrum-oberstdorf.de/; Rossbichlstrasse 2-6) The Eissportzentrum Oberstdorf, behind the Nebelhorn cable-car station, is the biggest ice-skating complex in Germany, with three separate rinks.

🛏 Sleeping

Oberstdorf is chock-full with private guesthouses, but owners are usually reluctant to rent rooms for just a single night, even in the quieter shoulder seasons.

DJH Hostel
HOSTEL €

(☎08322-987 50; www.oberstdorf.jugendherberge.de; Kornau 8; dm €28.90; ⬛) A relaxed, 200-bed chalet-hostel with commanding views of the Allgäu Alps. Take bus 1 from the bus station in front of the Hauptbahnhof to the Reute stop; it's in the suburb of Kornau, near the Söllereck chairlift.

Haus Edelweiss
APARTMENTS €€

(☎08322-959 60; www.edelweiss.de; Freibergstrasse 7; apt from €107; ⓟ⬛⬛) As crisp and sparkling as freshly fallen alpine snow, this new apartment hotel just a couple of blocks from the tourist office has 19 pristine, self-contained flats with fully equipped kitchens, ideal for stays of three nights or more. Generally the longer you tarry, the fewer euros per night you spend.

Weinklause
GUESTHOUSE €€

(☎08322-969 30; www.weinklause.de; Prinzenstrasse 10; s €73, d €110-172; ⓟ⬛) Willing to take one-nighters at the drop of a felt hat, this superb lodge offers all kinds of rooms and apartments, some with kitchenettes, others with jaw-dropping, spectacular alpine views. A generous breakfast is served in the restaurant, which comes to life most nights with local live music.

🍴 Eating & Drinking

Weinstube am Frohmarkt
TYROLEAN €€

(☎08322-3988; www.weinstube-oberstdorf.de; Am Frohmarkt 2; mains €10-19; ⏰5pm-midnight Mon-Sat) 'Where did Bavaria go?' you might exclaim at this intimate wine bar, where the musty-sweet aroma of wine, cheese and Tyrolean cured ham scents the air. Rub shoulders with locals downstairs over a plate of wild boar or Tessin-style turkey steak, or retreat upstairs for a quiet nip of wine.

Nordi Stüble
SWABIAN €€

(☎08322-7641; cnr Walserstrasse & Luitpoldstrasse; mains €9-20; ⏰11am-10pm Mon-Sat) Family owned and run, this intimate neighbourhood eatery, a small wood-panelled dining room bedecked in rural junk of yesteryear, is the place to enjoy local takes on schnitzel and *Maultaschen*. All dishes are prepared fresh, so be prepared to wait; a Stuttgart Dinkelacker beer is the way to wash it all down.

Oberstdorfer Dampfbierbrauerei
BREWERY

(www.dampfbierbrauerei.de; Bahnhofplatz 8; ⏰11am-1am) Knock back a few 'steamy ales' at Germany's southernmost brewery, right next to the train station.

ℹ Information

Tourist Office (☎08322-7000; www.oberstdorf.de; Prinzregenten-Platz 1; ⏰9am-5pm Mon-Fri, 9.30am-noon Sat) The tourist office and its branch office (Bahnhofplatz; ⏰10am-5pm daily) run a room-finding service.

ℹ Getting There & Away

There are at least five direct trains daily from Munich (€32.70, 2½ hours), otherwise change in Buchloe. The train station is a short walk north of the town centre on Bahnhofstrasse.

Andechs

Kloster Andechs
MONASTERY

(☎08152-376 253; www.andechs.de; admission free; ⏰8am-6pm Mon-Fri, 9am-6pm Sat, 9.45am-6pm Sun) Founded in the 10th century, the gorgeous hilltop monastery of Andechs has long been a place of pilgrimage, though today more visitors come to slurp the Benedictines' fabled ales.

The church owns two relics of enormous importance: branches that are thought to come from Christ's crown of thorns, and a victory cross of Charlemagne, whose army overran much of Western Europe in the 9th century. In the Holy Chapel, the votive candles, some of them over 1m tall, are among Germany's oldest. The remains of Carl Orff, the composer of *Carmina Burana,* are interred here as well.

Outside, soak up the magnificent views of the purple-grey Alps and forested hills before plunging into the nearby Bräustüberl (⏰10am-8pm), the monks' beer hall and garden. There are seven varieties of beer on offer, from the rich and velvety Doppelbock dark to the fruity unfiltered *Weissbier* (wheat beer). The place is incredibly popular and, on summer weekends, you may have to join a queue of day trippers at the door to get in.

The easiest way to reach Andechs from Munich is to take the S8 to Herrsching (49 minutes), then change to bus 951 or the private Ammersee-Reisen bus (€2.20, nine times daily). Alternatively, it's a pleasant 4km hike south from Herrsching through the protected woodland of the Kiental.

Bad Tölz

☑ 08041 / POP 18,000

Situated some 40km south of central Munich, Bad Tölz is a pretty spa town straddling the Isar River. The town's gentle inclines provide a delightful spot for its attractive, frescoed houses and the quaint shops of the old town. At weekends thousands flock here from Munich to enjoy the town's famous, ultramodern swimming complex, Alpine slide and hiking trips along the river. Bad Tölz is also the gateway to the Tölzer Land region and its emerald-green lakes, the Walchensee and the Kochelsee.

◉ Sights & Activities

Cobblestoned and car-free, Marktstrasse is flanked by statuesque town houses with ornate overhanging eaves that look twice as high on the sloping street.

Kalvarienberg   LANDMARK
Above the town, on Kalvarienberg, looms Bad Tölz' landmark, the twin-towered Kalvarienbergkirche (Cavalry Church). This enormous baroque structure stands side by side with the petite Leonhardikapelle (Leonhardi Chapel; 1718), the destination of the town's well-known Leonhardi pilgrimage.

Stadtmuseum   MUSEUM
(☑ 08041-793 5156; Marktstrasse 48; adult/concession €2/1.50; ☺10am-5pm Tue-Sun) The Stadtmuseum touches on practically all aspects of local culture and history, with a fine collection of painted armoires (the so-called Tölzer Kasten), a 2m-tall, single-stringed *Nonnengeige* (marine trumpet), examples of traditional glass painting and a cart used in the Leonhardifahrt.

Alpamare   SPA
(☑ 08041-509 999; www.alpamare.de; Ludwigstrasse 14; day pass adult/child €35/25; ☺9.30am-10pm) In the spa section of town, west of the Isar River, you'll find the fantastic water complex Alpamare, Europe's first covered aquapark. This huge centre has heated indoor and outdoor mineral pools, a wave and surfing pool, a series of wicked water slides (including Germany's longest, the 330m-long Alpabob-Wildwasser), saunas, solariums and its own hotel. Bus 9570 from the train station stops 100m away.

Blomberg   HIKING
Southwest of Bad Tölz, the Blomberg (1248m) is a family-friendly mountain that has a natural toboggan track in winter, plus easy hiking and a fun Alpine slide in summer. Unless you're walking, getting up the hill involves, weather permitting, a chairlift ride aboard the **Blombergbahn** (www.blomberg bahn.de; top station adult/child return €9.50/4; ☺11am-4pm Sat & Sun).

Over 1km long, the fibreglass Alpine toboggan track snakes down the mountain from the middle station. You zip down at up to 50km/h through the 17 hairpin bends on little wheeled bobsleds with a joystick to control braking. A long-sleeved shirt and jeans will provide a little protection. Riding up to the midway station and sliding down costs €5 per adult (€4 concession), with discounts for multiple trips.

To reach Blomberg, take RVO bus 9612 from the train station to the Blombergbahn stop.

★☆ Festivals & Events

Leonhardifahrt   RELIGIOUS
(www.bad-toelz.de) Every year on 6 November, residents pay homage to the patron saint of horses, Leonhard. The famous Leonhardifahrt is a pilgrimage up to the Leonhardi chapel on Kalvarienberg, where townsfolk dress up in traditional costume and ride dozens of garlanded horse carts to the strains of brass bands.

🛏 Sleeping & Eating

Posthotel Kolberbräu   HOTEL €€
(☑ 08041-768 80; www.kolberbraeu.de; Marktstrasse 29; s/d from €55/96; 🖳) Very well appointed 30-room inn amid the bustle of the main street, with hefty timber furniture, a classic Bavarian restaurant and a tradition going back over four centuries.

Gasthof Zantl   BAVARIAN €€
(www.gasthof-zantl.de; Salzstrasse 31; mains €8-18; ☺11.30am-2.30pm & 5pm-late, closed Thu) One of Bad Tölz' oldest buildings, this convivial tavern has a predictably pork-heavy menu, with ingredients sourced from local villages as much as possible. There's a sunny beer garden out front.

ⓘ Information

Tourist Office (☑ 08041-793 5156; www. bad-toelz.de; Marktstrasse 48; ☺10am-5pm Tue-Sun)

ℹ Getting There & Away

The private **Bayerische Oberlandbahn** (BOB; ☎ 08024-997 171; www.bayerischeoberland-bahn.de) runs at least hourly trains between Bad Tölz and Munich Hauptbahnhof (€12.50, 50 minutes). Alternatively, take the S2 from central Munich to Holzkirchen, then change to the BOB. In Holzkirchen make sure you board the Bad Tölz–bound portion of the train. The BOB/Alpamare KombiTicket (adult/child €39/28) entitles the holder to return 2nd class travel to/from Munich, bus travel from the train station to Alpamare and entry to Alpamare for four hours.

Chiemsee

☎ 08051

Most foreign visitors arrive at the shores of the Bavarian Sea – as Chiemsee is affectionately known – in search of King Ludwig II's Schloss Herrenchiemsee. This is Bavaria's biggest lake (if you don't count Bodensee which is only partially in the state) and its natural beauty and water sports make the area popular with de-stressing city dwellers, and many affluent Munich residents own weekend retreats by its shimmering waters.

The towns of Prien am Chiemsee and, about 5km south, Bernau am Chiemsee (both on the Munich–Salzburg rail line) are good bases for exploring the lake. Of the two towns, Prien is by far the larger and livelier. If you're day tripping to Herrenchiemsee, conveniently interconnecting transport is available. To explore further, you'll probably need a set of wheels.

◉ Sights

Schloss Herrenchiemsee CASTLE
(☎ 08051-688 70; www.herren-chiemsee.de; adult/concession €10/9; ⊙ tours 9am-6pm Apr-Oct, 9.40am-4.15pm Nov-Mar) An island just 1.5km across the Chiemsee from Prien, Herreninsel, is home to Ludwig II's Versailles-inspired castle. Begun in 1878, it was never intended as a residence, but as a homage to absolutist monarchy, as epitomised by Ludwig's hero, Louis XIV. Ludwig spent only 10 days here and even then was rarely seen, preferring to read at night and sleep all day. The palace is typical of Ludwig's creations, the product of his romantic obsessions and unfettered imagination.

Ludwig splurged more money on this palace than on Neuschwanstein and Linderhof combined, but when cash ran out in 1885, one year before his death, 50 rooms remained unfinished. Those that were completed outdo each other in opulence. The vast **Gesandtentreppe** (Ambassador Staircase), a double staircase leading to a frescoed gallery and topped by a glass roof, is the first visual knock-out on the guided tour, but that fades in comparison to the stunning **Grosse Spiegelgalerie** (Great Hall of Mirrors). This tunnel of light runs the length of the garden (98m, or 10m longer than that in Versailles). It sports 52 candelabra and 33 great glass chandeliers with 7000 candles, which took 70 servants half an hour to light. In late July it becomes a wonderful venue for classical concerts.

The **Paradeschlafzimmer** (State Bedroom) features a canopied bed that perches altar-like on a pedestal behind a golden balustrade. This was the heart of the palace, where morning and evening audiences were held. But it's the king's bedroom, the **Kleines Blaues Schlafzimmer** (Little Blue Bedroom), that really takes the cake. The decoration is sickly sweet, encrusted with gilded stucco and wildly extravagant carvings. The room is bathed in a soft blue light emanating from a glass globe at the foot of the bed. It supposedly took 18 months for a technician to perfect the lamp to the king's satisfaction.

Admission to the palace also entitles you to a spin around the **König-Ludwig II-Museum**, where you can see the king's christening and coronation robes, more blueprints of megalomaniac buildings and his death mask.

To reach the palace, take the hourly or half-hourly ferry from Prien-Stock (€7.60 return, 15 to 20 minutes) or from Bernau-Felden (€7.90, 25 minutes, May to October). From the boat landing on Herreninsel, it's about a 20-minute walk through pretty gardens to the palace. Palace tours, offered in German or English, last 30 minutes.

Fraueninsel ISLAND
A third of this tiny island is occupied by **Frauenwörth Abbey** (www.frauenwoerth.de) **FREE**, founded in the late 8th century, making it one of the oldest abbeys in Bavaria. The 10th-century church, whose free-standing campanile sports a distinctive onion-dome top (11th century), is worth a visit. Opposite the church is the AD 860 Carolingian **Torhalle** (admission €2; ⊙ 10am-6pm May-Oct). It houses medieval objets d'art, sculpture and changing exhibitions of regional paintings from the 18th to the 20th centuries.

Return ferry fare, including a stop at Herreninsel, is €8.60 from Prien-Stock and €8.90 from Bernau-Felden.

🏃 Activities

The swimming beaches at Chieming and Gstadt (both free) are the easiest to reach, on the lake's eastern and northern shores respectively. A variety of boats are available for hire at many beaches, for €13 to €25 per hour. In Prien, **Bootsverleih Stöffl** (www. stoeffl.de; Strandpromenade) is possibly the best company to turn to.

Prienavera   SWIMMING
(✆ 08051-609 570; www.prienavera.de; Seestrasse 120; 4hr pass adult/child €11/6, day pass €13/7; ⏰ 10am-10pm Mon-Fri, 9am-10pm Sat & Sun) The futuristic-looking glass roof by the harbour in Prien-Stock shelters Prienavera, a popular pool complex with a wellness area, water slides and a restaurant.

🛏 Sleeping

Panorama Camping Harras   CAMPGROUND €
(✆ 08051-904 613; www.camping-harras.de; Harrasser Strasse 135; per person/tent/car from €5.90/4.60/3) This camping ground is scenically located on a peninsula with its own private beach, and catamaran and surfboard hire. The restaurant has a delightful lakeside terrace.

Hotel Bonnschlössl   HOTEL €€
(✆ 08051-961 400; www.bonnschloessl.de; Ferdinand-Bonn-Strasse 2, Bernau; s €51-64, d €88-111; 🐾) Built in 1477, this pocket-size 21-room palace hotel with faux turrets once belonged to the Bavarian royal court. Rooms are stylish, if slightly overfurnished, and there's a wonderful terrace with a rambling garden. There's a small spa area, a library and a lobby bar, but no restaurant.

Hotel Garni Möwe   HOTEL €€
(✆ 08051-5004; www.hotel-garni-moewe.de; Seestrasse 111, Prien; d €59-128; 🐾🏊) This traditional Bavarian hotel right on the lakefront is excellent value, especially the loft rooms. It has its own bike and boat hire, plus a fitness centre, and the large garden is perfect for travellers with children.

Luitpold am See   HOTEL €€
(✆ 08051-609 100; www.herrenchiemsee-schloss-hotel.de; Seestrasse 101, Prien; s €57-79, d €112-150; 🐾) Right on the lake shore in Prien, the 54 rooms at this excellent choice offer a good price to standard ratio, with their pristine bathrooms, wood-rich furnishings and pretty views. There's an onsite restaurant and *Konditorei* (cafe-bakery) and reception can help out with travel arrangements, tours and such.

🍴 Eating

Alter Wirt   BAVARIAN €€
(Kirchplatz 9, Bernau; mains €9.50-17.50; ⏰ 11am-11pm Tue-Sun) This massive half-timbered inn with five centuries of history, situated on Bernau's main street, plates up south German meat blocks and international standards to a mix of locals and tourists. For dessert why not try 'Hot Love' (*Heisse Liebe*) – vanilla and chocolate ice cream with hot raspberry sauce and cream.

Badehaus   BAVARIAN €€
(✆ 08051-970 300; Rathausstrasse 11; mains €7-18; ⏰ 10am-late) Near the Chiemsee Info-Center and the lake shore, this fancy restaurant, contemporary beer hall and garden has quirky decor and gourmet-style fare priced for all wallet capacities. The Jazzkeller beneath the complex puts on regular jam sessions and other musical events in the evenings.

Westernacher am See   MODERN BAVARIAN €€
(✆ 08051-4722; www.westernacher-chiemsee.de; Seestrasse 115, Prien; mains €7.90-19.50) This lakeside dining haven has a multiple personality, with a cosy restaurant, cocktail bar, cafe, beer garden and glassed-in winter terrace. The long menu is an eclectic affair combining pizzas, Bavarian favourites, Italian pasta, Thai curries and Chiemsee fish dishes.

ℹ Information

Bernau Tourist Office (✆ 08051-986 80; www. bernau-am-chiemsee.de; Aschauer Strasse 10; ⏰ 8.30am-6pm Mon-Fri, 9am-noon Sat, shorter hours mid-Sep–Jun)
Chiemsee Tourist Office (✆ 08051-965 550; www.chiemsee-alpenland.de; Felden 10; ⏰ 10am-12.30pm & 1.30-6.30pm Mon-Fri) On the southern lake shore, near the Bernau-Felden autobahn exit.
Prien Tourist Office (✆ 08051-690 50; www. tourismus.prien.de; Alte Rathausstrasse 11; ⏰ 8.30am-5pm Mon-Fri, to 4pm Sat, closed Sat Oct-Apr)

ℹ Getting There & Around

Meridian trains run hourly from Munich to Prien (€17.90, 55 minutes) and Bernau (€19.80, one hour). Hourly RVO bus 9505 connects the two lake towns.

Local buses run from Prien Bahnhof to the harbour in Stock. You can also take the historic **Chiemseebahn** (www.chiemsee-schifffahrt.de; one-way/return €2.70/3.70) , the world's oldest narrow-gauge steam train (1887).

Chiemsee Schifffahrt (✆ 08051-6090; www. chiemsee-schifffahrt.de; Seestrasse 108) operates half-hourly to hourly ferries from Prien with stops at Herreninsel, Fraueninsel, Seebruck and Chieming on a schedule that changes seasonally. You can circumnavigate the entire lake and make all these stops (getting off and catching the next ferry that comes your way) for €12.20. Children aged six to 15 get a 50% discount.

Chiemgauer Radhaus (☑ 08051-4631; Bahnhofsplatz 6) and **Chiemgau Biking** (☑ 08051-961 4973; www.chiemgau-biking.de; Chiemseestrasse 84) hire out mountain bikes for between €12 and €22 per day.

Berchtesgaden

☑ 08652 / POP 7800

Wedged into Austria and framed by six formidable mountain ranges, the Berchtesgadener Land is a drop-dead-gorgeous corner of Bavaria steeped in myths and legends. Local lore has it that angels given the task of distributing the earth's wonders were startled by God's order to get a move on and dropped them all here. These most definitely included the Watzmann (2713m), Germany's second-highest mountain, and the pristine Königssee, perhaps Germany's most photogenic body of water.

Much of the area is protected by law within the Berchtesgaden National Park, which was declared a 'biosphere reserve' by Unesco in 1990. The village of Berchtesgaden is the obvious base for hiking circuits into the park.

Away from the trails, the main draws are the mountaintop Eagle's Nest, a lodge built for Hitler and now a major dark-tourism destination, and Dokumentation Obersalzberg, a museum that chronicles the region's sinister Nazi past.

◎ Sights

Eagle's Nest   HISTORIC SITE
(Kehlsteinhaus; ☑ 08652-2969; www.kehlstein-haus.de; Obersalzberg; adult/child €16.10/9.30; ⏱ buses 7.40am-4pm mid-May–Oct) The Eagle's Nest was built as a mountaintop retreat for Hitler, and gifted to him on his 50th birthday. It took some 3000 workers only two years to carve the precipitous 6km-long mountain road, cut a 124m-long tunnel and a brass-panelled lift through the rock, and build the lodge itself (now a restaurant). It can only be reached by special shuttle bus from the Kehlsteinhaus bus station.

On clear days, views from the top are breathtaking. If you're not driving, bus 838 makes the trip to the shuttle bus stop from

the Berchtesgaden Hauptbahnhof every half-hour.

At the mountain station, you'll be asked to book a spot on a return bus. Allow at least two hours to get through lines, explore the lodge and the mountaintop, and perhaps have a bite to eat. Don't panic if you miss your bus – just go back to the mountain station kiosk and rebook.

Königssee   LAKE
Crossing the serenely picturesque Königssee makes for some unforgettable memories and once-in-a-lifetime photo opportunities. Cradled by steep mountain walls some 5km south of Berchtesgaden, the emerald-green Königssee is Germany's highest lake (603m), with drinkably pure waters shimmering into fjordlike depths. Bus 841/842 makes the trip out here from the Berchtesgaden train station roughly every hour.

Escape the hubbub of the bustling lakeside tourist village of Schönau by taking an electric **boat tour** (☑ 08652-963 696; www.seenschifffahrt.de; Schönau; return boat adult/child €13.90/7; ⏱ boats 8am-5.15pm May–mid-Oct) to **St Bartholomä**, a quaint onion-domed chapel on the western shore. At some point, the boat will stop while the captain plays a horn towards the Echo Wall – the sound will bounce seven times. From St Bartholomä, an easy trail leads to the wondrous **Eiskapelle** (ice chapel) in about one hour.

You can also skip the crowds by meandering along the lake shore. It's a nice and easy 3.5km return walk to the secluded **Malerwinkel** (Painter's Corner), a lookout famed for its picturesque vantage point.

Dokumentation Obersalzberg   MUSEUM
(☑ 08652-947 960; www.obersalzberg.de; Salzbergstrasse 41, Obersalzberg; adult/concession €3/free, audioguide €2; ⏱ 9am-5pm daily Apr-Oct, 10am-3pm Tue-Sun Nov-Mar, last entry 1hr before closing) In 1933 the quiet mountain village of Obersalzberg (3km from Berchtesgaden) became the second seat of Nazi power after Berlin, a dark period that's given the full historical treatment at this excellent exhibit. It documents the forced takeover of the area, the construction of the compound and the daily life of the Nazi elite. All facets of Nazi terror are dealt with, including Hitler's near-mythical appeal, his racial politics, the resistance movement, foreign policy and the death camps.

A section of the underground bunker network is open for perusal. Hourly bus 838 from Berchtesgaden train station will get you there.

Salzbergwerk HISTORIC SITE
(www.salzzeitreise.de; Bergwerkstrasse 83; adult/
child €16/9.50; ⊙9am-5pm May-Oct, 11am-3pm
Nov-Apr) Once a major producer of 'white
gold', Berchtesgaden has thrown open its
salt mines for fun-filled 90-minute tours.
Kids especially love donning miners' garb
and whooshing down a wooden slide into
the depths of the mine. Down below, highlights include mysteriously glowing salt
grottoes and crossing a 100m-long subterranean salt lake on a wooden raft. Take hourly
bus 848 from Berchtesgaden train station.

🏃 Activities

Berchtesgaden National Park NATIONAL PARK
(www.nationalpark-berchtesgaden.de) The wilds
of this 210-sq-km park offer some of the best
hiking in Germany. A good introduction is
a 2km trail up from St Bartholomä beside
the Königssee to the notorious Watzmann-
Ostwand, where scores of mountaineers
have met their deaths. Another popular hike
goes from the southern end of the Königssee
to the Obersee.

For details of routes visit the **national
park office** (Haus der Berge; ☑08652-979
0600; Hanielstrasse 7; ⊙9am-5pm), or buy a
copy of the *Berchtesgadener Land* (sheet
794) map in the Kompass series.

Jenner-Königssee Area SKIING
(www.jennerbahn.de; daily pass €31.70) The Jenner-Königssee area at Königssee is the biggest and most varied of five local ski fields.
For equipment hire and courses, try **Skischule Treff-Aktiv** (☑08652-667 10; www.ski-
schule-treffaktiv.de; Jennerbahnstrasse 19).

Watzmann Therme SPA
(☑08652-946 40; www.watzmann-therme.de; Bergwerkstrasse 54; 2hr/4hr/day €10.50/13.90/15.50;
⊙10am-10pm Sun-Thu, to midnight Fri & Sat) The
Watzman Therme is Berchtesgaden's thermal wellness complex, with several indoor
and outdoor pools and various hydrother-
apeutic treatment stations, a sauna and inspiring Alpine views.

☞ Tours

Eagle's Nest Tours TOUR
(☑08652-649 71; www.eagles-nest-tours.com;
adult/child €53/35; ⊙1.15pm mid-May–Oct) This
highly reputable outfit offers a fascinating
overview of Berchtesgaden's Nazi legacy.
Guests are taken not only to the Eagle's Nest
but around the Obersalzberg area and into
the underground bunker system. The four-

hour English-language tour departs from
the tourist office, across the roundabout
opposite the train station. Booking ahead is
advisable in July and August.

🛏 Sleeping

DJH Hostel HOSTEL €
(☑08652-943 70; www.berchtesgaden.jugendher
berge.de; Struberberg 6; dm from €22.90; 🛜) This
265-bed hostel is situated in the suburb of
Strub, and has great views of Mt Watzmann.
It's a 25-minute walk from the Hauptbahnhof or a short hop on bus 839.

KS Hostel Berchtesgaden HOSTEL €
(☑08652-979 8420; www.hostel-berchtesgaden.
de; Bahnhofplatz 4; s/d/dm €26/52/22; 🛜) This
basic hostel above a Burger King is actually attached to the railway station, making
it good for arrival and departure as well as
for accessing buses to the sights. Rooms are
spartan but there are no bunks to climb up
into and you get 10% off a burger downstairs.

Hotel Krone HOTEL €€
(☑08652-946 00; www.hotel-krone-berchtesgaden.
de; Am Rad 5; s €47-56, d €78-112) Ambling distance from the town centre, this family-run
gem provides almost unrivalled views of the
valley and the Alps beyond. The wood-rich
cabin-style rooms are generously cut affairs,
with carved ceilings, niches and bedsteads all
in fragrant pine. Take breakfast on the sun-
trap terrace for a memorable start to the day.

Hotel Bavaria HOTEL €€
(☑08652-966 10; www.hotelbavaria.net;
Sunklergässchen 11; s/d €60/115; ℙ) In the same
family for over a century, this well-run hotel
offers a romantic vision of Alpine life with
rooms bedecked in frilly curtains, canopied
beds, heart-shaped mirrors and knotty wood
galore. Five of the pricier rooms have private
whirlpools. Breakfast is a gourmet affair,
with sparkling wine and both hot and cold
delectables.

Hotel Vier Jahreszeiten HOTEL €€
(☑08652-9520; www.hotel-vierjahreszeiten-
berchtesgaden.de; Maximilianstrasse 20; s €50-69,
d €79-94; ℙ🛜📶) For a taste of Berchtesgaden's storied past, stay at this traditional
lodge where Bavarian royalty once crumpled the sheets. Rooms have been updated
in the last decade and south-facing (more-
expensive) rooms offer dramatic mountain
views. After a day's sightseeing, dinner in
the hunting lodge-style Hubertusstube restaurant is a real treat.

✖ Eating

Gaststätte St Bartholomä   BAVARIAN €€
(☑ 08652-964 937; www.bartholomae-wirt.de; St
Bartholomä; mains €7-16; ☺ open according to the
boat tour timetable) Perched on the shore of
the Königssee, and accessible by boat tour
(p107), this is a tourist haunt that actually
serves delicious food made with ingredients
picked, plucked and hunted from the surrounding forests and the lake. Savour generous platters of venison in mushroom sauce
with dumplings and red sauerkraut in the
large beer garden or indoors.

Bräustübl   BAVARIAN €€
(☑ 08652-976 724; www.braeustueberl-berchtes
gaden.de; Bräuhausstrasse 13; mains €6.80-16;
☺10am-1am) Past the vaulted entrance painted in Bavaria's white and blue diamonds this
cosy beer hall-beer garden is run by the local brewery. Expect a carnivorous feast with
such favourite rib-stickers as pork roast and
the house speciality: breaded calf's head
(tastes better than it sounds). On Friday and
Saturday, an oompah band launches into
knee-slapping action.

Le Ciel   INTERNATIONAL €€€
(☑ 08652-975 50; www.restaurant-leciel.de; Hin-
tereck 1; mains €30-40; ☺ 6.30-10.30pm Wed-Sat)
Don't let the Hotel InterConti location turn
you off: Le Ciel really is as heavenly as its
French name suggests and it has the Michelin star to prove it. Testers were especially
impressed by Ulrich Heimann's knack for
spinning regional ingredients into inspired
gourmet compositions. Service is smooth
and the circular dining room is magical.
Only 32 seats, so book ahead if you can.

ℹ Information

Post Office (Franziskanerplatz 2)
Tourist Office (☑ 08652-896 70; www.bercht
esgaden.com; Königsseer Strasse; ☺8.30am-
6pm Mon-Fri, 9am-5pm Sat, 9am-3pm Sun,
reduced hours mid-Oct–Mar) Near the train
station, this very helpful office has detailed information on the entire Berchtesgaden region.

ℹ Getting There & Around

Travelling from Munich by train involves a
change from Meridian to BLB (Berchtesgadener
Land Bahn) trains at Freilassing (€33.80, 2½
hours, at least hourly connections). The best
option between Berchtesgaden and Salzburg is
RVO bus 840 (45 minutes), which leaves from
the train station in both towns roughly hourly.

Berchtesgaden is south of the Munich–Salzburg
A8 autobahn.

The train station in Berchtesgaden is around
15 minutes' walk from the village centre. The
Eagle's Nest, Königssee and Dokumentation
Obersalzberg all require trips by bus if you don't
have your own transport. Seeing all the sights
in a day without your own transport is virtually
impossible.

THE ROMANTIC ROAD

From the vineyards of Würzburg to the foot
of the Alps, the almost 400km-long Romantic Road (Romantische Strasse) draws two
million visitors every year, making it by
far the most popular of Germany's holiday
routes. This well-trodden trail cuts through
a cultural and historical cross-section of
southern Germany as it traverses Franconia
and clips Baden-Württemberg in the north
before plunging into Bavaria proper to end
at Ludwig II's crazy castles. Expect lots of
Japanese signs and menus, tourist coaches
and kitsch galore, but also a fair wedge of
Gemütlichkeit and geniune hospitality from
those who earn their living on this most romantic of routes.

ℹ Information

The Romantic Road runs north–south through
western Bavaria, covering 385km between
Würzburg and Füssen near the Austrian border.
It passes through more than two dozen cities
and towns, including Rothenburg ob der Tauber,
Dinkelsbühl and Augsburg.

ℹ Getting There & Away

Though Frankfurt is the most popular gateway
for the Romantic Road, Munich is a good choice
as well, especially if you decide to take the bus.

With its gentle gradients and bucolic flavour
between towns, the Romantic Road is ideal for
the holidaying cyclist. Bikes can be hired at
many train stations; tourist offices keep lists of
bicycle-friendly hotels that permit storage, or
check out **Bett und Bike** (www.bettundbike.de)
predeparture.

Direct trains run from Munich to Füssen
(€26.20, two hours) at the southern end of the
Romantic Road every two hours, more often if
you change in Buchloe. Rothenburg is linked by
train to Würzburg (€13.30, one hour), Munich
(from €40.60, three hours), Augsburg (€32.40,
2½ hours) and Nuremberg (€22, 1¼ to two
hours), with at least one change needed in Steinach to reach any destination.

ℹ Getting Around

It is possible to do this route using train connections and local buses, but the going is complicated, tedious and slow on weekdays, virtually impossible at weekends. The ideal way to travel is by car, though many foreign travellers prefer to take Deutsche Touring's **Romantic Road Coach** (www.romanticroadcoach.de), which can get incredibly crowded in summer. From April to October the special coach runs daily in each direction between Frankfurt and Füssen (for Neuschwanstein); the entire journey takes around 12 hours. There's no charge for breaking the journey and continuing the next day.

Tickets are available for short segments of the trip, and reservations are only necessary during peak-season weekends. Reservations can be made through travel agents, **Deutsche Touring** (www.touring.de, www.romantic-road.com) and Deutsche Bahn's Reisezentrum offices in the train stations. If you stayed on the coach all the way from Frankfurt to Füssen (a pointless exercise), the total fare would be €110. The average fare from one stop to the next is around €5.

Coaches can accommodate bicycles but you must give three working days' notice. Students, children, pensioners and rail-pass holders qualify for discounts of between 10% and 50%.

For detailed schedules and prices, see www.romanticroadcoach.de.

Würzburg

☑ 0931 / POP 133,800

'If I could choose my place of birth, I would consider Würzburg', wrote author Hermann Hesse, and it's not difficult to see why. This scenic town straddles the Main River and is renowned for its art, architecture and delicate wines. A large student population guarantees a lively scene, and plenty of hip nightlife pulsates through its cobbled streets.

Würzburg was a Franconian duchy when, in 686, three Irish missionaries tried to persuade Duke Gosbert to convert to Christianity, and ditch his wife. Gosbert was mulling it over when his wife had the three bumped off. When the murders were discovered decades later, the martyrs became saints and Würzburg was made a pilgrimage city, and, in 742, a bishopric.

For centuries the resident prince-bishops wielded enormous power and wealth, and the city grew in opulence under their rule. Their crowning glory is the Residenz, one of the finest baroque structures in Germany and a Unesco World Heritage Site.

Decimated in WWII when 90% of the city centre was flattened, the authorities originally planned to leave the ruins as a reminder of the horrors of war. But a valiant rebuilding project saw the city restored almost to its pre-war glory.

◉ Sights

★ **Würzburg Residenz**   PALACE
(www.residenz-wuerzburg.de; Balthasar-Neumann-Promenade; adult/concession/under 18yr €7.50/6.50/free; ⊘9am-6pm Apr-Oct, 10am-4.30pm Nov-Mar, 45-min English tours 11am & 3pm, also 4.30pm Apr-Oct) The vast Unesco-listed Residenz, built by 18th-century architect Balthasar Neumann as the home of the local prince-bishops, is one of Germany's most important and beautiful baroque palaces. Top billing goes to the brilliant zigzagging Treppenhaus (Staircase), lidded by what still is the world's largest fresco, a masterpiece by Giovanni Battista Tiepolo depicting

---

HITLER'S MOUNTAIN RETREAT

Of all the German towns tainted by the Third Reich, Berchtesgaden has a burden heavier than most. Hitler fell in love with nearby Obersalzberg in the 1920s and bought a small country home, later enlarged into the imposing Berghof.

After seizing power in 1933, Hitler established a part-time headquarters here and brought much of the party brass with him. They bought, or often confiscated, large tracts of land and tore down farmhouses to erect a 2m-high barbed-wire fence. Obersalzberg was sealed off as the fortified southern headquarters of the NSDAP (National Socialist German Workers' Party). In 1938, British prime minister Neville Chamberlain visited for negotiations (later continued in Munich) which led to the infamous promise of 'peace in our time' at the expense of Czechoslovakia's Sudetenland.

Little is left of Hitler's Alpine fortress today. In the final days of WWII, the Royal Air Force levelled much of Obersalzberg, though the Eagle's Nest, Hitler's mountaintop eyrie, was left strangely unscathed. The historical twists and turns are dissected at the impressive Dokumentation Obersalzberg (p107).

allegories of the four then-known continents (Europe, Africa, America and Asia).

The structure was commissioned in 1720 by prince-bishop Johann Philipp Franz von Schönborn, who was unhappy with his old-fashioned digs up in Marienberg Fortress, and took almost 60 years to complete. Today the 360 rooms are home to government institutions, university faculties and a museum, but the grandest 40 have been restored for visitors to admire.

Besides the Grand Staircase, feast your eyes on the ice-white stucco-adorned **Weisser Saal** (White Hall) before entering the **Kaisersaal** (Imperial Hall), canopied by another impressive Tiepolo fresco. Other stunners include the gilded stucco **Spiegelkabinett** (Mirror Hall), covered with a unique mirror-like glass painted with figural, floral and animal motifs (accessible by tour only).

In the residence's south wing, the **Hofkirche** (Court Church) is another Neumann and Tiepolo co-production. Its marble columns, gold leaf and profusion of angels match the Residenz in splendour and proportions.

Entered via frilly wrought-iron gates, the **Hofgarten** (Court Garden; ⊘until dusk; admission free) is a smooth blend of French- and English-style landscaping teeming with whimsical sculptures of children, mostly by court sculptor Peter Wagner. Concerts, festivals and special events take place here during the warmer months.

The complex also houses collections of antiques, paintings and drawings in the Martin-von-Wagner Museum (no relation to Peter) and, handily, a winery in the atmospheric cellar, the **Staatlicher Hofkeller Würzburg**, that is open for tours with tasting.

Festung Marienberg FORTRESS
(tour adult/concession €3.50/2.50; ⊘tours 11am, 2pm, 3pm & 4pm Tue-Sun, also 10am & 1pm Sat & Sun mid-Mar–Oct, 11am, 2pm & 3pm Sat & Sun Nov–mid-Mar) Enjoy panoramic city and vineyard views from this hulking fortress whose construction was initiated around 1200 by the local prince-bishops who governed here until 1719. Dramatically illuminated at night, the structure was only penetrated once, by Swedish troops during the Thirty Years' War, in 1631. Inside, the **Fürstenbaumuseum** (closed November to mid-March) sheds light on its former residents' pompous lifestyle, while the **Mainfränkisches Museum** presents city history and works by local late-Gothic master carver Tilmann Riemenschneider and other famous artists.

The fortress is a pleasant 25-minute walk uphill through the vineyards from the Alte Mainbrücke via the Tellsteige trail.

Neumünster CHURCH
(Schönbornstrasse; ⊘6am-6.30pm Mon-Sat, from 8am Sun) In the Altstadt, this satisfyingly symmetrical church stands on the site where three ill-fated Irish missionaries who tried to convert Duke Gosbert to Christianity in 686 met their maker. Romanesque at its core, it was given a thorough baroque restyle by the Zimmermann brothers and is typical of their work. The interior has busts of the three martyrs (Kilian, Colonan and Totnan) on the high altar, and the tomb of St Kilian lurks in the well-lit crypt.

Dom St Kilian CHURCH
(www.dom-wuerzburg.de; Domstrasse 40; ⊘8am-7pm Mon-Sat, 8am-8pm Sun) **FREE** Würzburg's highly unusual cathedral has a Romanesque core that has been altered many times over the centuries. Recently renovated, the elaborate stucco work of the chancel contrasts starkly with the bare whitewash of the austere Romanesque nave which is capped with a ceiling that wouldn't look out of place in a 1960s bus station.

The whole mishmash creates quite an impression and is possibly Germany's oddest cathedral interior. The **Schönbornkapelle** by Balthasar Neumann returns a little baroque order to things.

Museum Am Dom ART MUSEUM
(www.museum-am-dom.de; Kiliansplatz; adult/concession €3.50/2.50; ⊘10am-6pm Tue-Sun Apr-Oct, to 5pm Nov-Mar) Housed in a beautiful building by the cathedral, this worthwhile museum displays collections of modern art on Christian themes. Works of international renown by Joseph Beuys, Otto Dix and Käthe Kollwitz are on show, as well as masterpieces of the Romantic, Gothic and baroque periods.

Museum im Kulturspeicher ART MUSEUM
(✆0931-322 250; www.kulturspeicher.de; Veitshöchheimer Strasse 5; adult/concession €3.50/2; ⊘1-6pm Tue, 11am-6pm Wed & Fri-Sun, 11am-7pm Thu) In a born-again historic granary right on the Main River, you'll find this absorbing art museum with choice artworks from the 19th to the 21st centuries. The emphasis is on German impressionism, neo-realism and contemporary art, but the building also houses the post-1945 constructivist works of the Peter C Ruppert collection, a challenging assembly of computer art, sculpture, paintings and photographs.

Würzburg

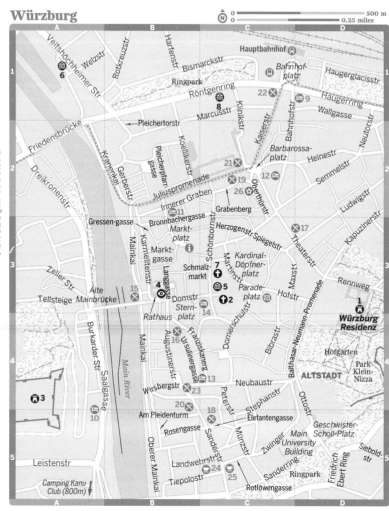

Grafeneckart MEMORIAL

(Domstrasse) FREE Adjoining the Rathaus, the 1659-built Grafeneckart houses a scale model of the WWII bombing, which starkly depicts the extent of the damage to the city following the night of 16 March 1945, when 1000 tonnes of explosives were dropped on the city and 5000 citizens lost their lives in just 20 minutes. Viewing it before you climb up to the fortress overlooking the city gives you an appreciation of Würzburg's astonishing recovery.

Röntgen Gedächtnisstätte MUSEUM

(www.wilhelmconradroentgen.de; Röntgenring 8; ⊙8am-8pm Mon-Fri, 8am-6pm Sat) FREE Win-

ner of the very first Nobel Prize in 1901, Wilhelm Conrad Röntgen discovered X-rays in 1895; his preserved laboratory forms the heart of this small exhibition which is complemented by a film on Röntgen's life and work in English.

★✦ Festivals & Events

Mozart Fest MUSIC

(☎0931-372 336; www.mozartfest-wuerzburg.de; ⊙mid-May–mid-Jun) Germany's oldest Mozart festival takes place at the Residenz.

Africa Festival CULTURAL
(☑0931-150 60; www.africafestival.org; ⊙early Jun) Held on the meadows northwest of the river at Mainwiesen, complete with markets, food stalls and, if it rains, lots of mud.

Hoffest am Stein WINE, MUSIC
(www.hoffest-am-stein.de; ⊙early Jul) Wine and music festival held in the first half of July at the Weingut am Stein.

🛏 Sleeping

Babelfish HOSTEL €
(☑0931-304 0430; www.babelfish-hostel.de; Haugerring 2; dm €17-23, s/d €45/70) With a name inspired by a creature in Douglas Adams' novel *The Hitchhiker's Guide to the Galaxy*, this uncluttered and spotlessly clean hostel has 74 beds spread over two floors and a sunny rooftop terrace. The communal areas are an inviting place to down a few beers in the evening and there's a well-equipped guest kitchen.

Breakfast is €4.90 extra; reception is open 8am to midnight.

DJH Hostel HOSTEL €
(☑0931-467 7860; www.wuerzburg.jugendherberge.de; Fred-Joseph-Platz 2; dm from €25.90) At the foot of the fortress, this well-equipped, wheelchair-friendly hostel has room for over 230 snoozers in three- to eight-bed dorms.

Camping Kanu Club CAMPGROUND €
(☑0931-725 36; www.kc-wuerzburg.de; Mergentheimer Strasse 13b; per person/tent €4/3) The closest camping ground to the town centre. Take tram 3 or 5 to the Judenbühlweg stop, which is on its doorstep.

Hotel Rebstock HOTEL €€
(☑0931-309 30; www.rebstock.com; Neubaustrasse 7; s/d from €92/113; ❄@🤖) Würzburg's top digs, in a squarely renovated rococo town house, has 70 unique, stylishly finished rooms with the gamut of amenities, impeccable service and an Altstadt location. A pillow selection and supercomfy 'gel' beds should ease you into slumberland, perhaps after a fine meal in the dramatic bistro or the slick Michelin-star restaurant.

Hotel Zum Winzermännle HOTEL €€
(☑0931-541 56; www.winzermaennle.de; Domstrasse 32; s €60-79, d €90-110; P🤖) This family-run converted winery is a feel-good retreat in the city's pedestrianised heart. Rooms are well-furnished if a little on the old-fashioned side; some among those fac-

ing the quiet courtyard have balconies. Communal areas are bright and often seasonally decorated. Breakfast costs €7.

Hotel Poppular HOTEL €€
(☑0931-322 770; www.hotelpoppular.de; Textorstrasse 17; r €72-100; P🤖) Relatively basic, city-centre hotel above a wine restaurant where rooms have a vague Scandinavian feel and are immaculately kept. An excellent deal for the location within suitcase-dragging distance of the Hauptbahnhof and often massively discounted on popular booking websites. For walkers-in: reception closes at 10pm.

Hotel Dortmunder Hof HOTEL €€
(☑0931-561 63; www.dortmunder-hof.de; Innerer Graben 22; s €42-65, d €76-100) This bike-friendly hotel occupies a brightly renovated building with spotless, en-suite rooms with cable TV. Parking can be arranged close by, and there's live music in the cellar bar.

✖ Eating

For a town of its size, Würzburg has an enticing selection of wine taverns, beer gardens, cafes and restaurants, with plenty of student hang-outs among them.

Uni-Café
CAFE €

(Neubaustrasse 2; snacks €3-9; ⊗8am-1am) Hugely popular cafe strung over two levels, with a student-priced, daily-changing menu of burgers and salads plus a buzzy bar.

Eva's
VEGETARIAN €

(Sanderstrasse 2a; dishes from €4; ⊗8.30am-4pm Mon-Fri;⏯) Come here for wholesome lactose-, meat- and gluten-free snacks and other healthy fare at simple wooden tables. Also runs the adjacent specialist grocery.

Denn's Bio Bistro
HEALTH FOOD €

(Juliuspromenade 64; dishes €2-6; ⊗9am-8pm Mon-Sat) Order healthy organic sandwiches, quiche, pizza, soup, cakes and other snacks at this self-service bistro then feel all those nutrients being absorbed as you browse the attached organic supermarket.

Capri & Blaue Grotto
ITALIAN €

(Elefantengasse 1; pizzas €5.90-8.30, other mains €6.90-10.90; ⊗11.30am-2pm & 6-10.30pm) This outpost of the *bel paese* has been plating up pronto pasta and pizza since 1952 – it was in fact Germany's first ever pizzeria.

Starback
BAKERY €

(Kaiserstrasse 33; snacks from €0.79; ⊗7am-7pm Mon-Fri, to 6pm Sat) No German-language skills are required to put together a budget breakfast or lunch at this no-frills self-service bakery opposite the train station.

★ Bürgerspital
Weinstube
WINE RESTAURANT €€

(☑0931-352 880; Theaterstrasse 19; mains €13-24; ⊗10am-11pm) If you are going to eat out just once in Würzburg, the aromatic and cosy nooks of this labyrinthine medieval place probably provide the top local experience. Choose from a broad selection of Franconian wines (some of Germany's best) and wonderful regional dishes and snacks, including *Mostsuppe* (a tasty wine soup).

Backöfele
FRANCONIAN €€

(☑0931-590 59; www.backoefele.de; Ursulinergasse 2; mains €7-19.50; ⊗noon-midnight Mon-Thu, to 1am Fri & Sat, to 11pm Sun) This old-timey warren has been serving hearty Franconian food for nearly 50 years. Find a table in the cobbled courtyard or one of four historic rooms,

each candlelit and uniquely furnished with local flair. Featuring schnitzel, snails, bratwurst in wine, wine soup with cinnamon croutons, grilled meat and other local faves, the menu makes for mouth-watering reading. Bookings recommended.

Juliusspital
WINE RESTAURANT €€

(Juliuspromenade 19; mains €11-22; ⊗10am-midnight) This attractive *Weinstube* (traditional wine tavern) features fabulous Franconian fish and even better wines. Ambient lighting, scurrying waiters and walls occupied by oil paintings make this the place to head to for a special do.

Alte Mainmühle
FRANCONIAN €€

(☑0931-167 77; www.alte-mainmuehle.de; Mainkai 1; mains €8-23; ⊗9.30am-midnight) Accessed straight from the old bridge, tourists and locals alike cram into this old mill to savour modern twists on Franconian classics (including popular river fish). In summer the double terrace beckons – the upper one delivers pretty views of the bridge and Marienberg Fortress; in winter retreat to the snug timber dining room. Year round, guests spill out onto the bridge itself, wine glass in hand.

♟ Drinking & Entertainment

For more options, grab a copy of the monthly listing magazine *Frizz* (in German). Look out for posters and flyers advertising big-name concerts that take place on the Residenzplatz.

Kult
CAFE, BAR

(Landwehrstrasse 10; ⊗6pm-1am Mon, from 10am Tue-Sun) Enjoy a tailor-made breakfast, much a cheap lunch or party into the wee hours at Würzburg's hippest cafe. The unpretentious interior, with its salvaged tables and old beige benches, hosts regular fancy-dress parties, table-football tournaments and other offbeat events. DJs take over at weekends.

MUCK
CAFE, BAR

(www.cafe-muck.de; Sanderstrasse 29; ⊗Sun-Thu 9am-1am, Fri & Sat till late) One of the earliest openers in town, and serving a hangover-busting breakfast, this long-established cafe morphs into something of an informal party after nightfall.

Standard
LIVE MUSIC

(Oberthürstrasse 11a; ⊗noon-1am Mon-Thu, to 2am Fri & Sat, 10am-late Sun) Soulful jazz spins beneath a corrugated-iron ceiling and stainless-steel fans, while bands and DJs play a couple of times or more a week in a second, dimly lit downstairs bar.

ℹ️ Information

Post Office (Paradeplatz 4)
Tourist Office (☑ 0931-372 398; www.wuerz burg.de; Marktplatz 9; ⊙10am-5pm Mon-Fri, 10am-2pm Sat & Sun, closed Sun Nov-Apr) Within the attractive Falkenhaus this efficient office can help you with room reservations and tour bookings.

ℹ️ Getting There & Away

BUS

The Romantic Road Coach (p110) stops at the main bus station next to the Hauptbahnhof, and at the Residenzplatz. Budget coach company **Meinfernbus** (www.meinfernbus.de) links Würzburg with numerous destinations across Germany and beyond including both Nuremberg and Munich.

TRAIN

Train connections from Würzburg:
➡ **Bamberg** €20.70, one hour, twice hourly
➡ **Frankfurt** €30 to €35, one hour, hourly
➡ **Nuremberg** €20.90 to €29, one hour, twice hourly
➡ **Rothenburg ob der Tauber** Change in Steinach; €13.30, one hour, hourly

ℹ️ Getting Around

The most useful service is bus 9 which shuttles roughly hourly between the Residenz and the Festung Marienberg. Otherwise Würzburg can be easily tackled on foot.

Rothenburg ob der Tauber

☑ 09861 / POP 10,900
A medieval gem, Rothenburg ob der Tauber (meaning 'above the Tauber River') is a top tourist stop along the Romantic Road. With its web of cobbled lanes, higgledy-piggledy houses and towered walls, the town is the fairy-tale Germany the hordes of tourists came to see. Urban conservation orders here are the strictest in Germany – and at times it feels like a medieval theme park – but all's forgiven in the evenings, when the yellow lamplight casts its spell long after the last tour buses have left.

⦿ Sights

Jakobskirche   CHURCH
(Church of St Jacob; Klingengasse 1; adult/concession €2.50/1.50; ⊙9am-5.15pm Mon-Sat,

10.45am-5.15pm Sun) One of the few places of worship in Bavaria to charge admission, Rothenburg's Lutheran parish church was begun in the 14th century and finished in the 15th. The building sports some wonderfully aged stained-glass windows, but the top attraction is Tilman Riemenschneider's **Heilig Blut Altar** (Altar of the Holy Blood). The gilded cross above the main scene depicting the Last Supper incorporates Rothenburg's most treasured reliquary – a rock crystal capsule said to contain three drops of Christ's blood.

Mittelalterliches Kriminalmuseum MUSEUM
(Medieval Crime & Punishment Museum; www.krim inalmuseum.eu; Burggasse 3; adult/concessions €5/3.50; ⊙10am-6pm May-Oct, shorter hours Nov-Apr) Medieval implements of torture and punishment are on show at this gruesomely fascinating museum. Exhibits include chastity belts, masks of disgrace for gossips, a cage for cheating bakers, a neck brace for quarrelsome women and a beer-barrel pen for drunks. You can even snap a selfie in the stocks!

Deutsches Weihnachtsmuseum MUSEUM
(Christmas Museum; ☑ 09861-409 365; www.weihnachtsmuseum.de; Herrngasse 1; adult/child/family €4/2.50/7; ⊙10am-5pm daily Easter-Christmas, shorter hours Jan–Easter) If you're glad Christmas comes but once every 365 days, then stay well clear of the Käthe Wohlfahrt Weihnachtsdorf (p118), a Yuletide superstore that also houses this Christmas Museum. This repository of all things 'Ho! Ho! Ho!' traces the development of various Christmas customs and decorations, and includes a display of 150 Santa figures, plus lots of retro baubles and tinsel – particularly surreal in mid-July when the mercury outside is pushing 30°C.

Not as big a hit with younger kids as you might predict, as they can't get their hands on anything.

Stadtmauer   HISTORIC SITE
(Town Wall) With time and fresh legs, a 2.5km circular walk around the unbroken ring of town walls gives a sense of the importance medieval man placed on defending his settlement. A great lookout point is the eastern tower, the **Röderturm** (Rödergasse; adult/child €1.50/1; ⊙9am-5pm Mar-Nov), but for the most impressive views head to the west side of town, where a sweeping view of the Tauber Valley includes the Doppelbrücke, a double-decker bridge.

Rothenburg ob der Tauber

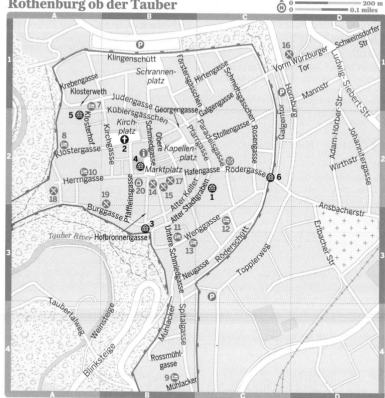

Alt-Rothenburger Handwerkerhaus
HISTORIC BUILDING

(Alter Stadtgraben 26; adult/concession €3/2.50; ⏰11am-5pm Mon-Fri, from 10am Sat & Sun Easter-Oct, 2-4pm daily Dec) Hidden down a little alley is the Alt-Rothenburger Handwerkerhaus, where numerous artisans – including coopers, weavers, cobblers and potters – have their workshops today, and mostly have had for the house's more than 700-year existence. It's half museum, half active workplace and you can easily spend an hour or so watching the craftsmen at work.

Reichsstadtmuseum
MUSEUM

(www.reichsstadtmuseum.rothenburg.de; Klosterhof 5; adult/concession €4.50/3.50; ⏰9.30am-5.30pm Apr-Oct, 1-4pm Nov-Mar) Highlights of the Reichsstadtmuseum, housed in a former Dominican convent, include the *Rothenburger Passion* (1494), a cycle of 12 panels by Martinus Schwarz, and the oldest convent kitchen in Germany, as well as weapons and armour. Outside the main entrance (on your right as you're facing the museum), you'll see a spinning barrel, where the nuns distributed bread to the poor – and where women would leave babies they couldn't afford to keep.

For a serene break between sightseeing, head to the **Klostergarten** (Monastery Garden) behind the museum (enter from Klosterhof).

Rathausturm
HISTORIC BUILDING

(Town Hall Tower; Marktplatz; adult/concession €2/0.50; ⏰9.30am-12.30pm & 1-5pm daily Apr-Oct, 10.30am-2pm & 2.30-6pm daily Dec, noon-3pm Sat & Sun rest of year) The Rathaus on Marktplatz was begun in Gothic style in the 14th century and was completed during the Renaissance. Climb the 220 steps of the medieval town hall to the viewing platform of the Rathausturm to be rewarded with widescreen views of the Tauber.

Rothenburg ob der Tauber

☞ Tours

The tourist office runs 90-minute walking tours (€7; in English) at 2pm from April to October. Every evening a lantern-toting *Nachtwächter* (Night Watchman) dressed in traditional costume leads an entertaining tour of the Altstadt; English tours (€7) meet at the Rathaus just before 8pm.

⚑ Festivals & Events

Historisches Festspiel 'Der Meistertrunk'   THEATRE
(www.meistertrunk.de; ⊘ late May) Takes place on Whitsuntide, with parades, dances and a medieval market. The highlight is the re-enactment of the mythical *Meistertrunk* story. The *Meistertrunk* play itself is performed three more times: once during the Reichsstadt-Festtage (early September), when the city's history is re-enacted in the streets, and twice during the Rothenburger Herbst, an autumn celebration (October).

Historischer Schäfertanz   DANCE
(Historical Shepherds' Dance; www.schaefertanz-rothenburg.de; Marktplatz) Featuring colourfully dressed couples; takes places on Marktplatz several times between April and October.

Christmas Market   MARKET
Rothenburg's Christmas market is one of the most romantic in Germany. It's set out around the central Marktplatz during Advent.

⛏ Sleeping

DJH Hostel   HOSTEL €
(☑ 09861-941 60; www.rothenburg.jugendherberge.de; Mühlacker 1; dm from €25.40; ⊛) Rothenburg's youth hostel occupies two enormous old buildings in the south of town.

It's agreeably renovated and extremely well equipped, but you can hear the screams of noisy school groups from outside.

Hotel Raidel   HOTEL €
(☑ 09861-3115; www.gaestehaus-raidel.de; Wenggasse 3; s/d €45/69; ⊛) With 500-year-old exposed beams studded with wooden nails, antiques throughout and a welcoming owner, as well as musical instruments for the guests to play, this is the place to check in if you're craving some genuine romance on the Romantic Road. Rates include breakfast.

Pension Birgit   B&B €
(☑ 09861-6107; www.birgit-pension.de; Wenggasse 16; s/d from €30/40; ⊛) Basic owner-run pension that offers Rothenburg's cheapest rooms in an epicentral location. Rates include a modest buffet breakfast.

Kreuzerhof Hotel Garni   GUESTHOUSE €
(☑ 09861-3424; www.kreuzerhof-rothenburg.de; Millergasse 2-6; s €45-52, d €62-78; ⊛) Away from the tourist swarms, this quiet family-run B&B has charming, randomly furnished rooms with antique touches in a medieval town house and annexe. There's free tea and coffee and the generous breakfast is an energy-boosting set-up for the day.

★ Burg-Hotel   HOTEL €€
(☑ 09861-948 90; www.burghotel.eu; Klostergasse 1-3; s €100-135, d €125-195; Ⓟ ⊜ ❄ ⊛) Each of the 17 elegantly furnished guest rooms at this boutique hotel built into the town walls has its own private sitting area. The lower floors shelter a decadent spa with tanning beds, saunas and rainforest showers, and a cellar with a Steinway piano; while phenomenal valley views unfurl from the breakfast room and stone terrace.

> ## SNOWBALLS
>
> **Diller's Schneeballen** (Hofbronnengasse 16; ⊙10am-6pm) Rothenburg's most obvious speciality is Schneeballen, ribbons of dough loosely shaped into balls, deep-fried then coated in icing sugar, chocolate and other dentist's foes. Some 27 different types are produced at Diller's Schneeballen.
>
> A more limited range is available all over town.

The owners have recently taken over the hotel across the road where there are 14 more modern rooms and a restaurant.

Altfränkische Weinstube   HOTEL €€
(⟋09861-6404; www.altfraenkische.de; Klosterhof 7; d €75-118; ☎) This characterful 650-year-old inn has eight wonderfully romantic rural-style rooms with exposed half-timber, bathtubs and most with four-poster or canopied beds. From 6pm onwards, the tavern serves up sound regional fare (mains €8.80 to €15.50) with a dollop of medieval cheer.

★Hotel Herrnschlösschen   HOTEL €€€
(⟋09861-873 890; www.herrnschloesschen.de; Herrngasse 20; r from €210) The most recent addition to Rothenburg's hotel stock has breathed life back into a 900-year-old mansion. The whole place is a blend of ancient and new, with Gothic arches leaping over faux-retro furniture and ageing oak preventing ceilings from crashing down onto chic 21st-century beds. The hotel's restaurant has established itself as one of the town's most innovative dining spots.

✗ Eating

TobinGo   KEBAB €
(Hafengasse 2; mains €3.50-8; ⊙10am-10pm) You can't say you've been to Bavaria until you've consumed a kebab in a twee medieval setting.

Zur Höll   FRANCONIAN €€
(⟋09861-4229; www.hoell.rothenburg.de; Burggasse 8; mains €6.80-20; ⊙5-11pm) This medieval wine tavern is in the town's oldest original building, with sections dating back to the year 900. The menu of regional specialities is limited but refined, though it's the superb selection of Franconian wines that people really come for.

Gasthof Goldener Greifen   FRANCONIAN €€
(⟋09861-2281; www.gasthof-greifen-rothenburg. de; Obere Schmiedgasse 5; mains €8-17; ⊙11am-9.30pm) Erstwhile home of Heinrich Toppler, one of Rothenburg's most famous medieval mayors (the dining room was his office), the 700-year-old Golden Griffin is the locals' choice in the touristy centre serving a hearty menu of Franconian favourites in an austere semi-medieval setting and out back in the sunny and secluded garden.

Mittermeier   BAVARIAN, INTERNATIONAL €€
(⟋09861-945 430; www.villamittermeier.de; Vorm Würzburger Tor 7; mains €12-19; ⊙6-10.30pm Tue-Sat; P ☎) Supporters of the slow food movement and deserved holders of a Michelin Bib Gourmand, this hotel restaurant pairs punctilious craftsmanship with top-notch ingredients, sourced regionally whenever possible. There are five different dining areas including a black-and-white tiled 'temple', an alfresco terrace and a barrel-shaped wine cellar. The wine list is one of the best in Franconia.

Weinstube zum Pulverer   FRANCONIAN €€
(⟋09861-976 182; Herrngasse 31; mains €5-16.50; ⊙5pm-late Mon & Wed-Fri, from noon Sat & Sun, closed Tue) The ornately carved timber chairs in this ancient wood-panelled wine bar (allegedly Rothenburg's oldest) are works of art. Its simple but filling dishes, like soup in a bowl made of bread, gourmet sandwiches and cakes, are equally artistic. There's also a piano for postprandial self-expression.

🛍 Shopping

Käthe Wohlfahrt Weihnachtsdorf   CHRISTMAS DECORATIONS
(www.wohlfahrt.com; Herrngasse 1; ⊙9am-6pm) With its mind-boggling assortment of Yuletide decorations and ornaments, this huge shop lets you celebrate Christmas every day of the year. Many of the items are handcrafted with amazing skill and imagination; prices are correspondingly high.

ℹ Information

Post Office (Rödergasse 11)
Tourist Office (⟋09861-404 800; www.tourismus.rothenburg.de; Marktplatz 2; ⊙9am-6pm Mon-Fri, 10am-5pm Sat & Sun May-Oct, 9am-5pm Mon-Fri, 10am-1pm Sat Nov-Mar) Helpful office offering free internet access.

ⓘ Getting There & Away

BUS
The Romantic Road Coach (p110) stops in the main bus park at the Hauptbahnhof and on the more central Schrannenplatz.

CAR
The A7 autobahn runs right past town.

TRAIN
You can go anywhere by train from Rothenburg, as long as it's Steinach. Change there for services to Würzburg (€13.30, one hour and 10 minutes). Travel to and from Munich (from €31, three hours) can involve up to three different trains.

ⓘ Getting Around
The city has five car parks right outside the walls. The town centre is essentially closed to nonresident vehicles, though hotel guests are exempt.

Dinkelsbühl

🄹 09851 / POP 11,300

Some 40km south of Rothenburg, immaculately preserved Dinkelsbühl proudly traces its roots to a royal residence founded by Carolingian kings in the 8th century. Saved from destruction in the Thirty Years' War and ignored by WWII bombers, this is arguably the Romantic Road's quaintest and most authentically medieval halt. For a good overall impression of the town, walk along the fortified walls with their 18 towers and four gates.

⊙ Sights

Haus der Geschichte   MUSEUM
(Altrathausplatz 14; adult/child €4/2; ⊙9am-6pm Mon-Fri, 10am-5pm Sat & Sun May-Oct, 10am-5pm daily Nov-Apr) Dinkelsbühl's history comes under the microscope at the Haus der Geschichte, which occupies the old town hall. There's an interesting section on the Thirty Years' War and a gallery with paintings depicting Dinkelsbühl at the turn of the century. Audioguides are included in the ticket price.

Münster St Georg   CHURCH
(Marktplatz 1) Standing sentry over the heart of Dinkelsbühl is one of southern Germany's purest late-Gothic hall churches. Rather austere from the outside, the interior stuns with an incredible fan-vaulted ceiling. A curiosity is the **Pretzl Window** donated by the bakers' guild; it's located in the upper section of the last window in the right aisle.

Museum of the 3rd Dimension   MUSEUM
(🄹 09851-6336; www.3d-museum.de; Nördlinger Tor; adult/concession/under 12yr €10/8/6; ⊙11am-5pm daily Apr-Oct, 11am-5pm Sat & Sun Nov-Mar) Located just outside the easternmost town gate, this is an engaging place to entertain young minds, bored with the Romantic Road's medieval pageant. Inside there are three floors of holographic images, stereoscopes and attention-grabbing 3-D imagery. The you-gotta-be-kidding admission includes a pair of red-green-tinted specs.

BAVARIA DINKELSBÜHL

BOTTOMS UP FOR FREEDOM

In 1631 the Thirty Years' War – pitching Catholics against Protestants – reached the gates of Rothenburg ob der Tauber. Catholic General Tilly and 60,000 of his troops besieged the Protestant market town and demanded its surrender. The town resisted but couldn't stave off the onslaught of marauding soldiers, and the mayor and other town dignitaries were captured and sentenced to death.

And that's about where the story ends and the legend begins. As the tale goes, Rothenburg's town council tried to sate Tilly's bloodthirstiness by presenting him with a 3L pitcher of wine. Tilly, after taking a sip or two, presented the men with an unusual challenge, saying 'If one of you has the courage to step forward and down this mug of wine in one gulp, then I shall spare the town and the lives of the councilmen!' Mayor Georg Nusch accepted – and succeeded! And that's why you can still wander through Rothenburg's wonderful medieval lanes today.

It's pretty much accepted that Tilly was really placated with hard cash. Nevertheless, local poet Adam Hörber couldn't resist turning the tale of the Meistertrunk into a play, which, since 1881, has been performed every Whitsuntide (Pentecost), the seventh Sunday after Easter. It's also re-enacted several times daily by the clock figures on the tourist office building.

✿ Festivals & Events

Kinderzeche   HISTORY, MUSIC
(www.kinderzeche.de; ⊘ Jul) In the third week
of July, the 10-day Kinderzeche celebrates
how, during the Thirty Years' War, the town's
children persuaded the invading Swedish
troops to spare Dinkelsbühl from a ran-
sacking. The festivities include a pageant,
re-enactments in the festival hall, lots of
music and other merriment.

🛏 Sleeping

DJH Hostel   HOSTEL €
(✆ 09851-9509; www.dinkelsbuehl.jugendherberge.
de; Koppengasse 10; dm from €22.50; ⊛) Un-
dergoing a complete refit at the time of research, Dinkelsbühl's hostel in the western
part of the Altstadt occupies a beautiful
15th-century granary.

**Campingpark 'Romantische
Strasse'**   CAMPGROUND €
(✆ 09851-7817; www.campingplatz-dinkelsbuehl.
de; Kobeltsmühle 6; per tent/person €9.30/4.40)
This camping ground is set on the shores
of a swimmable lake 1.5km northeast of the
Wörnitz Tor.

★ **Dinkelsbühler
Kunst-Stuben**   GUESTHOUSE €€
(✆ 09851-6750; www.kunst-stuben.de; Segringer
Strasse 52; s €60, d €80-85, ste €90; ⊜@⊛)
Personal attention and charm by the bucket-
load make this guesthouse, situated near the
westernmost gate (Segringer Tor), one of the
best on the entire Romantic Road. Furniture
(including the four-posters) is all handmade
by Voglauer, the cosy library is perfect for
curling up in with a good read, and the suite
is a matchless deal for travelling families.
The artist owner will show his Asia travel
films if enough guests are interested.

Gasthof Goldenes Lamm   HOTEL €€
(✆ 09851-6441; www.goldenes.de; Lange Gasse 26-
28; s €55-70, d €80-105; ℗⊛) Run by the same
family for four generations, this stress-free,
bike-friendly oasis has pleasant rooms at the
top of a creaky staircase, and a funky rooftop garden deck with plump sofas. The attached wood-panelled restaurant plates up
Franconian-Swabian specialities, including
a vegetarian selection.

Deutsches Haus   HOTEL €€
(✆ 09851-6058; www.deutsches-haus.net; Weinmarkt 3; s €80-99, d €116-129; ⊛) Concealed
behind the town's most ornate and out-of-

kilter facade, the 19 elegant rooms at this
central inn opposite the Münster St Georg
flaunt antique touches and big 21st-century
bathrooms. Downstairs Dinkelsbühl's haugh-
tiest restaurant serves game and fish prepared according to age-old recipes.

✖ Eating

Haus Appelberg   FRANCONIAN, INTERNATIONAL €€
(✆ 09851-582 838; www.haus-appelberg.de;
Nördlinger Strasse 40; dishes €6-11; ⊘ 6pm-
midnight Mon-Sat) At this 40-cover wine restaurant, the owners double up as cooks to
keep tables supplied with traditional dishes
such as local fish, Franconian sausages and
Maultaschen. On warm days swap the rustic interior for the secluded terrace, a fine
spot for some evening idling over a Franconian white.

The eight rooms upstairs are of a very
high standard and boast traditional antique
touches.

Weib's Brauhaus   PUB FOOD €€
(Untere Schmiedgasse 13; mains €5.70-14.60;
⊘ 11am-1am Thu-Mon, 6pm-1am Wed; ✍) A female brewmaster presides over the copper
vats at this half-timbered pub-restaurant,
which has a good-time vibe thanks to its
friendly crowd of regulars. Many dishes are
made with the house brew, including the
popular *Weib's Töpfle* ('woman's pot') – pork
in beer sauce with croquettes.

ⓘ Information

Tourist Office (✆ 09851-902 440; www.
dinkelsbuehl.de; Altrathausplatz 14; ⊘ 9am-
6pm Mon-Fri, 10am-5pm Sat & Sun May-Oct,
10am-5pm daily Nov-Apr)

ⓘ Getting There & Away

Despite a railway line cutting through the town,
Dinkelsbühl is not served by passenger trains.
Regional bus 501 to Nördlingen (50 minutes,
eight daily) stops at the new ZOB Schwedenwi-
ese bus station. Reaching Rothenburg is a real
test of patience without your own car. Change
from bus 805 to a train in Ansbach, then change
trains in Steinach. The Europabus stops right in
the Altstadt at Schweinemarkt.

Nördlingen

✆ 09081 / POP 19,400

Charmingly medieval, Nördlingen sees fewer tourists than its better-known neighbours
and manages to retain an air of authenticity,
which is a relief after some of the Romantic

Road's kitschy extremes. The town lies within the Ries Basin, a massive impact crater gouged out by a meteorite more than 15 million years ago. The crater – some 25km in diameter – is one of the best preserved on earth, and has been declared a special 'geopark'. Nördlingen's 14th-century walls, all original, mimic the crater's rim and are almost perfectly circular.

Incidentally, if you've seen the 1970s film *Willy Wonka and the Chocolate Factory*, you've already looked down upon Nördlingen from a glass elevator.

⊙ Sights

You can circumnavigate the entire town in around an hour by taking the sentry walk (free) on top of the walls all the way.

St Georgskirche
CHURCH
(tower adult/child €3/1.80; ⊙ tower 9am-6pm daily, to 7pm Jul & Aug, to 5pm Nov-Mar) Dominating the heart of town, the immense late-Gothic St Georgskirche got its baroque mantle in the 18th century. To truly appreciate Nördlingen's circular shape and the dished-out crater in which it lies, scramble up the 350 steps of the church's 90m-tall Daniel Tower.

Bayerisches Eisenbahnmuseum
MUSEUM
(www.bayerisches-eisenbahnmuseum.de; Am Hohen Weg 6a; adult/child €6/3; ⊙ noon-4pm Tue-Sat, 10am-5pm Sun May-Sep, noon-4pm Sat, 10am-5pm Sun Oct-Mar) Half museum, half junkyard retirement home for old locos, this trainspotter's paradise occupies a disused engine depot across the tracks from the train station (no access from the platforms). The museum runs steam and old diesel trains up to Dinkelsbühl, Feuchtwangen and Gunzenhausen several times a year; see the website for details.

Rieskrater Museum
MUSEUM
(Eugene-Shoemaker-Platz 1; adult/concession €4.50/2.50, ticket also valid for Stadtmuseum; ⊙10am-4.30pm Tue-Sun, closed noon-1.30pm Nov-Apr) Situated in an ancient barn, this unique museum explores the formation of meteorite craters and the consequences of such violent collisions with Earth. Rocks, including a genuine moon rock (on permanent loan from NASA), fossils and other geological displays shed light on the mystery of meteors.

Stadtmuseum
MUSEUM
(Vordere Gerbergasse 1; adult/concession €4.50/2.50, ticket also valid for Rieskrater Museum; ⊙1.30-4.30pm Tue-Sun Mar-early Nov) Nördlingen's worthwhile municipal museum covers

an ambitious sweep of human existence on the planet, from the early Stone Age to 20th-century art, via the Battle of Nördlingen during the Thirty Years' War, Roman endeavours in the area and the town's once-bustling mercantile life.

Stadtmauermuseum
MUSEUM
(Löpsinger Torturm; adult/concession €2/1.40; ⊙10am-4.30pm Tue-Sun Apr-Oct) Head up the spiral staircase of the Löpsinger Torturm for an engaging exhibition on the history of the town's defences, an apt place to kick off a circuit of the walls.

🛏 Sleeping & Eating

Hotel Altreuter
HOTEL €
(☏09081-4319; www.hotel-altreuter.de; Marktplatz 11; s/d from €36/52) Perched above a busy cafe and bakery, the bog-standard rooms here are of the could-be-anywhere type, but the epicentral location cannot be beaten. Bathrooms are private and breakfast is served downstairs in the cafe.

Jugend & Familengästehaus
GUESTHOUSE €
(JUFA; ☏09081-290 8390; www.jufa.eu; Bleichgraben 3a; d €50; P @ ⊛) Located just outside the town walls, this shiny, 186-bed hostel-guesthouse is spacious and clean-cut. There are two- to four-bed rooms, ideal for couples or families, and facilities include bicycle hire and a cafe with internet terminals. Unless you are travelling with an entire handball team in tow, dorms are off limits to individual travellers, no matter how hard you plead.

Kaiserhof Hotel Sonne
HOTEL €€
(☏09081-5067; www.kaiserhof-hotel-sonne.de; Marktplatz 3; s €55-75, d €80-120; P ⊛) Right on the main square, Nördlingen's top digs once hosted crowned heads and their entourages, but have quietly gone to seed in recent years. However, rooms are still packed with character, mixing modern comforts with traditional charm, and the atmospheric regional restaurant downstairs is still worth a shot.

La Fontana
ITALIAN €
(Bei den Kornschrannen 2; mains around €8; ⊙11am-11pm) Nördlingen's most popular restaurant is this large Italian pizza-pasta place occupying the terracotta Kornschrannen as well as tumbling tables out onto Schrannenstrasse. The menu is long, the service swift and when the sun is shining there's no lovelier spot to fill the hole.

Cafe-buch.de
CAFE €

(Weinmarkt 4; snacks from €2; ⊙10am-6pm Mon-Sat, from 11am Sun) That winning combination of coffee, cakes and secondhand books makes this new cafe a pleasing mid-stroll halt for literary types. No English is spoken.

Café Radlos
CAFE €€

(www.café-radlos.de; Löpsinger Strasse 8; mains €6.50-10; ⊙5pm-1am Mon-Fri, from noon Sat & Sun; 🛜🖊) More than just a place to tuck into tasty pizzas and pastas, this convivially random cafe, Nördlingen's coolest haunt, parades cherry-red walls that showcase local art and photography exhibits. Kids have their own toy-filled corner, while you relax with board games, soak up the sunshine in the beer garden, or surf the web.

ⓘ Information

Geopark Ries Information Centre (www.geopark-ries.de; Eugene-Shoemaker-Platz; ⊙10am-4.30pm Tue-Sun) Free exhibition on the Ries crater.

Tourist Office (☑09081-841 16; www.noerdlingen.de; Marktplatz 2; ⊙9.30am-6pm Mon-Thu, to 4.30pm Fri, 10am-2pm Sat Easter-Oct, plus 10am-2pm Sun Jul & Aug, closed Sat & Sun rest of year) Staff sell the Nördlinger TouristCard (€9.95) that saves you around €8 if you visit everything in town.

ⓘ Getting There & Away

BUS
The Europabus stops at the Rathaus. Bus 501 runs to Dinkelsbühl from the new bus station (50 minutes, eight daily).

TRAIN
Train journeys to and from Munich (€26.80, two hours) and Augsburg (€15.70, 1¼ hours) require a change in Donauwörth.

Donauwörth

☑0906 / POP 18,550

Sitting pretty at the confluence of the Danube and Wörnitz rivers, Donauwörth rose from its humble beginnings as a 5th-century fishing village to its zenith as a Free Imperial City in 1301. Three medieval gates and five town wall towers still guard it today, and faithful rebuilding – after WWII had destroyed 75% of the medieval old town – means steep-roofed houses in a rainbow of colours still line its main street, Reichstrasse.

Reichstrasse is around 10 minutes' walk north of the train station. Turn right onto Bahnhofstrasse and cross the bridge onto Ried Island.

⊙ Sights

Liebfraukirche
CHURCH

(Reichstrasse) At the western end of Reichstrasse rises this 15th-century Gothic church with original frescos and a curiously sloping floor that drops 120cm. Swabia's largest church bell (6550kg) swings in the belfry.

Käthe-Kruse-Puppenmuseum
MUSEUM

(www.kaethe-kruse.de; Pflegstrasse 21a; adult/child €2.50/1.50; ⊙11am-6pm Tue-Sun May-Sep, 2-5pm Thu-Sun Oct-Apr) This nostalgia-inducing museum fills a former monastery with old dolls and dollhouses by world-renowned designer Käthe Kruse (1883–1968).

Rathaus
HISTORIC BUILDING

(Rathausgasse) Work on the landmark town hall began in 1236, but it has seen many alterations and additions over the centuries. At 11am and 4pm daily, the carillon on the ornamented step gable plays a composition by local legend Werner Egk (1901–83) from his opera *Die Zaubergeige* (The Magic Violin). The building also houses the tourist office.

Heilig-Kreuz-Kirche
CHURCH

(Heilig-Kreuz-Strasse) Overlooking the grassy banks of the shallow River Wörnitz, this soaring baroque confection has for centuries lured the faithful to pray before a chip of wood, said to come from the Holy Cross, installed in the ornate-ceilinged **Gnadenkappelle** (Grace Chapel).

🛏 Sleeping & Eating

Drei Kronen
HOTEL €€

(☑09851-706 170; www.hotel3kronen.com; Bahnhofstrasse 25; s/d €82/115; 🅿🛜) Situated opposite the train station a little way along Bahnhofstrasse, the 'Three Crowns' has the town's most comfortable rooms and a lamplit restaurant. The reception is, inconveniently, closed in the evenings and all weekend, but staff are around in the restaurant.

Posthotel Traube
BAVARIAN €€

(Kapellstrasse 14-16; mains €5.50-17; ⊙11am-2pm & 5-10pm Mon-Fri & Sun, closed Sat) Choose from a cafe, coffee house, restaurant or beer garden at this friendly, multitasking hotel where Mozart stayed as a boy in 1777. The schnitzel, cordon bleu and local carp in beer sauce are where your forefinger should land on the menu.

Cafe Rafaello ITALIAN €€
(Fischerplatz 1; mains €6-24.50; ⊙10am-midnight daily) On Ried Island, this Italian job specialising in seafood uses Apennines kitsch to recreate *La Dolce Vita* to southern German tastes. The endless menu has something for everyone.

❶ Information

Tourist Office (☑09851-789 151; www.donauwoerth.de; Rathausgasse 1; ⊙9am-noon & 1-6pm Mon-Fri, 3-5pm Sat & Sun May-Sep, shorter hours Mon-Fri, closed Sat & Sun Oct-Apr)

❶ Getting There & Away

BUS
The Romantic Road Coach (p110) stops by the Liebfraukirche.

CAR & MOTORCYCLE
Donauwörth is at the crossroads of the B2, B16 and B25 roads.

TRAIN
Train connections from Donauwörth:
➡ **Augsburg** €6.60, 30 minutes, twice hourly
➡ **Harburg** €3.70, 11 minutes, twice hourly
➡ **Ingolstadt** €12.10, 45 minutes, hourly
➡ **Nördlingen** €6.10, 30 minutes, hourly

Augsburg

☑0821 / POP 276,500
The largest city on the Romantic Road (and Bavaria's third largest), Augsburg is also one of Germany's oldest, founded by the stepchildren of Roman emperor Augustus over 2000 years ago. As an independent city state from the 13th century, it was also one of Germany's wealthiest, free to raise its own taxes, with public coffers bulging on the proceeds of the textile trade. Banking families such as the Fuggers and the Welsers even bankrolled entire countries and helped out the odd skint monarch. However, from the 16th century, religious strife and economic decline plagued the city. Augsburg finally joined the Kingdom of Bavaria in 1806.

Shaped by Romans, medieval artisans, bankers, traders and, more recently, industry and technology, this attractive city of spires and cobbles is an easy day trip from Munich or an engaging stop on the Romantic Road, though one with a grittier, less quaint atmosphere than others along the route.

❍ Sights

Fuggerei HISTORIC SITE
(www.fugger.de; Jakober Strasse; adult/concession €4/3; ⊙8am-8pm Apr-Sep, 9am-6pm Oct-Mar) The legacy of Jakob Fugger 'The Rich' lives on at Augsburg's Catholic welfare settlement, the Fuggerei, which is the oldest of its kind in existence.

Around 200 people live here today and their rent remains frozen at 1 Rhenish guilder (now €0.88) per year, plus utilities and three daily prayers. Residents wave to you as you wander through the car-free lanes of this gated community flanked by its 52 pinneat houses (containing 140 apartments) and little gardens.

To see how residents lived before running water and central heating, one of the apartments now houses the **Fuggereimuseum** (Mittlere Gasse 14; admission incl with entry to the Fuggerei; ⊙9am-8pm Mar-Oct, 9am-6pm Nov-Apr), while there's a modern apartment open for public viewing at Ochsengasse 51. Interpretive panels are in German but you can ask for an information leaflet in English or download it from the website before you arrive.

Rathausplatz SQUARE
The heart of Augsburg's Altstadt, this large, pedestrianised square is anchored by the **Augustusbrunnen**, a fountain honouring the Roman emperor; its four figures represent the Lech River and the Wertach, Singold and Brunnenbach Brooks.

Rising above the square are the twin onion-domed spires of the Renaissance **Rathaus**, built by Elias Holl from 1615 to 1620 and crowned by a 4m-tall pine cone, the city's emblem (also an ancient fertility symbol). Upstairs is the **Goldener Saal** (Golden Hall; Rathausplatz; adult/concession €2.50/1; ⊙10am-6pm), a huge banquet hall with an amazing gilded and frescoed coffered ceiling.

For panoramic views over Rathausplatz and the city, climb to the top of the **Perlachturm** (Rathausplatz; adult/concession €2/1; ⊙10am-6pm daily Apr-Nov), a former guard tower, and also an Elias Holl creation.

St Anna Kirche CHURCH
(Im Annahof 2, off Annastrasse; ⊙noon-5pm Mon, 10am-12.30pm & 3-5pm Tue-Sat, 10am-12.30pm & 3-4pm Sun) Often regarded as the first Renaissance church in Germany, the rather plain-looking (and well-hidden) St Anna Kirche is accessed via a set of cloisters lined with tombstones. The church contains a bevy of treasures, as well as the sumptuous

WORTH A TRIP

HARBURG

Looming over the Wörnitz River, the medieval covered parapets, towers, turrets, keep and red-tiled roofs of the 12th-century **Schloss Harburg** (www.burg-harburg.de; adult/child €5/3; ⊙10am-5pm Tue-Sun mid-Mar–Oct) are so perfectly preserved they almost seem like a film set. Tours tell the building's long tale and evoke the ghosts that are said to use the castle as a hang-out.

From the castle, the walk to Harburg's cute, half-timbered **Altstadt** takes around 10 minutes, slightly more the other way as you're heading uphill. A fabulous panorama of the village and castle can be admired from the 1702 **Stone Bridge** spanning the Wörnitz.

The Europabus stops in the village (outside the Gasthof Grüner Baum) but not at the castle. Hourly trains run to Nördlingen (€4.40, 19 minutes) and Donauwörth (€3.70, 11 minutes). The train station is about a 30-minute walk from the castle. Harburg is on the B25 road.

Fuggerkapelle, where Jacob Fugger and some of his relatives lie buried, and the lavishly frescoed **Goldschmiedekapelle** (Goldsmiths' Chapel; 1420) – under renovation at the time of research.

The church played an important role during the Reformation. In 1518 Martin Luther, in town to defend his beliefs before the papal legate, stayed at what was then a Carmelite monastery. His rooms have been turned into the **Lutherstiege**, a recently revamped exhibition about the Reformation and Luther's life.

Maximilianmuseum   MUSEUM
(📞 0821-324 4102; www.kunstsammlungen-museen.augsburg.de; Philippine-Welser-Strasse 24; adult/concession €7/5.50; ⊙10am-5pm Tue-Sun) The Maximilianmuseum occupies two patrician town houses joined by a statue-studded courtyard covered by a glass-and-steel roof. Highlights include a fabulous collection of Elias Holl's original wooden models for his architectural creations, and a collection of gold and silver coins that can be viewed through sliding magnifying glass panels. However, the real highlights here are the expertly curated temporary exhibitions on a variety of Bavarian themes.

Bertolt-Brecht-Haus   MUSEUM
(📞 0821-324 2779; Auf dem Rain 7; adult/concession €2.50/2; ⊙10am-5pm Tue-Sun) Opened in 1998 to celebrate Brecht's 100th birthday, this house museum is the birthplace of the famous playwright and poet, where he lived from 1898 to 1900 before moving across town. Among the displays are old theatre posters and a great series of life-size chronological photos, as well as his mother's bedroom. The building is due for a revamp in 2016 so may be closed for some time.

Dom Mariä Heimsuchung   CHURCH
(Hoher Weg; ⊙7am-6pm) Augsburg's cathedral has its origins in the 10th century but was Gothicised and enlarged in the 14th and 15th centuries. The star treasures here are the so-called 'Prophets' Windows'. Depicting David, Daniel, Jonah, Hosea and Moses, they are among the oldest figurative stained-glass windows in Germany, dating from the 12th century. Look out for four paintings by Hans Holbein the Elder, including one of Jesus' circumcision.

Jüdisches Kulturmuseum   MUSEUM
(📞 0821-513 658; www.jkmas.de; Halderstrasse 6-8; adult/concession €4/2; ⊙9am-6pm Tue-Thu, to 4pm Fri, 10am-5pm Sun) About 300m east of the main train station, as you head towards the Altstadt, you'll come to the Synagoge Augsburg, an art-nouveau temple built between 1914 and 1917 and housing a worthwhile Jewish museum. Exhibitions here focus on Jewish life in the region, presenting religious artefacts collected from defunct synagogues across Swabia.

🛏 Sleeping

Augsburg is a good alternative base for Oktoberfest, though hotel owners pump up their prices just as much as their Munich counterparts.

Übernacht   HOSTEL €
(📞 0821-4554 2828; www.uebernacht-hostel.de; Karlstrasse 4; dm/d from €19/42; 🛜) Professionally run, 21st-century operation spread over three floors of an office block with a wide selection of bright dorms, doubles and apartments, some en suite, some with shared facilities. Amenities are hotel standard and there's a superb kitchen for guest use. Book ahead in summer and during Oktoberfest.

Gästehaus SLEPS   GUESTHOUSE €
(📞 0821-780 8890; www.sleps.de; Unterer Graben 6; s €42-49 d €59-69; 🛜) The SLEPS is simply

the singles and doubles at Augsburg's youth hostel *(Jugendherberge)*, rebranded as a guesthouse. Rooms still have that whiff of institutional occupation about them but are bright, clean and quiet. For these prices the decent buffet breakfast is a real bonus.

★ Dom Hotel   HOTEL €€

(☑ 0821-343 930; www.domhotel-augsburg.de; Frauentorstrasse 8; s €70-150, d €95-190; P ⊖ @ 🔊 🏊) Augsburg's top choice packs a 500-year-old former bishop's guesthouse (Martin Luther and Kaiser Maxmilian I stayed here) with 57 rooms, all different but sharing a stylishly understated air and pristine upkeep; some have cathedral views. However, the big pluses here are the large swimming pool, fitness centre and solarium. Parking is an extra €6.

Hotel am Rathaus   HOTEL €€

(☑ 0821-346 490; www.hotel-am-rathaus-augsburg.de; Am Hinteren Perlachberg 1; s €69-98, d €105-145; 🔊) Just steps from Rathausplatz and Maximilianstrasse, this central boutique hotel hires out 31 rooms with freshly neutral decor and a sunny little breakfast room. Attracts a business-oriented clientele, so watch out for special weekend deals (almost a third off normal rates).

Steigenberger Drei Mohren Hotel   HOTEL €€€

(☑ 0821-503 60; www.augsburg.steigenberger.de; Maximilianstrasse 40; r €125-280; P ⊖ ❄ @ 🔊) A proud Leopold Mozart stayed here with his prodigious offspring in 1766 and it remains Augsburg's oldest and grandest hotel. The punctiliously maintained rooms are the last word in soothing design and come with marble bathrooms and original art.

Dine in house at Maximilians, a great place to swing by for Sunday brunch.

✖ Eating

In the evening, Maximilianstrasse is the place to tarry, with cafes tumbling out onto the pavements and Augsburg's young and beautiful watching the world go by.

Barfüsser Café   CAFE €

(☑ 0821-450 4964; Barfüsserstrasse 10; snacks €2-7; ⊙ 11am-6pm Mon, Tue, Thu & Fri, from 9am Wed & Sat) Follow a short flight of steps down from the street through a covered passageway to uncover this pretty snack stop by a little canal. It's run by a team of staff with disabilities, for whom it provides work opportunities as part of a community project, and serves delectable homemade cakes, pastries, salads and light lunches. Tram 1 stops outside.

Anno 1578   CAFE €

(Fuggerplatz 9; mains €4.50-10; ⊙ 9am-7pm Mon-Sat; 🔊) Munch on blockbuster breakfasts, lunchtime burgers and sandwiches, or just pop by for a cappuccino or ice cream at this trendy cafe under ancient neon-uplit vaulting. The central table, a huge chunk of timber, is a great place to meet locals and other travellers.

Die Extra Veganten   VEGAN €

(Frauentorstrasse 4; mains €5-7; ⊙ 11am-7pm Tue-Sat; ✍) Modestly proportioned, 15-seat vegan cafe near the cathedral offering owner-prepared meat- and dairy-free wraps, kebabs, salads, *Käsespätzle* (egg noodles), cakes and smoothies. The name is a good example of German humour.

Bauerntanz   GERMAN €€

(Bauerntanzgässchen 1; mains €7-17; ⊙ 11am-11.30pm) Belly-satisfying helpings of creative Swabian and Bavarian food – *Spätzle* (noodles) and more *Spätzle* – are plated up by friendly staff at this prim Alpine tavern with lace curtains, hefty timber interior and chequered fabrics. When the sun makes an appearance, everyone bails for the outdoor seating.

Bayerisches Haus am Dom   BAVARIAN €€

(☑ 0821-349 7990; Johannisgasse 4; mains €7.20-16.50; ⊙ 11am-midnight Mon-Sat, to 11pm Sun) Enjoy an elbow massage from the locals at chunky timber benches, while refuelling on Bavarian and Swabian dishes, cheap lunch options (€6.50) or a sandwich served by dirndl-clad waitresses. Erdinger and Andechser are the frothy double act that stimulates nightly frivolity in the beer garden.

August   INTERNATIONAL €€€

(☑ 0821-352 79; Frauentorstrasse 27; dinner €130; ⊙ from 7pm Wed-Sat) Most Augsburgers have little inkling their city possesses two Michelin stars, both of which belong to chef Christian Grünwald. Treat yourself to some of Bavaria's most innovative cooking in the minimalist dining room, though with just 16 covers, reservations are essential.

🍷 Drinking

Elements   CAFE

(Frauentorstrasse 2) Knock back a cocktail or five at this trendy cafe-bistro which attracts the beautiful people of an eve. Weekend breakfast is ideal for those who rise at the crack of lunchtime.

Thing BEER GARDEN
(Vorderer Lech 45) Augsburg's coolest beer garden sports totem poles and often gets crowded in the evenings. Serves great burgers and beer.

☆ Entertainment

Augsburger Puppenkiste THEATRE
(☑ 0821-450 3450; www.augsburger-puppenkiste.de; Spitalgasse 15) The celebrated puppet theatre holds performances of modern and classic fairy tales that even non–German speakers will enjoy. Advance bookings are essential.

ℹ Information

Post Office (Halderstrasse 29) At the Hauptbahnhof.
Tourist Office (☑ 0821-502 0723; www.augsburg-tourismus.de; Rathausplatz; ⊘ 9am-6pm Mon-Fri, 10am-5pm Sat, 10am-3pm Sun) Doubles as citizen's advice point, so staff can be slightly distracted.

ℹ Getting There & Away

BUS
The Romantic Road Coach (p110) stops at the Hauptbahnhof and the Rathaus. Low-cost coach company **Meinfernbus** (www.meinfernbus.de) runs to Munich 11 times a day (one hour).

CAR & MOTORCYCLE
Augsburg is just off the A8 northwest of Munich.

TRAIN
Augsburg rail connections:
➻ **Füssen** €20.90, two hours, every two hours or change in Buchloe
➻ **Munich** €13.30 to €20, 30 to 45 minutes, three hourly
➻ **Nuremberg** €27.50, one to two hours, hourly
➻ **Ulm** €17.90 to €24, 45 minutes to one hour, three hourly

ℹ Getting Around

From the train station take tram 3, 4 or 6 (€1.30) to the central interchange at Königsplatz where all Augsburg's tram routes converge.

Landsberg am Lech

☑ 08191 / POP 28,100
Lovely Landsberg am Lech is often overlooked by Romantic Road trippers on their town-hopping way between Füssen to the south and Augsburg to the north. But it's for this very absence of tourists and a less commercial ambience that this walled town on the River Lech is worth a halt, if only brief.

Landsberg can claim to be the town where one of the German language's best-selling books was written. It was during Hitler's 264 days of incarceration in a Landsberg jail, following the 1923 beer-hall putsch, that he penned his hate-filled *Mein Kampf,* a book that sold an estimated seven million copies when published. The jail later held Nazi war criminals and is still in use.

◉ Sights

Landsberg's hefty medieval defensive walls are punctuated by some beefy gates, the most impressive of which are the 1425 **Bayertor** to the east and the Renaissance-styled **Sandauer Tor** to the north. The tall **Schmalztor** was left centrally stranded when the fortifications were moved further out and still overlooks the main square and the 500 listed buildings within the town walls.

Stadtpfarrkirche Mariä Himmelfahrt CHURCH
(Georg-Hellmair-Platz) This huge 15th-century church was built by Matthäus von Ensingen, architect of Bern Cathedral. The barrel nave is stuccoed to baroque perfection, while a cast of saints populates columns and alcoves above the pews. Gothic-era stained glass casts rainbow hues on the church's most valuable work of art, the 15th-century *Madonna with Child* by local sculptor Lorenz Luidl.

Johanniskirche CHURCH
(Vorderer Anger) If you've already seen the Wieskirche (p95) to the south, you'll instantly recognise this small baroque church as a creation by the same architect, Dominikus Zimmermann, who lived in Landsberg and even served as its mayor.

Heilig-Kreuz-Kirche CHURCH
(Von-Helfenstein-Gasse) Head uphill from the Schmalztor to view this beautiful baroque Jesuit church, the interior a hallucination in broodily dark gilding and glorious ceiling decoration.

Neues Stadtmuseum MUSEUM
(www.museum-landsberg.de; Von-Helfenstein-Gasse 426; adult/concession €3.50/2; ⊘ 2-5pm Tue-Fri, from 11am Sat & Sun May-Jan, closed Feb-Apr) Housed in a former Jesuit school, Landsberg's municipal museum chronicles the area's past from prehistory to the 20th century, and displays numerous works of local art, both religious and secular in nature.

🛏 Sleeping & Eating

Stadthotel Augsburger Hof HOTEL €€
(📞08191-969 596; www.stadthotel-landsberg.de;
Schlossergasse 378; s €40-65, d €80; 🅿 🛜) The
14 en-suite rooms at this highly recommended traditional inn are a superb deal, and
have chunky pine beds and well-maintained
bathrooms throughout. The owners and
staff are a friendly bunch, and the breakfast
is a filling set-up for the day. Cycle hire and
cycle friendly.

Lechgarten BAVARIAN €€
(www.lechgarten.de; Hubert-von-Herkomer-Strasse
73; mains €5-11; ⊙4-11pm Mon-Fri, 10am-11pm Sat
& Sun Apr-Oct) Lansberg's top beer garden on
the tree-shaded banks of the River Lech has
250 seats, beer from Andechs Monastery and
hearty beer-garden fare. Live music summer
weekends, pretty river views any time.

Schafbräu INTERNATIONAL €€
(Hinterer Anger 338; mains €6-16; ⊙11.30am-
11pm) This cosy Bavarian-styled tavern has
an international menu that leans firmly towards southern Europe. If you don't feel like
moving far afterwards, there are rooms to
rent upstairs.

ℹ Information

Tourist Office (📞08191-128 246; www.
landsberg.de; Rathaus, Hauptplatz 152; ⊙9am-
6pm Mon-Fri May-Oct, 11am-5pm Sat & Sun
Apr-Oct, shorter hours Mon-Fri, closed Sat &
Sun Nov-Mar)

ℹ Getting There & Away

BUS
The Romantic Road Coach (p110) makes an
epicentral stop on the Hauptplatz.

TRAIN
Landsberg has the following rail connections:
➡ **Augsburg** €8.10, 50 minutes, hourly
➡ **Füssen** Change at Kaufering; €15.70, 1½
hours, every two hours
➡ **Munich** Change at Kaufering; €13.30, 50
minutes, twice hourly

NUREMBERG & FRANCONIA

Somewhere between Ingolstadt and Nuremberg, Bavaria's accent mellows, the oompah
bands play that little bit quieter and wine
competes with beer as the local tipple. This
is Franconia (Franken) and, as every local
will tell you, Franconians, who inhabit the
wooded hills and the banks of the Main River in Bavaria's northern reaches, are a breed
apart from their brash and extrovert cousins
to the south.

In the northwest, the region's winegrowers produce some exceptional whites, sold in
a distinctive teardrop-shaped bottle called
the *Bocksbeutel*. For outdoor enthusiasts,
the Altmühltal Nature Park offers wonderful hiking, biking and canoeing. But it is
Franconia's old royalty and incredible cities
– Nuremberg, Bamberg and Coburg – that
draw the biggest crowds.

Nuremberg

📞0911 / POP 510,600
Nuremberg (Nürnberg), Bavaria's
second-largest city and the unofficial capital
of Franconia, is an energetic place where the
nightlife is intense and the beer is as dark as
coffee. As one of Bavaria's biggest draws it is
alive with visitors year-round, but especially
during the spectacular Christmas market.

For centuries, Nuremberg was the unde-
clared capital of the Holy Roman Empire
and the preferred residence of most German kings, who kept their crown jewels
here. Rich and stuffed with architectural
wonders, it was also a magnet for famous
artists, though the most famous of all, Albrecht Dürer, was actually born here. 'Nuremberg shines throughout Germany like a sun
among the moon and stars,' gushed Martin
Luther. By the 19th century, the city had become a powerhouse in Germany's industrial
revolution.

The Nazis saw a perfect stage for their
activities in working-class Nuremberg. It
was here that the fanatical party rallies were
held, the boycott of Jewish businesses began
and the infamous Nuremberg Laws outlaw-
ing German citizenship for Jewish people
were enacted. On 2 January 1945, Allied
bombers reduced the city to landfill, killing
6000 people in the process.

After WWII the city was chosen as the
site of the war crimes tribunal, now known
as the Nuremberg Trials. Later, the painstaking reconstruction – using the original
stone – of almost all the city's main buildings, including the castle and old churches
in the Altstadt, returned the city to some of
its former glory.

⊙ Sights

Most major sights are within the Altstadt.

★ Kaiserburg   CASTLE
(Imperial Castle; ☑ 0911-244 6590; www.kaiser burg-nuernberg.de; Auf der Burg; adult/concession incl Sinwell Tower €7/6, Palas & Museum €5.50/4.50; ⊙ 9am-6pm Apr-Sep, 10am-4pm Oct-Mar) This enormous castle complex above the Altstadt poignantly reflects Nuremberg's medieval might. The main attraction is a tour of the newly renovated **Palas** (residential wing) to see the lavish Knights' and Imperial Hall, a Romanesque double chapel and an exhibit on the inner workings of the Holy Roman Empire. This segues to the **Kaiserburg Museum**, which focuses on the castle's military and building history. Elsewhere, enjoy panoramic views from the **Sinwell Tower** or peer 48m down into the **Deep Well**.

For centuries the castle, which has origins in the 12th century, also sheltered the crown jewels (crown, sceptre, orb etc) of the Holy Roman Empire, which are now kept at Hofburg palace in Vienna. It also played a key role in the drawing up of Emperor Charles IV's Golden Bull, a document that changed the way Holy Roman Emperors were elected. The exhibition contains an original statue taken from Prague's Charles Bridge of Charles IV, who spent a lot of time in both Bohemia and Franconia during his reign.

★ Deutsche Bahn Museum   MUSEUM
(☑ 0800-3268 7386; www.db-museum.de; Lessingstrasse 6; adult/child €5/2.50; ⊙ 9am-5pm Tue-Fri, 10am-6pm Sat & Sun) Forget Dürer and Nazi rallies, Nuremberg is a railway town at heart. Germany's first passenger trains ran between here and Fürth, a fact reflected in the unmissable German Railways Museum which explores the history of Germany's legendary rail system. The huge exhibition which continues across the road is one of Nuremberg's top sights, especially if you have a soft spot for things that run on rails.

If you're with kids, head straight for KIBA-LA (Kinder-Bahnland – Children's Railway World), a recently refashioned part of the museum with lots of hands-on, interactive choo-choo-themed attractions. There's also a huge model railway, one of Germany's largest, set in motion every hour by a uniformed controller.

The main exhibition, charting almost two centuries of rail history, starts on the ground floor and continues with more recent exhibits on the 1st floor. Passing quickly through the historically inaccurate beginning (as every rail buff knows, the world's first railway was the Stockton–Darlington, not the Liverpool–Manchester), highlights include Germany's oldest railway carriage dating from 1835 and lots of interesting Deutsche Reichsbahn paraphernalia from East Germany.

However, the real meat of the show are the two halls of locos and rolling stock. The first hall contains Ludwig II's incredible rococo rail carriage, dubbed the 'Versailles of the rails', as well as Bismarck's considerably less ostentatious means of transport. There's also Germany's most famous steam loco, the Adler, built by the Stephensons in Newcastle-upon-Tyne for the Nuremberg–Fürth line. The second hall across the road from the main building houses some mammoth engines, some with their Nazi or Deutsche Reichsbahn insignia still in place.

Hauptmarkt   SQUARE
(Hauptmarkt) This bustling square in the heart of the Altstadt is the site of daily markets as well as the famous *Christkindlesmarkt* (Christmas Market). At the eastern end is the ornate Gothic **Frauenkirche** (church). Daily at noon crowds crane their necks to witness the clock's figures enact a spectacle called the *Männleinlaufen* (Little Men Dancing). Rising from the square like a Gothic spire is the sculpture-festooned **Schöner Brunnen** (Beautiful Fountain). Touch the golden ring in the ornate wrought-iron gate for good luck.

Memorium Nuremberg Trials   MEMORIAL
(☑ 0911-3217 9372; www.memorium-nuremberg. de; Bärenschanzstrasse 72; adult/concession incl audioguide €5/3; ⊙ 10am-6pm Wed-Mon) Göring, Hess, Speer and 21 other Nazi leaders were tried for crimes against peace and humanity by the Allies in **Schwurgerichtssaal 600** (Court Room 600) of this still-working courthouse. Today the room forms part of an engaging exhibit detailing the background, progression and impact of the trials using film, photographs, audiotape and even the original defendants' dock. To get here, take the U1 towards Bärenschanze and get off at Sielstrasse.

The initial and most famous trial, held from 20 November 1945 until 1 October 1946, resulted in three acquittals, 12 sentences to death by hanging, three life sentences and four long prison sentences. Hermann Göring, the Reich's field marshal, famously cheated the hangman by taking a cyanide capsule in his cell hours before his scheduled execution.

Although it's easy to assume that Nuremberg was chosen as a trial venue because of its role during the Nazi years, it was actually picked for practical reasons: the largely intact Palace of Justice was able to accommodate lawyers and staff from all four Allied nations.

Note that Court Room 600 is still used for trials and may be closed to visitors.

Reichsparteitagsgelände HISTORIC SITE
(Luitpoldhain; ☑ 0911-231 5666; www.museen-nuernberg.de; Bayernstrasse 110; grounds free, documentation centre adult/concession incl audioguide €5/3; ☺ grounds 24hr, documentation centre 9am-6pm Mon-Fri, 10am-6pm Sat & Sun) The infamous black-and-white images of ecstatic Nazi supporters hailing their Führer were taken here in Nuremberg. Much of the grounds were destroyed during Allied bombing raids, but enough remains to get a sense of the megalomania behind it, especially after visiting the excellent **Dokumentationszentrum** (Documentation Centre) served by tram 9 from the Hauptbahnhof.

In the north wing of the partly finished Kongresshalle (Congress Hall), the Documentation Centre examines various historical aspects, including the rise of the NSDAP, the Hitler cult, the party rallies and the Nuremberg Trials.

East of here is the **Zeppelinfeld**, where most of the big Nazi parades, rallies and events took place. It is fronted by a 350m-long grandstand, the Zeppelintribüne, where you can still stand on the very balcony from where Hitler incited the masses. It now hosts sporting events and rock concerts, though this rehabilitation has caused controversy.

The grounds are bisected by the 2km-long and 40m-wide **Grosse Strasse** (Great Road), which was planned as a military parade road. Zeppelinfeld, Kongresshalle and Grosse Strasse are all protected landmarks for being significant examples of Nazi architecture.

The Reichsparteitagsgelände is about 4km southeast of the city centre.

Germanisches Nationalmuseum MUSEUM
(German National Museum; ☑ 0911-133 10; www.gnm.de; Kartäusergasse 1; adult/concession €8/5; ☺ 10am-6pm Tue & Thu-Sun, to 9pm Wed) Spanning prehistory to the early 20th century, this museum is the German-speaking world's biggest and most important museum of Teutonic culture. It features works by German painters and sculptors, an archaeological collection, arms and armour, musical and scientific instruments, and toys.

Highlights of the eclectic collection include Dürer's anatomically detailed *Hercules Slaying the Stymphalian Birds* and the world's oldest terrestrial globe and pocket watch as well as 20th-century design classics and baroque dollhouses.

Neues Museum MUSEUM
(☑ 0911-240 269; www.nmn.de; Luitpoldstrasse 5; adult/child €4/3; ☺ 10am-6pm Fri-Wed, to 6pm Thu, closed Mon) The aptly named New Museum showcases contemporary art and design, with resident collections of paintings, sculpture, photography, video art and installations focusing on artists from Eastern Europe, as well as travelling shows. Equally stunning is the award-winning building itself, with a dramatic 100m curved glass facade that, literally and figuratively, reflects the stone town wall opposite.

Albrecht-Dürer-Haus MUSEUM
(☑ 0911-231 2568; Albrecht-Dürer-Strasse 39; adult/concession €5/3; ☺ 10am-5pm Fri-Wed, to 8pm Thu) Dürer, Germany's most famous Renaissance draughtsman, lived and worked at Albrecht-Dürer-Haus from 1509 until his death in 1528. After a multimedia show, there's an audioguide tour of the four-storey house, which is narrated by 'Agnes', Dürer's wife. Highlights are the hands-on demonstrations in the recreated studio and print shop on the 3rd floor and, in the attic, a gallery featuring copies and originals of Dürer's work.

Altes Rathaus HISTORIC BUILDING
(Rathausplatz 2) Beneath the Altes Rathaus (1616–22), a hulk of a building with lovely Renaissance-style interiors, you'll find the macabre **Mittelalterliche Lochgefängnisse** (Medieval Dungeons; ☑ 0911-231 2690; adult/concession €3.50/1.50; ☺ tours 10am-4.30pm Tue-Sun). This 12-cell death row and torture chamber must be seen on a 30-minute guided tour (held every half-hour) and might easily put you off lunch.

Stadtmuseum Fembohaus MUSEUM
(☑ 0911-231 2595; Burgstrasse 15; adult/child €5/3; ☺ 10am-5pm Tue-Fri, 10am-6pm Sat & Sun) Offering an entertaining overview of the city's history, highlights of the Stadtmuseum Fembohaus include the restored historic rooms of this 16th-century merchant's house. Also here, **Noricama** takes you on a flashy Hollywoodesque multimedia journey (in German and English) through Nuremberg's history.

Nuremberg

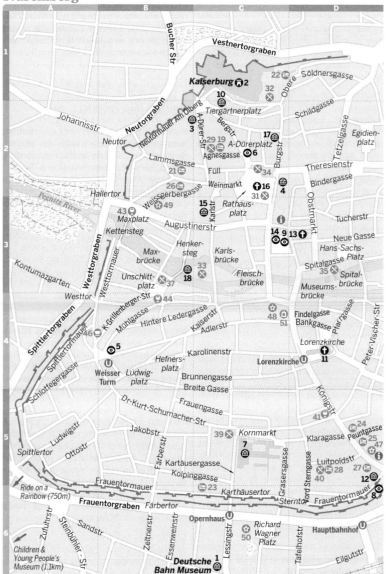

Jüdisches Museum Franken JEWISH, MUSEUM
(☎0911-770 577; www.juedisches-museum.org;
Königstrasse 89; adult/concession €3/2; ⊙10am-
5pm Wed-Sun, to 8pm Tue) A quick U-Bahn ride
away in the neighbouring town of Fürth is the
Jüdisches Museum Franken. Fürth once had
the largest Jewish congregation of any city in
southern Germany, and this museum, housed
in a handsomely restored building, chronicles
the history of Jewish life in the region from
the Middle Ages to today. To reach the museum, take the U1 to the Rathaus stop in Fürth.

tures and symbols; check out the ornate carvings over the **Bridal Doorway** to the north, showing the Wise and Foolish Virgins. Inside, the bronze shrine of St Sebald (Nuremberg's own saint) is a Gothic and Renaissance masterpiece that took its maker, Peter Vischer the Elder, and his two sons more than 11 years to complete (Vischer is in it, too, sporting a skullcap).

The church is free to enter, despite the misleading sign on the door.

Felsengänge HISTORIC SITE
(Underground Cellars; www.felsengaenge-nuernberg.de; Bergstrasse 19; tours adult/concession €6/5; ⊙tours 2.30pm daily, also 5.30pm Fri & Sat) Beneath the Albrecht Dürer Monument on Albrecht-Dürer-Platz are the chilly Felsengänge. Departing from the brewery shop at Bergstrasse 19, tours descend to this four-storey subterranean warren, which dates from the 14th century and once housed a brewery and a beer cellar. During WWII, it served as an air-raid shelter. Tours take a minimum of three people. Take a jacket against the chill.

Spielzeugmuseum MUSEUM
(Toy Museum; Karlstrasse 13-15; adult/child €5/3; ⊙10am-5pm Tue-Fri, to 6pm Sat & Sun) Nuremberg has long been a centre of toy manufacturing, and the large Spielzeugmuseum presents toys in their infinite variety – from innocent hoops to blood-and-guts computer games, historical wooden and tin toys to Barbie et al. Kids and kids at heart will delight in the imaginatively designed play area.

Ehekarussell Brunnen FOUNTAIN
(Am Weissen Turm) At the foot of the fortified Weisser Turm (White Tower; now the gateway to the U-Bahn station of the same name) stands this large and startlingly grotesque sculptural work depicting six interpretations of marriage (from first love to quarrel to death-do-us-part), all based on a verse by Hans Sachs, the medieval cobbler-poet. You soon realise why the artist faced a blizzard of criticism when the fountain was unveiled in 1984; it really is enough to put anyone off tying the knot.

Lorenzkirche CHURCH
(Lorenzplatz) Dark and atmospheric, the Lorenzkirche has dramatically downlit pillars, taupe stone columns, sooty ceilings and many artistic highlights. Check out the 15th-century tabernacle in the left aisle – the delicate carved strands wind up to the vaulted ceiling. Remarkable also are the stained

St Sebalduskirche CHURCH
(www.sebalduskirche.de; Albrecht-Dürer-Platz 1; ⊙9.30am-4pm Jan-Mar, to 6pm Apr-Dec) Nuremberg's oldest church was built in rusty pink-veined sandstone in the 13th century. Its exterior is replete with religious sculp-

Nuremberg

glass (including a rose window 9m in diameter) and Veit Stoss' *Engelsgruss* (Annunciation), a wooden carving with life-size figures suspended above the high altar.

Handwerkerhof   MARKET
(www.handwerkerhof.de; Am Königstor; ⊙9am-6.30pm Mon-Fri, 10am-4pm Sat mid-Mar–Dec) **FREE**
A recreation of an old-world Nuremberg crafts quarter, the Handwerkerhof is a self-contained tourist trap by the Königstor. It's about as quaint as a hammer on your thumbnail, but if you're in the market for souvenirs you may find some decent merchandise (and the bratwurst aren't bad here either).

⌖ Tours

Old Town Walking Tours   WALKING TOUR
(www.nuernberg-tours.de; adult/child €9/free; ⊙1.30pm May-Oct) English-language Old Town walking tours are run by the tourist office – tours leave from the Hauptmarkt branch and take two hours.

Geschichte für Alle   CULTURAL TOUR
(☑0911-307 360; www.geschichte-fuer-alle.de; adult/concession €8/7) Intriguing range of themed English-language tours by a non-profit association. The 'Albrecht Dürer' and 'Life in Medieval Nuremberg' tours come highly recommended.

Nuremberg Tours   WALKING TOUR
(www.nurembergtours.com; adult/concession €19/17; ⊙11.15am Mon, Wed & Sat Apr-Oct) Four-hour walking and public transport tours taking in the city centre and the Reichsparteitagsgelände (p129). Groups meet at the entrance to the Hauptbahnhof.

★☆ Festivals & Events

Christkindlesmarkt   CHRISTMAS MARKET
(www.christkindlesmarkt.de) From late November to Christmas Eve, the Hauptmarkt is taken over by the most famous Christkindlesmarkt in Germany. Yuletide shoppers descend on the 'Christmas City' from all over Europe to seek out unique gifts at the scores of colourful timber trinket stalls that fill the square.

The aroma of mulled wine and roast sausages permeates the chilly air, while special festive events take place across the city.

🛏 Sleeping

Accommodation gets tight and rates rocket during the Christmas market and the toy fair (trade only) in late January to early February. At other times, cheap rooms can be found, especially if you book ahead.

Five Reasons
HOSTEL €

(☑ 0911-9928 6625; www.five-reasons.de; Frauentormauer 42; dm/d from €23/69; @ 🛜) Crisply appointed, newly renovated and rebranded 90-bed hostel with spotless dorms, the trendiest hostel bathrooms you are ever likely to encounter, pre-made beds, card keys, fully equipped kitchen, a small bar and very nice staff. Breakfast is an extra €3.10 to €5.80, depending on what option you choose. Overall a great place to lay your head.

DJH Hostel
HOSTEL €

(☑ 0911-230 9360; www.nuernberg.jugendherberge.de; Burg 2; dm from €31.90) Open year round, this youth hostel is a real tripstopper with a standard of facilities many four-star hotels would envy. Fully revamped a few years ago, the old Kornhaus is a dramatic building itself, but now sports funky corridors, crisply maintained dorms with super-modern bathrooms, a canteen, bar and very helpful staff.

Be aware that in the summer months you can get a discounted single on popular booking sites for the price of a dorm bed in a four-bunk room here.

Probst-Garni Hotel
PENSION €

(☑ 0911-203 433; www.hotel-garni-probst.de; Luitpoldstrasse 9; s/d €56/75; 🛜) A creaky lift from street level takes you up to this realistically priced, centrally located guesthouse, run for 70 years by three generations of Probsts. The 33 gracefully old-fashioned rooms are multi-hued and high-ceilinged but some are more renovated than others. Furniture in the breakfast room is family made.

Hotel Drei Linden
HOTEL €

(☑ 0911-506 800; www.hotel-drei-linden-nuernberg.de; Äussere Sulzbacher Strasse 1-3; s/d €52/69; 🛜) A cheap-ish deal, rooms here are comfortable though not at all chic, and there's round-the-clock free tea and coffee. Breakfast is a whopping €9.50 extra. Located 1km east of the Altstadt; take tram 8 from the Hauptbahnhof to Deichlerstrasse.

Knaus-Campingpark
CAMPGROUND €

(☑ 0911-981 2717; www.knauscamp.de; Hans-Kalb-Strasse 56; per tent/person €5.50/7.90; 🛜) A camping ground near the lakes in the Volkspark, southeast of the city centre. Take the U1 to Messezentrum, then walk about 1km.

Hotel Elch
HOTEL €€

(☑ 0911-249 2980; www.hotel-elch.com; Irrerstrasse 9; s/d from €57/70; 🛜) Occupying a 14th-century, half-timbered house near the Kaiserburg, the Elch has seen big changes in recent years with a new boutique wing added and the reception and restaurant given a complete 21st-century makeover. The result is you now have a choice between fairy-tale 'historic' and slick 'boutique', the latter of which costs a bit more.

Hotel Deutscher Kaiser
HOTEL €€

(☑ 0911-242 660; www.deutscher-kaiser-hotel.de; Königstrasse 55; s/d from €92/109; @ 🛜) Epicentral in its location, aristocratic in its design and service, this treat of a historic hotel has been in the same family since the turn of the 20th century. Climb the castle-like granite stairs to find rooms of understated simplicity, flaunting oversize beds, Italian porcelain, silk lampshades and real period furniture (Biedermeier and *Jugendstil*).

The club-like reading room with newspapers and magazines in German and English is a welcome extra and the breakfast room is a study in soothing, early morning elegance. Renovation work is ongoing.

Art & Business Hotel
HOTEL €€

(☑ 0911-232 10; www.art-business-hotel.com; Gleissbühlstrasse 15; s/d from €74/105; 🛜) No need to be an artist or a businessperson to stay at this up-to-the-minute place, a short amble from the Hauptbahnhof. From the trendy bar to the latest in slate bathroom styling, design here is bold, but not overpoweringly so. From reception follow the wobbly carpet to your room, a well-maintained haven uninfected by traffic noise despite the city-centre frenzy outside.

Local Technicolor art and design brings cheer to the communal spaces and there's a small sculpture garden out back. Rates tumble at weekends.

Burghotel
HOTEL €€

(☑ 0911-238 890; www.burghotel-nuernberg.de; Lammsgasse 3; s/d from €66/77; @ 🛜 🏊) The mock-Gothic reception area and lantern-lit corridors (watch your head) indicate you're in for a slightly different hotel experience

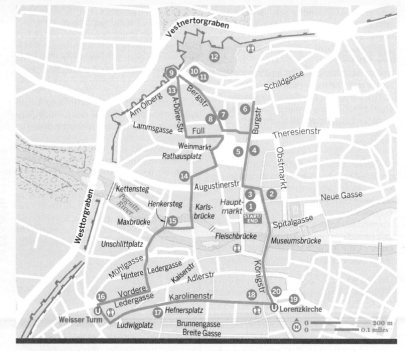

🏃 City Walk
Nuremberg Altstadt

START HAUPTMARKT
FINISH HAUPTMARKT
LENGTH 2.5KM, TWO HOURS

This circuit covers the historic centre's key sights over a leisurely 2.5km walk. The tour starts at the ① **Hauptmarkt**, the main square. At the eastern end is the ornate Gothic ② **Pfarrkirche Unsere Liebe Frau**. The ③ **Schöner Brunnen** (p128) rises up from the cobblestones like a buried cathedral. Walk north to the ④ **Altes Rathaus** (p129), the old town hall, with its medieval dungeons. Opposite stands the 13th-century ⑤ **St Sebalduskirche** (p131). Just up Burgstrasse is the ⑥ **Stadtmuseum Fembohaus** (p129). Backtrack south to Halbwachsengässchen and turn right into Albrecht-Dürer-Platz, with the ⑦ **Albrecht Dürer Monument**. Directly beneath are the ⑧ **Felsengänge** (p131), tunnels once used as an air-raid shelter.

Moving up Bergstrasse, you'll reach the massive ⑨ **Tiergärtnertor**, a 16th-century tower. Nearby is the half-timbered ⑩ **Pilatushaus**. A few steps east is the ⑪ **Histor-**

ischer Kunstbunker, where precious art was stored in WWII. Looming over the scene is the ⑫ **Kaiserburg** (p128). Go south to the ⑬ **Albrecht-Dürer-Haus** (p129). Continue south along Albrecht-Dürer-Strasse, turn left on Füll and skirt the back of Sebalduskirche to Karlsstrasse, where you'll reach the ⑭ **Spielzeugmuseum** (p131).

Cross the Karlsbrücke to enjoy a view of the ⑮ **Weinstadl**, an old wine depot overlooking the river. Continue across the Henkersteg and wend your way south to Vordere Ledergasse, which leads west to the amazing ⑯ **Ehekarussell Brunnen** (p131), with its shocking images of married life. Head east on Ludwigplatz past the ⑰ **Peter-Henlein-Brunnen**, with a statue of the first watchmaker, and proceed along Karolinenstrasse to reach the city's oldest house, ⑱ **Nassauer Haus** at No 2, and the massive ⑲ **Lorenzkirche** (p131). The ⑳ **Tugendbrunnen** (Fountain of the Seven Virtues) is on the north side of the church.

Continuing north up Königstrasse will return you to the Hauptmarkt, your starting point.

here. The small singles and doubles have strange '50s-style built-in timber furniture reminiscent of yesteryear train carriages, old-fashioned bedhead radios and chunky TVs, while some much larger 'comfort' rooms under the eaves have spacious sitting areas and more up-to-date amenities.

Apart from the medieval theme, the big draw here is the basement heated swimming pool, where all guests are free to make a splash.

Agneshof HOTEL €€
(☑0911-214 440; www.agneshof-nuernberg.de; Agnesgasse 10; s/d from €82/96; P 🛜) Tranquilly located in the antiques quarter near the St Sebalduskirche, the Agneshof's public areas have a sophisticated, artsy touch. The 74 box-ticking rooms have whitewashed walls and '90s furniture; some at the top have views of the Kaiserburg. There's a state-of-the-art wellness centre, and a pretty summer courtyard garden strewn with deckchairs. Breakfast is a cheeky extra €7.

Hotel Victoria HOTEL €€
(☑0911-240 50; www.hotelvictoria.de; Königstrasse 80; s/d from €82/98; P @ 🛜) A hotel since 1896, the Victoria is a solid option with a central location. With its early-21st-century bathrooms and now ever so slightly dated decor, the price is about right. Popular with business travellers. Parking costs €12.

Hotel Drei Raben BOUTIQUE HOTEL €€€
(☑0911-274 380; www.hoteldreiraben.de; Königstrasse 63; d incl breakfast from €150; P ✳ 🛜) The design of this classy charmer builds on the legend of the three ravens perched on the building's chimney stack, who tell stories from Nuremberg lore. Art and decor in the 'mythical theme' rooms reflect a particular tale, from the life of Albrecht Dürer to the first railway.

Valet parking available (€15).

BAVARIA NUREMBERG

NUREMBERG FOR KIDS

No city in Bavaria has more for kids to see and do than Nuremberg. In fact, keeping the little 'uns entertained in the Franconian capital is child's play.

Museums

Children & Young People's Museum (☑0911-600 040; www.kindermuseum-nuernberg.de; Michael-Ende-Strasse 17; adult/family €7/19; ⊙2-5.30pm Sat, 10am-5.30pm Sun Sep-Jun) Educational exhibitions and lots of hands-on fun – just a pity it's not open more often.

School Museum (☑0911-530 2574; Äussere Sulzbacher Strasse 62; adult/child €5/3; ⊙9am-5pm Tue-Fri, 10am-6pm Sat & Sun) Recreated classroom plus school-related exhibits from the 17th century to the Third Reich.

Deutsche Bahn Museum (p128) Feeds the kids' obsession for choo-choos.

Play

Playground of the Senses (www.erfahrungsfeld.nuernberg.de; Untere Talgasse 8; adult/child €8/6.50; ⊙9am-6pm Mon-Fri, 1-6pm Sat, 10am-6pm Sun May–mid-Sep) Some 80 hands-on 'stations' designed to educate children in the laws of nature, physics and the human body. Take the U2 or U3 to Wöhrder Wiese.

Toys

Playmobil (☑0911-9666 1700; www.playmobil-funpark.de; Brandstätterstrasse 2-10; admission €11; ⊙9am-7pm May-Sep, 9am-6pm Oct) This theme park has life-size versions of the popular toys. It's located 9km west of the city centre in Zirndorf; take the S4 to Anwanden, then change to bus 151. Free admission if it's your birthday. Special 'Kleine Dürer' (Little Dürer; €2.99) figures are on sale here and at the tourist office.

Käthe Wohlfahrt Christmas shop (www.wohlfahrt.com; Königstrasse 8) The Nuremberg branch of this year-round Christmas shop.

Spielzeugmuseum (p131) Some 1400 sq metres of Matchbox, Barbie, Playmobil and Lego, plus a great play area.

Germanisches Nationalmuseum (p129) Has a toy section and holds ocassional tours for children.

✗ Eating

Café am Trödelmarkt
CAFE €

(Trödelmarkt 42; dishes €4-8.50; ☺9am-6pm Mon-Sat, 11am-6pm Sun) A gorgeous place on a sunny day, this multilevel waterfront cafe overlooks the covered Henkersteg bridge. It's especially popular for its continental breakfasts, and has fantastic cakes, as well as good blackboard lunchtime specials between 11am and 2pm.

Naturkostladen Lotos
ORGANIC, BUFFET €

(www.naturkostladen-lotos.de; Am Unschlittplatz 1; dishes €3-6; ☺9.30am-6pm Mon-Fri, to 4pm Sat; 🖋) Unclog arteries and blast free radicals with a blitz of grain burgers, spinach soup or vegie pizza at this health-food shop. The fresh bread and cheese counter is a treasure chest of nutritious picnic supplies.

Suppdiwupp
CAFETERIA €

(Lorenzer Strasse 27; mains €3.50-7; ☺11am-6pm Mon-Thu, to 4pm Fri & Sat) This fragrantly spicy, recently revamped lunch halt has a weekly changing menu, outdoor seating and a choice of nonliquid mains (sandwiches, salads) if you don't fancy a bowl of broth. Very popular early afternoon so get there early.

Wurst Durst
GERMAN €

(Luitpoldstrasse 13; dishes €3-5; ☺11am-6pm Tue-Thu, to 5am Fri & Sat) Wedged between the facades of Luitpoldstrasse, this tiny snack bar offers munchies relief in the form of Belgian fries, sausages and trays of *Currywurst*.

Sushi Glas
SUSHI €

(Kornmarkt 5-7; sushi from €5; ☺noon-11pm Mon-Wed, noon-midnight Thu-Sat, 6-10pm Sun) Take a pew in this 21st-century sugar cube to watch the sushi chef deftly craft your order. When the mercury climbs high, enjoy your nigiri, sashimi and American sushi beneath the huge sunshades on the Kornmarkt.

★ Albrecht Dürer Stube
FRANCONIAN €€

(☑0911-227 209; www.albrecht-duerer-stube.de; cnr Albrecht-Dürer-Strasse & Agnesgasse; mains €7-15; ☺6pm-midnight Mon-Sat, 11.30am-2.30pm Fri & Sun) This unpretentious and intimate restaurant has a Dürer-inspired dining room, prettily laid tables, a ceramic stove keeping things toasty when they're not outside, and a menu of Nuremberg sausages, steaks, sea fish, seasonal specials, Franconian wine and *Landbier* (regional beer). There aren't many tables so booking ahead at weekends is recommended.

Goldenes Posthorn
FRANCONIAN €€

(☑0911-225 153; Glöckleinsgasse 2, cnr Sebalder Platz; mains €9-19; ☺11am-11pm; 🖋) Push open the heavy copper door to find a real culinary treat that has hosted royals, artists and professors (including Albrecht Dürer) since 1498. You can't go wrong sticking with the miniature local sausages, but the pork shoulder and the house speciality – vinegar-marinated ox cheeks – are highly recommended as well.

Heilig-Geist-Spital
BAVARIAN €€

(☑0911-221 761; Spitalgasse 16; mains €7-17; ☺11.30am-11pm) Lots of dark carved wood, a herd of hunting trophies and a romantic candlelit half-light make this former hospital, suspended over the Pegnitz, one of the most atmospheric dining rooms in town. Sample the delicious, seasonally changing menu inside or out in the pretty courtyard, a real treat if you are looking for somewhere traditional to dine.

Bratwursthäusle
GERMAN €€

(http://die-nuernberger-bratwurst.de; Rathausplatz 1; meals €7.20-12.90; ☺10am-10pm Mon-Sat) Seared over a flaming beech-wood grill, the little links sold at this rustic inn arguably set the standard across the land. You can dine in the timbered restaurant or on the terrace with views of the Hauptmarkt. Service can be flustered at busy times.

Marientorzwinger
GERMAN €€

(Lorenzer Strasse 33; mains €7-17; ☺11.30am-1am) The last remaining *Zwinger* eatery (taverns built between the inner and outer walls when they relinquished their military use) in Nuremberg is an atmospheric place to chomp on a mixed bag of sturdy regional specials in the simple wood-panelled dining room or the leafy beer garden. Fürth-brewed Tucher is the ale of choice here.

Burgwächter
FRANCONIAN, INTERNATIONAL €€

(☑0911-222 126; Am Ölberg 10; mains €9-15; ☺11am-11pm; 🖋) Refuel after a tour of the Kaiserburg with prime steaks, bratwurst with potato salad, and vegetarian-friendly Swabian filled pastas and salads, as you feast your eyes on the best terrace views from any Nuremberg eatery or drinking spot. With kiddies in tow, ask for *Kloss* (a simple dumpling with sauce).

American Diner
AMERICAN €€

(Gewerbemuseumsplatz 3; burgers €8-11; ☺11am-1am) For the juiciest burgers in town, head for this retro diner in the Cinecitta Cinema, Germany's biggest multiplex.

🍷 Drinking

Kettensteg
BEER GARDEN

(www.restaurant-biergarten-kettensteg.de; Maxplatz 35; ⊘11am-11pm) At the end of the chain bridge and in the shadow of the Halletor you'll find this classic Bavarian beer garden complete with its gravel floor, folding slatted chairs, fairylights, tree shade and river views. Zirndorfer, Lederer and Tucher beers are on tap and some of the food comes on heart-shaped plates.

Treibhaus
CAFE

(☑0911-223 041; Karl-Grillenberger-Strasse 28; light meals €5-10; ⊘9am to last customer; 🛜) Off the path of most visitors, this bustling cafe is a Nuremberg institution and one of the most happening places in town. Set yourself down in the sun on a yellow director's chair out front or warm yourself with something strong around the huge zinc bar inside.

Kloster
PUB

(Obere Wörthstrasse 19; ⊘5pm-1am) One of Nuremberg's best drinking dens is all dressed up as a monastery replete with ecclesiastic knick-knacks including coffins emerging from the walls. The monks here pray to the god of *Landbier* and won't be up at 5am for matins, that's for sure.

Cafe Katz
BAR

(Hans-Sachs-Platz 8; ⊘11am-1am Sun-Thu, to 2am Fri & Sat) From the outside this place looks like a secondhand furniture shop, the vitrines packed with 1970s coffee tables, old school desks and 1980s high-back chairs. But the La Marzocco espresso machine gives the game away as this is one of Nuremberg's coolest cafes, a hip spot to see, be seen and enjoy a drink and/or a vegie or vegan meal on retro furnishings.

Barfüsser Brauhaus
BEER HALL

(Königstrasse 60; ⊘11am-1am Mon-Fri, to 2am Sat) This beer hall deep below street level is a popular spot to hug a mug of site-brewed ale, bubbling frothily in the copper kettles that occupy the cavernous vaulted interior. The traditional trappings of the huge quaffing space clash oddly with the yellow polo shirts of the waiting staff, but that's our only criticism.

Meisengeige
BAR

(Am Laufer Schlagturm 3; ⊘30min before start of film to midnight Sun-Wed, to 1am Thu, to 2am Fri & Sat) Art- and foreign-film cinema with attached pub; it's a conversation-inspiring spot for a drink even if you're not going to see a film.

⭐ Entertainment

The excellent *Plärrer* (www.plaerrer.de), available at newsstands throughout the city and from the tourist office, is the best source of information on events around town.

Mata Hari Bar
LIVE MUSIC

(www.mataharibar.de; Weissgerbergasse 31; ⊘from 8pm Wed-Sun) This bar with live music and DJ nights is a Nuremberg institution. After 9pm it's usually standing room only and the party goes on well into the early hours.

Hirsch
LIVE MUSIC

(☑0911-429 414; www.der-hirsch.de; Vogelweiherstrasse 66) This converted factory, 2.5km south of the Hauptbahnhof, hosts live alternative music almost daily, both big-name acts and local names. Take the U1 or U2 to Plärrer, then change to tram 4, alighting at Dianaplatz.

Staatstheater
THEATRE

(www.staatstheater-nuernberg.de; Richard-Wagner-Platz 2) Nuremberg's magnificent state theatre serves up an impressive mix of dramatic arts. The renovated art-nouveau opera house presents opera and ballet, while the Kammerspiele offers a varied program of classical and contemporary plays. The Nürnberger Philharmoniker also performs here.

Filmhaus
CINEMA

(☑0911-231 5823; www.kunstkulturquartier.de; Königstrasse 93) This small indie picture house shows foreign-language movies, reruns of cult German flicks and films for kids.

Loop Club
CLUB

(www.loopclub.de; Klingenhofstrasse 52) With three dance areas and a languid chill-out zone with lounge music, this place attracts a slightly more mature crowd, meaning '80s and '90s hits plus student nights. Take the U2 to Herrnhütte, turn right and it's a five-minute walk.

Mach1
CLUB

(☑0911-246 602; www.macheins.club; Kaiserstrasse 1-9; ⊘Thu-Sat) This legendary dance temple has been around for decades, but still holds a spell over fashion victims. Don your best geek-chic, line up and be mustered.

ⓘ Information

Main Post Office (Bahnhofplatz 1)

ReiseBank (Hauptbahnhof)

Tourist Office (☏ 0911-233 60; www.tourismus.nuernberg.de; Königstrasse 93; ⊙ 9am-7pm Mon-Sat, 10am-4pm Sun) Publishes the excellent *See & Enjoy* booklet, a comprehensive guide to the city.

Tourist Office (☏ 0911-233 60; www.tourismus.nuernberg.de; Hauptmarkt 18; ⊙ 9am-6pm Mon-Sat year round, also 10am-4pm Sun Apr-Oct)

ⓘ Getting There & Away

AIR

Nuremberg's **Albrecht Dürer Airport** (www.airport-nuernberg.de) 5km north of the centre, is served by regional and international carriers, including Ryanair, Lufthansa, Air Berlin and Air France.

BUS

Buses to destinations across Europe leave from the main bus station (ZOB) near the Hauptbahnhof. There's a Touring/Eurolines office nearby. **Meinfernbus** (www.meinfernbus.de) links Nuremberg with countless destinations in Germany and beyond. Special Deutsche Bahn express coaches to Prague (€54, 3½ hours, nine daily) leave from outside the Hauptbahnhof.

TRAIN

Rail connections from Nuremberg:

➡ **Berlin** €100, five hours, at least hourly

➡ **Frankfurt** €55, 2½ hours, at least hourly

➡ **Hamburg** €130, 4½ hours, nine daily

➡ **Munich** €36 to €55, one hour, twice hourly

➡ **Vienna** €103, five hours, every two hours

ⓘ Getting Around

TO/FROM THE AIRPORT

U-Bahn 2 runs every few minutes from the Hauptbahnhof to the airport (€2.40, 13 minutes). A taxi to the airport will cost about €16.

ⓘ NÜRNBERG + FÜRTH CARD

Available to those staying overnight in the two cities, the Nürnberg + Fürth Card (€25) is good for two days of public transport and admission to all museums and attractions in both cities. It can only be purchased from tourist offices or online from Nuremberg's official tourism website.

BICYCLE

Nuremberg has ample bike lanes along busy roads and the Altstadt is pretty bike friendly. For bike hire, try the excellent **Ride on a Rainbow** (☏ 0911-397 337; www.ride-on-a-rainbow.de; Adam-Kraft-Strasse 55; per day from €9).

PUBLIC TRANSPORT

The best transport around the Altstadt is at the end of your legs. Timed tickets on the VGN bus, tram and U-Bahn/S-Bahn networks cost from €1.80. A day pass costs €5.40. Passes bought on Saturday are valid all weekend.

Bamberg

☏ 0951 / POP 71,200

A disarmingly beautiful architectural masterpiece with an almost complete absence of modern eyesores, Bamberg's entire Altstadt is a Unesco World Heritage Site and one of Bavaria's unmissables. Generally regarded as one of Germany's most attractive settlements, the town is bisected by rivers and canals and was built by archbishops on seven hills, earning it the inevitable sobriquet of 'Franconian Rome'. Students inject some liveliness into its streets, pavement cafes, pubs and no fewer than 10 breweries cooking up Bamberg's famous smoked beer, but it's usually wide-eyed tourists who can be seen filing through its narrow medieval streets. The town can be tackled as a day trip from Nuremberg, but, to really do it justice and to experience the romantically lit streets once most visitors have left, consider an overnight stay.

⊙ Sights

Bamberger Dom   CATHEDRAL

(www.erzbistum-bamberg.de; Domplatz; ⊙ 8am-6pm Apr-Oct, to 5pm Nov-Mar) FREE Beneath the quartet of spires, Bamberg's cathedral is packed with artistic treasures, most famously the life-size equestrian statue of the **Bamberger Reiter** (Bamberg Horseman), whose true identity remains a mystery. It overlooks the **tomb of cathedral founders**, Emperor Heinrich II and his wife Kunigunde, splendidly carved by Tilmann Riemenschneider. The **marble tomb of Clemens II** in the west choir is the only papal burial site north of the Alps. Nearby, the **Virgin Mary altar** by Veit Stoss also warrants closer inspection.

Founded by Heinrich II in 1004, the cathedral's current appearance dates to the early 13th century and is the outcome of a Romanesque-Gothic duel between church architects after the original and its immediate successor burnt down in the 12th century. The pillars have the original light hues of Franconian sandstone thanks to Ludwig I, who eradicated all postmedieval decoration in the early 19th century.

Altes Rathaus   HISTORIC BUILDING
(Old Town Hall; Obere Brücke; adult/concession €4.50/4; ⊙ 9.30am-4.30pm Tue-Sun) Like a ship in dry dock, Bamberg's 1462 Old Town Hall was built on an artifical island in the Regnitz River, allegedly because the local bishop had refused to give the town's citizens any land for its construction. Inside is a collection of precious porcelain, but even more enchanting are the richly detailed frescos adorning its facades – note the cherub's leg cheekily sticking out from the east facade.

Historisches Museum   MUSEUM
(📝 0951-519 0746; www.museum.bamberg.de; Domplatz 7; adult/concession €5/4.50; ⊙ 9am-5pm Tue-Sun May-Oct, occasionally open in winter for special exhibitions) Bamberg's main museum fills the Alte Hofhaltung (old court hall), a former prince-bishops' palace near the cathedral, with a mixed bag of exhibits. These include a model of the pilgrimage church Vierzehnheiligen and the Bamberger Götzen, ancient stone sculptures found in the region. Often of greater interest are the expertly curated special exhibitions, which examine aspects of the region's past in more detail.

Neue Residenz   PALACE
(New Residence; 📝 0951-519 390; Domplatz 8; adult/concession €4.50/3.50; ⊙ 9am-6pm Apr-Sep, 10am-4pm Oct-Mar) This splendid episcopal palace gives you an eyeful of the lavish lifestyle of Bamberg's prince-bishops who, between 1703 and 1802, occupied its 40-odd rooms that can only be seen on guided 45-minute tours (in German). Tickets are also good for the Bavarian State Gallery, with works by Lucas Cranach the Elder and other old masters. The baroque Rose Garden delivers fabulous views over Bamberg's sea of red-tiled roofs.

Fränkisches Brauereimuseum   MUSEUM
(📝 0951-530 16; www.brauereimuseum.de; Michaelsberg 10f; adult/concession €3.50/3; ⊙ 1-5pm Wed-Fri, 11am-5pm Sat & Sun Apr-Oct) Located in the Kloster St Michael, this comprehensive brewery museum exhibits over a thousand period mashing, boiling and bottling implements, as well as everything to do with local suds, such as beer mats, tankards, enamel

beer signs and lots of photos and documentation. If the displays have left you dry mouthed, quench your thirst in the small pub.

Kloster St Michael   MONASTERY
(Franziskanergasse 2; ⊙ 9am-6pm Apr-Oct) Above Domplatz, at the top of Michaelsberg, is the Benedictine Kloster St Michael, a former monastery and now an aged people's home. The monastery church is essential Bamberg viewing, both for its baroque art and the meticulous depictions of nearly 600 medicinal plants and flowers on the vaulted ceiling. The manicured garden terrace boasts a splendid city panorama.

🗘 Tours

BierSchmecker Tour   WALKING TOUR
(www.bier.bamberg.info; adult €22) Possibly the most tempting tour of the amazingly varied offerings at the tourist office is the self-guided BierSchmecker Tour. The price includes entry to the Fränkisches Brauereimuseum (depending on the route taken), plus five beer vouchers valid in five pubs and breweries, an English information booklet, a route map and a souvenir stein.

🛏 Sleeping

Backpackers Bamberg   HOSTEL €
(📝 0951-222 1718; www.backpackersbamberg. de; Heiliggrabstrasse 4; dm €17-20, s/d €29/44; 🛜) Bamberg's backpacker hostel is a funky but well-kept affair, with clean dorms, a fully functional kitchen and a quiet, family-friendly atmosphere. Make sure you let staff know when you're arriving, as it's left unmanned for most of the day.

Located 400m north along Luitpoldstrasse from the Luitpoldbrücke.

Alt Bamberg   HOTEL €
(📝 0951-986 150; www.hotel-alt-bamberg. de; Habergasse 11; s/d from €45/65) Often heavily discounted on popular booking websites, the no-frills rooms at this well-located, old-school hotel are digs of choice for euro-watching nomads. Some rooms share showers, the breakfast is free and there's a well-respected Greek restaurant downstairs.

Campingplatz Insel   CAMPGROUND €
(📝 0951-563 20; www.campinginsel.de; Am Campingplatz 1; tents €4-8, adult/car €6/4) If rustling nylon is your abode of choice, this well-equipped site, in a tranquil spot right on the

river, is the sole camping option. Take bus 918 to Campingplatz.

Hotel Sankt Nepomuk
HOTEL €€
(☑0951-984 20; www.hotel-nepomuk.de; Obere Mühlbrücke 9; s/d from €90/130; ℗⊜) Aptly named after the patron saint of bridges, this is a classy establishment in a half-timbered former mill right on the Regnitz. It has a superb restaurant (mains €15 to €30) with a terrace and 24 new-fangled rooms of recent vintage. Breakfast is an extra €5.

Barockhotel am Dom
HOTEL €€
(☑0951-540 31; www.barockhotel.de; Vorderer Bach 4; s/d from €84/99; ℗⊜) The sugary facade, a sceptre's swipe from the Dom, gives a hint of the baroque heritage and original details within. The 19 rooms have sweeping views of the Dom or the roofs of the Altstadt, and breakfast is served in a 14th-century vault.

Hotel Residenzschloss
HOTEL €€
(☑0951-609 10; www.residenzschloss.com; Untere Sandstrasse 32; r from €92; ℗⊜) Bamberg's grandest digs occupy a palatial building formerly used as a hospital. But have no fear, as the swanky furnishings – from the Roman-style steam bath to the flashy piano bar – have little in common with institutional care. High-ceilinged rooms are business standard though display little historical charm. Take bus 916 from the ZOB.

✕ Eating & Drinking

Zum Sternla
FRANCONIAN €
(☑0951-287 50; Lange Strasse 46; mains €5-10; ⊙11am-11pm Tue-Sun) Bamberg's oldest *Wirtshaus* (inn; established 1380) bangs down bargain-priced staples including pork dishes, steaks, dumplings and sauerkraut, as well as specials, but it's a great, nontouristy place for a traditional *Brotzeit* (snack), or just a pretzel and a beer. The menu is helpfully translated from Franconian into German.

Klosterbräu
BREWERY €
(Obere Mühlbrücke 1-3; mains €7-12; ⊙11.30am-10pm Mon-Sat, to 9pm Sun) This beautiful half-timbered brewery is Bamberg's oldest. It draws *Stammgäste* (regulars) and tourists alike who wash down filling slabs of meat and dumplings with its excellent range of ales in the unpretentious dining room.

Messerschmidt
FRANCONIAN €€
(☑0951-297 800; Lange Strasse 41; mains €12-25; ⊙11am-10pm) This stylish gourmet eatery may be ensconced in the house where

aviation engineer Willy Messerschmidt was born, but there's nothing 'plane' about dining here. The place oozes old-world charm, with dark woods, white linens and traditionally formal service. Sharpen your molars on platters of roast duck and red cabbage out on the alfresco terrace overlooking a pretty park, or in the attached wine tavern.

Schlenkerla
GERMAN €€
(☑0951-560 60; www.schlenkerla.de; Dominikanerstrasse 6; mains €6.50-13; ⊙9.30am-11.30pm) Beneath wooden beams as dark as the superb *Rauchbier* poured straight from oak barrels, locals and visitors dig into scrumptious Franconian fare at this legendary flower-festooned tavern near the cathedral.

Kornblume
ORGANIC €€
(☑0951-917 1760; www.kornblume-bamberg.de; Kapellenstrasse 22; mains €7-22; ⊙5.30pm-midnight Wed-Mon, plus 11.30am-2pm Sun) Don't be deterred by the somewhat style-absent decor at this family-run place 1.5km east of the centre, as the tasty food is lovingly prepared and strict organic and ecofriendly principles impeccably upheld. The menu reads like a vegetarian's antioxidant bible, though the occasional meat dish also makes an appearance. Take bus 905 to Wunderburg.

Spezial-Keller
GERMAN €€
(☑0951-548 87; www.spezial-keller.de; Sternwartstrasse 8; dishes €6-13; ⊙3pm-late Tue-Fri, from noon Sat, from 10am Sun) The walk into the hills past the cathedral to this delightful beer garden is well worth it, both for the malty *Rauchbier* and the sweeping views of the Altstadt. In winter the action moves into the cosy tavern warmed by a traditional wood-burning tiled stove.

Ambräusianum
PUB FOOD €€
(☑0951-509 0262; Dominikanerstrasse 10; mains €10-14; ⊙11am-11pm Tue-Sat, 11am-9pm Sun) Bamberg's only brewpub does a killer *Weisswurst* breakfast – parsley-speckled veal sausage served with a big freshly baked pretzel and a *Weissbier* (wheat beer) – as well as schnitzel, pork knuckle and *Flammkuchen* (Alsatian pizza) that'll have you waddling out the door like a Christmas goose.

Torschuster
BAR
(Obere Karolinenstrasse 10; ⊙from 6pm Tue-Sun) Beers from all of Bamberg's breweries, a good selection of whisky, old enamel ad-

Bamberg

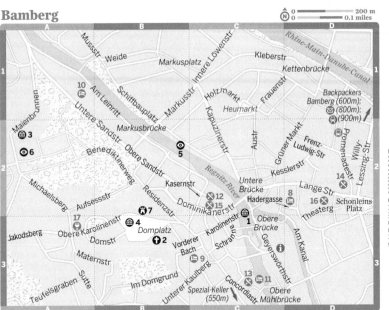

Bamberg

vertising signs and in particular owner Thomas' eclectic vinyl collection make up one of Bamberg's best nights out and an after-dark antedote to medieval tavern life. Thomas' collection doesn't go much past the mid-eighties – make of that what you will.

❶ Information

Post Office (Ludwigstrasse 25)

Tourist Office (✆ 0951-297 6200; www.bamberg.info; Geyerswörthstrasse 5; ◎ 9.30am-6pm Mon-Fri, to 4pm Sat, to 2.30pm Sun) Staff sell the Bambergcard (€12), valid for three days of free bus rides and free museum entry.

❶ Getting There & Around

BUS
Several buses, including 901, 902 and 931, connect the train station with the central bus station (ZOB). Bus 910 goes from the ZOB to Domplatz.

TRAIN
Bamberg has the following rail connections:
➡ **Berlin** €90, 4¼ hours, every two hours
➡ **Munich** €63, two hours, every two hours
➡ **Nuremberg** €21, 40 to 60 minutes, four hourly
➡ **Würzburg** €20.70, one hour, twice hourly

Bayreuth

📞 0921 / POP 71,600

Even without its Wagner connections, Bayreuth would still be an interesting detour from Nuremberg or Bamberg for its streets of baroque architecture and impressive palaces. But it's for the annual Wagner Festival that 60,000 opera devotees make a pilgrimage to this neck of the *Wald*.

Bayreuth's glory days began in 1735 when Wilhelmine, sister of King Frederick the Great of Prussia, was forced to marry stuffy Margrave Friedrich. Bored with the local scene, the cultured Anglo-oriented Wilhelmine invited the finest artists, poets, composers and architects in Europe to court. The period bequeathed some eye-catching buildings, still on display for all to see.

⊙ Sights

Outside of the Wagner Festival from late July to the end of August, most of Bayreuth slips into provincial slumber, although the town's strong musical traditions ensure there are good dramatic and orchestral performances all year.

Markgräfliches Opernhaus   THEATRE
(Opernstrasse 14; adult/concession €2.50/2; ⊙9am-6pm Apr-Sep, 10am-4pm Oct-Mar) Designed by Giuseppe Galli Bibiena, a famous 18th-century architect from Bologna, Bayreuth's opera house is one of Europe's most stunningly ornate baroque theatres. Germany's largest opera house until 1871, it has a lavish interior smothered in carved, gilded and marbled wood. However, Richard Wagner considered it too modest for his serious work and conducted here just once. The city has decided it's time this old dame had a facelift and until 2017 most of the building will be closed.

Neues Schloss   PALACE
(📞0921-759 690; Ludwigstrasse 21; adult/concession €5.50/4.50; ⊙9am-6pm daily Apr-Sep, 10am-4pm Tue-Sun Oct-Mar) Opening into the vast Hofgarten, the Neues Schloss lies a short distance south of the main shopping street, Maxmilianstrasse. A riot of rococo style, the margrave's residence after 1753 features a vast collection of 18th-century Bayreuth porcelain. The annual VIP opening of the Wagner Festival is held in the Cedar Room. Also worth a look is the **Spiegelscherben-kabinett** (Broken Mirror Cabinet), which is lined with irregular shards of broken mirror – supposedly Margravine Wilhelmine's response to the vanity of her era.

Richard Wagner Museum   MUSEUM
(Haus Wahnfried; www.wagnermuseum.de; Richard-Wagner-Strasse 48; admission €8; ⊙10am-6pm daily Jul & Aug, closed Mon rest of year) In the early 1870s King Ludwig II, Wagner's most devoted fan, gave the great composer the cash to build Haus Wahnfried, a mini-mansion on the northern edge of the Hofgarten. The building now houses the Richard Wagner Museum, which for three years was closed for complete renovation. It reopened in 2015.

At the back of the house is the unmarked, ivy-covered tomb containing Wagner and his wife Cosima. The sandstone grave of his loving canine companion Russ stands nearby.

Festspielhaus   THEATRE
(📞0921-787 80; Festspielhügel 1-2; adult/concession €7/5; ⊙tours 10am & 2pm daily Dec-Apr, 10am, 11am, 2pm & 3pm May, Sep & Oct, 2pm Sat Nov, closed Jun-Aug) North of the Hauptbahnhof, the main venue for Bayreuth's annual Wagner Festival is the Festspielhaus, constructed in 1872 with King Ludwig II's backing. The structure was specially designed to accommodate Wagner's massive theatrical sets, with three storeys of mechanical works hidden below stage. It's still one of the largest opera venues in the world. To see inside you must join a guided tour. Take bus 305 to Am Festspielhaus.

Eremitage   PARK
Around 6km east of the centre lies the Eremitage, a lush park girding the **Altes Schloss** (📞0921-759 6937; adult/concession €4.50/3.50; ⊙9am-6pm Apr-Sep), the summer residence that belonged to 18th-century Margrave Friedrich and his wife Wilhelmine. Visits to the palace are by guided tour only and take in the Chinese Mirror room where Countess Wilhelmine penned her memoirs.

Also in the park is horseshoe-shaped Neues Schloss (not to be confused with the one in town), which centres on the amazing mosaic Sun Temple with gilded Apollo sculpture. Take bus 302 from ZOH.

Maisel's Brauerei- &
Büttnerei-Museum   BREWERY, MUSEUM
(📞0921-401 234; www.maisel.com/museum; Kulmbacher Strasse 40; tours adult/concession €5/3; ⊙tours 2pm daily) For a fascinating look at the brewing process, head to this enormous museum next door to the brewery of one of Ger-

many's top wheat-beer producers – Maisel. The 90-minute guided tour takes you into the bowels of the 19th-century plant, with atmospheric rooms filled with 4500 beer mugs and amusing artefacts. Visits conclude with a glass of sweet-cloudy *Weissbier*.

🛏 Sleeping

Don't even think of attempting a sleepover in Bayreuth during the Wagner Festival, as rooms are booked out months in advance and rates are doubled and even tripled.

Goldener Löwe　　　　　　　HOTEL €
(✆0921-746 06; www.goldener-loewe.de; Kulmbacher Strasse 30; s €35-56.50, d €73-92; P ➊ 🕾) Outside the summer months (rates increase considerably mid-July to end of August) this is a great little deal within easy walking distance of the sights. Rooms are tiny but impeccably kept, the Michelin-reviewed restaurant downstairs is tempting and there's free parking. The owners seem to have a bit of a jam fetish, every guest receiving a free jar.

DJH Hostel　　　　　　　HOSTEL €
(✆0921-764 380; www.bayreuth.jugendherberge. de; Universitätsstrasse 28; dm from €20.40) This excellent 140-bed hostel near the university has comfortable, fresh rooms, a relaxed atmosphere and heaps of guest facilities.

Hotel Goldener Hirsch　　　HOTEL €€
(✆0921-1504 4000; www.bayreuth-goldener-hirsch. de; Bahnhofstrasse 13; s €68-85, d €85-110; P ➊ @ 🕾) Just across from the train station, the 'Golden Reindeer' looks a bit stuffy from the outside, but once indoors you'll discover crisp, well-maintained rooms with contemporary furniture and unscuffed, whitewashed walls. Some of the 40 rooms have baths. Parking is free.

Hotel Goldener Anker　　　HOTEL €€€
(✆0921-787 7740; www.anker-bayreuth.de; Opernstrasse 6; s €98-138, d €168-235; P ➊ 🕾) Bayreuth's top address just a few metres from the opera house oozes refined elegance, with many of the rooms decorated in heavy traditional style with swag curtains, dark woods and antique touches. There's a swanky restaurant at ground level, the service is impeccable and there is fresh fruit waiting for you on arrival.

🍴 Eating & Drinking

Kraftraum　　　　　　　CAFE €
(Sophienstrasse 16; mains €5.50-9; ⊙8am-1am Mon-Fri, from 9am Sat & Sun; 🖉) This vegetari-

KLEIN VENEDIG

A row of diminutive, half-timbered cottages once inhabited by fishermen and their families comprises Bamberg's **Klein Venedig** (Little Venice), which clasps the Regnitz's east bank between Markusbrücke and Untere Brücke. The little homes balance on poles set right into the water and are fronted by tiny gardens and terraces (wholly unlike Venice, but who cares).

Klein Venedig is well worth a stroll but looks at least as pretty from a distance, especially in summer when red geraniums spill from flower boxes. Good vantage points include the Untere Brücke near the Altes Rathaus, and Am Leinritt.

an eatery has plenty to tempt even the most committed meat eaters, including pastas, jacket potatoes, soups and huge salads. The retroish, shabby-chic interior empties on sunny days when everyone plumps for the alfresco seating out on the cobbles. Tempting weekend brunches (€13.50) always attract a large crowd.

Rosa Rosa　　　　　　　BISTRO €
(✆0921-685 02; Von-Römer-Strasse 2; mains €4-8; ⊙5pm-1am Mon-Fri, from 11am Sat, from 4pm Sun; 🖉) Join Bayreuth's chilled crowd at this bistro-cum-pub for belly-filling portions of salad, pasta and vegie fare, as well as seasonal dishes from the big specials board, or just a Frankenwälder beer in the evening. The poster-lined walls keep you up to date on the latest acts to hit town.

Hansl's Wood Oven Pizzeria　　PIZZA €
(Friedrichstrasse 15; pizzas €4.60-9.10; ⊙10am-10.30pm) The best pizza in town is found at this tiny place tucked away in a corner of the square near the Stadthalle. There's next to no chance of a seat at mealtimes, so grab a takeaway. No debit/credit card payments.

Oskar　　　　FRANCONIAN, BAVARIAN €€
(Maximilianstrasse 33; mains €7-15; ⊙8am-1am Mon-Sat, from 9am Sun) At the heart of the pedestrianised shopping boulevard, this multitasking, open-all-hours bar-cafe-restaurant is Bayreuth's busiest eatery. It's good for a busting Bavarian breakfast, a light lunch in the covered garden cafe, a full-on dinner feast in the dark-wood restaurant, or

a *Landbier* and a couple of tasty Bayreuth bratwursts anytime you feel like it.

Torten Schmiede CAFE
(Ludwigstrasse 10; ⊙12.30-6pm Tue-Fri, 10am-6pm Sat) Bayreuth has lots of cafes, but with its car-boot sale of retro furniture, home-made cakes and 'street art' on the walls, this tiny halt is something that's a bit different. Enjoy your shot of caffeine and cake on a 1960s living room chair, or streetside on a mini chaise longue.

❶ Information

The **Bayreuth Card** (72hr €12.90) is good for unlimited trips on city buses, entry to eight museums and a two-hour guided city walk (in German). The card covers one adult and up to two children under 15.

Post Office (Hauptbahnhof)

Tourist Office (✆0921-885 88; www.bayreuth-tourismus.de; Opernstrasse 22; ⊙9am-7pm Mon-Fri, 9am-4pm Sat all year, plus 10am-2pm Sun May-Oct) Has a train ticket booking desk and a worthwhile gift shop.

❶ Getting There & Away

Most rail journeys between Bayreuth and other towns in Bavaria require a change in Nuremberg.

➡ **Munich** Change in Nuremberg; €23 to €69, 2½ hours, hourly

➡ **Nuremberg** €21, one hour, at least hourly

➡ **Regensburg** Change in Nuremberg; €36, 2¼ hours, at least hourly

Coburg

✆09561 / POP 41,000

If marriage is diplomacy by another means, Coburg's rulers were surely masters of the art. Over four centuries, the princes and princesses of the house of Saxe-Coburg intrigued, romanced and ultimately wed themselves into the dynasties of Belgium, Bulgaria, Denmark, Portugal, Russia, Sweden and, most prominently, Great Britain. The crowning achievement came in 1857, when Albert of Saxe-Coburg-Gotha took his vows with first cousin Queen Victoria, founding the present British royal family. The British royals quietly adopted the less-German name of Windsor during WWI.

Coburg languished in the shadow of the Iron Curtain during the Cold War, all but closed in by East Germany on three sides, but since reunification the town has undergone a revival. Its proud Veste is one of Germany's finest medieval fortresses. What's

more, some sources contend that the original hot dog was invented here.

⊙ Sights & Activities

Veste Coburg FORTRESS, MUSEUM
(www.kunstsammlungen-coburg.de; adult/concession €6/3; ⊙9.30am-5pm daily Apr-Oct, 1-4pm Tue-Sun Nov-Mar) Towering above Coburg's centre is a story-book medieval fortress, the Veste Coburg. With its triple ring of fortified walls, it's one of the most impressive fortresses in Germany though it attracts few foreign visitors. It houses the vast collection of the **Kunstsammlungen**, with works by star painters such as Rembrandt, Dürer and Cranach the Elder. The elaborate Jagdintarsien-Zimmer (Hunting Marquetry Room) is a superlative example of carved woodwork.

Protestant reformer Martin Luther, hoping to escape an imperial ban, sought refuge at the fortress in 1530. His former quarters have a writing desk and, in keeping with the Reformation, a rather plain bed.

Marktplatz SQUARE
Coburg's epicentre is the magnificent Markt, a beautifully renovated square radiating a colourful, aristocratic charm. The fabulous Renaissance facades and ornate oriels of the **Stadthaus** (town house) and the **Rathaus** vie for attention, while a greening bronze of **Prince Albert**, looking rather more flamboyant and Teutonic medieval than the Brits are used to seeing Queen Victoria's husband, calmly surveys the scene.

Schloss Ehrenburg CASTLE
(✆09561-808 832; www.sgvcoburg.de; Schlossplatz; adult/concession €4.50/3.50; ⊙tours hourly 9am-5pm Tue-Sun Apr-Sep, 10am-4pm Tue-Sun Oct-Mar) The lavish Schloss Ehrenburg was once the town residence of the Coburg dukes. Prince Albert spent his childhood in this sumptuous, tapestry-lined palace, and his wife Queen Victoria stayed in a room with Germany's first flushing toilet (1860). The splendid **Riesensaal** (Hall of Giants) has a baroque ceiling supported by 28 statues of Atlas.

Coburger Puppenmuseum MUSEUM
(www.coburger-puppenmuseum.de; Rückerstrasse 2-3; adult/child €4/2; ⊙11am-4pm daily Apr-Oct, closed Mon Nov-Mar) Spanning 33 rooms, this delightfully old-fashioned museum displays a collection of 2000 dolls, dollhouses, miniature kitchens and chinaware, some from as far away as England and all dating from between

1800 and 1956. Aptly named 'Hallo Dolly', the stylish cafe next door is ideally situated for restoring calm after all those eerie glass eyes.

★彡 Festivals & Events

Samba Festival
MUSIC

(www.samba-festival.de) Believe it or not, Coburg hosts Europe's largest Samba Festival every year in mid-July, an incongruous venue if ever there was one. This orgy of song and dance attracts almost 100 bands and up to 200,000 scantily clad, bum-wiggling visitors, many from the Portuguese-speaking world.

🛏 Sleeping & Eating

The best place to experience Coburg's famous 30cm-long sausages grilled over pine-cone embers are the stands on Marktplatz.

Hotelpension Bärenturm
GUESTHOUSE €€

(☑09561-318 401; www.baerenturm-hotelpension. de; Untere Anlage 2; s €85, d €110-130; P 🛜) For those who prefer their complimentary pillow pack of gummy bears served with a touch of history, Coburg's most characterful digs started life as a defensive tower that was expanded in the early 19th century to house Prince Albert's private tutor. Each of the 15 rooms is a gem boasting squeaky parquet floors, antique-style furniture and regally high ceilings.

The Square
HOTEL €€

(☑09561-705 8520; www.hotelthesquare.com; Ketschengasse 1; s €69, d €79; P 🏧 @ 🛜) Right on the Marktplatz, what The Square lacks in character it more than makes up for in space and facilities. Each room has a kitchen, or corridor access to one, some have baths and the three large apartments cost the same as a double. You can also choose your view – the Prince Albert bronze out front or the pretty Stadtkirche out back.

Café Prinz Albert
CAFE €

(Ketschengasse 27; snacks & cakes €2-5; ⏱ 7.30am-6pm Mon-Fri, from 8am Sat) With a British royal theme throughout, this long-established cafe on newly renovated Albertsplatz is a good snack halt mid-sightseeing. The breakfast menu has a historical theme – the 'Martin Luther' (€2.90) is a sober, modest affair compared to the more lavish 'Prinz Albert' (€5.40).

Ratskeller
FRANCONIAN €

(Markt 1; mains €6-16.50; ⏱ 10am-midnight) Munch on regional dishes from Thuringia and Franconia while kicking back on well-padded leather benches under the heftily vaulted ceiling of Coburg's spectacular town hall.

Tie
VEGETARIAN €€€

(Leopoldstrasse 14; mains €9-19; ⏱ from 5pm Tue-Sun; 🍴) A five-minute walk east of the Marktplatz, this vegetarian restaurant serves up heavenly (if pricey) food crafted from fresh organic ingredients. Dishes range from vegetarian classics to Asian inspirations, with the odd fish or meat dish for the unconverted. Seasonally laid tables add colour to the simple decor.

ℹ Information

Tourist Office (☑09561-898 000; www. coburg-tourist.de; Herrngasse 4; ⏱ 9am-5pm Mon-Fri, 10am-2pm Sat & Sun) Helpful office where staff sell the CObook (€14.90), a five-day ticket good for 13 sights in Coburg and around as well as local public transport. English audioguides (€3.50) to the city are also available here.

ℹ Getting There & Away

Coburg has the following rail connections:
➡ **Bamberg** €12.10, one hour, hourly
➡ **Bayreuth** €17.90, 1½ hours, hourly
➡ **Nuremberg** €23.50, 1¾ hours, hourly

ℹ Getting Around

Veste-Express (one-way/return €3.50/4.50; ⏱ 10am-5pm Apr-Oct) This tourist train leaves the tourist office every 30 minutes for the Veste Coburg. Otherwise it's a steep, 3km climb.

Altmühltal Nature Park

The Altmühltal Nature Park is one of Germany's largest nature parks and covers some of Bavaria's most eye-pleasing terrain. The Altmühl River gently meanders through a region of little valleys and hills before joining the Rhine-Main Canal and eventually emptying into the Danube. Outdoor fun on well-marked hiking and biking trails is the main reason to head here, but the river is also ideal for canoeing. There's basic camping in designated spots along the river, and plenty of accommodation in the local area.

The park takes in 2900 sq km of land southwest of Regensburg, south of Nuremberg, east of Treuchtlingen and north of Eichstätt. The eastern boundaries of the park include the town of Kelheim.

MANIN RICHARD / GETTY IMAGES ©

1. Schloss Linderhof (p95) **2.** Würzburg Residenz (p110)
3. Schloss Neuschwanstein (p92)

Romantic Residences

Think Southern Germany and the Alps, think story-book castles and noble palaces, hilltop ruins and Renaissance splendour – few places on earth boast such a treasure trove of medieval and aristocratic architecture and visiting these stately piles is a key part of any visit to the region.

Neuschwanstein

One of the world's most romantic castles, King Ludwig II's 19th-century folly inspired Walt Disney's citadel as well as millions of tourists to visit this corner of the Alps. All turrets and pointed towers rising dreamily from the alpine forests, if Bavaria has a single unmissable sight, this is it.

Würzburg Residenz

Würzburg's Unesco-listed palace is one of the country's most exquisite chunks of aristocratic baroque, built by a stellar name of the period, Balthasar Neumann. The highlight of the huge building is without doubt the Grand Staircase whose ceiling boasts the world's largest fresco.

Schloss Linderhof

Another of Ludwig II's wistful follies, this lavish though compact palace was the only one of his creations he saw finished. The remote location in the foothills of the Alps only heightens the effect of the eye-pleasing symmetry of the outside and the quirkiness of the interior.

Kaiserburg

One of Bavaria's most historically significant fortresses, Nuremberg's Kaiserburg lords it over the old town of the state's second city. A tour takes you back to medieval times when Nuremberg was one of the key cities in the Holy Roman Empire, the castle used as a safe box for the empire's trinkets.

WALTER BIBIKOW / GETTY IMAGES ©

3

North of the river, activities focus around the towns of Kipfenberg, Beilngries and Riedenburg.

🏃 Activities

Canoeing & Kayaking

The most beautiful section of the river is from Treuchtlingen or Pappenheim to Eichstätt or Kipfenberg, about a 60km stretch that you can do lazily in a kayak or canoe in two to three days. There are lots of little dams along the way, as well as some small rapids about 10km northwest of Dollnstein, so make sure you are up for little bits of portaging. Signs warn of impending doom, but locals say that, if you heed the warning to stay to the right, you'll be safe.

You can rent canoes and kayaks in just about every town along the river. Expect to pay about €15/25 per day for a one-/two-person boat, more for bigger ones. Staff will sometimes haul you and the boats to or from your embarkation point for a small charge.

You can get a full list of boat-hire outlets from the Informationszentrum Naturpark Altmühltal (p149).

San-Aktiv Tours CANOEING
(☑ 09831-4936; www.san-aktiv-tours.com; Otto-Dietrich-Strasse 3, Gunzenhausen) San-Aktiv Tours is the largest and best-organised of the canoe-hire companies in the park, with a network of vehicles to shuttle canoes, bicycles and people around the area. Trips through the park run from April to October, and you can canoe alone or join a group. Packages generally include the canoe, swim vests, maps, instructions and transfer back to the embarkation point.

Cycling & Hiking

With around 3000km of hiking trails and 800km of cycle trails criss-crossing the landscape, foot and pedal are the best ways to strike out into the park. Cycling trails are clearly labelled and have long rectangular brown signs bearing a bike symbol. The hiking-trail markers are yellow. The most popular cycling route is the Altmühltal Radweg, which runs parallel to the river for 166km. The Altmühltal-Panoramaweg stretching 200km between Gunzenhausen and Kelheim is a picturesque hiking route, which crosses the entire park from west to east.

You can rent bikes in almost every town within the park, and prices are more or less uniform. Most bike-hire agencies will also store bicycles. Ask for a list of bike-hire outlets at the Informationszentrum Naturpark Altmühltal.

Located in Eichstätt, **Kanuuh** (☑ 08421-2110; www.kanuuh.de; Herzoggasse 3; €12/day) will bring the bikes to you, or take you and the bikes to anywhere in Altmühltal Nature Park for an extra fee.

Rock Climbing

The worn cliffs along the Altmühl River offer some appealing terrain for climbers of all skill levels. The medium-grade 45m-high rock face of Burgsteinfelsen, located between the towns of Dollnstein and Breitenfurt, has routes from the fourth to eighth climbing levels, with stunning views of the valley. The Dohlenfelsen face near the town of Wellheim has a simpler expanse that's more suitable for children. The Informationszentrum Naturpark Altmühltal can provide more details on the region's climbing options.

WAGNER FESTIVAL

The **Wagner Festival** (www.bayreuther-festspiele.de) has been a summer fixture in Bayreuth for over 140 years and is generally regarded as the top Wagner event anywhere in the world. The festival lasts for 30 days (from late July to late August), with each performance attended by an audience of just over 1900. Demand is insane, with an estimated 500,000 fans vying for less than 60,000 tickets.

Until a few years ago all tickets were allocated in a shady lottery with preference given to 'patrons' and 'Wagner enthusiasts'. Ordinary, unconnected fans sometimes had to wait five to 10 years before 'winning' a seat. However, in a bid to introduce a bit more transparency into proceedings, the festival organisers recently decided to release the vast majority of tickets onto the open market in an online free-for-all. Every ticket is snapped up in seconds, a fact that has angered many a Wagner society. Alternatively, it is still possible to lay siege to the box office two and a half hours before performances begin in the hope of snapping up cheap returned tickets, but there's no guarantee you'll get in.

RICHARD WAGNER

With the backing of King Ludwig II, Richard Wagner (1813–83), the gifted, Leipzig-born composer and notoriously poor manager of money, turned Bayreuth into a mecca of opera and high-minded excess. Bayreuth profited from its luck and, it seems, is ever grateful.

For Wagner, listening to opera was meant to be work and he tested his listeners wherever possible. *Götterdämmerung, Parsifal, Tannhäuser* and *Tristan & Isolde* are grandiose pieces that will jolt any audience geared for light entertainment. Four days of *The Ring of the Nibelung* are good for limbering up.

After poring over Passau and a few other German cities, Wagner designed his own festival hall in Bayreuth. The unique acoustics are bounced up from a below-stage orchestra via reflecting boards onto the stage and into the house. The design took the body density of a packed house into account, still a remarkable achievement today.

Wagner was also a notorious womaniser, an infamous anti-Semite and a hardliner towards 'non-Europeans'. So extreme were these views that even Friedrich Nietzsche called Wagner's works 'inherently reactionary, and inhumane'. Wagner's works, and by extension Wagner himself, were embraced as a symbol of Aryan might by the Nazis and, even today, there is great debate among music lovers about the 'correctness' of supporting Wagner's music and the Wagner Festival in Bayreuth.

ℹ Information

The park's main information centre is in Eichstätt, a charmingly historic town at the southern end of the park that makes an excellent base for exploring.

Informationszentrum Naturpark Altmühltal (☑ 08421-987 60; www.naturpark-altmuehltal. de; Notre Dame 1; ⊙ 9am-5pm Mon-Sat, 10am-5pm Sun Apr-Oct, 8am-noon & 2-4pm Mon-Thu, 8am-noon Fri Nov-Mar) Has information on, and help with planning an itinerary around, Altmühltal Nature Park. The website has tonnes of information on every aspect of the park, including activities and accommodation.

ℹ Getting There & Around

There are bus and train connections between Eichstätt and all the major milestones along the river including, from west to east, Gunzenhausen, Treuchtlingen and Pappenheim.

BUS

From mid-April to October the FreizeitBus Altmühltal-Donautal takes passengers and their bikes around the park. Buses normally run three times a day. Route 1 runs from Regensburg and Kelheim to Riedenburg on weekends and holidays only. Route 2 travels between Eichstätt, Beilngries, Dietfurt and Riedenburg, with all-day service on weekends and holidays and restricted service on weekdays. All-day tickets, which cost €10.50 for passengers with bicycles and €7.50 for those without (or €23.50/17.50 per family with/without bicycles) are bought from the driver.

TRAIN

Hourly trains run between Eichstätt Bahnhof and Treuchtlingen (€6.10, 25 minutes), and between Treuchtlingen and Gunzenhausen (€4.50, 15 minutes). RE trains from Munich that run through Eichstätt Bahnhof also stop in Dollnstein, Solnhofen and Pappenheim.

Eichstätt

☑ 08421 / POP 13,150

Hugging a tight bend in the Altmühl River, Eichstätt radiates a tranquil Mediterranean-style flair with cobbled streets meandering past elegantly Italianate buildings and leafy piazzas. Italian architects, notably Gabriel de Gabrieli and Maurizio Pedetti, rebuilt the town after Swedes razed the place during the Thirty Years' War (1618–48) and it came through WWII virtually without a graze. Since 1980 many of its baroque facades have played host to faculties belonging to Germany's sole Catholic university.

Eichstätt is pretty enough, but is really just a jumping-off and stocking-up point for flits into the wilds of Altmühltal Nature Park. You'll be chomping at the bit, eager to hit a trail or grab a paddle, if you stay more than a day.

⊙ Sights

Dom CHURCH
(www.bistum-eichstaett.de/dom; Domplatz; ⊙ 7.15am-7.30pm) Eichstätt's centre is dominated by the richly adorned Dom. Standout

features include an enormous 16th-century stained-glass window by Hans Holbein the Elder, and the carved sandstone Pappenheimer Altar (1489–97), depicting a pilgrimage from Pappenheim to Jerusalem. The seated statue is of St Willibald, the town's first bishop.

The adjoining **Domschatzmuseum** (Cathedral Treasury; ☑ 08421-507 42; Residenzplatz 7; adult/concession €3/1.50, Sun €1; ☺ 10.30am-5pm Wed-Fri, 10am-5pm Sat & Sun Apr-Nov) includes the robes of 8th-century English-born bishop St Willibald and baroque Gobelin tapestries.

Willibaldsburg   CASTLE
(☑ 08421-4730; Burgstrasse 19; adult/concession €4.50/3.50; ☺ 9am-6pm Tue-Sun Apr-Oct, 10am-4pm Tue-Sun Nov-Mar) The walk or drive up to the hilltop castle of Willibaldsburg (1355) is worth it for the views across the valley from the formally laid-out **Bastiongarten**; many locals also head up here on sunny days for the nearby beer garden. The castle itself houses two museums, the most interesting of which is the Jura-Museum, specialising in fossils and containing a locally found archaeopteryx (the oldest-known fossil bird), as well as aquariums with living specimens of the fossilised animals.

Kloster St Walburga   CONVENT
(www.abtei-st-walburg.de; Westenstrasse) The final resting place of St Willibald's sister, the Kloster St Walburga is a popular local pilgrimage destination. Every year between mid-October and late February, water oozes from Walburga's relics in the underground chapel and drips down into a catchment. The nuns bottle diluted versions of the so-called *Walburgaöl* (Walburga oil) and give it away to the faithful.

A staircase from the lower chapel leads to an off-limits upper chapel where you can catch a glimpse through the grill of beautiful ex-voto tablets and other trinkets left as a thank-you to the saint. The main St Walburga Church above has a glorious rococo interior.

Fürstbischöfliche Residenz   PALACE
(Residenzplatz; admission €1; ☺ Mon-Fri 7.30am-noon, 2-4pm Mon-Wed, 2-5.30pm Thu) The prince-bishops lived it up at the baroque Residenz, built between 1725 and 1736 by Gabriel de Gabrieli. Inside, the stunning main staircase and a hall of mirrors stick in the mind. In the square outside rises a late 18th-century golden statue of the Madonna atop a 19m-high column.

🛏 Sleeping & Eating

Fuchs   HOTEL €
(☑ 08421-6789; www.hotel-fuchs.de; Ostenstrasse 8; s €45-65, d €72-80; ☎) This central, family-run hotel, with under-floor heating in the bathrooms, adjoins a cake shop with a sunny dining area. It's convenient to a launch ramp on the river where you can put in, and you can lock your canoe or kayak in the garage.

DJH Hostel   HOSTEL €
(☑ 08421-980 410; www.eichstaett.jugendherberge.de; Reichenaustrasse 15; dm from €19.90; ☎) This comfy, 122-bed youth hostel provides pretty views of the Altstadt. As you might expect, the hostel is very bike- and canoe-friendly.

Municipal Camping Ground   CAMPGROUND €
(☑ 08421-908 147; www.eichstaett.info/wohnmobilstellplatz; Pirkheimerstrasse; per campsite €8) This basic camping ground is on the northern bank of the Altmühl River, about 1km southeast of the town centre. It's open year-round, but closes for 10 days during the Volksfest (a mini-Oktoberfest) in late August and early September.

Hotel Adler   HOTEL €€
(☑ 08421-6767; www.adler-eichstaett.de; Marktplatz 22; s €58-67, d €80-106; P ☎) A superb ambience reigns in this ornate 300-year-old building, Eichstätt's top digs. Sleeping quarters are bright and breezy and the generous breakfast buffet a proper set up for a day on the trail or river. Despite the posh feel, this hotel welcomes hiker and bikers.

Café im Paradeis   CAFE €€
(☑ 08421-3313; Marktplatz 9; mains €5-17; ☺ 8am-midnight) This open-all-hours spot on Markt is prime for people watching, wherever the hands of the clock may be. Recharge with a home-cooked meal or just a coffee, either in the olde-worlde antique-lined interior or out on the sunny terrace.

Trompete   BAVARIAN, ITALIAN €€
(www.braugasthof-trompete.de; Ostenstrasse 3; ☺ 7am-1am Mon-Fri, from 7.30am Sat & Sun) From breakfast to your last cocktail of the day, this friendly inn, just a short walk to the southeast of the centre, is a sure fire option at any time of day. The menu features some *echt*-Bavarian dishes such as *Ochsenbraten 'Altmühltaler Art'* (Altmühltaler roast beef) and *Krustenschäuferl* (roast pork with crispy skin) as well as Italian pizzas and pastas.

ℹ️ Information

Post Office (Domplatz 7)
Tourist Office (📞 08421-600 1400; www.eich-staett.de; Domplatz 8; ⏰ 9am-6pm Mon-Sat, 10am-1pm Sun Apr-Oct, 10am-noon & 2-4pm Mon-Thu, 10am-noon Fri Nov-Mar)

ℹ️ Getting There & Away

Eichstätt has two train stations. Mainline trains stop at the Bahnhof, 5km from the centre, from where coinciding diesel services shuttle to the Stadtbahnhof (town station). Trains run hourly between Ingolstadt and Eichstätt (€6.10, 25 minutes) and every two hours to Nuremberg (€19.80, 1½ hours).

REGENSBURG & THE DANUBE

The sparsely populated eastern reaches of Bavaria may live in the shadow of Bavaria's big-hitting attractions, but they hold many historical treasures to rival their neighbours. Top billing goes to Regensburg, a former capital, and one of Germany's prettiest and liveliest cities. From here the Danube gently winds its way to the Italianate city of Passau. Landshut was once the hereditary seat of the Wittelsbach family, and the region has also given the world a pope – Benedict XVI who was born in Marktl am Inn. Away from the towns, the Bavarian Forest broods in semi-undiscovered remoteness.

Eastern Bavaria was a seat of power in the Dark Ages, ruled by rich bishops at a time when Munich was but a modest trading post. A conquering Napoleon lumped Eastern Bavaria into river districts, and King Ludwig I sought to roll back these changes by recreating the boundaries of a glorified duchy from 1255. Though it brought a sense of renewed Bavarian identity, the area remained very much on the margins of things, giving rise to the odd and appealing mixture of ancient Roman cities, undulating farmland and rugged wilderness that it is today.

Regensburg

📞 0941 / POP 140,300

A Roman settlement completed under Emperor Marcus Aurelius, Regensburg was the first capital of Bavaria, the residence of dukes, kings and bishops, and for 600 years a Free Imperial City. Two millennia of history bequeathed the city some of the region's fin-est architectural heritage, a fact recognised by Unesco in 2006. Though big on the historical wow factor, today's Regensburg is a laid-back and unpretentious sort of place, and a good springboard into the wider region.

👁️ Sights

Schloss Thurn und Taxis CASTLE
(www.thurnundtaxis.de; Emmeramsplatz 5; tours adult/concession €13.50/11; ⏰ tours hourly 10.30am-4.30pm late Mar-early Nov, to 3.30pm Sat & Sun Nov-Mar) In the 15th century, Franz von Taxis (1459–1517) assured his place in history by setting up the first European postal system, which remained a monopoly until the 19th century. In recognition of his services, the family was given the former Benedictine monastery St Emmeram, henceforth known as Schloss Thurn und Taxis. It was soon one of the most modern palaces in Europe, and featured such luxuries as flushing toilets, central heating and electricity. Tours include the Basilika St Emmeram.

The palace complex also contains the Schatzkammer (Treasury). The jewellery, porcelain and precious furnishings on display belonged, for many years, to the wealthiest dynasty in Germany. The fortune, administered by Prince Albert II, is still estimated at well over €1 billion.

Dom St Peter CHURCH
(www.bistum-regensburg.de; Domplatz; ⏰ 6.30am-7pm Jun-Sep, to 6pm Apr, May & Oct, to 5pm Nov-Mar) It takes a few seconds for your eyes to adjust to the dim interior of Regensburg's soaring landmark, the Dom St Peter, one of Bavaria's grandest Gothic cathedrals with stunning kaleidoscopic stained-glass windows and an opulent, silver-sheathed main altar.

The cathedral is home of the Domspatzen, a 1000-year-old boys' choir that accompanies the 10am Sunday service (only during the school year). The Domschatzmuseum (Cathedral Treasury) brims with monstrances, tapestries and other church treasures.

Altes Rathaus HISTORIC BUILDING
(Old Town Hall; Rathausplatz; adult/concession €7.50/4; ⏰ tours in English 3pm Easter-Oct, 2pm Nov & Dec, in German every 30min) From 1663 to 1806, the Reichstag (imperial assembly) held its gatherings at Regensburg's old town, an important role commemorated by an exhibit in today's Reichstagsmuseum. Tours take in the lavish assembly hall and the original torture chambers in the cellar.

Buy tickets at the tourist office in the same building. Note that access is by tour only. Audioguides are available for English speakers in January and February.

Steinerne Brücke
BRIDGE

(Stone Bridge) An incredible feat of engineering for its day, Regensburg's 900-year-old Stone Bridge was at one time the only fortified crossing over the Danube. Damaged and neglected for centuries (especially by the buses that once used it) the entire expanse is currently under renovation. The design of the completed sections looks worryingly modern.

Golf Museum
MUSEUM

(www.golf-museum.com; Tändlergasse 3; adult/concession €7.50/5; ☉10am-6pm Mon-Sat) Claiming to be Europe's best golf museum (Scotland, home to the British Golf Museum, is strangely not counted as part of the continent), this unexpected repository of club, tee and score card (including one belonging to King George V of England) backswings its way through golf's illustrious past – interesting, even if you think a green fee is something to do with municipal recycling. The entrance is in an antiques shop.

Historisches Museum
MUSEUM

(Dachauplatz 2-4; adult/concession €5/2.50; ☉10am-4pm Tue-Sun) A medieval monastery provides a suitably atmospheric backdrop for the city's history museum. The collections plot the region's story from cave dweller to Roman, and medieval trader to 19th-century burgher.

Schottenkirche St Jakob
CHURCH

(Jakobstrasse 3) The sooty 12th-century main portal of the Schottenkirche St Jakob is considered one of the supreme examples of Romanesque architecture in Germany. Its reliefs and sculptures form an iconography that continues to baffle the experts. Sadly, it's protected from further pollution by an ageing glass structure that makes the whole thing an eyesore. However, this is more than made up for inside, where pure, tourist-free Romanesque austerity prevails.

Document Neupfarrplatz
HISTORIC SITE

(☑0941-507 3442; Neupfarrplatz; adult/concession €5/2.50; ☉tours 2.30pm Thu-Sat Sep-Jun, 2.30pm Thu-Mon Jul & Aug) Excavations in the mid-1990s revealed remains of Regensburg's once-thriving 16th-century Jewish quarter, along with Roman buildings, gold coins and a Nazi bunker. The subterranean Document Neupfarrplatz only provides access to a small portion of the excavated area, but tours feature a nifty multimedia presentation (in German) about the square's history. Back up above, on the square itself, a work by renowned Israeli artist Dani Karavan graces the site of the former synagogue.

Tickets are purchased from Tabak Götz at Neupfarrplatz 3.

Kepler-Gedächtnishaus
MUSEUM

(Kepler Memorial House; Keplerstrasse 5; adult/concession €2.20/1.10; ☉10.30am-4pm Sat & Sun) Disciples of astronomer and mathematician Johannes Kepler should visit the house he lived in while resident in Regensburg.

Alte Kapelle
CHURCH

(Alter Kornmarkt 8) South of the Dom, the humble exterior of the graceful Alte Kapelle belies the stunning interior with its rich rococo decorations. The core of the church, however, is about 1000 years old, although the vaulted ceilings were added in the Gothic period. The church is open only during services but you can always peek through the wrought-iron grill.

Roman Wall
HISTORIC SITE

The most tangible reminder of the ancient rectangular Castra Regina (Regen Fortress), where the name 'Regensburg' comes from, is the remaining Roman wall, which follows Unter den Schwibbögen and veers south onto Dr-Martin-Luther-Strasse. Dating from AD 179 the rough-hewn **Porta Praetoria** (Unter den Schwibbögen) arch is the tallest Roman structure in Bavaria and formed part of the city's defences for centuries.

MUSEUM OF BAVARIAN HISTORY

Regensburg is set to acquire a major attraction in 2018 – the Museum of Bavarian History. The architecturally striking building (other, less favourable, descriptions have been used) will be bolted together around 250m east of the Steinerne Brücke, altering the historical appearance of the river front. As well as the super-contemporary look of the structure, the wisdom of placing a major attraction in such a flood-prone location has been questioned.

⛵ Tours

Schifffahrt Klinger BOAT TOUR
(🖉 0941-521 04; www.schifffahrtklinger.de; cruises adult/child from €8.50/3.50; ⏱ Apr-late Oct) Offers short cruises on the Danube (50 minutes) and to the Walhalla monument.

Tourist Train Tours TRAIN
(depart Domplatz; adult/family €8/19; ⏱ 8 tours daily) Multilingual tourist train tours of the city centre take 45 minutes to complete a circuit from the south side of the cathedral. Fares include a free coffee at Haus Heuport.

✨ Festivals & Events

Dult FESTIVAL
Oktoberfest-style party with beer tents, carousel rides, entertainment and vendors on the Dultplatz, in May and late August or early September.

Weihnachtsmarkt MARKET
The Christmas market has stalls selling roasted almonds, gingerbread and traditional wooden toys. Held at Neupfarrplatz and Schloss Thurn und Taxis during December.

🛏 Sleeping

Regensburg has an unexpectedly wide choice of places to achieve REM, from blue-blooded antique-graced apartments to blood-red suites for fired-up honeymooners.

Brook Lane Hostel HOSTEL €
(🖉 0941-696 5521; www.hostel-regensburg.de; Obere Bachgasse 21; dm/s/d from €16/40/50, apt per person €55; 🛜) Regensburg's only backpacker hostel has its very own convenience store, which doubles up as reception, but isn't open 24 hours, so late landers should let staff know in advance. Dorms do the minimum required, but the apartments and doubles here are applaudable deals, especially if you're travelling in a twosome or more. Access to kitchens and washing machines throughout.

DJH Hostel HOSTEL €
(🖉 0941-466 2830; www.regensburg.jugendherberge.de; Wöhrdstrasse 60; dm from €25.40) Regensburg's 186-bed hostel occupies a beautiful old building on a large island about a 10-minute walk north of the Altstadt.

Hotel Am Peterstor HOTEL €
(🖉 0941-545 45; www.hotel-am-peterstor.de; Fröhliche-Türken-Strasse 12; s/d €40/50; ⏱ reception 7-11am & 4-10.30pm; 🛜) The pale-grey decor might be grim, and the recepetion hours silly, but the location is great, the price is right and staff go out of their way to assist. Make sure you get a nonsmoking room, as some pong of secondhand smoke. Breakfast is an optional €5 extra. Payment on arrival.

★ Elements Hotel HOTEL €€
(🖉 0941-3819 8600; www.hotel-elements.de; Alter Kornmarkt 3; d from €105; 🛜) Four elements, four rooms, and what rooms they are! 'Fire' blazes in plush crimson; while 'Water' is a wellness suite with a Jacuzzi; 'Air' is playful and light and natural wood; and stone and leather reign in colonial-inspired 'Earth.' Breakfast costs an extra €15.

Extras such as in-room massages, candlelit dinner (€65) and breakfast in bed (€25) can be booked.

Petit Hotel Orphée HOTEL €€
(🖉 0941-596 020; www.hotel-orphee.de; Wahlenstrasse 1; s €35-125, d €75-165; 🛜) Behind a humble door lies a world of genuine charm, unexpected extras and ample attention to detail. The striped floors, wrought-iron beds, original sinks and common rooms with soft cushions and well-read books give the feel of a lovingly attended home.

Check-in and breakfast is nearby in the Cafe Orphée at Untere Bachgasse 8. Additional rooms are available above the cafe.

Hotel Goldenes Kreuz HOTEL €€
(🖉 0941-558 12; www.hotel-goldeneskreuz.de; Haidplatz 7; s €85-110, d €105-135; 🛜) Surely the best deal in town, each of the nine fairy-tale rooms bears the name of a crowned head and is fit for a kaiser. Huge mirrors, dark antique and Bauhaus furnishings, four-poster beds, chubby exposed beams and parquet flooring produce a stylishly aristocratic opus in leather, wood, crystal and fabric. Breakfast is in the house chapel.

Hotel Roter Hahn HOTEL €€
(🖉 0941-595 090; www.roter-hahn.com; Rote-Hahnen-Gasse 10; s €80-105, d €100-135; 🅿🛜) A bulky beamed ceiling and a glassed-in Roman stone well (staff appear to be oblivious of its provenance) greet you in the lobby of the 'Red Rooster', contrasting with streamlined rooms offering freshly maintained amenities. Parking costs €12; request a room on the 2nd floor to access the free wi-fi.

Zum Fröhlichen Türken HOTEL €€
(🖉 0941-536 51; www.hotel-zum-froehlichen-tuerken.de; Fröhliche-Türken-Strasse 11; s/d €62/89) With its comfortable, clean quarters,

Regensburg

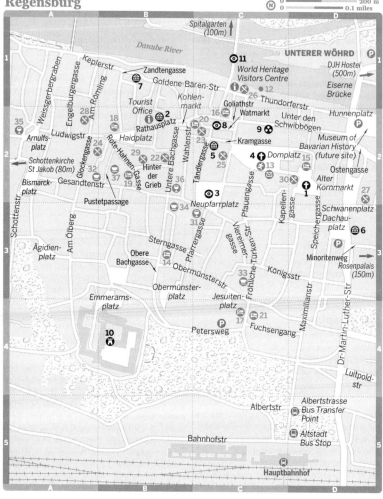

unstinting breakfast and mild-mannered staff, the 'Jolly Turk' will bring a smile to any price-conscious traveller's face. The pricier rooms have private bathrooms.

Goliath Hotel   HOTEL €€€
(☑0941-200 0900; www.hotel-goliath.de; Goliath-strasse 10; s/d from €130/160; P❀🛜) Right in the heart of the city centre, the 41 rooms at the Goliath are all differently conceived and pristinely serviced. Some have little extras, such as bathroom–bedroom windows and big baths. It's funky, but doesn't go the whole

boutique hog and staff are surprisingly old school. Parking costs €12.

🍴 Eating

'In Regensburg we ate a magnificent lunch, had a divine musical entertainment, an English hostess and a wonderful Moselle wine,' wrote Mozart to his wife Constance in 1790. Available in Mozart's day, but better washed down with a local Kneitinger Pils, is the delectable bratwurst and *Händlmaier's Süsser Hausmachersenf* (a distinctive sweet mustard).

Regensburg

Spaghetteria Aquino   ITALIAN €
(www.spaghetteria-regensburg.de; Am Römling 12; dishes €5.50-10; ⊙ 11am-2.30pm & 5.30pm-midnight) Get carbed up at this former 17th-century chapel, where you can splatter six types of pasta with 24 types of sauce, and get out the door for the cost of a cocktail in Munich. The all-you-can-eat buffets (€5 to €6.50) are a cheap way to fill up at lunchtime and there are pizzas, salads and antipasti to choose from.

Historische Wurstkuchl   GERMAN €
(🖉 0941-466 210; www.wurstkuchl.de; Thundorfer-strasse 3; 6 sausages €9; ⊙ 8am-7pm) Completely submerged several times by the Danube's fickle floods, this titchy eatery has been serving the city's traditional finger-size sausages, grilled over beech wood and dished up with sauerkraut and sweet grainy mustard, since 1135 and lays claim to being the world's oldest sausage kitchen.

Dampfnudel Uli   CAFE €
(Watmarkt 4; dishes €5-8; ⊙ 10.01am-6.01pm Wed-Fri, to 3.01pm Sat) This quirky, old-fashioned little noshery serves a mean *Dampfnudel* (steamed doughnut) with custard in a Gothic chamber lined with photos and beer steins (tankards) at the base of the Baumburger Tower.

★**Dicker Mann**   BAVARIAN €€
(www.dicker-mann.de; Krebsgasse 6; mains €8-19; ⊙ 7am-midnight) Stylish, tranquil, very traditional inn and plating up all the staples of

Bavarian sustenance, the 'Chubby Chappy' is one of the oldest restaurants in town, allegedly dating back to the 14th century. On a balmy eve, be sure to bag a table in the lovely beer garden out back.

★**Café Orphée**   FRENCH €€
(Untere Bachgasse 8; mains €11-24; ⊙ 8am-1am) Claiming to be the Frenchiest bistro east of the Rhine – and it is as if you've been teleported to 1920s Paris – this visually pleasing, always bustling eatery, is bedecked in faded red velvet, dark wood and art nouveau posters. Light-lunch fare populates a handwritten menu of appetising Gallic favourites with slight Bavarian touches for sturdiness.

Haus Heuport   INTERNATIONAL €€
(Domplatz 7; mains €8.50-20.50; ⊙ 10am-midnight Mon-Fri, from 9am Sat & Sun; 🖉) Enter an internal courtyard (flanked by stone blocks where medieval torches were once extinguished) and climb up the grand old wooden staircase to this space-rich Gothic dining hall for eye-to-eye views of the Dom St Peter and an internationally flavoured culinary celebration. The Sunday breakfast buffet runs to a hangover-busting 3pm. Always busy.

Vitus   FRENCH €€
(🖉 0941-526 46; Hinter der Grieb 8; mains €5.50-13.90; ⊙ 9am-11pm) Colourful canvases mix with ancient beamed ceilings at this bustling place serving provincial French food,

including delicious *Flammkuchen,* quiche, salads, meat and fish dishes, as well as a commendable number of meat-free options. Sit in the rustic bar area, the restaurant with linen-draped tables or the child-friendly cafe section.

Leerer Beutel
EUROPEAN €€

(☑0941-589 97; www.leerer-beutel.de; Bertoldstrasse 9; mains €10-23; ⊙6pm-1am Mon, 11am-1am Tue-Sat, 11am-3pm Sun) Subscriber to the slow-food ethos, the cavernous restaurant at the eponymous cultural centre offers an imaginatively mixed menu of Bavarian, Tyrolean and Italian dishes, served indoors or out on the car-free cobbles. From Tuesday to Friday, clued-in locals invade for the two-course lunches for €6.50.

Weltenburger am Dom
BAVARIAN €€

(☑0941-586 1460; www.weltenburger-am-dom. de; Domplatz 3; dishes €8.40-17.90; ⊙11am-11pm) Tightly packed gastropub with a mouth-watering menu card of huge gourmet burgers, sausage dishes, beer hall and garden favourites such as *Obazda* (cream cheese on pretzels) and *Sauerbraten* (marinated roast meat), dark beer goulash and a few token desserts. Make sure you are hungry before you come as portions are big.

🍷 Drinking

Spitalgarten
BEER GARDEN

(☑0941-847 74; www.spitalgarten.de; St Katharinenplatz 1; ⊙9am-midnight) A veritable thicket of folding chairs and slatted tables by the Danube, this is one of the best places in town for some alfresco quaffing. It claims to have brewed beer (today's Spital) here since 1350, so it probably knows what it's doing by now.

Félix
CAFE

(Fröhliche-Türken-Strasse 6; ⊙9am-2am Sun-Thu, 10am-3am Fri & Sat) Early birds breakfast, and after-dark trendoids leaf through the lengthy drinks menu behind the curvaceous neo-baroque frontage of this open-all-hours

---

SCHINDLER'S PLAQUE

Oskar Schindler Plaque (Am Watmarkt 5) Oskar Schindler lived in Regensburg for years, and today one of his houses bears a plaque to his achievements, as commemorated in Steven Spielberg's epic dramatisation *Schindler's List.*

---

cafe with a welcoming air. You'd be lucky to get a seat here at lunchtime so arrive early.

Kneitinger
PUB

(Arnulfsplatz 3; ⊙9am-midnight) This quintessential Bavarian brewpub is the place to go for some hearty home cooking, delicious house suds and outrageous oompah frolics. It's been in business since 1530.

Paletti
CAFE, BAR

(Gesandtenstrasse 6, Pustetpassage; ⊙8am-1am Mon-Sat, from 4pm Sun) Tucked into a covered passageway off Gesandtenstrasse, this buzzy Italian cafe-bar that has not changed since the 1960s teleports you back to the postwar years of the *Wirtschaftswunder* (economic miracle).

Cafebar
CAFE, BAR

(Gesandtenstrasse 14; ⊙8am-midnight Mon-Wed, to 1am Thu & Fri, 9am-1am Sat, 1pm-midnight Sun) This time-warped, tightly squeezed blast from the past in *Jugendstil* tile, cast iron and stained glass fills with newspaper-reading caffeine fans at first rays and ethanol fans after sundown.

Hemingway's
CAFE, BAR

(Obere Bachgasse 5; ⊙9am-1am Sun-Thu, to 2am Fri & Sat) Black wood, big mirrors and lots of photos of Papa himself add to the cool atmosphere of this art-deco-style cafe-bar.

Augustiner
BEER GARDEN

(Neupfarrplatz 15; ⊙10am-11.30pm) This popular fairy-lit beer garden and restaurant is ideally located in the heart of the city. Leave your beer-glass ring and pack away some traditional south German fare in the sprawling garden or cavernous interior.

Moritz
BAR

(Untere Bachgasse 15; ⊙7.30am-1am Mon-Sat, from 9am Sun) Take some Gothic cross vaulting, paint it high-visibility tunnel orange, throw in some killer cocktails and invite the iPad crowd – and you've got Moritz!

ℹ️ Information

Use the **Regensburg Card** (24/48hr €9/17) for free public transport and discounts at local attractions and businesses. Available at the tourist office.

Post Office (Domplatz) There's another branch next to the Hauptbahnhof.

Tourist Office (☑0941-507 4410; www.regensburg.de; Rathausplatz 4; ⊙9am-6pm Mon-Fri, 9am-4pm Sat, 9.30am-4pm Sun Apr-Oct, closes 2.30pm Sun Nov-Mar; 🛜) In the historic

Altes Rathaus. Sells tickets, tours, rooms and an audioguide for self-guided tours.

World Heritage Visitors Centre (☑ 0941-507 4410; www.regensburg-welterbe.de; Weisse-Lamm-Gasse 1; ☺ 10am-7pm) Brand-new visitors centre by the Steinerne Brücke, focusing on the city's Unesco World Heritage Sites. Interesting interactive multimedia exhibits.

ⓘ Getting There & Away

CAR

Regensburg is about an hour's drive southeast of Nuremberg and northwest of Passau via the A3 autobahn. The A93 runs south to Munich.

TRAIN

Train connections from Regensburg:

➡ **Frankfurt am Main** €71, three hours, every two hours, change in Nuremberg or Würzburg

➡ **Landshut** €13.30, 40 minutes, hourly

➡ **Munich** €27.50, 1½ hours, hourly

➡ **Nuremberg** €20.70, one to two hours, hourly

➡ **Passau** From €24.20 to €29, one to two hours, hourly or change in Plattling

ⓘ Getting Around

BICYCLE

Bikehaus (☑ 0941-599 8808; www.bikehaus.de; Bahnhofstrasse 18; bikes per day €12; ☺ 10am-7pm Mon-Sat) At Bikehaus you can rent anything from kiddies bikes to fully saddled tourers or even a rickshaw for a novel city tour.

BUS

On weekdays the Altstadtbus (€1.10) somehow manages to squeeze its way through the narrow streets between the Hauptbahnhof and the Altstadt every 10 minutes between 9am and 7pm. The bus transfer point is one block north of the Hauptbahnhof, on Albertstrasse. Tickets for all city buses (except the Altstadtbus) cost €2.30 for journeys in the centre; an all-day ticket costs €5 at ticket machines, €3.80 at weekends when valid for both days.

CAR & MOTORCYCLE

The Steinerne Brücke and much of the Altstadt are closed to private vehicles. Car parks in the centre charge from €1.50 per hour and are well signposted.

Around Regensburg

Walhalla

Walhalla NOTABLE BUILDING
(www.walhalla-regensburg.de; adult/concession €4/3; ☺ 9am-5.45pm Apr-Sep, 10-11.45am & 1-3.45pm Oct-Mar) Modelled on the Parthenon in Athens, the Walhalla is a breathtaking Ludwig I monument dedicated to the giants of Germanic thought and deed. Marble steps seem to lead up forever from the banks of the Danube to this dazzling marble hall, with a gallery of 127 heroes in marble.

The collection includes a few dubious cases, such as astronomer Copernicus, born in a territory belonging to present-day Poland. The most recent addition (2009) was romantic poet Heinrich Heine, whose works were set to music by Strauss, Wagner and Brahms.

To get there take the Danube Valley country road (unnumbered) 10km east from Regensburg to the village of Donaustauf, then follow the signs. Alternatively, you can take a two-hour boat cruise with Schifffahrt Klinger (p153), which includes a one-hour stop at Walhalla, or take bus 5 from Regensburg Hauptbahnhof.

Ingolstadt

☑ 0841 / POP 129,100

Even by Bavaria's elevated standards, Danube-straddling Ingolstadt is astonishingly affluent. Auto manufacturer Audi has its headquarters here, flanked by a clutch of oil refineries on the outskirts, but industry has left few marks on the medieval centre, with its cobblestone streets and historic, if slightly over-renovated, buildings. Ingolstadt's museum-church has the largest flat fresco ever made, and few people may know that its old medical school figured in the literary birth of Frankenstein's monster, the monster by which all others are judged.

⊙ Sights

Asamkirche Maria de Victoria CHURCH
(☑ 0841-305 1830; Neubaustrasse 11; adult/concession €2/1.50; ☺ 9am-noon & 12.30-5pm Tue-Sun Mar-Oct, 1-4pm Tue-Sun Nov-Feb) The Altstadt's crown jewel is the Asamkirche Maria de Victoria, a baroque masterpiece designed by brothers Cosmas Damian and Egid Quirin Asam between 1732 and 1736. The church's mesmerising trompe l'oeil ceiling, painted in just six weeks in 1735, is the world's largest fresco on a flat surface.

Visual illusions abound: stand on the little circle on the diamond tile near the door and look over your left shoulder at the archer with the flaming red turban – wherever you walk, the arrow points right at you. The fresco's Horn of Plenty, Moses' staff and the treasure chest also appear to dramatically alter as you move around the space.

Deutsches Medizinhistorisches Museum
MUSEUM

(German Museum of Medical History; ☑ 0841-305 2860; www.dmm-ingolstadt.de; Anatomiestrasse 18-20; adult/concession €5/2.50; ☺ 10am-5pm Tue-Sun) Located in the stately Alte Anatomie (Old Anatomy) at the university, this sometimes rather gory museum chronicles the evolution of medical science as well as the many (scary) instruments and techniques used. Unless you are, or have been, a medical student, pack a strong stomach for the visit.

The ground floor eases you into the exhibition with medical equipment such as birthing chairs, enema syringes, lancets used for bloodletting and other delightful paraphernalia guaranteed to make many go weak at the knees. Upstairs things get closer to the bone with displays of human skeletons, foetuses of conjoined twins, a pregnant uterus and a cyclops.

Neues Schloss
PALACE, MUSEUM

The ostentatious Neues Schloss (New Palace) was built for Duke Ludwig the Bearded in 1418. Fresh from a trip to wealth-laden France, Ludwig borrowed heavily from Gallic design and created a residence with 3m-thick walls, Gothic net vaulting and individually carved doorways. One guest who probably didn't appreciate its architectural merits was future French president Charles de Gaulle, held as prisoner of war here during WWI.

Today the building houses the **Bayerisches Armeemuseum** (Bavarian Military Museum; ☑ 0841-937 70; www.armeemuseum.de; Paradeplatz 4; adult/concession €3.50/3, Sun €2; ☺ 9am-5.30pm Tue-Fri, 10am-5.30pm Sat & Sun) with exhibits on long-forgotten battles, armaments dating back to the 14th century and legions of tin soldiers filling the rooms.

The second part of the museum is in the **Reduit Tilly** (adult/concession/child €3.50/3/ free, Sun €1; ☺ 9am-5.30pm Tue-Fri, 10am-5.30pm Sat & Sun) across the river. This 19th-century fortress has an undeniable aesthetic, having been designed by Ludwig I's chief architect. It was named after Johann Tilly – a field marshal of the Thirty Years' War who was known as the 'butcher of Magdeburg' – and features exhibits covering the history of WWI and post-WWI Germany.

The museum complex also houses the **Bayerisches Polizeimuseum** (Donaulände 1; adult/concession €3.50/3, Sun €1; ☺ 9am-5.30pm Tue-Fri, 10am-5.30pm Sat & Sun) which lives in the Turm Triva, built at the same time as the Reduit Tilly. Exhibitions trace the story of Bavarian police and their role in various episodes of history such as the Third Reich and the Cold War.

A combined ticket is available at each museum that covers entry to all three museums (adult/concession €7/5).

Museum Mobile
MUSEUM

(☑ 0800-283 4444; www.audi.de/foren; Ettinger Strasse 40; adult/child €4/free; ☺ 9am-6pm) This high-tech car museum is part of the Audi Forum complex. Exhibits on three floors chart Audi's humble beginnings in 1899 to its latest dream machines such as the R8. Some 50 cars and 20 motorbikes are on display, including prototypes that glide past visitors on an open lift. Bus 11 runs every 30 minutes from the Hauptbahnhof or central bus station (ZOB) to the Audi complex.

The two-hour tours of the **Audi factory** (☑ 0800-283 4444; adult/concession €7/3.50; ☺ Mon-Fri, 10.30am, 12.30pm & 2.30pm in German, 11.30am only in English) take you through the entire production process, from the metal press to the testing station.

THE BIRTH OF FRANKENSTEIN

Mary Shelley's *Frankenstein,* published in 1818, set a creepy precedent in the world of monster fantasies. The story is well known: young scientist Viktor Frankenstein travels to Ingolstadt to study medicine. He becomes obsessed with the idea of creating a human being and goes shopping for parts at the local cemetery. Unfortunately, his creature is a problem child and sets out to destroy its maker.

Shelley picked Ingolstadt because it was home to a prominent university and medical faculty. In the 19th century, a laboratory for scientists and medical doctors was housed in the Alte Anatomie (now the **Deutsches Medizinhistorisches Museum**, p158). In the operating theatre, professors and their students carried out experiments on corpses and dead tissue, though perhaps one may have been inspired to work on something a bit scarier...

Liebfrauenmünster
CHURCH

(Kreuzstrasse; ⊙ 8am-6pm) Ingolstadt's biggest church was established by Duke Ludwig the Bearded in 1425 and enlarged over the next century. This classic Gothic hall church has a pair of strangely oblique square towers that flank the main entrance. Inside, subtle colours and a nave flooded with light intensify the magnificence of the high-lofted vaulting and the blossoming stonework of several side chapels.

The high altar by Hans Mielich (1560) has a rear panel depicting St Katharina debating with the professors at Ingolstadt's new university, ostensibly in a bid to convert the Protestant faculty to Catholicism – a poke at Luther's Reformation. At the rear of the church, there's a small Schatzkammer (treasury) displaying precious robes, goblets and monstrances belonging to the diocese.

Museum für Konkrete Kunst
MUSEUM

(Museum of Concrete Art; ☑ 0841-305 1875; www.mkk-ingolstadt.de; Tränktorstrasse 6-8; adult/concession €3/1.50; ⊙ 10am-5pm Tue-Sun) This unique art museum showcases works and installations from the Concrete Movement, all of a bafflingly abstract nature. The movement was defined and dominated by interwar artists Max Bill and Theo van Doesburg whose works make up a large share of the collections.

Kreuztor
HISTORIC BUILDING

(Kreuzstrasse) The Gothic Kreuztor (1385) was one of the four main gates into the city until the 19th century and its redbrick fairy-tale outline is now the emblem of Ingolstadt. This and the main gate within the Neues Schloss are all that remain of the erstwhile entrances into the medieval city, but the former fortifications, now flats, still encircle the centre.

Lechner Museum
MUSEUM

(☑ 0841-305 2250; www.lechner-museum.de; Esplanade 9; adult/concession €3/1.50; ⊙ 11am-6pm Thu-Sun) This unusual art museum highlights works cast in steel, a medium that's more expressive than you might think. Exhibits are displayed in a striking glass-covered factory hall dating from 1953.

🛏 Sleeping

DJH Hostel
HOSTEL €

(☑ 0841-305 1280; www.ingolstadt.jugendherberge.de; Friedhofstrasse 4; dm from €19.20) This beautiful, well-equipped and wheelchair-friendly hostel is in a renovated redbrick fortress (1828), about 150m west of the Kreuztor.

Enso Hotel
HOTEL €€

(☑ 0841-885 590; www.enso-hotel.de; Bei der Arena 1; s/d from €99/129; P 🛜) Located just across the Danube from the city centre, the 176 business-standard rooms here come in bold dashes of lip-smacking red and soot black, with acres of retro faux veneer providing a funky feel. Traffic noise is barely audible despite the location at a busy intersection. Amenities include a commendable Italian restaurant-bar and a fitness room.

Hotel Anker
HOTEL €€

(☑ 0841-300 50; www.hotel-restaurant-anker.de; Tränktorstrasse 1; s/d €64/94) Bright rooms, a touch of surrealist art and a commendably central location make this family-run hotel a good choice, although the lack of English is a slight downside. Try to avoid arriving at mealtimes, when staff are busy serving in the traditional restaurant downstairs.

Bayerischer Hof
HOTEL €€

(☑ 0841-934 060; www.bayerischer-hof-ingolstadt.de; Münzbergstrasse 12; s €68-85, d €87-100) Located around a Bavarian eatery, the 34 rooms are a pretty good deal, and are filled with hardwood furniture, TVs and modern bathrooms. Rates come down at weekends and this is a good deal for lone travellers as almost half the rooms are singles.

Kult Hotel
DESIGN HOTEL €€€

(☑ 0841-951 00; www.kult-hotel.de; Theodor-Heuss-Strasse 25; d €189; P @ 🛜) The most eye-catching feature of rooms at this exciting design hotel, 2km northeast of the city centre, are the painted ceilings, each one a slightly saucy work of art. Otherwise fittings and furniture come sleek, room gadgets are the latest toys, and the restaurant constitutes a study in cool elegance.

🍴 Eating & Drinking

Local drinkers are proud that Germany's Beer Purity Law of 1516 was issued in Ingolstadt, the 500th anniversary of which the city celebrated in 2016. Herrnbräu, Nordbräu or Ingobräu are the excellent local brews.

For a quick bite head for the Viktualienmarkt, just off Rathausplatz, where fast-food stalls provide international flavour. Ingolstadt must have more Italian eateries per capita than any other Germany city!

Zum Daniel   BAVARIAN €€

(☑ 0841-352 72; Roseneckstrasse 1; mains €8-17; ⊙ 9am-midnight Tue-Sun) Ingolstadt's oldest inn is a lovingly run, Michelin-reviewed local institution serving what many claim to be the town's best pork roast and seasonal specials.

Stella D'Oro   ITALIAN €€

(☑ 0841-794 3737; www.stelladoro.de; Griesbadgasse 2; mains €8.20-30.90; ⊙ 11.30am-2.30pm & 5.30-11pm Mon-Sat) Ingolstadt has more Italian eateries than some Italian towns, so if you're going for *la dolce vita,* you might as well go for the best. The exquisite menu at this smart Italian job is divided into Terra (meat), Il Mare (fish), L'orot (vegetarian dishes) and Dolce (desserts) with the seafood a particularly refreshing change in meat-munching Bavaria.

Weissbräuhaus   PUB FOOD €€

(☑ 0841-328 90; Dollstrasse 3; mains €8.50-17.90; ⊙ 11am-midnight) This modern beer hall serves standard Bavarian dishes, including the delicious *Weissbräupfändl* (pork fillet with homemade *Spätzle*). There's a beer garden with a charming fountain out back.

Kuchlbauer   PUB

(☑ 0841-335 512; www.biermuseum-ingolstadt.de; Schäffbräustrasse 11a; ⊙ 11am-3pm & 5pm-1am) This unmissable brewpub, with oodles of brewing and rustic knick-knacks hanging from the walls and ceiling, really rocks (or should we say sways) when someone stokes up an accordion. Tipples include the house *Hefeweissbier* (unfiltered wheat beer) or you could try the Mass Goass, a 1L jug containing dark beer, cola and 4cL of cherry liqueur!

Neue Galerie Das MO   CAFE, BAR

(☑ 0841-339 60; Bergbräustrasse 7; ⊙ from 5pm) This trendy, evening-only place puts on occasional art exhibitions, but it's the walled beer garden in the shade of mature chestnut trees that punters really come for. The international menu offers everything from cheeseburgers to schnitzel and baked potatoes, and vegetarians are well catered for.

ℹ Information

Post Office (Am Stein 8; ⊙ 8.30am-6pm Mon-Fri, 9am-1pm Sat)

Sparkasse (Rathausplatz 6)

Tourist Office (☑ 0841-305 3005; www. ingolstadt-tourismus.de; Elisabethstrasse 3, Hauptbahnhof; ⊙ 8.30am-6.30pm Mon-Fri,

9.30am-1pm Sat) The other branch is at Rathausplatz (☑ 0841-305 3030; Rathausplatz 2; ⊙ 9am-6pm Mon-Fri, 10am-2pm Sat & Sun, shorter hours and closed Sun Nov-Mar).

ℹ Getting There & Away

When arriving by train from the north (from Eichstätt and Nuremberg), Ingolstadt Nord station is nearer to the historical centre than the Hauptbahnhof. Trains from the south arrive at the Hauptbahnhof. Ingolstadt has the following rail connections:

➡ **Munich** €17.90 to €28, one hour, twice hourly

➡ **Nuremberg** €20 to €31, 30 to 40 minutes, hourly

➡ **Regensburg** €15.70, two hours, twice hourly, change in Nuremberg

ℹ Getting Around

Buses 10, 11 and 18 run every few minutes between the city centre and the Hauptbahnhof, 2.5km to the southeast.

Landshut

☑ 0871 / POP 66,200

A worthwhile halfway halt between Munich and Regensburg, or a place to kill half a day before a flight from nearby Munich Airport, Landshut (pronounced *'lants*-hoot') was the hereditary seat of the Wittelsbach family in the early 13th century, and capital of the Dukedom of Bavaria-Landshut for over a century. Apart from a brief episode as custodian of the Bavarian University two centuries ago, Landshuters have since been busy retreating into provincial obscurity, but the town's blue-blooded past is still echoed in its grand buildings, a historical pageant with a cast of thousands and one seriously tall church.

◉ Sights

Coming from the train station, you enter Landshut's historical core through the broken Gothic arch of the stocky **Ländtor**, virtually the only surviving chunk of the town's medieval defences. From here, Theaterstrasse brings you to the 600m-long **Altstadt**, one of Bavaria's most impressive medieval marketplaces. Pastel town houses lining its curving cobbled length hoist elaborate gables, every one a different bell-shaped or saw-toothed creation in brick and plaster.

Burg Trausnitz   CASTLE

(☑ 0871-924 110; www.burg-trausnitz.de; adult/ concession €5.50/4.50; ⊙ tours 9am-6pm Apr-Sep, 10am-4pm Oct-Mar) Roosting high above the Altstadt is Burg Trausnitz, Landshut's star attraction. The 50-minute guided tour (in German with English text) takes you through the Gothic and Renaissance halls and chambers, ending at an alfresco party terrace with bird's-eye views of the town below. The tour includes the **Kunst- und Wunderkammer** (Room of Art and Curiosities), a typical Renaissance-era display of exotic curios assembled by the local dukes.

St Martin Church CHURCH
(www.st.martin-landshut.de; Altstadt; ☉ 7.30am-6pm Apr-Sep, to 5pm Oct-Mar) Rising in Gothic splendour at the southern end of the Altstadt is Landshut's record-breaking St Martin Church; its spire is the tallest brick structure in the world at 130.6m and took 55 years to build. It's by far Bavaria's tallest church with Regensburg's Dom a full 25m shorter.

Stadtresidenz PALACE
(🖉 0871-924 110; Altstadt 79; adult/concession €3.50/2.50; ☉ tours in German hourly 9am-6pm Apr-Sep, 10am-4pm Oct-Mar, closed Mon) Gracing the Altstadt is the Stadtresidenz, a Renaissance palace built by Ludwig X which hosts temporary exhibitions on historical themes. Admission is by guided tour only.

★ Festivals & Events

Landshuter Hochzeit MEDIEVAL
(www.landshuter-hochzeit.de) Every four years in July, the town hosts the Landshuter Hochzeit (next held in 2017 and 2021), one of Europe's biggest medieval bashes. It commemorates the marriage of Duke Georg der Reiche of Bavaria-Landshut to Princess Jadwiga of Poland in 1475.

🛏 Sleeping & Eating

DJH Hostel HOSTEL €
(🖉 0871-234 49; www.landshut.jugendherberge.de; Richard-Schirrmann-Weg 6; dm from €21; 🛜) This clean, well-run 100-bed hostel occupies an attractive old villa up by the castle, with views across town.

Goldene Sonne HOTEL €€
(🖉 0871-925 30; www.goldenesonne.de; Neustadt 520; s/d from €70/90; 🅿 🛜) True to its name, the 'Golden Sun' fills a magnificently gabled, six-storey town house with light. Rooms sport stylishly lofty ceilings, ornate mirrors, flat-screen TVs and renovated bathrooms. There's a fancy Bavarian restaurant on the premises.

Zur Insel HOTEL €€
(🖉 0871-923 160; www.insel-landshut.de; Badstrasse 16; s €60-95, d €75-110; 🛜) A good-value place to kip with 15 simple folksy rooms and a wood-panelled restaurant.

Augustiner an der St Martins Kirche BAVARIAN €€
(www.landshut-augustiner.de; Kirchgasse 251; mains €7.90-18.90; ☉ 10am-midnight) This dark wood tavern at the foot of the St Martin's spire is the best place in town to down a meat-dumpling combo, washed along with a frothy Munich wet one.

Alt Landshut BAVARIAN €€
(Isarpromenade 3; mains €6-14; ☉ 11am-11pm) Sunny days see locals linger over an Augustiner and some neighbourhood nosh outside by the Isar. In winter you can retreat to the simple whitewashed dining room.

ℹ Information

Tourist Office (🖉 0871-922 050; www.landshut.de; Altstadt 315; ☉ 9am-6pm Mon-Fri, 10am-4pm Sat Mar-Oct, 9am-5pm Mon-Fri, 10am-2pm Sat Nov-Feb)

ℹ Getting There & Away

TO/FROM THE AIRPORT
The airport bus (€13, 35 minutes) leaves hourly from near the tourist office and the train station between 3am and 10pm.

TRAIN
Landshut is a fairly major stop on the Munich–Regensburg mainline.
➡ **Munich** €15.70, 45 minutes, twice hourly
➡ **Passau** €23.50, 1½ hours, hourly
➡ **Regensburg** €13.30, 40 minutes, at least hourly

Passau

🖉 0851 / POP 49,500
Water has quite literally shaped the picturesque town of Passau on the border with Austria. Its Altstadt is stacked atop a narrow peninsula that jabs its sharp end into the confluence of three rivers: the Danube, the Inn and the Ilz. The rivers brought wealth to Passau, which for centuries was an important trading centre, especially for Bohemian salt, Central Europe's 'white gold'. Christianity, meanwhile, generated prestige as Passau evolved into the largest bishopric in the Holy Roman Empire. The Altstadt remains pretty much as it was when the powerful

WORTH A TRIP

MARKTL AM INN

On a gentle bend in the Inn River, some 60km southwest of Passau, sits the drowsy settlement of Marktl am Inn. Few people outside of Germany (or indeed Bavaria) had heard of it before 19 April 2005, the day when its favourite son, Cardinal Joseph Ratzinger, was elected **Pope Benedict XVI**. Literally overnight the community was inundated with reporters, devotees and the plain curious, all seeking clues about the pontiff's life and times. Souvenirs like mitre-shaped cakes, *Papst-Bier* (Pope's Beer) and religious board games flooded the local shops.

The pope's **Geburtshaus** (☑08678-747 680; www.papsthaus.eu; Marktplatz 11; adult/concession €3.50/2.50; ⊗10am-noon & 2-6pm Tue-Fri, 10am-6pm Sat & Sun Easter-Oct) is the simple but pretty Bavarian home where Ratzinger was born in 1927 and lived for the first two years of his life before his family moved to Tittmoning. The exhibition kicks off with a film (in English) tracing the pontiff's early life, career and the symbols he selected for his papacy. You then head into the house proper, where exhibits expand on these themes. The modest room where Ratzinger came into the world is on the upper floor.

The **Heimatmuseum** (☑08678-8104; Marktplatz 2; adult/concession €2/1.50) is in possession of a golden chalice and a skullcap that was used by Ratzinger in his private chapel in Rome, but is only open to groups of five or more by prior arrangement; visitors should call the **tourist office** (☑08678-748 820; www.marktl.de; Marktplatz 1; ⊗10am-noon & 2-4pm daily) at least a day ahead to arrange entry. His baptismal font can be viewed at the **Pfarrkirche St Oswald** (Marktplatz 6), which is open for viewing except during church services.

With immaculate rooms and a superb restaurant, family-run **Pension Hummel** (☑08678-282; www.gasthof-hummel.de; Hauptstrasse 34; s/d €44/63), a few steps from the train station, is the best spot to get some shut-eye. Wash down no-nonsense Bavarian fare with a *Papst-Bier* at **Gasthaus Oberbräu** (☑08678-1040; Bahnhofstrasse 2; mains €6-11; ⊗10am-midnight).

Marktl is a very brief stop on an Inn-hugging branch line of the train service between Simbach and the junction at Mühldorf (€6.10, 20 minutes), from where there are regular direct connections to Munich, Passau and Landshut.

prince-bishops built its tight lanes, tunnels and archways with an Italiante flourish, but the western end (around Nibelungenplatz) has received a modern makeover with shopping malls centred on the hang-glider-shaped central bus station (ZOB).

Passau is a Danube river-cruise halt and is often bursting with day visitors. It's also the convergence point of several long-distance cycling routes.

⊙ Sights

Dom St Stephan　　　　　　　　CHURCH
(www.bistum-passau.de; Domplatz; ⊗6.30am-7pm) There's been a church here since the late 5th century, but what you see today is much younger thanks to the fire of 1662, which ravaged much of the medieval town, including the cathedral. The rebuilding job went to a team of Italians, notably the architect Carlo Lurago and the stucco master Giovanni Battista Carlone. The result is a top-heavy baroque interior with a mob of saints and cherubs gazing down at the congregation from countless cornices and capitals.

The building's acoustics are perfect for its main attraction, the world's largest organ, which perches above the main entrance. This monster of a wind instrument contains an astonishing 17,974 pipes and it's an amazing acoustic experience to hear it in full puff. Half-hour organ recitals take place at noon daily Monday to Saturday (adult/child €4/2) and at 7.30pm on Thursday (adult/child €5/3) from May to October and for a week around Christmas. Show up at least 30 minutes early to ensure you get a seat.

Veste Oberhaus　　　　　　　　FORTRESS
(www.oberhausmuseum.de; adult/concession €5/4; ⊗9am-5pm Mon-Fri, 10am-6pm Sat & Sun mid-Mar–mid-Nov) A 13th-century defensive fortress, built by the prince-bishops, Veste Oberhaus towers over Passau with patriarchal pomp. Not surprisingly, views of the city and into Austria are superb from up here.

Inside the bastion is the **Oberhausmuseum**, a regional history museum where you can uncover the mysteries of medieval cathedral building, learn what it took to become a knight and explore Passau's period as a centre of the salt trade. Displays are labelled in English.

Altes Rathaus   TOWN HALL
(Rathausplatz 2) An entrance in the side of the Altes Rathaus (Old Town Hall) flanking Schrottgasse takes you to the **Grosser Rathaussaal** (Great Assembly Room; adult/concession €2/1.50; ⊙10am-4pm), where large-scale paintings by 19th-century local artist Ferdinand Wagner show scenes from Passau's history with melodramatic flourish. You can also sneak into the adjacent Small Assembly Room for a peek at the ceiling fresco, which again features allegories of the three rivers.

The rest of the Rathaus is a grand Gothic affair topped by a 19th-century painted tower. A carillon chimes several times daily (hours are listed on the wall, alongside historical flood-level markers).

Passauer Glasmuseum   MUSEUM
(☑0851-350 71; www.glasmuseum.de; Hotel Wilder Mann, Am Rathausplatz; adult/concession €7/5; ⊙10am-5pm) Opened by Neil Armstrong, of all people, Passau's warren-like glass museum is filled with some 30,000 priceless pieces of glass and crystal from the baroque, classical, art-nouveau and art-deco periods. Much of what you see hails from the glassworks of Bohemia, but there are also works by Tiffany and famous Viennese producers. Be sure to pick up a floor plan as it's easy to get lost.

Dreiflusseck   LANDMARK
The very nib of the Altstadt peninsula, the point where the rivers merge, is known as the Dreiflusseck (Three River Corner). From the north the little Ilz sluices brackish water down from the peat-rich Bavarian Forest, meeting the cloudy brown of the Danube as it flows from the west and the pale snowmelt jade of the Inn from the south to create a murky tricolour. The effect is best observed from the ramparts of the Veste Oberhaus.

Museum Moderner Kunst   ART MUSEUM
(☑0851-383 8790; www.mmk-passau.de; Bräugasse 17; adult/concession €5/3; ⊙10am-6pm Tue-Sun) Gothic architecture contrasts with 20th- and 21st-century artworks at Passau's Modern Art Museum. The rump of the permanent exhibition is made up of cubist and Expressionist works by Georg Philipp Wörlen, who died in Passau in 1954 and whose architect son, Hanns Egon Wörlen, set up the museum in the 1980s. Temporary exhibitions normally showcase big-hitting German artists and native styles and personalities from the world of architecture.

Römermuseum   MUSEUM
(☑0851-347 69; Lederergasse 43; adult/concession €4/2; ⊙10am-4pm Tue-Sun Mar–mid-Nov) Roman Passau can be viewed from the ground up at this Roman fort museum. Civilian and military artefacts unearthed here and elsewhere in Eastern Bavaria are on show and the ruins of **Kastell Boiotro**, which stood here from AD 250 to 400, are still in situ; some of the towers are still inhabited. There's a castle-themed kids' playground nearby.

🏃 Activities

Wurm + Köck   BOAT TOUR
(☑0851-929 292; www.donauschiffahrt.de; Höllgasse 26) From March to early November, Wurm + Köck operates cruises to the Dreiflusseck from the docks near Rathausplatz, as well as a whole host of other sailings to places along the Danube. The most spectacular vessels in the fleet are the sparkling *Kristallschiff* (Crystal Ship), *Kristallkönigin* (Crystal Queen) and *Kristallprinzessin* (Crystal Princess), all three decorated inside and out with Swarovski crystals.

🛌 Sleeping

Pension Rössner   GUESTHOUSE €
(☑0851-931 350; www.pension-roessner.de; Bräugasse 19; s/d €35/60; P 🛜) This immaculate place, in a restored mansion near the tip of the peninsula, offers great value for money and a friendly, cosy ambience. Each of the 16 rooms is uniquely decorated and many overlook the fortress. There's bike hire (€10 per day) and parking for €5 a day. Booking recommended.

Pension Vicus   GUESTHOUSE €
(☑0851-931 050; www.pension-vicus.de; Johann-Bergler-Strasse; s €38-44, d €62-69; P 🛜) Bright, family-run pension on the south side of the Inn. Rooms have small kitchenettes and there's a supermarket next door. Breakfast is an extra €7. Take frequent bus 3 or 4 from the ZOB to the Johann-Bergler-Strasse stop.

DJH Hostel   HOSTEL €
(☑0851-493 780; www.passau.jugendherberge.de; Oberhaus 125; dm from €23.40) Beautifully renovated 127-bed hostel right in the fortress.

HendlHouseHotel
HOTEL €

(☑ 0851-330 69; www.hendlhouse.com; Grosse Klingergasse 17; s/d €50/64; 🛜) With their light, unfussy decor and well-tended bathrooms, the 15 pristine rooms at this Altstadt inn offer a high quality-to-price ratio. Buffet breakfast is served in the downstairs restaurant.

Camping Passau
CAMPGROUND €

(☑ 0851-414 57; www.camping-passau.de; Halser Strasse 34; per person €9; ☺ May-Sep) Tent-only camping ground idyllically set on the Ilz River, 15 minutes' walk from the Altstadt. Catch bus 1 or 2 to Ilzbrücke.

★ Hotel Schloss Ort
BOUTIQUE HOTEL €€

(☑ 0851-340 72; www.hotel-schloss-ort.de; Im Ort 11; s €68-121, d €97-184; 🅿🛜) This 800-year-old medieval palace by the Inn River conceals a tranquil boutique hotel, stylishly done out with polished timber floors, crisp white cotton sheets and wrought-iron bedsteads. Many of the 18 rooms enjoy river views and breakfast is served in the vaulted restaurant. Parking is an extra €4.

Hotel König
HOTEL €€

(☑ 0851-3850; www.hotel-koenig.de; Untere Donaulände 1; s €69-90, d €89-130; 🅿🛜) This riverside property puts you smack in the heart of the Altstadt and near all the sights. The 41 timber-rich rooms – many of them enormous – are spread out over two buildings and most come with views of the Danube and fortress. One slight disadvantage is the lack of English. Parking is €10 a night.

Hotel Wilder Mann
HOTEL €€

(☑ 0851-350 71; www.wilder-mann.com; Höllgasse 1; s €55-77, d €88-200; 🅿🛜) Sharing space with the Glasmuseum (p163), this historic hotel boasts former guests ranging from Empress Elisabeth (Sisi) of Austria to Yoko Ono. In the rooms, folksy painted furniture sits incongrously with 20th-century telephones and 21st-century TVs. The building is a warren of staircases, passageways and linking doors, so make sure you remember where your room is. Guests receive a miserly discount to the museum.

✕ Eating & Drinking

Cafe Greindl
CAFE €

(www.greindl-passau.de; Wittgasse 8; meals €6-10; ☺ 7am-6pm Mon-Sat, from 11am Sun) The affluent *Kaffee-und-Torte* society meet daily at this bright, flowery cafe that oozes Bavarian *Gemütlichkeit*. Declared one of Germany's best in 2014 by *Feinschmecker* magazine,

the early opening makes this a sure-fire breakfast option.

Café Kowalski
CAFE €

(☑ 0851-2487; www.cafe-kowalski.de; Oberer Sand 1; dishes €4-11; ☺ 9.30am-1am Mon-Sat, from 10am Sun; 🛜) Chat flows as freely as the wine and beer at this retro-furnished cafe, a kicker of a nightspot. The giant burgers, schnitzels and big breakfasts are best consumed on the terrace overlooking the Ilz River.

★ Heilig-Geist-Stifts-Schenke
BAVARIAN €€

(☑ 0851-2607; www.stiftskeller-passau.de; Heilig-Geist-Gasse 4; mains €10-20; ☺ 11am-11pm, closed Wed; 🛜) Not only does this historical inn have a succession of walnut-panelled ceramic-stove-heated rooms, a candlelit cellar (from 6pm) and a vine-draped garden, but the food is equally inspired. Amid the river fish, steaks and seasonal dishes there are quite gourmet affairs such as beef fillet in flambéed cognac sauce. Help it all along with one of the many Austrian and German wines in stock.

Zum Grünen Baum
ORGANIC €€

(☑ 0851-356 35; Höllgasse 7; mains €7.20-13.80; ☺ 10am-1am; ✐) Take a seat in the newly renovated interior to savour risottos, goulash, schnitzel and soups, prepared as far as possible using organic ingredients, which are locally sourced as far as possible. Cosy, friendly and tucked away in the atmospherically narrow lanes between the Danube and the Residenzplatz.

Diwan
CAFE €€

(☑ 0851-490 3280; Niebelungenplatz 1, 9th fl, Stadtturm; mains €7-11; ☺ 9am-7pm Mon-Thu, to midnight Fri & Sat, 1-6pm Sun) Climb aboard the high-speed lift from street level to get to this trendy, high-perched cafe-lounge at the top of the Stadtturm, with by far the best views in town. From the tangled rattan and plush cappuccino-culture sofas you can see it all – the Dom St Stephan, the rivers, the Veste Oberhaus – while you tuck into the offerings of the changing seasonal menu.

Selly's Vegan Bar
VEGAN €€

(Grosse Klingergasse 10; mains €8; ☺ 11am-2am Mon-Thu, to 4am Fri & Sat, closed Sun; 🛜✐) Vegan cafe by day, slick drinking spot by night, the simple, 21st-century decor of this bar-restaurant is a world away from Bavaria's medieval inns. Burgers, curries, pastas and salads are served up meat- and dairy-free by the Czech owner.

STRAUBING

Some 30km southeast of Regensburg, Straubing enjoyed a brief heyday as part of a wonky alliance that formed the short-lived Duchy of Straubing-Holland. As a result, the centre is chock-a-block with historical buildings that opened new horizons in a small town. In August, the demand for folding benches soars during the **Gäubodenfest**, a 10-day blow-out that once brought together grain farmers in 1812, but now draws over 20,000 drinkers.

Lined with pastel-coloured houses from a variety of periods, the pedestrian square is lorded over by the Gothic **Stadtturm** (1316). It stands next to the richly gabled **Rathaus**, originally two merchant's homes but repackaged in neo-Gothic style in the 19th century. Just east of the tower is the gleaming golden **Dreifaltigkeitssäule** (Trinity Column), erected in 1709 as a nod to Catholic upheavals during the War of the Spanish Succession.

Straubing has about half a dozen historic churches. The most impressive is **St Jakobskirche** (Pfarrplatz), a late-Gothic hall church with original stained-glass windows; it was the recipient of a baroque makeover, courtesy of the frantically productive Asam brothers. The pair also designed the interior of the **Ursulinenkirche** (Burggasse), their final collaboration; its ceiling fresco depicts the martyrdom of St Ursula surrounded by allegorical representations of the four continents known at the time. Also worth a look is the nearby **Karmelitenkirche** (Hofstatt).

North of here is the former ducal residence **Herzogsschloss** (Schlossplatz), which overlooks the river. This rather austere 14th-century building was once the town's tax office.

One of Germany's most important repositories of Roman treasure is the intimate **Gäubodenmuseum** (☑ 09421-974 10; www.gaeubodenmuseum.de; Frauenhoferstrasse 23; adult/concession €4/3; ☉ 10am-4pm Tue-Sun). Displays include imposing armour and masks for both soldiers and horses, probably plundered from a Roman store.

If you fancy staying over, the **tourist office** (☑ 09421-944 307; www.straubing.de; Theresienplatz 2; ☉ 9am-5pm Mon-Wed & Fri, 9am-6pm Thu, 10am-2pm Sat) can find rooms.

Straubing has direct train connections to Regensburg (€10, 25 minutes, hourly). For Passau (€15.70, one hour and 10 minutes, hourly) and Munich (€23, two hours, hourly) change at Plattling or Neufahrn.

Andorfer Weissbräu BEER GARDEN
(☑ 0851-754 444; Rennweg 2) High on a hill 1.5km north of the Altstadt, this rural beer garden attached to the Andorfer brewery serves filling Bavarian favourites, but the star of the show is the outstanding *Weizen* and *Weizenbock* (strong wheat beer) brewed metres away. Take bus 7 from the ZOB to Ries-Rennweg.

Caffè Bar Centrale CAFE
(Rindermarkt 7) Venetian bar that has to spill out onto the cobbles of the Rindermarkt as it's so tiny inside. It may be small, but there's a huge drinks card and it's a fine place to head for a first or last drink. The Italian soundtrack fits nicely with the Italianate surroundings.

ⓘ Information

Post Office (Bahnhofstrasse 1; ☉ 9.30am-8pm Mon-Sat)

Tourist Office (☑ 0851-955 980; www.tourism.passau.de; Rathausplatz 3; ☉ 8.30am-6pm Mon-Fri, 9am-4pm Sat & Sun Easter–mid-Oct, shorter hours mid-Oct–Easter) Main tourist office in Passau, located in the Altstadt. There's another smaller office (Bahnhofstrasse 28; ☉ 9am-5pm Mon-Fri, 10.30am-3.30pm Sat & Sun Easter-Sep, shorter hours Oct-Easter) opposite the Hauptbahnhof. Both branches of the tourist office sell the PassauCard (one day per adult/child €16/13.50, three days €30/22), valid for several attractions, unlimited use of public transport and a city river cruise.

ⓘ Getting There & Away

BUS

Buses leave at 7.45am and 4.25pm to the Czech border village of Železná Ruda (2½ hours), from where there are connections to Prague. **Meinfernbus** (www.meinfernbus.de) links Passau with Vienna, Berlin Regensburg and Nuremberg.

TRAIN

Rail connections from Passau:

➡ **Munich** €35.70, 2¼ hours, hourly (change in Mühldorf or Regensburg)

➡ **Nuremberg** €48, two hours, every two hours

➡ **Regensburg** €24.20 to €29, one hour, every two hours or change in Plattling

➡ **Vienna** €55, 2¾ hours, every two hours

❶ Getting Around

Central Passau is sufficiently compact to explore on foot. The CityBus links the Bahnhof with the Altstadt (€1) up to four times an hour. Longer trips within Passau cost €1.80; a day pass costs €4 (€5.50 for a family).

The walk up the hill to the Veste Oberhaus or the DJH Hostel, via Luitpoldbrücke and Ludwig-steig path, takes about 30 minutes. From April to October, a shuttle bus operates every 30 minutes from Rathausplatz (€1.80).

There are several public car parks near the train station, but only one in the Altstadt at Römerplatz (€0.60/8.40 per 30 minutes/day).

Bavarian Forest

Together with the Bohemian Forest on the Czech side of the border, the Bavarian Forest (Bayerischer Wald) forms the largest continuous woodland area in Europe. This inspiring landscape of peaceful rolling hills and rounded tree-covered peaks is interspersed with little-disturbed valleys and stretches of virgin woodland, providing a habitat for many species long since vanished from the rest of Central Europe. A large area is protected as the surprisingly wild and remote Bavarian Forest National Park (National-park Bayerischer Wald).

Although incredibly good value, the region sees few international tourists and remains quite traditional. A centuries-old glass-blowing industry is still active in many of the towns along the Glasstrasse (Glass Road), a 250km holiday route connecting Waldsassen with Passau. You can visit the studios, workshops, museums and shops, and stock up on traditional and contemporary designs.

The central town of Zwiesel is a natural base, but other settlements along the Wald-bahn such as Frauenau and Grafenau are also good options if relying on public transport.

◉ Sights

Bavarian Forest National Park NATIONAL PARK
(Nationalpark Bayerischer Wald; www.national-park-bayerischer-wald.de) A paradise for out-door fiends, the Bavarian Forest National Park extends for around 24,250 hectares along the Czech border, from Bayerisch Eisenstein in the north to Finsterau in the south. Its thick forest, most of it mountain spruce, is criss-crossed by hundreds of kilometres of marked hiking, cycling and cross-country skiing trails, some of which now link up with a similar network across the border. The region is home to deer, wild boar, fox, otter and countless bird species.

Around 1km northeast of the village of Neu-schönau stands the **Hans-Eisenmann-Haus** (☑ 08558-96150; www.nationalpark-bayerischer-wald. de; Böhmstrasse 35; ⊙ 9am-6pm daily Apr-Oct, 9.30am-5pm daily Nov-Mar), the national park's main visitor centre. The free, but slightly dated, exhibition has hands-on displays designed to shed light on topics such as pollution and tree growth. There's also a children's discovery room, a shop and a library.

Glasmuseum MUSEUM
(☑ 09926-941 020; www.glasmuseum-frauenau. de; Am Museumspark 1, Frauenau; adult/concession €5/4.50; ⊙ 9am-5pm Tue-Sun) Frauenau's dazzlingly modern Glasmuseum covers four millennia of glassmaking history, starting with the ancient Egyptians and ending with modern glass art from around the world. Demonstrations and workshops for kids are regular features.

Museumsdorf Bayerischer Wald MUSEUM
(☑ 08504-8482; www.museumsdorf.com; Am Dreiburgensee, Tittling; adult/concession €6/4; ⊙ 9am-5pm Apr-Oct) Tittling, on the southern edge of the Bavarian Forest, is home to this 20-hectare open-air museum displaying 150 typical Bavarian Forest timber cottages and farmsteads from the 17th to the 19th centuries. Exhibitions inside the various buildings range from clothing and furniture to pottery and farming implements. Take frequent RBO bus 6124 to Tittling from Passau Hauptbahnhof.

Waldmuseum MUSEUM
(☑ 09922-503 706; www.waldmuseum.zwiesel. de; Kirchplatz 3; adult/concession €6/4; ⊙ 10am-5pm Wed-Mon) Housed in a former brewery, Zwiesel's 'Forest Museum' has exhibitions on local customs, flora and fauna, glassmaking and life in the forest.

🏃 Activities

Two long-distance hiking routes cut through the Bavarian Forest: the European Distance

Trails E6 (Baltic Sea to the Adriatic Sea) and E8 (North Sea to the Carpathian Mountains). There are mountain huts all along the way. Another popular hiking trail is the Gläserne Steig (Glass Trail) from Lam to Grafenau. Whatever route you're planning, maps produced by Kompass – sheets 185, 195 and 197 – are invaluable companions. They are available from tourist offices and the park visitor centre.

The Bavarian Forest has seven ski areas, but downhill skiing is low-key, even though the area's highest mountain, the Grosser Arber (1456m), occasionally hosts European and World Cup ski races. The major draw here is cross-country skiing, with 2000km of prepared routes through the ranges.

🛏 Sleeping

Accommodation in this region is a real bargain; Zwiesel and Grafenau have the best choices.

DJH Hostel   HOSTEL €
(📞08553-6000; www.waldhaeuser.jugendherberge. de; Herbergsweg 2, Neuschönau; dm from €21.90) The only hostel right in the Bavarian Forest National Park is an ideal base for hikers, bikers and cross-country skiers.

Ferienpark Arber   CAMPGROUND €
(📞09922-802 595; www.ferienpark-arber.de; Waldesruhweg 34, Zwiesel; per campsite €20.50) This convenient and well-equipped camping ground is about 500m north of Zwiesel train station.

★ Das Reiners   HOTEL €€
(📞08552-964 90; www.dasreiners.de; Grüb 20, Grafenau; s €66-75, d €112-190; P�🏊) Recently revamped and rebranded, this snazzily elegant hotel in Grafenau offers good value for the weary traveller. The stylish rooms are spacious and most have balconies. Guests

are treated to a pool and sauna, and scrumptious buffet meals. Prices are for half-board.

Hotel Zur Waldbahn   HOTEL €€
(📞09922-8570; www.zurwaldbahn.de; Bahnhofplatz 2, Zwiesel; s €60-66, d €80-100; P🐦) Opposite Zwiesel train station, many of the rooms at this characteristic inn, run by three generations of the same family, open to balconies with views over the town. The breakfast buffet is an especially generous spread and even includes homemade jams. The restaurant, serving traditional local fare, is the best in town.

ⓘ Information

Tourist Office (📞08552-962 343; www. grafenau.de; Rathausgasse 1, Grafenau; ⊙8am-5pm Mon-Thu, 8am-1pm Fri, 10-11.30am & 3-5pm Sat, 9.30-11.30am Sun)
Tourist Office (📞09922-840 523; www. zwiesel.de; Stadtplatz 27, Zwiesel; ⊙9am-noon & 1-4.30pm Mon-Fri)

ⓘ Getting There & Around

From Munich, Regensburg or Passau, Zwiesel is reached by rail via Plattling; most trains continue to Bayerisch Eisenstein on the Czech border, with connections to Prague. The scenic Waldbahn shuttles directly between Zwiesel and Bodenmais, and Zwiesel and Grafenau.

There's also a tight network of regional buses, though service can be infrequent. The Igel-Bus, operated by **Ostbayernbus** (www.ostbayernbus.de) navigates around the national park on five routes. A useful one is the Lusen-Bus (€5/12.50 per one/three days), which leaves from Grafenau Hauptbahnhof and travels to the Hans-Eisenmann-Haus, the DJH Hostel and the Lusen hiking area.

The best value is usually the Bayerwald-Ticket (€8), a day pass good for unlimited travel on bus and train across the forest area. It's available from the park visitor centre, stations and tourist offices throughout the area.

Salzburg & Around

Best Places to Eat

➡ Esszimmer (p186)

➡ Triangel (p185)

➡ Obauer (p195)

➡ Magazin (p186)

➡ The Green Garden (p185)

Best Places to Stay

➡ Haus Ballwein (p181)

➡ Pension Katrin (p182)

➡ Hotel Schloss Mönchstein (p184)

➡ Arte Vida (p183)

➡ Hotel & Villa Auersperg (p183)

Why Go?

One of Austria's smallest provinces, Salzburgerland is proof that size really doesn't matter. Well, not when you have Mozart, Maria von Trapp and the 600-year legacy of the prince-archbishops behind you. This is the land that grabbed the world spotlight and shouted 'visit Austria!' with Julie Andrews skipping joyously down the mountainsides. This is indeed the land of crisp apple strudel, dancing marionettes and high-on-a-hilltop castles. This is the Austria of your wildest childhood dreams.

Salzburg is every bit as grand as you imagine it: a baroque masterpiece, a classical music legend and Austria's spiritual heartland. But it is just the prelude to the region's sensational natural beauty. Just outside of the city, the landscape is etched with deep ravines, glinting ice caves, karst plateaus and mountains of myth – in short, the kind of alpine gorgeousness that no well-orchestrated symphony or yodelling nun could ever quite capture.

When to Go

Orchestras strike up at Mozart's birthday bash in January, Mozartwoche, and at the Easter Osterfestspiele. July to August is the best time to partake in the colossal feast of opera, classical music and drama that is the Salzburg Festival. Jazz festivals get into full swing from October, and late November sees Christmas markets fill Salzburg with festive sparkle.

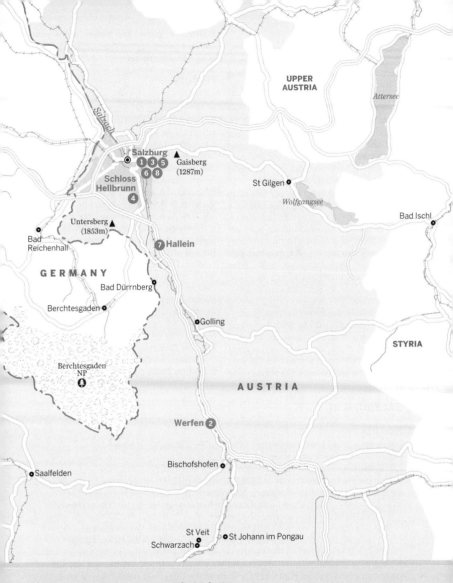

Salzburg & Around Highlights

1 Surveying Salzburg's baroque cityscape from 900-year-old **Festung Hohensalzburg** (p171)

2 Going subzero in the frozen depths of **Eisriesenwelt** (p194) in Werfen

3 Tuning into the life of a classical genius at Salzburg's **Mozart-Wohnhaus** (p176)

4 Getting drenched like a drunken prince-archbishop by fountains at **Schloss Hellbrunn** (p192)

5 Doing a Julie singing 'Do-Re-Mi' in the fountain-dotted gardens of Salzburg's **Schloss Mirabell** (p177)

6 Marvelling at puppetry magic at the smaller-than-life **Salzburger Marionettentheater** (p189)

7 Donning a boiler suit for a slippery-when-waxed ride at the **Salzwelten** (p193) salt mine in Hallein

8 Thanking heaven for small breweries and brimful steins at Salzburg's **Augustiner Bräustübl** (p187)

SALZBURG

☑ 0662 / POP 146,630 / ELEV 430M

The joke 'If it's baroque, don't fix it' is a perfect maxim for Salzburg: the storybook Old Town burrowed below steep hills looks much as it did when Mozart lived here 250 years ago. Standing beside the fast-flowing Salzach River, your gaze is raised inch by inch to its mosaic of graceful domes and spires, the formidable clifftop fortress and the mountains beyond. It's a view that never palls. It's a backdrop that did the lordly prince-archbishops and Maria proud.

Tempting as it is to spend every minute in the Unesco-listed Altstadt drifting from one baroque church and monumental square to the next in a daze of grandeur, Salzburg rewards those who venture further. Give Getreidegasse's throngs the slip, meander side streets where classical music wafts from open windows, linger decadently over coffee and cake, and let Salzburg slowly, slowly work its magic.

Beyond Salzburg's two biggest moneyspinners – Mozart and *The Sound of Music* – hides a city with a burgeoning arts and dining scene, manicured parks and concert halls that uphold musical tradition 365 days a year. Everywhere you go, the scenery, the skyline, the music, the history sends your spirits soaring higher than Julie Andrews octave-leaping vocals.

History

Salzburg has had a tight grip on the region as far back as 15 BC, when the Roman town Iuvavum stood on the site of the present-day city. This Roman stronghold came under constant attack from warlike Celtic tribes and was ultimately destroyed or abandoned due to disease.

The Frankish missionary St Rupert established the first Christian kingdom and founded St Peter's church and monastery in AD 696. As centuries passed, the successive archbishops of Salzburg gradually increased their power and were given the grandiose titles of princes of the Holy Roman Empire.

Wolf Dietrich von Raitenau, Salzburg's most influential prince-archbishop from 1587 to 1612, spearheaded the total baroque makeover of the city, commissioning many of its most beautiful churches, palaces and gardens. He fell from power after losing a fierce dispute over the salt trade with the powerful rulers of Bavaria, and died a prisoner.

Another of the city's archbishops, Paris Lodron (1619–53), managed to keep the

SALZBURG IN...

Two Days

Get up early to see **Mozarts Geburtshaus** (p176) and boutique-dotted Getreidegasse before the crowds arrive. Take in the baroque grandeur of **Residenzplatz** (p176) and the stately prince-archbishop's palace, **Residenz** (p174). Coffee and cake in the decadent surrounds of **Café Tomaselli** (p188) fuels an afternoon absorbing history at the hands-on **Salzburg Museum** (p171) or monastic heritage at **Erzabtei St Peter** (p176). Toast your first day with homebrews and banter in **Augustiner Bräustübl's** (p187) tree-canopied beer garden.

Begin day two with postcard views from 900-year-old **Festung Hohensalzburg's** (p171) ramparts, or cutting-edge art exhibitions at **Museum der Moderne** (p175). Have lunch at **M32** (p186) or bag Austrian goodies at the **Grünmarkt** (p187) for a picnic in **Schloss Mirabell's** (p177) sculpture-strewn gardens. Chamber music in the palace's sublime **Marble Hall** (p189) or enchanting puppetry at **Salzburger Marionettentheater** (p189) rounds out the day nicely.

Four Days

With another couple of days to explore, you can join a Mozart or *Sound of Music* tour. Hire a bike to pedal along the Salzach's villa-studded banks to summer palace **Schloss Hellbrunn** (p192) and its trick fountains. Dine in old-world Austrian style at **Zum Zirkelwirt** (p185) before testing the right-bank nightlife.

The fun-packed **salt mines** (p193) of Hallein and the Goliath of ice caves, **Eisriesenwelt** (p194) in Werfen, both make terrific day trips for day four. Or grab your walking boots or skis and head up to Salzburg's twin peaks: **Untersberg** (p193) and **Gaisberg** (p193).

principality out of the Europe-wide Thirty Years' War. Salzburg also remained neutral during the War of the Austrian Succession a century later, but bit by bit the province's power gradually waned and Salzburg came under the thumb of France and Bavaria during the Napoleonic Wars. In 1816 Salzburg became part of the Austrian Empire and was on the gradual road to economic recovery.

The early 20th century saw population growth and the founding of the prestigious Salzburg Festival in 1920. Austria was annexed to Nazi Germany in 1938 and during WWII some 40% of the city's buildings were destroyed by Allied bombings. These were restored to their former glory, and in 1997 Salzburg's historic Altstadt became a Unesco World Heritage site.

⊙ Sights

Salzburg's trophy sights huddle in the pedestrianised Altstadt, which straddles both banks of the Salzach River but centres largely on the left bank. Here the tangled lanes are made for a serendipitous wander, leading to hidden courtyards, medieval squares framed by burgher houses and baroque fountains.

Many of the places mentioned below close slightly earlier in winter and open longer – usually an hour or two – during the Salzburg Festival.

★ Festung Hohensalzburg FORT
(www.salzburg-burgen.at; Mönchsberg 34; adult/child/family €8/4.50/18.20, incl Festungsbahn funicular €11.30/6.50/26.20; ☺9am-7pm) Salzburg's most visible icon is this mighty 900-year-old cliff-top fortress, one of the biggest and best preserved in Europe. It's easy to spend half a day up here, roaming the ramparts for far-reaching views over the city's spires, the Salzach River and the mountains. The fortress is a steep 15-minute jaunt from the centre or a speedy ride in the glass Festungsbahn funicular (Festungsgasse 4; one way/return adult €6.70/8.30, child €3.70/4.50; ☺9am-8pm).

The fortress began life as a humble bailey, built in 1077 by Gebhard von Helffenstein at a time when the Holy Roman Empire was at loggerheads with the papacy. The present structure, however, owes its grandeur to spendthrift Leonard von Keutschach, prince-archbishop of Salzburg from 1495 to 1519 and the city's last feudal ruler. Highlights of a visit include the Golden Hall, where lavish banquets were once held, with a gold-studded ceiling imitating a starry night sky. Your ticket also gets you into

SALZBURG'S CATHEDRAL QUARTER
Salzburg shines more brightly than ever since the opening of the **DomQuartier** (www.domquartier.at; adult/child €12/5; ☺10am-5pm Wed-Mon) in 2014, showcasing the most fabulous baroque monuments and museums in the historic centre. A single ticket gives you access to the Residenz state rooms and gallery, the upper galleries of the Dom, the Dommuseum and Erzabtei St Peter. The multilingual audioguide whisks you through the quarter in an hour and a half, though you could easily spend half a day absorbing all of its sights.

the Marionette Museum, where skeleton-in-a-box Archbishop Wolf Dietrich steals the (puppet) show, as well as the Fortress Museum, which showcases a 1612 model of Salzburg, medieval instruments, armour and some pretty gruesome torture devices.

The Golden Hall is the backdrop for year-round Festungskonzerte (fortress concerts), which often focus on Mozart's works. See www.mozartfestival.at for times and prices.

★ Salzburg Museum MUSEUM
(www.salzburgmuseum.at; Mozartplatz 1; adult/child €7/3; ☺9am-5pm Tue-Sun, to 8pm Thu; ⊞) Housed in the baroque Neue Residenz palace, this flagship museum takes you on a fascinating romp through Salzburg past and present. Ornate rooms showcase everything from Roman excavations to prince-archbishop portraits. There are free guided tours at 6pm every Thursday.

A visit starts beneath the courtyard in the strikingly illuminated Kunsthalle, presenting rotating exhibitions of art.

Upstairs, prince-archbishops glower down from the walls at Mythos Salzburg, which celebrates the city as a source of artistic and poetic inspiration. Showstoppers include Carl Spitzweg's renowned *Sonntagsspaziergang* (Sunday Stroll; 1841) painting, the portrait-lined prince-archbishop's room and the Ständesaal (Sovereign Chamber), an opulent vision of polychrome stucco curling around frescoes depicting the history of Rome according to Titus Livius. The early 16th-century Millefiori tapestry, Archbishop Wolf Dietrich's gold-embroidered pontifical shoe and Flemish tapestries are among other attention-grabbers.

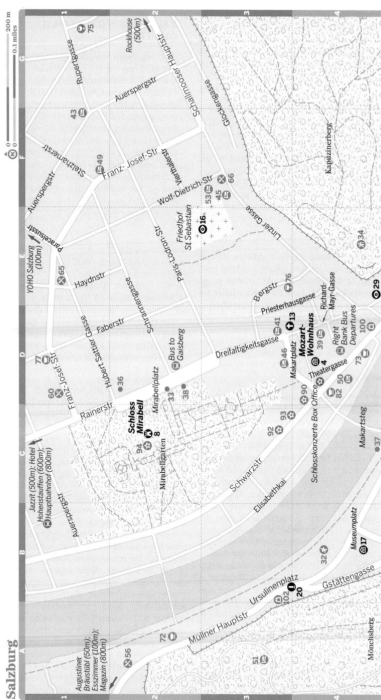

Salzburg

172

SALZBURG & AROUND

200 m
0.1 miles

Rockhouse
(500m)

YOHO Salzburg
(100m)

Jazzit (500m);
Hotel
Hohenstauffen (600m);
Haupthbahnhof (800m)

Augustiner
Bräustübl (50m);
Esszimmer (100m);
Magazin (800m)

Bus to
Gaisberg

Schloss
Mirabell

Mirabellgarten

Mirabellplatz

Friedhof
St Sebastian

Mozart-
Wohnhaus

Right
Bank Bus
Departures

Schlosskonzerte Box Office

Museumsplatz

Kapuzinerberg

Mönchsberg

Ursulinenplatz

Rupertgasse
Auerspergstr
Steinhamerstr
Franz-Josef-Str
Wolf-Dietrich-Str
Schallmooser Hauptstr
Glockengasse
Linzer Gasse
Paracelsusstr
Haydnstr
Schrannengasse
Paris-Lodron-Str
Bergstr
Priesterhausgasse
Richard-Mayr-Gasse
Hubert Sattler Gasse
Faberstr
Dreifaltigkeitsgasse
Theatergasse
Makartplatz
Franz-Josef-Str
Rainerstr
Schwarzstr
Elisabethkai
Makartsteg
Gstättengasse
Müllner Hauptstr
Auerspergstr

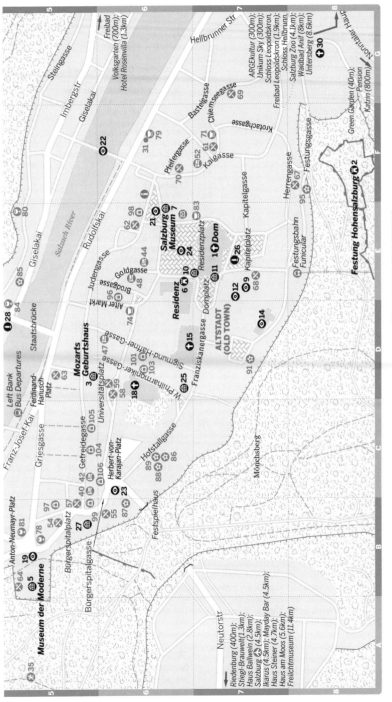

Salzburg

The **Panorama Passage** also provides some insight into Salzburg's past, with its Roman walls and potter's kiln and models of the city at different points in history.

Salzburg's famous 35-bell Glockenspiel, which chimes daily at 7am, 11am and 6pm, is on the western flank of the Neue Residenz.

★ Dom
CATHEDRAL

(Cathedral; Domplatz; donations accepted; ⊙ 8am-7pm Mon-Sat, 1-7pm Sun) Gracefully crowned by a bulbous copper dome and twin spires, the Dom stands out as a masterpiece of baroque art. Bronze portals symbolising faith, hope and charity lead into the cathedral. In the nave, intricate stucco and Arsenio Mascagni's ceiling frescoes recounting the Passion of Christ guide the eye to the polychrome dome.

Italian architect Santino Solari redesigned the cathedral during the Thirty Years' War and it was consecrated in 1628. Its origins, though, date to an earlier cathedral founded by Bishop Virgil in 767.

For more on the history, hook onto one of the free guided tours at 2pm Monday to Friday in July and August.

Dommuseum
MUSEUM

(www.domquartier.at; Kapitelplatz 6; DomQuartier adult/child €12/4; ⊙10am-5pm Wed-Mon) The Dommuseum is a treasure trove of sacred art. A visit whisks you past a cabinet of Renaissance curiosities crammed with crystals, coral and oddities such as armadillos and pufferfish, through rooms showcasing gem-encrusted monstrances, stained glass and altarpieces, and into the **Long Gallery**, which is graced with 17th- and 18th-century paintings, including Paul Troger's chiaroscuro *Christ and Nicodemus* (1739).

From the organ gallery, you get close-ups of the organ Mozart played and a bird's-eye view of the Dom's nave.

★ Residenz
PALACE

(www.domquartier.at; Residenzplatz 1; DomQuartier adult/child €12/5; ⊙10am-5pm Wed-Mon) The crowning glory of Salzburg's new Dom-

Quartier, the Residenz is where the prince-archbishops held court until Salzburg became part of the Habsburg Empire in the 19th century. An audioguide tour takes in the exuberant **state rooms**, lavishly adorned with tapestries, stucco and frescoes by Johann Michael Rottmayr. The 3rd floor is given over to the **Residenzgalerie**, where the focus is on Flemish and Dutch masters. Must-sees include Rubens' *Allegory on Emperor Charles V* and Rembrandt's chiaroscuro *Old Woman Praying*.

Nowhere is the pomp and circumstance of Salzburg more tangible than at this regal palace. A man of grand designs, Wolf Dietrich von Raitenau, prince-archbishop of Salzburg from 1587 to 1612, gave the go-ahead to build this baroque palace on the site of an 11th-century bishop's residence.

★**Museum der Moderne** GALLERY
(www.museumdermoderne.at; Mönchsberg 32; adult/child €8/6; ⊙10am-6pm Tue-Sun, to 8pm Wed) Straddling Mönchsberg's cliffs, this contemporary glass-and-marble oblong of a gallery stands in stark contrast to the fortress. The gallery shows first-rate temporary exhibitions of 20th- and 21st-century art. The works of Alberto Giacometti, Dieter Roth, Emil Nolde and John Cage have previously featured. There's a free guided tour of the gallery at 6.30pm every Wednesday. The **Mönchsberg Lift** (Gstättengasse 13; one

---

ℹ **SALZBURG CARD**

If you're planning on doing lots of sightseeing, it's seriously worth buying the money-saving **Salzburg Card** (1-/2-/3-day card €27/36/42). The card gets you entry to all of the major sights and attractions, a free river cruise, unlimited use of public transport (including the cable car to Untersberg) plus numerous discounts on tours and events. The card is half-price for children and €3 cheaper in the low season.

WALK OF MODERN ART

Eager to slip out of its baroque shoes and show the world that it can do cutting edge, too, Salzburg commissioned a clutch of public artworks between 2002 and 2011, many of which can be seen on a wander through the Altstadt. Internationally renowned artists were drafted to create contemporary sculptures that provide striking contrast to the city's historic backdrop.

On Mönchsberg you will find Mario Merz' 21 neon-lit **Numbers in the Woods** and James Turrell's elliptical **Sky Space** (⊙ 10am-8pm Apr-Oct, 10am-6pm Nov-Mar), the latter creating a play of light and shadow at dawn and dusk. Back in town, you will almost certainly stroll past Stephan Balkenhol's **Sphaera** on Kapitelplatz, a huge golden globe topped by a startlingly realistic-looking man. Tucked away on Ursulinenplatz is Markus Lüpertz' **Mozart – Eine Hommage**, an abstract, one-armed bronze sculpture of the genius, sporting trademark pigtail and the torso of a woman. Another tribute to Mozart stands across the river in the shape of Marina Abramovic's **Spirit of Mozart** (Schwarzstrasse), a cluster of chairs surrounding a 15m-high chair, which, as the name suggests, is said to embody the spirit of the composer.

For more, visit the **Salzburg Foundation** (www.salzburgfoundation.at), the driving force behind this display of open-air art installations and sculpture.

way/return €2.10/3.40, incl gallery adult/child €9.70/6.80; ⊙ 8am-7pm Thu-Tue, to 9pm Wed) whizzes up to the gallery year-round.

Mönchsberg commands broad outlooks across Salzburg's spire-dotted cityscape and its woodland walking trails are great for tiptoeing away from the crowds for an hour or two. While you're up here, take in the far-reaching views over Salzburg over coffee or lunch at M32 (p186).

★ **Mozarts Geburtshaus**   MUSEUM
(Mozart's Birthplace; www.mozarteum.at; Getreidegasse 9; adult/child €10/3.50, incl Mozart-Wohnhaus €17/5; ⊙ 9am-5.30pm) Wolfgang Amadeus Mozart, Salzburg's most famous son, was born in this bright yellow townhouse in 1756 and spent the first 17 years of his life here.

Today's museum harbours a collection of instruments, documents and portraits. Highlights include the mini-violin he played as a toddler, plus a lock of his hair and buttons from his jacket. In one room, Mozart is shown as a holy babe beneath a neon blue halo – we'll leave you to draw your own analogies...

★ **Mozart-Wohnhaus**   MUSEUM
(Mozart's Residence; www.mozarteum.at; Makartplatz 8; adult/child €10/3.50, incl Mozarts Geburtshaus €17/5; ⊙ 9am-5.30pm) Tired of the cramped living conditions on Getreidegasse, the Mozart family moved to this more spacious abode in 1773, where a prolific Mozart composed works such as the *Shepherd King* (K208) and *Idomeneo* (K366). Emanuel Schikaneder, a close friend of Mozart and the

librettist of *The Magic Flute*, was a regular guest here. An audioguide accompanies your visit, serenading you with opera excerpts. Alongside family portraits and documents, you'll find Mozart's original fortepiano.

Under the same roof and included in your ticket is the **Mozart Ton-und Filmmuseum**, a film and music archive of interest to the ultra-enthusiast, with some 25,000 audiovisual recordings.

Residenzplatz   SQUARE
With its horse-drawn carriages, palace and street entertainers, this stately baroque square is the Salzburg of a thousand postcards. Its centrepiece is the **Residenzbrunnen**, an enormous marble fountain ringed by four water-spouting horses and topped by a conch shell–bearing Triton. The plaza is the late-16th-century vision of Prince-Archbishop Wolf Dietrich von Raitenau who, inspired by Rome, enlisted Italian architect Vincenzo Scamozzi.

Erzabtei St Peter   MONASTERY
(St Peter's Abbey; St Peter Bezirk 1-2; catacombs adult/child €2/1.50; ⊙ church 8am-noon & 2.30-6.30pm, cemetery 6.30am-7pm, catacombs 10am-6pm) A Frankish missionary named Rupert founded this abbey church and monastery in around 700, making it the oldest in the German-speaking world. Though a vaulted Romanesque portal remains, today's church is overwhelmingly baroque, with rococo stucco, statues – including one of archangel Michael shoving a crucifix through the

throat of a goaty demon – and striking altar paintings by Martin Johann Schmidt.

Take a stroll around the **cemetery**, where the graves are mini works of art with their intricate stonework and filigree wrought-iron crosses. Composer Michael Haydn (1737–1806), opera singer Richard Mayr (1877–1935) and renowned Salzburg confectioner Paul Fürst (1856–1941) lie buried here; the last is watched over by skull-bearing cherubs.

The cemetery is home to the **catacombs**, cavelike chapels and crypts hewn out of the Mönchsberg cliff face.

★ **Schloss Mirabell**　PALACE
(Mirabellplatz 4; ⊘ Marble Hall 8am-4pm Mon, Wed & Thu, 1-4pm Tue & Fri, gardens 6am-dusk) **FREE**
Prince-Archbishop Wolf Dietrich built this splendid palace in 1606 to impress his beloved mistress Salome Alt. It must have done the trick because she went on to bear the archbishop some 15 children; sources disagree on the exact number – poor Wolf was presumably too distracted by spiritual matters to keep count himself. Johann Lukas von Hildebrandt, of Schloss Belvedere fame, remodelled the palace in baroque style in 1721. The lavish baroque interior, replete with stucco, marble and frescos, is free to visit.

The **Marmorsaal** (Marble Hall) provides a sublime backdrop for evening chamber concerts.

The flowery parterres, rose gardens and leafy arbours are less overrun first thing in the morning and early evening. The lithe *Tänzerin* (dancer) sculpture is a great spot to photograph the gardens with the fortress as a backdrop. *Sound of Music* fans will of course recognise the Pegasus statue, the steps and the gnomes of the Zwerglgarten (Dwarf Garden), where the mini von Trapps practised 'Do-Re-Mi'.

Rupertinum　GALLERY
(www.museumdermoderne.at; Wiener-Philharmoniker-Gasse 9; adult/child/family €6/4/8; ⊘ 10am-6pm Tue & Thu-Sun, to 8pm Wed) In the heart of the Altstadt, the Rupertinum is the sister gallery of the Museum der Moderne (p175) and is devoted to rotating exhibitions of modern art. There is a strong emphasis on graphic works and photography.

Friedhof St Sebastian　CEMETERY
(Linzer Gasse 41; ⊘ 9am-6.30pm) Tucked behind the baroque Sebastianskirche (St Sebastian's Church), this peaceful cemetery and its cloisters were designed by Andrea Berteleto in Italianate style in 1600. Mozart family members and well-known 16th-century physician Paracelsus are buried here, but out-pomping them all is Prince-Archbishop Wolf Dietrich von Raitenau's mosaic-tiled mausoleum, an elaborate memorial to himself.

Stift Nonnberg　CONVENT
(Nonnberg Convent; Nonnberggasse 2; ⊘ 7am-dusk)
A short climb up the Nonnbergstiege staircase from Kaigasse or along Festungsgasse brings you to this Benedictine convent, founded 1300 years ago and made famous as *the* nunnery in *The Sound of Music*. You can visit the beautiful rib-vaulted church, but the rest of the convent is off-limits. Take €0.50 to illuminate the beautiful Romanesque frescoes.

Steingasse　HISTORIC SITE
On the right bank of the Salzach River, this narrow, cobbled lane was, incredibly, the main trade route to Italy in medieval times. Look out for the 13th-century **Steintor** gate and the house of **Joseph Mohr**, who wrote the lyrics to that all-time classic of a carol 'Silent Night'. The street is at its most photogenic in the late morning when sunlight illuminates its pastel-coloured townhouses.

Kollegienkirche　CHURCH
(Universitätsplatz; ⊘ 8am-6pm) Johann Bernhard Fischer von Erlach's grandest baroque design is this late-17th-century university church, with a striking bowed facade. The high altar's columns symbolise the Seven Pillars of Wisdom.

SALZBURG & AROUND SIGHTS

TOP CULTURAL HIGHS

➡ The palatial state apartments and Old Master paintings at the **Residenz** (p174), once home to Salzburg's powerful prince-archbishops.

➡ The **Keltenmuseum** (p193) in Hallein, tracing regional heritage through Celtic artefacts and the history of salt extraction.

➡ Salzburg's **Altstadt** (p171), an early baroque masterpiece and Unesco World Heritage site, often hailed the 'Rome of the North'.

➡ The avant-garde art and architecture of **Museum der Moderne** (p175) atop Mönchsberg's cliffs.

➡ **Salzwelten** (p193) near Hallein, a cavernous salt mine that once filled Salzburg's princely coffers with 'white gold'.

Pferdeschwemme FOUNTAIN
(Horse Trough; Herbert-von-Karajan-Platz) Designed by Fischer von Erlach in 1693, this is a horse-lover's delight, with rearing equine pin-ups surrounding Michael Bernhard Mandl's statue of a horse tamer.

Franziskanerkirche CHURCH
(Franziskanergasse 5; ⊙ 6.30am-7.30pm) A real architectural hotchpotch, Salzburg's Franciscan church has a Romanesque nave, a Gothic choir with rib vaulting and a baroque marble altar (one of Fischer von Erlach's creations).

Dreifältigkeitskirche CHURCH
(Church of the Holy Trinity; Dreifaltigkeitsgasse 14; ⊙ 6.30am-6.30pm) Baroque master Johann Bernhard Fischer von Erlach designed this graceful right-bank church, famous for Johann Michael Rottmayr's dome fresco of the Holy Trinity.

Domgrabungsmuseum MUSEUM
(☑ 6208 081 31, 84 52 95; Residenzplatz; adult/child €2.50/1; ⊙ 9am-5pm Jul & Aug, on request Sep-Jun) Map out the city's past with a romp of the rocks at this subterranean archaeology museum beside the Dom. Particularly of interest are fragments of Roman mosaics, a milestone hewn from Untersberg marble and the brickwork of the former Romanesque cathedral.

🏃 Activities

There's an extensive network of cycling routes to explore: from a gentle 20-minute trundle along the Salzach River to Hellbrunn, to the highly scenic 450km Mozart Radweg through Salzburgerland and Bavaria. For maps and details, visit www.salzburgrad.at.

Mönchsberg WALKING
Rising sheer and rugged above the city, 540m Mönchsberg commands photogenic views over the Altstadt's spires and domes on one side and of the fortress perched high on a hill on the other. Trails head out in all directions, but arguably the most scenic is the 4km panoramic walking route from Stift Nonnberg to Augustiner Bräustübl, taking in Festung Hohensalzburg and Museum der Moderne en route, and commanding views deep into the Alps.

Kapuzinerberg WALKING
Presiding over the city, the serene, thickly wooded 640m peak of Kapuzinerberg is criss-crossed by walking trails up to a viewpoint that gazes across the river to the castle-topped Altstadt. Note the six baroque Way of the Cross chapels as you make the short trek uphill.

👉 Tours

If you would rather go it alone, the tourist office (p190) has four-hour iTour audioguides (€9), which take in big-hitters like the Residenz, Mirabellgarten and Mozartplatz.

Fräulein Maria's Bicycle Tours BICYCLE TOUR
(www.mariasbicycletours.com; Mirabellplatz 4; adult/child €30/18; ⊙ 9.30am May-Sep, plus 4.30pm Jun-Aug) Belt out *The Sound of Music* faves as you pedal on one of these jolly 3½-hour bike tours, taking in film locations, including the Mirabellgarten, Stift Nonnberg, Schloss Leopoldskron and Hellbrunn. No advance

---

A SUMMER SPLASH

Retreat from the summer madness at one of Salzburg's swimming areas. Here's our pick of the best:

Freibad Leopoldskron (Leopoldskronstrasse 50; adult/concession €4.60/2.60; ⊙ 9am-7pm May–mid-Sep) Salzburg's biggest outdoor pool, with laps for swimmers, kids' splash pools, diving boards, waterslides, table tennis, minigolf and volleyball. Bus 22 to Wartbergweg stops close by.

Waldbad Anif (Waldbadstrasse 1; adult/concession €6/4; ⊙ 9am-9pm May-Sep) A sylvan beauty of a turquoise, forest-rimmed lake. Go for a quiet dip or take part in activities such as canoeing, climbing, volleyball and table tennis. Take bus 25 or 28 to Maximarkt, a 1km walk from the lake.

Freibad Volksgarten (Hermann-Bahr-Promenade 2; adult/concession €4.60/2.60; ⊙ 9am-7pm May–mid-Sep) Just south of Kapuzinerberg, this park has decent-sized pools, plenty of space for sunbathing, plus a children's splash pool, table tennis and volleyball. Buses 6, 7 and 20 stop at Volksgarten.

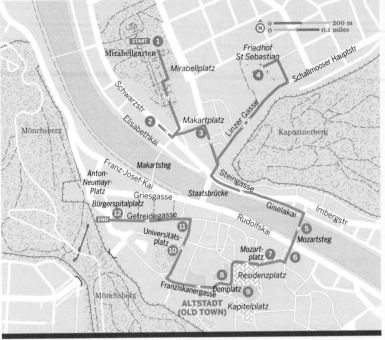

🏃 City Walk
In Mozart's Footsteps

START SCHLOSS MIRABELL
FINISH FÜRST
DISTANCE 3KM
DURATION 1½ HOURS

Mozart was the ultimate musical prodigy: he identified a pig's squeal as G sharp aged two, began to compose when he was five and first performed for Empress Maria Theresa at the age of six. Follow in his footsteps on this classic walking tour.

Begin at baroque **1** **Schloss Mirabell** (p177), where the resplendent *Marmorsaal* is often the backdrop for chamber concerts of Mozart's music. Stroll south through the fountain-dotted gardens, passing the strikingly angular **2** **Mozarteum** (p189), a foundation honouring Mozart's life and works, and the host of the renowned Mozartwoche festival in January. Just around the corner on Makartplatz is the 17th-century **3** **Mozart-Wohnhaus** (p176), where you can see how the Mozart family lived and listen to rare recordings of Mozart's symphonies. Amble north along Linzer Gasse to **4** **Friedhof St Sebastian** (p177),

the arcaded cemetery where Wolfgang's father Leopold and wife Constanze lie buried. Retrace your steps towards the Salzach River, turning left onto medieval Steingasse and crossing the art-nouveau **5** **Mozartsteg** (Mozart Bridge). Look out for the **6** **memorial plaque** at No 8, the house where Mozart's beloved Constanze died, as you approach **7** **Mozartplatz**. On this elegant square, Mozart is literally and metaphorically put on a pedestal. Across the way is the grand **8** **Residenz** (p174) palace where Mozart gave his first court concert at the ripe old age of six. Beside it rests the baroque **9** **Dom** (p174), where Mozart's parents were married in 1747 and Mozart was baptised in 1756. Mozart later composed sacred music here and was cathedral organist. Follow Franziskanergasse to reach the **10** **Kollegienkirche** (p177) on Universitätsplatz, where Mozart's D Minor Mass, K65, premiered in 1769. On parallel Getreidegasse, stop to contemplate the birthplace of a genius at **11** **Mozarts Geburtshaus** (p176) and buy some of **12** **Fürst's** (p190) famous chocolate *Mozartkugeln* (Mozart balls).

DIY SOUND OF MUSIC TOUR

Do a Julie and sing as you stroll your self-guided tour of *The Sound of Music* film locations. OK, let's start at the very beginning:

The Hills are Alive Cut! Make that *proper* mountains. The opening scenes were filmed around the jewel-coloured Salzkammergut lakes. Maria makes her twirling entrance on alpine pastures just across the border in Bavaria.

A Problem like Maria Nuns waltzing on their way to mass at Benedictine Stift Nonnberg (p177) is fiction, but it's fact that the real Maria von Trapp intended to become a nun here before romance struck.

Have Confidence Residenzplatz (p176) is where Maria belts out 'I Have Confidence' and playfully splashes the spouting horses of the Residenzbrunnen fountain.

Do-Re-Mi Oh the Pegasus fountain, the steps with fortress views, the gnomes...the Mirabellgarten (p177) might inspire a rendition of 'Do-Re-Mi', especially if there's a drop of golden sun.

Sixteen Going on Seventeen The loved-up pavilion of the century hides out in Hellbrunn (p192) Park, where you can act out those 'oh Liesl', 'oh Rolf' fantasies.

So Long, Farewell The grand rococo palace of Schloss Leopoldskron (www.schloss-leopoldskron.com; Leopoldskronstrasse 56-58), a 15-minute walk from Festung Hohensalzburg, is where the lake scene was filmed. Its Venetian Room was the blueprint for the Trapp's lavish ballroom, where the children bid their farewells.

Edelweiss and Adieu The Felsenreitschule (Summer Riding School; Hofstallgasse 1) is the dramatic backdrop for the Salzburg Festival in the movie, where the Trapp Family Singers win the audience over with 'Edelweiss' and give the Nazis the slip with 'So Long, Farewell'.

Climb Every Mountain To, erm, Switzerland. Or content yourself with alpine views from Untersberg (p193), which appears briefly at the end of the movie when the family flees the country.

booking is necessary; just turn up at the meeting point on Mirabellplatz.

Segway Tours TOUR
(www.segway-salzburg.at; Wolf-Dietrich-Strasse 3; City/Sound of Music tour €33/60; ☺tours 10.30am, 1pm & 3.30pm mid-Mar–Oct) These guided Segway tours take in the big sights by zippy battery-powered scooter. Trundle through the city on a one-hour ride or tick off *Sound of Music* locations on a 2½-hour tour.

Salzburg Schiffsfahrt BOAT TOUR
(www.salzburghighlights.at; Makartsteg; adult/child €15/7.50; ☺Apr-Oct) A boat ride along the Salzach is a leisurely way to pick out Salzburg's sights. Hour-long cruises depart from Makartsteg bridge, with some of them chugging on to Schloss Hellbrunn (adult/child €17/10, not including entry to the palace).

Stiegl-Brauwelt BREWERY TOUR
(www.brauwelt.at; Bräuhausstrasse 9; adult/child €11/6; ☺10am-5pm) Brewing and bottling since 1492, Stiegl is Austria's largest private brewery. A tour takes in the different stages of the brewing process and (woo hoo!) the world's tallest beer tower. A Stiegl beer and small gift are thrown in for the price of a ticket. The brewery is 1.5km southwest of the Altstadt; take bus 1 or 10 to Bräuhausstrasse.

Bob's Special Tours BUS TOUR
(☑84 95 11; www.bobstours.com; Rudolfskai 38; ☺office 8.30am-5pm Mon-Fri, 1-2pm Sat & Sun) Minibus tours to *Sound of Music* locations (€48), the Bavarian Alps (€48) and Grossglockner (€96). Prices include a free hotel pick-up for morning tours starting at 9am. Reservations essential.

Salzburg Panorama Tours BUS TOUR
(☑87 40 29; www.panoramatours.com; Mirabellplatz; ☺office 8am-6pm) Boasts the 'original *Sound of Music* Tour' (€40) as well as a huge range of others, including Altstadt walking tours (€16), Mozart tours (€25) and Bavarian Alps excursions (€40).

Salzburg Sightseeing Tours BUS TOUR
(☑88 16 16; www.salzburg-sightseeingtours.at; Mirabellplatz 2; ☺office 8am-6pm) Sells a 24-hour

ticket (adult/child €16/8) for a multilingual hop-on, hop-off bus tour of the city's key sights and *Sound of Music* locations.

✿ Festivals & Events

Mozartwoche   MUSIC
(Mozart Week; www.mozarteum.at; ☉ late Jan) World-renowned orchestras, conductors and soloists celebrate Mozart's birthday with a feast of his music in late January.

Osterfestspiele   MUSIC
(Easter Festival; www.osterfestspiele-salzburg.at; ☉ Mar/Apr) This springtime shindig brings orchestral highlights, under Christian Thielemann's sprightly baton, to the Festspielhaus.

SommerSzene   CULTURAL
(www.sommerszene.net; ☉ late Jun-early Jul) Boundary-crossing performing arts are the focus of this event held from late June to early July.

Jazz & the City   JAZZ
(www.salzburgjazz.com; ☉ late Oct) Salzburg gets its groove on at some 100 free concerts in the Altstadt in late October.

Christkindlmarkt   CHRISTMAS MARKET
(www.christkindlmarkt.co.at; ☉ Dec) Salzburg is at its storybook best during Advent, when Christmas markets bring festive sparkle and choirs to Domplatz and Residenzplatz.

🛏 Sleeping

Salzburg's accommodation is pricey by Austrian standards, but you can get a good deal if you're willing to go the extra mile or two. Ask the tourist office for a list of private rooms and pensions. Medieval guesthouses oozing history, avant-garde design hotels with river views and chilled-out hostels all huddle in the Altstadt, where booking ahead is advisable.

Bear in mind that the high-season prices below are jacked up another 10% to 20% during the Salzburg Festival. If Salzburg is booked solid, consider staying in Hallein or just across the border in Bavaria.

★ Haus Ballwein   GUESTHOUSE €
(☎ 82 40 29; www.haus-ballwein.at; Moosstrasse 69a; s €42-49, d €63-69, apt €98-120; P 🖨 ⛄) With its bright, pine-filled rooms, mountain views, free bike hire and garden, this place is big on charm. The largest, quietest rooms face the back and have balconies and kitchenettes. It's a 10-minute trundle from the Altstadt; take bus 21 to Gsengerweg. Breakfast is a wholesome spread of fresh rolls, eggs, fruit, muesli and cold cuts.

Haus Steiner   GUESTHOUSE €
(☎ 83 00 31; www.haussteiner.com; Moosstrasse 156; s/d €37/62; P 🖨 ⛄) Kind-natured Rosemarie runs a tight ship at this sunny yellow chalet-style guesthouse, that's ablaze with flowers in summer. The pick of the petite

---

FESTIVAL TIME

In 1920, dream trio Hugo von Hofmannsthal, Max Reinhardt and Richard Strauss combined creative forces and the **Salzburg Festival** (Salzburger Festspiele; www.salzburger festspiele.at; ☉ late Jul-Aug) was born. Now, as then, one of the highlights is the staging of Hofmannsthal's morality play *Jedermann* (Everyman) on Domplatz. A trilogy of opera, drama and classical concerts of the highest calibre have since propelled the five-week summer festival to international renown, attracting some of the world's best conductors, directors, orchestras and singers.

Come festival time Salzburg crackles with excitement, as a quarter of a million visitors descend on the city for some 200 productions. Theatre premieres, avant-garde works and the summer-resident Vienna Philharmonic performing Mozart works are all in the mix. The Festival District on Hofstallgasse has a spectacular backdrop, framed by Mönchsberg's cliffs. Most performances are held in the cavernous **Grosses Festpielhaus** (☎ 804 50; Hofstallgasse 1) accommodating 2179 theatre-goers, the **Haus für Mozart** (House for Mozart; ☎ 804 55 00; www.salzburgerfestspiele.at; Hofstallgasse 1) in the former royal stables and the baroque Felsenreitschule.

If you're planning on visiting during the festival, don't leave *anything* to chance – book your flights, hotel and tickets months in advance. Sometimes last-minute tickets are available at the **ticket office** (☎ 80 45-500; info@salzburgfestival.at; Herbert-von-Karajan-Platz 11; ☉ 10am-1pm & 2-5pm Mon-Sat early–mid-Jul, 10am-6pm daily mid-Jul–Aug), but they're like gold dust. Ticket prices range from €11 to €430.

rooms, furnished in natural wood, come with fridges, balconies and mood-lifting mountain views; family-sized apartments have kitchenettes. Breakfast is copious and the Altstadt is a 15-minute ride away on bus 21; get off at Hammerauerstrasse.

Haus am Moos GUESTHOUSE €
(☏82 49 21; www.ammoos.at; Moosstrasse 186a; s/d €30/60; P 🛜 🖂 👬) A slice of rural calm just a 15-minute ride from town on bus 21, this alpine-style chalet is a find. Many of the rooms have balconies with gorgeous mountain views and some come with canopy beds. A breakfast of muesli, cold cuts, eggs and fresh breads gears you up for the day, and there's an outdoor pool for an afternoon dip.

YOHO Salzburg HOSTEL €
(☏87 96 49; www.yoho.at; Paracelsusstrasse 9; dm €19-25, s €41, d €69-78; @🛜) Free wi-fi, se-cure lockers, comfy bunks, plenty of cheap beer and good-value schnitzels – what more could a backpacker ask for? Except, perhaps, a merry sing-along with *The Sound of Music* screened daily (yes, *every* day) at 7pm. The friendly crew can arrange tours, adventure sports such as rafting and canyoning, and bike hire. Breakfast is a bargain €3.50.

★Pension Katrin PENSION €€
(☏83 08 60; www.pensionkatrin.at; Nonntaler Hauptstrasse 49b; s €64-70, d €112-122, tr €153-168, q €172-188; P🛜👬) With its flowery garden, bright and cheerful rooms and excellent breakfasts, this *pension* is one of the homiest in Salzburg. The affable Terler family keeps everything spick and span, and nothing is too much trouble for them. They'll even help you with upstairs with your luggage. Take bus 5 from the Haupt-bahnhof to Wäschergasse.

SALZBURG FOR CHILDREN

With dancing marionettes, chocolate galore and a *big* fairy-tale-like fortress, Salzburg is kid nirvana. If the crowds prove unbearable with tots in tow, take them to the city's adventure playgrounds (there are 80 to pick from); the one on Franz-Josef-Kai is a central choice.

Salzburg's sights are usually half price for children and most are free for under six year olds. Many galleries, museums and theatres also have dedicated programs for kids and families. These include the **Museum der Moderne** (p175), which has regular art workshops at 3pm on Tuesdays (€4), and the matinée performances at the enchanting **Salzburger Marionettentheater** (p189). The **Salzburg Museum** (p171) has lots of hands-on displays, from harp-playing to old-fashioned quill writing. Pick up 'Wolf' Dietrich's cartoon guide at the entrance.

Other surefire kid-pleasers in and around Salzburg include the following:

Haus der Natur (www.hausdernatur.at; Museumsplatz 5; adult/child/family €8/5.50/20; ⏰9am-5pm) Kids will love the Haus der Natur, where they can bone up on dinosaurs and alpine crystals in the natural history rooms, gawp at snakes and crocs in the reptile enclosure, and glimpse piranhas and coral reefs in the aquarium. Blink-and-you'll-miss-them baby clownfish splash around in the 'Kinderstube'. Shark-feeding time is 10.15am on Mondays and Thursdays. On the upper levels is a science museum where budding scientists can race rowboats, take a biological tour of the human body and – literally – feel Mozart's music by stepping into a giant violin case.

Spielzeugmuseum (Toy Museum; www.salzburgmuseum.at; Bürgerspitalgasse 2; adult/child/family €4/1.50/8; ⏰9am-5pm Tue-Sun) On the arcaded Bürgerspitalplatz, the Spiel-zeugmuseum takes a nostalgic look at toys, with its collection of doll's houses and Steiff teddies. There's also dress-up fun, marble games and a little boy's dream of a Bosch workshop. Parents can hang out in the 'adult parking areas' and at the free tea bar while the little ones let off excess energy.

Freilichtmuseum (www.freilichtmuseum.com; Hasenweg; adult/child/family €10/5/20; ⏰9am-6pm Tue-Sun Apr-Oct) Outside Salzburg, near Untersberg, the open-air Freilichtmu-seum harbours around 100 archetypal Austrian farmhouses and has tractors to clamber over, goats to feed and a huge adventure playground.

Salzburg Zoo (www.salzburg-zoo.at; Anifer Landesstrasse 1; adult/child/family €10.50/4.50/24.50; ⏰9am-6.30pm, to 4.30pm in winter) Kids can come face to face with lions, flamingos and alpine ibex at Salzburg Zoo near Schloss Hellbrunn.

★ **Arte Vida** GUESTHOUSE €€
(⏰ 87 31 85; www.artevida.at; Dreifaltigkeitsgasse 9; s €59-129, d €86-140, apt €150-214; ☎) Arte Vida has the boho-chic feel of a Marrakech riad, with its lantern-lit salon, communal kitchen and serene garden. Asia and Africa have provided the inspiration for the rich colours and fabrics that dress the individually designed rooms, all with DVD players and iPod docks. Reinhold gives invaluable tips on Salzburg, and arranges yoga sessions and outdoor activities.

★ **Hotel & Villa Auersperg** BOUTIQUE HOTEL €€
(⏰ 88 94 40; www.auersperg.at; Auerspergstrasse 61; s €129-175, d €155-225, ste €235-325; ℗ @ ☎ ⓘ)
✎ This charismatic villa and hotel duo fuse late-19th-century flair with contemporary design. Guests can relax by the lily pond in the vine-strewn garden or in the rooftop wellness area with its sauna, tea bar and mountain views. Free bike hire is a bonus. Local organic produce features at breakfast.

Hotel Am Dom BOUTIQUE HOTEL €€
(⏰ 84 27 65; www.hotelamdom.at; Goldgasse 17; s €90-160, d €130-280; ❄ ☎) Antique meets boutique at this Altstadt hotel, where the original vaults and beams of the 800-year-old building contrast with razor-sharp design features. Artworks inspired by the musical legends of the Salzburg Festival grace the rooms, which sport caramel-champagne colour schemes, funky lighting, velvet throws and ultra-glam bathrooms.

Weisse Taube HISTORIC HOTEL €€
(⏰ 84 24 04; www.weissetaube.at; Kaigasse 9; s €99-109, d €125-159; ☎) Housed in a heritage-listed 14th-century building in a quiet corner of the Altstadt, the 'white dove' is a solid choice. Staff go out of their way to help and the warm-coloured rooms are large and well kept (some have fortress views). Breakfast is a generous spread.

Wolf Dietrich HISTORIC HOTEL €€
(⏰ 87 12 75; www.salzburg-hotel.at; Wolf-Dietrich-Strasse 7; s €70-130, d €113-250, ste €168-310; ℗ ☎ ⬛ ⓘ) For old-fashioned elegance you can't beat this central hotel, where rooms are dressed in polished wood furnishings and floral fabrics. There's even a suite based on Mozart's *Magic Flute*, with a star-studded ceiling and freestanding bath. By contrast, the spa and indoor pool are ultramodern. Organic produce is served at breakfast.

Hotel Goldgasse HISTORIC HOTEL €€
(⏰ 84 56 22; www.hotelgoldgasse.at; Goldgasse 10; s €98-160, d €165-260, ste €225-340, q €270-410; ❄ @ ☎ ⓘ) Bang in the heart of the Altstadt, this 700-year-old townhouse has oodles of charm – some rooms have four-poster beds, while paintings of Emperor Franz Josef guards over others. The sunny terrace overlooks the rooftops of the old town.

Gästehaus im Priesterseminar GUESTHOUSE €€
(⏰ 877 495 10; www.gaestehaus-priesterseminar-salzburg.at; Dreifaltigkeitsgasse 14; s €65, d €116-148) Ah, the peace is heavenly at this one-time seminary, tucked behind the Dreifältigkeitskirche. Its bright, parquet-floored rooms were recently given a total makeover, but the place still brims with old-world charm with its marble staircase, antique furnishings and fountain-dotted courtyard. It's still something of a secret, so whisper about it quietly...

Hotel Elefant HISTORIC HOTEL €€
(⏰ 84 33 97; www.elefant.at; Sigmund-Haffner-Gasse 4; s €129-208, d €127-402; ❄ ☎ ⓘ) Occupying a 700-year-old building and run by the good-natured Mayr family, this central Best Western hotel has loads of charm. Bright colours add a modern touch to the spacious, elegantly furnished rooms. A generous breakfast is available.

Hotel Amadeus HISTORIC HOTEL €€
(⏰ 87 14 01; www.hotelamadeus.at; Linzer Gasse 43-45; s €78-137, d €128-231, q €192-391; ☎) Centrally situated on the right bank, this 500-year-old hotel has a boutique feel, with bespoke touches such as chandeliers and four-poster beds in the vibrantly coloured rooms. Guests are treated to free tea or coffee in the afternoon.

Hotel Hohenstauffen HOTEL €€
(⏰ 87 21 93; www.hotel-hohenstauffen.at; Elisabethstrasse 19; s/d €107/145; ℗ @) Granted, it's not in the nicest part of town (erotica shops and all), but don't be put off. This genuinely friendly, family-run place has charmingly old-fashioned rooms and is geared up for cyclists, as the bicycle bell at reception confirms.

Hotel Rosenvilla GUESTHOUSE €€
(⏰ 62 17 65; www.rosenvilla.com; Höfelgasse 4; s €84-114, d €116-177, ste €166-253; ℗ ☎ ⓘ) This guesthouse goes the extra mile with its sharp-styled contemporary rooms, faultless service and incredible breakfasts with spreads, breads, cereals, eggs and fruit to

NO TOURIST TRAPP

Did you know that there were 10, not seven Trapp children, the eldest of whom was Rupert (so long Liesl)? Or that the captain was a gentle, family-loving man and Maria no soft touch? Or, perhaps, that in 1938 the Trapp family left quietly for the United States instead of climbing every mountain to Switzerland? For the truth behind the Hollywood legend, stay the night at **Villa Trapp** (☑ 63 08 60; www.villa-trapp.com; Traunstrasse 34; s €65-130, d €114-280, ste €290-580), tucked away in Salzburg's biggest private park in the Aigen district, 3km east of the Altstadt.

Marianne and Christopher have transformed the original von Trapp family home into a beautiful guesthouse (for guests only, we might add). The 19th-century villa is elegant, if not as palatial as in the movie, with tasteful wood-floored rooms and a balustrade for sweeping down à la Baroness Schräder. Family snapshots and heirlooms, including the baron's model ships and a photo of guest Pink Floyd guitarist David Gilmour strumming 'Edelweiss', grace the dining room. From the main station, take a train or bus 160 to Aigen.

jump-start your day. Take bus 7 to Finanzamt or walk 15 minutes along the tree-lined riverfront into the centre.

Hotel Mozart
HISTORIC HOTEL €€

(☑ 87 22 74; www.hotel-mozart.at; Franz-Josef-Strasse 27; s €80-110, d €120-190, tr €150-220; P 🛜 ♿) An antique-filled lobby gives way to spotless rooms with comfy beds and sizeable bathrooms at the Mozart. You'll have to fork out an extra €10 for breakfast, but it's a good spread with fresh fruit, boiled eggs, cold cuts and pastries.

★ Hotel Schloss Mönchstein
HERITAGE HOTEL €€€

(☑ 84 85 55-0; www.monchstein.at; Mönchsberg Park 26; d €350-650, ste €695-1900; P ❄ 🛜) On a fairy-tale perch atop Mönchsberg and set in hectares of wooded grounds, this 16th-century castle is honeymoon (and second mortgage) material. Persian rugs, oil paintings and Calcutta marble finish the rooms to beautiful effect. A massage in the spa, a candlelit tower dinner for two with Salzburg views, a helicopter ride – just say the word.

Hotel Sacher
HERITAGE HOTEL €€€

(☑ 88 97 70; www.sacher.com; Schwarzstrasse 5-7; s €226-336, d €241-651, ste €502-3898; P ❄ 🛜 ♿) Tom Hanks, the Dalai Lama and Julie Andrews have all stayed at this 19th-century pile on the banks of the Salzach. Scattered with oil paintings and antiques, the rooms have gleaming marble bathrooms, and fortress or river views. Compensate for indulging on chocolate *Sacher Torte* in the health club.

Goldener Hirsch
LUXURY HOTEL €€€

(☑ 808 40; www.goldenerhirschsalzburg.com; Getreidegasse 37; r €195-813; P ❄ @ 🛜) A skylight illuminates the arcaded inner courtyard of this 600-year-old Altstadt pile, where famous past guests include Queen Elizabeth and Pavarotti. Countess Harriet Walderdorff tastefully scattered the opulent rooms with objets d'art and hand-printed fabrics. Downstairs are two restaurants: beamed s'Herzl and vaulted Restaurant Goldener Hirsch.

Arthotel Blaue Gans
BOUTIQUE HOTEL €€€

(☑ 84 24 91; www.hotel-blaue-gans-salzburg.at; Getreidegasse 41-43; s €135-209, d €145-339, ste €269-499; ❄ 🛜 ♿) Contemporary design blends harmoniously with the original vaulting and beams of this 660-year-old hotel. Rooms are pure and simple, with clean lines, lots of white and streamlined furnishings. The restaurant is well worth a visit.

Hotel Bristol
LUXURY HOTEL €€€

(☑ 87 35 57; www.bristol-salzburg.at; Makartplatz 4; s/d/ste €250/395/690; P ❄ 🛜) The Bristol transports you back to a more decadent era. Chandelier-lit salons, champagne at breakfast, exquisitely crafted furniture, service as polished as the marble – this is pure class. Even Emperor Franz Josef and Sigmund Freud felt at home here.

🍴 Eating

Salzburg's eclectic dining scene skips from the traditional to the super-trendy to the downright touristy. This is a city where schnitzel is served with a slice of history in vaulted taverns, where you can dine in Michelin-starred finery or be serenaded by a warbling Maria wannabe. Save euros by taking advantage of the lunchtime *Tagesmenü* (fixed menu) served at most places.

Spicy Spices INDIAN €
(⏲87 07 12; Wolf-Dietrich-Strasse 1; day special €7.50, with soup €9; ⏰11am-9pm; ⚡) 'Healthy heart, lovely soul' is the mantra of this all-organic, all-vegetarian haunt. Service is slow but friendly. It's worth the wait for the good-value *thali* (appetisers) and curries mopped up with *paratha* (flat bread).

IceZeit ICE CREAM €
(Chiemseegasse 1; scoop €1.30; ⏰11am-8pm) Grab a cone at Salzburg's best ice-cream parlour, with flavours from salty peanut-caramel to passionfruit.

Heart of Joy CAFE €
(⏲89 07 73; Franz-Josef-Strasse 3; lunch €7.90-8.50, snacks & light meals €4.90-9.90; ⏰8am-7pm; ⏰⚡) This Ayurveda-inspired cafe has an all-vegetarian, part-vegan and mostly organic menu. It does great bagels, salads, homemade cakes and juices, creative breakfasts, plus day specials like curry and dhal with organic rice.

★The Green Garden VEGETARIAN €€
(⏲0662-841201; Nonntaler Hauptstrasse 16; mains €9.50-14.50; ⏰noon-3pm & 5.30-10pm Tue-Sat; ⚡) ✿ The Green Garden is a breath of fresh air for vegetarians and vegans. Locavore is the word at this bright, modern cottage-style restaurant, pairing dishes like wild herb salad, saffron risotto with braised fennel and vegan fondue with organic wines in a totally relaxed setting.

★Triangel AUSTRIAN €€
(⏲84 22 29; Wiener-Philharmoniker-Gasse 7; mains €10-32; ⏰11.30am-midnight Tue-Sat) The menu is market-fresh at this arty bistro, where the picture-clad walls pay tribute to Salzburg Festival luminaries. It does gourmet salads, a mean Hungarian goulash with organic beef, and delicious homemade ice cream. The lunch special costs €6.50.

Zum Zirkelwirt AUSTRIAN €€
(⏲84 27 96; www.zumzirkelwirt.at; Pfeifergasse 14; ⏰11am-midnight) A jovial inn serving good old-fashioned Austrian grub is what you get at Zum Zirkelwirt, which has a cracking beer garden on tucked-away Papagenoplatz and a cosy wood-panelled interior for winter imbibing. Go straight for classics like *Kaspressknödelsuppe* (cheese dumpling soup) and *Schweinsbraten im Weissbier-Kümmelsafterl* (pork roast in wheat beer-cumin sauce).

Hagenauerstuben AUSTRIAN €€
(⏲84 26 57; www.hagenauerstuben.at; Universitätsplatz 14; 2-course lunch €7.40, mains €9-18; ⏰10am-11pm Mon-Sat, to 6pm Sun) You'd be forgiven for thinking a restaurant tucked behind Mozarts Geburtshaus would have 'tourist trap' written all over it. Not so. The baroque-contemporary Hagenauerstuben combines a stylishly converted vaulted interior with a terrace overlooking the Kollegienkirche. Pull up a chair for good old-fashioned Austrian home cooking – pork medallions with herb mash, schnitzel with spinach *Knödel* (dumplings) and the like.

Bärenwirt AUSTRIAN €€
(⏲42 24 04; www.baerenwirt-salzburg.at; Müllner Hauptstrasse 8; mains €9.50-20; ⏰11am-11pm) Sizzling and stirring since 1663, Bärenwirt is Austrian through and through. Go for hearty *Bierbraten* (beer roast) with dumplings, locally caught trout or organic wild boar bratwurst. A tiled oven warms the woody, hunting-lodge-style interior in winter, while the river-facing terrace is a summer crowd-puller. The restaurant is 500m north of Museumplatz.

Zwettler's AUSTRIAN €€
(⏲84 41 99; www.zwettlers.com; Kaigasse 3; mains €12-21; ⏰11.30am-2am Tue-Sat, to 11pm Sun) This gastro-pub has a lively buzz on its pavement terrace. Local grub such as schnitzel with parsley potatoes and venison ragout goes well with a cold, foamy Kaiser Karl wheat beer. The two-course lunch is a snip at €7.90.

Afro Café AFRICAN €€
(⏲84 48 88; www.afrocoffee.com; Bürgerspitalplatz 5; lunch €8.20, mains €12-30; ⏰9am-midnight Mon-Sat; ⏰) Hot-pink walls, butterfly chairs and artworks made from beach junk...this afro-chic cafe is totally groovy. Staff keep the good vibes and food coming – from breakfasts (€14.60) to ostrich burgers and steaks sizzling hot from the grill. It also does a good line in coffee, rooibos teas and sweets.

Alter Fuchs AUSTRIAN €€
(⏲88 20 22; Linzer Gasse 47-49; mains €9.50-14.50; ⏰noon-midnight Mon-Sat; ⚡⏰) This sly old fox prides itself on no-nonsense Austrian fare – schnitzel, roast pork with dumplings, cordon bleu and the like. Bandana-clad foxes guard the bar in the vaulted interior, and there's a courtyard for good-weather dining. In the cosy *Stube* (parlour) out back, scribbling on

the walls (chalk only, please) is positively encouraged. Service can be hit or miss.

Gasthof Schloss Aigen
AUSTRIAN €€
(✉ 62 12 84; www.schloss-aigen.at; Schwarzenbergpromenade 37; mains €17-34.50, menus €44-54; ⊙ 11.30am-2pm & 5.30-9.30pm Thu & Fri, 11.30am-9.30pm Sat & Sun) A country manor with an elegantly rustic interior and a chestnut-shaded courtyard, this is Austrian dining at its finest. The Forstner family's house speciality is *Wiener Melange*, different cuts of meltingly tender Pinzgauer beef, served with apple horseradish, chive sauce and roast potatoes, best matched with robust Austrian wines. Bus 7 stops at Bahnhof Aigen, a 10-minute stroll away.

M32
FUSION €€
(✉ 84 10 00; www.m32.at; Mönchsberg 32; 2-course lunch €16, mains €26-36; ⊙ 9am-1am Tue-Sun; ✎⛵) Bold colours and a veritable forest of stag antlers reveal architect Matteo Thun's imprint at Museum der Moderne's ultra-sleek restaurant. The food goes with the seasons with specialities like tortellini of organic local beef with tomato ragout and tangy greenapple sorbet with cassis. The glass-walled restaurant and terrace take in the full sweep of Salzburg's mountain-backed skyline.

Pescheria Backi
SEAFOOD €€
(✉ 87 97 78; Franz-Josef-Strasse 16b; mains €9-15; ⊙ 9am-10pm Mon-Sat) A clapboard shed of a fishmonger-bistro dishing up fish, fresh and simple, to a hungry crowd of regulars.

K+K
AUSTRIAN €€
(✉ 84 21 56; Waagplatz 2; mains €16-30; ⊙ 11.30am-10pm; ⛵) This buzzy restaurant on the square is a warren of vaulted and wood-panelled rooms. Whether you go for crayfish tails, saddle of venison in morel sauce or good old bratwurst with lashings of potatoes and cabbage – the food here hits the mark.

St Paul's Stub'n
INTERNATIONAL €€
(✉ 43 33 203; Herrengasse 16; mains €11-22; ⊙ 5-11pm Mon-Sat) Up the cobbled Herrengasse lies this gloriously old-world tavern, with a darkwood interior crammed with antique curios, which attracts a regular crowd of locals. In summer, guests spill out into the beer garden to dig into authentically prepared classics such as roast pork in wheat beer sauce.

★ Esszimmer
FRENCH €€€
(✉ 87 08 99; www.esszimmer.com; Müllner Hauptstrasse 33; 3-course lunch €38, tasting menus €75-118; ⊙ noon-2pm & 6.30-9.30pm Tue-Sat) Andreas Kaiblinger puts an innovative spin on market-driven French cuisine at Michelin-starred Esszimmer. Eye-catching art, playful backlighting and a glass floor revealing the Almkanal stream keep diners captivated, as do gastronomic showstoppers such as Arctic char with calf's head and asparagus. Buses 7, 21 and 28 to Landeskrankenhaus stop close by.

★ Magazin
MODERN EUROPEAN €€€
(✉ 84 15 84; www.magazin.co.at; Augustinergasse 13a; 2-course lunch €16, mains €33-39, tasting menus €68-71, cookery classes €150; ⊙ 10am-midnight Tue-Sat) Gathered around a courtyard below Mönchsberg's sheer rock wall, Magazin shelters a deli, wine store, cookery school and restaurant. Chef Richard Brunnauer's menus fizz with seasonal flavours such as smoked alpine char with pickled root vegetables, saddle of venison with parsley potato purée and boletus mushrooms; are matched with wines from the 850-bottle cellar; and served alfresco or in the industro-chic, cavelike interior.

The three-hour, hands-on cookery classes are followed by a five-course dinner; prebooking is essential.

Ikarus
MODERN EUROPEAN €€€
(✉ 21 97 77; www.hangar-7.com; tasting menus €160-185; ⊙ noon-2pm & 7-10pm) At the space-age Hangar-7 complex at the airport, this glam Michelin-starred restaurant is the epitome of culinary globetrotting. Each month, Eckart Witzigmann and Martin Klein invite a world-famous chef to assemble an eight- to 12-course menu for a serious foodie crowd.

Carpe Diem Finest Finger Food
FUSION €€€
(✉ 84 88 00; www.carpediemfinestfingerfood.com; Getreidegasse 50; 3-course lunch €21.50, mains €37.50-39.50; ⊙ 8.30am-midnight) This avant-garde, Michelin-starred lounge-restaurant sits in pride of place on Getreidegasse. A food-literate crowd flocks here for cocktails and finger-food cones, mini taste sensations with fillings like tomato *panna cotta* with Jerusalem artichoke and scallop-rhubarb.

Riedenburg
MODERN EUROPEAN €€€
(✉ 83 08 15; www.riedenburg.at; Neutorstrasse 31; mains €20-33.50, 3-/4-/5-course menu €43/54/65; ⊙ noon-2pm & 6-10pm Tue-Sat) Helmut Schinwald works the stove at this gourmet restaurant with a romantic garden pavilion. His seasonally inflected flavours, such as homemade porcini ravioli with thyme butter and quail breast with pomegranate risotto, are expertly matched with top wines. The €15 two-course lunch is a bargain. Rieden-

CHRISTIANA SCHNEEWEISS, SALZBURG GUIDE

Best time to visit May when everything is in bloom and the mountains are still dusted with snow. September is lovely, too, with mild days and fewer crowds than in summer.

Salzburg Festival Even if you don't have tickets, you can still join in the fun. Opera and concert highlights are shown on a big screen against the spectacular backdrop of the fortress illuminated at the free Siemens Festival Nights on Kapitelplatz. If the weather is fine, little beats a performance of Jedermann on Domplatz – it is the very essence of the festival. Last-minute tickets are often available.

Great escapes Kapuzinerberg and Mönchsberg for shady strolls and magnificent panoramas of the Altstadt. For quiet contemplation, head to Friedhof St Sebastian or Stift Nonnberg, where the chapel choir contains wonderful 10th-century Byzantine frescoes, which are among Austria's oldest.

Top day trips Gaisberg and Untersberg for hiking in Alpine surrounds; the Bavarian lakes, such as Königsee just across the border; and Waldbad Anif for a swim in beautiful forested surrounds.

Sightseeing tips Avoid the groups by visiting the big sights after 4pm. To feel the true spirit of the Dom, attend Sunday morning mass. Don't overlook lesser-known sights: the Dommuseum, for instance, is fascinating and rarely crowded.

Christiana Schneeweiss is an official tour guide with Salzburg Guides (www. salzburgguides.at) with 20 years of experience as a tour guide in the city.

burg is a 10-minute walk southwest of the Altstadt along Neutorstrasse; take bus 1, 4 or 5 to Moosstrasse.

Blaue Gans Restaurant　　　AUSTRIAN €€€
(📞 84 24 91-50; www.blauegans.at; Getreidegasse 43; mains €19-25; ⏱ noon-1am Mon-Sat) In the 650-year-old vaults of Arthotel Blaue Gans, this restaurant is a refined setting for regional cuisine, such as pike-perch with fennel compote, braised lamb shanks and *Marillenknödel* (apricot dumplings), which are married with full-bodied wines. The olive-tree-dotted terrace is popular in summer.

Alt Salzburg　　　AUSTRIAN €€€
(📞 84 14 76; Bürgerspitalgasse 2; mains €19.50-30, tasting menus €43-58; ⏱ 11.30am-2pm & 6-10pm Mon-Sat) Tucked into a courtyard at the base of Mönchsberg, this supremely cosy restaurant has attentive service, hearty regional specialities like venison and veal knuckle, and fine Austrian wines.

Self-Catering

Grünmarkt　　　MARKET €
(Green Market; Universitätsplatz; ⏱ 7am-7pm Mon-Fri, to 3pm Sat) A one-stop picnic shop on one of Salzburg's grandest squares, for regional cheese, ham, fruit, bread and gigantic pretzels.

Kaslöchl　　　CHEESE €
(Hagenauerplatz 2; ⏱ 9am-6pm Mon-Fri, 8am-1pm Sat; 📷) A mouse-sized Austrian cheese shop,

crammed with creamy alpine varieties, holey emmental and fresh cheese with herbs.

Stiftsbäckerei St Peter　　　BAKERY €
(Kapitelplatz 8; ⏱ 7am-5pm Mon-Tue & Thu-Fri, to 1pm Sat) Next to the monastery where the watermill turns, this 700-year-old bakery bakes Salzburg's best sourdough loaves from a wood-fired oven.

🍷 Drinking

A stein-swinging beer hall, a sundowner on the Salzach, an intimate wine bar for appreciating the subtle nuances of Grüner Veltliner wines – all possible ideas for a good night out in Salzburg. Nobody's pretending this is rave city, but the days of lights out by 11pm are long gone. You'll find the biggest concentration of bars along both banks of the Salzach and some of the hippest around Gstättengasse. Rudolfskai can be on the rough side of rowdy at weekends.

★ Augustiner Bräustübl　　　BREWERY
(www.augustinerbier.at; Augustinergasse 4-6; ⏱ 3-11pm Mon-Fri, from 2.30pm Sat & Sun) Who says monks can't enjoy themselves? Since 1621, this cheery monastery-run brewery has been serving potent homebrews in Stein tankards in the vaulted hall and beneath the chestnut trees in the 1000-seat beer garden.

Get your tankard filled at the foyer pump and visit the snack stands for hearty, beer-swigging grub like *Stelzen* (ham hock), pork belly and giant pretzels.

Enoteca Settemila
WINE BAR

(Bergstrasse 9; ☺ 5-11pm Tue-Sat) This bijou wine shop and bar brims with the enthusiasm and passion of Rafael Peil and Nina Corti. Go to sample their well-edited selection of wines, including Austrian, organic and biodynamic ones, with *taglieri* – sharing plates of cheese and salumi from small Italian producers.

StieglKeller
BEER HALL

(Festungsgasse 10; ☺ 11am-11pm) For a 365-day taste of Oktoberfest, try this cavernous Munich-style beer hall, which shares the same architect as Munich's Hofbräuhaus. It has an enormous garden above the city's roof-tops and a menu of meaty mains (€11 to €18) such as fat pork knuckles and schnitzel. Beer is cheapest from the self-service taps outside.

Die Weisse
PUB

(www.dieweisse.at; Rupertgasse 10; ☺ pub 10am-midnight Mon-Sat, Sudwerk bar 5pm-2am Mon-Sat) The cavernous brewpub of the Salzburger Weissbierbrauerei, this is the place to guzzle cloudy wheat beers in the wood-floored pub and the shady beer garden out back. DJs work the decks in Sudwerk bar, especially at the monthly Almrausch when locals party in skimpy Dirndls and strapping Lederhosen.

Kaffee Alchemie
CAFE

(www.kaffee-alchemie.at; Rudolfskai 38; ☺ 7.30am-6pm Mon-Fri, 10am-6pm Sat & Sun) Making good coffee really is rocket science at this vintage-cool cafe down by the river, which plays up high-quality, fair-trade beans. Talented baristas knock up spot-on espressos, cappuccinos and speciality coffees, and the cake is pretty good too.

Steinterrasse
COCKTAIL BAR

(Giselakai 3; ☺ 7am-midnight Sun-Thu, to 1am Fri & Sat) Hotel Stein's chichi 7th-floor terrace attracts Salzburg's Moët-sipping socialites and anyone who loves a good view. It isn't cheap, but it is the best spot to see the Altstadt light up against the theatrical backdrop of the fortress.

Unikum Sky
CAFE

(Unipark Nonntal; ☺ 10am-7pm Mon-Fri, 8am-7pm Sat) For knockout fortress views and a full-on Salzburg panorama, head up to this sun-kissed terrace atop the new Unipark Nonntal campus, 300m south of Schanzlgasse in the Altstadt. It's a relaxed spot to chill over drinks and inexpensive snacks.

Köchelverzeichnis
WINE BAR

(Steingasse 27; ☺ 5-11pm Tue-Sat) This is a real neighbourhood bar with jazzy music, antipasti and great selection of wines. Taste

---

CAFE CULTURE

You can make yourself pretty *gemütlich* (comfy) over coffee and people-watching in Salzburg's cafes. Expect to pay around €4 for a slice of cake and €8 for a day special. Here are our six favourites:

220 Grad (Chiemseegasse 5; ☺ 9am-7pm Tue-Fri, to 6pm Sat) Famous for freshly roasted coffee, this retro-chic cafe serves probably the best espresso in town and whips up superb breakfasts.

Café Tomaselli (www.tomaselli.at; Alter Markt 9; ☺ 7am-8pm Mon-Sat, 8am-8pm Sun) Going strong since 1705, this marble and wood-panelled cafe is a former Mozart haunt. It's famous for having Salzburg's flakiest strudels, best *Einspänner* (coffee with whipped cream) and grumpiest waiters.

Sacher (www.sacher.com; Schwarzstrasse 5-7; ☺ 7.30am-midnight) Nowhere is the chocolate richer, the apricot jam tangier and cream lighter than at the home of the legendary *Sacher Torte*. The cafe is pure old-world grandeur, with its picture-lined walls and ruby-red banquettes. Sit on the terrace by the Salzach for fortress views.

Fingerlos (Franz-Josef-Strasse 9; ☺ 7.30am-7.30pm Tue-Sun) Salzburgers rave about the dainty petits fours, flaky pastries and creamy tortes served at this high-ceilinged cafe. Join a well-dressed crowd for breakfast or a lazy afternoon of coffee and newspapers.

Café am Kai (Müllner Hauptstrasse 4; ☺ 8.30am-8pm) On the banks of the Salzach River, this is a pleasantly low-key cafe to kick back over coffee and cake, ice cream or a cold beer.

Café Bazar (www.cafe-bazar.at; Schwarzstrasse 3; ☺ 7.30am-7.30pm Mon-Sat, 9am-6pm Sun) All chandeliers and polished wood, locals enjoy the same river views today over breakfast, cake and intelligent conversation, as Marlene Dietrich did in 1936.

citrusy Grüner Veltliners and rieslings from the family's vineyards in the Wachau.

Republic   BAR
(www.republic-cafe.at; Anton-Neumayr-Platz 2; ⊙8.30am-midnight Sun-Thu, to 4am Fri & Sat) One of Salzburg's most happening haunts, this backlit lounge-bar opens onto a popular terrace on the square. By night, DJs spin to a 20-something, cocktail-sipping crowd in the club. Check the website for free events from jazz, Latin and swing breakfasts to weekly salsa nights (9pm on Tuesdays).

Humboldt Stub'n   BAR
(www.humboldtstubn.at; Gstättengasse 4-6; ⊙11am-3am; ☏) Following a recent make-over, this rustic-cool bar is once again a prime gathering spot, with a pavement ter-race for sipping a cold, foamy one.

Mayday Bar   COCKTAIL BAR
(www.hangar-7.com; ⊙noon-midnight Sun-Thu, to 1am Fri & Sat) Peer down at Flying Bulls' aircraft through the glass walls at this crystalline bar, part of the airport's futuristic Hangar-7 com-plex. Strikingly illuminated by night, it's a unique place for a fresh fruit cocktail or 'smart food' appetisers served in Bodum glasses.

Salzburger Heimatwerk   CAFE
(Residenzplatz 9; ⊙9am-6pm Mon-Fri, to 5pm Sat) As well knocking fine fabrics into Dirndls and selling Austrian schnapps, preserves and honeys, Salzburger Heimatwerk has an uncrowded cafe terrace that offers prime views across Residenzplatz.

☆ Entertainment

★ Salzburger Marionettentheater   THEATRE
(☏87 24 06; www.marionetten.at; Schwarzstrasse 24; ♿) The red curtain goes up on a miniature stage at this marionette theatre, a lavish stuc-co, cherub and chandelier-lit affair, which cel-ebrated its centenary in 2013. The repertoire star is *The Sound of Music,* with a life-sized Mother Superior and a marionette-packed fi-nale. Other enchanting productions include Mozart's *The Magic Flute* and Strauss' *Die Fledermaus.* All have multilingual surtitles. Tickets cost between €15 and €35.

Landestheater   THEATRE
(☏87 15 12; www.salzburger-landestheater.at; Schwarzstrasse 22; ♿) Opera, ballet and mu-sicals dominate the stage at this elegant 18th-century playhouse. There's a strong em-phasis on Mozart's music, with the Mozarte-um Salzburg Orchestra often in the pit. There

are dedicated performances for kids, and *The Sound of Music* musical is a winner with all.

Schlosskonzerte   CLASSICAL MUSIC
(www.salzburger-schlosskonzerte.at; ⊙concerts 8pm) A fantasy of coloured marble, stucco and frescoes, Schloss Mirabell's baroque Marmorsaal (Marble Hall) is the exquisite setting for chamber-music concerts. Inter-nationally renowned soloists and ensembles perform works by Mozart and other well-known composers such as Haydn and Cho-pin. Tickets costing between €31 and €37 are available online or at the box office.

Mozarteum   CLASSICAL MUSIC
(☏87 31 54; www.mozarteum.at; Schwarzstrasse 26) Opened in 1880 and revered for its supreme acoustics, the Mozarteum highlights the life and works of Mozart through chamber music (October to June), concerts and opera. The annual highlight is Mozart Week in January.

ARGEkultur   CONCERT VENUE
(www.argekultur.at; Ulrike-Gschwandtner-Strasse 5) This alternative cultural venue was born out of protests against the Salzburg Festival in the 1980s. Today it's a bar and performing-arts hybrid. Traversing the entire arts spec-trum, the line-up features concerts, cabaret, DJ nights, dance, poetry slams and world music. It's at the Unipark Nonntal campus, a five-minute walk east of the Altstadt.

Rockhouse   LIVE MUSIC
(www.rockhouse.at; Schallmooser Hauptstrasse 46) Salzburg's hottest live music venue, Rock-house presents first-rate rock, pop, jazz, folk, metal and reggae concerts – see the website for details. There's also a tunnel-shaped bar that has DJs (usually free) and bands. Rock-house is 1km northeast of the Altstadt; take bus 4 to Canavalstrasse.

Jazzit   JAZZ
(☏88 32 64; www.jazzit.at; Elisabethstrasse 11; ⊙6pm-midnight Tue-Sat) Hosts regular con-certs from tango to electro alongside work-shops and club nights. Don't miss the free Tuesday-night jam sessions in Jazzit:Bar. It's 600m north of the Mirabellgarten along Elisabethstrasse.

Salzburg Arena   CONCERT VENUE
(☏24 04-0; www.salzburgarena.at; Am Messezen-trum 1) Under a domed wooden roof, this is Salzburg's premier stage for sporting events, musicals and big-name concerts (Santana and Bob Dylan have played here). The arena is 3km north of town; take bus 1 to Messe.

SALZBURG & AROUND ENTERTAINMENT

Das Kino
CINEMA

(www.daskino.at; Giselakai 11) Shows independent and art-house films from Austria and across the globe in their original language. The cinema hosts the mountain-focused Bergfilmfestival in November.

Sound of Salzburg Show
SHOW

(☑82 66 17; www.soundofsalzburgshow.com; Festungsgasse 10; tickets with/without dinner €48/33; ☻dinner 7.30pm, show 8.30pm May-Oct) This all-singing show at Sternbräu is a triple bill of Mozart, *The Sound of Music* and operetta faves performed in traditional costume. Kitsch but fun.

Mozart Dinner
CONCERT SHOW

(☑82 86 95; www.mozartdinnerconcert.com; Sankt-Peter-Bezirk 1; adult/child €54/33; ☻8pm) You'll love or hate this themed dinner, with Mozart music, costumed performers and (mediocre) 18th-century-style food. It's held in Stiftskeller St Peter's lavish baroque hall.

🔒 Shopping

Traditional wrought-iron signs hang above the shops on Getreidegasse, which has everything from designer fashion to hats. Goldgasse has accessories, antiques and porcelain. A popular street for a shop and stroll is Linzer Gasse.

★ Fürst
CONFECTIONERY

(www.original-mozartkugel.com; Getreidegasse 47; ☻10am-6.30pm Mon-Sat, 11am-5pm Sun) Pistachio, nougat and dark chocolate dreams, the *Mozartkugeln* (Mozart balls) here are still handmade to Paul Fürst's original 1890 recipe and cost €1 per mouthful. Other specialities include cube-shaped *Bach Würfel* – coffee, nut and marzipan truffles dedicated to yet another great composer.

Musikhaus Katholnigg
MUSIC

(Sigmund-Haffner-Gasse 16; ☻9am-6pm Mon-Fri, 9.30am-5pm Sat) Housed in a 16th-century townhouse and selling music since 1847, this is the place to pick up high-quality recordings of the Salzburg Festival. There's a huge selection of classical, jazz, chanson and folk CDs and DVDs.

Zotter
CHOCOLATE

(Herbert-von-Karajan-Platz 4; ☻10am-6pm Mon-Fri, 9.30am-6pm Sat) Made in Austria, Zotter's organic, Fairtrade chocolate – including unusual varieties like Styrian pumpkin, ginger-carrot and mountain cheese-walnut – is divine. Dip a spoon into the choc fountain and try samples from the conveyor belt.

Alte Hofapotheke
PHARMACY

(Alter Markt 6; ☻8am-6pm Mon-Fri, to noon Sat) For a whiff of nostalgia and a packet of sage throat pastilles, nip into this wonderfully old-fashioned, wood-panelled pharmacy, Salzburg's oldest, founded in 1591.

Salzburg Salz
GIFTS

(Wiener-Philharmoniker-Gasse 6; ☻10am-6pm Mon-Fri, to 4pm Sat) Pure salt from Salzburgerland and the Himalaya, herbal salts and rock-salt tea lights are among the high-sodium wonders here.

Drechslerei Lackner
GIFTS

(Badergasse 2; ☻9.30am-6.30pm Mon-Fri, to 5pm Sat) The hand-carved nutcrackers, nativity figurines and filigree Christmas stars are the real deal at this traditional craft shop.

Spirituosen Sporer
WINE

(Getreidegasse 39; ☻9.30am-7pm Mon-Fri, 8.30am-5pm Sat) In Getreidegasse's narrowest house, family-run Sporer has been intoxicating local folk with Austrian wines, herbal liqueurs and famous *Vogelbeer* (rowan berry) schnapps since 1903.

ℹ Information

EMERGENCY

Hospital (☑44 82; Müllner Hauptstrasse 48) Just north of Mönchsberg.

Police Headquarters (☑63 83; Alpenstrasse 90) Police headquarters.

MONEY

Bankomaten (ATMs) are all over the place. Exchange booths are open all day every day at the airport. There are also plenty of exchange offices downtown, but beware of potentially high commission rates.

POST

Main Post Office (Residenzplatz 9; ☻8am-6pm Mon-Fri)

Station Post Office (Südtiroler Platz 1; ☻8am-8.30pm Mon-Fri, to 2pm Sat)

TOURIST INFORMATION

Tourist Office (☑889 87 330; www.salzburg. info; Mozartplatz 5; ☻9am-6pm) Helpful tourist office with a ticket booking service.

Salzburgerland Tourismus (☑6688-0; www. salzburgerland.com; ☻8am-5.30pm Mon-Thu, to 5pm Fri) For information on the rest of the province, contact Salzburgerland Tourismus.

TRAVEL AGENCIES

STA Travel (☑45 87 33; www.statravel.at; Rainerstrasse 2; ☻9am-6pm Mon-Fri, 10am-2pm Sat) Student and budget travel agency.

RETURN OF THE TRACHT

Ever thought about purchasing a tight-fitting Dirndl or a pair of strapping Lederhosen? No? Well, Salzburg might just change your mind with its Trachten (traditional costume) stores adding alpine oomph to your wardrobe. If you have visions of old maids in gingham and men in feathered hats, you might be surprised. Walk the streets where 20-somethings flaunt the latest styles or hit the dance-floor at Die Weisse's Almrausch club night and you'll see that hemlines have risen and necklines have plunged over the years; that young Salzburgers are reinventing the style by teaming Lederhosen with T-shirts and trainers or pairing slinky off-the-shoulder numbers with ballet pumps. Their message? Trachten can be cool, even sexy.

The following stores are a very good place to start.

Ploom (www.ploom.at; Ursulinenplatz 5; ⊘11am-6pm Thu & Fri, to 5pm Sat) Embracing the *Trachten* trend is Ploom, where designer Pflaum has playfully and successfully reinvented the Dirndl. Her boutique is a wonderland of floaty femininity: a sky-blue bodice here, a frothy cotton blouse, a wisp of a turquoise *Schürze* (apron) or silk evening gown there.

Lanz Trachten (www.lanztrachten.at; Schwarzstrasse 4; ⊘9am-6pm Mon-Fri, to 5pm Sat) Just the place if it's a tight-fitting Dirndl or a snazzy felt hat you're after.

Stassny (www.stassny.at; Getreidegasse 30; ⊘9.30am-6pm Mon-Fri, to 5pm Sat) Upscale Stassny combines *Trachten*-making know-how with high-quality fabrics and age-old patterns (stag prints, polka dots, gingham etc).

Forstenlechner (www.salzburg-trachtenmode.at; Mozartplatz 4; ⊘9.30am-6pm Mon-Fri, to 5pm Sat) For a fusion of modern and traditional *Trachten* in myriad colours, try midrange Forstenlechner.

Wenger (www.wenger.at; Getreidegasse 29; ⊘10am-6pm Mon-Fri, to 5pm Sat) Wenger stocks figure-hugging Lederhosen for ladies and Dirndls from below-the-knee Heidi to thigh-flashing diva creations trimmed with ribbons and lace.

ⓘ Getting There & Away

AIR

Salzburg airport (☑ 662-858 00; www.salzburg-airport.com; Innsbrucker Bundesstrasse 95), a 20-minute bus ride from the centre, has regular scheduled flights to destinations all over Austria and Europe. Low-cost flights from the UK are provided by **Ryanair** (www.ryanair.com) and **EasyJet** (www.easyjet.com). Other airlines include **British Airways** (www.britishairways.com) and **Jet2** (www.jet2.com).

BUS

Buses depart from just outside the Hauptbahnhof on Südtiroler Platz, where timetables are displayed. Bus information and tickets are available from the information points on the main concourse. For more information on buses in and around Salzburg and an online timetable see www.svv-info.at and www.postbus.at.

CAR & MOTORCYCLE

Three motorways converge on Salzburg to form a loop around the city: the A1/E60 from Linz, Vienna and the east; the A8/E52 from Munich and the west; and the A10/E55 from Villach and the south. The quickest way to Tyrol is to take the road to Bad Reichenhall in Germany and continue to Lofer (B178) and St Johann in Tyrol.

TRAIN

Salzburg has excellent rail connections with neighbouring Bavaria in Germany and the rest of Austria on its recently revamped Hauptbahnhof.

Direct EC trains run at least hourly to Munich (€36, 1¾ hours) and every two hours to Stuttgart (€79, four hours). S-Bahn (suburban metro railway) trains operate twice hourly between the Hauptbahnhof and Bad Reichenhall (€6, 40 minutes). For timetables, see www.svv-info.at.

The quickest way to Innsbruck is by the 'corridor' train through Germany; trains depart at least every two hours (€44.90, two hours) and stop at Kufstein. Trains leave frequently for Vienna (€51.10, 2½ hours) and Linz (€25.30, 1¼ hours). There is a two-hourly express service to Klagenfurt (€38.90, three hours).

There are also several trains daily to Berlin (€142, eight hours), Budapest (€88, 5¾ hours), Prague (€73, seven hours) and Venice (€49.40 to €97.60, 6½ to nine hours).

❶ Getting Around

TO/FROM THE AIRPORT

Salzburg airport is around 5.5km west of the centre along Innsbrucker Bundesstrasse. Buses 2, 8 and 27 (€2.50) depart from outside the terminal roughly every 10 minutes and make several central stops near the Altstadt; buses 2 and 27 terminate at the Hauptbahnhof. Services operate roughly from 5.30am to 11pm. A taxi between the airport and the centre costs €15 to €20.

BICYCLE

Salzburg is one of Austria's most bike-friendly cities, with an extensive network of scenic cycling trails heading off in all directions, including along the banks of the Salzach River. See www.movelo.com (in German) for a list of places renting out electric bikes.

A Velo (Mozartplatz; half day/full day/week €12/18/55, e-bike €18/25/120; ⊙9am-6pm mid-Apr–Oct) Just across the way from the tourist office.

BUS

Bus drivers sell single (€2.50) and 24-hour (€5.50) tickets, but its around 20% cheaper if you buy them from the ticket machines. If you're planning on making several trips, *Tabak* (tobacconist) shops sell tickets even cheaper still (€1.80 each), but only in units of five. Week tickets (€15) can be purchased from machines and *Tabak* shops. Children under six travel free, while all other children pay half-price.

Bus routes are shown at bus stops and on some city maps; bus 1 starts from the Hauptbahnhof and skirts the pedestrian-only Altstadt. Another central stop is Hanuschplatz.

BUS TAXI

'Bus taxis' operate from 11.30pm to 1.30am (3am on weekends) on fixed routes, dropping off and picking up along the way, for a cost of €4.50. Ferdinand-Hanusch-Platz is the departure point for suburban routes on the left bank, and Theatergasse for routes on the right bank.

CAR & MOTORCYCLE

Parking places are limited and much of the Altstadt is only accessible on foot, so it's easier to leave your car at one of three park-and-ride points to the west, north and south of the city. The largest car park in the centre is the Altstadt Garage under Mönchsberg (€18 per day); some restaurants in the centre will stamp your ticket for a reduction. Rates are lower on streets with automatic ticket machines (blue zones); a three-hour maximum applies (€3, or €0.60 for 30 minutes) from 9am to 7pm on weekdays.

Avis (www.avis.com; Ferdinand-Porsche-Strasse 7)

Europcar (www.europcar.com; Gniglerstrasse 12)

Hertz (www.hertz.com; Ferdinand-Porsche-Strasse 7)

FIAKER

A *Fiaker* (horse-drawn carriage) for up to four people costs €44 for 25 minutes or €88 for a longer 50-minute ride. The drivers line up on Residenzplatz. Not all speak English, so don't expect a guided tour. All *Fiaker* horses are well-treated.

AROUND SALZBURG

Schloss Hellbrunn

⭐**Schloss Hellbrunn** PALACE
(www.hellbrunn.at; Fürstenweg 37; adult/child/family €10.50/5/25; ⊙9am-5.30pm, to 9pm Jul & Aug; ⊕) A prince-archbishop with a wicked sense of humour, Markus Sittikus built Schloss Hellbrunn in the early 17th century as a summer palace and an escape from his functions at the Residenz. The Italianate villa became a beloved retreat for rulers of state who flocked here to eat, drink and make merry. It was a Garden of Eden to all who beheld its exotic fauna, citrus trees and trick fountains – designed to sober up the clergy without dampening their spirits.

Domenico Gisberti, poet to the court of Munich, once gushed: 'I see the epitome of Venice in these waters, Rome reduced to a brief outline.'

While the whimsical palace interior – especially the oriental-style Chinese Room and frescoed Festsaal – is worth a peek, the eccentric *Wasserspiele* (trick fountains) are the big draw in summer. Be prepared to get soaked in the mock Roman theatre, the shell-clad Neptune Grotto and the twittering Bird Grotto. No statue here is quite as it seems, including the emblematic tongue-poking-out Germaul mask (Sittikus' answer to his critics). The tour rounds out at the 18th-century water-powered Mechanical Theatre, where 200 limewood figurines depict life in a baroque city. Tours run every 30 minutes.

Studded with ponds, sculptures and leafy avenues, the palace gardens are free and open until dusk year-round. Here you'll find *The Sound of Music* pavilion of 'Sixteen Going on Seventeen' fame.

❶ Getting There & Away

Hellbrunn is 4.5km south of Salzburg, a scenic 20-minute bike ride (mostly along the Salzach River) or a 12-minute ride on bus 25 (€2.50, every 20 minutes) from Mozartsteg/Rudolfskai in the Altstadt.

Untersberg

Untersberg   MOUNTAIN
(www.untersbergbahn.at; cable car up/down/return
€14/12.50/22, free with Salzburg Card; ⊙8.30-
5.30pm Jul-Sep, shorter hours rest of year, closed
early Nov–mid-Dec) Rising above Salzburg and
straddling the German border is the rugged
1853m peak of Untersberg. Spectacular views
of the city, the Rositten Valley and the Tyrolean, Salzburg and Bavarian alpine ranges
unfold from the summit. The mountain is
a magnet for local skiers in winter, and hikers, climbers and paragliders in summer.
From the cable car top station, short, easy
trails lead to nearby viewpoints at Geiereck
(1805m) and Salzburg Hochthron, while others take you much deeper into the Alps.

Temperatures can feel significantly cooler
up here than down in the valley and trails
are loose underfoot, so bring a fleece or jacket and sturdy footwear if you plan on doing
some walking.

A cable car runs every half hour to the peak.
To reach the cable car valley station, take bus
25 from Salzburg's Hauptbahnhof or Mirabellplatz to St Leonhard and the valley station.

Gaisberg

Gaisberg   MOUNTAIN
A road snakes up to 1287m Gaisberg, where
stellar views of the Salzburg Valley, Salzkammergut lakes, the limestone Tennengebirge
range and neighbouring Bavaria await. The
best way to appreciate all this is on the 5km
around-the-mountain circuit trail. Salzburgers also head up here for outdoor pursuits
from mountain biking to cross-country skiing. Bus 151 (€3.40, 18 minutes) operates a
twice daily direct service from Mirabellplatz
to Gaisberg in summer; or take the hourly bus number 2 (€4.70, 30 minutes) from
Mirabellplatz, which involves a change at
Obergnigl. From November to March the
bus only goes as far as Zistelalpe, 1.5km
short of the summit.

Hallein & Bad Dürrnberg

✈06245 / POP 20,380 / ELEV 460M
Too few people visit Hallein, but those who do
are pleasantly surprised. Beyond its industrial outskirts lies a pristine late-medieval town,
where narrow lanes are punctuated by courtyards, art galleries and boho cafes. Hotels
are cheaper and less sought-after here than

in Salzburg, a 25-minute train ride away – a
point worth considering during the Salzburg
Festival. Hallein's major family attraction, the
Salzwelten salt mine, is actually located in
Bad Dürrnberg, 6km southwest of town.

⦿ Sights

★**Salzwelten**   MINE
(www.salzwelten.at; Ramsaustrasse 3, Bad Dürrnberg; adult/child/family €19/9.50/48.50; ⊙9am-
5pm; ⊕) The sale of salt filled Salzburg's
coffers during its princely heyday. At Austria's biggest show mine, you can slip into
a boiler suit to descend to the bowels of the
earth. The tour aboard a rickety train passes
through a maze of claustrophobic passageways, over the border to Germany and down
a 27m slide – don't brake, lift your legs and
ask the guide to wax for extra speed! After
crossing a salt lake on a wooden raft, a 42m
slide brings you to the lowest point (210m
underground) and back to good old Austria.
Guided tours depart every half hour. Bus 41
runs from Hallein train station hourly on
weekdays, less often at weekends.

Keltenmuseum   MUSEUM
(Celtic Museum; www.keltenmuseum.at; Pflegerplatz
5; adult/child €6/2.50; ⊙9am-5pm; ⊕) Overlooking the Salzach, the glass-fronted Keltenmuseum runs chronologically through the region's heritage in a series of beautiful vaulted
rooms. It begins with Celtic artefacts, including Asterix-style helmets, an impressively reconstructed chariot, and a selection of bronze
brooches, pendants and buckles. The 1st floor

SILENT NIGHT

Hallein's festive claim to fame is as the
one-time home of Franz Xaver Gruber
(1787–1863) who, together with Joseph
Mohr, composed the carol 'Stille Nacht'
(Silent Night). Mohr penned the poem
in 1816 and Gruber, a schoolteacher at
the time, came up with the melody on
his guitar. You can see that fabled guitar
in Gruber's former residence, now the
Stille Nacht Museum (www.stille
nachthallein.at; Gruberplatz 1; adult/child
€2/0.70, free with entry to Keltenmuseum;
 ⊙3-6pm daily Jul & Aug, 3-6pm Fri-Sun rest
of year) next to Hallein's parish church.
The museum tells the story of the
carol through documents and personal
belongings.

traces the history of salt extraction in Hallein, featuring high points such as a miniature slide and the mummified Mannes im Salz (Man in Salt) unearthed in 1577. There is a pamphlet with English explanations.

✨ Festivals & Events

First-rate musicians and artists draw crowds to the two-week **Halleiner Stadtfestwoche** in mid-June. The festival is one of the headliners on the summer events program in Salzburgerland, with everything from classical concerts to live jazz, theatre, comedy acts, readings and exhibitions. For more details, see www.forum-hallein.at (in German).

🛏 Sleeping

Hallein can be visited on a day trip from Salzburg, but there are lots of value-for-money places to stay if you'd rather base yourself here, a point worth considering during the Salzburg Festival. The tourist office helps book private rooms.

Pension Sommerauer　　　　GUESTHOUSE €
(☑800 30; www.pension-hallein.at; Tschusistrasse 71; s €43-57, d €69-92, tr €92-120, q €117-152; Ⓟ⊗⛹) Housed in a 300-year-old farmhouse, the rustic rooms at this guesthouse are a bargain. There's a heated pool and conservatory as well as kiddie stuff including a playroom, sandpit and swings.

Pension Hochdürrnberg　　　GUESTHOUSE €
(☑751 83; Rumpelgasse 14, Bad Dürrnberg; s/d/tr/q €45/60/70/100; Ⓟ⛹) Surrounded by meadows, this farmhouse in Bad Dürrnberg has countrified rooms with warm pine furnishings and downy bedding. The furry residents (rabbits, sheep and cows) keep children amused.

Hotel Auwirt　　　　　　　HOTEL €€
(☑804 17; www.auwirt.com; Salzburgerstrasse 42; camp sites per adult/child/tent €8.50/6/5, s €60-88, d €90-145, tr €120-170, q €140-220; Ⓟ⚌⛹) Auwirt's light-filled rooms are a tad dated but comfy (ask for one with a balcony). The hotel is a good family base with its tree-shaded garden and playground. You can also pitch a tent here.

ℹ Information

Tourist Office (☑853 94; www.hallein.com; Mauttorpromenade 6; ⊙9am-5pm Mon-Fri) The tourist office is on the narrow Pernerinsel island adjoining the Stadtbrücke.

ℹ Getting There & Away

Hallein is close to the German border, 18km south of Salzburg via the B150 and A10/E55 direction Graz/Villach. It's a 25-minute bus or train journey from Salzburg, with departures roughly every 30 minutes (€2.40).

Werfen

☑06468 / POP 2960 / ELEV 525M

The world's largest accessible ice caves, the soaring limestone turrets of the Tennengebirge range and a formidable medieval fortress are but the tip of the superlative iceberg in Werfen. Such salacious natural beauty hasn't escaped Hollywood producers – Werfen stars in WWII action film *Where Eagles Dare* (1968) and makes a cameo appearance in the picnic scene of *The Sound of Music*.

◎ Sights & Activities

★**Eisriesenwelt**　　　　　　　CAVE
(www.eisriesenwelt.at; adult/child €11/6, incl cable car €22/12; ⊙8am-3.45pm May-Oct, to 4.45pm Jul & Aug) Billed as the world's largest accessible ice caves, Eisriesenwelt is a glittering ice empire spanning 30,000 sq m and 42km of narrow passages burrowing deep into the heart of the mountains. A tour through these Narnia-esque chambers of blue ice is a unique experience. As you climb up wooden steps and down pitch-black passages, with carbide lamps aglow, otherworldly ice sculptures shaped like polar bears and elephants, frozen columns and lakes emerge from the shadows.

A highlight is the cavernous **Eispalast** (ice palace), where the frost crystals twinkle when a magnesium flare is held up to them. A womblike tunnel leads to a flight of 700 steps, which descends back to the entrance. Even if it's hot outside, entering the caves in any season is like stepping into a deep freeze – bring warm clothing and sturdy footwear.

In summer, minibuses (return adult/child €6.50/4.10) run at 8.18am, 10.18am, 12.18pm and 2.18pm from Werfentrain station to Eisriesenwelt car park, which is a 20-minute walk from the bottom station of the cable car. The last return bus departs at 4.32pm. Allow roughly three hours for the return trip (including tour). You can walk the whole route, but it's a challenging four-hour ascent, rising 1100m above the village.

Burg Hohenwerfen　　　　　CASTLE
(adult/child/family €11/6/26.50, incl lift €14.50/8/34.50; ⊙9am-5pm Apr-Oct; ⛹) Slung high

A ROYAL RAVINE

One of the deepest and longest ravines in the Alps, the Liechtensteinklamm (Liechtenstein Gorge; www.liechtensteinklamm.at; adult/child €5.50/3.50; ⊘8am-6pm May-Sep, 9am-4pm Oct; ⓘ) is off the beaten track but well worth the detour. The jaw-dropping chasm was carved out during the last Ice Age and takes its name from Johann II, Prince of Liechtenstein, who poured plenty of money into making the gorge accessible in the 19th century. Following raging waters flanked by vertical 300m-high cliffs, the footpath crosses bridges and passes through tunnels gouged into slate cliffs veined with white granite.

The mossy boulders and crags glisten with spray from the water, which is at its most striking in the late afternoon when the sunlight turns it opal blue. The trail culminates at a spectacular 50m waterfall. Allow at least an hour to walk the gorge.

Trains run frequently between Werfen and St Johann im Pongau (€3.70, 18 minutes), a 4km walk from the gorge, where free parking is available.

on a wooded clifftop and cowering beneath the majestic peaks of the Tennengebirge range, Burg Hohenwerfen is visible from afar. For 900 years this fortress has kept watch over the Salzach Valley, its current appearance dating to 1570. The big draw is the far-reaching view over Werfen from the 16th-century belfry, though the dungeons (displaying the usual nasties such as the iron maiden and thumb screw) are also worth a look.

The entry fee also covers a falconry show in the grounds (11.15am and 3.15pm daily), where falconers in medieval costume release eagles, owls, falcons and vultures to wheel in front of the ramparts. There is commentary in English and German.

Both the fortress and the ice caves can be squeezed into a day trip from Salzburg; start early, visit the caves first and be at the fortress for the last falconry show. The brisk walk up from the village takes 20 minutes.

🛏 Sleeping & Eating

Nip into the tourist office for a list of nearby B&Bs, private rooms and campgrounds.

Camping Vierthaler   CAMPGROUND €
(☑565 74; www.camping-vierthaler.at; Reitsam 8; camp sites per adult/child/tent €6/3/6, bungalows d/tr/q €28/37/46; ⊘mid-Apr–Sep; ⓘ) This lovely campground on the bank of the Salzach River has a back-to-nature feel. Facilities include a snack bar and playground. Bungalows with kitchenettes, patios and barbecue areas are also available.

Mariannenschlössl   PENSION €
(☑420 93 80; Poststrasse 10; d €60-64) What a view! A five-minute uphill trot from the centre of the village, this family-run guest-

house offers an entrancing vista of the fortress and of the Tennengebirge's magnificent rock turrets and spires from its garden and the sweet, spotlessly kept rooms. A generous breakfast is served in a room adorned with hunting trophies.

★**Obauer**   MODERN EUROPEAN €€€
(☑52 12; www.obauer.com; Markt 46; 3-course lunch €35, dinner menus €40-120; ⊘noon-2pm & 7-9pm Wed-Sun; ⓘ) Culinary dream duo Karl and Rudi Obauer run the show at this highly-regarded, ingredient-focused restaurant. Sit in the rustic-chic restaurant or the garden, where most of the fruit and herbs are grown. Signatures like meltingly tender Werfen lamb and flaky trout strudel are matched with the finest of Austrian wines.

Oedlhaus   AUSTRIAN €€
(Eishöhlenstrasse; snacks €3.50-8, mains €8-12.50; ⊘9am-3.45pm May-Oct, to 4.45pm Jul & Aug) Next to Eisriesenwelt cable-car top station, this woodsy hut at 1574m fortifies walkers with mountain grub such as *Gröstl* (pan-fried potatoes, pork and onions topped with a fried egg). The terrace has views to rave about: looking across the Salzach Valley to the chiselled limestone peaks of the Hochkönig range.

ⓘ Information

Tourist Office (☑53 88; www.werfen.at; Markt 24; ⊘9am-5pm Mon-Fri) The friendly tourist office hands out information and maps.

ⓘ Getting There & Away

Werfen is 45km south of Salzburg on the A10/E55 motorway. Trains run frequently to Salzburg (€8.60, 40 minutes).

Stuttgart & the Black Forest

Best Places to Eat

➡ Valentin (p259)

➡ Olivo (p204)

➡ Kreuzblume (p237)

➡ Zur Forelle (p216)

➡ Weinstube im Baldreit (p222)

Best Places to Stay

➡ Hotel Scholl (p212)

➡ Hotel Schiefes Haus (p215)

➡ Weysses Rössle (p230)

➡ Die Reichstadt (p232)

➡ Parkhotel Wehrle (p243)

Why Go?

If one word could sum up Germany's southwesternmost region, it would be inventive. Baden-Würtemberg gave the world relativity (Einstein), DNA (Miescher) and the astronomical telescope (Kepler). It was here that Bosch invented the spark plug; Gottlieb Daimler the gas engine; and Count Ferdinand the zeppelin. And where would we be without black forest gateau, cuckoo clocks and the ultimate beer food, the pretzel?

Beyond the high-tech, urbanite pleasures of 21st-century Stuttgart lies a region still ripe for discovery. On the city fringes, country lanes roll into vineyards and lordly baroque palaces, spa towns and castles steeped in medieval myth. Swinging south, the Black Forest (*Schwarzwald* in German) looks every inch the Grimm fairy-tale blueprint. Hills rise sharply and wooded above church steeples, looming over half-timbered villages and a crochet of tightly woven valleys. It is a perfectly etched picture of sylvan beauty, a landscape refreshingly oblivious to time and trends.

When to Go

Snow dusts the heights from January to late February and pre-Lenten *Fasnacht* brings carnival shenanigans to the region's towns and villages. Enjoy cool forest hikes, riverside bike rides, splashy fun on Lake Constance and open-air festivals galore during summer. From late September to October the golden autumn days can be spent rambling in woods, mushrooming and snuggling up in Black Forest farmhouses.

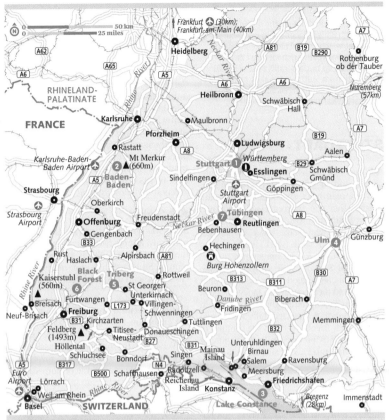

Stuttgart & the Black Forest Highlights

① Tuning into modern-day **Stuttgart** (p198)

② Wallowing in thermal waters and art nouveau grandeur in **Baden-Baden** (p218), belle of the Black Forest

③ Hopping between borders on **Lake Constance** (p247), straddling Switzerland, Germany and Austria

④ Being amazed by Einstein's birthplace, **Ulm** (p213), crowned by the world's tallest cathedral steeple

⑤ Going cuckoo for clocks, black forest gateau and waterfalls in **Triberg** (p243)

⑥ Roaming hill, dale and kilometre after pristine kilometre of woodland in the **Black Forest** (p218)

⑦ Cruising along the Neckar and living it up Goethe-style in postcard-pretty **Tübingen** (p208)

① Getting There & Around

AIR

Flights to the region serve Stuttgart Airport (p206), a major hub for Germanwings; Karlsruhe-Baden-Baden airport (p223), a Ryanair base; and Basel-Mulhouse EuroAirport (p238), where easyJet operates.

BUS

Trains, trams and/or buses serve almost every town and village, though public transport across the Black Forest can be slow, and long-distance trips (for instance, Freiburg to Konstanz) may involve several changes. Plan your journey with the help of www.efa-bw.de and www.bahn.de.

CAR & MOTORCYCLE

Motorways blazing through the region include the A5 from Baden-Baden south to Freiburg and Basel, which can get hellishly congested due to ongoing roadworks; www.swr.de (in German) has up-to-date traffic news. The A81 runs south from Stuttgart to Lake Constance via Villingen-Schwenningen, while the A8 links Stuttgart to Karlsruhe, Ulm and Munich.

STUTTGART

📞 0711 / POP 600,000

Ask many Germans their opinion of Stuttgarters and they will go off on a tangent: they are road hogs, speeding along the autobahn; they are sharp-dressed executives with a Swabian drawl; they are tight-fisted homebodies who slave away to *schaffe, schaffe, Häusle baue* (work, work, build a house). So much for the stereotypes.

The real Stuttgart is less superficial than legend. True, some good-living locals like their cars fast and their restaurants fancy, but most are just as happy getting their boots dirty in the surrounding vine-clad hills and hanging out with friends in the rustic confines of a *Weinstube* (wine tavern). In the capital of Baden-Württemberg, city slickers and down-to-earth country kids walk hand in hand.

History

Whether with trusty steeds or turbocharged engines, Stuttgart was born to ride – founded as the stud farm Stuotgarten around AD 950. Progress was swift: by the 12th century Stuttgart was a trade centre, by the 13th century a blossoming city and by the early 14th century the seat of the Württemberg royal family. Count Eberhard im Bart added sheen to Swabian suburbia by introducing the *Kehrwoche* in 1492, the communal cleaning rota still revered today.

ⓘ BADEN-WÜRTTEMBERG TICKET

Available at all train stations and online (www.bahn.de), the great-value Baden-Württemberg Ticket allows unlimited 2nd-class travel on IRE, RE, RB, S-Bahn trains and buses in the region. The one-day ticket costs €23 for an individual, plus €5 per extra person. Children aged 15 and under travel for free when accompanied by an adult.

The early 16th century brought hardship, peasant wars, plague and Austrian rulers (1520–34). A century later, the Thirty Years' War devastated Stuttgart and killed half its population.

In 1818, King Wilhelm I launched the first Cannstatter Volksfest to celebrate the end of a dreadful famine. An age of industrialisation dawned in the late 19th and early 20th centuries, with Bosch inventing the spark plug and Daimler pioneering the gas engine. Heavily bombed in WWII, Stuttgart was painstakingly reconstructed and became the capital of the new state of Baden-Württemberg in 1953. Today it is one of Germany's greenest and most affluent cities.

⊙ Sights

Stuttgart's main artery is the shopping boulevard Königstrasse, running south from the Hauptbahnhof. Steep grades are common on Stuttgart's hillsides: more than 500 city streets end in *Stäffele* (staircases).

Schlossplatz SQUARE

Stuttgart's central square is dominated by the exuberant three-winged Neues Schloss. Duke Karl Eugen von Württemberg's answer to Versailles, the baroque-neoclassical royal residence now houses state government ministries. A bronze statue of Emperor Wilhelm I graces nearby Karlsplatz.

Staatsgalerie Stuttgart GALLERY

(📞0711-470 400; www.staatsgalerie-stuttgart.de; Konrad-Adenauer-Strasse 30-32; adult/concession €7/5; ⊙10am-6pm Tue, Wed & Fri-Sun, to 8pm Thu) The neoclassical-meets-contemporary Staatsgalerie bears British architect James Stirling's curvy, colourful imprint. Alongside big-name exhibitions, the gallery harbours a representative collection of European art from the 14th to the 21st centuries as well as American post-WWII avantgardists.

Kunstmuseum Stuttgart GALLERY

(📞0711-2161 9600; www.kunstmuseum-stuttgart.de; Kleiner Schlossplatz 1; adult/concession €6/4; ⊙10am-6pm Tue-Thu, Sat & Sun, to 9pm Fri) Occupying a shimmering glass cube, this gallery presents high-calibre special exhibits alongside a permanent gallery filled with a prized collection of works by Otto Dix, Willi Baumeister and Alfred Höltzel. For a great view, head up to the Cube cafe.

Out front, the primary colours and geometric forms of Alexander Calder's mobile catch the eye.

Schlossgarten   GARDENS

The fountain-dotted **Mittlerer Schloss-garten** (Middle Palace Garden) draws thirsty crowds to its beer garden in summer. The **Unterer Schlossgarten** (Lower Palace Garden) is a ribbon of greenery rambling northeast to the Neckar River and the Rosensteinpark, home to the zoo. Sitting south, the **Oberer Schlossgarten** (Upper Palace Garden) is framed by eye-catching landmarks like the columned Staatstheater (p205) and the ultramodern **Landtag** (State Parliament), a glass rectangle housing the state parliament.

Turmforum   VIEWPOINT

(Hauptbahnhof; ⊘10am-6pm Mon-Thu & Sat & Sun, to 9pm Fri) FREE Some of the best views of Stuttgart are from the the top of the tower jutting out from the main train station. A free lift (elevator) deposits you right below the revolving Mercedes star. You also get a bird's-eye view of 'Stuttgart 21', a huge – and controversial – revamp of the main train station. Exhibits on floors 3, 5 and 7a explain the details.

Mercedes-Benz Museum   MUSEUM

(✆0711-173 0000; www.mercedes-benz-classic.com; Mercedesstrasse 100; adult/concession/under 15yr €8/4/free; ⊘9am-6pm Tue-Sun, last admission 5pm; ℝS1 to Neckarpark) A futuristic swirl on the cityscape, the Mercedes-Benz Museum takes a chronological spin through the Mercedes empire. Look out for legends like the 1885 Daimler Riding Car, the world's first gasoline-powered vehicle, and the record-breaking Lightning Benz that hit 228km/h at Daytona Beach in 1909.

Porsche Museum   MUSEUM

(✆0711-9112 0911; www.porsche.com/museum; Porscheplatz 1; adult/concession €8/4; ⊘9am-6pm Tue-Sun; ℝNeuwirtshaus) A pearly white spaceship preparing for lift-off, the barrier-free Porsche Museum is every little boy's dream. Groovy audioguides race you through the history of Porsche from its 1948 beginnings. Stop to glimpse the 911 GT1 that won Le Mans in 1998.

Landesmuseum Württemberg   MUSEUM

(www.landesmuseum-stuttgart.de; Schillerplatz 6; adult/concession €5.50/4.50; ⊘10am-5pm Tue-Sun) An archway leads to the turreted 10th-century Altes Schloss, where this museum features regional archaeology and architecture. The historic booty includes Celtic jewellery, neolithic pottery, diamond-encrusted crown jewels and rare artefacts. Time your visit to

GOING THE WHOLE HOG

Billing itself as the world's biggest pig museum, the **Schweinemuseum** (www.schweinemuseum.de; Schlachthofstrasse 2a; adult/concession €5.90/5; ⊘11am-7.30pm; ⓤSchlachthof) is one heck of a pigsty: 45,000 paintings, lucky trinkets, antiques, cartoons, piggy banks and a veritable mountain of cuddly toys cover the entire porcine spectrum. Since opening in 2010 in the city's 100-year-old former slaughterhouse, the kitsch-cool museum has drawn crowds to its exhibits spotlighting everything from pig worship to wild boar hunt rituals. In the adjacent beer garden (mains €12 to €19), you can pig out on schnitzel, pork knuckles and more.

see, from the arcaded courtyard, the rams above the clock tower lock horns on the hour.

Wilhelma Zoologisch-Botanischer Garten   ZOO

(www.wilhelma.de; Rosensteinpark; adult/concession €16/10, after 4pm & Nov-Feb €11/7; ⊘8.15am-dusk; ⓤWilhelma) Wilhelma Zoologisch-Botanischer Garten is a quirky mix of zoo and botanical gardens. Kid magnets include semi-striped okapis, elephants, penguins and a petting farm. Greenhouses sheltering tree ferns, camellias and Amazonian species are among the botanical highlights. Sniff out the gigantic bloom of the malodorous titan arum in the Moorish Villa.

Württembergischer Kunstverein   GALLERY

(www.wkv-stuttgart.de; Schlossplatz 2; adult/concession €5/3; ⊘11am-6pm Tue-Sun, to 8pm Wed) Identified by its copper cupola, this gallery stages thought-provoking contemporary art exhibitions.

Schillerplatz   SQUARE

Cobbled Schillerplatz is where the poet-dramatist **Friedrich Schiller** is immortalised in bronze.

Stiftskirche   CHURCH

(Collegiate Church; Stiftstrasse 12; ⊘10am-7pm Mon & Thu, 10am-4pm Fri & Sat, 10am-6pm Sun) FREE Topped by two mismatched towers, this largely 15th-century church has Romanesque origins.

Stuttgart

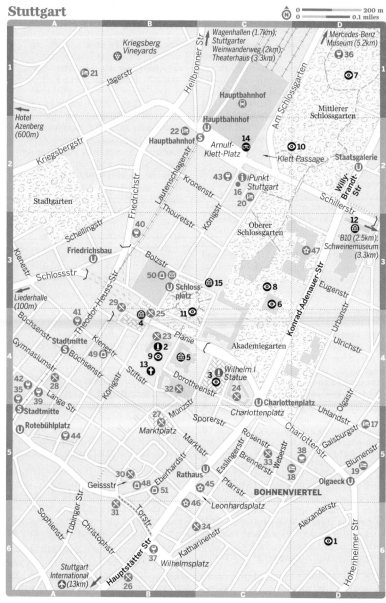

Tours

Pop into the tourist office for details on German-language guided tours, from vineyard ambles to after-work 'walk and wine' strolls.

CityTour Stuttgart BUS TOUR
(adult/concession €15/10; ☉10am-4pm) Departs roughly hourly from the tourist information and trundles past icons like Schlossplatz and the Mercedes-Benz Museum. Up to two

Stuttgart

children aged 14 and under go free when accompanied by an adult.

Neckar-Käpt'n BOAT TOUR
(www.neckar-kaeptn.de; Ⓤ Wilhelma) From early May to late October, Neckar-Käpt'n runs cruises on the Neckar River, departing from its dock at Wilhelma in Bad Cannstatt on the U14.

🎎 Festivals & Events

Sommerfest MUSIC
(www.sommerfest-stuttgart.de) Riverside parties, open-air gigs and alfresco feasting is what this four-day August shindig is all about.

Weindorf WINE
(www.stuttgarter-weindorf.de) A 10-day event where winemakers sell the year's vintages from hundreds of booths on Schlossplatz and the Oberer Schlossgarten. Begins on the last weekend in August.

Cannstatter Volksfest BEER
(www.cannstatter-volksfest.de) Stuttgart's answer to Oktoberfest, this beer-guzzling bash, held over three consecutive weekends from late September to mid-October, lifts spirits with oompah music, fairground rides and fireworks.

Weihnachtsmarkt CHRISTMAS MARKET
(www.stuttgarter-weihnachtsmarkt.de) One of Germany's biggest Christmas markets brings festive twinkle to Marktplatz, Schillerplatz and Schlossplatz from late November to 23 December.

🛏 Sleeping

Stuttgart is slowly upping the ante in slumberland but nondescript chains still reign supreme. Expect weekend discounts of 10% to 20% at hotels targeting business travellers. If you're seeking individual flair and a family welcome, stop by the tourist office for a list of private guesthouses and apartments.

DON'T MISS

BOHEMIAN BEANS

To really slip under Stuttgart's skin, mosey through one of the city's lesser-known neighbourhoods. Walk south to Hans-im-Glück Platz, centred on a fountain depicting the caged Grimm's fairytale character Lucky Hans, and you'll soon reach the boho-flavoured **Bohnenviertel** (Bean District; www.bohnenviertel. net), named after beans introduced in the 16th century. Back then they were grown everywhere as the staple food of the poor tanners, dyers and craftsmen who lived here.

A recent facelift has restored the neighbourhood's cobbled lanes and gabled houses, which harbour idiosyncratic galleries, workshops, bookshops, wine taverns and cafes. The villagey atmosphere is a refreshing tonic to the big-city feel of central Stuttgart.

Hostel Alex 30   HOSTEL $

(☑0711-838 8950; www.alex30-hostel.de; Alexanderstrasse 30; dm €25-29, s/d €43/64; P☎) Fun-seekers on a budget should thrive at this popular hostel within walking distance of the city centre. Rooms are spick and span, and the bar, sun deck and communal kitchen are ideal for swapping stories with fellow travellers. Light sleepers might want to pack earplugs for thin walls and street noise. Breakfast costs €8.

Hotel Azenberg   HOTEL $$

(☑0711-225 5040; www.hotelazenberg.de; Seestrasse 114-116; s €75-120, d €85-135; P☎☒; ☒43) This family-run choice has individually designed quarters with themes swinging from English country manor to Picasso. There's a pool, tree-shaded garden and mini spa for relaxing moments. Take bus 43 from Stadtmitte to Hölderlinstrasse.

City Hotel   HOTEL $$

(☑0711-210 810; www.cityhotel-stuttgart.de; Uhlandstrasse 18; s €87-95, d €101-119, incl breakfast; P☎) Eschew the anonymity of Stuttgart's cookie-cutter chains for this intimate hotel just off Charlottenplatz. Rooms are light, clean and modern, if slightly lacklustre. Breakfast on the terrace in summer is a bonus.

Ochsen Hotel   HISTORIC HOTEL $$

(☑0711-407 0500; www.ochsen-online.de; Ulmer Strasse 323; s €89-140, d €119-170; P☎; ☒Insel-

strasse) It's worth going the extra mile to this charismatic 18th-century hotel. Some of the spacious, warm-hued rooms have whirlpool tubs. The wood-panelled restaurant dishes up appetising local fare.

Kronen Hotel   HOTEL $$$

(☑0711-225 10; www.kronenhotel-stuttgart. de; Kronenstrasse 48; s €115-125, d €160-190; P☀@☎) Right on the lap of Königstrasse, this hotel outclasses most in Stuttgart with its terrific location, good-natured staff, well-appointed rooms and funkily lit sauna. Breakfast is above par, with fresh fruit, egg and bacon, smoked fish and pastries.

Steigenberger Graf Zeppelin   HOTEL $$$

(☑0711-204 80; www.stuttgart.steigenberger.de; Arnulf-Klett-Platz 7; r €140-311; P☀☎☒) While its concrete facade won't bowl you over, inside is a different story. This five-star pad facing the Hauptbahnhof is luxury all the way with snazzy rooms, Zen-style spa and Michelin-starred restaurant, Olivo (p204).

Der Zauberlehrling   BOUTIQUE HOTEL $$$

(☑0711-237 7770; www.zauberlehrling.de; Rosenstrasse 38; s €160-250, d €180-420; P☎) The dreamily styled rooms at the 'Sorcerer's Apprentice' offer soothing quarters after a day on the road. Each one interprets a different theme (Mediterranean siesta, sunrise, 1001 Nights), through colour, furniture and features such as canopy beds, clawfoot tubs, tatami mats or fireplaces. Breakfast costs €19.

Hotel am Schlossgarten   HOTEL $$$

(☑0711-202 60; www.hotelschlossgarten.com; Schillerstrasse 23; r €142-220, ste €204-600; P☀☎) Sidling up to the Schloss, this hotel has handsome, park-facing rooms flaunting the luxuries that justify the price tag. Book a table at Michelin-starred Zirbelstube (tasting menus €109 to €139) for classy French dining in subtly lit, pine-panelled surrounds.

✖ Eating

Stuttgart has raised the bar in the kitchen, with chefs putting an imaginative spin on local, seasonal ingredients. The city's half-dozen Michelin-starred restaurants prepare cuisine with enough gourmet panache to satisfy a food-literate crowd. For intimate bistro-style dining, explore the backstreets and the alleyways of Bohnenviertel.

Platzhirsch   INTERNATIONAL $

(☑0711-7616 2508; www.platzhirsch-stuttgart. de; Geissstrasse 12; mains €6.20-11.80; ⊙11am-

2am) Combining a breath of country air with a pinch of urban cool, wood-panelled Platzhirsch has a good buzz and, in summer, a packed terrace. Dig into mains such as parmesan *Knödel* (dumplings) in thyme-honey sauce and saffron risotto with prawns. Lunch specials go for a wallet-friendly €6.80 to €7.80.

Forum Café   CAFE $
(Gymnasiumstrasse 21; snacks €4-7.50; ☺3-11.30pm Mon-Fri, noon-11.30pm Sat; 🖉🚼) Wholesomely hip, kid-friendly cafe in the Forum Theatre, with yogi teas and organic snacks.

Stuttgarter Markthalle   MARKET $
(Market Hall; www.markthalle-stuttgart.de; Dorotheenstrasse 4; ☺7am-6.30pm Mon-Fri, 7am-5pm Sat) Olives, regional cheeses, spices, patisserie, fruit and veg, wine and tapas – you'll find it all under one roof at Stuttgart's art-nouveau market hall, which also has snack stands.

Food Market   MARKET $
(Marktplatz; ☺7.30am-1pm Tue, Thu & Sat) Self-caterers can pick up picnic fixings at the food market.

Reiskorn   INTERNATIONAL $$
(🖉0711-664 7633; Torstrasse 27; mains €11-15.50; ☺5-10pm Sun-Thu, 5-11pm Fri, noon-11pm Sat; 🖉) With an easygoing vibe and bamboo-green retro interior, this culinary globetrotter serves everything from aubergine schnitzel with feta cream to barramundi fillet in rice leaf with green curry. There are plenty of vegetarian and vegan choices.

Ochs'n'Willi   GERMAN $$
(🖉0711-226 5191; www.ochsn-willi.de; Kleiner Schlossplatz 4; mains €11-28; ☺11am-11.30pm) A warm, woody hunter's cottage restaurant just this side of twee, Ochs'n'Willi delivers gutsy portions of Swabian and Bavarian fare. Dig into pork knuckles with lashings of dumplings and kraut, spot-on *Maultaschen* (pasta pockets) or rich, brothy *Gaisburger Marsch* (beef stew). There's a terrace for warm-weather dining.

Weinhaus Stetter   GERMAN $$
(🖉0711-240 163; www.weinhaus-stetter.de; Rosenstrasse 32; snacks & mains €5-14.50; ☺3-11pm Mon-Fri, noon-3pm & 5.30-11pm Sat) This traditional wine tavern in the Bohnenviertel quarter serves up no-nonsense Swabian cooking, including flavoursome *Linsen und Saiten* (lentils with sausage) and beef roast with onion, in a convivial ambience. The attached wine shop sells 650 different vintages.

Weinstube Fröhlich   GERMAN $$
(🖉0711-242 471; www.weinstube-froehlich.de; Leonhardstrasse 5; mains €14-32; ☺5.30pm-midnight Sun-Thu, 5.30pm-1am Fri & Sat) True, it's in the heart of the red-light district, but don't be put off. This softly lit, dark-wood-panelled restaurant is an atmospheric choice for well-executed Swabian fare (cheese-rich *Käsespätzle, Maultaschen* with potato salad, wild boar ragout) and regional wines.

Amadeus   INTERNATIONAL $$
(🖉0711-292 678; Charlottenplatz 17; mains €10-26.50; ☺11.30am-11pm Mon-Fri, 9am-11pm Sat, 10am-9pm Sun) Once an 18th-century

---

SWABIAN MENU DECODER

As the Swabian saying goes: *Was der Bauer net kennt, frisst er net* (What the farmer doesn't know, he doesn't eat) – so find out before you dig in:

Bubespitzle Officially called *Schupfnudeln*, these short, thick potato noodles – vaguely reminiscent of gnocchi – are browned in butter and tossed with sauerkraut. Sounds appetising until you discover that *Bubespitzle* means 'little boys' penises'.

Gaisburger Marsch A strong beef stew served with potatoes and *Spätzle*.

Maultaschen Giant ravioli pockets, stuffed with leftover ground pork, spinach, onions and bread mush. The dish is nicknamed *Herrgottsbeschieserle* (God trickster) because it was a sly way to eat meat during Lent.

Saure Kuddle So who is for sour tripe? If you don't have the stomach, try potato-based, meat-free *saure Rädle* (sour wheels) instead.

Spätzle Stubby egg-based noodles. These are fried with onions and topped with cheese in the calorific treat *Käsespätzle*.

Zwiebelkuche Autumnal onion tart with bacon, cream and caraway seeds, which pairs nicely with *neuer Süsser* (new wine) or *Moschd* (cider).

DON'T MISS

THEODOR-HEUSS-STRASSE BAR CRAWL

Packed with clubs and hipper-than-thou lounges, Theodor-Heuss-Strasse is perfect for a late-night bar crawl.

7 Grad (Theodor-Heuss-Strasse 32; ⊘7pm-3am Tue-Sat) DJs work the crowd into a sweat spinning house and electro at charcoal-black 7 Grad.

Barcode (Theodor-Heuss-Strasse 30; ⊘11am-2am Mon-Thu, 11am-4pm Fri, 4pm-2am Sat) Barcode fuels the party with decadent cocktails in streamlined surrounds.

Rohbau (Theodor-Heuss-Strasse 26; ⊘9pm-4am Fri & Sat) Rohbau pumps out '80s disco and rock in retro-cool surrounds.

Muttermilch (Theodor-Heuss-Strasse 23; ⊘4pm-1am Wed & Thu, 4pm-5am Fri & Sat) Good-looking Stuttgarters dance to soul and funk at nouveau Alpine chic Muttermilch.

Ribingurūmu (Theodor-Heuss-Strasse 4; ⊘4.30pm-2am Mon-Sat) A chilled-out crowd hangs out over jam-jar cocktails in Ribingurūmu, which exudes an 'old-skool' vibe with its vintage furnishings.

orphanage dishing up gruel, this chic, bustling restaurant now serves glorious Swabian food such as *Maultaschen* and riesling-laced *Kutteln* (tripe), as well as salads and international dishes from wok noodles to burritos. The terrace is a big draw in summer.

Alte Kanzlei GERMAN $$
(☎0711-294 457; Schillerplatz 5a; mains €11-24.50; ⊘9.30am-midnight Mon-Thu, to 1am Fri & Sat, 9am-11pm Sun) Empty tables are rare as gold-dust at this convivial, high-ceilinged restaurant, with a terrace spilling out onto Schillerplatz. Feast on Swabian favourites like *Spanferkel* (roast suckling pig) and *Flädlesuppe* (pancake soup), washed down with regional tipples.

★**Olivo** MODERN EUROPEAN $$$
(☎0711-204 8277; www.olivo-restaurant.de; Arnulf-Klett-Platz 7; mains around €40, 4-course lunch/dinner €76/108; ⊘noon-2pm & 6.30-10pm Wed-Fri, 6.30-10pm Tue & Sat) Young, sparky chef Nico Burkhardt works his stuff at Steigenberger's Michelin-starred restaurant. The minimalist-chic restaurant is lauded

for exquisitely presented, French-inspired specialities such as Périgord goose liver with sheep's milk yoghurt, brioche crumble and woodruff, or beautifully cooked Breton turbot with ricotta and wild garlic.

Cube INTERNATIONAL $$$
(☎0711-280 4441; www.cube-restaurant.de; Kleiner Schlossplatz 1; 4-course lunch €29.80, mains €29-35; ⊘10am-midnight Sun-Thu, 10am-2am Fri & Sat) The food is stellar but it actually plays second fiddle to the dazzling decor, refined ambience and stunning views at this glass-fronted cube atop the Kunstmuseum. Lunches are perky, fresh and international, while dinners feature more complex Pacific Rim–inspired cuisine. The lunch special is a steal at €8.90.

Délice MODERN EUROPEAN $$$
(☎0711-640 3222; www.restaurant-delice.de; Hauptstätter Strasse 61; 5-course tasting menu €98; ⊘6.30pm-midnight Mon-Fri) Natural, integral flavours sing in specialities like medley of tuna with lemon vinaigrette and fried egg with parsnips and Périgord truffles at this vaulted Michelin-starred restaurant. The sommelier will talk you through the award-winning riesling selection.

Drinking & Nightlife

Ciba Mato LOUNGE
(www.ciba-mato.de; Wilhelmsplatz 11; ⊘5pm-1am Mon-Thu, 5pm-3am Fri & Sat, 10am-1am Sun) There's more than a hint of Buddha Bar about this scarlet-walled, Asia-infused space. It's a slinky spot to sip a gingertini or pisco punch, or to hang out Bedouin-style in the shisha tent and nibble on fusion food. The terrace deck is a summertime magnet.

Sky Beach BAR
(www.skybeach.de; Königstrasse 6, top fl Galeria Kaufhof; ⊘noon-12.30am Mon-Sat, 11am-midnight Sun Easter-Sep) When the sun comes out, Stuttgarters live it up at this urban beach, complete with sand, cabaña beds, DJs spinning mellow lounge beats and grandstand city views.

Biergarten im Schlossgarten BEER GARDEN
(www.biergarten-schlossgarten.de; ⊘10.30am-1am May-Oct; 🐾) Toast to summer with beer and pretzels at Stuttgart's best-loved, 2000-seat beer garden in the green heart of the Schlossgarten. Regular live music on Sundays gets steins a-swinging.

Hüftengold CAFE
(Olgastrasse 44; ⊘7am-midnight Mon-Fri, 9am-1am Sat, 10am-8pm Sun) Work on your own

Hüftengold (love handles) with cake and locally roasted coffee at this sylvan wonderland. The log stools and sheepskins create a wonderfully cosy vibe for brunch or evening chats by candlelight.

Zum Paulaner　　　　　　　　　　PUB
(Calwerstrasse 45; ⊘10am-midnight Sun-Thu, to 1am Fri & Sat) Freshly tapped Paulaner brews in a buzzy, tree-shaded beer garden.

Palast der Republik　　　　BEER GARDEN
(⟋0711-226 4887; www.facebook.com/Palast-Stuttgart; Friedrichstrasse 27; ⊘11am-3am; ⓤBörsenplatz) The palace in question is more like a little kiosk, but that's not stopping everyone from students to bankers making this *the* local hotspot for chilling under the trees, cold beer in hand.

Wagenhallen　　　　　　　　　　CLUB
(www.wagenhallen.de; Innerer Nordbahnhof 1; ⓤWagenhallen Nordbahnhof) Swim away from the mainstream at this post-industrial space 2km north of the centre, where club nights, gigs and workshops skip from Balkan-beat parties to poetry slams. There's a relaxed beer garden for summertime quaffing.

☆ Entertainment

For the low-down on events, grab a copy of German-language monthly *Lift Stuttgart* (www.lift-online.de) from the tourist office or news kiosks, or listings magazine *Prinz* (www.prinz.de/stuttgart.html). Events tickets can be purchased at the **i-Punkt desk** (⟋0711-222 8243; Königstrasse 1a; ⊘9am-8pm Mon-Fri, 9am-6pm Sat, 11am-6pm Sun).

Liederhalle　　　　　　CONCERT VENUE
(⟋0711-202 7710; www.liederhalle-stuttgart.de; Berliner Platz 1) Jimi Hendrix and Sting are among the stars who have performed at this culture and congress centre. The 1950s venue stages big-name classical and pop concerts, cabaret and comedy.

Staatstheater　　　　PERFORMING ARTS
(⟋0711-202 090; www.staatstheater-stuttgart. de; Oberer Schlossgarten 6) Stuttgart's grandest theatre presents a top-drawer program of ballet, opera, theatre and classical music. The Stuttgart Ballet (www.stuttgart-ballet. de) is hailed as one of Europe's best.

Bix Jazzclub　　　　　　LIVE MUSIC
(⟋0711-2384 0997; www.bix-stuttgart.de; Leonhardsplatz 28; ⊘7pm-2am Tue-Wed, 7pm-3am Thu-Sat) Suave chocolate-gold tones and soft lighting set the scene for first-rate jazz acts at Bix, swinging from big bands to soul and blues.

Kiste　　　　　　　　　　　　JAZZ
(www.kiste-stuttgart.de; Hauptstätter Strasse 35; ⊘6pm-1am Mon-Thu, to 2am Fri & Sat) Jampacked at weekends, this hole-in-the-wall bar is Stuttgart's leading jazz venue, with nightly concerts starting at 9pm or 10pm.

Theaterhaus　　　　　　　　THEATRE
(⟋0711-402 0720; www.theaterhaus.com; Siemensstrasse 11; ⓤMaybachstrasse) Stages live rock, jazz and other music genres, plus theatre and comedy performances.

🛍 Shopping

Mooch around plane-tree-lined Königstrasse, Germany's longest shopping mile, for high-street brands and department stores, Calwer Strasse for boutiques, and Stifftstrasse for designer labels. The casual Bohnenviertel is the go-to quarter for antiques, art galleries, vintage garb and Stuttgart-made crafts and jewellery.

Tausche　　　　　　　　ACCESSORIES
(Eberhardstrasse 51; ⊘11am-7pm Mon-Fri, to 6pm Sat) Berlin's snazziest messenger bags have

THROUGH THE GRAPEVINE

To taste the region's fruity Trollingers and citrusy rieslings, factor in a stroll through the vineyards surrounding Stuttgart. The **Stuttgarter Weinwanderweg** (www.stuttgarter-weinwanderweg. de) comprises several walking trails that thread through winegrowing villages. One begins at Pragsattel station (on the U5 or U6 line) and meanders northeast to Max-Eyth-See, affording fine views from Burgholzhofturm. Visit the website for alternative routes, maps and distances.

From October to March, look out for a broom above the door of *Besenwirtschaften* (Besa for short). Run by winegrowers, these rustic bolt-holes are atmospheric places to chat with locals while sampling the latest vintage and Swabian home cooking. Some operate every year but most don't. Check the Besen Kalender website (www.besen-kalender.de) during vintage season.

winged their way south. Tausche's walls are a technicolour mosaic of exchangeable flaps: from *die blöde Kuh* (the silly cow) to Stuttgart's iconic Fernsehturm (TV Tower). Pick one to match your outfit and mood.

Brunnenhannes FASHION
(Geissstrasse 15; ⊙ 11am-7pm Tue-Fri, 11am-6pm Sat) Nothing to wear to Oktoberfest? Biker-meets-Bavaria Brunnenhannes has the solution, with lederhosen for strapping lads, dirndls for buxom dames and gingham lingerie that is half-kitsch, half-cool.

Feinkost Böhm FOOD & DRINK
(Kronprinzstrasse 6; ⊙ 10am-8pm Mon-Thu, 9am-8pm Fri & Sat) Böhm is a foodie one-stop shop with regional wine, beer, chocolate and preserves, and an appetising deli.

Königsbau Passagen SHOPPING CENTRE
Overlooking Schlossplatz is the classical, colonnaded Königsbau, reborn as an upmarket shopping mall, the Königsbau Passagen.

ℹ Information

Königstrasse has many ATMs, including one in the tourist office.

Airport Tourist Office (☑ 0711-222 8100; ⊙ 8am-7pm Mon-Fri, 9am-1pm & 1.45-4.30pm Sat, 10am-1pm & 1.45-5.30pm Sun) The tourist office branch at Stuttgart International Airport is situated in Terminal 3, Level 2 (Arrivals).

Coffee Fellows (per 10min €0.50; ⊙ 8am-9pm; 🛜) Up the stairs opposite track 4 in the Hauptbahnhof.

iPunkt Stuttgart (☑ 0711-222 8100; www.stuttgart-tourist.de; Königstrasse 1a; ⊙ 9am-8pm Mon-Fri, 9am-6pm Sat, 10am-6pm Sun) The staff can help with room bookings (for a €3 fee) and public transport enquiries. Also has a list of vineyards open for tastings.

Klinikum Stuttgart (☑ 0711-278 01; Kriegsbergstrasse 60) The city's largest hospital.

Post Office (Bolzstrasse 3; ⊙ 10am-8pm Mon-Fri, 9am-4pm Sat) Just northwest of the Schlossplatz.

DISCOUNT CARDS

Get a **StuttCard** (24/48/72hr without VVS ticket €5/20/25, with VVS ticket €25/35/45) for free entry to most museums, plus discounts on events, activities and guided tours. Sold at the tourist office and some hotels.

Use a **VVS 3-Day Ticket** (72hr inner city/metropolitan area €12/17) for unlimited use of public transport, available to guests with a hotel reservation.

ℹ Getting There & Away

AIR
Stuttgart Airport (SGT; ☑ 0711-9480; www.stuttgart-airport.com) Stuttgart's airport, a major hub for Germanwings, is 13km south of the city. There are four terminals, all within easy walking distance of each other.

CAR & MOTORCYCLE
The A8 from Munich to Karlsruhe passes Stuttgart (often abbreviated to 'S' on highway signs), as does the A81 from Singen (near Lake Constance) to Heilbronn and Mannheim. Stuttgart is an Umweltzone (Green Zone; www.umwelt-plakette.de), where vehicles are graded according to their emissions levels. Expect to pay €6 to €10 for an *Umweltplakette* (environment sticker), which is obligatory in green zones and can be ordered online.

TRAIN
IC and ICE destinations include Berlin (€130 to €154, 5½ hours), Frankfurt (€47 to €63, 1¼ hours) and Munich (€53 to €57, 2¼ hours). There are frequent regional services to Tübingen (€13.30, one hour), Schwäbisch Hall (€17.90, 70 minutes) and Ulm (€19.80 to €26, one hour).

ℹ Getting Around

TO/FROM THE AIRPORT
S2 and S3 trains take about 30 minutes from the airport to the Hauptbahnhof (€3.90).

BICYCLE
Rent a Bike (www.rentabike-stuttgart.de; Lautenschlagerstrasse 22; adult 6½hr/full day €12/18, concession €9/14) delivers and picks up bikes. Stuttgart has 50 **Call-a-Bike** (☑ 0700-0522 2222; www.callabike.de) stands. The first 30 minutes are free and rental costs €4.80 per hour thereafter (€15 per day). Visit the website for maps and details.

It's free to take your bike on *Stadtbahn* lines, except from 6am to 8.30am and 4pm to 6.30pm Monday to Friday. Bikes are allowed on S-Bahn trains (S1 to S6) but you need a *Kinderticket* (child's ticket) from 6am to 8.30am Monday to Friday. You can't take bikes on buses or the *Strassenbahn* (tramway).

CAR & MOTORCYCLE
Underground parking costs about €2.50 for the first hour and €2 for each subsequent hour. See www.parkinfo.com (in German) for a list of car parks. The Park & Ride ('P+R') options in Stuttgart's suburbs offer cheap parking; convenient lots include Degerloch Albstrasse (on the B27; take the U5 or U6 into town), which is 4km south of the centre; and Österfeld (on the A81; take the S1, S2 or S3 into the centre).

Avis, Budget, Europcar, Hertz, National and Sixt have offices at the airport (Terminal 2, Level 2). Europcar, Hertz and Avis have offices at the Hauptbahnhof.

PUBLIC TRANSPORT

From slowest to fastest, Stuttgart's **VVS** (www. vvs.de) public transport network consists of a *Zahnradbahn* (rack railway), buses, the *Strassenbahn* (tramway), *Stadtbahn* lines (light-rail lines beginning with U; underground in the city centre), S-Bahn lines (suburban rail lines S1 through to S6) and *Regionalbahn* lines (regional trains beginning with R). On Friday and Saturday there are night buses (beginning with N) with departures from Schlossplatz at 1.11am, 2.22am and 3.33am.

For travel within the city, single tickets are €2.30 and four-ride tickets *(Mehrfahrtenkarte)* cost €8.70. For short hops of three stops or less, a *Kurzstrecken* ticket (€1.20) suffices. A day pass, good for two zones (including, for instance, the Mercedes-Benz and Porsche Museums), is better value at €6.60 for one person and €11.50 for a group of between two and five.

TAXI

To order a taxi call ☑ 0711-551 0000.

AROUND STUTTGART

Max-Eyth-See

Max-Eyth-See   LAKE
When temperatures soar, Stuttgarters head to Max-Eyth-See for pedalo fun on the lake and picnicking beside the Neckar River. Murky water rules out swimming but there's a worthwhile bike path, which is part of the Neckar-Radweg (www.neckarradweg.de). The terraced vineyards rising above the river are scattered with Wengerter-Häuschen (tool sheds); some are more than 200 years old and are protected landmarks.

The lake is 9km northeast of Stuttgart Hauptbahnhof on the U14 line.

Grabkapelle Württemberg

Grabkapelle Württemberg   CHAPEL
When King Wilhelm I of Württemberg's beloved wife Katharina Pavlovna, daughter of a Russian tsar, died at the age of 30 in 1819, the king tore down the family castle and built this domed burial chapel. The king was also interred in the classical-style Russian Orthodox chapel decades later. Scenically

perched on a vine-strewn hill, the grounds afford long views down to the valley.

Grapkapelle Württemberg is 10km southeast of Stuttgart's centre. Take bus 61 from Stuttgart-Untertürkheim station, served by the S1.

Ludwigsburg

☑ 07141 / POP 87,740
This neat, cultured town is the childhood home of the dramatist Friedrich Schiller. Duke Eberhard Ludwig put it on the global map in the 18th century by erecting a chateau to out-pomp them all – the sublime, Versailles-inspired Residenzschloss. With its whimsical palaces and gardens, Ludwigsburg is baroque in overdrive and a flashback to when princes wore powdered wigs and lords went a-hunting.

⊙ Sights & Activities

★**Residenzschloss**   PALACE
(www.schloss-ludwigsburg.de; tour adult/concession €7/3.50, museums incl audioguide €3.50/1.80; ⊙10am-5pm) Nicknamed the Swabian Versailles, the Residenzschloss is an extravagant 452-room baroque, rococo and Empire affair. The 90-minute chateau tours (in German) begin half-hourly; there's an English tour at 1.30pm.

The 18th-century feast continues with a spin of the staggeringly ornate Karl Eugen Apartment, and three museums showcasing everything from exquisite baroque paintings to fashion accessories and majolica.

Blühendes Barock   GARDENS
(Mömpelgardstrasse 28; adult/concession €8.50/4.20; ⊙gardens 7.30am-8.30pm, Märchengarten 9am-6pm, both closed early Nov–mid-Mar) Appealing in summer is a fragrant stroll amid the herbs, rhododendrons and gushing fountains of the Blühendes Barock gardens. Admission includes entry to the Märchengarten (adult/concession €8.50/4.20; ⊙9am-6pm), a fairy-tale theme park. Take the kids to see the witch with a Swabian cackle at the gingerbread house and admire your fairness in Snow White's magic mirror. Should you want Rapunzel to let down her hair at the tower, get practising: *Rapunzel, lass deinen Zopf herunter.* (The gold-tressed diva only understands well-pronounced German!)

Schloss Favorite   PALACE
(30min tour adult/concession €4/2; ⊙10am-noon & 1.30-5pm mid-Mar–Oct, 10am-noon & 1.30-4pm

DON'T MISS

MESSING ABOUT ON THE RIVER

There's nothing like a languid paddle along the sun-dappled Neckar River in summer.

Bootsvermietung Märkle (Eberhards-brücke 1; ⊘ 11am-6pm Apr-Oct, to 9pm in summer) At Bootsvermietung Märkle, an hour of splashy fun in a rowboat, canoe, pedalo or 12-person Stocherkähne (punt) costs €9, €9, €12 and €48 respectively.

Punting (adult/child €6/3; ⊘ 1pm daily, plus 5pm Sat Apr-Oct) You can sign up at the tourist office for an hour's punting around the Neckarinsel, beginning at the Hölderlinturm.

Stocherkahnrennen (www.stocherkah-nrennen.com) Students in fancy dress do battle on the Neckar at June's hilarious Stocherkahnrennen punt race, where jostling, dunking and even snapping your rival's oar are permitted. The first team to reach the Neckarbrücke wins the race, the title and as much beer as they can sink. The losers have to down half a litre of cod-liver oil. Arrive early to snag a prime spot on Platanenallee.

Tue-Sun Nov–mid-Mar) Sitting in parkland, a five-minute walk north of the Residenz-schloss, is the petit baroque palace Schloss Favorite, graced with Empire-style furniture. Duke Eugen held glittering parties here.

❶ Information

Tourist Office (☎ 07141-910 2252; www. mik-ludwigsburg.de; Eberhardtstrasse 1; ⊘ 10am-6pm) Ludwigsburg's tourist office has excellent material in English on lodgings, festivals and events such as the baroque Christmas market.

❶ Getting There & Around

S-Bahn trains from Stuttgart serve the Haupt-bahnhof, 750m southwest of the centre. The Residenzschloss, on Schlossstrasse (the B27) lies 400m northeast of the central Marktplatz.

Stuttgart's S4 and S5 S-Bahn lines go directly to Ludwigsburg's Hauptbahnhof (€3.90, nine to 15 minutes), frequently linked to the chateau by buses 421, 425 and 427. On foot, the chateau is 1km from the train station.

There are two large car parks 500m south of the Residenzschloss, just off the B27.

Maulbronn

Kloster Maulbronn MONASTERY
(Maulbronn Monastery; ☎ 07043-926 610; www. schloesser-und-gaerten.de; adult/concession/family €7/3.50/17.50; ⊘ 9am-5.30pm Mar-Oct, 9.30am-5pm Tue-Sun Nov-Feb) Billed as the best-preserved medieval monastery north of the Alps, the one-time Cistercian monastery Kloster Maul-bronn was founded by Alsatian monks in 1147. It was born again as a Protestant school in 1556 and designated a Unesco World Heritage Site in 1993. Its famous graduates include the astronomer Johannes Kepler. Aside from the Romanesque-Gothic portico in the monastery church and the weblike vaulting of the cloister, it's the insights into monastic life that make this place so culturally stimulating.

Maulbronn is 30km east of Karlsruhe and 33km northwest of Stuttgart, near the Pforzheim Ost exit on the A8. From Karlsru-he, take the S4 to Bretten Bahnhof and from there bus 700; from Stuttgart, take the train to Mühlacker and then bus 700.

SWABIAN ALPS & AROUND

Tübingen

☎ 07071 / POP 88,360

Liberal students and deeply traditional *Bur-schenschaften* (fraternities) singing ditties for beloved Germania, eco-warriors, artists and punks – all have a soft spot for this be-witchingly pretty Swabian city, where cobbled lanes lined with half-timbered town houses twist up to a turreted castle. It was here that Joseph Ratzinger, now Pope Benedict XVI, lectured on theology in the late 1960s; and here that Friedrich Hölderlin studied stan-zas, Johannes Kepler planetary motions, and Goethe the bottom of a beer glass.

The finest days unfold slowly in Tübingen: lingering in Altstadt cafes, punting on the plane-tree-lined Neckar River and pretending, as the students so diligently do, to work your brain cells in a chestnut-shaded beer garden.

◉ Sights & Activities

★ **Schloss Hohentübingen** CASTLE
(Burgsteige 11; ⊘ 7am-8pm) On its perch above Tübingen, this turreted 16th-century castle has a terrace overlooking the Neckar River,

the Altstadt's triangular rooftops and the vine-streaked hills beyond. An ornate Renaissance gate leads to the courtyard and the laboratory where Friedrich Miescher discovered DNA in 1869.

Museum Schloss Hohentübingen MUSEUM
(adult/concession €5/3; ⊙10am-5pm Wed-Sun, to 7pm Thu) Housed in Tübingen's hilltop castle, this archaeology museum hides the 35,000-year-old Vogelherd figurines, the world's oldest figurative artworks. These thumb-sized ivory carvings of mammoths and lions were unearthed in the Vogelherdhöhle caves in the Swabian Alps.

Am Markt SQUARE
Half-timbered town houses frame the Altstadt's main plaza Am Markt, a much-loved student hang-out. Rising above it is the 15th-century **Rathaus**, with a riotous baroque facade and an astronomical clock. Statues of four women representing the seasons grace the **Neptunbrunnen** (Am Markt) opposite. Keep an eye out for **No 15**, where a white window frame identifies a secret room where Jews hid in WWII.

Cottahaus LANDMARK
The Cottahaus is the one-time home of Johann Friedrich Cotta, who first published the works of Schiller and Goethe. A bit of a lad, Goethe conducted detailed research on Tübingen's pubs during his weeklong stay in 1797. The party-loving genius is commemorated by the plaque *'Hier wohnte Goethe'* (Goethe lived here). On the wall of the grungy student digs next door is perhaps the more insightful sign *'Hier kotzte Goethe'* (Goethe puked here).

Stiftskirche St Georg CHURCH
(Am Holzmarkt; ⊙9am-5pm) FREE The late-Gothic Stiftskirche shelters the tombs of the Württemberg dukes and some dazzling late-medieval stained-glass windows.

Platanenallee AREA
Steps lead down from Eberhardsbrücke bridge to Platanenallee, a leafy islet on the Neckar River canopied by sycamore trees, with views up to half-timbered houses in a fresco painter's palette of pastels and turreted villas nestled on the hillsides.

Hölderlinturm MUSEUM
(Bursagasse 6; adult/concession €2.50/1.50; ⊙10am-noon & 3-5pm Tue & Fri, 2-5pm Sat & Sun) You can see how the dreamy Neckar views from this silver-turreted tower fired

the imagination of Romantic poet Friedrich Hölderlin, resident here from 1807 to 1843. It now contains a museum tracing his life and work.

Kunsthalle GALLERY
(www.kunsthalle-tuebingen.de; Philosophenweg 76; adult/concession €9/7; ⊙10am-6pm Tue-Sun) The streamlined Kunsthalle stages first-rate exhibitions of mostly contemporary art. During our visit, Beuys, Polke and Warhol were in the spotlight. Buses 5, 13 and 17 stop here.

Botanischer Garten GARDENS
(Hartmeyerstrasse 123; ⊙8am-4.45pm daily, to 6.45pm Sat & Sun in summer) FREE Green-fingered students tend to the Himalayan cedars, swamp cypresses and rhododendrons in the gardens and hothouses of the serene Botanischer Garten, 2km northwest of the centre. Take bus 5, 13, 15 or 17.

Wurmlinger Kapelle WALKING
(⊙chapel 10am-4pm May-Oct) A great hike is the *Kreuzweg* (way of the cross) to the 17th-century Wurmlinger Kapelle, 6km southwest of Tübingen. A footpath loops up through well-tended vineyards to the whitewashed pilgrimage chapel, where there are long views across the Ammer and Neckar valleys. The tourist office has leaflets (€1).

🛏 **Sleeping**

The tourist office has a free booklet listing private rooms, holiday homes, youth hostels and camping grounds in the area.

STUTTGART & THE BLACK FOREST TÜBINGEN

★ **Hotel am Schloss** HISTORIC HOTEL **$$**
(☎07071-929 40; www.hotelamschloss.de; Burgsteige 18; s €78, d €125-148, tr/q €225/290; P 📶) So close to the castle you can almost touch it, this flower-bedecked hotel has dapper rooms ensconced in a 16th-century building. Rumour has it that Kepler was partial to the wine here; try a drop yourself before attempting the tongue twister above the bench outside: *dohoggeddiadiaemmerdohogged* (the same people sit in the same spot). And a very nice spot it is, too.

Hotel La Casa HOTEL **$$**
(☎07071-946 66; www.lacasa-tuebingen.de; Hechinger Strasse 59; d €156-182; 📶 ≋) Tübingen's swishest hotel is a 15-minute stroll south of the Altstadt. Contemporary rooms designed with panache come with welcome tea, coffee and soft drinks. Breakfast is a smorgasbord of mostly organic goodies. The crowning glory is the top-floor spa with tremendous city views.

Hotel Hospiz GUESTHOUSE **$$**
(☎07071-9240; www.hotel-hospiz.de; Neckarhalde 2; s/d €70/110; 📶) Huddled away in the Altstadt, this candy-floss-pink guesthouse has old-school, immaculately kept rooms, many looking across Tübingen's gables. Pastries, smoked fish and eggs are nice additions to the breakfast buffet. Parking costs an extra €7 per night.

✕ Eating

Kornblume VEGETARIAN **$**
(☎07071-527 08; Haaggasse 15; snacks & light meals €3-8; ⏲8.30am-6pm Mon-Fri, 8.30am-3pm Sat; ✍) Vegetarians and health-conscious locals squeeze into this hobbit-like cafe for wholesome soups, vitamin-rich juices and organic salads by the scoopful.

Samphat Thai THAI **$$**
(☎07071-566 7827; http://samphat-thai.de; Belthlestrasse 13; mains €14-19; ⏲5-11pm Tue-Sat, 11.30am-2pm & 5-11pm Sun) Slickly decorated in calming shades of lavender and violet, this sweet, petite Thai restaurant is the real deal. The smiley staff rustle up curries, noodles and wok dishes that are bang on the money and nicely presented. Veggie options are also available.

Mauganeschtle GERMAN **$$**
(☎07071-929 40; Burgsteige 18; mains €12-21.50; ⏲noon-2.30pm & 7-10pm) It's a stiff climb up to this restaurant at Hotel am Schloss, but worth every step. Suspended above the rooftops of Tübingen, the terrace is a scenic spot for the house speciality, *Maultaschen,* with fillings like lamb, trout, porcini and veal.

Neckarmüller PUB FOOD **$$**
(☎07071-278 48; Gartenstrasse 4; mains €7.50-15; ⏲10am-1am Mon-Sat, 10am-midnight Sun) Overlooking the Neckar, this cavernous microbrewery is a summertime magnet for its chestnut-shaded beer garden. Come for home brews by the metre and beer-laced dishes from (tasty) Swabian roast to (interesting) tripe stew.

Wurstküche GERMAN **$$**
(☎07071-927 50; Am Lustnauer Tor 8; mains €12.50-18.50; ⏲11.30am-11pm Mon-Sat) The rustic, wood-panelled Wurstküche brims with locals quaffing wine and contentedly munching *Schupfnudeln* (potato noodles) and *Spanpferkel* (roast suckling pig).

WORTH A TRIP

NATURPARK SCHÖNBUCH

For back-to-nature hiking and cycling, make for this 156-sq-km **nature reserve** (www.naturpark-schoenbuch.de), 8km north of Tübingen. With a bit of luck birdwatchers might catch a glimpse of black woodpeckers and yellow-bellied toads.

The nature reserve's beech and oak woods fringe the village of **Bebenhausen** and its well-preserved **Cistercian Abbey** (www.kloster-bebenhausen.de; adult/concession €4.50/2.20, incl guided tour €6/3, audioguide €1; ⏲9am-6pm Apr-Oct, 10am-noon & 1-5pm Nov-Mar, guided tours 2pm & 3pm Sat & Sun Apr-Oct). Founded in 1183 by Count Rudolph von Tübingen, the complex became a royal hunting retreat post-Reformation. A visit takes in the frescoed summer refectory, the Gothic abbey church and intricate star vaulting and half-timbered facades in the cloister.

Bebenhausen, 3km north of Tübingen, is the gateway to Naturpark Schönbuch. Buses run at least twice hourly (€2.30, 15 minutes).

🍷 Drinking

Weinhaus Beck BAR
(Am Markt 1; ⊙9am-11pm) There's rarely an empty table at this wine tavern beside the Rathaus. It's a convivial place to enjoy a local tipple or coffee and cake.

Storchen CAFE
(Ammergasse 3; ⊙3pm-1am, from 11am Sat) Mind your head climbing the stairs to this easygoing student hang-out, serving enormous mugs of milky coffee and cheap local brews under wooden beams.

Schwärzlocher Hof BEER GARDEN
(Schwarzloch 1; ⊙11am-10pm Wed-Sun; 🐾) Scenically perched above the Ammer Valley, a 20-minute trudge west of town, this creaking farmhouse is famous for its beer garden and home-pressed *Most* (cider). Kids love the resident horses, rabbits and peacocks.

ℹ️ Information

Find ATMs around the Hauptbahnhof, Eberhardsbrücke and Am Markt.

Post Office (Beim Nonnenhaus 14; ⊙9am-7pm Mon-Fri, 9am-6pm Sat) In the Altstadt.

Tourist Office (☑07071-913 60; www.tuebingen-info.de; An der Neckarbrücke 1; ⊙9am-7pm Mon-Fri, 10am-4pm Sat, plus 11am-4pm Sun May-Sep) Tourist information.

ℹ️ Getting There & Around

Tübingen is an easy train ride from Stuttgart (€13.30, one hour, at least two per hour) and Villingen (€23.80, 1¾ to two hours, hourly).

The centre is a maze of one-way streets with residents-only parking, so head for a multistorey car park. To drive into Tübingen, you need to purchase an environmentally friendly *Umweltplakette* (emissions sticker).

Radlager (Lazarettgasse 19-21; ⊙9.30am-6.30pm Mon, Wed & Fri, 2-6.30pm Tue & Thu, 9.30am-2.30pm Sat) rents bikes for €10 per day.

Burg Hohenzollern

Burg Hohenzollern CASTLE
(www.burg-hohenzollern.com; tour adult/concession €12/8, grounds admission without tour adult/concession €7/5; ⊙tour 10am-5.30pm mid-Mar–Oct, to 4.30pm Nov–mid-Mar) Rising dramatically from an exposed crag, with the medieval battlements and silver turrets often veiled in mist, Burg Hohenzollern is impressive from a distance, but up close it looks more contrived. Dating to 1867, this neo-Gothic cas-

TOP SNACK SPOTS

Eating on the hoof? Try these informal nosh spots.

Die Kichererbse (Metzgergasse 2; snacks €3.50-5; ⊙11am-9pm Mon-Fri; 🍴) All hail the 'chickpea' for its scrummy falafel. Grab one of the few tables to chomp on a classic.

X (Kornhausstrasse 6; snacks €2.70-3.50; ⊙11am-1am) Hole-in-the-wall joint rustling up Tübingen's crispiest fries, bratwurst and burgers.

Wochenmarkt (Am Markt; ⊙7am-1pm Mon, Wed & Fri) Bag glossy fruit and veg, oven-fresh bread and local honey and herbs at Tübingen's farmers market.

Eiscafé San Marco (Nonnengasse 14; cone €1; ⊙8.30am-11pm Mon-Sat, 10.30am-11pm Sun) Italian-run, with hands-down the best gelati in town.

tle is the ancestral seat of the Hohenzollern family, the first and last monarchical rulers of the short-lived second German empire (1871–1918).

History fans should take a 35-minute German-language tour, which takes in towers, overblown salons replete with stained glass and frescos, and the dazzling Schatzkammer (treasury). The grounds command tremendous views over the Swabian Alps.

Frequent trains link Tübingen, 28km distant, with Hechingen, about 4km northwest of the castle.

Schwäbisch Hall

☑0791 / POP 37,140
Out on its rural lonesome near the Bavarian border, Schwäbisch Hall is an unsung gem. This medieval time capsule of higgledy-piggledy lanes, soaring half-timbered houses built high on the riches of salt, and covered bridges that criss-cross the Kocher River, is story-book stuff.

Buzzy cafes and first-rate museums add to the appeal of this town, known for its rare black-spotted pigs and the jangling piggy banks of its nationwide building society.

⊙ Sights & Activities

A leisurely Altstadt saunter takes you along narrow alleys, among half-timbered hillside houses and up slopes overlooking the Kocher River. The islands and riverbank parks are great for picnics.

Am Markt
SQUARE

Am Markt springs to life with a farmers market every Wednesday and Saturday morning. On the square, your gaze is drawn to the baroque-style Rathaus (Town Hall; Am Markt), festooned with coats of arms and cherubs, and to the terracotta-hued Widmanhaus at No 4, a remnant of a 13th-century Franciscan monastery. Steps lead spectacularly up to the late-Gothic Kirche St Michael (Am Markt; ⊙ noon-5pm Mon, 10am-5pm Tue-Sat), which was built in place of the original three-aisled basilica. Note also the Gotischer Fischbrunnen (Am Markt; 1509), a large iron tub once used for storing fish before sale.

Neubau
LANDMARK

Towering above Pfarrgasse is the steep-roofed, 16th-century Neubau, built as an arsenal and granary and now used as a theatre. Ascend the stone staircase for dreamy views over red-roofed houses to the former city fortifications, the covered Roter Steg bridge and the Henkerbrücke (Hangman's Bridge).

★ Kunsthalle Würth
GALLERY

(www.kunst.wuerth.com; Lange Strasse 35; ⊙ 10am-6pm daily, guided tours 11.30am & 2pm Sun) FREE The brainchild of industrialist Reinhold Würth, this contemporary gallery is housed in a striking limestone building that preserves part of a century-old brewery. Stellar temporary exhibitions have recently spotlighted the precious silver of London's Victoria & Albert Museum and Op Art kinetics. Guided tours (in German) and audioguides cost €6.

Hällisch-Fränkisches Museum
MUSEUM

(adult/concession €2.50/2; ⊙ 10am-5pm Tue-Sun) This well-curated museum traces Schwäbisch Hall's history with its collection of shooting targets, Roman figurines, and rarities including an exquisite hand-painted wooden synagogue interior from 1738 and a 19th-century mouse guillotine.

Hohenloher Freilandmuseum
MUSEUM

(Wackershofen; adult/concession €7/5; ⊙ 9am-6pm May-Sep, 10am-5pm Tue-Sun rest of year; 🖶) One place you can be guaranteed of seeing a black-spotted pig is this open-air farming museum, a sure-fire hit with the kids with its traditional farmhouses, orchards and animals. It's 6km northwest of Schwäbisch Hall and served by bus 7.

🛏 Sleeping & Eating

★ Hotel Scholl
HOTEL $$

(☑ 0791-975 50; www.hotel-scholl.de; Klosterstrasse 2-4; s €79-109, d €124-169; 🛜) A charming pick behind Am Markt, this family-run hotel has rustic-chic rooms with parquet floors, flat-screen TVs and granite or marble bathrooms. Most striking of all is the attic penthouse with its beams, free-standing shower and far-reaching views over town. Breakfast is a fine spread of cold cuts, fruit and cereals.

Der Adelshof
HISTORIC HOTEL $$

(☑ 0791-758 90; www.hotel-adelshof.de; Am Markt 12; s €90-95, d €125-225, mains €15-34; 🅿🛜) This centuries-old pad is as posh as it gets in Schwäbisch Hall, with a wellness area and plush quarters, from the red-walled romance of the Chambre Rouge to the four-poster Turmzimmer. Its beamed Ratskeller knocks up spot-on local specialities, such as saddle of veal with mushrooms and pork tenderloin with lentils and Spätzle (egg noodles).

Entenbäck
BISTRO $$

(☑ 0791-9782 9182; Steinerner Steg 1; mains €11.50-29; ⊙ 11am-2.30pm & 5-11pm Tue-Sat, 11am-8pm Sun) This inviting bistro receives high praise for its Swabian-meets-Mediterranean menu, from cream of riesling soup to duck-filled Maultaschen and roast beef with onions and Spätzle.

Brauerei-Ausschank Zum Löwen
BREWPUB $$

(☑ 0791-204 1622; Mauerstrasse 17; mains €9-15.50; ⊙ 11.30am-2pm & 5.30-11pm Fri-Tue) Down by the river, this brewpub attracts a jovial bunch of locals who come for freshly tapped Haller Löwenbrauerei brews and hearty nosh-like pork cooked in beer-cumin sauce.

★ Rebers Pflug
INTERNATIONAL $$$

(☑ 0791-931 230; www.rebers-pflug.de; Weckriedener Strasse 2; mains €18.50-39, 4-course menu €59-78; ⊙ 6.30-9pm Mon & Tue, noon-2pm & 6-9pm Wed-Sat, 11.30am-2pm Sun) Hans-Harald Reber mans the stove at this 19th-century country house, one of Schwäbisch Hall's two Michelin-starred haunts. He puts his own imaginative spin on seasonal numbers such as local venison in a pumpernickel crust with sweet potato purée, asparagus and hazelnut Spätzle. Vegetarians are also well catered for. Dine in the chestnut-shaded garden in summer.

ℹ Information

Tourist Office (☏ 0791-751 246; www.schwaeb-ischhall.de; Am Markt 9; ⊙ 9am-6pm Mon-Fri, 10am-3pm Sat & Sun May-Sep, 9am-5pm Mon-Fri Oct-Apr) On the Altstadt's main square.

ℹ Getting There & Around

There are two train stations: trains from Stuttgart (€17.90, 1¼ hours, hourly) arrive at Hessental, on the right bank about 7km south of the centre and linked to the Altstadt by bus 1; trains from Heilbronn go to the left-bank Bahnhof Schwäbisch Hall, a short walk along Bahnhofstrasse from the centre.

Ulm

☏ 0731 / POP 122,800

Starting with the statistics, Ulm has the crookedest house (as listed in *Guinness World Records*) and one of the narrowest (4.5m wide), the world's oldest zoomorphic sculpture (aged 30,000 years) and tallest cathedral steeple (161.5m high), and is the birthplace of the physicist, Albert Einstein. Relatively speaking, of course.

This idiosyncratic city will win your affection with everyday encounters, particularly in summer as you pedal along the Danube, and the Fischerviertel's beer gardens hum with animated chatter. One *Helles* too many and you may decide to impress the locals by attempting the tongue twister: *'In Ulm, um Ulm, und um Ulm herum.'*

◎ Sights & Activities

Münster CATHEDRAL
(www.ulmer-muenster.de; Münsterplatz; organ concerts adult/concession €8/4, tower adult/concession €5/3.50; ⊙ 9am-6.45pm, to 4.45pm in winter) FREE 'Ooh, it's so big'... First-time visitors gush as they strain their neck muscles gazing up at the Münster. It is. And rather beautiful. Celebrated for its 161.5m-high steeple, the world's tallest, this Goliath of cathedrals took a staggering 500 years to build from the first stone laid in 1377. Note the hallmarks on each stone, inscribed by cutters who were paid by the block. Those intent on cramming the Münster into one photo, filigree spire and all, should lie down on the cobbles.

Only by puffing up 768 spiral steps to the 143m-high viewing platform of the tower can you appreciate the Münster's dizzying height. There are terrific views of the Black Forest and, on cloud-free days, the Alps.

The Israelfenster, a stained-glass window above the west door, commemorates Jews killed during the Holocaust. The Gothic-style wooden pulpit canopy eliminates echoes during sermons. Biblical figures, and historical characters such as Pythagoras, embellish the 15th-century oak choir stalls. The Münster's regular organ concerts are a musical treat.

Marktplatz SQUARE
Lording it over the Marktplatz, the 14th-century, step-gabled **Rathaus** sports an ornately painted Renaissance facade and a gilded astrological clock. Inside is a replica of Albrecht Berblinger's flying machine. In front is the **Fischkastenbrunnen** (Marktplatz), a fountain where fishmongers kept their catch alive on market days. The 36m-high glass pyramid behind the Rathaus is the city's main library, the **Zentralbibliothek** (Marktplatz), designed by Gottfried Böhm.

Stadtmauer AREA
South of the Fischerviertel, along the Danube's north bank, runs the red-brick Stadtmauer (city wall), the height of which was reduced in the 19th century after Napoleon decided that a heavily fortified Ulm was against his best interests. Walk it for fine views over the river, the Altstadt and the colourful tile-roofed **Metzgerturm**, doing a Pisa by leaning 2m off-centre.

East of the Herdbrücke, the bridge to Neu-Ulm, a bronze **plaque** marks where Albrecht Berblinger, a tailor who invented a flying machine, attempted to fly over the Danube in 1811. The so-called 'Tailor of Ulm' made an embarrassing splash landing but his design was later shown to be workable (his failure was caused by a lack of thermals on that day).

Fischerviertel AREA
The charming Fischerviertel, Ulm's old fishers' and tanners' quarter, is slightly southwest of the centre. Beautifully restored half-timbered houses huddle along the two channels of the Blau River. Harbouring art galleries, rustic restaurants, courtyards and the crookedest house in the world – as well as one of the narrowest – the cobbled lanes are ideal for a leisurely saunter.

Ulmer Museum MUSEUM
(www.ulmer-museum.ulm.de; Marktplatz 9; adult/concession €5/3.50, Fri free; ⊙ 11am-5pm Tue-Sun, to 8pm Thu) This museum is a fascinating

Ulm

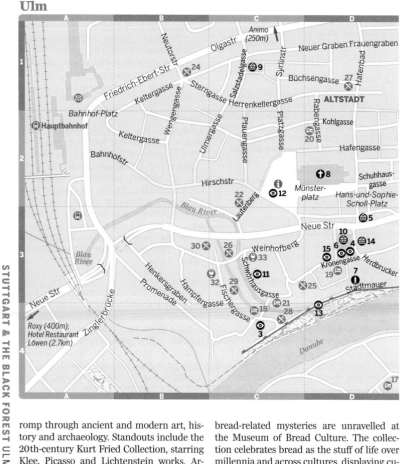

romp through ancient and modern art, history and archaeology. Standouts include the 20th-century Kurt Fried Collection, starring Klee, Picasso and Lichtenstein works. Archaeological highlights are tiny Upper Palaeolithic figurines, unearthed in caves in the Swabian Alps, including the 30,000-year-old ivory *Löwenmensch* (lion man), the world's oldest zoomorphic sculpture.

Kunsthalle Weishaupt   GALLERY
(www.kunsthalle-weishaupt.de; Hans-und-Sophie-Scholl-Platz 1; adult/concession €6/4; ⊙11am-5pm Tue-Sun, to 8pm Thu) The glass-fronted Kunsthalle Weishaupt contains the private collection of Siegfried Weishaupt. The accent is on modern and pop art, with bold paintings by Klein, Warhol and Haring.

Museum der Brotkultur   MUSEUM
(www.museum-brotkultur.de; Salzstadelgasse 10; adult/concession €4/3; ⊙10am-5pm) How grain grows, what makes a good dough and other bread-related mysteries are unravelled at the Museum of Bread Culture. The collection celebrates bread as the stuff of life over millennia and across cultures, displaying curios from mills to Egyptian corn mummies.

Stadthaus   LANDMARK
Designed by Richard Meier, the contemporary aesthetic of the concrete-and-glass Stadthaus is a dramatic contrast to the Münster. The American architect caused uproar by erecting a postmodern building alongside the city's Gothic giant, but the result is striking. The edifice stages exhibitions and events, and houses the tourist office and a cafe.

Schwörhaus   LANDMARK
(Oath House; Weinhof 12) On the third Monday of July, the mayor swears allegiance to the town's 1397 constitution from the 1st-floor loggia of the early-17th-century baroque Schwörhaus (Oath House), three blocks west of the Rathaus.

shows, splashy rides and a miniature world built from 25 million Lego bricks. It's in Günzburg, 37km east of Ulm, just off the A8.

🛏 Sleeping

The tourist office lists apartments and guesthouses charging around €25 per person.

Brickstone Hostel
HOSTEL $

(☎ 0731-708 2559; www.brickstone-hostel.de; Schützenstrasse 42; dm €18-22, s/d €30/44; 🛜) We love the homely vibe at this beautifully restored art-nouveau house in Neu-Ulm. The high-ceilinged rooms are kept spotless and backpacker perks include a self-catering kitchen with free coffee and tea, an honesty bar, bike rental and a cosy lounge with book exchange. Take bus 7 to Schützenstrasse from the Hauptbahnhof.

★ Hotel Schiefes Haus
B&B $$

(☎ 0731-967 930; www.hotelschiefeshausulm.de; Schwörhausgasse 6; s €125, d €148-160; 🛜) There was a crooked man and he walked a crooked mile...presumably to the world's most crooked hotel. But fear not, ye of little wonkiness, this early-16th-century, half-timbered rarity is not about to topple into the Blau River. And up those creaking wooden stairs, in your snug, beamed room, you won't have to buckle yourself to the bed thanks to spirit levels and specially made height adjusters. If you're feeling *really* crooked, plump straight for room No 6.

Das Schmale Haus
B&B $$

(☎ 0731-6027 2595; Fischergasse 27; s/d €119/149; P) Measuring just 4.5m across, the half-timbered 'narrow house' is a one-off. The affable Heides have transformed this slender 16th-century pad into a gorgeous B&B, with exposed beams, downy bedding and wood floors in the three rooms.

Hotel Restaurant Löwen
HOTEL $$

(☎ 0731-388 5880; www.hotel-loewen-ulm.de; Klosterhof 41; s €81-91, d €116-122; P 🛜) It's amazing what you can do with a former monastery and an eye for design. Exposed beams and stone add an historic edge to streamlined rooms with parquet floors and flat-screen TVs. The chestnut-canopied beer garden is a boon in summer. Take tram 1 from central Ulm to Söflingen.

Hotel Bäumle
HISTORIC HOTEL $$

(☎ 0731-622 87; www.hotel-baeumle.de; Kohlgasse 6; s €70-82, d €98-112, tr €140; 🛜) Big on old-world flair, the Bäumle can trace its history way

Einstein Fountain & Monument
FOUNTAIN

A nod to Ulm's most famous son, Jürgen Goertz's fiendishly funny bronze fountain shows a wild-haired, tongue-poking-out Albert Einstein, who was born in Ulm but left when he was one year old. Standing in front of the 16th-century **Zeughaus**, the rocket-snail creation is a satirical play on humanity's attempts to manipulate evolution for its own self-interest. Nearby, at Zeughaus 14, is a single stone bearing the inscription *Ein Stein* (One Stone).

Einstein Memorial
MEMORIAL

(Bahnhofstrasse) On Bahnhofstrasse sits Max Bill's memorial (1979) to the great physicist, a stack of red-granite pillars marking the spot where Einstein was born.

Legoland
AMUSEMENT PARK

(www.legoland.de; adult/concession €41.50/37; ⊙10am-6pm late Mar–early Nov) A sure-fire kid-pleaser, Legoland Deutschland is a pricey Lego-themed amusement park, with

Ulm

STUTTGART & THE BLACK FOREST ULM

back to 1522 and houses smart, immaculately kept rooms. Unless you class cathedral bells as 'noise', you're going to love the location. No lift.

Hotel am Rathaus & Hotel Reblaus HOTEL $$
(☏ 0731-968 490; www.rathausulm.de; Kronengasse 10; s €76-120, d €96-140, q €138-170, s/d without bathroom €64/76; 🛋) Just paces from the Rathaus, these twins ooze individual charm with flourishes like stucco and Biedermeier furnishings. Light sleepers take note: the walls are thin and the street can be noisy.

✗ Eating

Animo CAFE $
(☏ 0731-964 2937; www.cafe-animo.de; Syrlinstrasse 17; day specials around €7; ⊗ 7.30am-6pm Tue-Fri, 9am-6pm Sat & Sun; ✗) Snuggled away in a *Topferei* (potter's workshop), Animo is a relaxed cafe, with excellent homemade cakes and vegetarian specials (creative salads, pasta, risotto and the like) – all served in beautifully detailed porcelain. Also hosts regular cultural events.

★ Zur Forelle GERMAN $$
(☏ 0731-639 24; Fischergasse 25; mains €12-25; ⊗ 11am-3pm & 5pm-midnight Mon-Fri, 11am-midnight Sat, 11am-10pm Sun) Since 1626, this low-ceilinged tavern has been convincing wayfarers (Einstein included) of the joys of seasonal Swabian cuisine. Ablaze with flowers in summer, this wood-panelled haunt by the Blau prides itself on its namesake *Forelle* (trout), kept fresh under the bridge.

Barfüsser PUB FOOD $$
(☏ 0731-602 1110; Lautenberg 1; mains €8-21; ⊗ 10am-1am Sun-Wed, to 2am Thu-Sat) Hearty fare like *Käsespätzle* (cheese noodles) and pork roast soak up the prize-winning beer, microbrewed in Neu-Ulm, at this brewpub. The lunch special goes for €6.90.

Gerberhaus MEDITERRANEAN $$
(☏ 0731-677 17; Weinhofberg 9; mains €10-22; ⊗ 11.30am-2.30pm & 5.30-10pm) This warm, inviting woodcutter's cottage hits the mark with its Med-inspired dishes. Plump for a river-facing table and sample clean, bright flavours like home-smoked salmon carpaccio and lemongrass crème brûlée. Day specials go for as little as €7.

Zunfthaus der Schiffleute GERMAN $$
(☏ 0731-175 5771; Fischergasse 31; mains €11-28; ⊗ 11am-midnight) Looking proudly back on a 600-year tradition, this timber-framed restaurant sits by the river. The menu speaks of a chef who loves the region, with Swabian faves like *Katzagschroi* (beef, onions, egg and fried potatoes) and meaty one-pot *Schwäbisches Hochzeitssüppchen*.

Gaststätte Krone GERMAN $$
(☏ 0731-140 0874; www.krone-ulm.de; Kronengasse 4; mains €11-22.50; ⊗ 5pm-1am Mon-Fri, 10am-1am Sat & Sun; ⊕) Going strong since 1320, Ulm's oldest inn is now a delightfully cosy, wood-panelled affair. The regional grub is second to none, whether you opt for *Rin-*

DON'T MISS

SPOT THE SPARROW

You can't move for *Spatzen* (sparrows) in the German language. You can eat like one *(essen wie ein Spatz)* and swear like one *(schimpfen wie ein Rohrspatz);* there are *Spatzenschleuder* (catapults), *Spätzles* (little darlings) and *Spatzenhirne* (bird brains). Nicknamed *Spatzen*, Ulm residents are, according to legend, indebted to the titchy bird for the construction of their fabulous Münster.

The story goes that the half-baked builders tried in vain to shove the wooden beams for the minster sideways through the city gate. They struggled, until a sparrow fluttered past with straw for its nest. Enlightened, the builders carried the beams lengthways, completed the job and placed a bronze statue of a sparrow at the top to honour the bird.

Today there are sparrows everywhere in Ulm: on postcards, in patisseries, at football matches (team SSV Ulm are dubbed die Spatzen) and, above all, in the colourful sculptures dotting the Altstadt.

derbrühe mit Flädle (beef broth with sliced pancakes) or *Linsen mit Saitenwürste* (lentils with poached sausages).

Zur Lochmühle GERMAN $$
(☎0731-673 05; Gerbergasse 6; mains €9.50-22; 👪) The watermill has been churning the Blau since 1356 at this rustic half-timbered pile. Plant yourself in the riverside beer garden for Swabian classics like crispy roast pork, *Schupfnudeln* and brook trout with lashings of potato salad.

Da Franco ITALIAN $$$
(☎0731-305 85; Neuer Graben 23; mains €20-30; ⏰11am-midnight Tue-Sun) If you fancy a break from the norm, give this little Italian place a whirl. There is a seasonal touch to authentic dishes like swordfish with clams and veal escalope with asparagus, all cooked and presented with style.

Yamas GREEK $$$
(☎0731-407 8614; Herrenkellergasse 29; mains €13.50-30, lunch specials €8.90-13.90; ⏰11.30am-3pm & 5pm-midnight Tue-Sun; 👪) This classy Greek restaurant has a market-driven menu, lots of fresh seafood and a bulging wine cellar. Begin with some homemade dips and grilled octopus, before mains like sea bass with truffle mash and pork medallions with rosemary-thyme gravy.

Drinking & Entertainment

Naschkatze CAFE
(http://cafenaschkatze.de; Marienstrasse 6, Neu-Ulm; ⏰8am-7pm Mon-Fri, 9am-6pm Sat, 10am-6pm Sun) Naschkatze, or 'sweet-toothed', is a fitting name for this vintage-cool cafe, where Ulmers come to lap up the retro vibe, coffee and homemade cakes.

Café im Stadthaus CAFE
(Münsterplatz 50; ⏰8am-midnight Mon-Thu, 8am-1am Fri & Sat, 9am-midnight Sun) Go for coffee and linger for the mesmerising cathedral views at this glass cube.

Café im Kornhauskeller CAFE
(Hafengasse 19; ⏰8am-midnight Mon-Sat, 9am-10pm Sun) Arty cafe with an inner courtyard for drinks, breakfast, light bites or ice cream.

Zur Zill BAR
(Schwörhausgasse 19; ⏰10am-2am daily, to 4am Fri & Sat) Join a happy-go-lucky crowd for a cold beer or cocktail by the river.

Wilder Mann PUB
(Fischergasse 2; ⏰11.30am-1am Mon-Thu, to 3am Fri-Sun) Service is a lucky dip and the food is mediocre, but by all means head to the people-watching terrace for a drink.

Roxy CONCERT VENUE
(www.roxy.ulm.de; Schillerstrasse 1) This huge cultural venue, housed in a former industrial plant 1km south of the Hauptbahnhof, has a concert hall, cinema, disco, bar and special-event forum. Take tram line 1 to Ehinger Tor.

Information

Post Office (Bahnhofplatz 2; ⏰8.30am-6.30pm Mon-Fri, 9am-1pm Sat) To the left as you exit the Hauptbahnhof.

Tourist Office (☎0731-161 2830; www.tourismus.ulm.de; Münsterplatz 50, Stadthaus; ⏰9am-6pm Mon-Fri, 9am-4pm Sat, 11am-3pm Sun)

Getting There & Away

Ulm is about 90km southeast of Stuttgart and 150km west of Munich, near the intersection of the north–south A7 and the east–west A8.

ℹ CITY SAVER

If you're planning on ticking off most of the major sights, consider investing in a good-value **UlmCard** (1/2 days €12/18), which covers public transport in Ulm and Neu-Ulm, a free city tour or rental of the itour audioguide, entry to all museums, plus numerous other discounts on tours, attractions and restaurants.

Ulm is well-served by ICE and EC trains; major destinations include Stuttgart (€19.80 to €26, 56 minutes to 1¼ hours, several hourly) and Munich (€30 to €38, 1¼ to two hours, several hourly).

ℹ Getting Around

Ulm's ecofriendly trams run on renewable energy. There's a **local transport information counter** (www.swu-verkehr.de) in the tourist office. A single/day ticket for the bus and tram network in Ulm and Neu-Ulm costs €2.10/5.

Except in parking garages (€0.60 per 30 minutes), parking in the whole city centre is metered; many areas are limited to one hour (€1.80). There's a Park & Ride lot at Donaustadion, a stadium 1.5km northeast of the Münster and on tram line 1.

You can hire bikes from **Fahrradhandlung Ralf Reich** (☑ 0731-211 79; Frauenstrasse 34; per day €9; ⊙ 9am-12.30pm & 2-6.30pm Mon-Fri, 9am-2pm Sat), a five-minute stroll northeast of the Münsterplatz. Bike paths shadow the Danube.

THE BLACK FOREST

Baden-Baden

☑ 07221 / POP 54,500

Baden-Baden's air of old-world luxury and curative waters have attracted royals, the rich and celebrities over the years – Barack Obama and Bismarck, Queen Victoria and Victoria Beckham included. This Black Forest town boasts grand colonnaded buildings and whimsically turreted art-nouveau villas spread across the hillsides and framed by forested mountains.

The bon vivant spirit of France, just across the border, is tangible in the town's open-air cafes, chic boutiques and pristine gardens fringing the Oos River. And with its temple-like thermal baths – which put

the *Baden* (bathe) in Baden – and palatial casino, the allure of this grand dame of German spa towns is as timeless as it is enduring.

⊙ Sights

Trinkhalle   LANDMARK
(Pump Room; Kaiserallee 3; ⊙ 10am-5pm Mon-Sat, 2-5pm Sun) Standing proud above a manicured park, this neoclassical pump room was built in 1839 as an attractive addition to the Kurhaus. The 90m-long portico is embellished with 19th-century frescos of local legends. Baden-Baden's elixir of youth, some say, is the free curative mineral water that gushes from a faucet linked to the Friedrichsbad spring.

Kurhaus   LANDMARK
(www.kurhaus-baden-baden.de; Kaiserallee 1; tour €5) Corinthian columns and a frieze of mythical griffins grace the belle époque facade of the Kurhaus, which towers above well-groomed gardens. An alley of chestnut trees, flanked by two rows of boutiques, links the Kurhaus with Kaiserallee.

Casino   HISTORIC BUILDING
(www.casino-baden-baden.de; admission €5, guided tour €7; ⊙ 2pm-2am Sun-Thu, 2pm-3am Fri & Sat, guided tours 9.30-11.45am) The sublime casino seeks to emulate – indeed, outdo – the gilded splendour of Versailles. Marlene Dietrich called it 'the most beautiful casino in the world'. Gents must wear a jacket and tie. If you're not much of a gambler and want to simply marvel at the opulence, hook onto a 40-minute guided tour.

Museum Frieder Burda   GALLERY
(www.museum-frieder-burda.de; Lichtentaler Allee 8b; adult/concession €12/10; ⊙ 10am-6pm Tue-Sun) A Joan Miró sculpture guards the front of this architecturally innovative gallery, designed by Richard Meier. The star-studded collection of modern and contemporary art, featuring Picasso, Gerhard Richter and Jackson Pollock originals, is complemented by temporary exhibitions, such as recent ones spotlighting Neo-Expressionist Georg Baselitz and the striking light and shadow works of Heinz Mack.

Staatliche Kunsthalle   GALLERY
(www.kunsthalle-baden-baden.de; Lichtentaler Allee 8a; adult/concession €7/5, Fri free; ⊙ 10am-6pm Tue-Sun) Sidling up to the Museum Frieder Burda is this sky-lit gallery, which showcases rotating exhibitions of contempo-

Black Forest

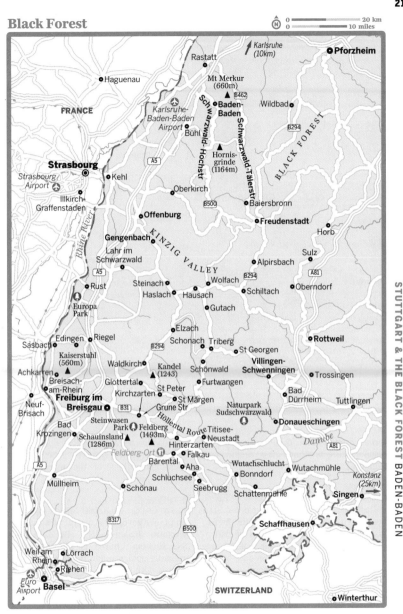

0   20 km
0   10 miles

Pforzheim

Karlsruhe (10km)

Rastatt

Haguenau

Mt Merkur (660m)

Baden-Baden

Wildbad

FRANCE

Karlsruhe-Baden-Baden Airport

Bühl

Hornisgrinde (1164m)

Strasbourg

Strasbourg Airport

Kehl

A5

Oberkirch

B500

Baiersbronn

Illkirch-Graffenstaden

Offenburg

Freudenstadt

Horb

Gengenbach

Lahr im Schwarzwald

Sulz

Alpirsbach

A81

A5

Rust

Steinach

Wolfach

B294

Schiltach

Oberndorf

Haslach

Hausach

Europa Park

Gutach

Edingen

Riegel

Elzach

Sásbach

Schonach

Triberg

St Georgen

Rottweil

Kaiserstuhl (560m)

Waldkirch

Kandel (1243)

Schönwald

Villingen-Schwenningen

Achkarren

Breisach-am-Rhein

Glottertal

Kirchzarten

St Peter

St Märgen

Furtwangen

Trossingen

Neuf-Brisach

Freiburg im Breisgau

B31

Grune Str

Naturpark Südschwarzwald

Bad Dürrheim

Tuttlingen

Bad Krozingen

Steinwasen Park

Schauinsland (1286m)

Feldberg (1493m)

Höllental Route

Titisee-Neustadt

Donaueschingen

A81

Danube

Feldberg-Ort

Hinterzarten

Falkau

A5

Bärental

Wutachschlucht

Wutachmühle

Konstanz (25km)

Müllheim

Schluchsee

Aha

Bonndorf

Schönau

Seebrugg

Schattenmühle

Singen

B317

B500

Schaffhausen

Weil am Rhein

Lörrach

Riehen

Euro Airport

Basel

SWITZERLAND

Winterthur

KINZIG VALLEY

Schwarzwald-Hochstr

Schwarzwald-Tälerstr

BLACK FOREST

B462

B294

B294

rary art in neoclassical surrounds. Recently it zoomed in on the highly experimental works of Czech artist Eva Kot'átková and the expressionistic painting of Beijing-based artist Li Songsong.

Stiftskirche   CHURCH

(Marktplatz; ⊙8am-6pm) The centrepiece of cobbled Marktplatz is this pink church, a hotchpotch of Romanesque, late-Gothic and, to a lesser extent, baroque styles. Its foundations incorporate some ruins of the

Baden-Baden

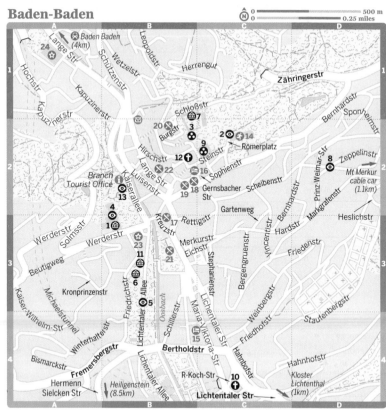

former Roman baths. Come in the early afternoon to see its stained-glass windows cast rainbow patterns across the nave.

Römische Badruinen
RUIN

(Römerplatz; adult/concession €2.50/1; ⊙11am-noon & 3-4pm mid-Mar–mid-Nov) The beauty-conscious Romans were the first to discover the healing properties of Baden-Baden's springs in the city they called Aquae Aureliae. Slip back 2000 years on a tour of the well-preserved ruins of their baths.

Lichtentaler Allee
GARDENS

This 2.3km ribbon of greenery, threading from Goetheplatz to Kloster Lichtenthal, is quite a picture: studded with fountains and sculptures and carpeted with flowers (crocuses and daffodils in spring, magnolias, roses and azaleas in summer). Shadowing the sprightly Oosbach, its promenade and bridges are made for aimless ambling. The avenue concludes at the **Kloster Lichten-**

thal (Lichtentaler Allee), a Cistercian abbey founded in 1245, with an abbey church where generations of the margraves of Baden lie buried.

Russische Kirche
CHURCH

(Russian Church; Lichtentaler Strasse 76; admission €1; ⊙10am-6pm) Beautiful, if a little incongrous, Baden-Baden's Byzantine-style 1882 Russian Church is topped with a brilliantly golden onion dome and lavishly adorned with frescos.

🏃 Activities

★ Friedrichsbad
SPA

(📞07221-275 920; www.carasana.de; Römerplatz 1; 3hr ticket €25, incl soap-&-brush massage €37; ⊙9am-10pm, last admission 7pm) If it's the body of Venus and the complexion of Cleopatra you desire, abandon modesty (and clothing) to wallow in thermal waters at this palatial 19th-century marble-and-mosaic-festooned

Contra Costa County Library
Orinda
6/9/2022 10:33:40 AM

- Patron Receipt -
- Charges -

ID: 21901013519107

Item: 31901066833700
Title: Germany /
Call Number: 914.30488 DI DUCA 2021
Due Date: 6/30/2022

Item: 31901059353526
Title: Munich, Bavaria & the Black Forest /
Call Number: 914.33048 CHRISTIANI 2016
Due Date: 6/30/2022

All Contra Costa County Libraries will be
closed Monday, July 4th. Items may be
renewed online at http://ccclib.org or by
calling 1-800-984-4636, menu option 1.
Book drops will be open for returns.
Book drops will be open for returns.

Baden-Baden

Sights

1 Casino ... B3
2 Fetquelle ... C2
3 Florentinerberg ... B2
4 Kurhaus ... B3
5 Lichtentaler Allee ... B3
6 Museum Frieder Burda ... B3
7 Neues Schloss ... B1
8 Paradies am Annaberg ... D2
9 Römische Badruinen ... C2
10 Russische Kirche ... C4
11 Staatliche Kunsthalle ... B3
12 Stiftskirche ... B2
13 Trinkhalle ... B2

Activities, Courses & Tours

14 Caracalla Spa ... C2
Friedrichsbad ... (see 9)

Sleeping

Hotel am Markt ... (see 12)
15 Hotel Belle Epoque ... B4
16 Rathausglöckel ... B2

Eating

17 Café König ... B3
18 Kaffeehaus Baden-Baden ... B2
19 La Casserole ... B2
20 La Provence ... B2
21 Rizzi ... B3
22 Weinstube im Baldreit ... B2

Entertainment

23 Baden-Baden Theater ... B3
Baden-Badener Philharmonie ... (see 1)
24 Festspielhaus ... A1

spa. As Mark Twain put it, 'after 10 minutes you forget time; after 20 minutes, the world', as you slip into the regime of steaming, scrubbing, hot-cold bathing and dunking in the Roman-Irish bath.

Caracalla Spa SPA
(☎07221-275 940; www.carasana.de; Römerplatz 11; 2/3/4hr €15/18/21; ⏰8am-10pm, last admission 8pm) This modern, glass-fronted spa has a cluster of indoor and outdoor pools, grottos and surge channels, making the most of the mineral-rich spring water. For those who dare to bare, saunas range from the rustic 'forest' to the roasting 95°C 'fire' variety.

Sleeping

Baden-Baden is crammed with hotels, but bargains are rare. The tourist office has a room-reservation service, for a 10% fee.

Hotel am Markt HISTORIC HOTEL $$
(☎07221-270 40; www.hotel-am-markt-baden.de; Marktplatz 18; s €35-65, d €90-120; P 📶) Sitting pretty in front of the Stiftskirche, this 250-year-old hotel has 23 homely, well-kept rooms. It's quiet up here apart from your wake-up call of church bells, but then you wouldn't want to miss out on the great breakfast.

Heiligenstein HOTEL $$
(☎07221-961 40; www.hotel-heiligenstein.de; Heiligensteinstrasse 19a; s €87-91, d €119-124; P) It's worth going the extra mile (or seven) to this sweet hotel overlooking vineyards. Slick, earthy-hued rooms come with balconies and guests can put their feet up in the spa and gardens. The highly regarded restaurant (mains €15 to €31) serves local, seasonally inspired fare, from freshly caught trout to venison with blackcurrant sauce and asparagus.

Rathausglöckel HOTEL $$
(☎07221-906 10; www.rathausgloeckel.de; Steinstrasse 7; s €80-100, d €115-139, ste €135-300; P 📶) Right in the thick of things, this family-run hotel occupies a 16th-century town house. The attractively renovated rooms (some with rooftop views) are dressed in muted tones with pine furniture – those on the 3rd floor command the best views over Baden-Baden's rooftops. Breakfast is a generous spread of fresh bread, fruit and pastries, homemade jam and bacon and eggs.

Hotel Belle Epoque LUXURY HOTEL $$$
(☎07221-300 660; www.hotel-belle-epoque.de; Maria-Viktoria-Strasse 2c; s €165-240, d €199-275,

DON'T MISS

TEN YEARS YOUNGER

Fettquelle (Römerplatz; ⏰24hr) Rheumatism, arthritis, respiratory complaints, skin problems – all this and a host of other ailments can, apparently, be cured by Baden-Baden's mineral-rich spring water. If you'd rather drink the stuff than bathe in it, head to the Fettquelle fountain at the base of a flight of steps near Römerplatz, where you can fill your bottle for free. It might taste like lukewarm bath water but who cares if it makes you feel 10 years younger?

SILENT HEIGHTS

Escape the crowds and enjoy the view at these Baden-Baden lookouts.

Neues Schloss (Schlossstrasse) Vine-swathed steps lead from Marktplatz to the 15th-century Neues Schloss, the former residence of the Baden-Baden margraves, which is set to reopen as a luxury hotel in late 2017. The lookout affords far-reaching views over Baden-Baden's rooftops and spires to the Black Forest beyond.

Mt Merkur (funicular one-way/return €2/4; ⊙10am-10pm) Though modest in height, 668m Mt Merkur commands wide-screen views of Baden-Baden and the Murg Valley. It's a popular spot for paragliding, gentle hiking and family picnics. Buses 204 and 205 stop near the funicular, which has been trundling to the top since 1913.

Florentinerberg The Romans used to cool off here; check out the ruins of the original baths at the foot of the hill. Nowadays, the serene botanical gardens nurture wisteria, cypress trees, orange and lemon groves.

Paradies am Annaberg These Italianate gardens are the perfect spot to unwind, with their soothing fountains and waterfalls. There are fine views of the Altstadt and wooded hills from these heights. Bus 205 to Friedrichshöhe runs nearby.

ste €325-695; 🗟) Nestling in manicured parkland, this neo-Renaissance villa is one of Baden-Baden's most characterful five-star pads. Antiques lend a dash of old-world opulence to the individually designed rooms. Rates include afternoon tea, with scones, cakes and fine brews served on the terrace or by the fireplace.

✖️ Eating

Café König   CAFE $
(Lichtentaler Strasse 12; cake €3.50-5; ⊙8.30am-6.30pm) Liszt and Tolstoy once sipped coffee at this venerable cafe, which has been doing a brisk trade in Baden-Baden's finest cakes, tortes, pralines and truffles for 250 years. Black forest gateau topped with clouds of cream, fresh berry tarts, moist nut cakes.

Kaffeehaus Baden-Baden   CAFE $
(Gernsbacherstrasse 24; snacks €3-6; ⊙9.30am-6pm Mon-Fri, 10.30am-6pm Sat, 1-6pm Sun) The aroma of freshly roasted coffee fills this artsy cafe, a laid-back spot for espresso and a slice of tart. Its shop sells organic preserves and handmade ceramics.

★**Weinstube im Baldreit**   GERMAN $$
(📞07221-231 36; Küferstrasse 3; mains €12.50-19; ⊙5-10pm Tue-Sat) Tucked down cobbled lanes, this wine-cellar restaurant is tricky to find, but worth looking for. Baden-Alsatian fare such as *Flammkuchen* (Alsatian pizza) topped with Black Forest ham, Roquefort and pears is expertly matched with local wines. Eat in the ivy-swathed courtyard in summer, and the vaulted interior in winter.

La Casserole   FRENCH $$
(📞07221-222 21; Gernsbacherstrasse 18; mains €12-18; ⊙5-11pm Mon, 11.30am-11pm Tue-Sat) Lace curtains, cheek-by-jowl tables and flickering candles create the classic bistro tableau at intimate La Casserole. Go for satisfying Alsatian specialities like beef cheeks braised in Pinot noir until tender, served with *Spätzle*.

La Provence   FRENCH $$$
(📞07221-255 50; Schlossstrasse 20; mains €14-38, 3-course menu €31; ⊙5-11pm Tue-Fri, noon-11pm Sat & Sun) Housed in the Neues Schloss wine cellar, the vaulted ceilings, art-nouveau mirrors and sense of humour at La Provence complement the French cuisine. Specialities like garlicky escargots and chateaubriand with truffle are spot-on.

Rizzi   INTERNATIONAL $$$
(📞07221-258 38; www.rizzi-baden-baden.de; Augaplatz 1; mains €18-48; ⊙noon-1am) A summertime favourite, this pink villa's tree-shaded patio is the place to sip excellent wines while tucking into choice steaks. Other menu faves include delicious burgers, homemade pastas and 'Rizzi-style sushi'.

⭐ Entertainment

Festspielhaus   CONCERT VENUE
(📞07221-301 3101; www.festspielhaus.de; Beim Alten Bahnhof 2, Robert-Schumann-Platz) Ensconced in an historic train station and fabled for its acoustics, the Festspielhaus is Europe's second biggest concert hall, seating 2500 theatre-goers, and a lavish tribute to

Baden-Baden's musical heritage. Under the direction of Andreas Mölich-Zebhauser, the grand venue hosts a world-class program of concerts, opera and ballet.

Baden-Badener Philharmonie   ORCHESTRA
(☑ 07221-932 791; www.philharmonie.baden-baden.de; Solms-Strasse 1) The revered Baden-Badener Philharmonie frequently performs in the Kurhaus.

Baden-Baden Theater   THEATRE
(☑ 07221-932 700; www.theater.baden-baden.de; Goetheplatz) The Baden-Baden Theater is a neo-baroque confection of white-and-red sandstone whose frilly interior looks like a miniature version of the Opéra-Garnier in Paris. It forms the gateway to Lichtentaler Allee and stages an eclectic line-up of German-language productions.

ⓘ Information

Branch Tourist Office (Kaiserallee 3; ⊘10am-5pm Mon-Sat, 2-5pm Sun) In the Trinkhalle. Sells tickets.

Main Tourist Office (☑ 07221-275 200; www.baden-baden.com; Schwarzwaldstrasse 52; ⊘9am-6pm Mon-Sat, 9am-1pm Sun) Situated 2km northwest of the centre. If you're driving from the northwest (from the A5) this place is on the way into town. Sells events tickets.

Post Office (Lange Strasse 44) Inside Kaufhaus Wagener.

ⓘ Getting There & Away

Karlsruhe-Baden-Baden Airport (Baden Airpark; ☑ 07229-66 20 00; www.badenairpark.de), 15km west of Baden-Baden, serves destinations including London Stansted, Rome and Malaga by Ryanair.

Buses to Black Forest destinations depart from the bus station, next to the Bahnhof.

Baden-Baden is close to the A5 (Frankfurt–Basel autobahn) and is the northern starting point of the zigzagging Schwarzwald-Hochstrasse, which follows the B500.

Baden-Baden is on a major north–south rail corridor. Twice-hourly destinations include Freiburg (€21 to €41, 45 to 90 minutes) and Karlsruhe (€11 to €16, 15 to 30 minutes).

ⓘ Getting Around

BUS

Local buses run by **Stadwerke Baden-Baden** (www.stadtwerke-baden-baden.de) cost €1.80/6 for a single/24-hour ticket. A day pass for up to five people is €9.80. Bus 201 (every 10 minutes) and other lines link the Bahnhof with

Leopoldsplatz. Bus 205 runs roughly hourly between the Bahnhof and the airport, less frequently at weekends.

CAR & MOTORCYCLE

The centre is mostly pedestrianised so it's best to park and walk. There is a free Park & Ride at the Bahnhof. Closer to the centre, the cheapest car park is at the Festspielhaus (€1 per hour). Michaelstunnel on the B500 routes traffic away from the centre, ducking underground west of the Festspielhaus and resurfacing just south of the Russische Kirche.

Karlsruhe

☑ 0721 / POP 295,000

When planning this radial city in 1715, the Margraves of Baden placed a mighty baroque palace smack in the middle – an urban layout so impressive it became the blueprint for Washington, DC.

Laid-back and cultured, Karlsruhe grows on you the longer you linger, with its rambling parks, museums crammed with futuristic

DON'T MISS

BLACK FOREST NATIONAL PARK

An outdoor wonderland of heather-speckled moors, glacial cirque lakes, deep valleys, mountains and near-untouched coniferous forest, the Nationalpark Schwarzwald (Black Forest National Park; ☑ 07449-9299 8444; www.schwarzwald-nationalpark.de; Schwarzwaldhochstrasse 2, Seebach; ⊘10am-6pm Tue-Sun May-Sep, 10am-5pm Tue-Sun Oct-Apr) , which finally got the seal of approval (national park status) on 1 January 2014, is the Schwarzwald at its wildest and untamed best. Nature is left to its own devices in this 100-sq-km pocket of forest in the northern Black Forest, tucked between Baden-Baden and Freudenstadt and centred on the Schwarzwaldhochstrasse (Black Forest High Road), the Murgtal valley and Mummelsee lake.

Hiking and cycling trails abound, as do discovery paths geared towards children. Stop by the information centre in Seebach for the low-down and to pick up maps. Details of guided tours and online maps are also available on the website.

gizmos and French Impressionist paintings. The suburbs dotted with art nouveau town houses are a reminder that France is just 15km away. Some 20,000 students keep the beer cheap and the vibe upbeat in the pubs, and the wheels of innovation in culture and technology turning.

◉ Sights & Activities

★ Schloss   PALACE

From the baroque-meets-neoclassical Schloss, Karlsruhe's 32 streets radiate like the spokes of a wheel. Karl Wilhelm Margrave of Baden-Durlach named his epicentral palace Karlsruhe (Karl's retreat) when founding the city in 1715. Destroyed during WWII, the grand palace was sensitively rebuilt. In warm weather, locals play pétanque on the fountain-strewn Schlossplatz parterre. The palace harbours the Badisches Landesmuseum.

Edging north, the Schlossgarten is a popular student hang-out and a relaxed spot for walks and picnics.

Badisches Landesmuseum   MUSEUM

(www.landesmuseum.de; adult/concession €4/3, after 2pm Fri free; ⊙10am-5pm Tue-Thu, 10am-6pm Fri-Sun) The treasure-trove Badisches Landesmuseum, inside the Schloss, shelters the jewel-encrusted crown of Baden's grand-ducal ruling family, and spoils of war from victorious battles against the Turks in the 17th century. Scale the tower for a better look at Karlsruhe's circular layout and for views stretching to the Black Forest.

Kunsthalle Karlsruhe   GALLERY

(www.kunsthalle-karlsruhe.de; Hans-Thoma-Strasse 2-6; adult/concession €12/9; ⊙10am-6pm Tue-Sun) The outstanding State Art Gallery presents a world-class collection: from the canvases of late-Gothic German masters like Matthias Grünewald and Lucas Cranach the Elder to Impressionist paintings by Degas, Monet and Renoir. Step across to the Orangerie to view works by German artists like Georg Baselitz and Gerhard Richter.

Zentrum für Kunst und
Medientechnologie   MUSEUM

(ZKM; www.zkm.de; Lorenzstrasse 19; entry to both museums €10/6.50, after 2pm Fri free; ⊙10am-6pm Wed-Fri, 11am-6pm Sat & Sun) Set in an historic munitions factory, the ZKM is a mammoth exhibition and research complex fusing art and emerging electronic media technologies. The interactive Medienmuseum has media art displays, including a computer-generated 'legible city' and real-time bubble simulations. The Museum für Neue Kunst hosts first-rate temporary exhibitions of post-1960 art. Served by tram 2, the ZKM is 2km southwest of the Schloss and a similar distance northwest of the Hauptbahnhof.

Marktplatz   SQUARE

The grand neoclassical Marktplatz is dominated by the Ionic portico of the 19th-century Evangelische Stadtkirche and the dusky-pink Rathaus. The iconic red-stone pyramid is an incongruous tribute to Karl Wilhelm Margrave of Baden-Durlach and marks his tomb.

Museum beim Markt   MUSEUM

(Karl-Friedrich-Strasse 6; adult/concession €2/1; ⊙11am-5pm Tue-Thu, 10am-6pm Fri-Sun) At the northern tip of Marktplatz, Museum beim Markt presents an intriguing stash of post-1900 applied arts, from art nouveau to Bauhaus.

Botanischer Garten   GARDENS

(Hans-Thoma-Strasse 6; garden admission free, greenhouses adult/concession €2/1; ⊙10am-6pm) Lush with exotic foliage, the Botanischer Garten is speckled with greenhouses – one with a giant Victoria waterlily.

Museum in der Majolika   MUSEUM

(Ahaweg 6; adult/concession €2/1; ⊙10am-1pm & 2-5pm Tue-Sun) A line of 1645 blue majolica tiles, called the Blaue Linie, connects the Schloss to the Museum in der Majolika, exhibiting glazed ceramics made in Karlsruhe since 1901.

🛏 Sleeping

Mainly geared towards corporate functions, Karlsruhe's hotels don't rank too highly on the charm-o-meter. Ask the tourist office for a list of private guesthouses.

Bed & Breakfast Karlsruhe   B&B $

(☑0157 850 730 50; www.bbkarlsruhe.de; Karlsstrasse 132a; dm/s/d €22/37/52) Artsy, individually decorated rooms, with a retro feel and paintings on the walls, make this one of Karslruhe's most enticing budget picks. Bathrooms are shared, as is the kitchen. It's a 10-minute walk northwest of the Hauptbahnhof. The nearest tram stop is Kolpingplatz.

Hotel Rio   HOTEL $$

(☑0721-840 80; www.hotel-rio.de; Hans-Sachs-Strasse 2; s €70-108, d €86-125; P ☎) Service can be brusque but this is still one of the best bets for spotless, contemporary quarters in Karlsruhe. Breakfast is worth the extra €6. Take the tram to Mühlburger Tor.

Acora Hotel
HOTEL $$$

(☑0721-850 90; www.acora.de; Sophienstrasse 69-71; s €91-134, d €117-169; P 🛜) Chirpy staff make you feel right at home at this apart-ment-hotel, featuring bright, modern rooms equipped with kitchenettes.

✕ Eating & Drinking

Die Kippe
PUB FOOD $

(Gottesauer Strasse 23; daily special €3.90; ⊙8am-1am, to 2am Fri & Sat) Every student has a tale about the 'dog end', named after the free to-bacco behind the bar. Wallet-friendly daily specials skip from schnitzel to plaice with potato salad. There's live music a couple of times weekly, as well as bingo and quiz nights. The beer garden has a great buzz in summer. Take tram 1 or 2 to Durlacher Tor.

Casa do José
PORTUGUESE $$

(☑0721-9143 8018; www.casadojose.de; Kriegsstrasse 92; mains €14-24; ⊙5-11pm Tue-Fri, 11.30am-11pm Sat & Sun) A slice of Portugal in the heart of Karlsruhe, Casa do José extends a heartfelt *bemvindo* (welcome). The look is modern rustic, with beams suspended above bistro tables in a light interior. *Petiscos* (Por-tuguese tapas) such as salt-cod fritters and fried garlic sausage are an appetising prelude to dishes like *cataplana de peixe e marisco* (paprika spiked fish and shellfish stew).

Vogelbräu
PUB FOOD $$

(Kapellenstrasse 50; mains €6.50-13; ⊙10am-1am) Quaff a cold one with regulars by the cop-per vats or in the leafy beer garden of this microbrewery. The unfiltered house pils washes down hale and hearty food such as Berlin-style beef liver with mash and onions.

Oberländer Weinstuben
GERMAN $$$

(☑0721-250 66; www.oberlaender-weinstube.de; Akademiestrasse 7; 3-course lunch/dinner €28/39, mains €18-26; ⊙noon-2pm & 6-10pm Tue-Sat) This highly atmospheric pick brings together an elegant wood-panelled tavern and a flowery courtyard. Fine wines marry perfectly with seasonal winners like stuffed ox-tail with spring leek and Pinot noir-shallot sauce – cooked with flair and served with finesse.

ℹ Information

Hauptbahnhof Tourist Office (☑0721-3720 5383; www.karlsruhe-tourism.de; Bahnhofplatz 6; ⊙8.30am-6pm Mon-Fri, 9am-1pm Sat, 10am-1pm Sun) Across the street from the Hauptbahnhof. The iGuide (€7.50) is a self-guided audiovisual walking tour of the centre lasting four hours. Also sells the Karlsruher WelcomeCard (24/48/72hr card €6.50/12.50/17.50) offering free or dis-counted entry to museums and other attractions.

Post Office (Poststrasse 3; ⊙9am-6.30pm Mon-Fri, 9am-1pm Sat) Just east of the Haupt-bahnhof.

ℹ Getting There & Away

Destinations well-served by train include Baden-Baden (€11 to €16, 15 to 30 minutes) and Frei-burg (€27 to €36, one hour).

Karlsruhe is on the A5 (Frankfurt–Basel) and is the starting point of the A8 to Munich. There are Park & Ride options outside of the city centre; look for 'P+R' signs.

ℹ Getting Around

The Hauptbahnhof is linked to the Marktplatz, 2km north, by tram and light-rail lines 2, 3, S1, S11, S4 and S41. Single tickets cost €2.30; a 24-Stunden-Karte (24-hour unlimited travel) costs €6 (€9.80 for up to five people).

A relaxed and ecofriendly way to explore Karls-ruhe is by bike. Deutsche Bahn has Call-a-Bike stands across the city.

Freudenstadt

☑07441 / POP 23,550

Duke Friedrich I of Württemberg built a new capital here in 1599, which was bombed to bits in WWII. The upshot is that Freuden-stadt's centre is underwhelming, though its magnificent setting in the Black Forest is anything but. Lovers of statistics will de-light in ticking off Germany's biggest square (216m by 219m, for the record), dislocated by a T-junction of heavily trafficked roads.

Freudenstadt marks the southern end of the Schwarzwald-Hochstrasse and is a terminus for the gorgeous Schwarzwald-Tälerstrasse, which runs from Rastatt via Alpirsbach.

◎ Sights

Stadtkirche
CHURCH

(⊙10am-5pm) In the southwest corner of Marktplatz looms the 17th-century red-sandstone Stadtkirche, with an ornate 12th-century Cluniac-style baptismal font, Gothic windows, Renaissance portals and baroque towers. The two naves are at right angles to each other, an unusual design by the geometrically minded duke.

A WALK IN THE BLACK FOREST

As locals will tell you, you need to hit the trails to really see the Black Forest. From gentle half-day strolls to multi-day treks, we've cherry-picked the region for a few of our favourites. Local tourist offices can help out with more info and maps, or check out the Schwarzwald Verein's free tour planner at www.wanderservice-schwarzwald.de.

It's also worth checking out the Schwarzwaldverein (www.schwarzwaldverein.de), whose well-marked paths criss-cross the darkest depths of the Black Forest.

Panoramaweg If you want to appreciate Baden-Baden and the northern Black Forest from its most photogenic angles, walk all or part of the 40km Panoramaweg, a high-level ridge trail weaving through orchards and woodlands past waterfalls and viewpoints.

Gütenbach-Simonswäldertal Gütenbach, 22km south of Triberg, is the trailhead for one of the Black Forest's most beautiful half-day hikes to Simonswäldertal, 13km distant. A forest trail threads to Balzer Herrgott, where a sandstone figure of Christ has grown into a tree. Walking downhill from here to Simonswälder Valley, fir-draped hills rise like a curtain before you.

Return by veering north to Teichsschlucht gorge, where a brook cascades through primeval forest lined with sheer cliffs and moss-strewn boulders. Head upstream to return to Gütenbach.

Westweg Up for an adventure? The 280km Westweg is a famous long-distance trail, marked with a red diamond, stretching from Pforzheim in the northern Black Forest to Basel in Switzerland. Highlights feature the steep Murg Valley, Titisee and 1493m Feldberg.

Wutachschlucht (www.wutachschlucht.de) This wild gorge, carved out by a fast-flowing river and flanked by near-vertical rock faces, lies near Bonndorf, close to the Swiss border and 15km east of Schluchsee. The best way to experience its unique microclimate, where you might spot orchids, ferns, rare butterflies and lizards, is on this 13km trail leading from Schattenmühle to Wutachmühle.

Feldberg Steig Orbiting the Black Forest's highest peak, 1493m Feldberg, this 12km walk traverses a nature reserve that's home to chamois and wildflowers. On clear days, the views of the Alps are glorious. It's possible to snowshoe part of this route in winter.

Martinskapelle A scenic and easygoing walk, this 10km loop begins at hilltop chapel Martinskapelle, 11km southwest of Triberg. The well-marked path wriggles through forest to tower-topped Brendturm (1149m) which affords views from Feldberg to the Vosges and the Alps on cloud-free days. Continue via Brendhäusle and Rosseck for a stunning vista of overlapping mountains and forest.

🏃 Activities

The deep forested valleys on Freudenstadt's fringes are worth exploring. Scenic hiking trails include a 12km uphill walk to **Knieb-is** on the Schwarzwald-Hochstrasse, where there are superb Kinzig Valley views. Ask the tourist office for details.

Jump on a mountain bike to tackle routes like the 85km **Kinzigtal-Radweg**, taking in dreamy landscapes and half-timbered villages, or the 60km **Murgtal-Radweg** over hill and dale to Rastatt. Both valleys have bike trails and it's possible to return to Freudenstadt by train.

Intersport Glaser　　　　　BICYCLE RENTAL
(Katharinenstrasse 8; bike rental per day €14-24; ⊙9.30am-6.30pm Mon-Fri, 9.30am-4pm Sat) A couple of blocks north of Marktplatz, this outlet hires mountain and electro bikes.

Panorama-Bad　　　　　　　SWIMMING
(www.panorama-bad.de; Ludwig-Jahn-Strasse 60; adult/concession 3hr pass €6.70/5.80; ⊙9am-10pm Mon-Sat, 9am-8pm Sun) The glass-fronted Panorama-Bad is a relaxation magnet with pools, steam baths and saunas.

🛏 Sleeping & Eating

At the heart of Freudenstadt, the sprawling, arcaded Marktplatz harbours rows of shops and cafes with alfresco seating.

Camping Langenwald　　　CAMPGROUND $
(☑07441-2862;　　www.camping-langenwald.de; Strasburger Strasse 167; per person/tent €8/9; ⊙Easter-Oct; ⊛) With a solar-heated pool and

nature trail, this leafy site has impeccable eco credentials. It's served by bus 12 to Kniebis.

Warteck
HOTEL **$$**
(☑07441-919 20; www.warteck-freudenstadt.de; Stuttgarterstrasse 14; s €60-78, d €98-105; P☎) In the capable hands of the Glässel family since 1894, this hotel sports modern, gleamingly clean rooms. The real draw, however, is the wood-panelled restaurant (mains €14.50 to €39), serving market-fresh fare like beetroot tortellini and rack of venison with wild mushrooms.

Hotel Adler
HOTEL **$$**
(☑07441-915 20; www.adler-fds.de; Forststrasse 15-17; s €54.50-81, d €80-105; P☎) This family-run hotel near Marktplace has well-kept, recently renovated rooms and rents out e-bikes for €9/16 per half-/full day. The restaurant (mains €12 to €17) dishes up appetising regional grub such as *Zwiebelrostbraten* (roast beef with onions).

Turmbräu
GERMAN **$$**
(Marktplatz 64; mains €8-28; ☾11am-midnight, to 3am Fri & Sat) This lively microbrewery doubles as a beer garden. Pull up a chair in ye-olde barn to munch *Maultaschen* and guzzle Turmbräu brews – a 5L barrel costs €39.

ⓘ Information

Tourist Office (☑07441-8640; www.freudenstadt.de; Marktplatz 64; ☾9am-6pm Mon-Fri, 10am-3pm Sat, 10am-1pm Sun; ☎) Hotel reservations are free.

ⓘ Getting There & Away

Freudenstadt's focal point is the Marktplatz on the B28. The town has two train stations: the Stadtbahnhof, five minutes' walk north of Marktplatz, and the Hauptbahnhof, 2km southeast of Marktplatz at the end of Bahnhofstrasse.

Trains on the Ortenau line, serving Offenburg and Strasbourg, depart hourly from the Hauptbahnhof and are covered by the 24-hour Europass. The pass represents excellent value at €11.50 for individuals and €18.40 for families. Trains go roughly hourly to Karlsruhe (€17.90, 1½ to two hours) from the Stadtbahnhof and Hauptbahnhof.

Kinzig Valley

Shaped like a horseshoe, the Kinzigtal (Kinzig Valley) begins south of Freudenstadt and shadows the babbling Kinzig River south to Schiltach, west to Haslach and north to Of-fenburg. Near Strasbourg, 95km downriver, the Kinzig is swallowed up by the mighty Rhine. The valley's inhabitants survived for centuries on mining and shipping goods by raft.

This Black Forest valley is astonishingly pretty, its hills brushed with thick larch and spruce forest and its half-timbered villages looking freshly minted for a fairy tale. For seasonal colour, come in autumn (foliage) or spring (fruit blossom).

ⓘ Getting There & Away

The B294 follows the Kinzig from Freudenstadt to Haslach, from where the B33 leads north to Offenburg. If you're going south, pick up the B33 to Triberg and beyond in Hausach.

An hourly train line links Freudenstadt with Offenburg (€15.70, 1¼ hours), stopping in Alpirsbach (€3.65, 16 minutes), Schiltach (€6.10, 27 minutes), Hausach (€8.10, 42 minutes), Haslach (€10, 50 minutes) and Gengenbach (€13.30, one hour). From Hausach, trains run roughly hourly southeast to Triberg (€6.10, 20 minutes), Villingen (€12.10, 47 minutes) and Konstanz (€29.60, two hours).

Alpirsbach
☑07444 / POP 6580

Lore has it that Alpirsbach is named after a quaffing cleric who, when a glass of beer slipped clumsily from his hand and rolled into the river, exclaimed: *All Bier ist in den Bach!* (All the beer is in the stream!). A prophecy, it seems, as today Alpirsbacher Klosterbräu is brewed from pure spring water. **Brewery tours** (☑07441-670; www.alpirsbacher.com; Marktplatz 1; tours €7; ☾2.30pm) are in German, though guides may speak English. Two beers are thrown in for the price of a ticket.

A few paces north, you can watch chocolate being made and scoff delectable beer-filled pralines at **Schau-Confiserie Heinzelmann** (Ambrosius-Blarer-Platz 2; ☾9am-noon & 2-6pm Mon-Fri, to 5pm Sat).

All the more evocative for its lack of adornment, the 11th-century former Benedictine **Kloster Alpirsbach** (Klosterplatz 1; adult/concession €5/2.50; ☾10am-5.30pm Mon-Sat, 11am-5.30pm Sun) sits opposite. The monastery effectively conveys the simple, spiritual life in its flat-roofed church, spartan cells and Gothic cloister, which hosts candlelit concerts (www.kreuzgangkonzerte.de) from late June to early August. It's amazing what you can find under the floorboards,

1. Lake at the base of Wettersteinspitze (p102) 2. Danube River, Passau (p161) 3. Bavarian Forest National Park (p166)

Dramatic Landscapes

From the high Alps to the Black Forest, the low dark hills of eastern Bavaria to the glassy mountain lakes of the Alpine foothill region, southern Germany has a photogenic menu of landscapes to suit every taste.

Mountains

Bavaria enjoys only a sliver of Europe's premier mountain range, the Alps, but it certainly packs a lot into its slice. Take a ride high into the thinning air in one of the region's countless cable cars, snap on skis, lace up hiking boots or just enjoy the views with a beer in hand.

Forests

Though there are plenty of trees in between, Southern Germany is a tale of two forests, one Bavarian in the east one Black in the west. The former is a dark, mysterious, sparsely populated area that spills over into neighbouring Czech Republic, the latter the location of Germany's newest national park.

Lakes

From soothing Lake Constance in the west to Munich's watery playground Lake Starnberg, the Black Forest's Titisee to the drama of Berchtesgaden's Königsee, southern Germany's lakes serve up some of the region's most astounding scenery and most serene views plus lots of fun both in and on the water.

Rivers

One of the world's most famous rivers, the Danube is born in the Black Forest before cutting through Bavaria and Baden-Württemberg at the beginning of its long journey to the Black Sea. The lesser-known Altmühl is a more tranquil affair flowing through Franconia, an ideal waterway for a lazy kayak trip.

as the museum reveals with its stash of 16th-century clothing, caricatures (of artistic scholars) and lines (of misbehaving ones).

The **tourist office** (☑ 07444-951 6281; www.stadt-alpirsbach.de; Krähenbadstrasse 2; ⊙ 9am-noon & 2-6pm Mon, 9am-noon & 2-5pm Tue & Thu, 9am-noon Wed, 9am-1pm & 2-5pm Fri, 10am-noon Sat) can supply hiking maps and, for cyclists, information on the 85km Kinzigtalradweg from Offenburg to Lossburg.

Schiltach

☑ 07836 / POP 3880

Sitting smugly at the foot of wooded hills and on the banks of the Kinzig and Schiltach Rivers, medieval Schiltach looks too perfect to be true. The meticulously restored half-timbered houses, which once belonged to tanners, merchants and raft builders, are a riot of crimson geraniums in summer.

◉ Sights & Activities

Because Schiltach is at the confluence of the Kinzig and Schiltach Rivers, logging was big business until the 19th century and huge rafts were built to ship timber as far as the Netherlands. The willow-fringed banks now attract grey herons and kids who come to splash in the shallow water when the sun's out.

Marktplatz   SQUARE

Centred on a trickling fountain, the sloping, triangular Marktplatz is Schiltach at its picture-book best. The frescos of its step-gabled, 16th-century Rathaus depict scenes from local history.

Schlossbergstrasse   STREET

Clamber south up Schlossbergstrasse, pausing to notice the plaques that denote the trades of one-time residents, such as the *Strumpfstricker* (stocking weaver) at No 6, and the sloping roofs where tanners once dried their skins. Up top there are views over Schiltach's red rooftops.

Museum am Markt   MUSEUM

(Marktplatz 13; ⊙ 11am-5pm Apr-Oct, Sat & Sun only Nov-Mar) FREE Museum am Markt is crammed with everything from antique spinning wheels to Biedermeier costumes. Highlights include the cobbler's workshop and an interactive display recounting the tale of the devilish Teufel von Schiltach.

Schüttesäge Museum   MUSEUM

(Gerbegasse; ⊙ 11am-5pm daily Apr-Oct, Sat & Sun only Nov-Mar) FREE The riverfront Schüttesäge Museum focuses on Schiltach's rafting tradition with reconstructed workshops, a watermill generating hydroelectric power for many homes in the area and touchy-feely exhibits for kids, from different kinds of bark to forest animals.

🛏 Sleeping & Eating

Campingplatz Schiltach   CAMPGROUND $

(☑ 07836-7289; Bahnhofstrasse 6; per person/tent/car €5.50/3.50/3; ⊙ Apr-Oct) Beautifully positioned on the banks of the Kinzig, this campground has impeccable eco credentials and a playground and sandpit for kids.

★Weysses Rössle   GUESTHOUSE $$

(☑ 07836-387; www.weysses-roessle.de; Schenkenzeller Strasse 42; s €55-59.50, d €78-96; P 🛜) Rosemarie and Ulrich continue the tradition of 19 generations in this 16th-century inn. Countrified rooms decorated with rosewood and floral fabrics also feature snazzy bathrooms and wi-fi. Its restaurant serves locally sourced, organic fare.

Zur Alten Brücke   GUESTHOUSE $$

(☑ 07836-2036; www.altebruecke.de; Schramberger Strasse 13; s/d/apt €60/90/110; P 🛜) You'll receive a warm welcome from Michael and Lisa at this riverside guesthouse. The pick of the bright, cheery rooms overlook the Schiltach. Michael cooks up seasonal, regional fare in the kitchen and there's a terrace for summer imbibing.

❶ Information

Tourist Office (☑ 07836-5850; www.schiltach.de; Marktplatz 6; ⊙ 9am-noon & 2-4pm Mon-Thu, 9am-noon Fri) The tourist office in the Rathaus can help find accommodation and offers free internet access. Hiking options are marked on an enamel sign just opposite.

Gutach

☑ 07831 / POP 2180

Worth the 4km detour south of the Kinzig Valley, the **Schwarzwälder Freilichtmuseum** (☑ 07831-935 60; www.vogtsbauernhof.org; adult/concession/child/family €9/8/5/25; ⊙ 9am-6pm late Mar-early Nov, to 7pm Aug, last entry 1hr before closing) spirals around the Vogtsbauernhof, an early-17th-century farmstead. Farmhouses shifted from their original locations have been painstakingly reconstructed, using techniques such as thatching and panelling, to create this authentic farming hamlet and preserve age-old Black Forest traditions.

REACH FOR THE STARS

Swinging along country lanes 6km north of Freudenstadt brings you to Baiersbronn. It looks like any other Black Forest town, snuggled among meadows and wooded hills. But on its fringes sit two of Germany's finest restaurants, both holders of the coveted three Michelin stars.

Schwarzwaldstube (07442-4920; www.traube-tonbach.de; Tonbachstrasse 237, Baiersbronn-Tonbach; 5-/7-course menu €80/210, cookery courses around €170; 7pm-midnight Wed, noon-4.30pm & 7pm-midnight Thu-Sun) Schwarzwaldstube commands big forest views from its rustically elegant dining room. Here Harald Wohlfahrt performs culinary magic, while carefully sourcing and staying true to French cooking traditions. The tasting menu goes with the seasons, but you might begin with a palate-awakening variation of mackerel with cucumber-oyster relish, followed by saddle of venison with juniper crust and caramelised *chicorée* (chicory).

If you fancy getting behind the stove, sign up for one of the cookery classes, which revolve around a theme such as cooking with crustaceans, asparagus, goose or truffles, or techniques like pasta-making and preparing pâtés.

Restaurant Bareiss (07442-470; www.bareiss.com; Gärtenbühlweg 14, Baiersbronn-Mitteltal; lunch menu €95, dinner menus €168-210; noon-2pm & 7-9.30pm Wed-Sun) Claus-Peter Lumpp has consistently won plaudits for his brilliantly composed, French-inflected menus at Restaurant Bareiss. On paper, dishes such as sautéed langoustine with almond cream and fried fillet of suckling calf and sweetbreads with chanterelles seem deceptively simple; on the plate they become things of beauty, rich in textures and aromas and presented with an artist's eye for detail.

Explore barns filled with wagons and horn sleds, *Rauchküchen* (kitchens for smoking fish and meat) and the Hippenseppenhof (1599), with its chapel and massive hipped roof constructed from 400 trees. It's a great place for families, with inquisitive farmyard animals to pet, artisans on hand to explain their crafts and frequent demonstrations, from sheep shearing to butter-making.

The self-controlled bobs of the **Schwarzwald Rodelbahn** (Black Forest Toboggan Run; Singersbach 4; adult/child €2.50/2; 10am-6pm Apr-early Nov), 1.5km north of Gutach, are faster than they look. Lay off the brakes for extra speed.

Haslach

 07832 / POP 6980

Back in the Kinzig Valley, Haslach's 17th-century former Capuchin monastery houses the **Schwarzwälder Trachtenmuseum** (Black Forest Costume Museum; www.trachtenmuseum-haslach.de.vu; Im Alten Kapuzinerkloster; adult/concession €2/1.50; 10am-12.30pm & 1.30-4pm Tue-Fri), showcasing flamboyant costumes and outrageous hats, the must-have accessories for the well-dressed Fräulein of the 1850s. Look out for the Black Forest *Bollenhut,* a straw bonnet topped with pompons (red for unmarried women, black for married) and the *Schäppel,* a fragile-looking crown made from hundreds of beads and weighing up to 5kg.

Gengenbach

 07803 / POP 11,020

If ever a Black Forest town could be described as chocolate box, it would surely be Gengenbach, with its scrumptious Altstadt of half-timbered town houses framed by vineyards and orchards. It's fitting, then, that director Tim Burton made this the home of gluttonous Augustus Gloop in the 2005 blockbuster *Charlie and the Chocolate Factory* (though less so that he called it Düsseldorf).

Sights & Activities

The best way to discover Gengenbach's historic centre is with a saunter through its narrow backstreets, such as the gently curving Engelgasse, off Hauptstrasse, lined with listed half-timbered houses draped in vines and bedecked with scarlet geraniums.

Between the town's two tower-topped gates sits the triangular Marktplatz, dominated by the Rathaus, an 18th-century pink-and-cream confection. The fountain bears a

STUTTGART & THE BLACK FOREST HASLACH

statue of a knight, a symbol of Gengenbach's medieval status as a Free Imperial City.

Amble east along Klosterstrasse to spy the former Benedictine monastery. The calm Kräutergarten is behind its walls.

The tourist office has info on the hour-long Weinpfad, a wine trail beginning in the Altstadt that threads through terraced vineyards to the Jakobskapelle, a 13th-century chapel commanding views that reach as far as Strasbourg on clear days. The free, lantern-lit Nachtwächterrundgang (night watchman's tour) starts at the Rathaus on Wednesday and Saturday at 10pm from May to July and at 9pm from August to October.

🛏 Sleeping & Eating

DJH Hostel   HOSTEL $
(☑ 07803-317 49; www.jugendherberge-schloss-ortenberg.de; Burgweg 21; dm €23-29) The Hogwarts gang would feel at home in the 12th-century Schloss Ortenberg, rebuilt in whimsical neo-Gothic style complete with lookout tower and wood-panelled dining hall. A staircase sweeps up to dorms with Kinzig Valley views. From Gengenbach station, take bus 7134 or 7160 to Ortenberg, and get off at the 'Schloss/Freudental' stop.

Pfeffermühle   B&B $$
(☑ 07803-933 50; www.pfeffermuehle-gengenbach. de; Oberdorfstrasse 24; s/d €54/84) In a snug half-timbered house dating to 1476, close to one of the Altstadt gate towers, this neat-and-tidy B&B is a bargain. Decorated with antique knick-knacks, the wood-panelled restaurant (mains €14 to €22) features among

CHRISTMAS COUNTDOWN

Every December, Gengenbach rekindles childhood memories of opening tiny windows when the Rathaus morphs into the world's biggest advent calendar. At 6pm daily, one of 24 windows is opened to reveal a festive scene. In the past, the tableaux have been painted by well-known artists and children's-book illustrators such as Marc Chagall and Tomi Ungerer.

From late November to 23 December, a Christmas market brings extra yuletide sparkle, mulled wine and carols to the Marktplatz.

the town's best, dishing out regional favourites like Black Forest trout and *Sauerbraten* (pot roast).

⭐ **Die Reichstadt**   BOUTIQUE HOTEL $$$
(☑ 07803-966 30; www.die-reichsstadt.de; Engelgasse 33; s €140-160, ste €190-210, 4-course half-board per person €35; 🅿 🛜) This boutique stunner on Engelgasse wings you to storybook heaven. Its 16th-century exterior conceals a pure, contemporary aesthetic, where clean lines, natural materials and subtle cream-caramel shades are enlivened with eye-catching details. A spa, sparkling wine on arrival, free fruit in your room and one of the top restaurants in town, with a season-driven menu, complete this pretty picture.

Holzofen-Bäckerei Klostermühle   BAKERY $
(Klosterstrasse 7; ⊙ 7am-6pm Mon-Fri, 7am-noon Sat) Opposite the Benedictine monastery, the stuck-in-time Holzofen-Bäckerei Klostermühle fills the lanes with wafts of freshly baked bread from its wood-fired oven. Buy a loaf to munch in the calm Kräutergarten.

ℹ Information

Tourist Office (☑ 07803-930 143; www. stadt-gengenbach.de; Im Winzerhof; ⊙ 9am-5pm Mon-Fri) The tourist office is in a courtyard just off Hauptstrasse.

Freiburg
☑ 0761 / POP 224,190

Sitting plump at the foot of the Black Forest's wooded slopes and vineyards, Freiburg is a sunny, cheerful university town, its medieval Altstadt a story-book tableau of gabled town houses, cobblestone lanes and cafe-rimmed plazas. Party-loving students spice up the local nightlife.

Blessed with 2000 hours of annual sunshine, this is Germany's warmest city. Indeed, while neighbouring hilltop villages are still shovelling snow, the trees in Freiburg are clouds of white blossom, and locals are already imbibing in canalside beer gardens. This eco-trailblazer has shrewdly tapped into that natural energy to generate nearly as much solar power as the whole of Britain, making it one of the country's greenest cities.

⦿ Sights

Freiburg's medieval past is tangible in backstreets like wisteria-draped Konviktstrasse and in the canalside Fischerau and Gerberau, the former fishing and tanning quarters. The Dreisam River runs along the Altstadt's southern edge.

Keep an eye out for the cheerful pavement mosaics in front of many shops – a cow is for a butcher, a pretzel for a baker, a diamond marks a jewellery shop, and so on.

★ **Freiburger Münster** CATHEDRAL
(Freiburg Minster; ☑0761-202 790; www.freiburgermuenster.info; Münsterplatz; tower adult/concession €2/1.50; ☉9.30am-5pm, tower 9.30am-4.45pm Mon-Sat, 1-5pm Sun) With its lacy spires, cheeky gargoyles and intricate entrance portal, Freiburg's 11th-century minster cuts an impressive figure above the central market square. It has dazzling kaleidoscopic stained-glass windows that were mostly financed by medieval guilds and a high altar with a masterful triptych by Dürer protégé Hans Baldung Grien. Square at the base, the tower becomes an octagon higher up and is crowned by a filigreed 116m-high spire. On clear days you can spy the Vosges Mountains in France.

Closer to the ground, near the main portal in fact, note the medieval wall measurements used to ensure that merchandise (eg loaves of bread) were of the requisite size.

Note that the cathedral is closed for visits during services (exact times are available at the info desk inside).

Augustinermuseum MUSEUM
(☑0761-201 2531; Auginerplatz 1; adult/concession/under 18yr €6/4/free; ☉10am-5pm Tue-Sun) Dip into the past as represented by artists working from the Middle Ages to the 19th century at this superb museum in a sensitively modernised monastery. The Sculpture Hall on the ground floor is especially impressive for its fine medieval sculpture and masterpieces by Renaissance artists Hans Baldung Grien and Lucas Cranach the Elder. Head upstairs for eye-level views of mounted gargoyles.

There is a cafe overlooking the cloister where you can sip a drink and soak up the monastic vibe. A €7/5 ticket includes temporary exhibitions and is valid for all museums in Freiburg.

Historisches Kaufhaus HISTORIC BUILDING
(Münsterplatz) Facing the Münster's south side and embellished with polychrome tiled turrets is the arcaded brick-red Historisches Kaufhaus, an early-16th-century merchants' hall. The coats of arms on the oriels and

the four figures above the balcony symbolise Freiburg's allegiance to the House of Habsburg.

City Gates GATE
(Kaiser-Joseph-Strasse) Freiburg has two intact medieval gates. The **Martinstor** (Martin's Gate) rises above Kaiser-Joseph-Strasse, while the 13th-century **Schwabentor**, on the Schwabenring, is a massive city gate with a mural of St George slaying the dragon and tram tracks running under its arches.

Schlossberg VIEWPOINT
(Schlossbergring; cable car one way/return €3/5; ☉9am-10pm, shorter hours in winter) The forested Schlossberg dominates Freiburg. Take the footpath opposite the Schwabentor, leading up through sun-dappled woods, or hitch a ride on the recently restored Schlossbergbahn cable car. For serious hikers, several trails begin here including those to St Peter (17km) and Kandel (25km).

The little peak is topped by the ice-cream-cone-shaped Aussichtsturm (lookout tower). From here, Freiburg spreads photogenically before you – the spire of the Münster soaring above a jumble of red gables, framed by the dark hills of the Black Forest.

Rathausplatz SQUARE
(Town Hall Square) Join locals relaxing in a cafe by the fountain in chestnut-shaded Rathausplatz, Freiburg's prettiest square. Pull out your camera to snap pictures of the ox-blood-red 16th-century Altes Rathaus (Old Town Hall) with the tourist office, the step-gabled 19th-century Neues Rathaus

Freiburg

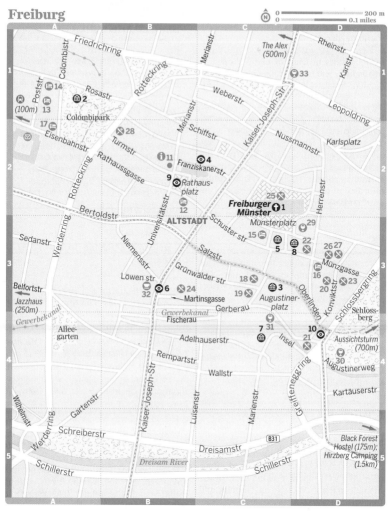

(New Town Hall) and the medieval Martins-kirche with its modern interior.

Haus zum Walfisch   LANDMARK
(House of the Whale; Franziskanerstrasse) The marvellously extravagant Haus zum Wal-fisch sports a late-Gothic oriel garnished with two impish gargoyles.

Archäologisches Museum   MUSEUM
(www.museen.freiburg.de; Rotteckring 5; adult/concession €3/2; ⏰10am-5pm Tue-Sun) In a sculpture-dotted park sits the neo-Gothic Colombischlössle. Built for the Countess of Colombi in 1859, the whimsical red-sandstone villa now harbours this archaeology-focused museum. From the skylit marble entrance, a cast-iron staircase ascends to a stash of finds from Celtic grave offerings to Roman artefacts.

Museum für Stadtgeschichte   MUSEUM
(Münsterplatz 30; adult/concession €3/2; ⏰10am-5pm Tue-Sun) The sculptor Christian Wentzinger's baroque town house, east of the Historisches Kaufhaus, now shelters this museum, spelling out in artefacts Freiburg's eventful past. Inside, a wrought-iron staircase guides the eye to an elaborate ceiling fresco.

Freiburg

◎ Top Sights
1 Freiburger Münster C2

◎ Sights
2 Archäologisches Museum A1
3 Augustinermuseum............................... C3
    Colombischlössle...........................(see 2)
4 Haus zum Walfisch C2
5 Historisches Kaufhaus C3
6 Martinstor B3
7 Museum für Neue Kunst...................... C4
8 Museum für Stadtgeschichte D3
9 Rathausplatz B2
10 Schwabentor D4

◎ Activities, Courses & Tours
11 Freiburg Kultour................................... B2

◎ Sleeping
12 Hotel am Rathaus B2
13 Hotel Barbara A1
14 Hotel Minerva A1
15 Hotel Oberkirch.................................... C3
16 Hotel Schwarzwälder Hof.................... D3

17 Park Hotel Post.....................................A2

◎ Eating
18 Chang...C3
19 Edo's Hummus Küche C3
20 Englers Weinkrügle D3
21 Enoteca Trattoria D4
22 Gasthaus zum Kranz............................D3
23 Kreuzblume..D3
24 Markthalle...B3
    Martin's Bräu ....(see 24)
25 Münsterplatz Food Market C2
26 Rücker Käse und Wein..........................D3
27 Wolfshöhle...D3
28 Zirbelstube B2

◎ Drinking & Nightlife
29 Alte Wache D3
30 Greiffenegg-Schlössle D4
31 Hausbrauerei Feierling C4
    Isle of Innisfree ....(see 19)
32 Schlappen...B3
33 White Rabbit Club D1

Museum für Neue Kunst   GALLERY
(Marienstrasse 10; adult/concession €3/2; ☉10am-5pm Tue-Sun) Across the Gewerbeka-nal, this gallery highlights 20th-century Expressionist and abstract art, including emotive works by Oskar Kokoschka and Otto Dix.

☞ Tours

Freiburg Kultour   GUIDED TOUR
(www.freiburg-kultour.com; Rathausplatz 2-4; adult/concession €9/7; ☉10.30am Mon-Fri, 10am Sat in German, 11.30am Sat in English) Kultour offers 1½- to two-hour walking tours of the Altstadt and the Münster in German and English.

Fahrradtaxi   GUIDED TOUR
(🖉0172-768 4370; www.fahrradtaxi-freiburg.de; An der Höhlgasse 5; ☉mid-Apr–Oct) Fahrra-dtaxi charges €7.50 for a 15-minute, two-person spin of the Altstadt in a pedicab. Call ahead or look for one on Rathausplatz or Münsterplatz.

🛏 Sleeping

Charismatic hotels abound in the Altstadt but it's wise to book ahead in summer. The tourist office offers a booking service (€3) and has a list of good-value private guesthouses.

Black Forest Hostel   HOSTEL $
(🖉0761-881 7870; www.blackforest-hostel.de; Kartäuserstrasse 33; dm €17-27, s/d €35/58, linen €4; ☉reception 7am-1am; @) Boho budget digs with chilled common areas, a shared kitch-en, bike rental and spacey stainless-steel showers. It's a five-minute walk from the town centre.

Hirzberg Camping   CAMPGROUND $
(🖉0761-350 54; www.freiburg-camping.de; Kartäuserstrasse 99; campsites per adult/tent/car €8.80/4.70/2.70; P🖀) This year-round campground sits in a quiet woodland spot 1.5km east of Schwabentor. It has cooking facilities and bike rental. Take tram 1 to Musikhochschule.

The Alex   BOUTIQUE HOTEL $$
(🖉0761-296 970; www.the-alex-hotel.de; Rhein-strasse 29; s €103-142, d €112-151; P❄🖀) This welcome newcomer to Freiburg's hotel scene has a clean, sleek aesthetic, with lots of plate glass, blonde wood, natural materials and a muted palette of colours. Besides contempo-rary-style rooms with rain showers, there's a bar, Winery29, where you can try locally produced wines.

Hotel Schwarzwälder Hof   HOTEL $$
(🖉0761-380 30; www.schwarzwaelder-hof.com; Herrenstrasse 43; s €68-80, d €99-125; @) This bijou hotel has an unrivalled style-for-euro

ratio. A wrought-iron staircase sweeps up to snazzy rooms furnished in classic, modern or traditional style. Some have postcard views of the Altstadt.

Hotel am Rathaus
HOTEL $$

(☑0761-296 160; www.am-rathaus.de; Rathausgasse 4-8; s €93-95, d €110-129; P🐾🛜) Just steps away from the bustle of Rathausplatz, this neat-and-tidy hotel has spacious, neutral-toned rooms with homely touches like CD and DVD players; ask for a rear-facing room if you're a light sleeper.

Hotel Minerva
HOTEL $$

(☑0761-386 490; www.minerva-freiburg.de; Poststrasse 8; s €65-95, d €130-155, tr €165; P🛜) All curvaceous windows and polished wood, this art nouveau charmer is five minutes' trudge from the Altstadt. The sleek, contemporary rooms feature free wi-fi. The sauna (€8) is another plus.

Hotel Barbara
HISTORIC HOTEL $$

(☑0761-296 250; www.hotel-barbara.de; Poststrasse 4; s €80-94, d €110-151, apt €135-205; 🛜) A grandfather clock, curvy staircases and high ceilings give this art nouveau town house a nostalgic feel. It's a homely, family-run place with old-fashioned, pastel-hued rooms and homemade jams at breakfast.

Park Hotel Post
HISTORIC HOTEL $$

(☑0761-385 480; www.park-hotel-post.de; Am Colombipark; s €109-159, d €139-199; P🛜) Slip back to the more graceful age of art nouveau at this refined pile overlooking Colombipark, with summery rooms decorated in blues and yellows. Attentive service and generous breakfasts sweeten the deal.

★ Hotel Oberkirch
HISTORIC HOTEL $$$

(☑0761-202 6868; www.hotel-oberkirch.de; Münsterplatz 22; s €75-104, d €154-174; P) Wake up to Münster views at this green-shuttered hotel. The country-style rooms feature floral wallpaper and half-canopies over the beds. Oberkirch has an intoxicating 250-year history; during a fire in WWII the hotelier doused the blaze with wine from his cellar. The dark-wood downstairs tavern (mains €13 to €23) does a roaring trade in hearty Badisch fare such as venison ragout with Knödel (dumplings).

✗ Eating

The Altstadt is stacked with cafes, wine taverns, brewpubs and restaurants, many spilling out onto pavement terraces. You can find cheap bites on Martinstor and Kartäuserstrasse.

Edo's Hummus Küche
VEGETARIAN $

(http://thehummuscorner.com; Atrium Auginerplatz; light meals €2.50-8.50; ⊙11.30am-9pm Mon-Sat; 🍴) Edo's pulls in the midday crowds by doing what it says on the tin – superb homemade hummus served with warm pitta, as well as lentil salad and falafel. The basic hummus plate for €4.30 is a meal in itself.

Chang
THAI $

(Grünwälderstrasse 21; mains €6-9.50; ⊙noon-11pm) Sweet little Thai place for inexpensive daily specials, from green curry to pad thai.

Münsterplatz Food Market
MARKET $

(⊙7.30am-1.30pm Mon-Fri, to 2pm Sat) Bag local goodies (honey, cheese, fruit and the like), or snack on a wurst-in-a-bun, topped with fried onions.

Markthalle
MARKET $

(www.markthalle-freiburg.de; Martinsgasse 235; light meals €4-8; ⊙8am-8pm Mon-Thu, to midnight Fri & Sat) Eat your way around the world – from curry to sushi, oysters to antipasti – at the food counters in this historic market hall, nicknamed 'Fressgässle'.

Rücker Käse und Wein
DELI $

(Münzgasse 1; ⊙10am-6.30pm Mon-Fri, 9am-3pm Sat) For wine and cheese.

Gasthaus zum Kranz
GERMAN $$

(☑0761-217 1967; www.gasthauszumkranz.de; Herrenstrasse 40; mains €13-24; ⊙11.30am-3pm & 5.30pm-midnight Mon-Sat, noon-3pm & 5.30pm-midnight Sun) There's always a good buzz at this quintessentially Badisch tavern. Pull up a chair at one of the wooden tables for well-prepared regional faves like roast suckling pig, Maultaschen and Sauerbraten (beef pot roast with vinegar, onions and peppercorns).

Englers Weinkrügle
GERMAN $$

(☑0761-383 115; Konviktstrasse 12; mains €9-19; ⊙11.30am-2pm & 5.30pm-midnight Tue-Sun) A warm, woody Baden-style Weinstube with wisteria growing out front and regional flavours on the menu. The trout in various guises (for instance, with riesling or almond-butter sauce) is delicious.

Enoteca Trattoria
ITALIAN $$

(☑0761-389 9130; www.enoteca-freiburg.de; Schwabentorplatz 6; mains €16-30; ⊙6pm-midnight Mon-Sat) This is the trattoria of the two Enoteca twins (the more formal restaurant is at

Gerberau 21). The chef here hits the mark with authentic Italian dishes such as Taleggio ravioli with Frascati sauce and glazed pear.

Martin's Bräu
PUB FOOD $$

(www.martinsbräu-freiburg.de; Fressgässle 1; mains €9-18; ⊙11am-midnight, to 2am Fri & Sat) Homebrewed pilsners wash down meaty snacks from ox-tongue salad to half-metre bratwursts. Lunch is a snip at €5.50. It's off Kaiser-Joseph-Strasse.

★ Kreuzblume
INTERNATIONAL $$$

(☑0761-311 94; www.hotel-kreuzblume.de; Konviktstrasse 31; 2-/3-/4-course dinner €32.50/39/47; ⊙6-10pm Wed-Sun) On a flower-festooned lane, this pocket-sized restaurant with clever backlighting and a menu fizzing with bright, sunny flavours attracts a rather food-literate clientele. Each dish combines just a few hand-picked ingredients in bold and tasty ways. Service is tops.

Zirbelstube
FRENCH $$$

(☑0761-210 60; www.colombi.de; Rotteckring 16; mains €45-59; ⊙noon-2pm & 7pm-midnight Mon-Sat) Freiburg's bastion of fine dining is this candlelit restaurant, decorated in warm Swiss pine. Chefs of exacting standards allow each ingredient to shine in specialities like Black Forest chateaubriand with red wine jus and chanterelles and Breton turbot filet with artichoke-octopus salsa – all perfectly matched with quality wines.

Wolfshöhle
MEDITERRANEAN $$$

(☑0761-303 03; Konviktstrasse 8; mains €21-36, 3-course lunch/dinner €33/54; ⊙6-10pm Mon, noon-2pm & 6-10pm Tue-Sat) With tables set up on a pretty square, Wolfshöhle is a summer-evening magnet. The menu whisks you off on a gastro tour of the Mediterranean, with well-executed dishes such as Iberian pork with wild-garlic purée and scampi with saffron-infused risotto.

🍸 Drinking & Entertainment

Freiburg's restless student population keep steins a-swinging in the beer gardens and bars and clubs pumping until the wee hours.

Schlappen
CAFE, PUB

(Löwenstrasse 2; ⊙11am-1am Mon-Wed, to 2am Thu, to 3am Fri & Sat, 3pm-1am Sun) In historic digs and crammed with antiques and vintage theatre posters, this evergreen pub has made the magic happen for generations of students. Check out the skeleton in the men's toilet. Summer terrace.

COLD FEET OR WEDDED BLISS?

As you wander the Altstadt, watch out for the gurgling *Bächle*, streamlets once used to water livestock and extinguish fires. Today they provide welcome relief for hot feet on sweltering summer days. Just be aware that you could get more than you bargained for: legend has it that if you accidentally step into the *Bächle*, you'll marry a Freiburger or a Freiburgerin.

Alte Wache
WINE BAR

(Münsterplatz 38; ⊙10am-9pm Mon-Sat) Right on the square, this 18th-century guardhouse serves local Müller-Thurgau and Pinot noir wines at the tasting tables. If they sharpen your appetite, you can order tapas on Thursdays.

Hausbrauerei Feierling
BEER GARDEN

(Gerberau 46; ⊙11am-midnight, to 1am Fri & Sat Mar-Oct) This stream-side beer garden is a relaxed spot to quaff a cold one under the chestnut trees in summer. Pretzels and sausages (snacks €3 to €9.50) soak up the malty brews.

Greiffenegg-Schlössle
BEER GARDEN

(Schlossbergring 3; ⊙11am-midnight Mar-Oct) All of Freiburg is at your feet from this chestnut-shaded beer garden atop Schlossberg. Perfect sunset spot.

Isle of Innisfree
PUB

(Atrium Auginerplatz; ⊙6pm-midnight Mon-Thu, 5pm-2am Fri, 4pm-2am Sat, 7pm-midnight Sun) Find Guinness and the craic at this lively Irish watering hole, with a weekly line-up of quizzes, karaoke and live music.

White Rabbit Club
CLUB

(www.white-rabbit-club.de; Leopoldring 1; ⊙9pm-3am Mon-Thu, 10pm-5am Fri & Sat) A student wonderland of cheap beers, DJs and gigs. Things get even curiouser at Wednesday night's open jam sessions.

Jazzhaus
LIVE MUSIC

(☑0761-349 73; www.jazzhaus.de; Schnewlinstrasse 1) Under the brick arches of a wine cellar, this venue hosts first-rate jazz, rock and world-music concerts (€20 to €30) at 7pm or 8pm at least a couple of nights a week (see the website for details). It morphs into a club from 11pm to 3am on Friday and Saturday nights.

STUTTGART & THE BLACK FOREST FREIBURG

ℹ Information

Available at the tourist office, the three-day WelcomeKarte, covering all public transport and the Schauinslandbahn, costs €25/15 per adult/child.

Police Station (Rotteckring) Freiburg's police station.

Post Office (Eisenbahnstrasse 58-62; ⊙ 8.30am-6.30pm Mon-Fri, 9am-2pm Sat) Main post office.

Tourist Office (📞 0761-388 1880; www.freiburg.de; Rathausplatz 2-4; ⊙ 8am-8pm Mon-Fri, 9.30am-5pm Sat, 10.30am-3.30pm Sun) Pick up the three-day WelcomeKarte at Freiburg's central tourist office.

ℹ Getting There & Around

AIR

Freiburg shares **EuroAirport** (BSL; 📞 in France 03 89 90 31 11; www.euroairport.com) with Basel (Switzerland) and Mulhouse (France). Low-cost airline easyJet flies from here to destinations including London, Berlin, Rome and Alicante.

BICYCLE

Bike paths run along the Dreisam River, leading westward to Breisach and then into France.

Freiburg Bikes (📞 0761-202 3426; Wentzingerstrasse 15; city bike 4hr/day €8/16, mountain/e-bike per day €20/25; ⊙ 9.30am-1pm & 2-7pm Mon-Sat, 10am-1pm & 2-6pm Sun, shorter hours in winter), in a glass-enclosed pavilion across the bridge from the Hauptbahnhof, rents bikes and sells cycling maps.

BUS

The **airport bus** (📞 0761-500 500; www.freiburger-reisedienst.de; one-way/return €26/42) goes hourly from Freiburg's bus station to EuroAirport.

Südbaden Bus (www.suedbadenbus.de) and **RVF** (www.rvf.de) operate bus and train links to towns and villages throughout the southern Black Forest. Single tickets for one/two/three zones cost €2.20/3.80/5.40; a 24-hour Regio24 ticket costs €5.50 for one person and €11 for two to five people.

Bus and tram travel within Freiburg is operated by **VAG** (www.vag-freiburg.de) and charged at the one-zone rate. Buy tickets from the vending machines or from the driver and validate upon boarding.

CAR & MOTORCYCLE

The Frankfurt–Basel A5 passes just west of Freiburg. The scenic B31 leads east through the Höllen Valley to Lake Constance. The B294 goes north into the Black Forest.

Car-hire agencies include **Europcar** (📞 0761-515 100; Lörracher Strasse 10) and **Avis** (📞 0761-197 19; St Georgener Strasse 7).

About 1.5km south of Martinstor, there's unmetered parking on some side streets (eg Türkenlouisstrasse). Otherwise, your best bet is to park at a free Park & Ride, such as the one at Bissierstrasse, a 10-minute ride from the centre on tram 1.

TRAIN

Freiburg is on a major north–south rail corridor, with frequent departures for destinations such as Basel (€19 to €24.20, 45 minutes) and Baden-Baden (€18.10 to €25.80, 45 minutes to one hour). Freiburg is also the western terminus of the Höllentalbahn to Donaueschingen via Neustadt (€5.40, 38 minutes, twice an hour). There's a local connection to Breisach (€5.40, 26 minutes, at least hourly).

Schauinsland

Freiburg seems tiny as you drift up above the city and into a tapestry of meadows and forest on the Schauinslandbahn (return adult/concession €12/11, one way €8.50/8; ⊙ 9am-5pm Oct-Jun, to 6pm Jul-Sep) to the 1284m Schauinsland peak (www.bergwelt-schauinsland.de). The lift provides a speedy link between Freiburg and the Black Forest highlands.

Up top there's a lookout tower commanding astounding views to the Rhine Valley and Alps, plus walking, cross-country and cycling trails that allow you to capture the scenery from many angles. Or you can bounce downhill on the 8km off-road scooter track (www.rollerstrecke.de; €22; ⊙ 2pm & 5pm Sun May-Jun, Sat & Sun Jul & Sep-Oct, Wed-Sun Aug), one of Europe's longest; it takes around an hour from top to bottom station. To reach Schauinslandbahn from Freiburg, take tram 2 to Günterstal and then bus 21 to Talstation.

On its quiet perch above the rippling hills of the Black Forest, Die Halde (📞 07602-944 70; www.halde.com; Oberried-Hofsgrund; d €124-157, mains €16-26.50; 🅿 @ 🏊) is a rustic-chic retreat, with an open fire crackling in the bar, calm rooms dressed in local wood and a glass-walled spa overlooking the valley. Martin Hegar cooks market-fresh dishes from trout to wild boar with panache in the wood-panelled restaurant.

Steinwasen Park

Steinwasen Park   AMUSEMENT PARK
(www.steinwasen-park.de; Steinwasen 1; adult/concession €23/19; ⊙ 9am-6pm late Mar-early Nov) Buried deep in the forest, the nature-focused Steinwasen Park is a big hit with families. A trail weaves past animal-friendly

enclosures, home to wild boar, ibex and burrowing marmots. One of the top attractions is a 218m-long hanging bridge, one of the world's longest. Steinwasen also has a bobsled run and a handful of whizzy rides such as Gletscherblitz and River Splash.

Todtnauer Wasserfall

Todtnauer Wasserfall WATERFALL
(☉ daylight hours) FREE Heading south on the Freiburg–Feldberg road, you'll glimpse the roaring Todtnauer Wasserfall. While the 97m falls are not as high as those in Triberg, they're every bit as spectacular – tumbling down sheer rock faces and illuminating the velvety hills with their brilliance. Hike the zigzagging 9km trail to Aftersteg for views over the cataract. Take care on paths in winter when the falls often freeze solid. The waterfall car park is on the L126.

St Peter

📞 07660 / POP 2550
The folk of the bucolic village of St Peter, on the southern slopes of Mt Kandel (1243m), are deeply committed to time-honoured traditions. On religious holidays, villagers still proudly don colourful, handmade Trachten (folkloric costumes).

The most outstanding landmark is the **Ehemaliges Benedikterkloster** (Former Benedictine Abbey; guided tours adult/concession €6/2; ☉ tours 11.30am Sun, 11am Tue, 2.30pm Thu), a rococo jewel designed by Peter Thumb of Vorarlberg. Many of the period's top artists collaborated on the sumptuous interior of the twin-towered red-sandstone church, including Joseph Anton Feuchtmayer, who carved the gilded Zähringer duke statues affixed to pillars. Guided tours (in German) to the monastery complex include the rococo library.

The **tourist office** (📞 07660-910 224; www.st-peter-schwarzwald.de; Klosterhof 11; ☉ 9am-noon & 3-5pm Mon-Fri) is under the archway leading to the Klosterhof (the abbey courtyard). A nearby information panel shows room availability.

By public transport, the best way to get from Freiburg to St Peter is to take the train to Kirchzarten (13 minutes, twice hourly) and then bus 7216 (23 minutes, twice hourly). St Peter is on the **Schwarzwald Panoramastrasse**, a 70km-long route from Waldkirch (17km northeast of Freiburg) to Feldberg with giddy mountain views.

Breisach

📞 07667 / POP 14,500
Rising above vineyards and the Rhine, Breisach is where the Black Forest spills into Alsace. Given its geographical and cultural proximity to France, it's little surprise that the locals share their neighbours' passion for a good bottle of plonk.

From the cobbled streets lined with pastel-painted houses you'd never guess that 85% of the town was flattened in WWII, so successful has been the reconstruction. Vauban's star-shaped French fortress-town of Neuf-Brisach (New Breisach), which made the Unesco World Heritage list in 2008, sits 4km west of Breisach.

◉ Sights & Activities

St Stephansmünster CHURCH
(☉ 9am-5pm Mon-Sat) High above the centre, the Romanesque and Gothic St Stephansmünster shelters a faded fresco cycle, Martin Schongauer's *The Last Judgment* (1491), and a magnificent altar triptych (1526) carved from linden wood. From the tree-shaded square outside, the Schänzletreppe leads down to Gutgesellentor, the gate where Pope John XXIII was scandalously caught fleeing the Council of Constance in 1415.

BFS BOAT TOUR
(www.bfs-info.de; Rheinuferstrasse; ☉ Apr-Sep) Boat excursions along the Rhine are run by BFS. A one-hour harbour tour costs €9.

🛏 Sleeping

DJH Hostel HOSTEL $
(📞 07667-7665; www.jugendherberge-breisach. de; Rheinuferstrasse 12; dm 1st/subsequent night €30.40/27) On the banks of the Rhine, this hostel has first-rate facilities, including a barbecue hut, volleyball court and access to the swimming pool next door.

ℹ Information

Tourist Office (📞 07667-940 155; http:// tourismus.breisach.de; Marktplatz 16; ☉ 9am-12.30pm & 1.30-6pm Mon-Fri, 10am-3pm Sat) The tourist office can advise on wine tasting and private rooms in the area.

ℹ Getting There & Around

Breisach's train station, 500m southeast of Marktplatz, serves Freiburg (€5.40, 25 minutes, at least hourly) and towns in the Kaiserstuhl. Buses go to Colmar, 22km west.

Breisach is a terrific base for free-wheeling over borders. Great rides include crossing the Rhine to the delightful French town of Colmar, or pedalling through terraced vineyards to Freiburg. Hire wheels from **Funbike** (☑ 07667-7733; Metzgergasse 1; 1/3 days €10/25; ⊙ 9am-noon & 5-7pm) opposite the tourist office.

Feldberg

☑ 07655 / POP 1880

At 1493m Feldberg is the Black Forest's highest mountain, and one of the few places here with downhill skiing. The actual mountaintop is treeless and not particularly attractive but on clear days the view southward towards the Alps is mesmerising.

Feldberg is also the name given to a cluster of five villages, of which Altglashütten is the hub.

Around 9km west of Altglashütten is Feldberg-Ort, in the heart of the 42-sq-km nature reserve that covers much of the mountain. Most of the ski lifts are here, including the scenic Feldbergbahn chairlift to the Bismarckdenkmal (Bismarck monument).

🏃 Activities

The Feldberg ski area comprises 28 lifts, all accessible with one ticket. Four groomed cross-country trails are also available. To hire skis, look out for the signs reading 'Skiverleih' or enquire at the tourist office.

Feldbergbahn CABLE CAR, VIEWPOINT
(www.feldbergbahn.de; adult/concession return €9.50/6.60; ⊙ 9am-5pm Jul-Sep, 9am-4.30pm May, Jun & Oct) This cable car whisks you to the 1450m summit of Feldberg in minutes. The panorama unfolding at the top reaches across the patchwork meadows and woods of the Black Forest all the way to the Vosges, Swiss and French Alps on clear days.

Haus der Natur HIKING
(☑ 07676-933 610; www.naturpark-suedschwarzwald.de; Dr-Pilet-Spur 4; ⊙ 10am-5pm) The eco-conscious Haus der Natur can advise on some of the area's great hiking opportunities, such as the rewarding 12km Feldberg–Steig (p226) to Feldberg summit. In winter, Feldberg's snowy heights are ideal for a stomp through twinkling woods. Strap on snowshoes to tackle the pretty 3km Seebuck-Trail or the more challenging 9km Gipfel-Trail. The Haus der Natur rents lightweight snowshoes for €10/5 per day for adults/children.

🛏 Sleeping

Naturfreundehaus HOSTEL $
(☑ 07655-336; www.jugendherberge-feldberg.de; Am Baldenweger Buck; dm €15) 🌿 In a Black Forest farmhouse a 30-minute walk from Feldberg's summit, this back-to-nature hostel uses renewable energy and serves fairtrade and organic produce at breakfast (€6). Surrounding views of wooded hills and comfy, pine-clad dorms make this a great spot for hiking in summer, and skiing and snowshoeing in winter.

Landhotel Sonneck HOTEL $$
(☑ 07655-211; www.sonneck-feldberg.de; Schwarzenbachweg 5; d €96-116; 🐾) Immaculate, light-filled rooms with pine furnishings and balconies are features at this hotel. The quaint restaurant (mains €8 to €15) dishes up hearty local fare.

ℹ Information

Tourist Office (Kirchgasse 1; ⊙ 8am-noon & 1-5pm Mon-Fri) Altglashütten's Rathaus harbours the tourist office, with stacks of information on activities and Nordic walking poles for rent.

ℹ Getting There & Away

Bärental and Altglashütten are stops on the Dreiseenbahn, linking Titisee with Seebrugg (Schluchsee). From the train station in Bärental, bus 7300 makes trips at least hourly to Feldberg-Ort (€2.20, 21 minutes).

From late December until the end of the season, shuttle buses run by Feldberg SBG link Feldberg and Titisee with the ski lifts (free with a lift ticket or Gästekarte).

If you're driving, take the B31 (Freiburg–Donaueschingen) to Titisee, then the B317. To get to Altglashütten, head down the B500 from Bärental.

Titisee-Neustadt

☑ 07651 / POP 11,860

Titisee is a cheerful summertime playground with a name that makes English-speaking travellers giggle. The shimmering bluegreen glacial lake, ringed by forest, has everyone diving for their cameras.

🏃 Activities

The forest trails around Titisee are hugely popular for Nordic walking, which, for the uninitiated, is walking briskly with poles to simultaneously exercise the upper body and legs. Snow transforms Titisee into a winter wonderland and a cross-country skiing magnet, with *Loipen* (tracks) threading through the hills and woods, including a 3km floodlit track for a starlit skate. The tourist office map highlights cross-country and Nordic walking trails in the area.

Seepromenade
WALKING, WATER SPORTS

Wander along the flowery Seestrasse promenade and you'll soon leave the crowds and made-in-China cuckoo clocks behind to find secluded bays ideal for swimming and picnicking. A lap of the lake is 7km. A laid-back way to appreciate its soothing beauty is to hire a rowing boat or pedalo at one of the set-ups along the lakefront; expect to pay around €6 per hour.

Strandbad Titisee
SWIMMING

(Strandbadstrasse 1; adult/concession €3.50/1.90; ⊙9am-7pm May-Sep) This lakefront lido has a pool and children's pool, a slide, floating raft and a volleyball area, as well as lawns for sunbathing. You can also rent kayaks and stand-up paddle boards here for €10/18 per half/full hour.

Badeparadies
SPA

(www.badeparadies-schwarzwald.de; Am Badeparadies 1; 3hr €18, incl sauna complex €22; ⊙10am-10pm Mon-Thu, 10am-11pm Fri, 9am-10pm Sat & Sun) This huge, glass-canopied leisure and wellness centre is a magnet year-round. You can lounge, cocktail in hand, by palm-fringed lagoons in Palmenoase, race down white-knuckle slides with gaggles of overexcited kids in Galaxy, or strip off in themed saunas with waterfalls and Black Forest views in the adults-only Wellnessoase.

🛏 Sleeping & Eating

Neubierhäusle
PENSION $

(☑07651-8230; www.neubierhaeusle.de; Neustädterstrasse 79; d €74-94, apt €134-174; 🅿🖰) Big forest views, piny air and pastures on the doorstep – this farmhouse is the perfect country retreat. Dressed in local wood, the light-filled rooms are supremely comfy, while apartments have space for families. Your hosts lay on a hearty breakfast spread and you can help yourself to free tea and fruit. It's on the L156, 3km northeast of the station.

Action Forest Active Hotel
GUESTHOUSE $$

(☑07651-825 60; www.action-forest-hotel.de; Neustädter Strasse 41; s €60-75, d €100-130, tr €130-180, q €160-230; 🅿🖰) You can't miss this green-fronted guesthouse, snuggled

up against the forest. It's run by a friendly family and contains spacious, light-filled rooms fitted out with country-style pine furnishings. It makes a great base for outdoorsy holidays, offering the whole shebang of activities – a climbing park, bike academy, winter sports school, guided hikes and stand-up paddle boarding.

Alemannenhof
HOTEL $$$

(☑07652-911 80; www.hotel-alemannenhof.de; Bruderhalde 21, Hinterzarten am Titisee; d €129-259; 🅿🖰🖰) A pool, private beach and contemporary rooms with transparent shower stalls and balconies overlooking Titisee await at this farmhouse-style hotel. Opening onto a lakefront terrace, the alpine restaurant (mains €22 to €34) serves regional cuisine with a twist, such as local beef with potato-rosemary purée and wild-garlic pasta.

❶ Information

Tourist Office (☑07652-1206 8120; www.titisee-neustadt.de; Strandbadstrasse 4; ⊙9am-6pm Mon-Fri, 10am-1pm & 3-6pm Sat, 10am-1pm Sun) The tourist office in the Kurhaus, 500m southwest of the train station, stocks walking and cycling maps.

❶ Getting There & Around

Train routes include the twice-hourly Höllentalbahn to Freiburg (€5.40, 40 minutes) and hourly services to Donaueschingen (€10, 50 minutes), Feldberg (€2.20, 12 minutes) and Schluchsee (€2.20, 22 minutes).

From Titisee train station, there are frequent services on bus 7257 to Schluchsee (€2.20, 40 minutes) and bus 7300 to Feldberg–Bärental (€2.20, 13 minutes).

Ski-Hirt (☑07651-922 80; Titiseestrasse 28; ⊙9am-6.30pm Mon-Fri, 9am-4pm Sat) rents reliable bikes and ski equipment, and can supply details on local cycling options.

Schluchsee

☑07656 / POP 2540

Photogenically poised above its namesake petrol-blue lake – the Black Forest's largest – and rimmed by forest, Schluchsee tempts you outdoors with pursuits such as swimming, windsurfing, hiking, cycling and, ahem, skinny-dipping from the secluded bays on the western shore. The otherwise sleepy resort jolts to life with sun-seekers in summer and cross-country skiers in winter.

KAISERSTUHL

Squeezed between the Black Forest and French Vosges, these low-lying volcanic hills in the Upper Rhine Valley yield highly quaffable wines, including fruity *Spätburgunder* (Pinot noir) and *Grauburgunder* (Pinot gris) varieties.

The grapes owe their quality to a unique microclimate, hailed as Germany's sunniest, and fertile loess (clay and silt) soil that retains heat during the night. Nature enthusiasts should look out for rarities like sand lizards, praying mantis and European bee-eaters.

The Breisach tourist office can advise on cellar tours, wine tastings, bike paths like the 55km **Kaiserstuhl-Tour** circuit, and trails such as the **Winzerweg** (Wine Growers' Trail), an intoxicating 15km hike from Achkarren to Riegel.

The Kaiserstuhlbahn does a loop around the Kaiserstuhl. Stops (where you may have to change trains) include Sasbach, Endingen, Riegel and Gottenheim.

Vitra Design Museum (www.design-museum.de; Charles-Eames-Strasse 1, Weil am Rhein; adult/concession €10/8, architectural tour €13/11; ⊙10am-6pm) Sharp angles contrast with graceful swirls on Frank Gehry's strikingly postmodern Vitra Design Museum. The blindingly white edifice hosts thought-provoking contemporary design exhibitions. Buildings on the nearby Vitra campus, designed by prominent architects like Nicholas Grimshaw, Zaha Hadid and Alvaro Siza, can be visited on a two-hour architectural tour, held in English at noon and 2pm daily.

Europa-Park (www.europapark.de; adult/concession €42.50/37; ⊙9am-6pm Apr-early Nov, to 8pm Aug–mid-Sep, 11am-7pm late Nov-early Jan) Germany's largest theme park, 35km north of Freiburg near Rust, is Europe in miniature. Get soaked fjord-rafting in Scandinavia before nipping across to England to race at Silverstone, or Greece to ride the water roller coaster Poseidon. Aside from white-knuckle thrills, Welt der Kinder amuses tots with labyrinths and Viking ships. When Mickey waltzed off to Paris, Europa-Park even got its own mousy mascot, Euromaus.

Shuttle buses (hourly in the morning) link Ringsheim train station, on the Freiburg–Offenburg line, with the park. By car, take the A5 exit to Rust (57b).

🏃 Activities

Aqua Fun Strandbad　　　　　　SWIMMING
(Strandbadstrasse; adult/concession €4/2.70; ⊙9am-7pm Jun-Sep) Popular with families, this lakefront lido has a heated pool, water slide and rapid river, sandy beach and volleyball court.

T Toth　　　　　　　　　　BOAT TOUR
(www.seerundfahrten.de) T Toth runs boat tours around Schluchsee, with stops in Aha, Seebrugg and the Strandbad. An hour-long round trip costs €9.50 (less for single stops). You can hire rowing boats and pedalos for €5/8 per half/full hour.

🛏 Sleeping & Eating

Decent beds are slim pickings in Schluchsee, though there are a few good-value pensions and farmstays – ask the tourist office.

Gasthof Hirschen　　　　　GUESTHOUSE $
(☑07656-989 40; www.hirschen-fischbach.de; Schluchseestrasse 9; s €49-51, d €74-92; 🅿🛜) It's worth going the extra mile to this farmhouse prettily perched on a hillside in Fischbach, 4km north of Schluchsee. The simple, quiet rooms are a good-value base for summer hiking and modest winter skiing. There's also a sauna, playground and a restaurant (mains €13 to €21) dishing up regional fare.

Seehof　　　　　　　INTERNATIONAL $$
(☑07656-988 9965; Kirchsteige 4; mains €8-18; ⊙11.30am-10.30pm) An inviting spot for a bite to eat, with a terrace overlooking the lake, Seehof has a menu packed with local fish and meat mains, salads, pizzas and ice cream.

ℹ Information

The train tracks and the B500 shadow the lake's eastern shore between the lakefront and the Schluchsee's town centre. The lake's western shore is accessible only by bike or on foot.

Tourist Office (☑07652-1206 8500; www. schluchsee.de; Fischbacher Strasse 7, Haus des Gastes; ⊙8am-5pm Mon-Thu, 9am-5pm Fri) Situated 150m uphill from the church, with maps and info on activities and accommodation.

❶ Getting There & Around

Trains go hourly to Feldberg–Altglashütten (€2.10, 11 minutes) and Titisee (€2.10, 22 minutes). Bus 7257 links Schluchsee three or four times daily with the Neustadt and Titisee train stations (€2.10, 40 minutes).

City, mountain and e-bikes can be rented for €11/12/23 per day at **Müllers** (An der Staumauer 1; ☺10am-6pm Apr-Oct). An hour's pedalo/rowing boat/motor boat hire costs €8/8/17.

Triberg

☏ 07722 / POP 5000

Home to Germany's highest waterfall, heir to the original 1915 black forest gateau recipe and nesting ground of the world's biggest cuckoos, Triberg leaves visitors reeling with superlatives. It was here that in bleak winters past folk huddled in snowbound farmhouses to carve the clocks that would drive the world cuckoo, and here that in a flash of brilliance the waterfall was harnessed to power the country's first electric street lamps in 1884.

◎ Sights & Activities

★ **Triberger Wasserfälle**   WATERFALL

(adult/concession/family €4/3.50/9.50; ☺9am-7pm Mar-early Nov, 25-30 Dec) Niagara they ain't but Germany's highest waterfalls do exude their own wild romanticism. The Gutach River feeds the seven-tiered falls, which drop a total of 163m and are illuminated until 10pm.

A paved trail accesses the cascades. Pick up a bag of peanuts at the ticket counter to feed the tame squirrels.

1. Weltgrösste Kuckucksuhr   LANDMARK

(First World's Largest Cuckoo Clock; ☏ 07722-4689; www.1weltgroesstekuckucksuhr.de; Untertalstrasse 28, Schonach; adult/concession €1.20/0.60; ☺9am-noon & 1-6pm) The 'world's oldest-largest cuckoo clock' kicked into gear in 1980 and took local clockmaker Joseph Dold three years to build by hand. A Dold family member is usually around to the explain the mechanism.

Haus der 1000 Uhren   CLOCK MUSEUM

(www.hausder1000uhren.de;   Hauptstrasse 79; ☺9.30am-6pm summer, to 5.30pm winter) A glockenspiel bashes out melodies and a cuckoo greets his fans with a hopelessly croaky squawk on the hour at the kitschy House of 1000 Clocks, a wonderland of clocks from traditional to trendy. The latest

quartz models feature a sensor that sends the cuckoo to sleep after dark!

Sanitas Spa   .   SPA

(☏07722-860 20; www.sanitas-spa.de; Gartenstrasse 24; 2hr pass €15, half-day €26-30, full-day €45-50; ☺9.30am-8pm) Fronted by wraparound windows overlooking Triberg's forested hills, Parkhotel Wehrle's day spa is gorgeous. This is a serene spot to wind down, with its spacily lit kidney-shaped pool, exquisitely tiled hammams, steam rooms, whirlpool and waterbed meditation room. Treatments vary from rhassoul clay wraps to reiki. Admission is cheaper on weekdays. Towel and robe hire is available for €8.

🛏 Sleeping & Eating

Kukucksnest   B&B $

(☏07722-869 487; Wallfahrtstrasse 15; d €64) Above the shop of master woodcarver Gerald Burger, is the beautiful nest he has carved for his guests, featuring blonde-wood rooms with flat-screen TVs. The *Wurzelsepp* (faces carved into fir tree roots) by the entrance supposedly ward off evil spirits.

★ **Parkhotel Wehrle**   HISTORIC HOTEL $$$

(☏07722-860 20; www.parkhotel-wehrle.de; Gartenstrasse 24; s €95-105, €145-179; [P][🎧][❄]) This 400-year-old hotel has a recommended integrated day spa. Often with a baroque or Biedermeier touch, quarters are roomy and beautifully furnished with antiques; the best have Duravit whirlpool tubs. Hemingway once waxed lyrical about the trout he ordered at the hotel's venerable **restaurant** (www.parkhotel-wehrle.de; Gartenstrasse 24; mains €13-32; ☺6-9pm daily, noon-2pm Sun).

★ **Café Schäfer**   CAFE $

(☏07722-4465;   www.cafe-schaefer-triberg.de; Hauptstrasse 33; cake €3-4; ☺9am-6pm Mon, Tue, Thu & Fri, 8am-6pm Sat, 11am-6pm Sun) Confectioner Claus Schäfer uses the original 1915 recipe for black forest gateau to prepare this sinful treat that layers chocolate cake perfumed with cherry brandy, whipped cream and sour cherries and wraps it all in more cream and shaved chocolate. Trust us, it's worth the calories.

❶ Information

Triberg's main drag is the B500, which runs more or less parallel to the Gutach River. The town's focal point is the Marktplatz, a steep 1.2km uphill walk from the Bahnhof.

Triberg markets itself as Das Ferienland (The Holiday Region; www.dasferienland.de).

STUTTGART & THE BLACK FOREST TRIBERG

DRIVE TIME

The Schwarzwald may be a forest but it sure is a big 'un and you'll need a car to reach its out-of-the-way corners.

Schwarzwald-Hochstrasse (Black Forest Highway; www.schwarzwaldhochstrasse.de) Swoon over views of the mist-wreathed Vosges Mountains, heather-flecked forests and glacial lakes like Mummelsee on this high-altitude road, meandering 60km from Baden-Baden to Freudenstadt on the B500.

Badische Weinstrasse (Baden Wine Road; www.deutsche-weinstrassen.de) From Baden-Baden south to Lörrach, this 160km route corkscrews through the red-wine vineyards of Ortenau, the Pinot noir of Kaiserstuhl and Tuniberg, and the white-wine vines of Markgräflerland.

Schwarzwald-Tälerstrasse (Black Forest Valley Road) What scenery! Twisting 100km from Rastatt to Alpirsbach, this road dips into the forest-cloaked hills and half-timbered towns of the Murg and Kinzig valleys.

Deutsche Uhrenstrasse (German Clock Road; www.deutscheuhrenstrasse.de) A 320km loop starting in Villingen-Schwenningen that revolves around the story of clockmaking in the Black Forest. Stops include Furtwangen and cuckoo-crazy Triberg.

Grüne Strasse (Green Road; www.gruene-strasse.de) Linking the Black Forest with the Rhine Valley and French Vosges, this 160km route zips through Kirchzarten, Freiburg, Breisach, Colmar and Münster.

Tourist Office (☑ 07722-866 490; www.triberg.de; Wallfahrtstrasse 4; ⏰ 9am-5pm Mon-Fri, 10am-5pm Sat & Sun) Inside the Schwarzwald-Museum. Stocks walking (€3), cross-country ski trail (€2) and mountain bike (€6.90) maps.

ⓘ Getting There & Away

The Schwarzwaldbahn train line loops southeast to Konstanz (€23.50, 1½ hours, hourly), and northwest to Offenburg (€12.10, 46 minutes, hourly).

Bus 7150 travels north through the Gutach and Kinzig Valleys to Offenburg; bus 7265 heads south to Villingen via St Georgen. Local buses operate between the Bahnhof and Marktplatz, and to the nearby town of Schonach (hourly).

Stöcklewaldturm

Triberg's waterfall is the trailhead for an attractive 6.5km walk to Stöcklewaldturm (1070m). A steady trudge through spruce forest and pastures brings you to this 19th-century **lookout tower** (admission €0.50; ⏰ 10am-8pm Wed-Mon), where the 360-degree views stretch from the Swabian Alps to the snowcapped Alps. Footpaths head off in all directions from the summit, where the woodsy **cafe** (snacks €2.50-7; ⏰ 10am-8pm Wed-Mon) is an inviting spot for a beer and snack or, in winter, hot chocolate. The car park on the L175 is a 10-minute stroll from the tower.

Martinskapelle

Named after the tiny chapel at the head of the Breg Valley, **Martinskapelle** attracts cross-country skiers in winter and hikers when the snow melts. The steep road up to the 1100m peak negotiates some pretty hairy switchbacks, swinging past wood-shingle farmhouses that cling to forested slopes.

To immerse yourself in the solace and wonderful views, stay the night at family-run **Höhengasthaus Kolmenhof** (☑ 07723-931 00; www.kolmenhof.de; An der Donauquelle; s/d €55/88; P 🛜 🐾). Sitting right at the main source of the Danube, the guesthouse has e-bike rental, a sauna for post-hiking or skiing relaxation and a rustic restaurant (mains €9 to €19). The speciality is fresh trout, served smoked, roasted in almond butter or poached in white wine.

Bus 7270 runs roughly hourly from the Marktplatz in Triberg to Escheck (€2.10, 20 minutes); from here it's a 4.5km walk to Martinskapelle. If you're driving, take the B500 from Triberg following signs to Schwarzenbach, Weissenbach and the K5730 to Martinskapelle.

Villingen-Schwenningen

☑ 07721 / POP 81,020

Villingen and Schwenningen trip simultaneously off the tongue, yet each town has its own flavour and history. Villingen once belonged to the Grand Duchy of Baden and Schwenningen to the duchy of Württemberg, conflicting allegiances that apparently can't be reconciled. Villingen, it must be said, is the more attractive of the twin towns.

Encircled by impenetrable walls that look as though they were built by the mythical local giant Romäus, Villingen's Altstadt is a late-medieval time capsule, with cobbled streets and handsome patrician houses. Though locals nickname it the *Städtle* (little town), the name seems inappropriate during February's mammoth weeklong *Fasnet* celebrations.

◉ Sights & Activities

Münster   CATHEDRAL
(Münsterplatz; ◷9am-6pm) The main crowd-puller in Villingen's Altstadt is the red-sandstone, 12th-century Münster with its disparate spires: one overlaid with colour-ed tiles, the other spiky and festooned with gargoyles. The Romanesque portals with haut-relief doors depict dramatic biblical scenes.

Münsterplatz   SQUARE
The Münsterplatz is presided over by the step-gabled Altes Rathaus (Old Town Hall) and Klaus Ringwald's Münsterbrunnen, a bronze fountain and a tongue-in-cheek portrayal of characters that have shaped Villingen's history. The square throngs with activity on Wednesday and Saturday mornings when market stalls are piled high with local bread, meat, cheese, fruit and flowers.

Franziskaner Museum   MUSEUM
(Rietgasse 2; adult/concession €5/3; ◷1-5pm Tue-Sat, 11am-5pm Sun) Next to the 13th-century Riettor and occupying a former Franciscan monastery, the Franziskaner Museum skips merrily through Villingen's history and heritage. Standouts include Celtic artefacts unearthed at Magdalenenberg, 30 minutes' walk south of Villingen's centre. Dating to 616 BC, the mystery-enshrouded site is one of the largest Hallstatt burial chambers ever discovered in Central Europe, and is shaded by a 1000-year-old oak tree.

Spitalgarten   GARDENS
Tucked behind the Franziskaner is the Spitalgarten, a park flanked by the original city walls. Here your gaze will be drawn to Romäusturm, a lofty 13th-century thieves' tower named after fabled local leviathan Remigius Mans (Romäus for short).

Kneippbad   SWIMMING
(Am Kneippbad 1; adult/child €4.20/2.80; ◷6.30am-8pm Mon-Fri, 8am-8pm Sat & Sun mid-May–early Sep) If the sun's out, take a 3km walk northwest of the Altstadt to this forest lido, a family magnet with its outdoor pools, slides and volleyball courts.

🛏 Sleeping & Eating

Haus Bächle   GUESTHOUSE $
(☑07721-597 29; Am Kneippbad 5; s/d €16/32; 🅿) This half-timbered house overlooks the flowery Kurgarten. The tidy rooms are an absolute bargain and the Kneippbad is next door for early-morning swims.

Rindenmühle   HOTEL $$
(☑07721-886 80; www.rindenmuehle.de; Am Kneippbad 9; s €78-105, d €120-145; 🅿🛜) Next to the Kneippbad, this converted watermill houses one of Villingen's smartest hotels, with forest walks right on its doorstep. Rooms are slick and decorated in muted hues. In the restaurant (mains €26 to €36), Martin Weisser creates award-winning flavours using home-grown organic produce, including chickens, geese and herbs from his garden.

Zampolli   CAFE $
(Rietstrasse 33; ice-cream cone €1; ◷9.30am-10.30pm Mon-Sat, 10.30am-10.30pm Sun Feb–mid-Nov) For an espresso or creamy gelati, head to this Italian-run cafe. By night, the pavement terrace facing Riettor is a laid-back spot for a drink.

Schlachthof   GERMAN $$
(☑07721-878 7935; www.schlachthof-vs.de; Schlachthausstrasse 11; mains €11-22; ◷11.45am-2pm & 6pm-midnight Tue-Fri, 6pm-midnight Sat, 11.45am-2pm Sun; ♿) Wine-red walls, globe lights and wood panelling set the scene at this smart brasserie-style restaurant, a 10-minute stroll south of the Altstadt. The cooking is a regional-Mediterranean mix, with dishes such as chicken breast in rosemary butter with market veg and *Tafelspitz* (boiled beef). The €8.40 two-course lunch is a bargain.

❶ Information

Post Office (Bahnhofstrasse 6)

Villingen Tourist Office (☑07721-822 525; www.tourismus-vs.de; Rietgasse 2; ◷10am-5pm Mon-Sat, 11am-5pm Sun) In the Franziskaner Museum. You can pick up the itour audioguide in English; up to three hours costs €5. E-bikes are also available for rent for €10/20 per half/full day.

CLAUS SCHÄFER, CONFECTIONER

Want to whip up your own black forest gateau back home? Claus Schäfer reveals how.

All About Cake Baking a black forest gateau isn't rocket science but it involves time, practice and top-quality ingredients. Eat the cake the day you make it, when it is freshest, and never freeze it or you will lose the aroma.

Secrets in the Mix Whip the cream until silky, blend in gelatine and two shots of quality kirsch. Mine comes from a local distillery and is 56% proof. The compote needs tangy cherries, sugar, cherry juice and a pinch of cinnamon. The bottom layer of sponge should be twice as thick as the other two, so it can support the compote without collapsing.

Finishing Touches These are important: spread the gateau with cream, then decorate with piped cream, cherries, chocolate shavings and a dusting of icing sugar.

Other Regional Flavours When in the Black Forest, try the fresh trout, smoked ham and *Kirschwasser* sold locally by farmers. The quality is higher and prices lower than elsewhere.

❶ Getting There & Around

Villingen's Bahnhof is on the scenic Schwarzwaldbahn train line from Konstanz (€19.80, 70 minutes) to Triberg (€6.10, 22 minutes) and Offenburg (€17.90, 70 minutes). Trains to Stuttgart (€27.90 to €29.50, 1¾ hours) involve a change in Rottweil, and to Freiburg (€19.80 to €29.60, two hours) a change in Donaueschingen.

From Villingen, buses 7265 and 7270 make regular trips north to Triberg. Frequent buses (eg line 1) link Villingen with Schwenningen.

Villingen-Schwenningen is just west of the A81 Stuttgart–Singen motorway and is also crossed by the B33 to Triberg and the B27 to Rottweil.

Rottweil

☑ 0741 / POP 25,660

Baden-Württemberg's oldest town is the strapline of Roman-rooted Rottweil, founded in AD 73. But a torrent of bad press about the woofer with a nasty nip means that most folk readily associate the town with the Rottweiler, which was indeed bred here as a hardy butchers' dog until recently. Fear not, the Rottweiler locals are much tamer.

The sturdy 13th-century Schwarzes Tor is the gateway to Hauptstrasse and the well-preserved Altstadt, a cluster of red-roofed, pastel-painted houses. Nearby at No 6, the curvaceous Hübschen Winkel will make you look twice with its 45-degree kink. Just west on Münsterplatz, the late Romanesque Münster-Heiliges-Kreuz features some striking Gothic stonework and ribbed vaulting. Equally worth a peek is the Roman bath (Hölderstrasse; ⊙ daylight hours) FREE, a

45m-by-42m bathing complex unearthed in 1967, about 1km south of the Altstadt.

The tourist office (☑ 0741-494 280; www.rottweil.de; Hauptstrasse 21; ⊙ 9.30am-5.30pm Mon-Fri, 9.30am-12.30pm Sat) can advise on accommodation, tours and biking the Neckartal-Radweg.

Rottweil is just off the A81 Stuttgart–Singen motorway. Trains run at least hourly to Stuttgart (€22.70, 1½ hours) and Villingen (€3.40, 25 minutes).

Unterkirnach

☑ 07721 / POP 2730

Nestled among velvety green hills, low-key Unterkirnach appeals to families and outdoorsy types. Kids can slide and climb to their heart's content at the all-weather play centre Spielscheune (Schlossbergweg 4; admission €4.50; ⊙ 2-7pm Mon-Fri, 11am-7pm Sat & Sun), or toddle uphill to the farm to meet inquisitive goats and Highland cattle (feeding time is 3pm). In summer, the village is a great starting point for forest hikes, with 130km of marked walking trails, while in winter there are 50km of *Loipen* (cross-country ski tracks) and some terrific slopes to sledge.

Picturesquely perched above Unterkirnach, Ackerloch Grillschopf (www.ackerloch.de; Unteres Ackerloch; light meals €4-11; ⊙ 11.30am-midnight Wed-Mon) is a rickety barn, brimming with rustic warmth in winter and with a beer garden overlooking a broad valley in summer. Occasionally there is a suckling pig roasting on the spit and you can grill your own steaks and sausages on the barbecue.

Bus 61 runs roughly hourly between Unterkirnach and Villingen (€3.30, 18 minutes).

LAKE CONSTANCE

Nicknamed the *schwäbische Meer* (Swabian Sea), Lake Constance is Central Europe's third-largest lake and it straddles three countries: Germany, Austria and Switzerland. Formed by the Rhine Glacier during the last ice age and fed and drained by that same sprightly river today, this whopper of a lake measures 63km long by 14km wide and up to 250m deep. There is a certain novelty effect in the fact that this is the only place in the world where you can wake up in Germany, cycle across to Switzerland for lunch and make it to Austria in time for afternoon tea, strudel and snapshots of the Alps.

Taking in meadows and vineyards, orchards and wetlands, beaches and Alpine foothills, the lake's landscapes are like a 'greatest hits' of European scenery. Culture? It's all here, from baroque churches to Benedictine abbeys, Stone Age dwellings to Roman forts, and medieval castles to zeppelins.

Come in spring for blossoms and autumn for new wine, fewer crowds and top visibility when the warm *föhn* blows. Summers are crowded, but best for swimming and camping. Almost everything shuts from November to February, when fog descends and the first snowflakes dust the Alps.

🛈 Getting There & Around

The most enjoyable way to cross the lake is by ferry. Konstanz is the main hub but Meersburg and Friedrichshafen also have plentiful ferry options.

Although most towns have a train station (Meersburg is an exception), in some cases buses provide the only land connections. **Euregio Bodensee** (www.euregiokarte.com), which groups all Lake Constance–area public transport, publishes a free *Fahrplan* with schedules for all train, bus and ferry services.

The **Euregio Bodensee Tageskarte** (www.euregiokarte.com; €18/24/31 for one/two/all zones) gets you all-day access to land transport around Lake Constance, including areas in Austria and Switzerland. It's sold at train stations and ferry docks. Children pay half price.

CAR FERRY

The roll-on roll-off **Konstanz–Meersburg car ferry** (www.sw.konstanz.de; car up to 4m incl driver/bicycle/pedestrian €9.30/5.20/2.80) runs 24 hours a day, except when high water levels prevent it from docking. The ferry runs every 15 minutes from 5.35am to 8.50pm, every 30 minutes from 8.50pm to midnight and every hour from midnight to 5.35am. The crossing, affording superb views from the top deck, takes 15 minutes.

DON'T MISS

CELEBRATE THE FIFTH SEASON

Boisterous and totally bonkers, the Swabian-Alemannic Fasnacht or *Fasnet* (not to be confused with Carnival) is a 500-year-old rite to banish winter and indulge in pre-Lenten feasting, parades, flirting and all-night drinkathons. Starting on Epiphany, festivities reach a crescendo the week before Ash Wednesday. Dress up to join the party, memorise a few sayings to dodge the witches, and catch the flying sausages – anything's possible, we swear. For *Fasnacht* at its traditional best, try the following:

Rottweil Fasnacht (www.narrenzunft.rottweil.de; Rottweil) At Monday's 8am *Narrensprung,* thousands of jester-like *Narros* in baroque masks ring through Baden-Württemberg's oldest town. Look out for the devil-like Federhannes and the Guller riding a cockerel.

Schramberg Fasnacht (www.narrenzunft-schramberg.de; Schramberg) Parade protagonists include the *hoorige Katz* (hairy cat) and the hopping Hans. Even more spectacular, however, is Da-Bach-Na-Fahrt, where characters hurtle down the river in wooden bathtubs.

Elzach Fasnacht (www.schuttig.info; Elzach) *Trallaho!* Wearing a hand-carved mask and a tricorn hat adorned with snail shells, *Schuttige* (ghoulish masked characters) dash through Elzach's streets cracking *Saublodere* (pig bladders) – dodge them unless you wish for many children! Sunday's torchlit parade and Shrove Tuesday's afternoon *Schuttigumzug* are the must-sees.

NATURPARK OBERE DONAU

Upper Danube Valley Nature Reserve (www.naturpark-obere-donau.de) Theatrically set against limestone, cave-riddled cliffs, dappled with pine and beech woods that are burnished gold in autumn, and hugging the Danube's banks, the Upper Danube Valley Nature Reserve bombards you with rugged splendour. Stick to the autobahn, however, and you'll be none the wiser. To fully explore the nature reserve, slip into a bicycle saddle or walking boots, and hit the trail.

One of the finest stretches is between Fridingen and Beuron, a 12.5km ridge-top walk of three to four hours. The signposted, easy-to-navigate trail runs above ragged cliffs, affording eagle's-eye views of the meandering Danube, which has almost 2850km to go before emptying into the Black Sea. The vertigo-inducing outcrop of Laibfelsen is a great picnic spot. From here, the path dips in and out of woodlands and meadows flecked with purple thistles. In Beuron the big draw is the working Benedictine abbey, one of Germany's oldest, dating to 1077. The lavish stucco-and-fresco church is open to visitors. See the website www.beuron.de for more details.

Fridingen and Beuron lie on the L277, 45km east of Villingen.

The dock in Konstanz, served by local bus 1, is 4km northeast of the centre along Mainaustrasse. In Meersburg, car ferries leave from a dock 400m northwest of the old town.

PASSENGER FERRY

The most useful lines, run by German **BSB** (www.bsb-online.com) and Austrian **OBB** (www.bodenseeschifffahrt.at), link Konstanz with ports such as Meersburg (€5.90, 30 minutes), Friedrichshafen (€12.70, 1¾ hours), Lindau (€16.70, three hours) and Bregenz (€17.80, 3½ hours); children aged six to 15 years pay half-price. The website lists timetables in full.

Der Katamaran (www.der-katamaran.de; adult/6-14yr €10.20/5.10) is a sleek passenger service that takes 50 minutes to make the Konstanz–Friedrichshafen crossing (hourly from 6am to 7pm, plus hourly from 8pm to midnight on Fridays and Saturdays from mid-May to early October).

Konstanz

📞 07531 / POP 84,690

Sidling up to the Swiss border, bisected by the Rhine and outlined by the Alps, Konstanz sits prettily on the northwestern shore of Lake Constance. Roman emperors, medieval traders and the bishops of the 15th-century Council of Constance have all left their mark on this alley-woven town, mercifully spared from the WWII bombings that obliterated other German cities.

When the sun comes out, Konstanz is a feel-good university town with a lively buzz and upbeat bar scene, particularly in the cobbled Altstadt and the harbour where the voluptuous *Imperia* turns. In summer the lo-

cals, nicknamed *Seehasen* (lake hares), head outdoors to the leafy promenade and enjoy lazy days in lakefront lidos.

◎ Sights

⭐ **Münster**   CATHEDRAL
(tower adult/child €2/1; ⊙10am-6pm Mon-Sat, 10am-6pm Sun, tower 10am-5pm Mon-Sat, 12.30-5.30pm Sun) Crowned by a filigreed spire and looking proudly back on 1000 years of history, the sandstone Münster was the church of the diocese of Konstanz until 1821. Its interior is an architectural potpourri of Romanesque, Gothic, Renaissance and baroque styles. Standouts include the 15th-century Schnegg, an ornate spiral staircase in the northern transept, to the left of which a door leads to the 1000-year-old crypt. From the crypt's polychrome chapel, you enter the sublime Gothic cloister.

On cloudless days, it's worth ascending the tower for broad views over the city and the lake.

Römersiedlung   RUIN
(Münsterplatz; tour €1; ⊙6pm Sun) The glass pyramid in front of the Münster shelters the Römersiedlung, the 3rd-century-AD remains of the Roman fort Constantia, which gave the city its name. You'll only get a sneak peek from above, so join one of the guided tours that begin at the tourist office for a touch of magic as a staircase opens from the cobbles and leads down to the ruins.

Rathaus   HISTORIC BUILDING
(City Hall; Kanzleistrasse) Slightly south of the Münster, the flamboyantly frescoed Renais-

Lake Constance

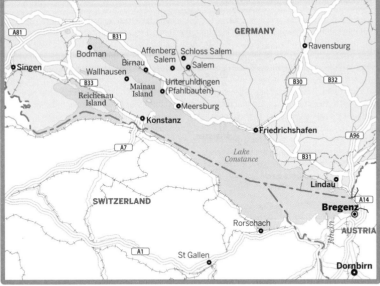

sance Rathaus occupies the former linen weavers' guildhall. Behind it you'll find a peaceful arcaded courtyard.

Niederburg
AREA

Best explored on foot, Konstanz' cobbled heart, Niederburg, stretches north from the Münster to the Rhine. The twisting lanes lined with half-timbered houses are the place to snoop around galleries and antique shops.

Rosgartenmuseum
MUSEUM

(www.rosgartenmuseum-konstanz.de; Rosgartenstrasse 3-5; adult/concession €3/1.50, 1st Sun of the month & after 2pm Wed free; ⊙10am-6pm Tue-Fri, 10am-5pm Sat & Sun) The one-time butchers' guildhall now harbours the Rosgartenmuseum, spotlighting regional art and history, with an emphasis on medieval panel painting and sculpture.

Sea Life
AQUARIUM

(www.visitsealife.com/konstanz; Hafenstrasse 9; adult/child €17.50/12.95; ⊙10am-5pm) Running a dragnet through your wallet, the borderline kitsch Sea Life immerses you in an underwater world. Highlights include a shipwreck where you can handle starfish and get stingray close-ups, a shark tunnel, penguins, and a creepy corner blubbing with oddities like frogfish and, ugh, giant isopods.

Kloster Zoffingen
CONVENT

(Brückengasse 15) The 13th-century Kloster Zoffingen is Konstanz' only remaining convent, still in the hands of Dominican nuns.

Rheintorturm
TOWER

(Rhine Gate Tower; Rheinsteig) On the Rheinsteig is the medieval Rheintorturm, a defensive tower with a pyramid-shaped red-tile roof.

Pulverturm
TOWER

(Gunpowder Tower; Rheinsteig) About 200m west along the river is the squat 14th-century Pulverturm tower, with 2m-thick walls.

Domprobstei
HISTORIC BUILDING

(Rheingasse 20) The orange-red, baroque Domprobstei was once the residence of the cathedral provosts.

Konzilgebäude
HISTORIC BUILDING

(Council Building; Konzilstrasse) Look out for the white dormered Konzilgebäude, built in 1388, which served as a granary and warehouse before Pope Martin V was elected here in 1417. Today it's a conference and concert hall.

Zeppelin Monument
MONUMENT

(Stadtgarten) The Zeppelin Monument shows the airship inventor Count Ferdinand von Zeppelin in an Icarus-like pose. He was born in 1838 on the Insel islet.

Konstanz

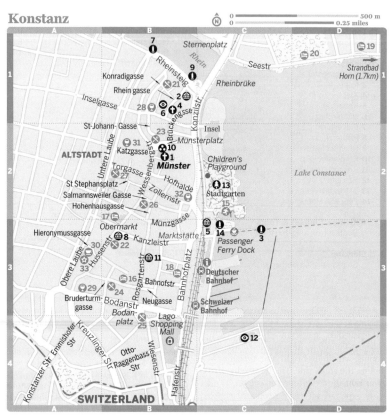

Stadtgarten
PARK

With its landscaped flower beds, plane trees and children's playground, the Stadtgarten is a fine place to kick back and enjoy dreamy views out over Lake Constance.

🏃 Activities

For some ozone-enriched summer fun, grab your bathers and head to the lake.

Strandbad Horn
BEACH

(Eichhornstrasse 100; ⊙mid-May–Sep) **FREE** This lakefront beach, 4km northeast of the centre, has sunbathing lawns, a kiddie pool, playground, volleyball courts and even a naturist area.

La Canoa
CANOEING

(www.lacanoa.com; Robert-Bosch-Strasse 4; canoe/kayak 3hr €14/18, per day €21/27; ⊙10am-12.30pm & 2-6pm Tue-Fri, 10am-4pm Sat) La Canoa has canoe rental points in all major towns on the lake; see the website for details.

Bootsvermietung Konstanz
BOATING

(Stadtgarten; per hr €12-32; ⊙11am-7pm Easter–mid-Oct) This boat rental in the Stadtgarten has pedalos for trundling across the lake.

🛌 Sleeping

Rock up between November and mid-March and you may find some places closed. The tourist office has a free booking service and a list of private rooms.

Glückseeligkeit Herberge
GUESTHOUSE **$**

(☏07531-902 2075; www.herberge-konstanz.de; Neugasse 20; s €30-50, d €50-70; 🖎) What a sweet deal this little guesthouse is. Housed in a period building in the Altstadt, it shelters petite but attractively decorated rooms. The attic room has direct access to the roof terrace, which peers over a jumble of rooftops to the cathedral spire. There's also a shared lounge, kitchen and patio. E-bikes are available for rental.

Konstanz

Hotel Barbarossa   HISTORIC HOTEL $$

(☑ 07531-128 990; www.barbarossa-hotel.com; Obermarkt 8-12; s €59-79, d €99-140; ☎) This 600-year-old patrician house features parquet-floored, individually decorated rooms, which are bright and appealing if a tad on the small side. The terrace has views over Konstanz' rooftops and spires.

Hotel Halm   HOTEL $$

(☑ 07531-1210; www.hotel-halm-konstanz.de; Bahnhofplatz 6; s €110-145, s €130-220; ☎) A joyous hop and skip from the lake and Altstadt, this late-19th-century pile has warm, elegantly furnished rooms with marble bathrooms; upgrade if you want a balcony with lake view. Skip the €17 breakfast and hit a nearby bakery instead.

Villa Barleben   HISTORIC HOTEL $$$

(☑ 07531-942 330; www.hotel-barleben.de; Seestrasse 15; s €75-165, d €95-255; ☎) Gregariously elegant, this 19th-century villa's sunny rooms and corridors are sprinkled with antiques and ethnic art. The rambling lakefront gardens are ideal for dozing in a *Strandkorb* (wicker beach lounger), G&T in hand, or enjoying lunch on the terrace.

Riva   BOUTIQUE HOTEL $$$

(☑ 07531-363 090; www.hotel-riva.de; Seestrasse 25; s €110-230, d €200-320; P ☎ ☒) This ultra-chic contender has crisp white spaces, glass walls and a snail-like stairwell. Zenlike rooms with hardwood floors feature perks such as (like it!) free minibars. A rooftop pool, spa area and gym, and a gourmet restaurant and terrace overlooking the lake, seal the deal.

✖ Eating

Münsterplatz and Markstätte are peppered with pizzerias, snack bars and gelaterias. Watch out for rip-offs around Stadtgarten.

Voglhaus   CAFE $

(Wessenbergstrasse 8; light meals €5-8; ⊙ 9am-6.30pm Mon-Sat, 11am-6pm Sun; ☑) Locals flock to the 'bird house' for its chilled vibe and contemporary wood-and-stone interior, warmed by an open fire in winter. Wood-oven bread with spreads, wholegrain

---

ⓘ BODENSEE ERLEBNISKARTE

The three-day **Bodensee Erlebniskarte** (adult/child €72/37, not incl ferries €40/20), available at area tourist and ferry offices from late March to mid-October, allows free travel on almost all boats and mountain cableways on and around Lake Constance (including its Austrian and Swiss shores). It also includes free entry to more than 160 tourist attractions and museums. There are also seven-day (adult/child €97/48) and 14-day (adult/child €140/70) versions.

ONE LAKE, TWO WHEELS, THREE COUNTRIES

Bodensee Radweg (www.boden-see-radweg.com) When the weather warms, there is no better way to explore Bodensee (Lake Constance) than with your bum in a saddle. The well-marked Bodensee Cycle Path is a 273km loop of Lake Constance, taking in vineyards, meadows, orchards, wetlands and historic towns. There are plenty of small beaches where you can stop for a refreshing dip in the lake. See the website for itineraries and maps. Bike hire is available in most towns for between €10 and €20 per day. While the entire route takes roughly a week, ferries and trains make it possible to cover shorter chunks, such as Friedrichshafen–Konstanz–Meersburg, in a weekend.

bagels, wraps and cupcakes pair nicely with smoothies and speciality coffees like Hansel and Gretel (with gingerbread syrup).

Zeitlos GERMAN $
(☑07531-189 384; St Stephansplatz 25; snacks €4-10; ☺10am-1am Mon-Fri, 10am-6pm Sat & Sun) Behind Stephanskirche, this beamed, stone-walled bistro overflows with regulars. It's a cosy spot for brunch or filling snacks like *Wurstsalat* (sausage salad) and *Maultaschen*, the local take on ravioli. Sit in the ivy-draped courtyard in summer. Gluten-free dishes are available.

Maximilian's DELI $
(Hussenstrasse 9; cakes €2.50, lunch specials €7.90-12.80; ☺10am-7pm Mon-Fri, 10am-6.30pm Sat) Fancy a picnic by the lake? Stop by this central deli for fresh bread, cheese, ham, wine and other goodies. It's also a snug spot for coffee and cake or light lunch specials.

La Bodega TAPAS $$
(☑07531-277 88; Schreibergasse 40; tapas €5-10.50; ☺5-11pm Tue-Sat) Squirrelled away in Niederburg, this candy-bright bodega with tiny terrace whips up tapas from *papas canarias* (Canarian potatoes) to stuffed calamari.

Münsterhof GERMAN $$
(☑07531-363 8427; Münsterplatz 3; mains €9-22; ☺11.30am-1am Sun-Thu, to 2am Fri, to 3am Sat; ☑⊕) Tables set up in front of the Münster, a slick bistro interior and a lunchtime buzz

have earned Münsterhof a loyal local following. Dishes from cordon bleu with pan-fried potatoes to asparagus-filled *Maultaschen* in creamy chive sauce are substantial and satisfying. The €7.90 lunch is great value.

Tolle Knolle INTERNATIONAL $$
(☑07531-175 75; Bodanplatz 9; mains €10-18; ☺11am-11pm; ⊕) On a fountain-dotted square with alfresco seating, this art-slung restaurant lives up to its 'great potato' moniker. Potatoes come in various guises: with Wiener schnitzel, beer-battered fish and on the signature pizza.

San Martino INTERNATIONAL $$$
(☑07531-284 5678; www.san-martino.net; Bruderturmgasse 3; mains €26-36, menus €56-115; ☺11.30am-2pm & 5.30-10pm Tue-Sat) A class act, this Michelin-starred restaurant slumbers against the old city walls. Exposed stone, muted colours, soft light and bistro seating create an understated yet elegant feel. Jochen Fecht's beautifully cooked food has a seasonal touch – be it sesame-crusted yellowfin tuna with asparagus or wine-braised veal cheeks with creamy polenta. Vegans are also well catered for.

🍷 Drinking & Entertainment

A vibrant student population fuels Konstanz' after-dark scene. For the low-down, see www.party-news.de (in German). Head to the harbour for drinks with a lake view.

Klimperkasten BAR
(Bodanstrasse 40; ☺6pm-1am Mon-Thu, 6pm-2am Fri & Sat) Indie kids, garage and old-school fans all hail this retro cafe, which gets clubbier after dark when DJs work the decks. Occasionally hosts gigs.

Schwarze Katz BAR
(Katzgasse 8; ☺9.30am-midnight Tue-Sat, 9.30am-6pm Sun) With its relaxed mood, friendly crowd and reasonably priced drinks (including Black Forest Alpirsbacher beer), the Black Cat is a Konstanz favourite.

nikOlala CAFE
(Hieronymusgasse 6; ☺11am-6pm) A tiny pocket of vintage cool in the heart of the Altstadt, nikOlala brings together a craft shop and cafe. It's a nicely chilled spot for a coffee and *pastel de nata* (Portuguese custard tart) between sightseeing.

Brauhaus Johann Albrecht PUB
(Konradigasse 2; ☺11.30am-1pm) This stepgabled microbrewery is a relaxed haunt for

quaffing wheat beer or hoppy lager by the glass or metre. There's a terrace for summer imbibing.

Seekuh PUB

(Konzilstrasse 1; 5pm-1am Sun-Thu, 5pm-2am Fri & Sat) The rough and ready 'lake cow' is a Konstanz favourite for its beer garden, cheapish drinks and occasional gigs.

K9 CULTURAL CENTRE

(www.k9-kulturzentrum.de; Obere Laube 71) Once a medieval church, this is now Konstanz' most happening cultural venue, with a line-up skipping from salsa nights and film screenings to gigs, club nights and jive nights. See the website for schedules.

ℹ Information

ReiseBank (Hauptbahnhof; 8am-6pm Mon-Fri, 8am-3pm Sat) Currency exchange, including Swiss francs.

Tourist Office (07531-133 030; www.konstanz-tourismus.de; Bahnhofplatz 43; 9am-6.30pm Mon-Fri, 9am-4pm Sat, 10am-1pm Sun Apr-Oct, 9.30am-6pm Mon-Fri Nov-Mar) Just north of the train stations. Inside you can pick up a walking-tour brochure (€1) and city map (€0.50); outside there's a hotel reservation board and free hotel telephone.

ℹ Getting There & Away

Konstanz is the main ferry hub for Lake Constance.

By car, Konstanz can be reached via the B33, which links up with the A81 to and from Stuttgart near Singen. Or you can take the B31 to Meersburg and then catch a car ferry.

Konstanz' Hauptbahnhof is the southern terminus of the scenic Schwarzwaldbahn, which trundles hourly through the Black Forest, linking Offenburg with towns such as Triberg and Villingen. To reach Lake Constance's northern shore, you usually have to change in Radolfzell. The Schweizer Bahnhof has connections to destinations throughout Switzerland.

ℹ Getting Around

The city centre is a traffic headache, especially on weekends. Your best bet is the free Park & Ride lot 3km northwest of the Altstadt, near the airfield on Byk-Gulden-Strasse, where your only outlay will be for a bus ticket.

Local buses (www.sw.konstanz.de) cost €2.30 for a single ticket; day passes are €4.50/7.80 for an individual/family. Bus 1 links the Meersburg car-ferry dock with the Altstadt. If you stay in Konstanz for at least two nights,

your hotelier will give you a Gästekarte entitling you to free local bus travel.

Bicycles can be hired from **Kultur-Rädle** (07531-273 10; Bahnhofplatz 29; per day/week €13/70; 9am-12.30pm & 2.30-6pm Mon-Fri, 10am-4pm Sat year-round, plus 10am-12.30pm Sun Easter-Sep), close to the tourist office.

Mainau Island

Mainau GARDENS

(www.mainau.de; adult/concession €19/11 summer, €9.50/5.50 winter; 10am-7pm late Mar-late Oct, 10am-5pm rest of year) Jutting out over the lake and bursting with flowers, the lusciously green islet of Mainau is a 45-hectare Mediterranean garden dreamed up by the Bernadotte family, relatives of the royal house of Sweden.

Around two million visitors flock here every year to admire sparkly lake and mountain views from the baroque castle, and wander sequoia-shaded avenues and hothouses bristling with palms and orchids. Crowd-pullers include the Butterfly House, where hundreds of vivid butterflies flit amid the dewy foliage, an Italian Cascade integrating patterned flowers with waterfalls, and a petting zoo. Tulips and rhododendrons bloom in spring, hibiscus and roses in summer. Avoid weekends, when the gardens get crowded.

You can drive, walk or cycle to Mainau, 8km north of Konstanz. Take bus 4 from Konstanz' train station or hop aboard a passenger ferry.

Reichenau Island

Reichenau ISLAND

(www.reichenau.de) In AD 724 a missionary named Pirmin founded a Benedictine monastery on Reichenau, a 4.5km-by-1.5km island (Lake Constance's largest) about 11km west of Konstanz. During its heyday, from 820 to 1050, the so-called Reichenauer School produced stunning illuminated manuscripts and vivid frescos. Today, three surviving churches provide silent testimony to Reichenau's Golden Age. Thanks to them, this fertile islet of orchards and wineries was declared a Unesco World Heritage Site in 2000.

Bring walking boots and binoculars to explore Wollmatinger Ried, a marshy nature reserve that attracts butterflies, migratory birds including kingfishers, grey herons and cuckoos, and even the odd beaver.

DON'T MISS

IMPERIA RULES

At the end of the pier, giving ferry passengers a come-hither look from her rotating pedestal, stands Imperia. Peter Lenk's 9m-high sculpture of a buxom prostitute, said to have plied her trade in the days of the Council of Constance, is immortalised in a novel by Honoré de Balzac. In her clutches are hilarious sculptures of a naked (and sagging) Pope Martin V and Holy Roman Emperor Sigismund, symbolising religious and imperial power.

A 2km-long tree-lined causeway connects the mainland with the island, which is served by bus 7372 from Konstanz. The Konstanz–Schaffhausen and Konstanz–Radolfzell ferries stop off at Reichenau.

Meersburg

☎07532 / POP 5630

Tumbling down vine-streaked slopes to Lake Constance and crowned by a perkily turreted medieval castle, Meersburg lives up to all those clichéd knights-in-armour, damsel-in-distress fantasies. And if its tangle of cobbled lanes and half-timbered houses filled with jovial banter doesn't sweep you off your feet, the local Pinot noir served in its cosy *Weinstuben* will.

Sights & Activities

Altes Schloss CASTLE

(adult/concession €9.50/6.50; ⏲9am-6.30pm Mar-Oct, 10am-6pm Nov-Feb) Looking across Lake Constance from its lofty perch, the Altes Schloss is an archetypal medieval stronghold, complete with keep, drawbridge, knights' hall and dungeons. Founded by Merovingian king Dagobert I in the 7th century, the fortress is among Germany's oldest, which is no mean feat in a country with a *lot* of old castles. The bishops of Konstanz used it as a summer residence between 1268 and 1803.

Neues Schloss CASTLE

(www.schloesser-und-gaerten.de; adult/concession €5/2.50; ⏲9am-6.30pm May-Oct, 11am-4pm Sat & Sun Nov-Apr) In 1710 Prince-Bishop Johann Franz Schenk von Stauffenberg, perhaps tired of the dinginess and rising damp, swapped the Altes Schloss for the dusky-pink, lavishly baroque Neues Schloss. A visit to the now state-owned palace takes in the extravagant bishops' apartments replete with stucco work and frescos, Bathasar Neumann's elegant staircase, and gardens with inspirational lake views.

Lakefront HARBOUR

Stroll the harbour for classic snaps of Lake Constance or to hire a pedalo. On the jetty, you can't miss – though the pious might prefer to – Peter Lenk's satirical Magische Säule (Magic Column). The sculpture is a hilarious satirical depiction of characters who have shaped Meersburg's history, including buxom wine-wench Wendelgart and poet Annette von Droste-Hülshoff (the seagull).

Meersburg Therme SPA

(☎07532-440 2850; www.meersburg-therme.de; Uferpromenade 12; thermal baths 2hr adult/concession €9/8.50, incl sauna 3hr €18/17.50; ⏲10am-10pm Mon-Thu, 10am-11pm Fri & Sat, 9am-10pm Sun) It's a five-minute walk east along the Uferpromenade to this lakefront spa, where the 34°C thermal waters, water jets and Swiss Alp views are soothing. Those who dare to bare all can skinny-dip in the lake and steam in saunas that are replicas of Unteruhldingen's Stone Age dwellings.

Sleeping & Eating

Meersburg goes with the seasons, with most places closing from November to Easter. Pick up a brochure listing good-value apartments and private rooms at the tourist office.

Characterful wine taverns line Unterstadtstrasse, while the lakefront Seepromenade has wall-to-wall pizzerias, cafes and gelaterias with alfresco seating.

Landhaus Ödenstein GUESTHOUSE **$$**

(☎07532-6142; www.oedenstein.de; Droste-Hülshoff-Weg 25; s €62-80, d €92-150; P) Spectacularly plonked on a hill above vine-cloaked slopes, this family-run guesthouse has knockout views of Lake Constance and spotless, light-filled rooms with pine furnishings – the pick of which have balconies. A pretty garden, warm welcome and generous breakfasts sweeten the deal.

Gasthof zum Bären GUESTHOUSE **$$**

(☎07532-432 20; www.baeren-meersburg.de; Marktplatz 11; s €50, d €88-110; P 📶) Straddling three 13th- to 17th-century buildings, this guesthouse near Obertor receives glowing reviews for its classic rooms, spruced up with stucco work, ornate wardrobes and lustrous wood; corner rooms No 13 and 23 are the most romantic.

The rustic tavern (mains €9 to €18) serves Lake Constance fare such as *Felchen* (whitefish).

Romantik Residenz
am See
BOUTIQUE HOTEL $$$

(☑ 07532-800 40; www.hotel-residenz-meersburg. com; Uferpromenade 11; s €87-122, d €150-288, apt €210-348; 🕾) Sitting with aplomb on the promenade, this romantic hotel is a class act. The higher you go, the better the view in the warm-hued rooms facing the vineyards or lake. In the hotel's Michelin-starred restaurant, Casala (Uferpromenade 11; tasting menus €78-146), chef Markus Philippi brings sophisticated Mediterranean cuisine to the table.

Valentino
PIZZA $

(☑ 07532-807 690; www.valentino-meersburg.de; Seepromenade 10; pizza €8-12; ⊙ 11am-11pm) The pizzas and light, crisp *Flammkuchen* are the stars of the menu at this friendly Italian job. Nab a spot on the terrace when the sun's out.

Winzerstube zum Becher
GERMAN $$

(☑ 07532-9009; Höllgasse 4; mains €10.50-26; ⊙ noon-2pm & 6-10pm Tue-Sun) Vines drape the facade of this wood-panelled bolt-hole, run by the same family since 1884. Home-grown Pinot noirs accompany Lake Constance classics such as whitefish in almond-butter sauce. The terrace affords Altes Schloss views.

Badische Weinstube
GERMAN $$

(☑ 07532-496 42; www.badische-weinstube.com; Unterstadtstrasse 17; mains €13-25; ⊙ 5-11pm) Close to the lakefront, this wine tavern combines a mock-rustic interior with a pavement terrace. Try the homemade fish soup flavoured with saffron and garlic, followed, say, by Bodensee *Felchen* in almond butter or *Zwiebelrostbraten* (onion beef roast) with *Spätzle*.

❶ Information

Tourist Office (☑ 07532-440 400; www.meersburg.de; Kirchstrasse 4; ⊙ 9am-12.30pm & 2-6pm Mon-Fri, 10am-3pm Sat, 10am-1pm Sun) Housed in a one-time Dominican monastery.

❶ Getting There & Away

Meersburg, which lacks a train station, is 18km west of Friedrichshafen.

From Monday to Friday, eight times a day, express bus 7394 makes the trip to Konstanz (€3.25, 40 minutes) and Friedrichshafen (€3.45, 26 minutes). Bus 7373 connects Meersburg with Ravensburg (€5.90, 40 minutes, four daily Monday to Friday, two Saturday). Meersburg's main bus stop is next to the church.

❶ Getting Around

The best and only way to get around Meersburg is on foot. Even the large pay car park near the car-ferry port (€1.20 per hour) is often full in high season. You might find free parking north of the old town along Daisendorfer Strasse.

Hire bikes at **Hermann Dreher** (☑ 07532-5176; Stadtgraben 5; per day €5; ⊙ rental 8am-noon), down the alley next to the tourist office.

Pfahlbauten

Pfahlbauten
ARCHAEOLOGICAL SITE

(Pile Dwellings; www.pfahlbauten.de; Strandpromenade 6, Unteruhldingen; adult/concession €9/6.50; ⊙ 9am-6.30pm Apr-Sep, 9am-5pm Oct, 9am-5pm Sat & Sun Nov; 👶) Awarded Unesco World Heritage status in 2011, the Pfahlbauten represent one of 11 prehistoric pile dwellings around the Alps. Based on the findings of local excavations, the carefully reconstructed dwellings catapult you back to the Stone and Bronze Ages, from 4000 to 850 BC. A spin of the lakefront complex takes in stilt dwellings that give an insight into the lives of farmers, fishermen and craftsmen. Kids love the hands-on activities from axe making to fire-starting using flints.

Birnau

Wallfahrtskirche Birnau
HISTORIC BUILDING

(Pilgrimage Church; Uhldingen-Mühlhofen; ⊙ 7.30am-7pm, to 5.30pm in winter) The exuberant, powder-pink Birnau pilgrimage church is one of Lake Constance's architectural highlights. It was built by the rococo master Peter Thumb of Vorarlberg in 1746. The decor is so intricate and profuse you won't know where to look first. At some point your gaze will be drawn to the ceiling, where Gottfried Bernhard Göz worked his usual fresco magic.

Affenberg Salem

Affenberg Salem
ZOO

(www.affenberg-salem.de; adult/child €8.50/5.50; ⊙ 9am-6pm Mar-Oct) No zoo-like cages, no circus antics, just happy Barbary macaques free to roam in a near-to-natural habitat: that's the concept behind conservation-oriented Affenberg Salem. Trails interweave the 20-hectare woodlands, where you can feed tail-less monkeys one piece of special popcorn at a time, observe their behaviour (you scratch my back, I'll scratch yours…) and get primate close-ups at hourly feedings. The park is also home to storks; listen for bill clattering and look out for their nests near the entrance.

Schloss Salem

Schloss Salem PALACE
(www.salem.de; adult/concession €9/4.50; ⊙ 9.30am-6pm Mon-Sat, 10.30am-6pm Sun Apr-Oct) Founded as a Cistercian monastery in 1134, the immense estate known as Schloss Salem was once the largest and richest of its kind in southern Germany. The Grand Duchy of Baden sold out to the state recently, but you can still picture the royals swanning around the hedge maze, gardens and extravagant rococo apartments dripping with stucco. The west wing shelters an elite boarding school, briefly attended by Prince Philip (Duke of Edinburgh and husband of Queen Elizabeth II).

Friedrichshafen

📞 07541 / POP 59,000

Zeppelins, the cigar-shaped airships that first took flight in 1900 under the stewardship of high-flying Count Ferdinand von Zeppelin, will forever be associated with Friedrichshafen. An amble along the flowery lakefront promenade and a visit to the museum that celebrates the behemoth of the skies are the biggest draws of this industrial town, which was heavily bombed in WWII and rebuilt in the 1950s.

◉ Sights & Activities

★ **Zeppelin Museum** MUSEUM
(www.zeppelin-museum.de; Seestrasse 22; adult/concession €8/4; ⊙ 9am-5pm daily May-Oct, 10am-5pm Tue-Sun Nov-Apr) Near the eastern end of Friedrichshafen's lakefront promenade is the Zeppelin Museum, housed in the Bauhaus-style former Hafenbahnhof, built in 1932. The centrepiece is a full-scale mock-up of a 33m section of the *Hindenburg* (LZ 129), the largest airship ever built, measuring an incredible 245m long and outfitted as luxuriously as an ocean liner. The hydrogen-filled craft tragically burst into flames, killing 36, while landing in New Jersey in 1937.

Other exhibits provide technical and historical insights, including an original motor

gondola from the famous Graf Zeppelin, which made 590 trips and travelled around the world in 21 days in 1929.

The top-floor art collection stars brutally realistic works by Otto Dix.

Lakefront AREA
A promenade runs through the lakefront, sculpture-dotted Stadtgarten park along Uferstrasse, a great spot for a picnic or stroll. Pedal and electric boats can be rented at the Gondelhafen (€9 to €23 per hour).

The western end of Friedrichshafen's promenade is anchored by the twin-onion-towered baroque Schlosskirche. It's the only accessible part of the Schloss and is still inhabited by the ducal family of Württemberg.

🛏 Sleeping & Eating

The tourist office has a free booking terminal. For lake-view snacks, hit Seestrasse's beer gardens, pizzerias and ice-cream parlours.

Gasthof Rebstock GUESTHOUSE $
(📞 07541-950 1640; www.gasthof-rebstock-fn. de; Werastrasse 35; s/d/tr/q €65/80/95/110; 🛜) Geared up for cyclists and offering bike rental (€7 per day), this family-run hotel has a beer garden and humble but tidy rooms with pine furnishings. It's 750m northwest of the Stadtbahnhof.

Hotel Restaurant Maier HOTEL $$
(📞 07541-4040; www.hotel-maier.de; Poststrasse 1-3, Friedrichshafen-Fischbach; s €59-95, d €89-160; 🅿🛜) The light-drenched rooms are immaculately kept at this family-run hotel, 5km west of Friedrichshafen and an eight-minute hop on the train. The mini spa invites relaxing moments, with its lake-facing terrace, steam room and sauna. Championing slow food, the wood-panelled restaurant is hailed far and wide for its regional food.

Brot, Kaffee, Wein CAFE $
(Karlstrasse 38; snacks €3-8; ⊙ 8.30am-8pm Mon-Fri, 9am-8pm Sat, 9.30am-8pm Sun) Slick and monochrome, this deli-cafe has a lakeside terrace for lingering over a speciality coffee, breakfast, homemade ice cream or sourdough bread sandwich.

Beach Club TAPAS $
(Uferstrasse 1; snacks €6-8; ⊙ 9am-midnight Apr-Oct) This lakefront shack is the place to unwind on the deck, mai tai in hand, admiring the *Klangschiff* sculpture and the not-so-distant Alps. Revive over tapas, salads and antipasti.

ℹ Information

Post Office (Bahnhofplatz 1; ⊘9am-6pm Mon-Fri, 9am-1pm Sat) To the right as you exit the Stadtbahnhof.

Tourist Office (☑07541-300 10; www.frie-drichshafen.info; Bahnhofplatz 2; ⊘9am-1pm & 2-6pm Mon-Fri, 9am-1pm Sat) On the square outside the Stadtbahnhof. Staff can book accommodation and zeppelin flights.

ℹ Getting There & Around

There are ferry options, including a catamaran to Konstanz. Sailing times are posted on the waterfront just outside the Zeppelin Museum.

From Monday to Friday, seven times a day, express bus 7394 makes the trip to Konstanz (1¼ hours) via Meersburg (30 minutes). Birnau and Meersburg are also served almost hourly by bus 7395.

Friedrichshafen is on the Bodensee–Gürtelbahn train line, which runs along the lake's northern shore from Radolfzell to Lindau. There are also regular services on the Bodensee-Oberschwaben-Bahn to Ravensburg (€4.30, 20 minutes).

Ravensburg

☑0751 / POP 49,780

Ravensburg has puzzled the world for the past 125 years with its jigsaws and board games. The medieval Altstadt has toy-town appeal, studded with turrets, robber-knight towers and gabled patrician houses. For centuries dukes and wealthy merchants polished the cobbles of this Free Imperial City – now it's your turn.

◎ Sights & Activities

Marienplatz SQUARE
The heart of Altstadt is the elongated, pedestrianised Marienplatz, framed by sturdy towers, like the round Grüner Turm, with its lustrous tiled roof, and frescoed patrician houses, such as the late-Gothic, step-gabled Waaghaus. The 15th-century **Lederhaus**, with its elaborate Renaissance facade, was once the domain of tanners and shoemakers.

Blaserturm TOWER
(adult/concession €1.50/1; ⊘11am-4pm early Apr-early Oct) The 51m-high Blaserturm is a part of the original fortifications and has superb views over the Altstadt from up top.

Liebfrauenkirche CHURCH
(Church of Our Lady; Marienplatz) Rising high above Marienplatz, the weighty, late-Gothic Liebfrauenkirche conceals some fine examples of 15th-century stained glass and a gilt altar.

Ravensburger Spieleland AMUSEMENT PARK
(www.spieleland.de; Mecklenbeuren; adult/concession €29/27; ⊘10am-6pm Apr-Oct) Kids in tow? Take them to this board-game-inspired theme park, with attractions from giant rubber-duck racing and cow milking against the clock to rodeos and Alpine rafting. It's a 10-minute drive south of Ravensburg on the B467.

Museum Humpis MUSEUM
(www.museum-humpis-quartier.de; Marktstrasse 45; adult/concession €4/2; ⊘11am-6pm Tue-Sun, to 8pm Thu) Seven exceptional late-medieval houses set around a glass-covered courtyard shelter a permanent collection and rotating exhibitions focusing on Ravensburg's past as a trade centre. Free audioguides provide some background.

Mehlsack TOWER
The all-white Mehlsack (Flour Sack) is a tower marking the Altstadt's southern edge. A steep staircase leads up to the **Veitsburg**, a quaint baroque castle, which now harbours the restaurant of the same name, with outlooks over Ravensburg's mosaic of red-tiled roofs.

🍴 Sleeping & Eating

Waldhorn HISTORIC HOTEL $$
(☑0751-361 20; http://waldhorn.de; Marienplatz 15; s €75-125, d €135-150; 🛜) The Waldhorn creaks with history and its light, appealingly restored rooms make a great base for exploring the Altstadt. Lodged in the 15th-century vintners' guildhall, its wood-beamed restaurant (mains €12 to 25), Rebleutehaus,

DON'T MISS

COME FLY WITH ME

Zeppelin NT (☑07541-590 00; www.zeppelinflug.de; 30/45/60/90/120-minute flights €200/295/395/565/745) Real airship fans will justify the splurge on a trip in a high-tech, 12-passenger Zeppelin NT. Shorter trips cover lake destinations such as Schloss Salem and Lindau, while longer ones drift across to Austria or Switzerland. Take-off and landing are in Friedrichshafen. The flights aren't cheap but not much can beat floating over Lake Constance with the Alps on the horizon, and so slowly that you can make the most of legendary photo ops.

STUTTGART & THE BLACK FOREST RAVENSBURG

turns out spot-on seasonal dishes like tender corn-fed chicken with herb gnocchi.

Gasthof Obertor
GUESTHOUSE $$

(☑0751-366 70; www.hotelobertor.de; Marktstrasse 67; s €75-95, d €120-130; P🐾) The affable Rimpps take pride in their lemon-fronted patrician house. It stands high above most Altstadt guesthouses, with spotless rooms, a sauna area and generous breakfasts.

Mohren
INTERNATIONAL $$

(☑0751-1805 4310; www.mohren-ravensburg.de; Marktstrasse 61; mains €9-21.50; ⊘5pm-midnight Mon, 10.30am-2.30pm & 5.30pm-midnight Tue-Sat) Contemporary rustic best sums up Mohren, with its bright feel, exposed red brick and log piles. The slow food menu wings you from antipasti to steaks and Thai curries – all playfully presented and revealing the chef's pride in careful sourcing.

❶ Information

Tourist Office (☑0751-828 00; www.ravensburg.de; Kirchstrasse 16; ⊘9am-5.30pm Mon-Fri, 10am-1pm Sat) A block northeast of Marienplatz.

❶ Getting There & Away

The train station is six blocks west of the tourist office along Eisenbahnstrasse. Ravensburg is on the train line linking Friedrichshafen (€4.30, 20 minutes, at least twice hourly) with Ulm (€20.90, 1¼ hours, at least hourly) and Stuttgart (€36.20, 2½ hours, at least hourly).

Lindau

☑08382 / POP 24,800

Brochures rhapsodise about Lindau being Germany's 'Garden of Eden' and the 'Bavarian Riviera'. Paradise and southern France it ain't, but it is pretty special. Cradled in the southern crook of Lake Constance and almost dipping its toes into Austria, this is a good-looking, outgoing little town, with a candy-coloured postcard of an Altstadt, clear-day Alpine views and lakefront cafes that use every sunray to the max.

◉ Sights

Seepromenade
AREA

In summer the harbourside promenade has a happy-go-lucky air, with its palms, bobbing boats and folk sunning themselves in pavement cafes.

Out at the harbour gates, looking across to the Alps, is Lindau's signature 36m-high Neuer Leuchtturm (New Lighthouse; adult/concession €1.80/0.70; ⊘10am-7.30pm) and, just in case you forget which state you're in, a statue of the Bavarian lion. The square tile-roofed, 13th-century Mangturm (Old Lighthouse) guards the northern edge of the sheltered port.

Altes Rathaus
LANDMARK

(Old Town Hall; Bismarckplatz) Lindau's biggest architectural stunner is the 15th-century step-gabled Altes Rathaus, a frescoed frenzy of cherubs, merry minstrels and galleons.

Stadtmuseum
MUSEUM

(Marktplatz 6; adult/concession €7.50/3.50; ⊘10am-6pm) Lions and voluptuous dames dance across the trompe l'oeil facade of the flamboyantly baroque Haus zum Cavazzen, which contains this museum, showcasing a fine collection of furniture, weapons and paintings. The museum also showcases stellar temporary exhibitions, such as recent ones featuring works of Picasso, Chagall, Matisse and Emil Nolde.

Peterskirche
CHURCH

(Schrannenplatz; ⊘daily) Looking back on a 1000-year history, this enigmatic church is now a war memorial, hiding exquisite time-faded frescos of the Passion of Christ by Hans Holbein the Elder. The cool, dimly lit interior is a quiet spot for contemplation. Next door is the turreted 14th-century Diebsturm, once a tiny jail.

🛏 Sleeping

Lindau virtually goes into hibernation from November to February, when many hotels close. Nip into the tourist office for a list of good-value holiday apartments.

Hotel Anker
GUESTHOUSE $$

(☑08382-260 9844; www.anker-lindau.com; Bindergasse 15; s €55-69, d €99-169; 🐾) Shiny parquet floors, citrus colours and artwork have spruced up the charming and peaceful rooms at this central guesthouse, tucked down a cobbled lane. Rates include a hearty breakfast.

Hotel Garni-Brugger
HISTORIC HOTEL $$

(☑08382-934 10; www.hotel-garni-brugger.de; Bei der Heidenmauer 11; s €60-88, d €94-130; 🐾) Our readers rave about this 18th-century hotel, with bright rooms done up in floral fabrics and pine. The family bends over backwards to please. Guests can unwind in the little spa with steam room and sauna (€10) in the cooler months.

Alte Post
HOTEL **$$**

(☏ 08382-934 60; www.alte-post-lindau.de; Fischergasse 3; s €70-95, d €120-190) This 300-year-old coaching inn was once a stop on the Frankfurt–Milan mail run. Well-kept, light and spacious, the rooms are fitted out with chunky oak furnishings. Downstairs is a beer garden and a highly regarded restaurant (mains €12 to €23), with dishes like *Tafelspitz* (boiled beef) and *Maultaschen,* and local wines.

Reutemann & Seegarten
LUXURY HOTEL **$$$**

(☏ 08382-9150; www.reutemann-lindau.de; Ludwigstrasse 23; s €99-183, d €142-262; 🛜 🌊) Wow, what a view! Facing the harbour, lighthouse and lion statue, this hotel has plush, spacious rooms done out in sunny shades, as well as a pool big enough to swim laps, a spa, gym and refined restaurant.

✖ Eating & Drinking

For a drink with a cool view, head to Seepromenade. The crowds on the main thoroughfare, Maximilianstrasse, can be dodged in nearby backstreets, where your euro will stretch further.

37°
CAFE **$**

(Bahnhofplatz 1; snacks €4-11; ⏰ 10am-11pm Tue-Sun) Part boutique, part boho-chic cafe, 37° combines a high-ceilinged interior with a lake-facing pavement terrace. Pull up a candy-coloured chair for cold drinks and light bites such as tapas, quiche and soups.

Engelstube
GERMAN **$$**

(www.engel-lindau.de; mains €13-19; ⏰ 11am-2pm & 5-11pm) Dark wood panelling keeps the vibe cosy at this smart wine tavern, which spills out onto a pavement terrace in summer. Regional dishes like Bodensee fish with herbs and roast Bavarian ox are cooked to a T.

★ Valentin
MEDITERRANEAN **$$$**

(☏ 08382-504 3740; In der Grub 28; mains €20-31, day specials €11.50-13.50; ⏰ noon-2pm & 6-10pm Wed-Mon) The chef carefully sources the local ingredients that go into his Med-style dishes at this sleek vaulted restaurant. Dishes like spinach and pecorino ravioli and locally caught trout with creamy lentils are beautifully cooked and presented.

Weinstube Frey
GERMAN **$$$**

(☏ 08382-947 9676; Maximilianstrasse 15; mains €16-22; ⏰ 11.30am-10pm) This 500-year-old wood-panelled wine tavern oozes Bavarian charm with its cosy nooks. Dirndl-clad waitresses serve up regional wines and fare such as Lake Constance whitefish with market veg and *Zwiebelrostbraten.* Sit out on the terrace when the sun's out.

Marmor Saal
BAR

(Bahnhofplatz 1e; ⏰ 10am-2am) The lakefront 'marble hall' once welcomed royalty and still has a feel of grandeur with its soaring columns, chandeliers and Biedermeier flourishes. Nowadays it's a relaxed cafe-bar with occasional live music and a chilled terrace.

ⓘ Information

Post Office (Obere Schrannenplatz 4; ⏰ 9am-6.30pm Mon-Fri, 9am-3pm Sat)

Tourist Office (☏ 08382-260 030; www.lindau.de; Alfred-Nobel-Platz 1; ⏰ 10am-6pm Mon-Sat, 10am-1pm Sun, shorter hours in low season)

ⓘ Getting There & Away

Lindau is on the B31 and connects to Munich by the A96. The precipitous Deutsche Alpenstrasse (German Alpine Rd), which winds giddily eastward to Berchtesgaden, begins here.

Lindau is at the eastern terminus of the train line, which goes along the lake's north shore via Friedrichshafen (€6.10, 20 minutes) westward to Radolfzell, and the southern terminus of the Südbahn to Ulm (€25.70, 1¾ hours) via Ravensburg (€10, 44 minutes).

ⓘ Getting Around

The compact, walkable Insel (island), home to the town centre and harbour, is connected to the mainland by the Seebrücke, a road bridge at its northeastern tip, and by the Eisenbahndamm, a rail bridge open to cyclists and pedestrians. The Hauptbahnhof lies to the east of the island, a block south of the pedestrianised, shop-lined Maximilianstrasse.

Buses 1 and 2 link the Hauptbahnhof to the main bus hub, known as ZUP. A single ticket costs €2.10, a 24-hour pass is €5.40.

To get to the island by car follow the signs to 'Lindau-Insel'. It's easiest and cheapest to park at the large metered car park (€0.80 per hour) just before you cross the bridge to the island.

Bikes and tandems can be rented at **Unger's Fahrradverleih** (Inselgraben 14; per day bikes €6-12, tandems €18, electro bikes €20; ⏰ 9am-1pm & 3-6pm Mon-Fri, 9am-1pm Sat & Sun).

Understand Munich, Bavaria & the Black Forest

Munich, Bavaria & the Black Forest Today

A high-voltage economy and thigh-slapping traditions, green energy and the world's greatest luxury car industry, supermarkets of organic food, and sausages and beer for breakfast – southern Germany's contradictions continue to baffle outsiders. But what is clear is that the whole caboodle is based on three sound principles – a Bavarian electorate that has returned the same conservative-minded party to power every time since 1958, a focus on manufacturing and respect for the traditions of yesteryear.

Best in Print

Massacre in Munich: Manhunt for the Killers Behind the 1972 Olympics Massacre (Michael Bar Bar-Zohar and Eitan Haber, 2005) The title says it all really.

Lola Montez: A Life (Bruce Seymour, 1998) A superbly written account of the life of Bavaria's most outrageous courtesan who brought down a king.

Ludwig II of Bavaria (Martha Schad, 2001) One of the most readable and compact biographies of Bavaria's most flamboyant monarch, and available throughout the state.

Best on Film

Sophie Scholl – The Final Days (Marc Rothmund, 2005) Extremely moving account of the capture, trial and execution of members of the White Rose anti-Nazi group.

Ludwig (Luchino Visconti, 1973) The reign of Ludwig II.

Hierankl (Hans Steinbichler, 2003) Family drama set against the backdrop of the Alps.

The Nasty Girl (Michael Verhoeven, 1990) A woman digging up her town's Nazi past gets more than she bargains for.

Normality Resumed

In September 2013 it was back to political business as usual following the *Landtagswahl* (regional election) which saw the Bavarian Christlich-Soziale Union (CSU) receive over 60% of the vote for the first time since 1998. This decade and a half represented the greatest period of political 'turmoil' experienced by the state since the early 1950s. The CSU was even forced to enter a coalition between 2008 and 2013 with the Freie Demokratische Partei (FDP), something it hadn't done since the early 1960s. But as the whole of Europe lurches to the right, the CSU is back with Bavarian prime minister Horst Seehofer at the helm.

It's the Economy, Stupid!

Even the most militant anti-capitalist might, just for a moment, agree that Bavaria is a rampant success story of postwar free enterprise. Just one stat says it all – if Bavaria was an independent country (and not a small number of locals secretly wish it were), its economy would be the world's 19th largest (equally affluent Baden-Württemberg would rank around 22nd), bigger than Sweden or Austria and more than twice the size of neighbouring Czech Republic. Germany's economic powerhouse is cooking with gas, and probably on an ecofriendly stove of sturdy design, proudly stamped with 'Hergestellt in Bayern' (Made in Bavaria). Even after the slump in the euro and the Greek debt crisis, Germany's south still looks like one of the best investments in the world.

So what underpins the south's economic triumph? Good 'ole manufacturing seems to be the 'secret', with a motor industry second to none leading the way. The most desirable names of the Teutonic luxury car world – BMW, Audi, Porsche and Mercedes – are all based in the south, pumping billions of euros into the economy and employing hundreds of thousands. Other local corporate behemoths include Siemens, Allianz, Grundig and Adidas.

Tourism also generates a solid chunk of the south's wealth. In 2014 Munich alone saw well over five million foreign guests crumple hotel bed sheets, and blockbuster sights such as Schloss Neuschwanstein and Regensburg's Unesco-listed city centre attract millions.

Green Giant

With local plants boxing up everything from R8s to locos, you'd expect a toxic murk to envelope you at the airplane door. But it doesn't. In fact by 2025 Munich is set to become the world's first major city powered solely using renewable energy sources, and in the countryside some small towns look very different from one direction than from the other as south-facing roofs bear the weight of millions of solar panels (you see this odd phenomenon best from trains). Farmers have turned over considerable acreage to accommodate vast swathes of buzzing solar panels, wind turbines are a common sight and biking has been in fashion for decades. The plan to switch off Germany nuclear power stations by 2020 is still on track, with Berlin's politicians seemingly still on board with the policy first drafted in 2011.

Traditional Success Story

It must feel good to be a German from the south – a high-octane economy; sun and wind powering your latest gadgetry; the cultural and historic delights of Germany's secret capital (Munich); an Alpine playground a swift train ride away; your country top of the Continent's (shaky) euro-pile; and the German Chancellor Merkel now the most powerful figure in Europe. So why all the glum faces on the S-Bahn you may wonder? What do these people have to be grumpy about? As throughout the Western world, even flourishing southern Germany is not immune to an underlying angst about the future. But the difference here may be that on the evenings and weekends, locals retreat to the unglobalised world of thigh-slapping tradition – the beer hall, the Alpine tavern, a baroque theatre or a folk bash – to celebrate their astounding successes, whatever the future may bring.

MUNICH & BAVARIA

AREA: **70,549 SQ KM**

POPULATION: **12.6 MILLION**

GDP: **€487 BILLION**

UNEMPLOYMENT: **3.1%**

if Southern Germany were 100 people

92 would be German
3 would be Turkish
2 would be from the former Yugoslavia
1 would be Italian
2 would be other

belief systems
(% of population)

54.4 — Catholic

4 — Muslim

21.2 — Other

20.4 — Evangelical

population per sq km

BADEN-WURRTEMBERG   BAVARIA   GERMANY

= 180 people

History

One of Europe's oldest states, with origins dating back to the 6th century, it's safe to say that Bavaria, Germany's largest *Land* (province), has enjoyed a long and eventful past, one populated by a weird-and-*wunderbar* cast of oddball kings, scandalous courtesans and infamous Nazis. Having suffered war and revolution, mad monarchs and even madder dictators, you could say all's well that ends well, with Bavaria and Southern Germany in general one of the world's most prosperous and peaceful places.

On Bavaria's coat of arms, 'Old Bavaria' is represented by a blue panther, the Franconians by a red-and-white rake, the Swabians by three black lions, and the Upper Palatinate (no longer part of today's Bavaria) by a golden lion.

The Bavaria of today is a relatively new territorial entity, its three distinct tribes – the Bajuwaren (Bavarians), the Franken (Franconians) and the Schwaben (Swabians) – each having developed quite separately until thrown in together by Napoleon as the Kingdom of Bavaria in 1806. Munich was founded in 1158 by Duke Heinrich der Löwe (Henry the Lion), granted town rights in 1175 and declared capital of Bavaria in 1506. Although never really at the centre of European power, Bavaria was a key player in continental politics for centuries. Governed by the same family, the colourful Wittelsbachs, for over 700 years, it was able to form a distinct culture that continues to shape its image and identity to this day. The most famous member of the House of Wittelsbach was King Ludwig II, who frittered away the family silver on blockbuster castles, thus creating Bavaria's modern tourist industry.

Of course Bavaria of the 20th century is synonymous with the rise of Hitler and the Nazis who found fertile ground for their ideas in the working class neighbourhoods of Munich and Nuremberg. The area is littered with reminders of those stormy decades when mass rallies were held in Nuremberg, and Dachau became the Nazis' first concentration camp.

After WWII Bavaria firmly established itself as Germany's economic engine, with high-tech industries and car production in particular making this region one of Europe's most successful. In more recent times Bavaria has given the world an Olympic games, which ended in tragedy, and a controversial pope, as well as playing a memorable part in the 2006 FIFA World Cup soccer championships.

TIMELINE	15 BC	AD 555–788	7th–8th centuries
	Nero Claudius Drusus and Tiberius Claudius Nero, stepsons of Roman emperor Augustus, conquer the Celtic tribes north of the Alps, calling their new colony Raetia. Augusta Vindelicorum (today's Augsburg) is capital.	The Agilofinges dynasty founds the first Bavarian duchy with Garibald I (r 555–91) its first-known duke. They remain in power until absorbed into the Frankish Empire in 788 by Charlemagne.	Christianity takes hold as roving missionaries arrive in Bavaria from Ireland, Scotland and the Frankish Empire. In 738 St Boniface creates the dioceses of Salzburg, Freising, Passau and Regensburg.

Tribal Melting Pot

The first recorded inhabitants of Bavaria were the Celts, who proved to be a pushover for the Romans who began swarming across the Alps in the 1st century AD. The invaders founded the province of Raetia with Augusta Vindelicorum (Augsburg) as its capital. By the 5th century the tables were turned on the Romans by marauding eastern Germanic tribes pushing up the Danube Valley in search of pastures new.

As with all central Europe's peoples, the precise origin of the Bavarian tribe is obscure, but it's widely assumed that it coalesced from the remaining Romans, Romanised Celts and the newcomers from the east. The name 'Bajuwaren' may be derived from 'men from Bohemia', the neighbouring region of today's Czech Republic.

The Franken began forming in the 3rd century AD from several western Germanic tribes who settled along the central and lower Rhine, on the border with the Roman Empire. The Schwaben, meanwhile, are a subtribe of the population group of the Alemannen (Alemannic tribes) who spread across the southwestern corner of Germany around the 2nd century AD. In the 3rd century they took on the Romans, eventually pushing as far east as the Lech River.

For a comprehensive overview of Bavarian history (partly in English) see the website of the government-financed Haus der Bayerischen Geschichte at www.hdbg.de.

Church Dominance

Religion, especially of the Roman Catholic variety, has shaped all aspects of Bavarian history and culture for nearly two millennia. Following the decline of the Roman Empire, missionaries from Ireland and Scotland swarmed across Europe to spread the gospel. They found open arms and minds among the Agilofinges, the dynasty who had founded the first Bavarian duchy in the 6th century. They adopted the faith eagerly and Christianity quickly took root. By 739 there were bishoprics in Regensburg, Passau, Freising and Salzburg, and monasteries had been founded in Tegernsee, Benediktbeuern, Weltenburg and several other locations.

For almost the next 800 years, the Church dominated daily life as the only major religion in the land. Until 1517, that is. That's when a monk and theology professor named Martin Luther sparked the Reformation with his 95 theses critiquing papal infallibility, clerical celibacy, selling indulgences and other elements of Catholic doctrine.

Despite the Church's attempt to quash Luther, his teachings resonated widely, especially in Franconia and Swabia, though not in Bavaria proper where local rulers instantly clamped down on anyone toying with conversion. They also encouraged the newly founded Jesuit order to make Ingolstadt the hub of the Counter-Reformation. The religious strife eventually escalated into the Thirty Years' War (1618–48), which left Europe's soil drenched with the blood of millions. During the conflict, Bavaria's Duke Maximilian I (r 1598–1651) fought firmly on the side of Catholic

Bavaria is made up of seven historical *Regierungsbezirken* (administrative areas) – Unterfranken, Oberfranken, Mittelfranken, Oberpfalz, Schwaben, Niederbayern and Oberbayern.

962	1158	1180	1214
The pope crowns the Saxon King Otto I Kaiser (emperor), marking the beginning of the Holy Roman Empire, which remains a major force in European history until 1806.	Duke Heinrich der Löwe establishes Munich as a market town in a bid to take control of the lucrative central European trade in salt, known then as 'white gold'.	The Wittelsbachs' 738-year reign begins with Otto von Wittelsbach's appointment as duke of Bavaria by Emperor Friedrich Barbarossa, marking the transition from tribal duchy to territorial state.	Emperor Friedrich II grants the fiefdom of the Palatinate along the Rhine River to Duke Otto II von Wittelsbach, thereby significantly enlarging the family's territory and increasing its power.

WE ARE POPE!

'*Habemus papam.*' It was a balmy spring evening in Rome when the world – Catholics and non-Catholics – held its collective breath. Who would follow in the footsteps of the charismatic Pope John Paul II who had led the church for 27 years? The man was Cardinal Joseph Ratzinger, henceforth known as Benedict XVI and born on 16 April 1927 in Bavaria's Marktl am Inn. For the first time in nearly 500 years a German had been elected pope. The following day the headline of the tabloid German daily *Bild* screamed proudly: '*Wir sind Papst!*' (We are Pope!).

Ratzinger's election met with a mix of elation and disappointment. Those who had hoped for a more progressive and liberal church leader were stunned to find that the job had gone to this fierce and uncompromising cardinal who for 24 years had been John Paul II's enforcer of church doctrine. He was known to be opposed to abortion, homosexuality and contraception, and ruthless in his crackdowns on dissident priests. 'Panzer cardinal' and 'God's Rottweiler' were just two of his nicknames.

Yet, even his staunchest critics could not deny that Ratzinger was well prepared for the papal post. A distinguished theologian, he spoke seven languages and had written more than 50 books. He could look back on a long career as a university professor, archbishop of Freising and Munich, and 24 years as John Paul II's main man.

If pope Benedict's election was a surprise, it was nothing compared to the way he left the papacy. In February 2013 he resigned citing old age, the first pope to do so in over 700 years. He was succeeded by Argentine Jesuit pope Francis, but many fretted that having two popes alive at the same time might cause problems. However, so far this has not proved to be the case.

emperor Ferdinand II of Habsburg, who thanked him by expanding Max's territory and promoting him to *Kurfürst* (prince-elector). With calm restored in 1648 following the signing of the Peace of Westphalia, Bavaria – along with much of the rest of central Europe – lay in ruins.

The treaty permitted each local ruler to determine the religion of his territory and essentially put the Catholic and Lutheran churches on equal legal footing. Bavaria, of course, remained staunchly Catholic. In fact, if the baroque church-building boom of the 17th century is any indication, it seemed to positively revel in its religious zeal.

But beyond Bavaria times were a-changing. The Enlightenment spawned reforms throughout Europe, first leading to the French Revolution, then the Napoleonic Wars and ultimately to the demise of the Holy Roman Empire. The ancient Church structure collapsed along with it, prompting the secularisation of Bavarian monasteries after 1803 and, finally, religious parity. Although Ludwig I restored the monasteries, Protestants have since enjoyed equal rights throughout Bavaria, even though it remains predominantly Catholic to this day.

1506	1516	1517	1555
To further prevent Bavaria from being split into ever-smaller territories, Duke Albrecht the Wise introduces the law of primogeniture. Possessions now pass automatically to first-born sons.	On 23 April the Reinheitsgebot (Purity Law) is passed in Ingolstadt, which limits the ingredients used in the production of beer to water, barley and hops.	Martin Luther splits the Christian church by kicking off the Reformation with his 95 theses posted on the door of the cathedral in the eastern German town of Wittenberg.	Emperor Karl V signs the Peace of Augsburg allowing each local ruler to decide which religion to adopt in their principality, ending decades of religious strife and officially recognising Lutherism.

Much to the delight and pride of the population, Bavarian-born Joseph Cardinal Ratzinger was elected Pope Benedict XVI in 2005 (he resigned in early 2013). The previous German pope was Adrian VI who ruled from 1522 to 1523.

Keep it in the Family – the Wittelsbachs

From 1180 to 1918, a single family held Bavaria in its grip, the House of Wittelsbach. Otto von Wittelsbach was a distant relative of Emperor Friedrich Barbarossa who, in 1180, appointed him duke of Bavaria, which at that time was a fairly small and insignificant territory. Ensuing generations of Wittelsbachs focused on expanding their land – and with it their sphere of influence – through wheeling and dealing, marriage, inheritance and war.

Being granted the fiefdom of the Palatinate, an area along the Rhine River northwest of present-day boundaries, was a good start back in 1214, but the family's fortunes peaked when one of their own, Ludwig the Bavarian, became Holy Roman Emperor in 1328. As the first Wittelsbach on the imperial throne, Ludwig used his powerful position to bring various far-flung territories, including the March of Brandenburg (around Berlin), the Tyrol (part of today's Austria) and several Dutch provinces, under Bavarian control.

The Thirty Years' War brought widespread devastation but, by aligning themselves with Catholic emperor Ferdinand II, the Wittelsbachs managed not only to further expand their territory but to score a promotion from duchy to *Kurfürstentum* (electorate), giving them a say in the election of future emperors.

Not all alliances paid off so handsomely. In the 1680s Maximilian II Emanuel (r 1679–1726) – a man of great ambition but poor judgement – battled the Turks alongside the Habsburg Kaiser in an attempt to topple the Ottoman Empire. Much to his dismay, his allegiance did not lead to the rewards he had expected. So he tried again, this time switching sides and fighting with the French against Austria in the War of the Spanish Succession (1701–14). The conflict ended in a disastrous Franco-Bavarian loss and a 10-year occupation of Bavaria by Habsburg troops. Not only had Max Emanuel failed to achieve his personal goals, his flip-flop policies had also seriously weakened Bavaria's political strength.

Max Emanuel's son, Karl Albrecht (r 1726–45), was determined to avenge his father's double humiliation. Through some fancy political manoeuvring, he managed to take advantage of the confusion caused by the War of Succession and, with the backing of Prussia and France, ended up on the imperial throne as Karl VII in 1742. His triumph, however, was short-lived as Bavaria was quickly reoccupied by Austrian troops. Upon Karl Albrecht's death in 1745, his son Maximilian III Joseph (r 1745–77) was forced to renounce the Wittelsbachs' claims to the imperial crown forever.

The most prominent Wittelsbach descendant is Prince Luitpold of Bavaria who runs his own brewery, the Schlossbrauerei Kaltenberg, and hosts a popular jousting tournament, the Kaltenberger Ritterturnier. Learn more at www.kaltenberg.com.

Top Five Wittelsbach Residences

Schloss Neuschwanstein

Munich Residenz

Schloss Herrenchiemsee

Schloss Nymphenburg

Schloss Linderhof

1618–48	1806	1810	1835
The Thirty Years' War involves most European nations, but is fought mainly on German soil, bringing murder, starvation and disease, and decimating Europe's population from 21 million to 13.5 million.	Bavaria becomes a kingdom and nearly doubles its size when handed Franconia and Swabia. Sweeping reforms result in the passage of the state's first constitution in 1808.	Ludwig I marries Princess Therese von Sachsen-Hildburghausen with a horse race and lavish festivities that mark the beginning of the tradition of the annual Munich Oktoberfest.	Drawn by a steam locomotive called Adler (Eagle), Germany's first railway commences operations between Nuremberg and nearby Fürth, transporting newspapers, beer and people. It ploughs on until 1922.

The Accidental Kingdom

Modern Bavaria, more or less as we know it today, was established in the early 19th century by Napoleon. At the onset of the Napoleonic Wars (1799–1815), Bavaria initially found itself on the losing side against France. Tired of war and spurred on by his powerful minister Maximilian Graf von Montgelas, Maximilian IV Joseph (r 1799–1825) decided to put his territory under Napoleon's protection.

In 1803, after victories over Austria and Prussia, Napoleon set about re-mapping much of Europe. Bavaria fared rather well, nearly doubling its size when it received control over Franconia and Swabia. In 1806 Napoleon created the kingdom of Bavaria and made Maximilian I his new best buddy.

Alas, keeping allegiances had never been Bavaria's strong suit and, in 1813, with Napoleon's fortunes waning, Montgelas shrewdly threw the new kingdom's support behind Austria and Prussia. After France's defeat, the victorious allies again reshaped European boundaries at the Congress of Vienna (1814–15) and Bavaria got to keep most of the territory it had obtained with Napoleon's help.

> Germany's first ever postage stamp was issued in Bavaria in November 1849 and was called the *Schwarze Einser* (Black Penny). Not as rare as Britain's Penny Black, a used copy only fetches around €1300 when auctioned.

Reluctant Reformers

During the 18th century, the ideas of the Enlightenment that had swept through other parts of Europe had largely been ignored in Bavaria. Until Elector Maximilian III Joseph (r 1745–77) arrived on the scene, that is. Tired of waging war like his predecessors, he made peace with Austria and busied himself with reforming his country from within. He updated the legal system, founded the Bavarian Academy of Sciences and made school attendance compulsory. Max Joseph's reign also saw the creation of the Nymphenburg porcelain factory and the construction of the Cuvilliés-Theater at the Munich Residenz.

Now that the reforms had begun, there was no going back, especially after Bavaria became a kingdom in 1806. The architect of modern Bavaria was King Maximilian I's minister, Maximilian Graf von Montgelas. He worked feverishly to forge a united state from the mosaic of 'old Bavaria', Franconia and Swabia, by introducing sweeping political, administrative and social changes, including the secularisation of the monasteries. The reforms ultimately led to Bavaria's first constitution in 1808, which was based on rights of freedom, equality and property ownership, and the promise of representative government. Ten years later Bavaria got its first *Landtag* (two-chamber parliament).

Under Max I's son, Ludwig I (r 1825–48), Bavaria flourished into an artistic and cultural centre, an 'Athens on the Isar'. Painters, poets and philosophers gathered in Munich, where Leo von Klenze and Friedrich von Gärtner were creating a showcase of neoclassical architecture. Königsplatz with the Glyptothek and Propyläen, flashy Ludwigstrasse with the

> At economic odds today, Bavaria and Greece once shared a ruler when Otto I of Bavaria became modern Greece's first monarch in 1832. The biggest headache of his reign – Greece's ailing economy.

1848	1865	1869	1870-71
A man with a weakness for the arts and beautiful women, King Ludwig I is forced to resign after his affair with Lola Montez causes a public scandal.	Wagner's opera *Tristan and Isolde* premieres at Munich's Nationaltheater on 10 June during the composer's 18 months in the city under the patronage of Ludwig II.	Building work on Neuschwanstein castle is begun by architect Eduard Riedel. Due to lack of funds, work was halted in 1892 and Ludwig II's fairytale pile was never completed.	Through brilliant diplomacy and the Franco-Prussian War, Bismarck creates a unified Germany. However, Bavaria keeps much of its sovereignty and many of its own institutions.

MILESTONES IN BLACK FOREST HISTORY

In the beginning the Black Forest was just that: a huge, dark, dense clump of trees so impenetrable that even the Romans didn't dare colonise it, although they couldn't resist taking advantage of the thermal mineral springs in Baden-Baden on the forest's edge. Around the 7th century, a band of intrepid monks took a stab at taming the area, but it would be another few centuries until the ruling Zähringer clan founded Freiburg in 1120. In order to solidify their claim on the land, they moved farmers into the valleys to clear the trees and create small settlements. This led to the discovery of natural resources and, up until the 15th century, the extraction of iron, zinc, lead and even silver were major industries.

While their feudal lords enjoyed the spoils of their subjects' labour, the lot of the miners and farmers steadily deteriorated. In the 16th century unrest fomenting in the Black Forest eventually grew into the Peasant Rebellion that swept through much of southern Germany. Poorly equipped and haphazardly organised, the farmers were, of course, no match for the authorities who brought the uprising to a bloody conclusion.

In the following centuries the people of the Black Forest experienced a series of hardships of Biblical proportions. The Thirty Years' War left about 70% of the population dead, and plague and crop failures did much the same for the rest. Unsurprisingly, many of the survivors left for greener pastures in other parts of Europe.

The Black Forest stayed out of the spotlight for well over a century until the Baden Revolution of 1848–49. Inspired by the democratic movement in France and the declaration of the French Republic in February 1848, local radical democratic leaders Friedrich Hecker and Gustav von Struve led an armed rebellion against the archduke of Baden in April 1848, demanding freedom of expression, universal education, popular suffrage and other democratic ideals. Struve was arrested and Hecker fled into exile, but their struggle inspired the population and spilled over into other parts of Germany. Eventually Prussian troops cracked down on the revolutionaries in a fiery showdown at Rastatt in July 1849.

Nearly 100 years later, Freudenstadt and Freiburg were among the regional cities bombed to bits during WWII. In 1952 the Black Forest became part of the newly formed German state of Baden-Württemberg. Still largely agrarian, tourism is the single biggest source of income today.

Siegestor triumphal arch, and the Ludwig Maximilian University were all built on Ludwig I's watch, as was the Alte Pinakothek. The king was also keen on new technology and heavily supported the idea of a nationwide railway. The first short line from Nuremberg to Fürth opened during his reign in 1835.

Politically though, Ludwig I brought a return to authority from the top as revolutionary rumblings in other parts of Europe coaxed out his reactionary streak. An arch-Catholic, he restored the monasteries, introduced press censorship and authorised arrests of students, journalists and university professors whom he judged subversive. Bavaria was

1886	1914–18	1919	1923
King Ludwig II is declared mentally unfit and confined to Schloss Berg (Berg Palace) on Lake Starnberg where he drowns in mysterious circumstances in shallow water, alongside his doctor.	WWI: Germany, Austria, Hungary and Turkey go to war against Britain, France, Italy and Russia. Germany is defeated, the monarchy overthrown and Bavaria declared a 'free state'.	Left-leaning intellectuals proclaim the Münchner Räterepublik on 4 April, hoping to create a Soviet-style regime. The movement never spreads beyond Munich and is quashed by government forces on 3 May.	Hitler's failed putsch attempt lands him in jail where he takes just nine months to pen his vitriolic rant, *Mein Kampf*. It sells between eight and nine million copies.

LOLA MONTEZ, FEMME FATALE BY JEREMY GRAY

A whip-toting dominatrix and seductress of royalty, Lola Montez (1818–61) would show today's celebs what sex scandals are all about. Born as Eliza Gilbert in Ireland, to a young British army officer and a 13-year-old Creole chorus girl, Lola claimed to be the illegitimate daughter of poet Lord Byron (or, depending on her mood, of a matador). When her actual father died of cholera in India, her mother remarried and then shipped the seven-year-old Eliza off to Scotland. During her time in Scotland she was occasionally seen running stark naked through the streets. She then finished her schooling in Paris and after an unsuccessful stab at acting, reinvented herself as the Spanish dancer Lola Montez.

She couldn't dance either but her beauty fascinated men, who fell at her feet – sometimes under the lash of her ever-present riding crop. One time she fired a pistol at a lover who'd underperformed, but he managed to escape with his trousers around his knees.

Those succumbing to her charms included the tsar of Russia, who paid her 1000 roubles for a 'private audience'; novelist Alexandre Dumas; and composer Franz Liszt. Liszt eventually tired of Lola's incendiary temper, locked his sleeping mistress in their hotel room and fled – leaving a deposit for the furniture Lola would demolish when she awoke.

When fired by a Munich theatre manager, Lola took her appeal to the court of Ludwig I himself. As the tale goes, Ludwig asked casually whether her lovely figure was a work of nature or art. The direct gal she was, Lola seized a pair of scissors and slit open the front of her dress, leaving the ageing monarch to judge for himself. Predictably, she was rehired (and the manager sacked).

The king fell head over heels for Lola, giving her a huge allowance, a lavish palace and even the doubtful title of Countess of Landsfeld. Her ladyship virtually began running the country, too, and when Munich students rioted during the 1848 revolution, Lola had Ludwig shut down the university. This was too much for the townsfolk, who joined the students in revolt. Ludwig was forced to abdicate and Lola was chased out of town.

Lola cancanned her way around the world; her increasingly lurid show was very popular with gold miners in California and Australia. Next came a book of 'beauty secrets' and a lecture tour featuring topics such as 'Heroines of History and Strong-Minded Women'. She shed her Spanish identity, but in doing so, Lola – who had long publicly denied any link to her alter ego, Eliza – became a schizophrenic wreck. She spent her final two years as a pauper in New York, dying of pneumonia and a stroke aged 43.

becoming restrictive, even as French and American democratic ideas flourished elsewhere in Germany.

On 22 March 1848 Ludwig I abdicated in favour of his son, Maximilian II (r 1848–64), who finally put into place many of the constitutional reforms his father had ignored, such as abolishing censorship and introducing the right to assemble. Further progressive measures passed by his son Ludwig II (r 1864–86) early in his reign included welfare for the poor, liberalised marriage laws and free trade.

1933	1938	1939–45	1943
Hitler becomes chancellor of Germany and creates a dictatorship, making Munich the 'capital of the movement' and Obersalzberg, near Berchtesgaden, a second seat of government.	The Munich Agreement allows Hitler to annex the Sudetenlands, a mostly German-speaking region of Czechoslovakia. British Prime Minister Neville Chamberlain declares there will be 'peace in our time'.	WWII: Hitler invades Poland; Britain, France and, in 1941, the US, declare war on Germany; Jews are murdered en masse in concentration camps throughout Eastern Europe during the Holocaust.	Members of the Nazi resistance group Die Weisse Rose (The White Rose) are caught distributing anti-Nazi leaflets at Ludwig Maximilian University and executed a few days later, following a sham trial.

The Mystique of Ludwig II

No other Bavarian king stirs the imagination quite as much as Ludwig II, the fairy-tale king so tragically at odds with a modern world that had no longer any use for an absolutist, if enlightened, monarch. Ludwig was a sensitive soul, fascinated by romantic epics, architecture and the music of Richard Wagner. When he became king at 18, he was at first a rather enthusiastic leader; however, Bavaria's days as a sovereign state were numbered. After it was absorbed into the Prussian-led German Reich in 1871, Ludwig became little more than a puppet king (albeit one receiving regular hefty allowances from Berlin).

Disillusioned, the king retreated to the Bavarian Alps to drink, draw castle plans, and enjoy private concerts and operas. His obsession with French culture and the Sun King, Louis XIV, inspired the fantastical palaces of Neuschwanstein, Linderhof and Herrenchiemsee (more were planned) – lavish projects that spelt his undoing.

In January 1886 several ministers and relatives arranged a hasty psychiatric test that diagnosed Ludwig as mentally unfit to rule. He was dethroned and taken to Schloss Berg on Lake Starnberg (Starnbergersee). Then, one evening, the dejected bachelor and his doctor took a lakeside walk and several hours later were found dead – mysteriously drowned in just a few feet of water.

No-one knows with certainty what happened that night. There was no eyewitness or proper criminal investigation. The circumstantial evidence was conflicting and incomplete. Reports and documents were tampered with, destroyed or lost. Conspiracy theories abound. That summer the authorities opened Neuschwanstein to the public to help pay off Ludwig's huge debts. King Ludwig II was dead, but a tourist industry was just being born.

King Ludwig II was born at half past midnight on 25th August 1845 in Munich's Nymphenburg Castle.

Nazi Legacy

If Berlin was the head of the Nazi government, its heart beat in Bavaria. This was the birthplace of the movement, born out of the chaos and volatility of a post-WWI Germany wracked by revolution, crippling reparations and runaway inflation. Right-wing agitation resonated especially among Bavarians who deeply resented losing much of their sovereignty to a centralised national government in Berlin.

In Munich, a failed artist and WWI corporal from Austria – Adolf Hitler – had quickly risen to the top of the extreme right-wing Nationalsozialistische Arbeiterpartei (NSDAP). On 8 November 1923 he led his supporters in a revolt aimed at overthrowing the central government following a political rally in the Bürgerbräukeller (near today's Gasteig arts centre). The so-called Beer Hall Putsch was an abysmal failure, poorly planned and amateurishly executed. The following day a ragtag bunch of would-be armed revolutionaries marched through Munich's streets but

In 1923 a postage stamp cost 50 billion marks, a loaf of bread cost 140 billion marks and US$1 was worth 4.2 trillion marks. In November the new Rentenmark was traded in for one trillion old marks.

1945	1945–46	1958	1950s-1980s
Hitler commits suicide in his Berlin bunker. A broken Germany surrenders to the Allies and is divided into four zones. Bavaria falls into the US Zone.	The Allies hold a series of trials against Nazi leaders accused of crimes against peace and humanity in a courthouse at Nuremberg. Ten of the accused are executed by hanging.	The Munich air disaster kills 23 of the Manchester United Busby Babes, journalists and supporters on a slushy runway at Riem airfield.	Bavaria leads the way in the nation's *Wirtschaftswunder* (economic miracle) with huge companies such as Adidas, Puma and Playmobil established in the state.

only got as far as the Feldherrnhalle where a shoot-out with police left 16 Nazis and four policemen dead.

The NSDAP was banned and Hitler was sentenced to five years in prison for high treason. While in Landsberg jail, west of Munich, he began work on *Mein Kampf* (My Struggle), dictated in extended ramblings to his secretary Rudolf Hess. Incredibly, Hitler was released after only nine months in 1924 on grounds of 'good behaviour'.

After Hitler took control of Germany in January 1933, Bavaria was assigned a special status. Munich was declared the 'Capital of the Movement' and Nuremberg became the site of the Nazi party's mass rallies. In 1935 the party brass enacted the Nuremberg Laws, which ushered in the systematic repression of the Jews. In Dachau, north of Munich, Germany's first concentration camp was built in 1933. In addition, many Nazi honchos hailed from Bavaria, including *Sturmabteilung* (SA) chief Ernst Röhm (later killed by Hitler), Heinrich Himmler and Hermann Göring. Hitler himself was born just across the border in Austria's Braunau. The Nazis enjoyed almost universal support in Bavaria, but there were also some pockets of resistance, most famously the Munich-based group Die Weisse Rose (The White Rose).

In 1938 Hitler's troops met no resistance when they marched into Austria and annexed it to Nazi Germany. The same year, the UK's Neville Chamberlain, Italy's Benito Mussolini and France's Édouard Daladier, in an attempt to avoid another war, continued their policy of appeasement by handing Hitler control over large portions of Czechoslovakia in the Munich Agreement. Chamberlain's naive hope that such a move would bring 'peace in our time' was destroyed on 1 September 1939 when Nazi troops marched into Poland, kicking off WWII.

The Munich Air Disaster

One of Europe's worst sporting tragedies happened on a freezing February afternoon in 1958 at Munich Riem Airport. The Manchester United football team, the much-lauded Busby Babes, along with journalists and supporters were returning from a UEFA European Cup (the forerunner to today's Champions League) fixture in Belgrade when their flight had to land in Munich to refuel. With fuel tanks full, two take-off attempts were made but engine trouble meant they were unsuccessful. The passengers were offloaded, a solution to the problem found and the passengers got back on. However, on the third attempt, the plane never reached take-off speed on the slushy runway and slid off the end, hitting a house and other buildings. Some 23 people died, including eight players, eight journalists and three coaching staff. Bobby Charlton was one of the survivors – he went on to lift the World Cup for England in 1966. The German authorities opened an investigation against the one pilot who survived, captain James Thain – this dragged on until 1968 when the case was dropped.

Hitler called his regime the 'Third Reich' because he thought of the Holy Roman Empire and Bismarck's German empire as the first and second Reichs, respectively.

Bavaria's Most Visited Nazi Sites

Eagle's Nest, Berchtesgaden

Dachau concentration camp

Reichsparteitagsgelände, Nuremberg

Nuremberg Trials courtroom, Nuremberg

Dokumentation Obersalzberg, Berchtesgaden

1972	1974	1992	2005
Bavaria shows off its prosperity, friendliness and cutting-edge architecture during the Olympic Games, although the event is overshadowed by the so-called Munich Massacre, a deadly terrorist attack on Israeli athletes.	Just two years after the tragic events of the Munich Olympics, the city hosts the final of the FIFA World Cup. West Germany defeat Holland 2:1 at the Olympic Stadium.	The Munich airport begins operations, becoming the second-busiest airport in Germany and the seventh-busiest in Europe. It's named after former Bavarian minister-president Franz Josef Strauss, who helped establish Airbus.	Cardinal Joseph Ratzinger, who was born in 1927 in the town of Marktl am Inn near the Austrian border, is elected Pope Benedict XVI.

A State Apart

Modern Bavaria may be integrated thoroughly within the German political construct, but its people take great pride in their distinctiveness. Its history, traditions, attitudes, political priorities and culture are, in many ways, quite different from the rest of Germany. While seeing themselves as Germans, Bavarians are Bavarians first. This is not true over the 'border' in Baden-Württemberg.

After WWII Bavaria became part of the American occupation zone and was allowed to pass its own constitution in December 1946. In 1949 it became the only German state that didn't ratify the German constitution because, in its opinion, it put unacceptable limitations on state powers. Bavaria did, however, agree to honour and abide by the federal constitution and has always done so. However, to underscore its independent streak it calls itself 'Freistaat' (free state) Bayern, even though this has no real political meaning.

Since 1946 a single party, the archconservative Christlich-Soziale Union (CSU; Christian Social Union) has dominated Bavarian politics at every level of government, from communal to state. Although peculiar to Bavaria, it is closely aligned with its national sister party, the Christlich-Demokratische Union (CDU; Christian Democratic Union).

Powerful CSU figures include Franz-Josef Strauss, who served as Bavarian *Ministerpräsident* (minister-president, ie governor) from 1978 until his death in 1988, and his protégé, Edmund Stoiber, who clung to the job from 1999 until 2007. Although hugely popular and successful in Bavaria, both failed in their attempts to become federal chancellor: Strauss when losing to Helmut Schmidt in 1980, and Stoiber when outmanoeuvred by Gerhard Schröder in 2002. Since October 2008, Bavaria has been led by Horst Seehofer.

No other German state has been more successful in its postwar economic recovery than Bavaria. Within decades it transformed from an essentially agrarian society into a progressive, high-tech state. The upturn was at least in part fuelled by the arrival of two million ethnic German expellees mainly from the Sudetelands of Bohemia and Moravia, who brought much-needed manpower. Bavaria is now synonymous with state-of-the-art engineering, quality manufacturing and top of the range cars. But much of the past lives on in its traditional ways and in the treasure trove of architecture bequeathed by its erstwhile rulers.

Part travelogue, part history *Germania* (2010), by Simon Winder, is arguably the most digestible account of Germany's past to be published in recent decades, a fair share of the book dealing with Bavaria.

HISTORY A STATE APART

2006	2007	2008-13	2016
Munich's new Allianz Arena hosts the first match of the FIFA World Cup soccer championships. Hosts Germany beat Costa Rica 4:2 in an exciting curtain raiser.	After 14 years, Edmund Stoiber steps down as minister-president of Bavaria and party chairman of the CSU, after his leadership skills are called into question.	The CSU is forced into a coalition (with the FDP) for the first time since the early 1960s. Normality is resumed in 2013 when the party regained its overall majority in the *Landtag*.	The Free State of Bavaria's rights to Hitler's *Mein Kampf* run out. The text can now be reproduced freely by any publishing house in the world.

People & Culture

The culture of southern Germany is truly a vibrant mixed bag. Where else on earth can you find beer hall oompah bands alongside Gothic sculpture, galleries of cutting-edge contemporary art next door to shops selling strapping folk costumes (that people still actually wear). The ebb and flow of history has left many cultural tide marks here, some from the bucolic past, others from darker and more recent chapters in the region's history. Whatever cultural experience floats your boat, Bavaria is bound to intrigue.

Regional Identity

Few other states in Germany can claim as distinct an identity as Bavaria. The country's southernmost state has always been a crossroads of trading routes to the Mediterranean and southeast Europe, and as the Alps never formed a truly impassable barrier, Bavaria early on absorbed the influences of Mediterranean culture. This gave the Bavarian character an easygoing outlook but one tempered with a Germanic respect for law and order. Patriotic feeling runs high, and at any hint of an affront Bavarians close ranks, at least until the next party or festival. People here claim to be Bavarians first, Germans second, though this feeling weakens the further north into Franconia you head.

Indigenous Bavarians still strongly identify with their tribal heritage and call everyone not born in this neck of the *Wald* a *Zuagroaste* ('newcomer' in Bavarian dialect).

For outsiders, the marriage of traditional rural Bavaria with modern-day industrial efficiency and wealth are hard to see as one entity – the two just don't seem to fit together. A popular slogan once coined by the state government dubbed Bavaria 'the land of Lederhosen and laptops', conjuring up images of farmers and computer scientists happily working hand in virtual hand. Modern Bavaria is indeed the land of Oktoberfest, beer and tradition, but it's also about cutting-edge glass-and-steel architecture, bright-lights nightlife, hipster fashion, sophisticated dining and world-class sport. It's youthful, dynamic and with only a hint of the brooding introspection you may encounter elsewhere in Germany.

Only created in 1952 out of the small states of Württemberg-Baden, Württemberg-Hohenzollern and Baden, today's Baden-Württemberg has none of the national feeling of Bavaria. Region is more important there, with Swabia and the Allgäu possessing their own traditions.

Lifestyle

So who exactly is the average inhabitant of Germany's south? Statistically speaking, they are in their early 30s, white and married, have at least some higher education and live in a 90-sq-metre rented apartment in a midsize town. They drive a midsize car, but use public transport to commute to work in the service industry, where they earn about €3300 per month. About 40% of that evaporates in tax and social security deductions. The average Bavarian or Baden-Württemberger tends to vote conservative, but would not rule out giving another party the nod. Sorting and recycling rubbish is done religiously and, speaking of religion, Bavarians tend to be Roman Catholic while those from Baden-Württemberg are more likely to be Lutherans, though neither are regular churchgoers. A southern German feels comfortable on the hiking trail and ski slopes,

The distinctive Bavarian flag is made up of at least 21 blue and white diamonds.

MULTICULTURALISM

Despite a high level of tolerance, few groups mix on a day-to-day basis and racial tensions are increasing, at least in the cities. Government 'integration courses' for immigrants on welfare payments have done little to break down barriers and neo-Nazism is on the rise with a growing number of cases of intimidation of non-white foreigners reported.

but is not fitness-obsessed and could actually stand to lose a few pounds. When they decide to have a family, they will have exactly 1.38 children.

Religion

Bavaria is overwhelmingly Roman Catholic with over 50% claiming to be followers of the Vatican. However, pockets of Lutherans can be found in such cities as Munich, Augsburg and Nuremberg, and in the Bavarian regions of Oberfranken and Mittelfranken they are marginally in the majority. Munich has a growing Jewish community of around 10,000 people, most of them arrivals from former Soviet republics from the last three decades. Muslims account for about 4.2% of the population and this number is growing fast.

Baden-Württemberg is divided into the Lutheran north/middle and the Catholic south – the split between the two is around 50/50. Islam is the state's third religion with 6% of the population claiming to be followers of the Prophet.

The website www. kulturportal-bayern.de is your guide to Bavarian culture, with sections on fine arts, film, museums, traditions and much, much more.

Conventions

Bavarians (and their counterparts in the Black Forest) are a culturally conservative bunch. When in business mode, at fancy social gatherings or at high-brow cultural events, such as opera and theatre performances, you'll probably feel more comfortable if dressed in smart casual clothes. However chic threads may be needed to get past face control at fancier Munich nightclubs.

Locals are generally accommodating and fairly helpful towards visitors, and many will volunteer assistance if you look lost. This politeness does not necessarily extend to friendliness, however, and in public people usually maintain a degree of reserve towards strangers – you won't find many conversations striking up on the bus or in the supermarket checkout queue. On the other hand, in younger company it's easy to chat with just about anyone, particularly in student hang-outs.

Shaking hands is common among both men and women, as is a hug or a kiss on the cheek, especially among young people. When making a phone call, start by giving your name (eg 'Smith, Grüss Gott'). Not doing so is considered impolite.

Importance is placed on the formal '*Sie*' form of address, especially in business situations. Among younger people and in social settings, though, people are much more relaxed about using '*Sie*' and '*Du*'.

Germany's most successful golfer, Bernhard Langer, is the son of a Russian prisoner of war who jumped off a Siberia-bound train and settled in Bavaria.

Sport

Football

Mention *Fussball* (football, soccer) in Bavaria and passions will flare. FC Bayern München has dominated the Bundesliga on and off for the past two decades and has won the German championship 21 times, most recently in 2015. It's also had some success in the UEFA Champion's League, reaching the final five times since 1999, but winning the competition only twice. The team packs plenty of actual and financial muscle and attracts some of Europe's best players.

Bayern may dominate proceedings but there are several other good teams in southern Germany. FC Augsburg, Ingolstadt 04 and VfB Stuttgart currently play in the top flight; SpVgg Greuther Fürth and 1. FC Nürnberg play in the second tier.

In 2015 women's football came to the fore in Bavaria when Bayern Munich won the women's Bundesliga for the first time since 1976.

The football season runs from September to June, with a winter break from Christmas to mid-February.

Skiing

If you want to follow the thrills, spills and manager tantrums in Germany's top soccer league, it's all online at www.bundesliga.de (in English).

Bavarian slopes still lure the sport's elite to annual World Cup races held in such resorts as Garmisch-Partenkirchen, Reit im Winkl and Berchtesgaden. On New Year's Day, Garmisch-Partenkirchen is also a stop on the four-part Vierschanzen-Tournee, the World Cup ski-jumping competition. Famous female champions from Bavaria include Rosi Mittermaier, a two-time Olympic gold-medal winner in 1976, and more recently Martina Ertl and Hilde Gerg. In early 2005 Alois Vogl ended the men's drought by snagging the World Cup for slalom.

Arts

Literature

Quite a few German writers of the 18th and 19th centuries, including Jean Paul and ETA Hoffmann, lived in southern Germany, but the golden age of Bavarian literature kicked off in the second half of the 19th century. Some of the finest writers of the time, Thomas Mann and Frank Wedekind (famous for his coming-of-age tale *Spring Awakening,* 1891) among them, contributed to *Simplicissimus,* a satirical magazine founded in 1896 with a cover bearing a trademark red bulldog. A few of its barbs about Emperor Wilhelm II were so biting that the magazine was censored and some of its writers (Wedekind among them) were sent to jail. During his 40 years in Munich, Thomas Mann wrote an entire bookcase of acclaimed works and picked up a Nobel prize in the process. His Bavarian gems include the short story *Gladius Dei* (1902), a clever parody of Munich's pretensions to being the Florence of Bavaria.

More contemporary names are/were an eclectic, label-defying bunch. Herbert Rosendorfer (b 1934–2012), a former Munich judge, has a long list of credits, including a legal satire, a history of the Thirty Years' War and travel guides. Anna Rosmus (b 1960) has turned her investigation of the Third Reich period in Passau, her birthplace, into several best-selling novels, including *Against the Stream: Growing Up Where Hitler Used to Live* (2002). Munich-based Patrick Süskind (b 1949) achieved international acclaim with *Das Parfum* (Perfume; 1985), his extraordinary tale of a psychotic 18th-century perfume-maker, which was made into a film by Tom Tykwer in 2006.

Catholic Bavaria has produced few Jewish writers of note. A major exception is Jakob Wassermann (1873–1934), a popular novelist of the early 20th century.

Although he lived mostly in Switzerland, Nobel Prize–winner Hermann Hesse (1877–1962) is originally a Black Forest boy whose most famous novels, *Siddhartha* and *Steppenwolf,* became hippie-era favourites. The philosopher Martin Heidegger (1889–1976), author of *Being and Time,* one of the seminal works of German existentialism, also hailed from the Black Forest, as did Hans Jacob Christoffel von Grimmelshausen (1622–76), a 17th-century literary genius and author of the earliest German adventure novel, *Simplicissimus* (Adventures of a Simpleton; 1668), which later inspired the name of the aforementioned satirical magazine.

Bavaria's greatest playwright of international stature was the ever-abrasive Bertolt Brecht (1898–1956) from Augsburg. After WWII, writers throughout Germany either dropped out of sight ('inner exile' was the

HEIMATFILM

Southern Germany's dreamy Alpine landscapes helped spawn the *Heimatfilm* (homeland film), the only film genre to have been created in Germany. It reached its zenith in the 1950s and helped spread many of today's cosy clichés about Bavaria.

Most *Heimatfilms* show a world at peace with itself, focusing on basic themes such as love, family and the delights of traditional rural life. An interloper, such as a priest, creates some kind of conflict for the main characters – perhaps a milkmaid and her boyfriend or a poacher fighting local laws – who then invoke traditional values to solve the problem. Stories are set in the mountains of Austria, Bavaria or Switzerland, with predictable plots and schmaltzy film scores.

If you'd like to experience the *Heimatfilm* genre, titles to look out for include *Die Fischerin vom Bodensee* (The Fisher Girl of Lake Constance; 1956), *Hoch Droben auf dem Berg* (High Up On the Mountain; 1957) and *Die Landärztin von Tegernsee* (Lady Country Doctor; 1958), though these often cheap flicks were made by the dozen.

favoured term) or, as Hans Carossa and Ernst Wiechert did, attempted some kind of political and intellectual renewal.

Cinema & Television

OK, so Germany's last true international success, the Oscar-winning *Das Leben der Anderen* (The Lives of Others; 2006), was filmed in Berlin, but Munich's Bavaria Film studio is no slouch in the movie scene. Successes cranked out this side of the millennium include Marc Rothemund's Oscar-nominated *Sophie Scholl – The Final Days* (2005) and Tom Twyker's *Perfume: Story of a Murderer* (2006).

The studio pegs its pedigree back to 1919 and has lured many well-known directors, including Alfred Hitchcock (*The Pleasure Garden;* 1925), Billy Wilder (*Fedora;* 1978), Rainer Werner Fassbinder (*Bolwieser;* 1977) and, most famously, Wolfgang Petersen *Das Boot* (The Boat, 1981, and *The Neverending Story,* 1984). Many made-for-German-TV features, detective series such as *Polizeiruf 110* and popular soaps such as *Marienhof* are also produced in Munich. Part of the studio complex is Bavaria Filmstadt, a movie-themed film park with original sets and props from *Das Boot* and other famous flicks.

In Anna Rosmus' *Against the Stream: Growing Up Where Hitler Used to Live,* a teenage girl writes an essay and uncovers shocking crimes in prewar Passau.

Music

Ironically, the composer most commonly associated with Bavaria didn't hail from Bavaria at all. Richard Wagner (1813–83) was born in Leipzig and died in Venice but his career took a dramatic turn when King Ludwig II became his patron in 1864 and financed the *Festspielhaus* (opera house) in Bayreuth, which was completed in 1872. Strongly influenced by Beethoven and Mozart, Wagner is most famous for his operas, many of which dealt with mythological themes (eg *Lohengrin* or *Tristan und Isolde*). His great achievement was a synthesis of visual, musical, poetic and dramatic components into a *Gesamtkunstwerk* (single work of art). Wagner's presence also drew other composers to Bayreuth, most notably Anton Bruckner and Franz Liszt, Wagner's father-in-law.

As the scores for symphonies became more complex, not the least thanks to Wagner, Bavarian composers hastened to join in. Richard Strauss (1864–1949), who hailed from Munich, created such famous symphonies as *Don Juan* and *Macbeth* but later focused on operas, including the successful *Der Rosenkavalier* (The Knight of the Rose).

Last, but not least, there's Munich-born Carl Orff (1895–1982), who achieved lasting fame with just a single work: his life-embracing 1935 cantata *Carmina Burana,* a work characterised by simple harmonies,

Florian von Donnersmarck, celebrated director of the Oscar-winning *The Lives of Others* (2006), learned his craft at the Munich film school.

VOLKSMUSIK

No other musical genre is as closely associated with Bavaria as *Volksmusik* (folk music). Every village has its own proud brass band or choir, and the state government puts serious euros into preserving this traditional music. More than 600,000 Bavarians, mostly lay musicians, belong to some 11,000 music groups, most of them in the Alpine regions. The basic musical form is the ¾-time *Landler,* which is also a dance involving plenty of hopping and stomping; men sometimes slap themselves on their knees in what is called *Platteln*. Typical instruments are the accordion and the zither and some songs end in a yodel. Popular performers of traditional *Volksmusik* are the Rehm Buam, Sepp Eibl and Ruperti Blech.

In the 1970s and '80s, small stages in Munich such as the Fraunhofer pub gave birth to a new style of *Volksmusik*. Performers infused the folklore concept with a political edge, freed it from conservative ideology and merged it with folk music from countries as diverse as Ireland and Ghana. Among the pioneers was the Biermösl Blosn, a band known for its satirical and provocative songs. Also keep an ear out for the Fraunhofer Saitenmusik, a chamber folk music ensemble that plays traditional tunes on acoustic instruments and which used to be the Fraunhofer pub's house band.

Since the '90s the scene has gone even further and now champions wacky crossovers of Bavarian folk with pop, rock, punk, hip-hop and techno in what has been dubbed 'Alpine New Wave'. Look for the folk rockers Hundsbuam, or the jazzy Munich trio Die Interpreten. Rudi Zapf uses the hammered dulcimer to take you on a musical journey around the world. The wildest band of them all is the hardcore folk-punk band Attwenger.

rhythms and hypnotic repetition. Kloster Andechs, where he is buried, holds an annual Orff festival.

The most illustrious name in music to emerge from just across the border in Austria was Wolfgang Amadeus Mozart, born in Salzburg in 1756. On their travels, the Mozart family visited several places in Bavaria and played at the court of the prince-elector Maximilian III in Munich in 1762. Mozart's birthplace and his family house can both be visited in Salzburg.

First stop for fans of 'serious music' should be Munich where the Münchner Philharmoniker is the chart topper thanks to music director Lorin Maazel. Equally respected is the Bayerische Staatsoper, currently helmed by California wunderkind Kent Nagano. Nuremberg's highbrow scene perked up in 2005 when the Bavarian state government elevated the municipal theatre to the Staatstheater Nuremberg, whose opera, concert and ballet productions also get high marks.

Southern Germany maintains a busy festival schedule, but the granddaddy of them all is the Richard Wagner Festival in Bayreuth. Opened by the maestro himself in 1876 with the *Ring des Nibelungen* opera marathon, it was run by the composer's grandson, Wolfgang Wagner, from 1951 until his death in 2010. Although still a major societal and artistic event, the festival stagnated under his long leadership and is still emerging from his shadow with a recent shake-up of the ticket allocation system and number of other improvements to the visitor experience.

One of the few Bavarian names to have made it in the pop era is Harold Faltermeyer, born in Munich in 1952. He is best known for composing the 'Axel F' theme tune for the 1984 film *Beverly Hills Cop* and the 'Top Gun Anthem', both of which earned him a Grammy. In the 1980s he worked as a session musician and producer with some of the biggest names of the era such as Billy Idol, Barbra Streisand and the Pet Shop Boys.

Painting & Sculpture
Early Works

Frescoes and manuscript illumination were early art forms popular between the 9th and 13th centuries. The oldest frescoes in Bavaria are in the crypt of the Benedictine Abbey of St Mang in Füssen. Stained glass emerged around 1100; the 'Prophet's Windows' in Augsburg's cathedral are the earliest example in Central Europe.

Gothic

Portraiture and altar painting hit the artistic stage around 1300 AD. Top dog here was Jan Polack, whose work can be admired in such churches as Munich's Schloss Blutenburg.

A major Gothic sculptor was Erasmus Grasser, whose masterpieces include the St Peter altar in St Peterskirche in Munich and the *Morris Dancers* in the Munich Stadtmuseum. Another is Veit Stoss, a Franconian who imbued his sculptures with dramatic realism. In 1503 Stoss spent a stint in jail for forgery, but restored his reputation with the main altar in Bamberg's cathedral, his crowning achievement.

Renaissance

The Renaissance saw the rise of human elements in painting: religious figures were now depicted alongside mere mortals. The heavyweight – quite literally – in Germany was the Nuremberg-born Albrecht Dürer, who excelled both as a painter and graphic artist. His subjects ranged from mythology to religion to animals, all in fantastic anatomical detail, natural perspective and vivid colours. The Alte Pinakothek in Munich has several famous works, and his Nuremberg house is now a museum.

Dürer influenced Lucas Cranach the Elder, a major artist of the Reformation. Cranach's approach to landscape painting, though, grew out of the Donauschule (Danube School), an artistic movement based in Passau and Regensburg. The amazing details of these landscapes seethed with dark movement, making them the focal point of the painting rather than a mere backdrop.

The brightest of stars among Renaissance sculptors was Tilman Riemenschneider. His skills were formidable, allowing his stone to mimic wood and featuring compositions playing on light and shadow. Mustsees include the altars in the Jakobskirche in Rothenburg ob der Tauber and in the Herrgottskirche in Creglingen, both on the Romantic Road. The Mainfränkisches Museum in Würzburg also has an outstanding Riemenschneider collection.

TRACHTEN

If the tourist bumf is to be believed, Bavaria is full of locals cavorting around in *Trachten* (folk costume), the men in Lederhosen, the women in figure-hugging, cleavage-baring, aproned dresses called Dirndl. You may not see many such exotic folk on the streets of Nuremberg, Ingolstadt or Passau, but travel to the Alpine region, and you'll be in cliché heaven. Many young Munich city dwellers own these traditional outfits, but most only leave the closet for Oktoberfest and special occasions, but things are different in rural areas, especially among older generations. If you want to see real *Trachten* on parade, go to any folk festival or even just a Sunday morning church service in Oberammergau or Berchtesgaden.

Munich has several *Trachten* emporia selling everything from the real hand-embroidered deal to made-heaven-knows-where imitations. Getting garbed up for a beer festival or a night in a beer hall is an essential part of the fun in the Bavarian capital.

Baroque & Rococo

The sugar-iced styles of the baroque and rococo periods left their mark throughout Bavaria, especially in church art. Illusionary effects and contrast between light and shadow are typical features, and surfaces are often bewilderingly ornate.

The Goethe Institut website, www.goethe.de, is a superb place to start for detailed info on all aspects of German culture.

Arguably the finest and most prolific artists of the period, the brothers Cosmas and Egid Asam were of a generation of Germans educated in Rome in the Italian baroque tradition. Their father, Hans Georg, was a master fresco artist who transformed the Basilika St Benedikt in Benediktbeuern. Word of their supreme talent, along with the family's connections in the Benedictine order, meant the duo were always swamped with work. Cosmas was primarily a fresco painter while Egid used his considerable talents as an architect and stucco sculptor. Examples of their brilliant collaboration can be found throughout Bavaria, mostly notably in the Asamkirche in central Munich and the Asamkirche Maria de Victoria in Ingolstadt.

Another set of brothers who dominated the baroque period was Dominikus and Johann Baptist Zimmermann, whose collaboration reached its pinnacle in the Unesco-listed Wieskirche, a short stop on the Romantic Road. Johann Baptist also worked on Munich's St Peterskirche and Schloss Nymphenburg. Both were members of the so-called Wessobrunner School, which counted architect and stucco artist Josef Schmuzer among its founding members. Schmuzer's work can be admired at Kloster Ettal and in the Alte St Martinskirche in Garmisch-Partenkirchen.

The 19th Century

Heart-on-your-sleeve Romanticism that drew heavily on emotion and a dreamy idealism dominated the 19th century. Austria-born Moritz von Schwind is noted for his moody scenes of German legends and fairy tales. His teacher, Peter Cornelius, was a follower of the Nazarenes, a group of religious painters who drew from the old masters for inspiration. There's a giant fresco of his in Munich's Ludwigskirche, although for the full survey of Romantic art you should swing by the nearby Sammlung Schack.

Romanticism gradually gave way to the sharp edges of realism and, later on, the meticulous detail of naturalism. Major practitioners were Wilhelm Leibl, who specialised in painting Bavarian country scenes, and Hans Thoma, who joined Leibl in Munich but favoured the landscapes of his native Black Forest. Look for their works in Munich's Städtische Galerie im Lenbachhaus.

Munich Secession & Jugendstil

During the 1890s a group of about 100 artists shook up the art establishment when they split from Munich's Künstlergesellschaft (Artists' Society), a traditionalist organisation led by portrait artist Franz von

---

MORE FAMOUS BAVARIANS

➡ Franz Beckenbauer (b 1945 in Munich) – 'Der Kaiser' is the Germany's most famous footballer and manager

➡ Pope Benedikt XVI (b 1927 in Marktl am Inn) – Served as pope from 2005 until his resignation in 2013.

➡ Edmund Stoiber (b 1941 in Oberaudorf) – The most influential politician in postwar Bavaria.

➡ Uschi Disl (b 1970 in Bad Tölz) – Bavaria's most successful Olympian with two golds, four silvers and three bronzes in the biathlon.

CORNELIUS GURLITT – NO ORDINARY ART COLLECTOR

Thousands of pieces of art were looted by the Nazis across Europe during WWII and many remain missing. However, the mystery of what happened to some of them was solved in March of 2012 when almost 1400 works were discovered in the Schwabing apartment of Cornelius Gurlitt. They included paintings by Chagall, Matisse, Dix and Lieberman among countless others. Cornelius was the son of art dealer and collector Hildebrand Gurlitt who had been responsible for selling art deemed degenerate by the Nazis for foreign currency. He was captured by the US Army with 20 boxes of artworks after WWII but released due to his Jewish heritage and the art returned to him. Hildebrand died in 1956 and Cornelius hid the works in his Munich flat, occasionally selling the odd painting abroad to make ends meet. It was on one of these sales trips that he was rumbled – German customs officers undertook a random inspection of a train crossing the Swiss-German border and Cornelius was discovered with €9000 in readies. Suspicious of how the unemployed Bavarian could have so much cash, Munich's prosecutor ordered a search of his flat.

Lenbach. Secessionists were not linked by a common artistic style, but by a rejection of reactionary attitudes towards the arts that stifled new forms of expression. They preferred scenes from daily life to historical and religious themes, shunned studios in favour of natural outdoor light and were hugely influential in inspiring new styles.

One of them was *Jugendstil* (art nouveau), inspired by printmaking and drawing on functional, linear ornamentation partly inspired by Japanese art. The term originated from the weekly trendsetting art-and-literature magazine *Die Jugend,* published in Munich from 1896 until 1940. In Munich the Neue Pinakothek is the place to head for some fine examples of this most elegant of styles.

Expressionism

In the early 20th century German artists looked for a purer, freer approach to painting through abstraction, vivid colours and expression. In Bavaria the trailblazer was the artist group Der Blaue Reiter (The Blue Rider), founded by Wassily Kandinsky and Franz Marc in 1911, and joined later by Paul Klee, Gabriele Münter and other top artists. The Städtische Galerie im Lenbachhaus has the most comprehensive collection, much of it donated by Münter, who managed to hide her colleagues' paintings from the Nazis. A good selection of Münter's own paintings is on view at the Schlossmuseum Murnau, a town in the Alps. At the Buchheim Museum on Starnberger See, the focus is on the equally avant-garde artist group called Die Brücke (The Bridge), founded in 1905 in Dresden by Ernst Ludwig Kirchner, Erich Heckel and Karl Schmidt-Rottluff.

Nazi Era

After the creative surge in the 1920s, the big chill of Nazi conformity sent Germany into an artistic deep freeze in the 1930s and '40s. Many internationally famous artists, including Paul Klee and Max Beckmann, were classified as 'degenerate' and their paintings confiscated, sold off or burned.

Modern & Contemporary

Post-1945 creativity revived the influence of Nolde, Kandinsky and Schmidt-Rottluff, but also spawned a new abstract expressionism in the work of Willi Baumeister. The completely revamped and enlarged Franz Marc Museum in Kochel am See traces the evolution of pre- and post-WWII expressionism.

HISTORICAL INVENTIONS

Over the past five centuries, Bavaria has been a bit of a hotbed when it comes to inventors and inventions, giving the world some of its most essential gadgets and machines. If you've put on a pair of jeans, listened to an MP3 or driven a diesel powered car recently, they're all Bavarian inventions (Levi Strauss, Karlheinz Brandenburg and Rudolf Diesel respectively). The globe (Martin Bahaim in 1493), the watch (Peter Henlein in 1505) and the plane engine (Gustav Weisskopf in 1901) are other things we just couldn't imagine the world lacking. That may no longer be the case with steerable oxcarts (Georg Lankensperger in 1816) and the board game Ludo (Josef Schmidt in 1908).

An edgy genre that has found major representation in Bavaria is concrete art, which emerged in the 1950s and takes abstract art to its extreme, rejecting any natural form and using only planes and colours. See what this is all about at the Museum für Konkrete Kunst in Ingolstadt and the Museum im Kulturspeicher in Würzburg.

The Bavarian photorealist Florian Thomas is among the influential artists whose work is now in the Museum Frieder Burda in Baden-Baden. Other good spots to plug into the contemporary art scene are the Neues Museum in Nuremberg, and the Pinakothek der Moderne and the superb Museum Brandhorst in Munich.

The website www. theaterparadies-deutschland. de (in German) is the ultimate thespian's portal with links to hundreds of theatres throughout the German-speaking world.

Theatre

Theatre in its various forms enjoys a wide following in Bavaria, especially in Munich, which has the famous Münchener Kammerspiele, but also in Nuremberg, Regensburg and Bamberg. Bavaria's longest-running drama is the *Passionsspiele* (Passion Play), which has been performed in Oberammergau once every decade since the 17th century.

For a dose of local colour, head to a *Bauerntheater* (literally, 'peasant theatre'), which usually presents silly and rustic tales in dialect so thick that it's basically incomprehensible to all non-Bavarians. But never mind, because the story lines are so simplistic, you'll probably be able to follow the plot anyway. The oldest *Bauerntheater* is in Garmisch-Partenkirchen.

If you're travelling with kids, don't miss one of the many excellent marionette theatres starring endearing and often handmade puppets. The most famous is the Augsburger Puppenkiste in Augsburg, but the Marionettentheater Bad Tölz and the Münchener Marionetten Theater will also take you on a magic carpet ride.

Stuttgart's Staatstheater hosts the Stuttgart Ballet, generally regarded as one of Europe's best companies.

Food & Drink

Sausages with foaming wheat beer in rollicking Munich beer halls, snowball-sized dumplings with an avalanche of sauerkraut and roast pork in the Alps, Black Forest gateau slathered in chocolate, cream and cherries – calorific excess still abounds in southern Germany. But while country menus revel in tradition, in the cities things have changed. Munich can easily switch from pig-trotter–chomping rusticity to the chic flavours of Michelin-starred fine dining. Meanwhile menus in Nuremberg and Freiburg go beyond the obvious, with a world of street food and new chefs wowing critics.

Regional & Seasonal

Classic Mains

The Chinese say you can eat every part of the pig bar the 'oink', and Bavarian chefs seem to be in full agreement. No part of the animal is spared their attention as they cook up its *Schweinshaxe* (knuckles), *Rippchen* (ribs), *Züngerl* (tongue) and *Wammerl* (belly). Pork also appears as *Schweinebraten* (roast pork) and the misleadingly named *Leberkäse* (liver cheese), a savoury meatloaf that contains neither liver nor cheese. The Black Forest contributes the famous *Schwarzwälder Schinken* – ham that's been salted, seasoned and cured for around two weeks.

Non-pork-based dishes include *Hendl* (roast chicken) and *Fleischpflanzerl*, the Bavarian spin on the hamburger. Fish is often caught fresh from the lakes. *Forelle* (trout) is especially popular in the Black Forest and served either *Forelle Müllerin* (baked), *Forelle Blau* (boiled) or *Räucherforelle* (smoked). In Bavarian beer gardens, you'll often find *Steckerlfisch* – skewers of grilled mackerel.

Originating in Swabia but now served throughout southern Germany are *Maultaschen*, which are ravioli-like stuffed pasta pockets, and *Kässpätzle*, stubby noodle-dumpling hybrids topped with melted cheese.

Side Orders

The humble *Kartoffel* (potato) is 'vegetable *Nummer Eins*' in any meat-and-three-veg dish and can be served as *Salzkartoffeln* (boiled),

Opening Hours

Cafes: 8am-8pm

Bars: 6pm-1am minimum

Price Ranges

€ – Under €8

€€ – €8 to €18

€€€ – More than €18

SEASON'S GREETINGS

May is peak season for *Spargel* (white asparagus), which is classically paired with boiled potatoes, hollandaise sauce and sometimes *Schinken* (smoked or cooked ham). In spring, look for *Bärlauch*, a wild-growing garlic that is often turned into a delicious pesto sauce. Wild mushrooms peak in late summer and early autumn when you find many dishes revolving around *Pfifferlinge* (chanterelles) and *Steinpilze* (cep or porcini). Other autumn delights include pumpkins, game and *Zwiebelkuchen* (onion tart), especially in rural Swabia, where it is paired with sweet *Neuer Süsser* (new wine) or *Most* (cider).

Bavaria is beer festival country. At Oktoberfest in September, between six and seven million partygoers wash down entire farms of pigs, oxen and chickens with *Mass* litres of beer. In March, the city throws festivals for pre-Lenten *Starkbier* (strong beer), where you can quaff the malty 7.5% brews monks once dubbed *flüssiges Brot* (liquid bread).

Bratkartoffeln (fried), *Kartoffelpüree* (mashed) or shaped into *Knödel* (dumplings). Dumplings can be made of bread *(Semmelknödel)* and there's also a meaty version made with liver *(Leberknödel)*. Pickled cabbage is another common vegetable companion and comes as either sauerkraut (white) or *Rotkohl* and *Blaukraut* (red). Rice is a semi-traditional side you might occasionally encounter.

Bavaria's World of Sausages

While travelling around Bavaria you might find yourself thinking 'another town, another sausage' – it must be said that nowhere else on earth offers so much sausage variety as Bavaria does. Bavaria's flagship sausage is the veal Weisswurst. In Eastern Bavaria and Franconia the smaller mildly spicy Bratwurst rules. Nuremberg and Regensburg make the most famous versions: finger-sized and eaten by the half dozen or dozen – or ask for '*drei im Weggla*' (three in a bun). When it comes to size, Coburg has the king of the *Wurst*, a 30cm affair, grilled over pine cone embers and served in a miniature airline-style bun with a dollop of mustard. Bayreuth also gets in on the act with its own Bratwurst, as do many other small towns in Franconia.

Sausages that do not hail from southern Germany, but make for tasty snacks all the same, include the Bockwurst, a mixture of ground veal and pork flavoured with herbs; the Thüringer, a kind of large Bratwurst with a lower fat content and PGI (protected geographical indication) status from the EU; the Frankfurter; the Krakauer and the hot dog–like Wiener.

Whatever shape of sausage arrives on your table or is handed to you in a flimsy napkin from a kiosk window, it will invariably be served with *Senf* (mustard). Even this comes in a number of varieties and pairing sausage to mustard in Bavaria is a bit like matching wines to food in France and Italy. *Weisswurst* is traditionally served with *süsser* (sweet whole-grain mustard), others normally come with *mittelscharfer Senf* (medium strength). English-style mustard is rare. Common side dishes that may come with your sausage are tangy sauerkraut, potato salad and/or a simple slice of bread.

You can get a sausage at almost anywhere human beings gather in numbers across the south of Germany, but each town has its own kiosk, cafe or restaurant traditionally considered the best place to eat the local sausages. In Nuremberg this is the Bratwursthäusle (p136) and Goldenes Posthorn (p136), in Munich it's the Weisses Brauhaus (p75) and in Coburg and Bayreuth simple, unassuming kiosks on their main squares.

In June 2015 *Obatzda* cheese was given Protected Geographical Indication (PGI) by the European Commission.

Bavarians like to 'pig out' and the numbers prove it: of the 60kg of meat consumed by the average resident each year, about two-thirds are pork. Oink!

WEISSWURST ETIQUETTE

Bavarians love sausage and there is no sausage more Bavarian than the *Weisswurst*. It's so Bavarian, in fact, that there's even an imaginary boundary – the *Weisswurst* equator – beyond which it is no longer served (ie roughly north of Frankfurt, though you'll rarely find it even in Franconia where the Bratwurst rules supreme). Unlike most sausages, which are pork-based, this one's made from veal and pork fat and flavoured with onions and parsley, and sometimes lemon, mace, ginger and cardamom. Before refrigeration *Weisswurst* had to be eaten before noon to prevent them going off, but now they're available all day long. They're brought to the table still swimming in hot water. The way to eat them is to strip them of their skin and eat only with fresh pretzels, sweet mustard and, preferably, paired with a mug of Weissbier (wheat beer). This unlikely combination is a popular breakfast choice among those who rise at the crack of brunch. No preservatives are used in the production of Bavaria's oddest sausage, hence its white-ish grey hue.

Just Desserts

You will never forget your first forkful of real *Schwarzwälder Kirschtorte* (Black Forest cake): a three-layered chocolate sponge cake filled with cream, morello cherries and Kirsch (cherry liqueur). The real thing is nothing like the frozen versions you might have tried back home.

Usually served with a dollop of ice cream is *Apfelstrudel* (apple strudel), which actually originated in Austria but is now eaten all over southern Germany. Tasty alternatives include *Dampfnudeln*, steamed doughy dumplings drenched in custard sauce, and Allgäu's *Apfelkrapfen*, sugar-sprinkled apple fritters. Nuremberg is famous for its *Lebkuchen* (gingerbread) made with nuts, fruit peel, honey and spices, while in Rothenburg ob der Tauber, *Schneeballen* (snowballs) are spherical nests of linguine-like dough sprinkled with sugar and/or dipped in a variety of sweet flavourings. *Bayerische Creme* is a cream and gelatin custardy creation, flavoured with liqueur and normally served with strawberries or raspberries. *Prinzregententorte* from Munich has at least seven layers of sponge glued together with chocolate butter cream and iced with chocolate.

In beer halls and beer gardens it must be said that the desserts are a bit of an afterthought. The situation is slightly better in restaurants, but the sweet-toothed should really head to a cafe bakery or coffeehouse to get their sugar high.

From *Allerseelenzopf* (a sweet bread loaf) to *Zwickelbier* (unfiltered beer), all of the mysteries behind Bavaria's regional culinary secrets are revealed on www.food-from-bavaria.de.

Ethnic Food

Munich is naturally the place where taking a break from the beer and pork comes easiest. You don't have to be in the Bavaria metropolis long to realise the Bavarians are bonkers about Italian food. Italian *trattorie, ristoranti* and *pizzerie* are so common that in some parts of the city it's almost easier to get a lasagna than *Leberkäse*! Many of these places are Italian owned and the standard of the food is high with ingredients shipped in from all over the Alps. This may contribute to prices being higher than in the *bel paese*. French restaurants are also a feature of Munich's more gentrified neighbourhoods, while Thai, Korean and Indian food is becoming increasingly popular. One unusual culinary experience you can have in Munich is going Afghan – Munich has a large Afghan population and there are several Afghan restaurants in the city.

Cookery Schools

The region's fledgling cookery school scene has started to spread its wings of late. On average, anticipate paying between €140 and €240 for a day at the stove, which usually includes lunch and recipes to take home. We've picked three favourites, but you can search by region for a course to suit you on www.kochschule.de or www.die-kochschulen.de (both in German). The annual Munich restaurant review magazine *Munich Geht Aus* (Munich Goes Out) also has a comprehensive listings section for the Bavarian capital.

If you want to train your tummy for your trip to Bavaria, try any of the recipes – roast pork to liver dumplings – detailed on www.bavariankitchen.com.

➡ **Schwarzwaldstube** (p231) Three Michelin–starred legend in Baiersbronn in the Black Forest. Classes revolve around a theme such as cooking with asparagus or pasta making.

➡ **Wirthaus in der Au** (☑089-448 14 00; http://wirtshausinderau.de; Lilienstrasse 51) Munich's king of *Knödel* since 1901 runs an English-language dumpling-making workshop.

➡ **Magazin** (p186) Hop over the border to Salzburg for hands-on, small-group classes spotlighting cookery themes from fish and crustaceans to Austrian desserts.

BEER GARDEN GRUB

In beer gardens, tables laid with a cloth and utensils are reserved for people ordering food. If you're only planning to down a mug of beer, or have brought along a picnic, don't sit there.

If you do decide to order food, you'll find very similar menus at all beer gardens. Typical dishes include roast chicken, spare ribs, *Schweinebraten* (roast pork) and schnitzel.

Radi is a huge, mild radish that's eaten with beer. You can buy a prepared radish or buy a radish at the market and a *Radimesser* at any department store, stick it down in the centre and twist the handle round and round, creating a radish spiral. If you do it yourself, smother the cut end of the radish with salt until it weeps to reduce the bitterness (and increase your thirst!).

Obatzda (oh-batsdah) is Bavarian for 'mixed up'. This cream cheese–like speciality is made of butter, ripe Camembert, onion and caraway. Spread it on *Brezn* (a pretzel) or bread. It's a bit of an acquired taste for the uninitiated.

Presssack (yes that triple 's' is correct) is ham and other cooked meat in aspic, served with horse radish and sliced onion. *Saure Zipfel* or *Blaue Zipfel* is Bratwurst cooked in vinegar and spices and served with a pretzel. It's mostly found in Franconia.

Grape & Grain

Here's to Beer!

Bavarians have made beer-making a science, and not just since the passage of the *Reinheitsgebot* (Purity Law) in Ingolstadt in 1516, which stipulates brewers may use only three ingredients – yeast, hops and water. It stopped being a legal requirement in 1987 when the EU struck it down as uncompetitive, but many Bavarian brewers still conform to it anyway, making local brews among the best in the world. Many traditional family-run concerns have been swallowed up by the big brewers – in 1960 there were over 1500 breweries in Bavaria, but by 2010 that figure had fallen to 'just' 600. Some smaller operations have survived, including those set up in monasteries. Kloster Weltenburg in the Altmühltal and Kloster Andechs near Munich are especially famous.

The northern Bavarian region of Oberfranken has 163 breweries –that's three times more than neighbouring Czech Republic.

Bavaria's beer consumption figures are simply astounding. The estimated per capita intake is around 170L per year, around 20L per person more than the neighbouring Czechs who lead the world country rankings by around 50L (Austria is second, Germany third). Bavaria produces around 22.3 million hectolitres of *bier* every year, a certain share of which goes for export.

Beer aficionados face a bewildering choice of labels, especially in Franconia where almost every village has its own brewery. The following is a small glossary of the most commonly encountered varieties. Note that most Bavarian beer has an alcohol content between 4.5% and 5.5%, although some can be as strong as 8%.

Beer Glossary

Freising's Weihenstaphan Brewery claims to be the world's oldest having been pumping out ales since 1040. The millennium celebrations in 2040 promise to be quite a bash!

➡ **Alkoholfreies Bier** Nonalcoholic beer

➡ **Bockbier/Doppelbock** Strong beer (*doppel* meaning even more so), either pale, amber or dark in colour with a bittersweet flavour

➡ **Dampfbier (steam beer)** Originating from Bayreuth, it's top-fermented (this means the yeast rises to the top during the fermentation process) and has a fruity flavour

➡ **Dunkles (dark lager)** A reddish-brown, full-bodied lager, malty and lightly hopped

➡ **Helles (pale lager)** A lightly hopped lager with strong malt aromas and a slightly sweet taste

➡ Hofbräu – type of brewery belonging to a royal court

➡ Klosterbräu – type of brewery belonging to a monastery

➡ Malzbier – sweet, aromatic, full-bodied malt beer

➡ Märzen – full bodied with strong malt aromas and traditionally brewed in March

➡ Pils (pilsener) – a bottom-fermented lager with strong hop flavour

➡ Rauchbier (smoke beer) – dark beer with a fresh, spicy or 'smoky' flavour, found mostly in Bamberg

➡ Weissbier/Weizen (wheat beer) – around 5.4% alcohol. A cloudy *Hefeweizen* has a layer of still-fermenting yeast on the bottom of the bottle, whereas *Kristallweizen* is clearer with more fizz. These wheat beers are fruity and spicy, often recalling bananas and cloves. Decline offers of a slice of lemon as it ruins the head and – beer purists say – the flavour.

If you want to go easy on the booze, order a sweetish *Radler,* which comes in half or full litres and mixes *Helles Lagerbier* and lemonade. A *Russe* (Russian) is generally a litre-sized concoction of *Helles Weissbier* and lemonade.

> With roughly 14,000 distillers, the Black Forest has the highest density of schnapps makers in the world.

FOOD & DRINK GRAPE & GRAIN

Riesling to Pinot

Bavaria's only wine-growing region is located in Franconia in and around Würzburg. Growers here produce some exceptional dry white wines, which are bottled in distinctive green flagons called *Bocksbeutel.* If *Silvaner* is the king of the grape here, then *Müller-Thurgau* is the prince, and riesling, *Weissburgunder* (Pinot grigio) and *Bacchus* the courtiers. The latter three thrive especially on the steep slopes flanking the Main River. Red wines play merely a supporting role. Nearly 80% of all wine produced is consumed within the region.

Kaiserstuhl is the major wine-growing area in the Black Forest. It produces mainly *Spätburgunder* (Pinot noir) and *Grauburgunder* (Pinot gris).

> For more information about German grape varieties, growing regions, wine festivals and courses, check out the pages of the German Wine Institute at www.deutsche weine.de.

Kaffee und Kuchen

Anyone who has spent any length of time in Bavaria or the Black Forest knows the reverence bestowed on the three o'clock weekend ritual of *Kaffee und Kuchen* (coffee and cake). More than just a chance to devour delectable cakes and tortes – though it's certainly that, too – locals see it as a social event. You'll find *Cafe-Konditoreien* (cafe–cake shops) pretty much everywhere – in castles, in the middle of the forest, even plopped on top of mountains. Track down the best by asking sweet-toothed locals where the cake is *hausgemacht* (homemade). Coffee is usually brewed fresh and all the usual varieties are on offer, including cappuccinos, espressos and milky coffee called *Milchkaffee.*

Except in posh cafes, tea is usually a teabag in a glass or pot of hot water, served with a slice of lemon. If you want milk, ask for *Tee mit Milch.*

DARE TO TRY

Feeling daring? Why not give these three regional faves a whirl.

➡ **sauere Kuttlen/Nierle/Lüngerl** (sour tripe/kidneys/lung) No beer fest would be complete without these offal faves, simmered in vinegar or wine, bay, laurel, juniper and spices.

➡ **Bubespitzle** Otherwise known as *Schupfnudeln,* this Swabian dish's ingredients are innocuous: potato noodles tossed in butter, served with sauerkraut and speck. But the name (literally, 'little boys' penises') certainly isn't.

➡ **Leberknödelsuppe** Hearty beef broth with beef, veal or pork liver dumplings, flavoured with onions, parsley and marjoram.

Festive Food

Major holidays are feast days and usually spent at home with family, gorging and guzzling way more than everyone knows is good for them. At Easter roast lamb is often the star of the show. Easter is preceded by Lent, a period of fasting when sweet dishes such as *Rohrnudeln* (browned yeasty buns served with plum compote and vanilla sauce) are enjoyed and fish replaces meat in Catholic households. Carp, served boiled, baked or fried, is popular at Christmas time, although more people roast up a goose or a turkey as the main event. *Lebkuchen* (gingerbread) and *Spekulatius* (spicy cookies) are both sweet staples of *Advent* (the pre-Christmas season). For drinks, *Glühwein* (spicy mulled wine), best consumed at a Christmas market, is a favoured seasonal indulgence.

> www.biergarten guide.com (in German) is the definitive guide to all of Munich's beer gardens. The printed version is available at bookshops across the state.

Where to Eat & Drink

➡ **Gaststätte & Gasthöfe** Rural inns with a laid-back feel, local crowd and solid menu of *gutbürgerliche Küche* (home cooking). There's sometimes a beer garden out the back.

➡ **Eiscafé** Italian or Italian-style cafes, where you can grab an ice cream or cappuccino and head outside to slurp and sip.

➡ **Stehcafé** A stand-up cafe for coffee and snacks at speed and on the cheap. Be prepared to share a table with strangers at busy times.

➡ **Cafe-Konditorei** A traditional cake shop doubling as a cafe.

➡ **Ratskeller** Atmospheric town-hall basement restaurant, generally more frequented by tourists than locals nowadays.

➡ **Restaurant** These serve everything from informal meals to *gehobene Küche* (gourmet meals). The *Tagesmenü* (fixed daily menu) often represents good value.

➡ **Bierkeller & Weinkeller** The emphasis is on beer and wine respectively, with a little food (sausages and pretzels, cold cuts etc) on the side.

➡ **Imbiss** Handy speed-feed stops for savoury fodder from wurst-in-a-bun to kebabs and pizza, normally with no seating.

When to Eat

> In Bavaria beer is officially defined not as alcohol but as a staple food, just like bread.

Traditionally *Frühstück* (breakfast) is a sweet and savoury smorgasbord of bread, cheese, salami, wurst, preserves, yoghurt and muesli. At weekends, it's an altogether more leisurely, family-oriented affair. Many cafes have embraced the brunch trend, serving all-you-can-eat buffets with fresh rolls, eggs, smoked fish, fruit salad and even prosecco. The ultimate Bavarian breakfast involves *Weisswurst*, pretzels and beer.

Traditionally, *Mittagessen* (lunch) has been the main meal of the day, but modern working practices have changed this considerably, at least in the cities. However, many restaurants still tout lunch-time dishes or a fixed lunch menu (*Mittagsmenü* or *Tagesmenü*), which can be an affordable way of dining even at upscale restaurants.

WHAT'S HOT

➡ Gourmet burgers are all the rage in Munich.

➡ Asian fusion eateries with designer edge.

➡ Vegan and vegetarian food done creatively.

➡ Imaginative Italian *ristoranti* – it would seem Munich has more than some Italian cities of comparable size.

➡ Slow food (locally sourced food).

DOS & DON'TS

⇒ Do bring a small gift – flowers or a bottle of wine – when invited to a meal.

⇒ Do say *Guten Appetit!* (bon appetit!) before starting to eat.

⇒ Do offer to help with clearing the table and washing the dishes afterwards.

⇒ Don't start eating until everyone has been served.

⇒ Don't expect to get a glass of tap water at a restaurant.

⇒ Don't assume you can pay by credit card when eating out.

⇒ Do watch out for 'no prams' signs in Munich if travelling with kiddies.

Dinner is dished up at home around 7pm. For those who have already eaten heartily at midday, there is *Abendbrot,* bread with cold cuts. Bar the cities with their late-night dining scenes, Germans head to restaurants earlier than elsewhere in Europe, and many kitchens in rural areas stop serving around 9pm. At home, meals are relaxed and require few airs and graces beyond the obligatory *'Guten Appetit'* (literally 'good appetite'), exchanged before eating.

Dining Etiquette

On the Menu

English menus are not a given, even in big cities, though the waiter or waitress will almost invariably be able to translate for you. The more rural and remote you go, the less likely it is that the restaurant will have an English menu, or multilingual staff for that matter. It helps to know a few words of German. That said, a good share of Bavaria's waiters are not from Germany at all and might just know your language!

Paying the Bill

Sometimes the person who invites pays, but generally locals split the bill evenly between them. This might mean everyone chipping in at the end of a meal or asking to pay separately *(getrennte Rechnung).* Buying rounds in bars British-style is not usually the done thing, though friends might buy each other the odd drink. In bars and beer halls, table service is still quite common and waiting staff often come around to *abkassieren* (cash up). Always make sure you can pay by card before you tuck in – most restaurants now take cards, but it's by no means a given.

Table Reservations

If you want to dine at formal or popular restaurants, it is wise to make table reservations a day or two ahead. Michelin-starred restaurants are often booked up weeks in advance, especially at weekends and some have a compulsory reservation policy. Most *Gasthöfe, Gaststätten,* cafes and beer halls should be able to squeeze you in at a moment's notice, except on Saturday nights when things are normally chock-a-block.

Prost! (with beer) or *Zum Wohl!* (with wine) are typical drinking toasts.

Tipping

Tipping is quite an individual matter and you could easily get round the whole of Bavaria without giving a single one. As a rule of thumb, most Germans round up the bill to the nearest €5 or €10 in restaurants, cafes and bars. Do whatever you're comfortable with, given the service and setting. Give any tip directly to the server when paying your bill. Say either the amount you want to pay, or *'Stimmt so'* if you don't want change. Only tip if you were really satisfied with the service and your server has gone out of his or her way to make the experience a pleasant one. Levels of service vary greatly across the south of Germany.

Landscapes & Wildlife

From Alpine peaks to the Danube plain, from the Black Forest to the lakes of southern Bavaria, southern Germany provides diverse central-European vistas by the bucket and is a joy to explore. This diversity has also been recognised on a national level with three national parks now functioning in the region, the most recent addition to the list being the Nationalpark Schwarzwald (Black Forest National Park) in 2014. Germany's south also has some pretty accessible wild animal populations, so get those binoculars and cameras ready.

The Land

In Bavaria and the Black Forest nature has been as prolific and creative as Picasso in his prime. The most dramatic region is the Bavarian Alps, a phalanx of craggy peaks created by tectonic uplift some 770 million years ago and chiselled and gouged by glaciers and erosion ever since. Several limestone ranges stand sentinel above the rest of the land, including, west to east, the Allgäuer Alps, the glaciated Wetterstein/Karwendel Alps (with Germany's highest mountain, the Zugspitze at 2962m) and the Berchtesgadener Alps. Many peaks tower well above 2000m and are capped with a snowy mantle year-round.

North of here, the Alpine Foothills are a lush mosaic of moorland, rolling hills, gravel plains and pine forests dappled with glacial lakes, including the vast Chiemsee, Starnberger See and the Ammersee. The foothills are book-ended by Lake Constance in the west and the Inn and Salzach Rivers in the east.

The Bavarian Forest in eastern Bavaria is a classic *Mittelgebirge,* a mid-size mountain range, and one of Germany's greatest unknowns. Its highest peak, the Grosse Arber (1456m), juts out like the tall kid in your school photo. Much of it is blanketed by dark, dense forests that fade into the thinly populated Frankenwald and Fichtelgebirge areas further north. The forest continues just as thick on the other side of the border in the Czech Republic.

The Black Forest, in Germany's southwestern corner, is another *Mittelgebirge,* a storied quilt that enwraps waterfalls, rolling hills, sparkling lakes, lush vineyards, and oak, pine and beech forests into one mystique-laden package. The little Kinzig River divides the north from the much higher south, where the Feldberg is the highest elevation at 1493m.

Much of Franconia and Swabia is a complex patchwork of low ranges, rifts and deep meandering valleys. A Jurassic limestone range is responsible for bizarre rock formations, such as those in the Franconian Switzerland region north of Nuremberg.

Southern Germany is traversed by several major rivers, of which the Danube, which originates in the Black Forest, and the Main are the longest. The Inn and the Isar flow down from the Alps into the Danube, the former at Passau, the latter near Deggendorf on the edge of the Bavarian Forest. Germany's main south–north river, the mighty Rhine, divides the Black Forest from France and Switzerland.

Wildlife

The most common large forest mammal is the red deer, a quick-footed fellow with skinny legs supporting a chunky body. Encounters with wild

Statistically Speaking

Highest peak: Zugspitze (2962m) in the Bavarian Alps

Biggest lake: Lake Constance (536 sq km), Europe's third largest

Tallest waterfall: Triberger Wasserfälle (163m)

Longest border: 815km with Austria

Bavaria sprawls over 70,550 sq km, making it bigger than Ireland, Portugal or Denmark. The Black Forest is comparatively small at only 13,500 sq km.

boar, a type of wild pig with a keen sense of smell but poor eyesight, are also possible, especially in the Bavarian Forest.

Beavers faced extinction in the 19th century not only because they were coveted for their precious pelts (beaver hats were all the rage), but also because they were cooked up in strict Catholic households each Friday since the good people considered them to be 'fish'. Reintroduced in the mid-1960s, beavers are thriving once again, especially along the Danube, between Ingolstadt and Kelheim, and its tributaries.

Lynxes actually died out in Germany in the 19th century but in the 1980s Czech authorities released 17 lynxes in the Bohemian Forest, and a small group of brave souls have since tried their luck again in the Bavarian Forest right across the border. There have even been rare sightings around the Feldberg in the southern Black Forest.

In the Alps, the Alpine marmot, a sociable animal that looks like a fat squirrel, lives in burrows below the tree line, while wild goats make their home in the upper mountains. The snow hare, whose fur is white in winter, is also a common Alpine denizen. The endangered *Auerhuhn* (capercaillie), a grouselike bird, also makes its home here and in the Bavarian Forest. Lizards, praying mantids and European bee-eaters live in the sunny Kaiserstuhl area.

Local skies are home to over 400 bird species, from white-backed woodpeckers and pygmy owls to sparrowhawks, grey herons, jays and black redstarts. The Wutach Gorge in the Black Forest is a unique habitat that supports such rare birds as treecreepers and kingfishers, as well as many species of butterflies, beetles and lizards.

Get up to speed on German flora and fauna browsing www.bund-naturschutz.de, www.heimische-tiere.de, www.baumkunde.de and www.deutsche wildtierstiftung.de (all in German).

Plants

Despite environmental pressures, southern German forests remain beautiful and commendably tranquil places to escape the crowds. At lower altitudes, they usually consist of a jumbled mix of beech, oak, birch, chestnut, lime, maple and ash that erupt into a riot of colour in autumn. Up at the higher elevations, fir, pine, spruce and other conifers are more prevalent. Canopies often shade low-growing ferns, heather, clover and foxglove.

In spring, Alpine regions burst with wildflowers – orchid, cyclamen, gentian, pulsatilla, Alpine roses, edelweiss and buttercups – which brighten meadows. Minimise your impact by sticking to trails.

The true king of the skies is the golden eagle. If you're lucky, you might spot one patrolling the mountain peaks in Nationalpark Berchtesgaden (p108).

Wild Food

Bavaria and the Black Forest's woods brim with berries, herbs and mushrooms, many of which are perfectly edible. Summer and autumn yield rich forest pickings, with bilberries, raspberries, blackberries and wild strawberries; wild herbs like bear's garlic, dandelion, dill, buckhorn and sorrel fringe meadows and woodlands. The fungi-foraging season kicks off with apricot-hued, trumpet-shaped *Pfifferlinge* (chanterelles) in June/July, peaks with the prized *Steinpilz* (cep or porcini) around August and ends with autumnal delights like button-topped *Maronen* (Bay Bolete).

Tourist offices can point you towards local *Kräuterwanderungen* and *Pilzwanderung* (herb and mushroom walks), such as those run by the German Alpine Club (www.alpenverein.de) or Schwarzwaldverein (www.schwarzwaldverein.de); you'll need to join as a member first. A word of warning, however – several people a year die in southern Germany from consuming, and sometimes just touching, poisonous mushrooms. It's better to go mushrooming with a local first, one who knows what to pick and what to leave on the forest floor. Never let children touch any mushroom.

Of course many of the forest's inhabitants end up on restaurant plates. Venison and wild boar are common dishes, especially in Bavaria's east. Often a pricey meat in other countries, venison costs only a little bit more then beef and pork and tastes best with forest berry sauce and dumplings, an unmissable culinary experience in these parts.

Germany's 15 Unesco Biosphere Reserves include the Bavarian Forest, the Berchtesgaden Alps and the Swabian Alb. For the lowdown, visit www.unesco.org.

National & Nature Parks

For the inside scoop on the region's nature and national parks, surf the German-language websites www. naturparke. de and www. nationalpark-deutschland.com.

Bavaria is home to Germany's oldest national park, the Nationalpark Bayerischer Wald, which was founded in 1970. There is only one more of Germany's 16 national parks in Bavaria, but it's a good one: the National-park Berchtesgaden on the Austrian border, a ravishing mountainscape of big-shouldered Alps and jewel-coloured, fjordlike lakes. Both parks preserve places of outstanding natural beauty, rare geographical features and various wildlife species.

In 2014 Germany's newest national park was created in Baden-Württemburg – the Black Forest National Park (Nationalpark Schwarzwald). At 100 sq km it's a small affair split into two parts roughly 3.5km apart. The creation of a national park here was opposed by logging companies, two of the state's big political parties, the CDU and the FDP, and many locals. The park represents just 0.7% of the state's considerable forest, but is an area now left entirely to nature.

The Black Forest also has two nature parks, which enjoy a lower degree of environmental protection and are essentially outdoor playgrounds. These are sprawling rural landscapes criss-crossed by roads and dotted with villages. Selective logging (no clear-cutting) and agriculture here is done in a controlled and environmentally friendly fashion.

NATIONAL & NATURE PARKS

PARK	FEATURES	ACTIVITIES	BEST TIME TO VISIT	WEBSITE
Nationalpark Bayerischer Wald (p166)	mountain forest, bogs, streams (243 sq km); deer, hazel grouse, fox, otter, pygmy owl, three-toe woodpecker	hiking, mountain biking, cross-country skiing	year-round	www. nationalpark-bayerischer-wald.de
Nationalpark Berchtesgaden (p108)	lakes, mixed forest, cliffs, meadows (210 sq km); eagle, chamois, marmot, blue hare, salamander	hiking, skiing, wildlife-watching	year-round	www.national park-berchtes gaden.de
Naturpark Altmühltal (p149)	mixed forest, streams, rock formations, Roman ruins (2962 sq km)	hiking, cycling, canoeing, kayaking, rock climbing, cross-country skiing, fossil digging	late spring to autumn	www.naturpark-altmuehltal.de
Naturpark Bayerischer Wald	largest continuous forest in Germany (includes the smaller Nationalpark Bayerischer Wald), moorland, meadows, rolling hills (3077 sq km)	hiking, cycling, cross-country skiing, Nordic walking	late spring to autumn	www.naturpark-bayer-wald.de
Naturpark Schwarzwald Mitte/Nord	mixed forest, deep valleys, lakes (3750 sq km); deer, wild boar, raven, capercaillie	hiking, Nordic walking, mountain biking	late spring to autumn	www.naturpark schwarzwald.de
Naturpark Südschwarzwald	mixed forest, pastures, lake, moorland (3700 sq km); capercaillie, deer, lynx	hiking, Nordic walking, snowshoeing, mountain biking	year-round	www.naturpark-suedschwarz wald.de
Nationalpark Schwarzwald (p223)	mixed forest, moorland plateaux and lakes (100 sq km)	walking	year-round	www. schwarzwald-nationalpark.de

Survival
Guide

Directory A–Z

Accommodation

Bavaria and the Black Forest offer all types of places to unpack your suitcase, from hostels, campsites and traditional taverns to chains, business hotels and luxury resorts. Reservations are a good idea between June and September, around major holidays and festivals and, in business-oriented cities, during trade shows.

➡ The website www. sightsleeping.by is a booking portal for rooms in some of Bavaria's most magnificent properties such as castles, palaces and other historical buildings.

➡ Many tourist office and hotel websites let you check room availability and make reservations. Staff can also help you in person or, if you arrive after office hours, have vacancies posted in the window or a display case.

➡ Electronic reservation boards, especially common in the Alps, connect you directly to local properties for free, but don't always work reliably.

➡ Properties with designated nonsmoking rooms are now the norm, but before committing to a room at midrange and budget level, go and smell it first.

➡ If heading to the region in late September (during Oktoberfest) accommodation of any kind may be very difficult to book at short notice.

➡ Rooms with air-con are rare.

➡ Wherever you stay, breakfast always appears on price lists as a separate item, not included in room rates. This is due to finicky local tax laws.

➡ Another extra charge is the Kurtaxe (resort tax), particularly common in the Alps. Between €1 and €3, it's not included in the room rate but does often gain you a discount card for local transport and sights.

➡ Wi-fi at every standard of accommodation is virtually guaranteed and almost always free. However, web connection can be patchy at lower standard accommodation, the exception being hostels where it is usually excellent.

Camping

Almost every town in southern Germany has a campsite a short bus ride away. German campsites are normally well maintained and offer a wide range of facilities.

➡ The core season runs from May to September with only a few campsites open year-round. July and August are naturally the busiest months.

➡ There are usually separate charges per person, tent and car, and additional fees for resort tax, electricity and sewage disposal.

➡ A Camping Card International may yield some savings.

➡ The *ADAC Camping & Caravanning Führer,* available from bookshops, is a comprehensive camping guide, in German. Other handy sources include www. alanrogers.com and www. eurocampings.eu.

➡ It's a grey area, but wild camping in Germany is illegal. Farmers may be willing to let you camp on their land if you ask permission first.

Farm Stays

A holiday on a working farm is a big hit with kids who love interacting with barnyard animals and helping with everyday chores. Accommodation ranges from bare-bones rooms with shared facilities to fully furnished holiday flats. Minimum stays of three days are common. For details, check www.landtourismus.de (in German).

Hostels

Bavaria has many hostels of both the indie and youth

BOOK YOUR STAY ONLINE

For more accommodation reviews by Lonely Planet authors, check out http://lonelyplanet.com/hotels/. You'll find independent reviews, as well as recommendations on the best places to stay. Best of all, you can book online.

varieties. While dorm rooms are the cheapest form of accommodation available (even cheaper than camping at certain times of the week/year), private rooms can cost the same or even more than midrange hotel rooms booked online or last minute.

➡ There are backpacker hostels across the region, though fewer in Baden-Württemberg than Bavaria. This type of hostel attracts a convivial, international crowd to mixed dorms and private rooms. Facilities usually include communal kitchens, lockers, internet access, laundry and a common room.

➡ When booking hostels the best places to start are international booking systems such as www.hostelworld.com and www.hostelbookers.com.

➡ Most hostels offer inexpensive sightseeing and themed tours.

➡ Classic Hostelling International–affiliated hostels are run by the Deutsches Jugendherbergswerk (www.jugendherberge.de) and cater primarily to German school groups and families.

➡ Most DJH hostels have been modernised but can't quite shake that institutional feel. Some can be noisy with harried, grumpy staff.

➡ Rates in gender-segregated dorms or in family rooms range from €17 to €27 per person, including linen and breakfast. People over 27 are charged an extra €2 to €4. In Bavaria, if space is tight, priority is given to people under 27, except for those travelling as a family.

➡ Unless you're a member of your home country's HI association, you either need to buy a Hostelling

International Card for €15.50 (valid for one year) or six individual stamps costing €3.10 per night. Both are available at any DJH hostel.

➡ DJH hostels can now be booked online.

Hotels

Hotels range from small family-run establishments to comfortable midsized properties to luxurious international chains. Expect even budget establishments to be well run and clean. In most older, privately run hotels rooms may vary dramatically in terms of size, décor and amenities. The cheapest share bathroom facilities, while others may come with a shower cubicle installed but no private toilet; only pricier ones have en suite bathrooms. If possible, ask to see several rooms before committing.

Top-end establishments offer deluxe amenities, perhaps a scenic location, special decor or historical ambience. Many also have pools, saunas, business centres and other upmarket facilities.

Standards of service across the board may be low-

er than those you are used to back home.

Pensions, Inns & Private Rooms

➡ *Pensionen* (guesthouses) and *Gasthöfe* or *Gasthäuser* (inns) are smaller, less formal and cheaper than hotels; the latter usually have a restaurant. Expect clean rooms but only minimal amenities – maybe a radio, sometimes a small TV, rarely a phone. Facilities may be shared. What rooms lack in amenities, they often make up for in charm and authenticity.

➡ *Privatzimmer* (essentially guestrooms in private homes) are ubiquitous and great for catching a glimpse into how locals live, although privacy seekers may find these places a bit too intimate. Tourist offices list rooms available, or look around for *Zimmer Frei* (rooms available) signs in house or shop windows. Per person prices range from €25 to €40.

Rental Accommodation

Renting a *Ferienwohnung* (furnished flat) for a week or longer is a sensible option for self-caterers, families and small groups. Stays under a week usually incur a surcharge, and there's almost always a 'cleaning fee' payable at the end.

PRACTICALITIES

Newspapers The Monday edition of *Süddeutsche Zeitung* has a *New York Times* supplement; the *International Herald Tribune* is also available, especially in cities.

Magazines *Der Spiegel* and *Focus* magazines are popular German news weeklies, which, along with the *Economist, Time* and *Newsweek,* are sold at train stations and major newsstands.

Radio Stations are regional with most featuring a mix of news, talk and music.

Weights & Measures Germany uses the metric system.

Smoking As of 2010 a proper smoking ban in all public indoor spaces took effect in Bavaria. Baden-Württemberg has had a ban since 2007.

Customs Regulations

Most articles that you take into Germany for your personal use may be imported free of duty and tax. The following allowances apply to duty-free goods purchased in a non-European Union country. In addition, you can bring in other products up to a value of €430, including tea, coffee and perfume. Bringing meat and milk, as well as products made from them, into the EU is prohibited.

➡ **Alcohol** 1L of strong liquor or 2L of less than 22% alcohol by volume and 4L of wine

➡ **Tobacco** 200 cigarettes or 100 cigarillos or 50 cigars or 250g of loose tobacco

Electricity

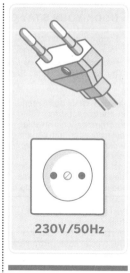

230V/50Hz

220V/50Hz

Climate

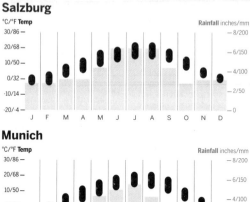

Salzburg

°C/°F **Temp**   Rainfall inches/mm

Munich

°C/°F **Temp**   Rainfall inches/mm

Zugspitze

°C/°F **Temp**   Rainfall inches/mm

Embassies & Consulates

Most foreign embassies are in Berlin but many countries have consular offices in Munich (only Australia and New Zealand in the list below don't). For other foreign missions in Germany see www.auswaertiges-amt.de.

Australian Consulate (☑0308 800 880; Wallstrasse 76-79, Berlin)

Austrian Consulate (☑089 998 150; Ismaninger Strasse 136)

Belgian Consulate (☑089 2104 1603; Pacellistrasse 16)

Canadian Consulate (☑089-219 9570; Tal 29)

Czech Republic Consulate (☑089-9583 7232; Libellenstrasse 1)

French Consulate (☑089-419 4110; Heimeranstrasse 10)

Irish Honorary Consulate (☑089 2080 5990; Denninger Strasse 15)

Netherlands (☑089 206 026 710; Nymphenburger Str 20a)

New Zealand Embassy (☑030-206 210; www.nzembassy.com; Friedrichstrasse 60; ⑤Stadtmitte)

Polish Consulate (☑089 418 6080; Röntgenstrasse 5)

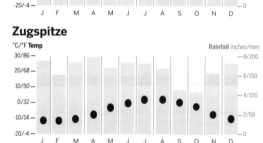

UK Consulate (☎089 211 090; Möhlstrasse 5)

US Consulate (☎089 288 80; Königinstrasse 5)

Gay & Lesbian Travellers

Homosexuality is legal in Bavaria and the Black Forest, but the scene, even in Munich, is tiny compared to, say, Berlin or Cologne. Nuremberg, Regensburg and Freiburg are a little more relaxed as well, but in rural areas gays and lesbians tend to keep a low profile. There are websites aplenty but most are in German only. Try www.gayscape. com, www.gay-web.de or, for women, www.lesarion.de.

Insurance

No matter how long your trip is, make sure you have travel insurance covering you for medical expenses, luggage theft or loss, and against cancellations or delays of your travel arrangements. Check your existing insurance policies at home (medical, homeowners etc), since some policies may already provide worldwide coverage.

Worldwide travel insurance is available at www. lonelyplanet.com/bookings. You can buy, extend and claim online anytime – even if you're already on the road.

Internet Access

Getting online is fairly easy in Germany's south, as is the case across Europe internet cafes are almost a thing of the past, with perhaps a sole survivor hanging on in each town.

➡ Public libraries offer free terminals and sometimes wi-fi access, but downsides may include time limits, reservation requirements and queues.

➡ Some tourist information centres lay on free web access.

➡ Internet access is available at slightly seedy telephone call shops, which cluster near train stations in some big cities.

➡ Hotels and hostels often have high-speed access and wi-fi (W-LAN in German – the word wi-fi is not generally understood), which is usually free. At some business hotels you can pay for faster internet speed. The lower down the hotel food chain you go, the less likely it is that wi-fi will work. Hostels, however, often have excellent wi-fi.

➡ Some cafes and pubs offer wi-fi access, often at no charge with purchase.

➡ There are free hotspots in Germany's south but these often require pre-registration. Airports offer a limited number of free minutes – for example at Nuremberg Airport you have quarter of an hour free to check emails. After that charges are steep.

Language Courses

Several Munich schools offer quality German language courses.

DESK (☎089 263 334; www. desk-sprachkurse.de; Blumenstrasse 1) Tried and tested school with almost three decades of experience behind it and a central location.

Deutschakademie (☎089 2601 8989; www.deutschakademie.de; Sonnenstrasse 8) Small groups, qualified teachers and courses throughout the day.

Inlingua (☎089 231 1530; www.inlingua-muenchen. de; Sendlinger-Tor-Platz 6) A national chain serving a more corporate clientele.

Ludwig-Maximilians-Universität München (☎089 2180 2143; www. sprachenzentrum.uni-muenchen.de; Schellingstrasse 3) Summer and term-time courses at the university.

Legal Matters

By law, you must carry photo identification such as your passport or national identity card (a driving licence may or may not be acceptable to the police). If you are arrested, you have the right to make a phone call and are presumed innocent until proven guilty.

Maps

Most tourist offices distribute free (but often very basic) city maps, but for driving around you'll need a detailed road map or atlas such as those published by Falkplan, Freytag & Berndt, RV Verlag or ADAC. Look for them at bookshops, tourist offices, newsagents and petrol stations. Find downloadable maps and driving directions at www.viamichelin.com and www.stadtplandienst.de.

Money

➡ Germany is one of the 17 countries in the European Union that uses the euro as its national currency.

➡ Euros come in seven notes (five, 10, 20, 50, 100, 200 and 500 euros) and eight coins (one and two euro coins, and one, two, five, 10, 20 and 50 cent coins). You're unlikely ever to set eyes on a 200 or 500 euro note.

➡ Exchange money at airports, some banks and currency exchange offices, such as Reisebank, American Express and TravelEx. In rural areas, such facilities are rare, so take plenty of cash.

ATMs

ATMs are ubiquitous, accessible 24/7 and the easiest and quickest way to obtain cash. However not all machines take all cards. Check with your bank or credit-card company about fees.

Cash

Bavaria is still very much a cash culture and making sure you have ample supply of the stuff will avoid embarrassing situations, such as trying to pay for a beer in a pub or a sausage at the railway station with your credit card. Even at the supermarket cashiers (and the queue behind you) can still get a bit huffy if you don't have readies, especially when spending small sums.

Credit Cards

A piece of plastic can be vital in emergencies and also useful for phone or internet bookings. Avoid getting cash on your credit card via ATMs since fees are steep and you'll be charged interest immediately (in other words, there's no grace period as with purchases). Report lost or stolen cards to the following:

American Express ☏069 9797 1000

MasterCard ☏0800 819 1040

Visa ☏0800 814 9100

Travellers Cheques

Travellers cheques are really not worth the hassle for the security they offer and have become virtually obsolete in the age of network-linked ATMs. German businesses generally don't accept them, and banks charge exorbitant fees for cashing them (currency exchange offices are usually better). American Express offices cash Amex cheques free or for a very low commission rate.

Opening Hours

Museums usually take Monday off but stay open late one evening a week. Many eateries observe a *Ruhetag* (day of rest), usually Monday or Tuesday. All supermarkets close on Sundays, a real headache if you are self-catering.

Banks 8.30am-4pm Mon-Wed & Fri, 8.30am-5.30pm or 6pm Thu

Bars around 6pm-1am minimum

Clubs around 11pm-early morning hours

Post offices 9am-6pm Mon-Fri, 9am-1pm Sat

Restaurants 11am-11pm (varies)

Major stores and supermarkets 9.30am-8pm Mon-Sat (varies)

Post

➡ The postal service in Germany is operated by Deutsche Post (www.

deutschepost.de) and is very reliable.

➡ Main post offices are often near train stations.

➡ Busy offices often have a dedicated desk/window for letters and postcards, avoiding the need to stand in lengthy queues with locals paying bills etc.

➡ Avoid the post office by printing out *Internetmarke* (internet stamps) from the Deutsche Post website.

Public Holidays

Businesses and offices are closed on the following public holidays:

➡ **Neujahrstag** (New Year's Day) 1 January

➡ **Heilige Drei Könige** (Epiphany) 6 January

➡ **Ostern** (Easter) March/April – Good Friday, Easter Sunday and Easter Monday

➡ **Maifeiertag** (Labour Day) 1 May

➡ **Christi Himmelfahrt** (Ascension Day) 40 days after Easter

➡ **Pfingsten** (Whitsun/Pentecost) mid-May to mid-June – Whit Sunday and Whit Monday

➡ **Fronleichnam** (Corpus Christi) 10 days after Pentecost

➡ **Mariä Himmelfahrt** (Assumption Day, Bavaria only) 15 August

➡ **Tag der Deutschen Einheit** (Day of German Unity) 3 October

➡ **Allerheiligen** (All Saints Day) 1 November

➡ **Weihnachtstag** (Christmas Day) 25 December

➡ **Sankt Stephanstag** (Boxing/St Stephen's Day) 26 December

Telephone

Domestic & International Calls

German phone numbers consist of an area code,

which starts with 0, and the local number. Area codes can be up to six numbers and local numbers up to nine digits long. If dialling from a landline within the same city, you don't need to dial the area code. If using a mobile, you must dial it.

➡ If calling Germany from abroad, first dial your country's international access code, then 49 (Germany's country code), the area code (dropping the initial 0) and the local number. Germany's international access code is 00.

➡ Numbers starting with 0800 are toll-free but numbers starting with 0190 or 900 are charged at exorbitant rates. Direct-dialled calls made from hotel rooms are also usually charged at a premium.

➡ If you have access to a private phone, you can benefit from cheaper rates by using a call-by-call access code. Rates can be found online at www.billiger-telefonieren.de.

➡ With a high-speed internet connection, you can talk PC to PC for free via Skype (www.skype.com), or, for a small per-minute charge, to landlines and mobiles direct from your computer.

Mobile Phones

➡ Mobile phones operate on GSM 900/1800. If your home country uses a different standard, you'll need a multiband GSM phone in Germany.

➡ If you have an unlocked multiband phone, a prepaid rechargeable SIM card from a German telecom provider is cheaper than using your own network. Cards are available at any mobile phone store (eg T-Mobile, Vodafone, E-Plus or O2) and will give you a local number without signing a contract.

➡ If you have a SIM card from anywhere in the EU, rates are now low and are set to come into line with national tariffs in June 2017.

Phonecards

Most public payphones only work with Deutsche Telecom (DT) phonecards, available in denominations of €5, €10 and €20 from DT stores, post offices, newsagents and tourist offices.

For long-distance and international calls, prepaid calling cards issued by other providers tend to offer better rates. Look for them at newsagents and telephone call shops. There may be a connection fee. Most cards work with payphones with a surcharge.

Time

Clocks in Germany are set to central European time (GMT/UTC plus one hour). Daylight-saving time kicks in at 2am on the last Sunday in March and ends on the last Sunday in October. The use of the 24-hour clock (eg where 6.30pm is 18.30) is common.

Toilets

➡ Men's toilets are marked 'Herren' (or just 'H'), the ladies' 'Damen' (or just 'D').

➡ Public toilets in southern Germany's city centres are almost nonexistent. Instead use facilities in department stores, railway stations, markets, beer halls and other public places.

➡ Toilets are rarely free and those at large railway stations can charge a silly €1 to spend a penny. At some facilities payment is by donation, thus you pay as much as you like. At others there's a price list.

➡ Toilets are normally clean, well maintained and not of the squat variety, though some are of the slightly off-putting 'reverse bowl design', not common in the UK or US.

Tourist Information

Every reasonable-sized town in southern Germany (even those with no tourists) has a municipally-funded tourist information centre, some of which are stand-alone operations, while others are twinned with a local residents' information point. Only very occasionally will you come across staff who don't speak English and the vast majority of those charged with aiding tourists on their way are knowledgeable, friendly and efficient. Websites operated by tourist boards vary wildly in quality.

Good websites for your pre-trip research are www.bayern.by and www.germany-tourism.de.

Each region/product/*Land* also has its own dedicated website:

Black Forest Tourism Association (www.schwarzwald-tourismus.info)

Baden-Württemberg Tourist Association (www.tourism-bw.com)

Eastern Bavarian Tourism Association (www.ostbayern-tourismus.de, in German)

Franconian Tourism Association (www.frankentourismus.org)

Tourism Association Allgäu-Bavarian Swabia (www.bavarian-alps.info)

Upper Bavarian Tourism Association (www.oberbayern-tourismus.de, in German)

Romantic Road Tourism Association (www.romantische-strasse.de)

Travellers with Disabilities

➡ Generally speaking, southern Germany caters well for the needs of the *Behinderte* (disabled).

➡ You'll find access ramps and/or lifts in many public buildings, including train stations, museums, theatres and cinemas.

➡ New hotels and some renovated establishments have lifts and rooms with extra-wide doors and accessible bathrooms.

➡ Nearly all trains are accessible, and local buses and U-Bahns are becoming increasingly so. Seeing-eye dogs are allowed on all forms of public transport.

➡ Many local and regional tourism offices have special brochures for people with disabilities, although usually in German. Good general resources include the following:

Deutsche Bahn Mobility Service Centre (☑0180 599 6633512; www.bahn.com) Train access information and route planning assistance. The website has useful information in English (search for 'barrier-free travel' under 'Services').

German National Tourism Office (www.germany.travel) Your first port of call, with inspirational information in English.

Munich for Physically Challenged Tourists (www.munich.de) Searching the official Munich tourism website will produce gigabytes of info for travellers with disabilities from Oktoberfest to local clubs and organisations to special ride services.

Natko (www.natko.de) Central clearing house for enquiries about barrier-free travel in Germany.

Visas

Most EU nationals only need their national identity card or passport to enter, stay and work in Germany. Citizens of Australia, Canada, Israel, Japan, New Zealand and the US are among those countries that need only a valid passport (no visa) if entering as tourists for up to three months within a six-month period. Passports should be valid for at least another four months from the planned date of departure from Germany.

Nationals from other countries need a so-called Schengen Visa, named after the 1995 Schengen Agreement that enables passport controls between most countries in the Europe Union to be abolished (all except the UK and Ireland have signed up). For full details, see www.auswaertiges-amt.de or check with a German consulate in your country.

Transport

GETTING THERE & AWAY

If coming from anywhere in Europe, southern Germany's central position means excellent transport connections to the rest of the Continent. Air, rail and bus are all options and Germany's autobahn (motorways) make car journeys fast and inexpensive when compared to other countries. From other continents, air is the best option with many big-name flag-carrier airlines operating in and out of Munich airport.

Flights, tours and rail tickets can all be booked online at www.lonelyplanet.com/bookings.

Entering the Country

Entering Germany is normally a straightforward procedure. Citizens of most Western countries don't need a visa, but even if you do, you'll be through checks swiftly.

When arriving in Germany from any of the Schengen countries (all Germany's neighbours), you no longer have to go through passport and customs checks, regardless of your nationality.

Air

Airports

Southern Germany is served by several airports:

➤ The main regional hub is **Flughafen München** (MUC; $\varnothing$089-975 00; www.munich-airport.de), 30km northeast of Munich's city centre.

➤ Although Munich is well served by transcontinental flights, most land at **Frankfurt Airport** (FRA; www.frankfurt-airport.com; ☎; ☒Flughafen Regionalbahnhof), which is closer to northern Bavaria and the beginning of the Romantic Road.

➤ **Salzburg Airport** ($\varnothing$662-858 00; www.salzburg-airport.com; !Innsbrucker Bundesstrasse 95) is convenient for the southeast of the region and the Alps.

➤ Despite the name, **Frankfurt-Hahn** (HHN; www.hahn-airport.de) is about 100km west of Frankfurt – not at all convenient for southern Germany.

➤ The main airport in Franconia is **Nuremberg** (NUE; www.airport-nuernberg.de).

➤ The two airports serving the Black Forest are **Karlsruhe-Baden-Baden** (Baden Airpark; $\varnothing$07229 66 20 00; www.badenairpark.de) for the north and **EuroAirport Basel-Mulhouse-Freiburg** (BSL; $\varnothing$+33 (0)3 89 90 31 11; www.euroairport.com) for Freiburg and the south.

➤ Ryanair uses **Allgäu Airport** (FMM; $\varnothing$08331-984 2000; www.allgaeu-airport.de)

CLIMATE CHANGE & TRAVEL

Every form of transport that relies on carbon-based fuel generates CO_2, the main cause of human-induced climate change. Modern travel is dependent on aeroplanes, which might use less fuel per kilometre per person than most cars but travel much greater distances. The altitude at which aircraft emit gases (including CO_2) and particles also contributes to their climate change impact. Many websites offer 'carbon calculators' that allow people to estimate the carbon emissions generated by their journey and, for those who wish to do so, to offset the impact of the greenhouse gases emitted with contributions to portfolios of climate-friendly initiatives throughout the world. Lonely Planet offsets the carbon footprint of all staff and author travel.

125km west of Munich near the town of Memmingen.

Airlines

The main airline serving Germany, **Lufthansa** (www.lufthansa.com) operates a huge network of domestic and international flights and has a good safety record. Munich is also a major hub for **Air Berlin** (www.airberlin.com) and **Germanwings** (www.germanwings.com).

Many of the world's major national carriers fly into Munich while budget airlines prefer the region's smaller airports.

Tickets

➡ Bagging a flight any time around Oktoberfest (late September to early October) is nigh on impossible, even well in advance. Other busy times include late August, Christmas and New Year.

➡ When flights to Munich are unavailable or beyond budget, many travellers buy cheaper tickets to other airports such as Frankfurt, Salzburg or Nuremberg, then hop on a train to their final destination.

➡ Don't assume budget airline tickets to Germany will be cheaper than those offered by other airlines. Lufthansa often has some great deals and doesn't charge for all those extras like luggage and credit card payment as the no-frills carriers usually do.

➡ If travelling from North America, Australia or Asia via Frankfurt, save money (and time) and take the train south, rather than another domestic flight to Munich. Frankfurt airport has its own train station.

Land

Border Crossings

Germany is bordered (anticlockwise) by Denmark, the Netherlands, Belgium, Luxembourg, France, Switzerland, Austria, the Czech Republic and Poland. The Schengen Agreement abolished passport and customs formalities between Germany and all bordering countries.

Bus

➡ Eurolines is the umbrella organisation of European coach operators connecting over 500 destinations across Europe. Its website has links to each national company's site, with detailed fare and route information, promotional offers, contact numbers and, in many cases, an online booking system. In Germany, Eurolines is represented by **Deutsche Touring** (www.eurolines.de).

➡ If Germany's south is part of your European-wide itinerary, a Eurolines Pass (15-/30-day peak-travel pass travellers over 26 €320/425, under 26 €270/350) can save you money. It allows for unlimited travel between 53 European cities within a 15- or 30-day period. Buy online or from travel agents.

➡ **Busabout** (www.busabout.com) is a hop-on, hop-off service that runs coaches along several interlocking European loops between May and October. Six out of the seven loops include Munich and four take in Stuttgart and Salzburg.

➡ Low-cost coach company **Meinfernbus/Flixbus** (☑ 0180 515 9915; www.meinfernbus.de; Zentraler Omnibusbahnhof, Arnulfstrasse 21) links the region with many cities in neighbouring countries.

Boat

The Romanshorn-Friedrichshafen ferry provides the quickest way across Lake Constance between Switzerland and Germany. Ferries operated by **SBS Schifffahrt** (www.sbsag.ch) take 40 minutes.

Car & Motorcycle

➡ When bringing your own vehicle to Germany, you need a valid driving licence, your car registration certificate and proof of insurance.

➡ Foreign cars must display a nationality sticker unless they have official Euro-plates.

➡ Equipment you need to have in your car by law includes a first-aid kit, spare bulbs and a warning triangle.

➡ Between Novermber and May, even away from the Alps, make sure your vehicle is fitted with winter tyres and carry snow chains in the boot. Spiked tyres are prohibited.

➡ Be aware that if driving to Germany via France, you must now have a breathalyser approved by the French authorities in the car, as well as other equipment not required in Germany. The Czech Republic also has some finicky requirements, so see www.theaa.com (click through to 'Driving', then 'Driving Abroad') for the full rundown.

Train

➡ Long-distance trains connecting major German cities with those in other countries are called EuroCity (EC) trains. Seat reservations are highly recommended, especially during the peak summer season and around major holidays.

➡ Linking the UK with continental Europe, the Eurostar (www.eurostar.com) takes less than three hours from London-St Pancras to Paris, where you can get a high-speed TGV service to Munich taking another six hours.

➡ There are direct overnight trains to Munich from Amsterdam, Copenhagen, Belgrade, Budapest, Bucharest, Florence, Milan, Rome, Venice and Vienna.

➡ Use the Deutsche Bahn website (www.bahn.de) or The Man in Seat 61 site (www.seat61.com) to plan your journey to southern Germany.

GETTING AROUND

Getting around Bavaria and the Black Forest is most efficient by car or by train. Regional bus services fill the gaps in areas not well served by the rail network.

Air

Although it is possible to fly, say, from Frankfurt to Munich or Salzburg, the time and cost involved don't make air travel a sensible way to get around southern Germany.

Unless you're travelling to Bavaria or the Black Forest from northern Germany, planes are only marginally faster than trains if you factor in the time it takes to travel to and from the airports. **Lufthansa** (www.lufthansa.com), **Air Berlin** (www.airberlin.com) and **Germanwings** (www.germanwings.com) are among the airlines flying domestically.

Bicycle

Cycling is one of the most popular ways to get around for both locals and visitors, making southern Germany one of Europe's most bike-friendly regions.

➡ Cycling is allowed on all roads and highways but not on the autobahn (motorway). Cyclists must follow the same rules of the road as vehicles.

➡ Cycle paths are ubiquitous in large cities.

➡ Lights are compulsory but helmets aren't, not even for children. Wearing one is still a good idea, though.

➡ Bicycles may be taken on most trains but usually require a separate *Fahrradkarte* (bicycle ticket). However, they're not allowed on high-speed ICE trains. For specifics inquire at a local station or call Deutsche Bahn (DB) on the **DB Radfahrer-Hotline** (Bicycle Hotline; ☎0180-599 6633; ⏰8am-8pm).

➡ Many regional bus companies use vehicles with special bike racks. Bicycles are also allowed on practically all lake and river boats.

➡ Around 250 train stations throughout the country hire bikes. All information can be found at www.bahn.de.

➡ Cycle hire centres are common – rates range between €10 and €25 per day.

➡ Bett & Bike (Bed & Bike; www.bettundbike.de) lists accommodation with facilities for bikes (storage, tools, washing amenities).

Bus

Basically, wherever there is a train, take it. Buses are generally slower, less dependable and more polluting than trains, but in some rural areas they may be your only option. This is especially true of the Bavarian Forest and the Black Forest, sections of the Alpine foothills and the Alpine region. Separate bus companies, each with its

own tariffs and schedules, operate in the different regions, but with a bit of practice all timetables and fares can be looked up using the Deutsche Bahn website (www.bahn.de).

In cities, buses generally converge at the *Busbahnhof* or *Zentraler Omnibus Bahnhof/ZOB* (central bus station), often near the Hauptbahnhof (main train station). The frequency of service varies from 'rarely' to 'constantly'. Commuter-geared routes offer limited or no service in the evenings and on weekends. It's always a good idea to ask about special fare deals, such as day or weekly passes or tourist tickets.

Car & Motorcycle

➡ German autobahns are generally of a good standard though they do possess some quirks such as excessively bendy slip roads and many two-lane sections.

➡ The extensive network of *Bundesstrassen* (secondary 'A' and 'B' roads) is also good, though perhaps not up to the standard you are used to back home.

➡ As yet no tolls are charged on public roads, though this may soon change for the motorways.

➡ Traffic can be heavy on *Bundesstrassen* at busy times of the day.

➡ Up-to-the-minute travel and roadwork information in English is available at www.bayerninfo.de. Traffic reports on the radio (in German) usually follow on-the-hour news summaries and should trigger your car radio's TIM (Traffic Information Message) system.

➡ Well-equipped service areas appear every 40km to 60km on autobahns with petrol stations, toilet facilities and restaurants; some are open 24 hours. In between are *Rastplätze* (rest stops), which usually

---

ROMANTIC ROAD COACH

The **Romantic Road Coach** (www.romanticroadcoach.de) is geared towards individual travellers on the Romantic Road between Würzburg and Füssen from April to October.

There's one coach in either direction daily. Tickets can be purchased by phone or online and are available either for the entire distance or for segments between any of the stops. Various discounts are available.

have picnic tables and toilet facilities. Toilets at service stations are never free and you'll need change to access them.

Automobile Associations

Germany's main motoring organisation, the **Allgemeiner Deutscher Automobil-Club** (Allgemeiner Deutscher Automobil-Club; ☎ for information 0800 510 1112, for roadside assistance 0180 222 2222; www.adac.de) has offices in all major cities and many smaller ones.

Driving Licence

Drivers need a valid driving licence. International Driving Permits (IDP; issued by your local automobile association) for non-EU drivers are not compulsory but having one may help Germans make sense of your home licence (always carry that one too) and may simplify the car hire process.

Hire

➡ Southern Germany has an excellent public transport system meaning car hire isn't absolutely necessary. One exception is the trip along the Romantic Road where a car makes travel a lot easier.

➡ As anywhere, rates for car hire vary quite considerably by model, pick-up date and location.

➡ Mini-economy class vehicles start from around €35 per day, but expect surcharges for additional drivers and one-way hire.

➡ Pre-booking through websites such as www.auto-europe.co.uk, www.rentalcars.com and www.holidayautos.com can bring daily rates down to less than €20 depending on how long you need the car.

➡ Child or infant seats are usually available for free or for a symbolic charge. Satellite-navigation units can be hired for a small fee per

day. Both should be reserved at the time of booking.

➡ To pick up your car you'll probably need to be at least 21 years old with a valid driving licence as well as a major credit card.

➡ Taking your car into an Eastern European country, such as the Czech Republic or Poland, is usually not allowed. Check in advance if that's where you're heading.

➡ All the main international companies maintain branches at airports, major train stations and in large towns.

Insurance

➡ German law requires that all registered vehicles carry minimum third-party liability insurance. Don't even think of driving uninsured or under-insured.

➡ When hiring a vehicle, make sure your contract includes adequate liability insurance at the very minimum.

➡ Optional Collision Damage Waiver (CDW) for hire cars is extra and is charged when you pick up the vehicle.

Road Rules

➡ Driving is on the right-hand side of the road and standard international signs are in use. If you're unfamiliar with these, contact your local motoring organisation.

➡ Obey the road rules carefully: speed and red-light cameras are common and notices are sent to the car's registration address, wherever that may be. If you're renting a car, the police will obtain your home address from the rental agency and fines may be chased up by debt collectors where you live.

➡ There's a long list of other actions that may incur a fine, including using abusive language or gestures and running out of petrol on the autobahn.

➡ Speed limits are 50km/h in built up areas, 100km/h on highways and country roads and 130km/h on the autobahn unless otherwise indicated. There are sections of autobahn where there's no speed limit, but always keep an eye out for signs indicating that slower speeds must be observed.

➡ Drivers unaccustomed to the high speeds on autobahns should be extra careful when passing another vehicle. It takes only seconds for a car in the rear-view mirror to close in at 200km/h. Pass as quickly as possible, then quickly return to the right lane.

➡ Ignore drivers who flash their headlights to make you drive faster and get out of the way. It's an illegal practice, as is passing on the right.

➡ If you break down, pull over to the side of the road immediately and set up your warning triangle about 100m behind the car. Emergency call boxes are spaced about 2km apart or, if you have a mobile phone, call the ADAC and wait for assistance.

➡ The highest permissible blood-alcohol level for drivers is 0.05%, which for most people equates to roughly one glass of wine or two small beers. The limit for drivers under 21 and for those who have held their license for less than two years is 0%.

➡ Pedestrians at crossings have right of way over all motor vehicles. Always watch out for cyclists when turning right; they too have the right of way. Right turns at a red light are only legal if there's also a green arrow pointing to the right.

Hitching & Ride-Share

Trampen (hitching) is never entirely safe and, frankly, we don't recommend it. Travellers who hitch should understand that they are taking a small but potentially serious risk. That said, in some remote parts of Bavaria and the Black Forest – such as sections of the Alpine foothills and the Bavarian Forest – that are poorly served by public transport, you will occasionally see people thumbing for a ride. Remember that it's safer to travel in pairs and be sure to let someone know where you're planning to go.

A safer and more predictable form of travelling is ride-shares, where you travel as a passenger in exchange for some petrol money. Most arrangements are now made via online ride-boards at www.mitfahrzentrale.de, www.mitfahrgelegenheit.de or www.drive2day.de. You can advertise a ride yourself or link up with a driver going to your destination.

Local Transport

➡ Most towns have efficient public transport systems. Bigger cities, such as Munich

and Nuremberg, integrate buses, trams, and U-Bahn (underground) and S-Bahn (suburban) trains into a single network.

➡ Tickets are generally bought in advance from ticket machines before boarding any mode of transport and must be stamped before or upon boarding in order to be valid.

➡ Fares are either determined by zones or time travelled, or sometimes by both. *Tageskarten* (day passes) generally offer better value than single-ride tickets.

➡ The fine if you're caught without a valid ticket is €40.

➡ Taxis are metered and charged at a base rate (flag fall) plus a per-kilometre fee. These are fixed but vary across cities. Some charge extra for bulky luggage or night-time rides. Rarely can you flag down a taxi. Rather, you board at a taxi rank or order one by phone.

Train

Southern Germany's rail system is mostly operated by Deutsche Bahn (www.bahn.com) though private operators such as BLB (www.blb.info), Meridian (www.

SAMPLE FARES

Permanent rail deals include:

Ticket	Cost	Validity
Bayern-Ticket	€23+€5 per extra person	9am-3am Mon-Fri, midnight-3am weekends
Baden-Württemberg-Ticket	€23+€5 per extra person	9am-3am Mon-Fri, midnight-3am weekends
Bayern-Ticket Nacht	€23+€2 per extra person	6pm-6am
Baden-Württemberg-Ticket Nacht	€20+€5 per extra person	6pm-6am

All of the above tickets are good for 2nd-class travel on IRE, SE, RB and S-Bahn trains, as well as all public buses, trams, U-Bahns and privately run railways across the given *Land* for which they are valid. Always buy them from vending machines as there's a €2 surcharge if you purchase from a service desk. Remember, with the daytime tickets you can save tens of euros by putting off your journey until after 9am, especially when travelling long distances within Bavaria. The Bayern-Ticket is also valid as far as Salzburg Hauptbahnhof.

der-meridian.de) and Agilis (www.agilis.de) oversee an ever-increasing number of lines. Deutsche bahn operates a bamboozling 'alphabet soup' of train types serving just about every corner of the region and country. The system is efficient, but largely automated and unmanned. This can cause problems when things go wrong as there are often no staff members around to whom you can turn for information.

Most train stations have coin-operated lockers charging from €1.50 to €4 for 24 hours.

➡ Long-distance trains are either called ICE (InterCity Express), which travel at high speeds, or the only slightly slower IC (InterCity) or EC (EuroCity) trains. Both run at hourly or bi-hourly intervals.

➡ Regional service is provided by the IRE (InterRegio Express), the RB (RegionalBahn), the SE (StadtExpress) and the S-Bahn.

Tickets

➡ Large train stations have a *Reisezentrum* (travel centre) where staff sell tickets and can help you plan an itinerary (ask for an English-speaking agent). Smaller stations may only have a few ticket windows or no staff at all.

➡ Sometimes you will have no choice but to buy your ticket from a vending machine. These are plentiful at staffed and unstaffed stations and convenient if you don't want to queue at a ticket counter. Instructions are in English and the ticket

TRAIN PASSES

If residing permanently outside Europe, you qualify for the German Rail Pass (www.germanrailpasses.com), which entitles you to unlimited travel for four to 10 days within a one-month period. Sample prices for four/seven/10 days of travel are €178/237/303 in 2nd class (half-price for children ages six to 11). The pass is valid on all trains within Germany, plus Salzburg and Basel as well as some river services, and entitles you to discounts on the Europabus along the Romantic Road and the Bayerische Zugspitzbahn.

The German Rail Youth Pass for people between 12 and 25, and the German Rail Twin Pass for two adults travelling together are variations on the scheme. If Bavaria is part of a wider European itinerary, look into a Eurail Pass (www.eurail.com).

A great resource for rail passes wherever you live is Rail Europe (www.raileurope.com), a major agency specialising in train travel around Europe.

purchasing system has been greatly simplified though can still bamboozle the uninitiated.

➡ Both ticket windows and machines accept major credit cards, but machines don't take €50 notes. Tickets sold on board (cash only) incur a service fee (€3 to €8) unless the station where you boarded was unstaffed or had a broken vending machine.

➡ Tickets are also available online up to 10 minutes before departure but need to be printed out.

➡ Tickets and passes are almost always checked. The fine for not holding a valid travel document is €40.

➡ Standard, non-discounted train tickets are expensive, but promotions, discount tickets and special offers

become available all the time. Check the website or ask at the train station.

ON BOARD

German trains have 1st- and 2nd-class cars, both of them modern and comfortable. Seating is either in compartments of up to six people or in open-plan carriages with panoramic windows. Trains are now completely nonsmoking. ICE, IC and EC trains are fully air-conditioned and have a restaurant or self-service bistro.

RESERVATIONS

Seat reservations (€4.50 per person) for long-distance travel are recommended, especially on a Friday or Sunday afternoon, around holidays or in summer. They can be made up to 10 minutes before departure by phone, online or at ticket counters.

Language

German belongs to the West Germanic language family, with English and Dutch as close relatives, and has around 100 million speakers. It is commonly divided into two forms – Low German (*Plattdeutsch*) and High German (*Hochdeutsch*). Low German is an umbrella term used for the dialects spoken in Northern Germany. High German is considered the standard form and is understood throughout German-speaking communities; it's also the variety used in this chapter.

German is easy for English speakers to pronounce because almost all of its sounds are also found in English. If you read our coloured pronunciation guides as if they were English, you'll have no problems being understood. Note that kh is like the 'ch' in 'Bach' or the Scottish 'loch' (pronounced at the back of the throat, r is also pronounced at the back of the throat (almost like a g, but with some friction), zh is pronounced as the 's' in 'measure', and ü as the 'ee' in 'see' but with rounded lips.The stressed syllables are indicated with italics.

BASICS

Hello.	*Guten Tag.*	goo·ten tahk
Goodbye.	*Auf Wiedersehen.*	owf vee·der·zay·en
Yes./No.	*Ja./Nein.*	yah/nain
Please.	*Bitte.*	bi·te
Thank you.	*Danke.*	dang·ke
You're welcome.	*Bitte.*	bi·te
Excuse me.	*Entschuldigung.*	ent·shul·di·gung
Sorry.	*Entschuldigung.*	ent·shul·di·gung

How are you?
Wie geht es Ihnen/dir? (pol/inf) vee gayt es ee·nen/deer

Fine. And you?
Danke, gut. *Und Ihnen/dir?* (pol/inf) dang·ke goot unt ee·nen/deer

What's your name?
Wie ist Ihr Name? (pol) vee ist eer *nah*·me

Wie heißt du? (inf) vee haist doo

My name is ...
Mein Name ist ... (pol) main *nah*·me ist ...
Ich heiße ... (inf) ikh *hai*·se ...

Do you speak English?
Sprechen Sie Englisch? (pol) shpre·khen zee eng·lish
Sprichst du Englisch? (inf) shprikhst doo eng·lish

I don't understand.
Ich verstehe nicht. ikh fer·*shtay*·e nikht

ACCOMMODATION

campsite	*Campingplatz*	kem·ping·plats
guesthouse	*Pension*	pahng·*zyawn*
hotel	*Hotel*	ho·*tel*
inn	*Gasthof*	gast·hawf
room in a private home	*Privatzimmer*	pri·*vaht*·tsi·mer
youth hostel	*Jugend-herberge*	yoo·gent·her·ber·ge

Do you have a ... room?	*Haben Sie ein ...?*	hah·ben zee ain ...
double	*Doppelzimmer*	do·pel·tsi·mer
single	*Einzelzimmer*	ain·tsel·tsi·mer
How much is it per ...?	*Wie viel kostet es pro ...?*	vee feel kos·tet es praw ...
night	*Nacht*	nakht
person	*Person*	per·*zawn*

Is breakfast included?
Ist das Frühstück inklusive? ist das frü·shtük in·kloo·*zee*·ve

DIRECTIONS

Where's ...?
Wo ist ...? vaw ist ...

What's the address?
Wie ist die Adresse?   vee ist dee a·dre·se

How far is it?
Wie weit ist es?   vee vait ist es

Can you show me (on the map)?
Können Sie es mir   ker·nen zee es meer
(auf der Karte) zeigen?   (owf dair kar·te) tsai·gen

How can I get there?
Wie kann ich da   vee kan ikh dah
hinkommen?   hin·ko·men

Turn ...	Biegen Sie ... ab.	bee·gen zee ... ab
at the corner	an der Ecke	an dair e·ke
at the traffic lights	bei der Ampel	bai dair am·pel
left	links	lingks
right	rechts	rekhts

EATING & DRINKING

I'd like to reserve a table for ...	Ich möchte einen Tisch für ... reservieren.	ikh merkh·te ai·nen tish für ... re·zer·vee·ren
(eight) o'clock	(acht) Uhr	(akht) oor
(two) people	(zwei) Personen	(tsvai) per·zaw·nen

I'd like the menu, please.
Ich hätte gern die   ikh he·te gern dee
Speisekarte, bitte.   shpai·ze·kar·te bi·te

What would you recommend?
Was empfehlen Sie?   vas emp·fay·len zee

What's in that dish?
Was ist in diesem   vas ist in dee·zem
Gericht?   ge·rikht

I'm a vegetarian.
Ich bin Vegetarier/   ikh bin ve·ge·tah·ri·er/
Vegetarierin. (m/f)   ve·ge·tah·ri·e·rin

That was delicious.
Das hat hervorragend   das hat her·fawr·rah·gent
geschmeckt.   ge·shmekt

Cheers!
Prost!   prawst

Please bring the bill.
Bitte bringen Sie   bi·te bring·en zee
die Rechnung.   dee rekh·nung

Key Words

bar (pub)	Kneipe	knai·pe
bottle	Flasche	fla·she
bowl	Schüssel	shü·sel
breakfast	Frühstück	frü·shtük
cold	kalt	kalt

KEY PATTERNS

To get by in German, mix and match these simple patterns with words of your choice:

When's (the next flight)?
Wann ist (der   van ist (dair
nächste Flug)?   naykhs·te flook)

Where's (the station)?
Wo ist (der Bahnhof)?   vaw ist (dair bahn·hawf)

Where can I (buy a ticket)?
Wo kann ich (eine   vaw kan ikh (ai·ne
Fahrkarte kaufen)?   fahr·kar·te kow·fen)

Do you have (a map)?
Haben Sie   hah·ben zee
(eine Karte)?   (ai·ne kar·te)

Is there (a toilet)?
Gibt es (eine Toilette)?   gipt es (ai·ne to·a·le·te)

I'd like (a coffee).
Ich möchte   ikh merkh·te
(einen Kaffee).   (ai·nen ka·fay)

I'd like (to hire a car).
Ich möchte   ikh merkh·te
(ein Auto mieten).   (ain ow·to mee·ten)

Can I (enter)?
Darf ich   darf ikh
(hereinkommen)?   (her·ein·ko·men)

Could you please (help me)?
Könnten Sie   kern·ten zee
(mir helfen)?   (meer hel·fen)

Do I have to (book a seat)?
Muss ich (einen Platz   mus ikh (ai·nen plats
reservieren lassen)?   re·zer·vee·ren la·sen)

cup	Tasse	ta·se
daily special	Gericht des Tages	ge·rikht des tah·ges
delicatessen	Feinkostgeschäft	fain·kost·ge·sheft
desserts	Nachspeisen	nahkh·shpai·zen
dinner	Abendessen	ah·bent·e·sen
drink list	Getränkekarte	ge·treng·ke·kar·te
fork	Gabel	gah·bel
glass	Glas	glahs
grocery store	Lebensmittelladen	lay·bens·mi·tel·lah·den
hot (warm)	warm	warm
knife	Messer	me·ser
lunch	Mittagessen	mi·tahk·e·sen
market	Markt	markt
plate	Teller	te·ler
restaurant	Restaurant	res·to·rahng
set menu	Menü	may·nü

spicy	würzig	vür·tsikh
spoon	Löffel	ler·fel
with/without	mit/ohne	mit/aw·ne

Meat & Fish

beef	Rindfleisch	rint·flaish
carp	Karpfen	karp·fen
fish	Fisch	fish
herring	Hering	hay·ring
lamb	Lammfleisch	lam·flaish
meat	Fleisch	flaish
pork	Schweinefleisch	shvai·ne·flaish
poultry	Geflügelfleisch	ge·flü·gel·flaish
salmon	Lachs	laks
sausage	Wurst	vurst
seafood	Meeresfrüchte	mair·res·frükh·te
shellfish	Schaltiere	shahl·tee·re
trout	Forelle	fo·re·le
veal	Kalbfleisch	kalp·flaish

Fruit & Vegetables

apple	Apfel	ap·fel
banana	Banane	ba·nah·ne
bean	Bohne	baw·ne
cabbage	Kraut	krowt
capsicum	Paprika	pap·ri·kah
carrot	Mohrrübe	mawr·rü·be
cucumber	Gurke	gur·ke
fruit	Frucht/Obst	frukht/awpst
grapes	Weintrauben	vain·trow·ben
lemon	Zitrone	tsi·traw·ne
lentil	Linse	lin·ze
lettuce	Kopfsalat	kopf·za·laht
mushroom	Pilz	pilts
nuts	Nüsse	nü·se
onion	Zwiebel	tsvee·bel

Signs

Ausgang	Exit
Damen	Women
Eingang	Entrance
Geschlossen	Closed
Herren	Men
Toiletten (WC)	Toilets
Offen	Open
Verboten	Prohibited

orange	Orange	o·rahng·zhe
pea	Erbse	erp·se
plum	Pflaume	pflow·me
potato	Kartoffel	kar·to·fel
spinach	Spinat	shpi·naht
strawberry	Erdbeere	ert·bair·re
tomato	Tomate	to·mah·te
vegetable	Gemüse	ge·mü·ze
watermelon	Wassermelone	va·ser·me·law·ne

Other

bread	Brot	brawt
butter	Butter	bu·ter
cheese	Käse	kay·ze
egg/eggs	Ei/Eier	ai/ai·er
honey	Honig	haw·nikh
jam	Marmelade	mar·me·lah·de
pasta	Nudeln	noo·deln
pepper	Pfeffer	pfe·fer
rice	Reis	rais
salt	Salz	zalts
soup	Suppe	zu·pe
sugar	Zucker	tsu·ker

Drinks

beer	Bier	beer
coffee	Kaffee	ka·fay
juice	Saft	zaft
milk	Milch	milkh
orange juice	Orangensaft	o·rang·zhen·zaft
red wine	Rotwein	rawt·vain
sparkling wine	Sekt	zekt
tea	Tee	tay
water	Wasser	va·ser
white wine	Weißwein	vais·vain

EMERGENCIES

Help!
Hilfe! — hil·fe

Go away!
Gehen Sie weg! — gay·en zee vek

Call the police!
Rufen Sie die Polizei! — roo·fen zee dee po·li·tsai

Call a doctor!
Rufen Sie einen Arzt! — roo·fen zee ai·nen artst

Where are the toilets?
Wo ist die Toilette? — vo ist dee to·a·le·te

I'm lost.
Ich habe mich verirrt. ikh *hah*·be mikh fer·*irt*

I'm sick.
Ich bin krank. ikh bin krangk

It hurts here.
Es tut hier weh. es toot heer vay

I'm allergic to ...
Ich bin allergisch ikh bin a·*lair*·gish
gegen ... gay·gen ...

SHOPPING & SERVICES

I'd like to buy ...
Ich möchte ... kaufen. ikh *merkh*·te ... *kow*·fen

I'm just looking.
Ich schaue mich nur um. ikh *show*·e mikh noor um

Can I look at it?
Können Sie es mir *ker*·nen zee es meer
zeigen? *tsai*·gen

How much is this?
Wie viel kostet das? vee feel *kos*·tet das

That's too expensive.
Das ist zu teuer. das ist tsoo *toy*·er

Can you lower the price?
Können Sie mit dem *ker*·nen zee mit dem
Preis heruntergehen? prais he·*run*·ter·gay·en

There's a mistake in the bill.
Da ist ein Fehler dah ist ain *fay*·ler
in der Rechnung. in dair *rekh*·nung

ATM	*Geldautomat*	*gelt*·ow·to·maht
post office	*Postamt*	*post*·amt
tourist office	*Fremden-*	*frem*·den·
	verkehrsbüro	fer·kairs·bü·raw

TIME & DATES

What time is it? *Wie spät ist es?* vee shpayt ist es

It's (10) o'clock. *Es ist (zehn) Uhr.* es ist (tsayn) oor

At what time? *Um wie viel Uhr?* um vee feel oor

At ... *Um ...* um ...

morning	*Morgen*	*mor*·gen
afternoon	*Nachmittag*	*nahkh*·mi·tahk
evening	*Abend*	*ah*·bent
yesterday	*gestern*	*ges*·tern
today	*heute*	*hoy*·te
tomorrow	*morgen*	*mor*·gen
Monday	*Montag*	*mawn*·tahk
Tuesday	*Dienstag*	*deens*·tahk
Wednesday	*Mittwoch*	*mit*·vokh

Question Words

How?	*Wie?*	vee
What?	*Was?*	vas
When?	*Wann?*	van
Where?	*Wo?*	vaw
Who?	*Wer?*	vair
Why?	*Warum?*	va·*rum*

Thursday	*Donnerstag*	*do*·ners·tahk
Friday	*Freitag*	*frai*·tahk
Saturday	*Samstag*	*zams*·tahk
Sunday	*Sonntag*	*zon*·tahk
January	*Januar*	*yan*·u·ahr
February	*Februar*	*fay*·bru·ahr
March	*März*	merts
April	*April*	a·*pril*
May	*Mai*	mai
June	*Juni*	*yoo*·ni
July	*Juli*	*yoo*·li
August	*August*	ow·*gust*
September	*September*	zep·*tem*·ber
October	*Oktober*	ok·*taw*·ber
November	*November*	no·*vem*·ber
December	*Dezember*	de·*tsem*·ber

TRANSPORT

Public Transport

boat	*Boot*	bawt
bus	*Bus*	bus
metro	*U-Bahn*	*oo*·bahn
plane	*Flugzeug*	*flook*·tsoyk
train	*Zug*	tsook
At what time's the ... bus?	*Wann fährt der ... Bus?*	van fairt dair... bus
first	*erste*	*ers*·te
last	*letzte*	*lets*·te
A ... to (Berlin).	*Eine ... nach (Berlin).*	*ai*·ne ... nahkh (ber·*leen*)
1st-class ticket	*Fahrkarte erster Klasse*	*fahr*·kar·te *ers*·ter *kla*·se
2nd-class ticket	*Fahrkarte zweiter Klasse*	*fahr*·kar·te *tsvai*·ter *kla*·se
one-way ticket	*einfache Fahrkarte*	*ain*·fa·khe *fahr*·kar·te
return ticket	*Rückfahrkarte*	*rük*·fahr·kar·te

Numbers

1	eins	ains
2	zwei	tsvai
3	drei	drai
4	vier	feer
5	fünf	fünf
6	sechs	zeks
7	sieben	zee·ben
8	acht	akht
9	neun	noyn
10	zehn	tsayn
20	zwanzig	tsvan·tsikh
30	dreißig	drai·tsikh
40	vierzig	feer·tsikh
50	fünfzig	fünf·tsikh
60	sechzig	zekh·tsikh
70	siebzig	zeep·tsikh
80	achtzig	akht·tsikh
90	neunzig	noyn·tsikh
100	hundert	hun·dert
1000	tausend	tow·sent

At what time does it arrive?
Wann kommt es an? — van komt es an

Is it a direct route?
Ist es eine direkte — ist es ai·ne di·rek·te
Verbindung? — fer·bin·dung

Does it stop at (Freiburg)?
Hält es in (Freiburg)? — helt es in (frai·boorg)

What station is this?
Welcher Bahnhof — vel·kher bahn·hawf
ist das? — ist das

What's the next stop?
Welches ist der — vel·khes ist dair
nächste Halt? — naykh·ste halt

I want to get off here.
Ich möchte hier — ikh merkh·te heer
aussteigen. — ows·shtai·gen

Please tell me when we get to (Kiel).
Könnten Sie mir bitte — kern·ten zee meer bi·te
sagen, wann wir in — zah·gen van veer in
(Kiel) ankommen? — (keel) an·ko·men

Please take me to (this address).
Bitte bringen Sie mich — bi·te bring·en zee mikh
zu (dieser Adresse). — tsoo (dee·zer a·dre·se)

platform — Bahnsteig — bahn-shtaik

ticket office — Fahrkarten- — fahr·kar·ten-
verkauf — fer·kowf
timetable — Fahrplan — fahr·plan

Driving & Cycling

I'd like to — Ich möchte — ikh merkh·te
hire a ... — ein ... mieten. — ain ... mee·ten
  4WD — Allrad- — al·raht-
fahrzeug — fahr·tsoyk
  bicycle — Fahrrad — fahr·raht
  car — Auto — ow·to
  motorbike — Motorrad — maw·tor·raht

How much — Wie viel kostet — vee feel kos·tet
is it per ...? — es pro ...? — es praw ...
  day — Tag — tahk
  week — Woche — vo·khe

bicycle pump — Fahrradpumpe — fahr·raht·pum·pe
child seat — Kindersitz — kin·der·zits
helmet — Helm — helm
petrol — Benzin — ben·tseen

Does this road go to ...?
Führt diese Straße — fürt dee·ze shtrah·se
nach ...? — nahkh ...

(How long) Can I park here?
(Wie lange) Kann ich — (vee lang·e) kan ikh
hier parken? — heer par·ken

Where's a petrol station?
Wo ist eine Tankstelle? — vaw ist ai·ne tangk·shte·le

I need a mechanic.
Ich brauche einen — ikh brow·khe ai·nen
Mechaniker. — me·khah·ni·ker

My car/motorbike has broken down (at ...).
Ich habe (in ...) eine — ikh hah·be (in ...) ai·ne
Panne mit meinem — pa·ne mit mai·nem
Auto/Motorrad. — ow·to/maw·tor·raht

I've run out of petrol.
Ich habe kein — ikh hah·be kain
Benzin mehr. — ben·tseen mair

I have a flat tyre.
Ich habe eine — ikh hah·be ai·ne
Reifenpanne. — rai·fen·pa·ne

Are there cycling paths?
Gibt es Fahrradwege? — geept es fahr·raht·vay·ge

Is there bicycle parking?
Gibt es Fahrrad- — geept es fahr·raht·
Parkplätze? — park·ple·tse

GLOSSARY

(pl) indicates plural

Abtei – abbey

ADAC – Allgemeiner Deutscher Automobil Club (German Automobile Association)

Allee – avenue

Altstadt – old town

Apotheke – pharmacy

Ärzt – doctor

Ausgang – exit

Bad – spa, bath

Bahnhof – train station

Basilika – basilica

Bedienung – service; service charge

Berg – mountain

Bibliothek – library

Biergarten – beer garden

Bierkeller – cellar pub

Brauerei – brewery

Brotzeit – literally bread time, typically an afternoon snack featuring bread with cold cuts, cheeses or sausages

Brücke – bridge

Brunnen – fountain, well

Burg – castle

Busbahnhof – bus station

Christkindlmarkt – Christmas food and craft market; sometimes spelt Christkindlesmarkt

DB – Deutsche Bahn (German national railway)

Denkmal – memorial

Deutsche Reich – German empire; refers to the period 1871–1918

DJH – Deutsches Jugendherbergswerk (German youth hostel association)

Dom – cathedral

Dorf – village

Eingang – entrance

Fahrrad – bicycle

Ferienwohnung, Ferienwohnungen (pl) – holiday flat or apartment

Fest – festival

Flohmarkt – flea market

Flughafen – airport

Krankenhaus – hospital

Kunst – art

Kurhaus – literally spa house, but usually a spa towns central building, used for social gatherings and events

Kurort – spa resort

Kurtaxe – resort tax

Kurverwaltung – spa resort administration

Kurzentrum – spa centre

Land, Länder (pl) – state

Landtag – state parliament

Markgraf – margrave; German nobleman ranking above a count

Markt – market; often used instead of Marktplatz

Marktplatz – marketplace or square; often abbreviated to Markt

Mass – 1L tankard or stein of beer

Mensa – university cafeteria

Milchcafé – coffee with milk

Münster – minster, large church, cathedral

Nord – north

Notdienst – emergency service

NSDAP – National Socialist German Workers Party, Nazi party

Ost – east

Pension, Pensionen (pl) – inexpensive boarding house

Pfarrkirche – parish church

Platz – square

Postamt – post office

Radwandern – bicycle touring

Rathaus – town hall

Ratskeller – town hall restaurant

Reisezentrum – travel centre in train or bus stations

Ruhetag – rest day; closing day at a shop or restaurant

Saal, Säle (pl) – hall, room

Sammlung – collection

S-Bahn – Schnellbahn; suburban-metropolitan trains

Schatzkammer – treasury

Schloss – palace

Schnellimbiss – fast-food stall or restaurants

See – lake

Seilbahn – cable car

Speisekarte – menu

Stadt – city, town

Stadtbad, Stadtbäder (pl) – public pool

Staumauer – dam

Strasse – street; often abbreviated to Str

Süd – south

Tal – valley

Tor – gate

Tracht, Trachten (pl) – traditional costume

Turm – tower

U-Bahn – underground train

Verboten – forbidden

Viertel – quarter, district

Volksmusik – folk music

Wald – forest

Wasserfall – waterfall

Weg – way, path

Weinstube – traditional wine bar or tavern

West – west

Zimmer Frei – room available (for accommodation purposes)

Behind the Scenes

SEND US YOUR FEEDBACK

We love to hear from travellers – your comments keep us on our toes and help make our books better. Our well-travelled team reads every word on what you loved or loathed about this book. Although we cannot reply individually to your submissions, we always guarantee that your feedback goes straight to the appropriate authors, in time for the next edition. Each person who sends us information is thanked in the next edition – the most useful submissions are rewarded with a selection of digital PDF chapters.

Visit **lonelyplanet.com/contact** to submit your updates and suggestions or to ask for help. Our award-winning website also features inspirational travel stories, news and discussions.

Note: We may edit, reproduce and incorporate your comments in Lonely Planet products such as guidebooks, websites and digital products, so let us know if you don't want your comments reproduced or your name acknowledged. For a copy of our privacy policy visit lonelyplanet.com/privacy.

OUR READERS

Many thanks to the travellers who used the last edition and wrote to us with helpful hints, useful advice and interesting anecdotes: Christian Ebner, Federica Gallo, Carmen Goodwin, Guy Migneron, Michelle Renaud.

AUTHOR THANKS

Kerry Christiani

A heartfelt *dankeschön* to friends and family in the Schwarzwald, especially Hans and Monika in Villingen and Anja at the Brickstone Hostel, Ulm. Big thanks to Claus Schäfer in Triberg and Christiana Schneeweiss in Salzburg for the interviews. I'd also like to thank all the tourist board pros I met on the road and my Lonely Planet coauthors for being great to work with. Finally, thanks to my husband for his ongoing support and for introducing me to the Black Forest all those years ago.

Marc Di Duca

Huge thanks go to my parents-in-law Mykola and Vira for looking after the boys while I was away. Also much gratitude goes to Oleksandr in Erding for a night 'researching' the output of Bavaria's breweries, Andrea in Nuremberg and the staff at tourist offices across the region, but in particular those in Coburg, Passau, Regensburg and Bayreuth.

ACKNOWLEDGEMENTS

Climate map data adapted from Peel MC, Finlayson BL & McMahon TA (2007) 'Updated World Map of the Köppen-Geiger Climate Classification', *Hydrology and Earth System Sciences*, 11, 163344.

Cover photograph: Great Hall of Schloss Nymphenburg in Munich, Claudio Cassaro/4Corners/©Bayerische Schlösserverwaltung.

THIS BOOK

This 5th edition of Lonely Planet's *Munich, Bavaria & the Black Forest* guidebook was researched and written by Kerry Christiani and Marc Di Duca, who also wrote the 4th edition. This guidebook was produced by the following:

Destination Editor
Gemma Graham

Product Editor Elin Berglund, Kathryn Rowan

Senior Cartographer
Valentina Kremenchutskaya

Book Designer Wibowo Rusli

Assisting Editors Melanie Dankel, Jeanette Wall

Cover Researcher
Naomi Parker

Thanks to Ryan Evans, Andi Jones, Anne Mason, Karyn Noble, Kirsten Rawlings, Diana Saengkham, Ellie Simpson, Lyahna Spencer, Lauren Wellicome, Tony Wheeler

BEHIND THE SCENES

Index